کتابشناسی برگزیدهء ایرج افشار

کتابها، مقالات و رسالات و چاپکرده ها در کتابهای دیگران و در فرهنگ *ایران زمین*

۱۳۳۰/۱۹۵۱-۲

- *نثر فارسی معاصر : منتخباتی از بهترین آثار مورخین و محققین نامی ایران از صدر مشروطیت تا معاصر.* تهران : کانون معرفت.

۱۳۳۱/۱۹۵۲-۳

- *حالات و سخنان شیخ ابوسعیدابوالخیر* / یکی از احفاد شیخ. تهران : کتابفروشی دانش.
- *سمریه : (مزرات سمرقند)* / ابوطاهر سمرقندی. تهران : کتابفروشی دانش.
  - چاپ ۲. تهران : فرهنگ ایران زمین.

۱۳۳۲/۱۹۵۳-٤

- رسالهء مادة الحیوة / نوراالله، آشپز شاه عباس صفوی. فرهنگ *ایران زمین*، ۲۰۵-۷۰.

- *قندیه : (در بیان مزرات سمرقند)* / محمد بن عبدالجلیل سمرقندی. تهران : کتابفروشی طهوری.
- *یادداشتهای قزوینی*. جلد ۱. تهران : دانشگاه تهران.

۱۳۳۳/۱۹۵٤-٥

- *تاریخ عالم آرای عباسی* / اسکندر بیك منشی. جلد ۱. تهران : امیرکبیر.
- *فردوس المرشدیة فی اسرار الصمدیه* / محمود بن عثمان. تهران : کتابفروشی دانش.

۱۳۳٤/۱۹٥٥-٦

- وقفنامهء سه دیه در کاشان. *فرهنگ ایران زمین*، ۳۸-۱۲۲.
- *یادداشتهای قزوینی*. جلد ۲. تهران : دانشگاه تهران.

۱۳۳٥/۱۹٥٦-۷

- *آغاز و انجام* / نصیرالدین طوسی. تهران : دانشگاه تهران.
- *تاریخ عالم آرای عباسی* / اسکندر بیك منشی. جلد ۲. تهران : امیرکبیر.
- *تاریخ کاشان : (مرآة القاسان)* / عبدالرحیم کلانتر ضرابی. تهران : فرهنگ ایران زمین.
- چند فصل از تاریخ کبیر / جعفر بن محمد بن حسن جعفری. *فرهنگ ایران زمین*، ۱٥۸-۸۹.

۱۳۳۶/۱۹۵۷-۸

- بیان الصناعات / حبیش بن ابراهیم بن محمد تفلیسی. فرهنگ *ایران زمین*، ۴۵۷-۲۷۹.
- *یادداشتهای قزوینی*. جلد ۳. تهران : دانشگاه تهران.

۱۳۳۷/۱۹۵۸-۹

- *کتابشناسی فهرستهای نسخه های خطی فارسی در کتابخانه های دنیا*. تهران : دانشگاه تهران.
- *یادداشتهای قزوینی*. جلد ۱. چاپ ۲. تهران : دانشگاه تهران.
- *یادداشتهای قزوینی*. جلد ٤. تهران : دانشگاه تهران.

۱۳۳۸/۱۹۵۹-۶۰

- *تاریخ یزد* / جعفر بن محمد بن جعفری. تهران : بنگاه ترجمه و نشر کتاب.

۱۳۳۹/۱۹۶۰-۱

- کارنامهء اوقاف / تاج الدین نسائی. فرهنگ *ایران زمین*، ۲۲-۵.
- *یادداشتهای قزوینی*. جلد ۵. تهران : دانشگاه تهران.

۱۳٤۰/۱۹٦۱-۲

- پند نامهء ماتریدی. *فرهنگ ایران زمین*، ٦۷-٤٦.
- جامع الخیرات : (وقفنامهء سید رکن الدین). باهمکاری محمد تقی دانش پژوه. *فرهنگ ایران زمین*، ۲۷۷-٦۸.
- *جامع مفیدی* / محمود مفید مستوفی بافقی. جلد ۱. تهران : کتابفروشی اسدی.
- *فهرست مقالات فارسی*. جلد ۱. تهران : دانشگاه تهران.
- *مسالك و ممالك : ترجمهء فارسی المسالك و الممالك از قرن پنجم-ششم هجری* /ابواسحق ابراهیم اصطخری. تهران : بنگاه ترجمه و نشر کتاب.
- *میرزا تقی خان امیرکبیر* / عباس اقبال آشتیانی. تهران : دانشگاه تهران.

Safi-al-din Bākharzi. In *A locust's leg*. London : Percy Lund, Humphries & Co. Ltd., 21-7.

۱۳٤۱/۱۹٦۲-۳

- *تاریخ کاشان* / عبدالرحیم کلانتر ضرابی (سهیل کاشانی). بانضمام یادداشتهایی از الهیار صالح. چاپ ۲. فرهنگ ایران زمین : ابن سینا.
- *حالات و سخنان شیخ ابوسعید ابو الخیر میهنی : متن بازمانده از قرن ششم هجری* / *یکی از احفاد شیخ*. چاپ ۲. تهران : کتابفروشی فروغی.
- کتابچهء موقوفات یزد / عبدالوهاب طراز. *فرهنگ ایران زمین*،

۱۲۳-۵.

- *یادداشتهای قزوینی*. جلد ٦. تهران : دانشگاه تهران.
- *یادگار زندگی* / حسین امین الضرب مهدوی. تهران : مجلهء یغما.

۱۳٤۲/۱۹٦۳-٤

- اصول و قواعد خطوط سته / فتح الله سبزواری. *فرهنگ ایران زمین*، ۳۳-۱۰۳.
- جزئی از جلد دوم جامع مفیدی / محمد مفید مستوفی. فرهنگ *ایران زمین*، ۲۲۸-۱۹۳.
- چند فرمان مربوط به یزد. *فرهنگ ایران زمین*، ۷٤-۱٦۹.
- *فهرست نامهء کتابشناسی های ایران*. تهران : دانشکدهء ادبیات دانشگاه تهران.
- *مجموعهء اسناد و مدارک چاپ نشده دربارهء سید جمال الدین مشهور به افغانی*. باهمکاری اصغر مهدوی. تهران : دانشگاه تهران.

۱۳٤۳/۱۹٦٤-٥

- *اسکندر نامه : روایت فارسی کالیستنس دروغین*، پرداختهء میان قرون ۸-٦ هجری. تهران : بنگاه ترجمه و نشر کتاب.
- تاریخ مختصر اصفهان / حیدر علی ندیم الملك اصفهانی. *فرهنگ ایران زمین*، ۷۳-۱٤٥.
- *تاریخ یزد* / جعفر بن محمد بن جعفری. چاپ ۲. تهران : بنگاه ترجمه و نشر کتاب.

- *جامع مفیدی* / محمود مفید مستوفی بافقی. جلد ۲. تهران : کتابفروشی اسدی.
- *کتابهای درسی : نظرآزمایی مجلهء راهنمای کتاب و جواب نویسندگان و دانشمندان*. تهران : انجمن کتاب.
- *یادداشتهای قزوینی*. جلد ۷. تهران : دانشگاه تهران.

۱۳۴٤/۱۹٦٥-٦

- *اصول سادهء کتابداری*. باهمکاری حسین بنی آدم، هوشنگ اعلم، علی اکبر جانا. تهران : ادارهء کل نگارش وزارت آموزش و پرورش.
- تذکرهء جلالی / عبدالغفور طاهری. فرهنگ *ایران زمین*، ٥٤-۱۰۱.
- ذخیرهء *خوارزمشاهی* / اسماعیل بن حسین جرجانی. جلد ۱. باهمکاری محمد تقی دانش پژوه. تهران : دانشگاه تهران.
- رسائلی از مؤلف ارشاد الزراعه : [قواعد ضرب و قسمت]، [طریق قسمت آب از قلب]. فرهنگ *ایران زمین*، ٦٧-٧.
- روزنامهء خراسان و سیستان / محمد ابراهیم خدابنده لو. فرهنگ *ایران زمین*، ٤٤-۱۲۲.
- سفرنامهء تهران به شیراز نظام الملك. فرهنگ *ایران زمین*، ۲۷۸-۱۸۸.
- *سواد و بیاض*. جلد ۱. تهران : کتابفروشی دهخدا.
- *سیر کتاب در ایران*. تهران : امیرکبیر.
- *کتابخانه های ایران و مقدمه ای در بارهء کتابخانه های قدیم*. تهران : ادارهء کل نگارش وزارت آموزش و پرورش.
- کتابی مهم از عبدالقادر اهری تألیف سال ٦۲۹ و رباعیات خیام

در آن. باهمکاری محمد تقی دانش پژوه. *فرهنگ ایران زمین*، ۲۲-۳۱۱.

۱۳۴۵/۱۹۶۶-۷

- *اوراد الاحباب و فصوص الاداب* / ابوالمفاخر یحیی باخرزی. جلد ۲. تهران : دانشگاه تهران.
- *تاریخ جدید یزد* / احمد بن حسین بن علی کاتب. تهران : فرهنگ ایران زمین : ابن سینا.
- *دو رساله‌ء عرفانی* : [شرایط مریدی / ابوجعفر محمد کاتب]، [فصل در عرفان / مجدالدین اسفزاری]. تهران : فرهنگ ایران زمین، ۳۷-۳۱۹.
- *رمز الریاحین* / رمزی کاشانی. تهران : مجله‌ء وحید.
- روزنامه‌ء *خاطرات اعتمادالسلطنه*. تهران : امیرکبیر.
- *عرائس الجواهر و نفائس الاطایب* / ابوالقاسم عبدالله کاشانی. تهران : انجمن آثار ملی.
- *فهرست نسخه های خطی کتابخانه مجلس شورای ملی*. جلد ۱۱. باهمکاری محمد تقی دانش پژوه، علینقی منزوی، احمد منزوی. تهران : کتابخانه.
- وقفنامه‌ء آب فرات از عهد شاه طهماسب. *فرهنگ ایران زمین*، ۸-۳۱۳.
- *یادداشتهای قزوینی*. جلد ۸. تهران : دانشگاه تهران.

۱۳۴۶/۱۹۶۷-۸

- *خوابگزاری : متن قدیمی بر اساس نسخه ای منحصر*. تهران :

۱۳٤۸/۱۹٦۹-۷۰

- *استرآبادنامه* / مسیح ذبیحی. باهمکاری محمد تقی دانش پژوه. تهران : فرهنگ ایران زمین : ابن سینا.
- *دیوان کهنهء حافظ*. تهران : فرهنگ ایران زمین : ابن سینا.
- رسالهء جلد سازی، (صحافی) / سید یوسف حسین. فرهنگ *ایران زمین*، ٤۳-۱.
- سفرنامهء کلنل لوات. در *استرآبادنامه*. باهمکاری مسیح ذبیحی. تهران : ابن سینا.
- *فهرست مقالات حقوقی*. باهمکاری یوسف موسی زادهء فصیح، ابراهیم صمدانی. تهران : دانشگاه تهران.
- *فهرست مقالات فارسی : فهرست موضوعی تحقیقات و مطالعات ایرانشناسی بزبان فارسی که در نشریات ادواری چاپ ایران و ممالك دیگر تا پایان سال ۱۳۳۸ شمسی چاپ شده است*. جلد ۱ : ۱۳۲۸ ق۱۳۳۸ ش. چاپ ۲. تهران : کتابهای جیبی.
- *فهرست مقالات فارسی*. جلد ۲ : ۱۳۳۹-۱۳٤٥. تهران : دانشگاه تهران.
- قصه ای از اسکندر : عجائب الدنیا در تاریخ. *فرهنگ ایران زمین*، ۳۱-۲۲۱.
- *کتابشناسی ده سالهء ۱۳۳۳-۱۳٤۲ : (کتابهای ایران)*. باهمکاری حسین بنی آدم. تهران : انجمن کتاب.
- هدایة التصدیق الی حکایة الحریق [چاپ عکسی] / فضل الله ابن روزبهان خنجی. در *یادنامهء ایرانی مینورسکی*. تهران : دانشگاه تهران.
- *یادنامهء ایرانی مینورسکی : شامل مقالات تحقیقی مربوط به مطالعات ایرانی*. باهمکاری مجتبی مینوی. تهران : دانشگاه

بنیاد فرهنگ ایران.

- *فرخنامه* / ابوبکر مطهر بن محمد جمالی یزدی. تهران : امیرکبیر.
- *کتابشناسی ده ساله‌ء ۱۳۴۲-۱۳۳۳ : کتابهای ایران*. باهمکاری حسین بنی آدم. تهران : انجمن کتاب.
- *یادداشتهای قزوینی*. جلد ۱. چاپ ۳. تهران : دانشگاه تهران.

۱۳۴۷/۱۹۶۸-۹

- دو اثر از حسین ابیوردی : [چار تخت]، [انیس العاشقین]. *فرهنگ ایران زمین*، ۱۶۰-۵.
- *فهرست مقالات حقوقی*. با همکاری یوسف موسی زاده فصیح، ابراهیم صمدانی. تهران : دانشگاه تهران.
- *کتابشناسی فردوسی : فهرست آثار و تحقیقات درباره‌ء فردوسی و شاهنامه*. تهران : انجمن آثار ملی.
- *گزیده در اخلاق و تصوف* / ابونصر طاهر بن محمد الخانقاهی. تهران : بنگاه ترجمه و نشر کتاب.
- *مسالك و ممالك : ترجمه‌ء فارسی المسالك و الممالك از قرن پنجم-ششم هجری* /ابواسحق ابراهیم اصطخری. چاپ ۲. تهران : بنگاه ترجمه و نشر کتاب.
- *یادداشتهای قزوینی*. جلد ۲. چاپ ۲. تهران : دانشگاه تهران.
- *یادداشتهای قزوینی*. جلد ۹. تهران : دانشگاه تهران.
- *یادگارهای یزد : معرفی ابنیه‌ء تاریخی و آثار باستانی*. جلد ۱ : خاك یزد. تهران : انجمن آثار ملی.

تهران.

١٣٤٩/١٩٧٠-١

- *اصطلاحات الصوفيه* / نورالدين جعفر بدخشانی. تهران : فرهنگ ایران زمین.
- اوقاف رشیدی در یزد / رشید الدین فضل الله همدانی. فرهنگ *ایران زمین*، ٢٤٨-١٤٩.
- تحفة العشاق [چاپ عکسی]. فرهنگ *ایران زمین*، ٢٦-١.
- *حالات و سخنان شیخ ابوسعید ابو الخیر میهنی : متن بازمانده از قرن ششم هجری* / یکی از احفاد شیخ. چاپ ٣. تهران : کتابفروشی فروغی.
- *دافع الغرور* / عبدالعلی ادیب الملك. تهران : خوارزمی.
- *راهنمای تحقیقات ایرانی*. تهران : مرکز بررسی ومعرفی فرهنگ ایران.
- *رشید الدین فضل الله : (مجموعهء چند مقاله)*. تهران : کتابخانهء مرکزی و مرکز اسناد دانشگاه تهران.
- سرگذشت محمد حسن خان ملك الحکماء به قلم خود او. فرهنگ *ایران زمین*، ٤٨-١١٨.
- *سواد و بیاض*. جلد ٢. تهران : کتابفروشی دهخدا.
- مرگ تقی زاده نه کاری است خرد. در *یادنامهء تقی زاده*. تهران : انجمن آثار ملی، ٥٦-١٤٠.
- *مقالات تقی زاده*. جلد ١ : تحقیقات و نوشته های تاریخی. تهران : [شکوفان].

۱۳۵۰/۱۹۷۱-۲

- *انیس الناس : تألیف سال ۸۳۰ هجری* / شجاع. تهران : بنگاه ترجمه و نشر کتاب.
- *مقالات تقی زاده*. جلد ۲ : شرقشناسیها ، سرگذشتها ، کتابها. تهران : [شکوفان].
- *تاریخ عالم آرای عباسی* / اسکندر بیك منشی. ۲ جلد. چاپ ۲. تهران : امیرکبیر ؛ اصفهان : کتابفروشی تأیید.
- تقویم و پنجهء کاشان. *فرهنگ ایران زمین*، ۵۶-۱۳۸.
- *دیوان کهنهء حافظ*. چاپ ۲. تهران : امیرکبیر.
- *ذخیرهء خوارزمشاهی* / اسماعیل بن حسین جرجانی. جلد ۲. باهمکاری محمد تقی دانش پژوه. تهران : دانشگاه تهران.
- *روزنامهء خاطرات اعتمادالسلطنه*. چاپ ۲. تهران : امیرکبیر.
- سفرنامهء طالب اف. در *نامهء مینوی*. تهران : [بی نا]، ۴۷-۳۷.
- قسمت اضافی تحفة الملوك / سید حسن تقی زاده. *فرهنگ ایران زمین*، ۳۷-۱۳۰.
- *مجموعه خطابه های تحقیقی دربارهء رشید الدین فضل الله همدانی*. تهران : دانشکدهء ادبیات و علوم انسانی دانشگاه تهران.
- منتخباتی از آثار عبید زاکانی : از روی نسخهء خطی مورخ ۸۶۸ هجری. *فرهنگ ایران زمین*، ۸۵-۱.
- *نامهء مینوی : مجموعهء سی و هشت گفتار در ادب و فرهنگ ایرانی به پاس پنجاه سال تحقیقات و مطالعات مجتبی مینوی*. با همکاری حبیب یغمایی، محمد روشن. تهران : [بی نا].
- *نوادر التبادر لتحفة البهادر* / شمس الدین محمد دنیسری. با

همکاری محمد تقی دانش پژوه. تهران : بنیاد فرهنگ ایران.

- *وقفنامهء ربع رشیدی = الوقفیة الرشدیة*[چاپ عکسی] / رشید الدین فضل الله همدانی. با همکاری مجتبی مینوی. تهران : انجمن آثار ملی.
- *یادداشتهای قزوینی*. جلد ۳. چاپ ۲. تهران : دانشگاه تهران.

۱۳۵۱/۱۹۷۲-۳

- *آثاردرویش محمد طبسی*. با همکاری محمد تقی دانش پژوه. تهران : خانقاه نعمة اللهی.
- *خاطرات و اسناد ظهیرالدوله*. جلد ۱. تهران : سازمان کتابهای جیبی.
- *روزنامهء اخبار مشروطیت و انقلاب ایران* / حاجی میرزا سید احمد تفرشی. تهران : امیرکبیر.
- *مقالات تقی زاده*. جلد ۳ : زبان و فرهنگ - تعلیم و تربیت. تهران : [شکوفان].

۱۳۵۲/۱۹۷۳-٤

- ترتیب القاب [چاپ عکسی] / محمود خان ملك الشعراء صبا. فرهنگ *ایران زمین*، ۸۸-۶۲.
- تشخیص و ترقیم القاب [چاپ عکسی]. فرهنگ *ایران زمین*، ۶۱-٤۹.
- سفرنامهء تلگرافچی فرنگی. باهمکاری عباس سایبانی. فرهنگ *ایران زمین*، ۲۶۰-۱۸۳.
- *صیدنه* / ابوریحان بیرونی. ترجمه ابوبکر بن علی بن عثمان

کاشانی. با همکاری منوچهر ستوده. جلد ۱. تهران : شورای عالی فرهنگ و هنر.

- *فهرست کتابهای خطی کتابخانهء ملی ملك، وابسته به آستان قدس*. با همکاری محمد تقی دانش پژوه، محمد باقر حجتی، احمد منزوی. جلد ۱ : کتابهای عربی و ترکی. تهران : کتابخانه.

۱۳۵۳/۱۹۷٤-۵

- *بیاض تاج الدین احمد وزیر : (۸۷۲ هجری)*. باهمکاری مرتضی تیموری. اصفهان : دانشگاه اصفهان.
- جامع جعفری : *تاریخ یزد در دوران نادری، زندی و عصر فتحعلیشاه* / محمد جعفر بن محمد حسین نائینی متخلص به طرب. تهران : انجمن آثار ملی.
- خوابگزاری امام فخر رازی. در جشن *نامهء محمد پروین گنابادی*. تهران : توس، ۵۸-٤۷.
- فرائد الفوائد در احوال مدارس و مساجد. در عامری *نامه*. تهران : یغما، ۸۳-۱۷۲.
- فرامین میرزا رضا علی نایب الوزاره. فرهنگ *ایران زمین*، ٤٤-۱۲۳.
- کتب درسی قدیم / میرزا طاهر تنکابنی. فرهنگ *ایران زمین*، ۸۲-۳۹.
- *مقالات تقی زاده*. جلد ٤ : جوهر تاریخ و مباحث اجتماعی و مدنی بانضمام بازیافته ها در زمینه های ادب تاریخ. تهران : شکوفان.
- *نامه های قزوینی به تقی زاده : ۱۹۳۹-۱۹۱۲ : یادگارنمای دوستی و همکاری دو دانشمند طراز اول ایران*. تهران : جاویدان.

- وصایای سیف الدین باخزری برای سید شمس الدین محمد بن حسن بن علی حسینی. فرهنگ *ایران زمین*، ۲۳-۳۱۶.

۱۳۵۴/۱۹۷۵-۶

- *ابونصر فارابی : (مجموعه‌ء بحث و تحقیق درباره‌ء ابونصر فارابی)*. تهران : کتابخانه مرکزی و مرکز اسناد دانشگاه تهران.
- *بیاض سفر : یادداشت های سفر در زمینه‌ء ایرانشناسی، کتابشناسی، و نسخه شناسی*. تهران : توس.
- *التحبیر فی علم التعبیر* / فخرالدین محمد بن عمر رازی. تهران : بنیاد فرهنگ ایران.
- ترغیب المتعلمین [چاپ عکسی] / محرم بن محمد بن یزید القسطمونی. فرهنگ *ایران زمین*، ۷۸-۴۱.
- عمدة الکتاب و عدة ذوی الالباب : فیه صفة الخط و الارقام و المداد و اللیق و البحر و الاصباغ و آلة التجلید [چاپ عکسی] / معز ابن بادیس تمیمی. فرهنگ *ایران زمین*، ۱۹۱-۷۹.
- صورت انتظامات باغ و خلوت ناصری در سال ۱۲۹۸ قمری [چاپ عکسی]. فرهنگ *ایران زمین*، ۲۱۰-۱۹۳.
- *فهرست کتابهای خطی کتابخانه‌ء ملی ملك، وابسته به آستان قدس رضوی*. با همکاری محمد تقی دانش پژوه، محمد باقر حجتی، احمد منزوی. جلد ۲ : کتابهای فارسی از آداب جنگ تا ذخیره‌ء خوارزمشاهی. تهران : کتابخانه.
- مجموعه‌ء کمینه : *مقاله هایی در نسخه شناسی و کتابشناسی*. تهران : فرهنگ ایران زمین.
- *مقالات تقی زاده*. جلد ۱ : تحقیقات و نوشته های تاریخی. چاپ ۲. تهران : شکوفان.

- *نامه های ادوارد براون به سید حسن تقی زاده*. با همکاری عباس زریاب. تهران : کتابهای جیبی.
- وقفیهء کججی [چاپ عکسی] / ابواب البر شیخ غیاث الدین محمد کججی. *فرهنگ ایران زمین*، ۳۸-۱.
- *یادداشتهای قزوینی*. جلد ۱۰. تهران : دانشگاه تهران.
- *یادگارهای یزد : معرفی ابنیهء تاریخی و آثار باستانی شهر یزد*. جلد ۲ و ضمیمهء جلد ۲. تهران : انجمن آثار ملی.

۱۳۵۵/۱۹۷۶-۷

- *رصد خانهء مراغه* [چاپ عکسی] / علیقلی میرزا اعتضاد السلطنه. تهران : کتابخانه سرکزی و مرکز اسناد دانشگاه تهران.
- *شاهنامه از خطی تا چاپی*. تهران : مجلهء هنر و مردم.
- فوائدی از ترجمهء فارسی تنبیه الغافلین. در *همائی نامه*. تهران : انجمن استادان زبان و ادبیات فارسی، ۴۲-۱۳۵.
- *فهرست مقالات فارسی در زمینهء تحقیقات ایرانی*. جلد ۳ : ۱۳۴۶-۱۳۵۰. تهران : سازمان کتابهای جیبی.
- قیمت اجناس در سفرنامهء ناصر خسرو. در *یادنامهء ناصر خسرو*. مشهد : دانشگاه فردوسی، ۷۰-۵۹.
- *کاوه : با مقدمه و فهرست مندرجات*. با همکاری جعفر صمیمی، کاوس جهانداری. تهران : توزیع امیرکبیر.
- *کتابشناسی فردوسی : فهرست آثار و تحقیقات دربارهء فردوسی و شاهنامه*. چاپ ۲. تهران : انجمن آثار ملی.
- *المختارات من الرسائل : مجموعهء منشأت و فرامین و احکام دیوانی و شرعی و عرفی از قرون پنجم و ششم و هفتم هجری از روی نسخهء کتابخانهء وزیری (یزد)*. تهران : انجمن آثار ملی.

- *مقالات تقی زاده*. جلد ۵ : تاریخ، اجتماع، سیاست : بانضمام تاریخ مختصر مجلس ملی ایران. تهران : شکوفان.
- موزونان. در *ارمغانی برای زرین کوب*. [لرستان] : اداره کل فرهنگ و هنر لرستان، ۸-۲٤.
- *میرزا تقی خان امیرکبیر* / عباس اقبال. چاپ ۲. تهران : توس.

۱۳۵٦/۱۹۷۷-۸

- اطلاعات کتابداری و نسخه شناسی در تذکرهء نصرآبادی. در *جشن نامهء استاد مدرس رضوی*. تهران : انجمن استادان زبان و ادبیات فارسی، ۳۳-٤۳.
- *انیس الناس : تألیف سال ۸۳۰ هجری* / شجاع. چاپ ۲. تهران : بنگاه ترجمه و نشر کتاب.
- *پانزده گفتار دربارهء مجتبی مینوی*. تهران : کتابخانه مرکزی و مرکز اسناد دانشگاه تهران.
- *تاریخ کاشان* / عبدالرحیم کلانتر ضرابی (سهیل کاشانی). بانضمام یادداشتهایی از الهیار صالح. چاپ ۳. تهران : فرهنگ ایران زمین : امیرکبیر.
- راپورت مسافرت سال ۱۳۰۸ قمری از شیراز به فسا و دارابجرد و جهرم و خفر و کوار / محمد حسن مهندس قاجار. *فرهنگ ایران زمین*، ۹٦-٤۵۹.
- رساله در معنی شمشیر و قلم : (مناظرة بین السیف و القلم) / ابو صاعد محمد بن ابی الفتوح الیعقوبی الطوسی. در *یادگارنامهء حبیب یغمایی*. تهران : توس، ۲۷-۵٤.
- *روزنامهء خاطرات اعتمادالسلطنه*. چاپ ۳. تهران : امیرکبیر.
- *فهرست مقالات ایرانشناسی در زبان عربی : فهرست انتخابی*.

تهران : انجمن کتاب.

- مختصر جغرافیای کاشان / عبدالحسین سپهر. *فرهنگ ایران زمین*، ۵۸-۴۳۰.
- منتخب الزمان در بیان تیراندازی /محمد زمان مشهور به چراغ بیك. در *یادنامهء شادروان سپهبد فرج الله آق اولی، رئیس پیشین هیئت مدیرهء انجمن آثار ملی*. تهران : انجمن آثار ملی، ٤٤-۱۲۱.
- منتخباتی از سه شاعر شیعی قرن هشتم : (نصرة علوی رازی، حمزهء کوچك ورامینی، شهاب سمنانی). در *جشن نامهء هانری کربن*. مونترال، کانادا : دانشگاه مك گیل ؛ تهران : مؤسسهء مطالعات اسلامی با همکاری دانشگاه تهران و انجمن شاهنشاهی فلسفهء ایران، ۶۹-۱۵۰.
- *مقالات تقی زاده*. جلد ٦ : تحقیقات ایرانی (به زبانهای خارجی) ؛ ۷ : نوشته های سیاسی (به زبانهای خارجی) ؛ ۹ : بانضمام از پرویز تا چنگیز - مانی و دین او. تهران : شکوفان.
- *نامه های قزوینی به تقی زاده : ۱۹۱۲-۱۹۳۹ : یادگارنمای دوستی و همکاری دو دانشمند طراز اول ایران*. چاپ ۲. تهران : جاویدان.
- *وقفنامهء ربع رشیدی = الوقفیة الرشدیة* / رشید الدین فضل الله همدانی. با همکاری مجتبی مینوی، عبدالعلی کارنگ. تهران : انجمن آثار ملی.
- *یادگارنامهء حبیب یغمایی : به پاس پنجاه سال نگاهبانی از ادب فارسی و به مناسبت سی امین سال انتشار مجله یغما*. با همکاری غلامحسین یوسفی، محمد ابراهیم باستانی پاریزی. تهران : فرهنگ ایران زمین : توس.

۱۳۵۷/۱۹۷۸-۹

- اسنادی از علما از اوراق "رکورد آفیس" انگلیس [چاپ عکسی]. *فرهنگ ایران زمین*، ٦٤-٤٥٧.
- بیاضی از مکاتب عصر صفوی [چاپ عکسی]. *فرهنگ ایران زمین*، ۳۳٦-۱۷۹.
- *تاریخ جدید یزد* / احمد بن حسین بن علی کاتب. چاپ ۲. تهران : فرهنگ ایران زمین : امیرکبیر.
- تفریظات توضیحات رشیدی [چاپ عکسی] / عباس اقبال. *فرهنگ ایران زمین*، ۸-٤۳.
- حجازیه (یا) سفرنامهء حج / ابوالاشرف محمد بن الحسین بن علی الحسینی الیزدی. در *محیط ادب*. تهران : مجلهء یغما.
- *خطای نامه : شرح مسافرت سید علی اکبر خطایی معاصر شاه اسماعیل صفوی در چین*. تهران : مرکز اسناد فرهنگی آسیا.
- سفرنامهء راه تبریز به طهران [چاپ عکسی] / میرزا علی سررشته دار. *فرهنگ ایران زمین*، ٤۷-۱۰۷.
- *آزادی و سیاست* / عبدالرحیم طالبوف تبریزی. تهران : سحر.
- شجرهء طیبه [چاپ عکسی] / حسین بن هبة الله رضوی کاشانی. *فرهنگ ایران زمین*، ٤٥۳-۳۳۷.
- *صحافی سنتی : (مجموعه پانزده گفتار و کتابشناسی دربارهء وراقی، صحافی، وصالی، مجلدگری از یادگارهای هنر ایرانی و اسلامی)*. تهران : کتابخانهء مرکزی و مرکز اسناد دانشگاه تهران.
- فایدهء زیارت : مباحثات علامهء حلی و رشیدالدین فضل الله همدانی [چاپ عکسی] / رشیدالدین فضل الله همدانی. *فرهنگ ایران زمین*، ۹۳-۷۳.

- قلعهء کرفتو [چاپ عکسی] / عبد المجید ملك الکلامی. فرهنگ *ایران زمین*، ۷۲-۴۸.
- قواعد دفاتر و حساب [چاپ عکسی] / سلمان فراهانی (بیانی). فرهنگ *ایران زمین*، ۷۷-۱۴۹.
- *محیط ادب : مجموعهء سی گفتار به پاس پنجاه سال تحقیقات و مطالعات سید محمد محیط طباطبایی*. با همکاری حبیب یغمایی، سید جعفر شهیدی، محمد ابراهیم باستانی پاریزی. تهران : مجلهء یغما.
- معرفی کتابهای درسی قدیم [چاپ عکسی] / میرزا فضلعلی آقا تبریزی؟ فرهنگ *ایران زمین*، ۴۱-۱.
- *مقالات تقی زاده*. جلد ۱۰ : گاه شماری در ایران قدیم : تجدید چاپ از روی چاپ ۱۳۱۶ شمسی به انضمام اصلاحات به خط مؤلف. تهران : شکوفان.
- وقفنامه مدرسهء سلطانی کاشان [چاپ عکسی]. فرهنگ *ایران زمین*، ۱۰۷-۹۵.

۱۳۵۸/۱۹۷۹-۸۰

- *اوراد الاحباب و فصوص الاداب* / ابوالمفاخر یحیی باخرزی. ۲ جلد. تهران : فرهنگ ایران زمین : سازمان کتاب.
- چراغان : جغرافیای قصبهء بیدگل [چاپ عکسی] / محمد رضا بن جعفر وصاف. فرهنگ *ایران زمین*، ۱۶۳-۱.
- سواد وقفنامه و تقسیم نامهء آب شاه [چاپ عکسی]. فرهنگ *ایران زمین*، [۱۴-۱].
- *صیدنه* / ابوریحان بیرونی. ترجمه ابوبکر بن علی بن عثمان کاشانی. ۲ جلد. چاپ ۲. با همکاری منوچهر ستوده. تهران :

سازمان ملی خدمات اجتماعی.
- فتوت نامهء آهنگران. در *فرخنده پیام*. مشهد : دانشگاه مشهد، ۹-۵۳.
- *فردوس المرشدیة فی اسرار الصمدیه : به انضمام روایت ملخص آن موسوم به انوار المرشدیة فی اسرار الصمدیة* / محمود بن عثمان. چاپ ۲. تهران : انجمن آثار ملی.
- مجموعهء چاپی اسناد عصر فتحعلی شاه / [از اسناد سید حسن تقی زاده]. *فرهنگ ایران زمین*، [۲۹-۱].
- *مصدق و مسائل حقوق و سیاست : مجموعهء ۹ مقاله و رساله از محمد مصدق*. تهران : زمینه.
- *مقالات تقی زاده*. جلد ۸ : نوشته های چاپ نشده (به زبانهای خارجه). تهران : شکوفان.
- مکتوب مسیو شوستر خزانه دار کل ایران بعنوان روزنامهء طایمس راجع بمناسبات دولت ایران با دولتین روس و انگلیس [چاپ عکسی]. *فرهنگ ایران زمین*، [۱۵ صفحه].
- *نامه های سیاسی دهخدا در موضوع مبارزه با محمد علی شاه، نشر صور اسرافیل در اروپا، انتخابات مجلس دوم، راهسازی شوسهء خراسان*. تهران : روزبهان.
- یعقوبی و نسطوری و ملکائی [چاپ عکسی] / محمد قزوینی. *فرهنگ ایران زمین*، [۷۹-۱۶۵].

۱۳۵۹/۱۹۸۰-۱

- *اوراق تازه یاب مشروطیت مربوط به سالهای ۱۳۲۵-۱۳۳۰ قمری*. تهران : جاویدان.
- *تقریرات مصدق در زندان دربارهء حوادث زندگی خویش* /

یادداشت شده توسط جلیل بزرگمهر. تهران : فرهنگ ایران زمین : سازمان کتاب.

- *دو رسالهء عرفانی در عشق* / احمد غزالی، سف الدین باخرزی. تهران : کتابفروشی منوچهری.
- *دیوان کهنهء حافظ : از روی نسخه خطی نزدیك به زمان شاعر.* [ویرایش ۲]. تهران : امیرکبیر.
- *مبارزه با محمد علی شاه : اسنادی از فعالیتهای آزادیخواهان ایران در اروپا و استانبول در سالهای ۱۳۲۶-۱۳۲۸ قمری.* تهران : فرهنگ ایران زمین : سازمان کتاب.

۱۳۶۰/۱۹۸۱-۲

- *سه رساله در تصوف : لوامع و لوایح در شرح قصیدهء خمریهء ابن فارض و در بیان معارف و معانی عرفانی، بانضمام شرح رباعیات در وحدت وجود* / عبدالرحمان جامی. تهران : فرهنگ ایران زمین : کتابفروشی منوچهری.
- *کارنامه و مادة الحیوة : متن دو رساله در آشپزی از دورهء صفوی : عصر سلطنت شاه اسماعیل اول و شاه عباس اول.* تهران : سروش.

۱۳۶۱/۱۹۸۲-۳

- اشعار به لهجه های محلی [چاپ عکسی]. *فرهنگ ایران زمین*، ۹۵-۳۸۲.
- چند لغت و ترکیب و تعبیر و اصطلاح کمیاب در تذکرهء نصرآبادی. در *آرام نامه*. تهران : انجمن استادان زبان و ادبیات

فارسی، ٥٤-٢٤٣.

- *خاطرات و اسناد مستشارالدوله‌ء صادق*. مجموعه‌ء ۱ : یادداشتهای تاریخی و اسناد سیاسی. تهران : فردوسی.
- *دو رساله‌ء عرفانی در عشق* / احمد غزالی، سف الدین باخرزی. چاپ ۲. تهران : کتابفروشی منوچهری.
- *دیوان کهنه‌ء حافظ : از روی نسخه خطی نزدیك به زمان شاعر*. چاپ ۳. تهران : امیرکبیر.
- سه فرمان و یك حکم مربوط به یزد. *فرهنگ ایران زمین*، ٤٠٣-٣٩٦.
- صحافی سنتی در ماوراء النهر. *فرهنگ ایران زمین*، ٩-٤٠٦.
- *فهرست کتابهای خطی کتابخانه‌ء ملی ملك، وابسته به آستان قدس*. با همکاری محمد تقی دانش پژوه، محمد باقر حجتی، احمد منزوی. جلد ۱ : کتابهای عربی و ترکی. چاپ ۳. تهران : کتابخانه.
- *فهرست کتابهای خطی کتابخانه‌ء ملی ملك، وابسته به آستان قدس*. با همکاری محمد تقی دانش پژوه، محمد باقر حجتی، احمد منزوی. جلد ۳، بخش ۱ : کتابهای فارسی. تهران : کتابخانه.

Some remarks on the early history of photography in Iran. In *Qajar Iran*. Edinburgh : Edinburgh University Press, 261-90.

١٣٦٢/١٩٨٣-٤

- کنیه، لقب، نسبت عشایر و ذکر آنها در متون فارسی. در *ایلات* و

عشایر. تهران : آگاه، ۵۰-۲٤۰.

- *مناقب الصوفیه* / قطب الدین ابوالمظفر منصور بن اردشیر سنجی عبادی مروزی. با همکاری محمد تقی دانش پژوه. تهران : فرهنگ ایران زمین : کتابفروشی منوچهری.
- *خاطرات و اسناد مستشارالدوله‌ء صادق*. مجموعه‌ء ۲: اسناد مشروطه، ۱۳۲۵-۱۳۳۰. تهران : فردوسی.

۱۳٦۳/۱۹۸٤-۵

- اسناد گرفتاری محسن خان امین الدوله در جنگل. در *یادگارنامه [فخرائی]*. تهران : نشر نو، ۷۸-۳٦۱.
- *تذکره‌ء انجمن ناصری به همراه تذکره‌ء مجدیه*[چاپ عکسی] / میرزا ابراهیم خان مدایح نگار تفرشی. تهران : بابك.
- *چهل سال تاریخ ایران : المآثر و الآثار* / محمد حسن خان اعتماد السلطنه. تهران : اساطیر.
- *خاطرات و اسناد ناصر دفتر روایی : (انقلاب مشروطیت - نهضت جنگل - دوره‌ء نا امنی خلخال)*. با همکاری بهزاد رزاقی. تهران : فردوسی.
- *دیوان وثوق* / وثوق الدوله. تهران : نشریات ما.
- *رجال عصر مشروطیت* / سید ابوالحسن علوی. با همکاری حبیب یغمایی. تهران : اساطیر.
- *سفرنامه‌ء عتبات، (سال ۱۲۸۷ ق)* / ناصرالدین شاه قاجار. تهران : فردوسی.
- *سفرنامه‌ء فرنگستان، "سفر دوم"* / ناصرالدین شاه قاجار. چاپ ۲. تهران : شرق.
- *فهرست نسخه های خطی کتابخانه ملی ملك، وابسته به آستان*

قدس. با همکاری محمد تقی دانش پژوه، محمد باقر حجتی، احمد منزوی. جلد ۵ : مجموعه ها و جنگ ها. تهران : کتابخانه.

- *گرگان نامه* / مسیح ذبیحی. تهران : فرهنگ ایران زمین : بابك.
- *مخابرات استراباد : گزارشهای حسینقلی مقصودلو وکیل الدوله.* با همکاری محمد رسول دریاگشت. ۲ جلد. تهران : نشر تاریخ ایران.
- *میرزا تقی خان امیر کبیر* / عباس اقبال آشتیانی. چاپ ۳، همراه با ۵ پیوست تازه. تهران : توس.
- *یادداشتهای قزوینی.* ۱۰ جلد در ۵ مجلد. چاپ ۳. تهران : علمی.

۱۳٦٤/۱۹۸۵-٦

- *تاریخ ایران در دوره‌ء قاجار* / کلمنت مارکام ؛ ترجمه از میرزا رحیم فرزانه. تهران : نشر فرهنگ ایران.
- *خاطرات و تألمات دکتر محمد مصدق* / محمد مصدق. تهران : علمی.
- سخنی مقدماتی در باب طرح کتابشناسی سعدی و حافظ. در *حافظ شناسی*. جلد ۱. تهران : گنج کتاب، ۲٦-۱۱۳.
- سوگ آل احمد. در *یادنامه جلال آل احمد*. تهران : پاسارگاد، ٦۲-۱۵۹.
- *فهرست نسخه های خطی کتابخانه ملی ملك، وابسته به آستان قدس*. با همکاری محمد تقی دانش پژوه، محمد باقر حجتی، احمد منزوی. جلد ٤ : نسخه های فارسی از کلیات شوقی تا یوسف و زلیخا. تهران : کتابخانه.
- *ناموارهء دکتر محمود افشار*. با همکاری کریم اصفهانیان. جلد ۱

: دربرگیرنده‌ء سی و چهار مقاله. تهران : موقوفات دکتر محمود افشار.

۱۳۶۵/۱۹۸۶-۷

- امیرنامه. *فرهنگ ایران زمین*، ۷۰-۲۵۳.
- *خاطرات و تألمات دکتر محمد مصدق* / محمد مصدق. چاپ ۲. تهران : علمی و چاپ افست در لندن.
- *رجال وزارت خارجه در عصر ناصری و مظفری* / میرزا مهدی خان ممتحن الدوله‌ء شقاقی، میرزا هاشم خان. تهران : اساطیر.
- مزار حافظ در سفرنامه‌ء کمپفر. در *حافظ شناسی*. جلد ۳. تهران : پاژنگ، ۴۰-۲۲۹.
- *ناموارهء دکتر محمود افشار*. با همکاری کریم اصفهانیان. جلد ۲ : دربرگیرنده‌ء سی مقاله. تهران : موقوفات دکتر محمود افشار.

۱۳۶۶/۱۹۸۷-۸

- ترجمه منتخب کتاب مرآة الزمان / محمد سعید الشریف القاضی القمی. *فرهنگ ایران زمین*، ۸۷-۱۴۶.
- *جامع التواریخ حسنی : بخش تیموریان پس از تیمور* / تاج الدین حسن بن شهاب یزدی. با همکاری حسین مدرسی طباطبایی. کراچی : مؤسسه‌ء تحقیقات علوم آسیای میانه و غربی.
- *دیوان کهنه‌ء حافظ : از روی نسخه خطی نزدیك به زمان شاعر*. چاپ ۴. تهران : امیرکبیر.
- زیارتگه رندان جهان. در *حافظ شناسی*. جلد ۷. تهران : پاژنگ، ۸۱-۱۰۹.

- *فهرست نسخه های خطی کتابخانه ملی ملك، وابسته به آستان قدس.* با همکاری محمد تقی دانش پژوه، محمد باقر حجتی، احمد منزوی. جلد ٦ : مجموعه ها و جنگ ها. تهران : کتابخانه.
- مقاله شناسی برای حافظ شناسی. در *حافظ شناسی.* جلد ٥. تهران : پاژنگ، ٢٧-٢٠٥.
- *منتخب التواریخ* / میرزا ابراهیم شیبانی (صدیق الممالك). تهران : علمی.
- *ناموارهٔ دکتر محمود افشار.* با همکاری کریم اصفهانیان. جلد ٣ : دربرگیرندهٔ بیست و چهار مقاله. تهران : موقوفات دکتر محمود افشار.

١٣٦٧/١٩٨٨-٩

- *آثار و احیاء : متن فارسی دربارهٔ فن کشاورزی* / خواجه رشید الدین فضل الله همدانی. با همکاری منوچهر ستوده. تهران : مؤسسه مطالعات اسلامی دانشگاه مك گیل با همکاری دانشگاه تهران.
- *تاریخ ایران در دورهٔ قاجار* / کلمنت مارکام ؛ ترجمه از میرزا رحیم فرزانه. چاپ ٢. تهران : نشر فرهنگ ایران.
- چند نکته. در *حافظ شناسی.* جلد ١٠. تهران : پاژنگ، ٦٦-٧٩.
- *چهل سال تاریخ ایران : ضمائم و فهرستهای چندگانه.* تهران : اساطیر.
- *چهل سال تاریخ ایران : یادداشتها و تعلیقات* / حسین محبوبی اردکانی. تهران : اساطیر.
- *خاطرات و اسناد ظهیرالدوله.* چاپ ٢. تهران : زرین.

- *خاطرات و اسناد مستشارالدوله صادق*. مجموعهء ۳ : راپرتهای پلیس مخفی از شایعات شهری، (سالهای ۱۳۳۳ و ۱۳۳۵ قمری). تهران : طلایه.
- *قندیه و سمریه : دو رساله در تاریخ مزرات و جغرافیای سمرقند* : قندیه / محمد بن عبدالجلیل سمرقندی ؛ سمریه / ابوطاهر خواجه سمرقندی. تهران : مؤسسه فرهنگی جهانگیری.
- کتابشناسی کتابهای فارسی چاپ شده در ایران دربارهء گویشهای ایرانی. در *مطالعات ایرانی-آریایی تقدیمی به ژیلبر لازار*. پاریس : انجمن پیشبرد مطالعات ایرانی، ۲۷-۳.
- *ناموارهء دکتر محمود افشار*. با همکاری کریم اصفهانیان. جلد ٤ : دربرگیرندهء چهل و چهار مقاله. تهران : موقوفات دکتر محمود افشار.

۱۳٦۸/۱۹۸۹-۹۰

- بیاض ۷۸۸-۷۵٤ و بعد. در *عابدی نامه*. دهلی : گروه زبان و ادبیات فارسی دانشگاه دهلی و انجمن فارسی، ۱۱٦-۲۰.
- جغرافیا و تاریخ بلوچستان : تألیف سال ۱۲۸۹ قمری. باهمکاری خالقداد آریا. *فرهنگ ایران زمین*، ۲۰۲-۷۸.
- جغرافیای بلوچستان : نوشتهء سال ۱۳۰٤ قمری، ظاهرا از مهدی. *فرهنگ ایران زمین*، ۲۷۹-۹۳.
- *خلاصة السیر : تاریخ روزگار شاه صفی صفوی* / محمد معصوم بن خواجگی اصفهانی. تهران : علمی.
- *زبان فارسی در آذربایجان*. جلد ۱. تهران : موقوفات دکتر محمود افشار.
- *زندگی طوفانی : خاطرات سید حسن تقی زاده*. تهران : علمی؛ و

چاپ افست در لوس آنجلس.

- *قباله‌ء تاریخ : نمونه هایی از اعلامیه ها ، بیانیه ها ، شب نامه ها ، روزنامه ها و فوق العاده های دولتی، حزبی، سیاسی، بازرگانی، فرهنگی در دوره‌ء مشروطیت تا پایان سلطنت احمد شاه.* تهران : طلایه.
- غرائب روزگار و عجائب آثار. فرهنگ *ایران زمین*، ۷۲-۱۵۵.
- *مسالك و ممالك : ترجمه‌ء فارسی قرن پنجم-ششم هجری /* ابواسحق ابراهیم اصطخری. چاپ ۳، با الحاقات جدید. تهران : شرکت انتشارات علمی و فرهنگی.
- *ناموارهء* دکتر محمود *افشار*. با همکاری کریم اصفهانیان. جلد ۵ : دربرگیرنده‌ء سی و شش مقاله. تهران : موقوفات دکتر محمود افشار.
- *واژه نامه‌ء* یزدی. به کوشش محمد رضا محمدی. تهران : فرهنگ ایران زمین : کتابفروشی تاریخ.

۱۳۶۹/۱۹۹۰-۱

- *فهرست مقالات فارسی در زمینه‌ء تحقیقات ایرانی.* جلد ٤ : ۱۳۵۱-۱۳٦۰. تهران : شرکت انتشارات علمی و فرهنگی.
- *فهرست نسخه های خطی کتابخانه ملی ملك، وابسته به آستان* قدس. با همکاری محمد تقی دانش پژوه، محمد باقر حجتی، احمد منزوی. جلد ۸-۷ : مجموعه ها و جنگ ها. تهران : کتابخانه.
- نامه‌ء کاشانی به مصدق از نگاه سندشناسی. در *هفتاد مقاله*. جلد ۱. تهران : اساطیر، ۸۰-۲۷۰.
- *هفتاد مقاله : ارمغان فرهنگی به دکتر غلامحسین صدیقی.* جلد

۱. باهمکاری یحیی مهدوی. تهران : اساطیر.

۲-۱۹۹۱/ ۱۳۷۰

- امانت دادن کتاب و چند نکته و نمونهء تاریخی. در *یکی قطره باران*. تهران : [بی نا]، ٤٥-۲۳۵.
- *خاطرات و اسناد مستشارالدوله*. مجموعهء ٤ : مشروطیت در آذربایجان : تلگرافهای ۱۳۲۵-۱۳۲۹. تهران : طلایه.
- دوست سخنسرای ایراندوستمان. در *باغ بی برگی*. تهران : نشر ناشران، ۳-۹۲.
- زندگینامه و فهرستنامهء آثار حبیب یغمائی. در *یغمای سی و دوم*. تهران : انتشارات ایران، ٤۰-٦۳۳.
- شهرآشوب پیشه های ساختمانی. در *نامگانی استاد علی سامی*. جلد ۱. شیراز : نوید، ٦-۳۳۳.
- *عالم آرای شاه طهماسب : زندگی داستانی دومین پادشاه دورهء صفوی*. تهران : دنیای کتاب.
- *قانون قزوینی : انتقاد اوضاع اجتماعی ایران دورهء ناصری* / محمد شفیع قزوینی. تهران : طلایه.
- محمد بن محمود زنگی بخاری. در *قافله سالار سخن*، خانلری. تهران : نشر البرز، ٦٤-٤٧.
- *ناموارهء دکتر محمود افشار*. با همکاری کریم اصفهانیان. جلد ٦ : دربرگیرندهء سی مقاله. تهران : موقوفات دکتر محمود افشار.
- *یغمای سی و دوم : یادنامهء حبیب یغمایی*. با همکاری قدرت الله روشنی زعفرانلو. تهران : انتشارات ایران.

۱۳۷۱/۱۹۹۲-۳

- ابیات حافظ شیرازی در ظفرنامهء یزدی. در *حافظ شناسی*. جلد ۱۵. تهران : پاژنگ، ٦-۱۳٤.
- دو مطلب دربارهء زیارتگه رندان جهان. در *حافظ شناسی*. جلد ۱۵. تهران : پاژنگ، ۳۳-۱۲۹.
- *زبان فارسی در آذربایجان*. جلد ۲. تهران : موقوفات دکتر محمود افشار.
- *فهرست نسخه های خطی کتابخانه ملی ملك، وابسته به آستان قدس*. با همکاری محمد تقی دانش پژوه، محمد باقر حجتی، احمد منزوی. جلد ۹ : مجموعه ها و جنگ ها. تهران : کتابخانه.
- *گنجینهء عکسهای ایران : همراه تاریخچهء ورود عکاسی به ایران*. تهران : نشر فرهنگ ایران.
- *نامه های ادوارد براون به سید حسن تقی زاده*.چاپ ۲. با همکاری عباس زریاب. تهران : کتابهای جیبی.
- نهضت جنگل و استراباد و مازندران. در *گیلان نامه*. جلد ۳. رشت : طاعتی، ۱۵-۷.
- *هفتاد مقاله : ارمغان فرهنگی به دکتر غلامحسین صدیقی*. جلد ۲. باهمکاری یحیی مهدوی. تهران : اساطیر.
- *یزدنامه*. جلد ۱. تهران : فرهنگ ایران زمین.

Zīlū. *Iranian studies* 25, nos. 1-2: 31-6.

Le Taẕkera-ye Naṣrābādi. Ses données socio-économiques et culturelles. In *Etudes safavides*. Paris : Institut français de recherche en Iran, 1-12.

۱۳۷۲/۱۹۹۳-٤

- *خاطرات سردار اسعد بختیاری*، *جعفر قلی خان امیر بهادر*. تهران : اساطیر.
- *خطای نامه : شرح مشاهدات سید علی اکبر خطایی معاصر شاه اسماعیل صفوی در چین*. چاپ ۲. تهران : مرکز اسناد فرهنگی آسیا با همکاری مؤسسهء مطالعات و تحقیقات فرهنگی (پژوهشگاه).
- *ذیل تاریخ گزیده* / زین الدین بن حمدالله مستوفی. تهران : موقوفات دکتر محمود افشار.
- *زندگی طوفانی : خاطرات سید حسن تقی زاده*. چاپ ۲، برافزوده شده. تهران : علمی.
- *زنگی نامه : شش رساله و مقامه و مناظره* / محمد بن محمود بن محمد زنگی بخاری. تهران : توس.
- *فهرست نسخه های خطی کتابخانه ملی ملك، وابسته به آستان قدس رضوی*. با همکاری محمد تقی دانش پژوه، قدرت الله پیشنمازاده. جلد ۱ : فهرست ترتیبی شمارهء نسخه ها. تهران : کتابخانه.
- *کلیات آثار ادیب قاسمی کرمانی*. کرمان : مرکز کرمان شناسی.
- *ناموارهء دکتر محمود افشار*. با همکاری کریم اصفهانیان. جلد ۷ : دربرگیرندهء سی و دو مقاله. تهران : موقوفات دکتر محمود افشار.

۱۳۷۳/۱۹۹٤-٥

- رسالهء خط خلیل تبریزی. در *پند و سخن*. تهران : معین : انجمن

ایرانشناسی فرانسه در ایران، ۳۱-۳۰۹.

- *فهرستوارهء کتابخانهء مینوی : (خطی، عکسی، میکروفیلم، یادداشتها)*. با همکاری محمد تقی دانش پژوه. تهران : پژوهشگاه علوم انسانی و مطالعات فرهنگی.
- *گزارشها و نامه های دیوانی و نظامی امیرنظام گروسی دربارهء وقایع کردستان در سال ۱۲۹۷ هجری*. تهران : بنیاد موقوفات دکتر محمود افشار.
- *مقاله ها و رساله ها* / غلامرضا رشید یاسمی. با همکاری محمد رسول دریاگشت. تهران : موقوفات دکتر محمود افشار.
- *ممالك و مسالك* / ابواسحق ابراهیم اصطخری ؛ ترجمه محمد بن اسعد بن عبدالله تستری. تهران : موقوفات دکتر محمود افشار.
- *نامورهء دکتر محمود افشار*. با همکاری کریم اصفهانیان. جلد ۸ : دربرگیرندهء بیست و پنج مقاله. تهران : موقوفات دکتر محمود افشار.

۱۳۷٤/۱۹۹٥-٦

- *انیس الناس : تألیف سال ۸۳۰ هجری* / شجاع. چاپ ۳. تهران : شرکت انتشارات علمی و فرهنگی.
- *خاطرات و اسناد مستشارالدوله*. مجموعهء ۵ : گوشه هایی از سیاست داخلی ایران. تهران : طلایه.
- *روزنامهء خاطرات بصیرالملك شیبانی : ۱۳۰۱-۱۳۰۶ قمری، در روزگار پادشاهی ناصرالدین شاه قاجار*. با همکاری محمد رسول دریاگشت. تهران : دنیای کتاب.
- *روزنامهء خاطرات عین السلطنه*. جلد ۱ : روزگار پادشاهی ناصرالدین شاه. با همکاری مسعود سالور. تهران : اساطیر.

- *روزنامهء سفر خراسان به همراهی ناصرالدین شاه* (۱۳۰۰) / میرزا قهرمان امین لشکر. با همکاری محمد رسول دریاگشت. تهران : اساطیر.
- شهیدی در قلمرو زبان فارسی. در *نامهء شهیدی*. تهران : طرح نو، ۸–۵۵.
- عقول عشره. در سعی مشکور. تهران : مؤسسهء فرهنگی و انتشاراتی پایا، ۹–۵۵.
- فهرست کتابخانهء صدرالدین قونوی. در *یادنامهء دکتر عباس زریاب*. در *تحقیقات اسلامی*، ۱۰: شماره های ۲–۱، ۵۰۲–۴۷۷.
- *فهرست مقالات فارسی در زمینهء تحقیقات ایرانی*. جلد ۵ : ۱۳۶۱–۱۳۷۰. تهران : شرکت انتشارات علمی و فرهنگی.
- *گزیده در اخلاق و تصوف* / ابونصر طاهر بن محمد الخانقاهی. چاپ ۲. تهران : شرکت انتشارات علمی و فرهنگی.
- *یادگارهای یزد*. ۳ جلد. چاپ ۲. تهران : انجمن آثار و مفاخر فرهنگی : خانهء کتاب یزد.

Similar Farmans from the reign of Shah Safi. In *Safavid Persia*. London : I.B. Tauris, 285-304.

۱۳۷۵/۱۹۹۶-۷

- *بستان العقول فی ترجمان المنقول* / محمد بن محمود بن محمد زنگی بخاری. با همکاری محمد تقی دانش پژوه. تهران : پژوهشگاه علوم انسانی و مطالعات فرهنگی.

- *فهرست نسخه های خطی کتابخانه ملی ملك، وابسته به آستان قدس رضوی*. با همکاری محمد تقی دانش پژوه، قدرت الله پیشنمازززاده. جلد ۱۱ : فهرست الفبائی، مؤلفان، مصنفان، گردآورندگان. تهران : کتابخانه.
- فهرستواره، مجموعه، ناصری. *فرهنگ ایران زمین*، ۴۳-۱۳۳.
- *مجمل الحکمه : ترجمه گونه ای کهن از رسائل اخوان الصفا*. با همکاری محمد تقی دانش پژوه. تهران : پژوهشگاه علوم انسانی و مطالعات فرهنگی.
- *ناموارهء دکتر محمود افشار*. با همکاری کریم اصفهانیان. جلد ۹ : دربرگیرندهء چهل و یك مقاله. تهران : موقوفات دکتر محمود افشار.
- *نامه های دوستان* / گردآوری محمود افشار. تهران : موقوفات دکتر محمود افشار.
- *نامه های لندن از دوران سفارت تقی زاده در انگلستان*. تهران : نشر و پژوهش فرزان روز.
- نامه های نجومی سید جلال الدین طهرانی [چاپ عکسی]. *فرهنگ ایران زمین*، [۶۳۱-۵۶۴].

۱۳۷۶/۱۹۹۷-۸

- *روزنامهء خاطرات عین السلطنه*. جلد ۲ : روزگار پادشاهی مظفرالدین شاه. با همکاری مسعود سالور. تهران : اساطیر.
- *سخنواره : پنجاه و پنج گفتار پژوهشی به یاد دکتر پرویز ناتل خانلری*. باهمکاری هانس روبرت رویمر. تهران : توس.
- کاغذ و کتاب و نسخه در شعر اشرف. در درخت معرفت. تهران : سخن، ۸۴-۱۵۹.

۱۳۷۷/۱۹۹۸

- روزنامهء *خاطرات عین السلطنه*. جلد ۳ : روزگار پادشاهی محمد علی و انقلاب مشروطه. با همکاری مسعود سالور. تهران : اساطیر.

Iran and Iranian Studies

Essays in Honor of Iraj Afshar

Edited by Kambiz Eslami

ZAGROS
Princeton, New Jersey

Jacket illustration: binding for a *Būstān* of Sa'dī, copied in 1026/1617,
Art and History Trust Collection, courtesy of the Arthur M. Sackler Gallery,
Smithsonian Institution, Washington, DC

First edition 1998

Library of Congress Catalog Card Number 98-84316

Iran and Iranian studies : essays in honor of Iraj Afshar / edited by Kambiz Eslami.
p. cm.
English, French, and Persian.
Includes bibliographical references.
ISBN 0-966-34420-0
1. Iran—Civilizaton. I. Afshār, Īraj.
II. Eslami, Kambiz, 1956–
III. Title.
DS252.4.I67 1998
955.219—dc20
98-84316 CIP

ISBN 0-966-34420-0 (cloth : alk. paper)

Manufactured in the United States of America

Zagros Press
P.O. Box 1556
Princeton, NJ 08542-1556

The publication of this volume has been made possible by grants from The Program in Near Eastern Studies, Princeton University and the Yarshater Fund

CONTENTS

* The bibliography appears at the end of the volume

ILLUSTRATIONS

CONTRIBUTORS

Janet Afary, Purdue University, West Lafayette, Indiana

Sheila S. Blair, Richmond, New Hampshire

François de Blois, Royal Asiatic Society, London, England

Jerome W. Clinton, Princeton University, Princeton, New Jersey

Kambiz Eslami, Princeton University Library, Princeton, New Jersey

Willem Floor, World Bank, Washington, DC

C.-H. de Fouchécour, Paris, France

M. R. Ghanoonparvar, University of Texas at Austin, Austin, Texas

Ulrich W. Haarmann, Keil University, Keil, Germany

Gilbert Lazard, Paris, France

Rudi Matthee, University of Delaware, Newark, Delaware

Charles Melville, University of Cambridge, Cambridge, England

John R. Perry, University of Chicago, Chicago, Illinois

Angelo Michele Piemontese, Rome, Italy

B. W. Robinson, London, England

Geoffrey Roper, Cambridge University Library, Cambridge, England

Roger M. Savory, Toronto, Canada

Priscilla P. Soucek, New York University, New York, New York

Abolala Soudavar, Houston, Texas

Paul Sprachman, Rutgers University, New Brunswick, New Jersey

Faridun Vahman, University of Copenhagen, Copenhagen, Denmark

Jan Just Witkam, Leiden University Library, Leiden, The Netherlands

EDITOR'S NOTE

For over fifty years, Iraj Afshar has been writing and publishing on Iran. The sheer volume of his output (more than 130 books, 500 articles, and growing) is prodigious and its impact on current and future studies on Iran is indisputable. Sometimes as a bibliographer, sometimes as an editor or a publisher, but always as a resourceful scholar, he has made tremendous contributions in such fields as Persian manuscripts and bibliographies, Timurid, Safavid, and Qajar history, as well as local histories of Iran. He has been the editor of several important periodicals, one of which, *Farhang-i Irān zamīn*, is still active.[1] Most students of Iranian studies are indebted to his informative and illuminating work in one way or another.

The twenty-two essays gathered in this volume represent a sincere acknowledgment of the importance of Iraj Afshar's body of work, and a mark of respect for a truly remarkable scholar of Iranian studies. As some of the contributions are actually based on, or closely related to, specific projects carried out by Iraj Afshar,[2] they also attest to the wide-ranging and significant effect of his work. The scope of the essays reflects as diverse a scope as *Ustād*'s own interests and achievements, and ranges over such general rubrics as Iranian historiography (Melville), local history (de Blois), foreign relations (Piemontese, Matthee, Vahman, Floor, Savory), fine arts and cultural studies (Soucek, de Fouchécour, Eslami, Haarmann, Soudavar, Blair, Ghanoonparvar, Robinson, Witkam, Roper), as well as political, literary, and linguistic studies (Afary, Clinton, Lazard, Perry, Sprachman). Mainly because of this varied makeup, I found another form of presentation (one based on a more-or-less chronological order of the subject matters covered) to be more appropriate.

[1] Periodically, he was the editor, co-editor, or managing editor of *Mihr* (1331–2 Sh./1942–4), *Sukhan* (1332–6 Sh./1953–7), *Kitābhā-yi māh* (1334–40 Sh./1955–61), *Rāhnamā-yi kitāb* (1337–57 Sh./1958–78), *Nuskhah'hā-yi khaṭṭī* (1339–62 Sh./1960–83), *Īrānshināsī* (1349–50 Sh./1970–1), and *Āyandah* (1358–72 Sh./1979–94).

[2] I.e., essays by C. Melville, C.-H. de Fouchécour, U. Haarmann, M.R. Ghanoonparvar, R. Savory, and J. Afary.

The transliteration system used here for Persian and Arabic words is that of the Library of Congress.[3] Non-Roman place and proper names have in general been transliterated, with very few exceptions (e.g., Tehran for Tihrān; or Iraj Afshar for Īraj Afshār). Vernacular terms and honorific titles have also been transliterated according to the specific context in which they appear, so the reader will find *vaẕīr*, *waẕīr*, and *veẕir* appearing where the text refers to Persian, Arabic, and Turkish chief ministers, respectively. Throughout the book, an oblique stroke is used to separate the *Hijrī* date from its Christian equivalent. Where only a Christian date was available or known, corresponding *Hijrī* date(s) was/were supplied following the stroke.

I am deeply grateful to all the authors of the essays for their support and willingness in participating in this project. My thanks go also to Svat Soucek who translated the contributions by C.-H. de Fouchécour and Angelo Piemontese, and to Mark Farrell who made very helpful stylistic suggestions for some of the essays. I would also like to thank Ehsan Yarshater, Heath Lowry, Hossein Modarressi, Bernard O'Kane, Farhad Eslami, Yaḥyá Ẕukā', Mark Becker, and Heshmat Moayyad, whose assistance is acknowledged at appropriate points in the book. I am particularly thankful to Farhad who also compiled a bibliography of Iraj Afshar and was gracious enough to allow me to include only a selection of it here.[4] Karim Emami, Jochen Twele, and Fred Plank helped me to have access to certain resources, and Maryam Zandi kindly provided the photograph of Iraj Afshar. I am indebted to Jalal Matini who was extremely helpful in answering my questions about two very difficult Persian texts. Finally, for giving so willingly of her expertise to help design the format of the volume, I am very grateful to Marion Carty.

Kambiz Eslami
Princeton
March 1998

[3] For a full description of those schemes, see *ALA-LC romanization tables : transliteration schemes for non-Roman scripts*, Washington, 1997, pp. 10–9, 171–7. One minor deviation from the LC scheme for Persian transliteration is the interchangeable usage of *va* and *u* in certain titles and poetic citations.

[4] Considerations of space and balance forced me to limit the bibliography to titles published in book format and in monographic collections of articles, as well as those published in the journal *Farhang-i Īrān zamīn*.

Iran and Iranian Studies

Ḥamd Allāh Mustawfī's *Ẓafarnāmah* and the Historiography of the Late Ilkhanid Period

*Charles Melville**

NO STUDENT OF 14TH-CENTURY PERSIAN HISTORY CAN get far without resorting to the *Ẕayl-i Jāmi' al-tavārīkh-i Rashīdī*, a continuation of Rashīd al-Dīn Faẕl Allāh's "Compendium of chronicles" written by the Timurid historian Ḥāfiẓ-i Abrū (d. 833/1430).[1] Though perhaps best known for his contemporary works on Tīmūr and the reign of Shāhrukh, his patron, Ḥāfiẓ-i Abrū is also the essential source for the history of the turbulent period between the end of the Ilkhanate and Tīmūr's campaigns in Iran.[2] Indeed, Ḥāfiẓ-i Abrū is apparently the sole authority for a mass of information about the reign of the last Ilkhanid ruler, Abū Sa'īd Bahādur Khān (r. 717–36/1317–35), as well as subsequent events in western Iran.

In his critical review of Bayānī's first edition of the *Ẕayl-i Jāmi' al-tavārīkh*, Felix Tauer noted that Ḥāfiẓ-i Abrū's continuation of Rashīd al-Dīn's *Jāmi' al-tavārīkh* could be divided into three parts: (1) the reign of Öljeytü; (2) the reign of Abū Sa'īd, and (3) the years 735–95/1334–93. While his principal authority for the first part was considered to be Kāshānī's *Tārīkh-i Ūljāytū*, the sources for the reign of Abū Sa'īd and the later period were still unidentified.[3]

So what were Ḥāfiẓ-i Abrū's sources? Among Iraj Afshar's myriad services to the study of Persian history is his recent edition of the *Ẕayl-i Tārīkh-i guzīdah* of Zayn al-Dīn, son of Ḥamd Allāh Mustawfī Qazvīnī, based on two manuscript copies, one (MS 153, inv. no. 1647, pp. 469–513), dated 813/1411,

* I am very grateful to Kambiz Eslami for his care in editing this contribution and in particular for the additional bibliographical details and sources that he has supplied.

[1] French translation by Khānbābā Bayānī (Ḥāfiẓ-i Abrū 1936), followed by an edition of the Persian text (Ḥāfiẓ-i Abrū 1939), the inadequacy of which was comprehensively demonstrated by Felix Tauer 1952–5. Many years later, Bayānī published a revised edition of the text, see Ḥāfiẓ-i Abrū 1972.

[2] See also Ḥāfiẓ-i Abrū 1959.

[3] Tauer 1952–5, pt. 1, 40. The subtitle of the second edition of *Ẕayl-i Jāmi' al-tavārīkh-i Rashīdī* (Ḥāfiẓ-i Abrū 1972) misleadingly states that it covers the period 703–81 [1303–80].

in the Saint Petersburg State University Library, and one (MS 2402, pp. 239–86), undated, in Kitābkhānah-i Markazī va Markaz-i Asnād-i Dānishgāh-i Tihrān.[4] From this it becomes clear to those previously unaware of the fact, how greatly Ḥāfiẓ-i Abrū relied on this text in compiling the "third part" of his continuation of Rashīd al-Dīn's work.[5]

Zayn al-Dīn's chronicle covers the period from 742/1341–2 to 794/1391–2. In his introduction he writes that since his father, Ḥamd Allāh Mustawfī (d. ca. 750/1349), had brought the *Tārīkh-i guzīdah* down to the start of Malīk Ashraf's time, he now wished to carry on the story to Tīmūr's second Persian campaign.[6] This gives the misleading impression that Zayn al-Dīn's book is a continuation of the *Tārīkh-i guzīdah*, whereas it actually follows a separate work by Mustawfī. Although untitled, the work is referred to by Mustawfī himself as a continuation of his *Ẓafarnāmah*, and therefore it may appropriately be called "*Ẕayl-i Ẓafarnāmah*." In fact, in both the Saint Petersburg and Tehran manuscripts, this "*Ẕayl-i Ẓafarnāmah*" precedes Zayn al-Dīn's text.[7]

Ḥamd Allāh Mustawfī's continuation of his *Ẓafarnāmah* covers the events immediately surrounding the death of Abū Sa'īd in 736/1335, up to the murder

[4] Zayn al-Dīn Qazvīnī 1993. I am grateful to Iraj Afshar for a copy of this book. Previously, two Azerbaijani scholars, M. D. Kazymov and V. Z. Piriiev, had used the Saint Petersburg manuscript to publish a facsimile edition of the text of Zayn al-Dīn's *Ẕayl-i Tārikh-i guzīda* as well as Russian and Azeri translations of the work, see Zayn al-Dīn Qazvīnī 1990.

[5] As correctly observed by Afshar in his introduction (Zayn al-Dīn Qazvīnī 1993, 9–11), where attention is also drawn to similarities with Aharī's *Tārīkh-i Shaykh Uvays*.

[6] Zayn al-Dīn Qazvīnī 1993, 25.

[7] The text of Mustawfī's "*Ẕayl-i Ẓafarnāmah*" appears on pp. 433–68 of the same MS 153 in the Saint Petersburg State University Library, between *Tārīkh-i guzīdah* and *Ẕayl-i Tārīkh-i guzīdah*. It was first published in 1978 in facsimile by V. Z. Piriiev (1978), who eight years later published—with the cooperation of M. D. Kazymov—Russian and Azeri translations of it under the erroneous title *Zeil-e Tarikh-e gozide* (Mustawfī 1986). As mentioned before, the two scholars later collaborated further to publish Zayn al-Dīn's *Ẕayl*, see footnote no. 4. The Tehran manuscript, which seems to be later than the copy in Saint Petersburg, follows the same content format, except that at least its "*Ẕayl-i Ẓafarnāmah*" and *Ẕayl-i Tārīkh-i guzīdah* portions lack the author and title information found in the Saint Petersburg copy. The Iranian scholar, Rukn al-Dīn Humāyūnfarrukh, had in his possession an earlier (800/1397–8) manuscript of the *Tārīkh-i guzīdah* which seems to contain this "*Ẕayl-i Ẓafarnāmah*" as well (he published portions of the latter in his *Ḥāfiẓ-i kharābāṭī*, see Humāyūnfarrukh 1990–1, 1:49–53). The new owner of this manuscript is the Kitābkhānah-i Majlis-i Shūrā-yi Islāmī (this information from Dr. Humāyūnfarrukh). There is still another later manuscript copy of the *Ẕayl-i Tārīkh-i guzīdah*, dated 1024/1615, in a volume in the Institute of the Peoples of Asia, also in Saint Petersburg, which seems to have been copied from the MS 153, and which also follows a copy of *Tārīkh-i guzīdah*, see Storey and Bregel' 1972, 1:330 and 1983, 2:486. Reference to "*Ẕayl-i Ẓafarnāmah*" is made throughout the present article to both the facsimile edition and its Russian version, which was translated into English by Richard Sigee of Pembroke College at my request and before I was able to locate a copy of the facsimile edition. I am most grateful to him for his willingness to take on this task and the care with which he accomplished it.

of Ḥasan-i Kūchik and the end of the year 744/1344. He includes a considerable amount of autobiographical information, which, though of some interest, is not my concern here. It will readily be seen that Ḥāfiẓ-i Abrū also adopted Mustawfī's narrative, excluding the autobiographical material, for the years in question. Although I have not collated these texts in any detail, Ḥāfiẓ-i Abrū generally follows Mustawfī very closely and adds little new material. The Timurid historian also repeats many of the lines of poetry found in Mustawfī's "*Ẕayl-i Ẓafarnāmah*," which appear to have been composed by the author himself [8]; this shows that the borrowing is direct, rather than from a third source common to both works.[9]

If this largely disposes of the question of sources for the period after the death of Abū Sa'īd, there remains the problem of his reign itself, the "second part" of the continuation. Though other chronicles are known, such as Mustawfī's *Tārīkh-i guzīdah*, Shabānkārah'ī's *Majma' al-ansāb* and the later *Tārīkh-i Shaykh Uvays* by Aharī, these are all brief compilations and, while occasionally confirming Ḥāfiẓ-i Abrū in points of detail, clearly cannot have been the source for the large amount of information preserved only in the later work.[10] Of the three, Ḥāfiẓ-i Abrū is nearest to Mustawfī's *Tārīkh-i guzīdah*, completed in 730/1329–30. For many incidents in the first part of Abū Sa'īd's reign, Ḥāfiẓ-i Abrū seems to present an expanded version of Mustawfī's narrative; the relationship between the two, though not quite direct, is unmistakable.[11]

The *Tārīkh-i guzīdah* was written as a summary of another larger work, on which Mustawfī was then still engaged. This is his *Ẓafarnāmah*, eventually completed five years later in 735/1334–5, just before the end of Abu Sa'īd's reign.[12] Although Rieu, who cataloged the British Library manuscript, noted its possible importance,[13] a damning but misguided verdict on its value was passed by Blochet:

[8] See, for instance, Ḥāfiẓ-i Abrū 1972, 191, 192, 194, 195, 196, 197, 198, 203, 206, 210, 211, 212, 214, 216, 218; cf. Mustawfī 1978, 116, 117, 118, 120, 125, 127, 139, 141, 142, 145 / Mustawfī 1986, 93, 94, 95, 96, 98, 99, 104, 107, 123, 125, 127, 128, 131.

[9] Ḥāfiẓ-i Abrū's use of the work was also noted by the Azerbaijani editors (Mustawfī 1986, 85–6), who also draw attention to the fact that he concentrated only on the narrative of political events.

[10] See Jackson 1985, 376b–7a, for a recent summary of the sources available for Abū Sa'īd's reign.

[11] For example, in the treatment of the revolt of the *amīr*s in 719/1319, for which see my contribution to *Iran face à la domination mongole*, still awaiting publication in Damascus (Melville forthcoming).

[12] Mustawfī [1960] 1983, 3, 5. At the time of writing, Mustawfī had written just over 50,000 *bayt*s and was aiming for a total of 75,000.

[13] *Ẓafarnāmah*, British Library, London, MS Or. 2833, dated Ramaḍān 807/March 1405; cf. Rieu 1895, 172–4, echoed by Browne [1902–24] 1928, 3:95–8.

> This work has virtually no literary value...It is obvious that Ḥamd Allāh is vainly trying to reach to the level of his incomparable model [i.e., Firdawsī's *Shāhnāmah*]; and in the meantime he is making a fool of himself; like the versified chronicle [of *Tārīkh-i mubārak-i Ghāzānī*] by Shams al-Dīn Kāshānī, it too fell into oblivion the day after its composition, and had it not been for the Timurid renaissance which for a short period of time revived them, they would have disappeared altogether.[14]

The literary merits or otherwise of the *Ẓafarnāmah* are of course irrelevant to its status as a work of historiography, but although both Karl Jahn and John A. Boyle have since drawn attention to its potential value,[15] it has always been completely ignored by historians of the Mongols, if not by literary research.[16] However, on inspection it is immediately obvious that here is the work on which Ḥāfiẓ-i Abrū chiefly relied for the last two reigns of the Ilkhanate.

In summary, therefore, Ḥāfiẓ-i Abrū's *Ẕayl-i Jāmi' al-tavārīkh* is indebted first, to Ḥamd Allāh's *Ẓafarnāmah* to 735/1334–5; secondly, to his "*Ẕayl-i Ẓafarnāmah*" to 744/1343–4, and finally to Zayn al-Dīn's continuation of the latter for the period to 794/1391–2.

That Mustawfī's *Ẓafarnāmah* has not received the attention it deserves I attribute to various causes. First, it is written in verse, which may have branded it as primarily a literary composition; but anyway, historians seem to be generally uneasy about poetry and reluctant to believe that a verse chronicle can be "real history" because of the constraints imposed by the demands of rhyme and metre, as well as the need to achieve "poetic" effects. Secondly, most historians of the Mongols in Iran have been preoccupied with the early period of Ilkhanid rule, culminating in the reign of Ghāzān, and dazzled by Rashīd al-Dīn and all his works. For this period, Mustawfī's *Ẓafarnāmah* is indeed of very restricted (but still not totally negligible) value, for it is closely based on the *Jāmi' al-tavārīkh*, as is humbly acknowledged by Mustawfī himself. Thirdly, the ready availability of Kāshānī's *Tārikh-i Ūljāytū* and Ḥāfiẓ-i Abrū's *Ẕayl-i Jāmi' al-tavārīkh* have evidently seemed sufficient for the treatment of the later Ilkhanid period.

However, Mustawfī's *Ẓafarnāmah* has not been entirely neglected, for one of Boyle's last students, L. J. Ward, produced a translation of the part dealing with the Mongols in Iran as his doctoral dissertation in 1983.[17]

14 Blochet 1910, 107–8.

15 Jahn 1963, 200; Boyle 1974, 186. Neither can have looked at the work very closely themselves. M. Murtaẕavī (1991, 559–62) merely quotes the opinions of Blochet and Rieu.

16 Cf. Rastegar 1989, with references.

17 Ward 1983. I am grateful to Sandy Morton for this belated discovery on my part, and to David Morgan (external examiner of the thesis) and Paul Luft (who took over from Boyle as superviser), for helping me track it down.

Unfortunately, Boyle died before the work was completed and Ward himself died prematurely, without making his research more widely known. When I received the dissertation from Manchester in June 1995, I noticed that I was the first person to have consulted it, a sorry comment on the current state of activity in this area of research. Ward is mainly concerned with Mustawfī's own sources of information and is strangely unalert to the significance of the *Ẓafarnāmah* for the reign of Abū Sa'īd, though he does briefly note Ḥāfiẓ-i Abrū's use of the work.[18]

In the remainder of this essay I aim first to demonstrate the extent of Ḥāfiẓ-i Abrū's dependence on Mustawfī's *Ẓafarnāmah*, and secondly to assess the implications for the historiography of the late Ilkhanid period.

The simplest way to demonstrate Ḥāfiẓ-i Abrū's dependence on the *Ẓafarnāmah*, without comparing whole passages of both works, is to follow their section headings. For the reign of Abū Sa'īd, there is a complete correspondence between the two works, both in the order of chapter headings and in their wording, except for the first two or three years of the reign; *Ẕayl-i Jāmi' al-tavārīkh* contains long sections on events involving Prince Yasavur up to his death in 720/1320, not found in the *Ẓafarnāmah*.[19] For these episodes in Khurāsān, Ḥāfiẓ-i Abrū used a different source, Sayf ibn Muḥammad Haravī's *Tārīkh'nāmah-'i Harāt*.[20] Thereafter, and following the failure of the revolt against Chūpān in 719/1319, the differences are few and minor. For example:

Ẓafarnāmah	*Ẕayl-i Jāmi' al-tavārīkh*
Mukhālifat-i Timurtāsh-i Jūbān bi-Rūm va bi iṭā'at āmadan (fol. 729v)	Ẕikr-i mukhālifat-i Tīmūrtāsh ibn Chūpān dar Rūm va bāz bih iṭā'at āmadan (p. 160)
Vafāt-i Khvājah Tāj al-Dīn 'Alīshāh (fol. 730r)	Ẕikr-i vafāt-i Khvājah Tāj al-Dīn 'Alīshāh (p. 161)
Vizārat-i Malik Nuṣrat al-Dīn 'Ādil Nasavī (fol. 730r)	Ẕikr-i vizārat-i Malik Nuṣrat al-Dīn 'Ādil (p. 162)
Raftan-i Amīr Jūbān bi-Ulūs-i Bādshāh-i Uzbak (fol. 730v)	Ẕikr-i raftan-i Amīr Chūpān bi-Ulūs-i Uzbak (p. 163)

[18] Ibid., 1:40.

[19] Ḥāfiẓ-i Abrū 1972, culminating on 158–9.

[20] Haravī 1944; cf. the editor's comments, xvi–xix. Almost all the verses noted by Ward (1983, 1:51) as occurring in *Ẕayl-i Jāmi' al-tavārīkh* but not in the *Ẓafarnāmah* can be identified from Haravī's history.

The next section is differently headed, Ḥāfiẓ-i Abrū being rather more coy in treating this delicate subject:

Mihrvarzī-i Sulṭān Abū Sa'īd bā Baghdād Khātūn (fol. 730v)	Ẕikr-i sabab-i taghyīr-i mizāj-i Sulṭān Abū Sa'īd bar Chūpān va Chūpāniyān (p. 163)

As we shall see, it is in precisely this section also that Ḥāfiẓ-i Abrū departs from his total dependence on Mustawfī.

Mustawfī has one long section on the flight of Chūpān and the fall of the family, which Ḥāfiẓ-i Abrū breaks into two, with a separate section on the fate of Chūpān's sons, but the material contained in these passages is very similar.[21] The last event covered by Mustawfī is the revolt of Maḥmūd Shāh Īnjū in 734/1333–4 reported in a little more detail by Ḥāfiẓ-i Abrū, who mentions particularly the fortresses in which the rebels were incarcerated.[22]

The same close correspondence in the section headings is found for the reign of Öljeytü, which is interesting in view of the assertion that Kāshānī's *Tārīkh-i Ūljāytū* is Ḥāfiẓ-i Abrū's principal source for this "first part" of the continuation of Rashīd al-Dīn's work. Here again additional material about events in the east is taken from the *Tārīkh'nāmah-'i Harāt*.

The lines of poetry that Ḥāfiẓ-i Abrū frequently introduces into his narrative provide the second important clue to the extent of his debt to Mustawfī's *Ẓafarnāmah*.[23] Between Öljeytü's Gīlān campaign in 706/1307 and Shaykh Ḥasan-i Buzurg's exile to Kamākh castle in 732/1331–2, nearly 40 *bayt*s from the *Ẓafarnāmah* are interspersed, without acknowledgment, throughout the text.[24] This on its own, without the striking similarity of information presented, would be sufficient to illustrate Ḥāfiẓ-i Abrū's close familiarity with Mustawfī's verse chronicle. This is equally true for the reigns of both Öljeytü and Abū Sa'īd.

There is insufficient space here to demonstrate the relationship between the Ḥāfiẓ-i Abrū's *Ẕayl-i Jāmi' al-Tavārīkh* and Mustawfī's *Ẓafarnāmah* by a

[21] *Ẓafarnāmah*, fol. 733v; cf. Ḥāfiẓ-i Abrū 1972, 176, 180.

[22] *Ẓafarnāmah*, fols. 735r–v; cf. Ḥāfiẓ-i Abrū 1972, 187–8.

[23] This point was also noted by Ward 1983, 1:51. He refers, rather surprisingly, to the first edition of the *Ẕayl-i Jāmi' al-tavārīkh-i Rashīdī*.

[24] Ḥāfiẓ-i Abrū 1972, 70, 74, 75, 76, 95, 118, 119–20, 122, 146, 149, 150, 164, 168, 173, 174, 183, 187; cf. *Ẓafarnāmah*, fols. 713r, 715v, 716v, 717r, 721r, 722r, 724r, 727v, 728v, 731r, 731v, 733r, 734r–v, 735r; the list is perhaps incomplete. Not all the lines are quoted in the same order as found in the *Ẓafarnāmah*.

detailed comparison of their accounts of specific episodes. A number of general observations on the implications of this study may, however, provide a starting point for further work.

First, for the reign of Öljeytü, Kāshānī's *Tārīkh-i Ūljāytū* remains an important source of information. However, it is clear even from a superficial comparison between the two, that *Tārīkh-i Ūljāytū* is not Ḥāfiẓ-i Abrū's principal source, except in as much as it was certainly available to and used by Mustawfī.[25] On the other hand, it would be interesting to pursue the relationship between Kāshānī's *Tārīkh-i Ūljāytū* and Mustawfī's *Ẓafarnāmah*. On some occasions—such as Öljeytü's Gīlān campaign—their accounts are very similar, but it would be incorrect to regard the *Ẓafarnāmah* as merely a selective verse rendering of *Tārīkh-i Ūljāytū*.

Secondly, for the reign of Abū Sa'īd, Ḥāfiẓ-i Abrū's close dependence on the *Ẓafarnāmah* does not make the *Ẕayl-i Jāmi' al-tavārīkh* redundant. There are several passages in which Ḥāfiẓ-i Abrū provides a fuller account of events than Mustawfī, one example being the behavior of Chūpān's son, Amīr Dimashq, at court around the time of Abū Sa'īd's infatuation with Baghdād Khātūn.[26] It is clear that the Timurid historian was not indebted exclusively to Mustawfī.

Here again, the poetry cited by Ḥāfiẓ-i Abrū helps to reveal his source, namely another neglected verse chronicle, the *Shahanshāhnāmah* by Aḥmad Tabrīzī.[27] Fourteen lines from this chronicle are quoted (again without acknowledgment) in the space of a few pages.[28] Doubtless other presently unidentified verses may also be found to originate from the same work, or elsewhere. In general terms, a more detailed comparison between the *Ẓafarnāmah* and the *Ẕayl-i Jāmi' al-tavārīkh* would help to isolate material for which Ḥāfiẓ-i Abrū was not indebted to Mustawfī.

In this context, mention must be made of yet another recension of the *Ẕayl-i Jāmi' al-tavārīkh*, covering only the reigns of Öljeytü and Abū Sa'īd,

25 Mustawfī lists Kāshānī's *Zubdat al-tavārīkh* among his sources, see Mustawfī [1960] 1983, 7.

26 Ḥāfiẓ-i Abrū 1972, 163–73; cf. *Ẓafarnāmah*, fols. 730v–1r.

27 *Shahanshāhnāmah*, British Library, London, MS Or. 2780, dated 14 Rajab 800/2 April 1398, for which see Jahn 1963, 202–3 (A. Zeki Velidi Togan's assertion, relayed by Jahn, that *Shahanshāhnāmah* is "almost identical" to Nūr al-Dīn ibn Shams al-Dīn Muḥammad's *Ghāzān'nāmah* is not true); see also Boyle 1974, 186–7. Besides the *Shahanshāhnāmah*, the British Library MS Or. 2780 contains three other poems, *Garshāsb'nāmah*, *Bahman'nāmah*, and *Kūsh'nāmah*. The *Shāhnāmah* MS 114 in the Chester Beatty Library too was once part of this volume, see Rieu 1895, 133–7; and Arberry, Minovi, and Blochet 1959–62, 1:30–2.

28 Ḥāfiẓ-i Abrū 1972, 163–6; cf. *Shahanshāhnāmah*, fol. 122v.

which contains quite a significant amount of material not included in Bayānī's edition of the text. This recension, still in manuscript, was extensively used by E. M. Quatremère and the Baron C. D'Ohsson in their seminal works on the history of Mongol Iran.[29] Though these scholars did not associate this anonymous continuation of Rashīd al-Dīn's *Jāmi' al-tavārīkh* with Ḥāfiẓ-i Abrū, Tauer's attribution of his authorship seems sound. The important point, in the present context, is that the additional material found in the manuscript recension does *not* derive from Mustawfī's *Ẓafarnāmah*, so that at least one other presently unknown source remains to be identified for this period. Furthermore, in its account of Öljeytü's Gīlān campaign, for example, this recension clearly does take material directly from Kāshānī's *Tārīkh-i Ūljāytū*, rather than indirectly via the *Ẓafarnāmah*.[30]

Thirdly, just as Ḥāfiẓ-i Abrū's continuation is not made redundant by Mustawfī's *Ẓafarnāmah*, so the latter is not diminished by the existence of the more convenient and readily accessible printed text of Bayānī's edition of the *Ẕayl*. Further work must be undertaken to identify material in the *Ẓafarnāmah* that was not incorporated by Ḥāfiẓ-i Abrū. Even if the latter omitted nothing of major significance, there remains the opportunity to discover better and more authoritative readings in Mustawfī's work, particularly in the case of proper names, and to verify dates or other minor details. The same is equally true of the third part of Ḥāfiẓ-i Abrū's continuation, for which Mustawfī's own continuation and that of his son Zayn al-Dīn are available for comparison.[31]

The identification of the link between the two works provides an opportunity to re-evaluate their significance. The value of Ḥāfiẓ-i Abrū's continuation is enhanced, because it can be shown to rest on identifiable contemporary authorities for the period before his own time. In addition, further light can be thrown on Ḥāfiẓ-i Abrū's methods as a historian and compiler, through the

[29] Rashīd al-Dīn Faẕl Allāh [1836] 1968 and D'Ohsson 1834–5, vol. 4, using Paris manuscript supplément persan 255. Other copies exist in İstanbul (MS 3271 in Nuruosmaniye Mosque), London (MS Or. 2885 in the British Library, attached to a copy of the first volume of *Jāmi' al-tavārīkh* copied in 1030/1621), and Saint Petersburg, see Storey and Bregel' 1972, 1:343 and 1983, 2:501–2; see also Tauer 1932, 251–2, where Ḥāfiẓ-i Abrū's authorship is proposed.

[30] I have a paper in preparation on Öljeytü's Gīlān campaign, which addresses the historiography of the event.

[31] Two chronological examples may be noted: Ḥāfiẓ-i Abrū 1972, 73, has Öljeytü's advance into Gīlān in Dhū al-Ḥijjah 706, whereas *Ẓafarnāmah*, fol. 715r, has Dhū al-Qa'dah; Ḥāfiẓ-i Abrū 1972, 217, puts Ḥasan-i Kūchik's death on 20 Rajab 744, Mustawfī 1978, 145 / 1986, 130 has 27 Rajab.

use he made of these sources and the way he moulded them into his own narrative.

As for Mustawfī, his importance as a historian of the late Ilkhanid period certainly needs revision. Even for later generations of Persian historians, Mustawfī's reputation depended on the *Tārīkh-i guzīdah*, which appears not to have been held in great esteem.[32] However, this is only a digest of his major work, completed five years later.

Although Blochet's evaluation of the *Ẓafarnāmah*, quoted above, fails to discern its importance as a historical source, he is at least largely right in explaining both its disappearance and its survival. Whether the poor quality of the verse is the sole reason for its subsequent neglect, or whether the confusion and disorder following the collapse of the Ilkhanate is also to blame, can be argued by those better equipped than I to appreciate Mustawfī's efforts to emulate the *Shāhnāmah*. One might speculate that manuscript(s) of the *Ẓafarnāmah* perished along with other works in the library of Ghiyās̱ al-Dīn ibn Rashīd al-Dīn, to whom the work was dedicated, when the Rashidīyah was sacked in 736/1336.[33] The history of the text is not known until it was copied, almost certainly in Shīrāz, in 807/1405, the date of the earliest surviving manuscript, possibly directly from Mustawfī's own copy. Although he visited Shīrāz in 740/1339–40, it was not a fortunate experience, but it is not impossible that he left a copy of his work there.[34]

Of the rescue act carried out by the Timurid princes, there is no doubt, for both the London manuscript of *Ẓafarnāmah* and Aḥmad Tabrīzī's *Shahanshāhnāmah* were copied during Pīr Muḥammad's governorship of Fārs, probably by the same scribe,[35] and Zayn al-Dīn's Saint Petersburg copy of the *Ẕayl* was copied a few years later, in 813/1411, though not necessarily in

[32] See, for example, the view of Faẕl Allāh ibn Rūzbihān Khunjī Iṣfahānī in his *Tārīkh-i 'ālam'ārā-yi Amīnī* (Khunjī 1992, 87–8). Khunjī rightly puts Rashīd al-Dīn and Ḥāfiẓ-i Abrū in a different class; although ironically this is, at least in part, unwitting praise also for Mustawfī.

[33] Mustawfī 1978, 118 / 1986, 96–7; for the dedication, see idem [1960] 1983, 4.

[34] For his time in Shīrāz, see idem 1978, 131–7 / 1986, 112–20.

[35] See Ward 1983, 1:41–9; other manuscripts of the *Ẓafarnāmah* date from 808/1405–6 and 838/1434–5 (MSs 2042 and 2041, respectively), both in the Museum of Turkish and Islamic Art (Türk ve Islam Eserleri Müzesi), İstanbul, see Jahn 1963, 200. As mentioned earlier, the British Library manuscript copy of *Shahanshāhnāmah* was completed on 14 Rajab 800/2 April 1398. It has been discussed by B. W. Robinson 1967, 40–1 and other art historians, who tend to associate it with the patronage of Iskandar Sulṭān. However, on his death in 796/1394, 'Umar Shaykh was succeeded as governor of Fārs by his eldest son, Pīr Muḥammad, until the latter's temporary disgrace in 802/1400; he was reinstated in 805/1403, see Yazdī 1957, 1:475; 2:166–7, 367. I am grateful to Barbara Brend for pointing me in the right direction here.

Shīrāz.[36] Timurid interest in preserving the Mongol heritage of the Ilkhanid period, and Ḥāfiẓ-i Abrū's role in this, take us beyond the scope of the present essay. Nevertheless, Ḥāfiẓ-i Abrū was fully aware of the value of Mustawfī's *Ẓafarnāmah* in the historiography of the last Ilkhans, and the work now calls for more serious consideration than it has received from anyone since Ḥāfiẓ-i Abrū made it his own within a century of its composition.

[36] The calligrapher was a certain 'Alī ibn Shaykh Maḥmūd al-Abīvardī (Zayn al-Dīn Qazvīnī 1993, 149), brother of another scribe of the period, Aḥmad ibn Shaykh Maḥmūd al-Abīvardī, who in 826/1422–3 copied the famous Paris manuscript supplément persan 1443 of Shams al-Dīn Kāshānī's versified *Tārīkh-i mubārak-i Ghāzānī*, see Murtaẓavī 1991, 591. Zayn al-Dīn may himself have provided his Timurid patrons with a copy of his own and his father's work. On Iskandar Sulṭān's patronage at this period, see Aubin 1957.

BIBLIOGRAPHY

ARBERRY, A., MINOVI, M., and BLOCHET, E. 1959–62. *The Chester Beatty Library : a catalogue of the Persian manuscripts and miniatures*. Ed. J. V. S. Wilkinson. 3 vols. Dublin : Hodges Figgis & Co. LTD.

AUBIN, JEAN. 1957. Le mécénat timouride à Chiraz. *Studia Islamica* 8: 71–88.

BLOCHET, E. 1905–34. *Catalogue des manuscrits persans de la Bibliothèque nationale*. 4 vols. Paris : Imprimerie nationale (v. 1–2) : Réunion des bibliothèques nationales (v. 3) : Bibliothèque nationales (v. 4).

—— 1910. *Introduction à l'Histoire des Mongols de Fadl Allah Rashid ed-din*. Leiden : E. J. Brill ; London : Luzac & Co.

BOYLE, JOHN ANDREW. 1974. Some thoughts on the sources for the Il-khanid period of Persian history. *Iran* 12: 185–8.

BROWNE, EDWARD G. [1902–24] 1928. *A literary history of Persia*. 4 vols. Reprint, Cambridge, [Cambridgeshire] : The University Press.

D'OHSSON, C. 1834–5. *Histoire des Mongols, depuis Tchinguiz-Khan jusqu' à Timour Bey, ou Tamerlan*. 4 vols. The Hague : Les frères Van Cleef.

ḤĀFIẒ-I ABRŪ. 1936. *Chronique des rois mongols en Iran*. Tr. Khānbābā Bayānī. Published as vol. 2 of ḤĀFIẒ-I ABRŪ 1939. Paris : Adrien-Maisonneuve.

—— 1939. *Ẕayl-i Jami' al-tavārīkh-i Rashīdī*. Ed. Khānbābā Bayānī. Published as vol. 1 of ḤĀFIẒ-I ABRŪ 1936. Tehran : Shirkat-i Taẓāminī-i 'Ilmī, Day 1317 Sh.

—— 1959. *Cinq opuscules de Ḥāfiẓ-i Abrū concernant l'histoire de l'Iran au temps de Tamerlan*. Ed. Felix Tauer. Prague : Académie Tchécoslovaque des sciences.

—— 1972. *Ẕayl-i Jāmi' al-tavārīkh-i Rashīdī : shāmil-i vaqā''-i 703–781 Hijrī-i Qamarī*. 2nd ed. Ed. Khānbābā Bayānī. Tehran : Anjuman-i Āṣār-i Millī, Isfand 1350 Sh.

HARAVĪ, SAYF IBN MUḤAMMAD. 1944. *The Ta'ríkh náma-i-Harát : the history of Harát*. Ed. Muḥammad Zubayr al-Ṣiddīqī. Calcutta : Khān Bahādur Khalīfah Muḥammad Asad Allāh, [Persian t.p. has 1943 as date of publication].

HUMĀYŪNFARRUKH, RUKN AL-DĪN. 1990–1. *Ḥāfiẓ-i kharābātī*. 2nd ed. 9 vols. Tehran : Asāṭīr, 1369–70 Sh.

JACKSON, P. 1985. Abū Sa'īd Bahador Khan. *Encyclopaedia Iranica*. Vol. 1. London : Routledge & Kegan Paul: 374b–7a.

JAHN, KARL. 1963. Study on supplementary Persian sources for the Mongol history of Iran. In *Aspects of Altaic civilization : proceedings of the Fifth Meeting of the Permanent International Altaistic Conference held at Indiana University, June 4–9, 1962*. Ed. Denis Sinor. Bloomington : Indiana University ; The Hague : Mouton & Co., 197–204.

KĀSHĀNĪ, ABŪ AL-QĀSIM. 1969. *Tārīkh-i Ūljāytū : tārīkh-i pādshāh Sa'īd Ghiyāṣ al-Dunyā va al-Dīn Ūljāytū Sulṭān Muḥammad*. Ed. Mahīn Hamblī. Tehran : Bungāh-i Tarjumah va Nashr-i Kitāb, 1348 Sh.

KHUNJĪ, FAẔL ALLĀH IBN RŪZBIHĀN. 1992. *Tārīkh-i 'ālam-ārā-yi Amīnī : with the abridged English translation by Vladimir Minorsky [entitled] Persia in A.D. 1478–1490*. Ed. John E. Woods. London : Royal Asiatic Society.

MELVILLE, CHARLES. Forthcoming. Abū Sa'īd and the revolt of the amirs in 719/1319. In *Iran face à la domination mongole*. Ed. D. Aigle. Damascus.

MURTAẒAVĪ, MANŪCHIHR. 1991. *Masā'il-i 'aṣr-i Īlkhānān*. 2nd ed. Tehran : Āgāh, 1370 Sh.

MUSTAWFĪ, ḤAMD ALLĀH. [1960] 1983. *Tārīkh-i guzīdah*. Ed. 'Abd al-Ḥusayn Navā'ī. Reprint, Tehran : Amīr Kabīr, 1362 Sh.

—— 1986. *Zeil-e Tarikh-e gozide : Sechilmish tarikha alava*. Ed. & tr. M. D. Kazymov, V. Z. Piriiev. Baku : Elm.

PIRIIEV, V. Z. 1978. *Azarbaijan Hulakular dovlatinin tanazzulu dovrunda : 1316–1360- jy illar*. Baku : Elm Nashriiiaty.

RASHĪD AL-DĪN FAẒL ALLĀH. [1836] 1968. *Histoire des Mongols de la Perse*. Ed. & tr. M. Quatremère. Reprint, Amsterdam : Oriental Press.

RASTEGAR, NOSRATOLLAH. 1989. Ḥamdu'llah Mustawfīs historisches Epos Ẓafarnāme. *Wiener Zeitschrift für die Kunde des Morgenlandes* 79: 185–95.

RIEU, CHARLES. 1895. *Supplement to the catalogue of the Persian manuscripts in the British Museum*. London : The Trustees of the British Museum.

ROBINSON, B. W. 1967. *Persian miniature painting from collections in the British Isles*. London : Victoria and Albert Museum.

STOREY, C. A. and BREGEL', I͡U. Ė. 1972. Persidskai͡a literatura : bio-bibliograficheskiĭ obzor. Ed. I͡U. E. Borshchevskiĭ. 3 vols. Moscow : Nauka.

—— 1983. *Adabiyāt-i Fārsī bar mabnā-yi ta'līf-i Istūrī*. Tr. Yaḥyá Āryan'pūr, Sīrūs Īzadī, Karīm Kishāvarz. Ed. Aḥmad Munzavī. 2 vols. Tehran : Mu'assasah-'i Muṭāla'āt va Taḥqīqāt-i Farhangī, 1362 Sh.

TAUER, FELIX. 1932. Vorbericht über die Edition des Ẓafarnāma von Niẓām Šāmī und der Wichtigsten Teile der Geschichtswerke Ḥāfiẓ-i Abrū's. *Archiv Orientální* 4, no. 2 (August): 250–6.

—— 1952–5. Le Ẕail-i Ǧāmi'u-t-tawārīḫ-i Rašīdī de Ḥāfiẓ-i Abrū et son édition par K. Bayani. *Archiv Orientální* 20, no. 1–2: 39–52 (pt. 1); 21: 206–17 (pt. 2); 22: 88–98 (pt. 3); 23: 99–108 (pt. 4).

WARD, L. J. 1983. *The Ẓafar-nāmah of ḤamdAllāh Mustaufī and the Il-khān dynasty of Iran*. 3 vols. Ph.D. diss. University of Manchester.

YAZDĪ, SHARAF AL-DĪN 'ALĪ. 1957. *Ẓafarnāmah : tārīkh-i 'umūmī-i mufaṣṣal-i Īrān dar dawrah-'i Tīmūriyān*. Ed. Muḥammad 'Abbāsī. 2 vols. Tehran : Amīr Kabīr, 1336 Sh.

ZAYN AL-DĪN QAZVĪNĪ. 1990. *Zeil-e Tarikh-e gozide : Sechilmish tarikha-a alava*. Ed. & tr. M. D. Kazymov, V. Z. Piriiev. Baku : Elm.

—— 1993. *Ẕayl-i Tārīkh-i guzīdah*. Ed. Iraj Afshar. Tehran : Mawqūfāt-i Duktur Maḥmūd Afshār Yazdī, 1372 Sh.

The Iftikhāriyān of Qazvīn

François de Blois

THE IFTIKHĀRIYĀN WERE A FAMILY OF LOCAL notables who played a significant if fairly short-lived part in the history of Qazvīn, as well as in that of the Ilkhanid empire as a whole, during the greater part of the 7th/13th century. A fairly substantial sketch of their fortunes is given by Ḥamd Allāh Mustawfī Qazvīnī in the final chapter of his *Tārīkh-i guzīdah*, where the 8th/14th-century author, having completed his survey of the history of the world down to his own time, turns his attention to the glories of his native town, in the course of which he gives an account of some of its illustrious families. Mustawfī's potted history of the Iftikhāriyān[1] can be supplemented by the information of other, for the most part earlier, authors and, more significantly, by the fact that one member of the family is the author of an extant Persian *dīvān*. It is hoped that the present provisional attempt to gather together some of the printed and unprinted material connected with this family might be of interest to this volume's distinguished dedicatee, who has contributed so much to the discovery and publication of forgotten documents of the history of Iran.

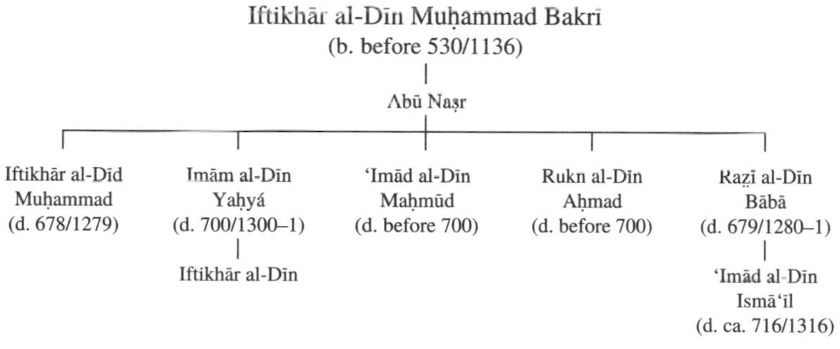

[1] Mustawfī [1960] 1983, 798–800. The text in the old facsimile edition published by Browne is considerably shorter and contains various scribal errors, the most significant of which is doubtless the fact that the family's *nisbah* "Iftikhārī" is more than once miscopied as "al-Bukhārī" (idem 1910–3, 1:824, 833, 841), an error reproduced, among other places, in the article "Ḳazwīn" in *The Encyclopaedia of Islam* (new edition); in fact, this family has no known connection with Bukhārā.

The family claimed descent from Abū Bakr, the first caliph, and this is reflected by their use of the *nisbah* Bakrī. The first member about whom we have as yet any information was one Iftikhār al-Dīn Muḥammad Bakrī, about whom Mustawfī tells us only that he was "a learned and pious man who studied with the blessed Imām Muḥammad ibn Yaḥyá Nayshābūrī."[2] The latter is evidently the Shāfi'ī religious scholar Abū Sa'd Muḥammad ibn Yaḥyá ibn Abī Manṣūr al-Nayshābūrī, who was born in 476/1083–4, studied with the famous al-Ghazālī, and died, according to our most reliable informant, in the year 550/1155, killed by the Ghuzz in the course of their rebellion against the Seljuks.[3] His pupil Iftikhār al-Dīn can consequently not have been born much later than 530/1136.

It is, however, only with his grandchildren[4] and notably with another Iftikhār al-Dīn Muḥammad, the son of Abū Naṣr, that the family came to prominence, their change of fortune being the result of the fact that they were among those Persian notables who entered the service of the Mongols. Already at the time of the Great Khān Ögedei, who succeeded his father Chingiz Khān in 624/1227, Iftikhār al-Dīn attached himself to the Mongol court and served as a tutor to the future Great Khān Möngke and his brothers. When Möngke came to the throne, he remembered his former teacher and in 651/1253–4 appointed him governor of Qazvīn and for the next quarter of a century Iftikhār and his brother Imām al-Dīn Yaḥyá were undisputed masters of the town.[5] In 653/1255 Qazvīn came under attack by the Ismā'īlīs, whereupon

[2] Idem [1960] 1983, 798.

[3] Ibn al-Athīr 1851–76, 11:133 includes the death of Muḥammad ibn Yaḥyá in his enumeration of the events of the year 550/1155–6. To be sure, the same historian, in his general account of the rebellion of the Ghuzz against Sanjar, which he includes among the events of 548/1153–4 (the year in which the rebellion got under way), says twice (11:118, 120) that the Ghuzz slaughtered many religious dignitaries and scholars, among them Muḥammad ibn Yaḥyá. It is doubtless from this rather misleading formulation that later authors deduced that 548/1153–4 was in fact the year of this scholar's death; thus Ibn Khallikān ([1968–72], 4:223–4, no. 591) who also mentions, and rejects, an alternative date for his death, 553/1158, followed, with largely identical wording, by Subkī (1964–76, 7:25–8), where the name is partially garbled, Ṣafadī (1931–, 5:197, no. 2253), and others. For further references, see the notes in the editions of the three last-mentioned works and add: Rāvandī 1921, 181; 'Awfī 1903–6, 1:229–30, and Qazvīnī's note on p. 349 of the latter (with references to further sources).

[4] "*Aḥfād*" (Mustawfī [1960] 1983, 798) can of course mean "descendants," but it is likely that it has here its literal meaning "grandsons." If the elder Iftikhār was born ca. 530/1136, his son Abū Naṣr could have been born in say 570/1174 and his grandson, the younger Iftikhār, in about 600/1204; the latter would then have been fifty-one when he became governor of Qazvīn and seventy-eight when he died.

[5] Ibid., 797.

the *Muslim* qāẕī of the town, Shams al-Dīn Aḥmad Mākī Qazvīnī, petitioned the *pagan* Mongol ruler to send an army to drive out the *Muslim* heretics; thereupon Möngke sent his brother Hülegü to suppress the Ismā'īlīs. Ibn al-Ṭiqṭaqā quotes an eye-witness account of these events which he himself had heard from "al-Malik Imām al-Dīn Yaḥyá ibn al-Iftikhārī," Iftikhār's brother.[6] At the beginning of the reign of Abaqa in 663/1265 Iftikhār was, according to his contemporary Rashīd al-Dīn Faẕl Allāh (d. 718/1318),[7] appointed (that is to say, confirmed) as governor of Qazvīn and part of Iraq, but in 676/1277–8 Iftikhār was accused of embezzlement and resigned his post and spent the last two years of his life "miserably" (*maflūk*) at the Mongol camp (*ūrdū*).[8] It is interesting that the local patriot Mustawfī passes over the governor's disgrace in silence, but he does confirm the date given by Rashīd al-Dīn for Iftikhār's death, quoting an elegy by the governor's nephew 'Imād al-Dīn Ismā'īl (to whom we shall return), putting this event in Jumādá I 678/June 1279.[9] Mustawfī praises Iftikhār's wise government, adds that he was an expert in the Mongolian and Turkish languages and scripts,[10] and that he translated *Kalīlah va Dimnah* into Mongolian and *Sindbādnāmah* into Turkish. We have no other information about these translations, which, if they had survived, would have been of immense interest for the history of literature.[11]

As mentioned, Iftikhār shared power in Qazvīn with Imām al-Dīn Yaḥyá. It was presumably some years after his brother's disgrace that Imām al-Dīn was appointed the governor of "the whole of 'Irāq-i 'ajam . . . from Tabrīz to Yazd," and then "at the end of his life for about ten years he was also governor of 'Irāq-i 'arab," i.e., in Baghdād; he died in Rabī' II 700/December 1300–January 1301 "after all his brothers."[12] Some further details of Imām al-Dīn's governorship in Baghdād are provided by an anonymous local chronicle[13]

[6] Ibn al-Ṭiqṭaqā 1895, 40. The author does not give the date of this incident, but it (and the full name of the Qāẕī) are indicated by Mustawfī [1960] 1983, 588–9; see also Rashīd al-Dīn Faẕl Allāh 1994, 2:991.

[7] Rashīd al-Dīn Faẕl Allāh 1994, 2:1061.

[8] Ibid., 2:1107.

[9] Mustawfī [1960] 1983, 799.

[10] Ibid. "*Khaṭṭ-i Turkī*" can at the time in question hardly refer to anything other than Uighur alphabet.

[11] The translation of *Kalīlah va Dimnah* is mentioned also by late authors such as Ḥājjī Khalīfah (Kâtib Çelebi 1835–58, 5:239), evidently in direct or indirect dependence on Mustawfī.

[12] Mustawfī [1960] 1983, 799–800.

[13] I.e., the Arabic chronicle wrongly identified on the title-page and in the introduction of the printed edition as *al-Ḥawādith al-jāmi'ah* of Ibn al-Fuwaṭī, quoted here as Ibn al-Fuwaṭī [pseud.] 1932. For the authorship, see the editor's introduction in Ibn al-Fuwaṭī 1962–7, 1:62–6.

which specifies that Imām al-Dīn Yaḥyá was appointed co-regent of Baghdād in 693/1294, but was recalled at the end of the year.[14] He assumed sole command of the same province in 698/1298–9,[15] died in 700/1300–1 in al-Ḥillah, and was buried in the *madrasah* which he had founded in Darb Firāshā; he was succeeded by his son, yet another Iftikhār al-Dīn.[16] The *madrasah* in question, which was located to the east of Baghdād, is mentioned also by Ṣafadī, who says that Imām al-Dīn had founded it for his compatriot al-Qāẕī Tāj al-Dīn Abū al-Ḥasan ʻAlī ibn Abī al-Qāsim ibn Aḥmad al-Qazvīnī al-Shāfiʻī, thus underlining once again the family's connection with the Shāfiʻī clergy.[17]

Three further brothers held governorships at one time or another: ʻImād al-Dīn Maḥmūd in Māzandarān, Rukn al-Dīn Aḥmad in Gurjistān (Georgia) and Raẕī al-Dīn Bābā in Diyār Bakr (Eastern Anatolia)[18] and, evidently later, in Mawṣil.[19] His stint in Mawṣil was dramatic; unfortunately, the sources disagree about the chronology. What seems clear is that some years after his first appointment to this position, Raẕī al-Dīn was replaced as civil governor by a Christian by the name of Masʻūd, from the village of Bar Qūṭā, who was seconded by the military governor (*shiḥnah*) Ashnūṭ or Ashmūṭ,[20] a Mongol Christian.[21] Two years later, Raẕī al-Dīn returned to power and had both Masʻūd

[14] Ibn al-Fuwaṭī [pseud.] 1932, 478.

[15] Ibid., 498.

[16] Ibid., 504.

[17] Ṣafadī 1911, 204.

[18] Mustawfī [1960] 1983, 800. Rashīd al-Dīn Faẕl Allāh (1994, 2:1061) similarly says that at the beginning of the reign of Abaqa, i.e., around 663/1265, the governorship of Diyār Bakr was conferred on Malik Raẕī al-Dīn Bābā and on Jalāl al-Dīn Ṭarīr; the latter is perhaps identical with Jalāl al-Dīn Sarā'ī Khutanī, who took over as governor on Diyār Bakr after Raẕī al-Dīn's dismissal, according to Mustawfī [1960] 1983, 733.

[19] Ibn al-Fuwaṭī (1962–70, 2:683) calls Raẕī al-Dīn "the *walī* of Mawṣil and Diyār Rabīʻah" and Ṣafadī (1931–, 10:61, no. 4502) similarly styles him "*walī* of Mawṣil." Ibn al-Fuwaṭī [pseud.] (1932, 354) states that Raẕī al-Dīn was appointed *walī* of Mawṣil in 663/1265, replacing al-Zakī al-Irbilī, but this date is difficult to reconcile with Rashīd al-Dīn's statement (quoted in the previous footnote) which at the time in question makes Raẕī al-Dīn governor of Diyār Bakr. As we shall see in what follows, the dates in Ibn al-Fuwaṭī [pseud.] are often unreliable. The mentioned al-Zakī al-Irbilī became governor of Mawṣil in 1575 Seleucid (October 1263–September 1264), according to the Syriac chronicle of Bar Hebraeus (1890, 520–1) or in 661 *Hijrī* (November 1262–November 1263), according to the same author's Arabic chronicle (Bar Hebraeus 1663, 543).

[20] The former spelling is used consistently in Ibn al-Fuwaṭī [pseud.], the latter in Bar Hebraeus; see also *Tashʻīthā dh-mār(y) Ya(h)bhallāhā* 1895, 40, 48, where the military governor is called Amīr Ashmūt (with -t; wrong word-division in both passages).

[21] Ibn al-Fuwaṭī [pseud.] 1932, 361, who puts this event in 666/1267–8. The appointment of Masʻūd and Ashmūṭ (but not the removal of Raẕī al-Dīn) is mentioned also by Bar Hebraeaus (1890, 535), but he says that this was in 1587 Seleucid/1275–6.

and Ashnūṭ arrested for financial impropriety,[22] but these men appealed to Abaqa, who appointed two of his relatives to investigate the matter, found the Christians innocent, and had Raẕī al-Dīn put to death. Once reinstated in their posts, the civil and military governors "returned to Mawṣil with Raẕī al-Dīn's head, paraded it about the town, and hung it up on the Bāb al-Jisr."[23] This was in 679/1280–1.[24] The story is interesting as evidence for the rivalry between Muslim and Christian bureaucrats for the favor of the pagan rulers, but it also shows that the Mongols at least sometimes actually investigated abuses rather than beheading people for no other reason than that they had been denounced by their enemies.

Raẕī al-Dīn was also a poet. In his *Mu'nis al-aḥrār fī daqā'iq al-ash'ār*, the 8th/14th-century anthologist Muḥammad ibn Badr Jājarmī quotes two Persian odes by Raẕī Bābā al-Qazvīnī addressing a *vazīr* by the name of Muḥammad ibn Muḥammad, evidently the famous Ṣāḥib al-Dīvān Shams al-Dīn Juvaynī,[25] while Mustawfī quotes a quatrain of his mocking that same minister at the time when the poet was dismissed from his post as governor of Diyār Bakr.[26] A much later author, Amīn ibn Aḥmad Rāzī in his *Haft iqlīm*, quotes, evidently from Mustawfī, the same quatrain and adds a short *ghazal* by this poet.[27]

[22] Ibn al-Fuwaṭī [pseud.] (1932, 367) puts this among the events of 668/1269, but Bar Hebraeaus (1890, 549) puts it in the winter of 1589 Seleucid/1277–8. Thus both sources agree in putting the arrest of the two Christians two years after their appointment. It is noteworthy that Bar Hebraeus spells Raẕī al-Dīn's personal name consistently as Pāpā (not Bābā; *p* and *b* are distinct in Syriac script).

[23] Ibn al-Fuwaṭī [pseud.] 1932, 397–8. The incident is related also, in more detail, in the chronicle of Bar Hebraeus (1890, 542–3), which describes also (in the section apparently added after the author's death) the later adventures of Mas'ūd Barqūṭī.

[24] Rashīd al-Dīn (1994, 2:1113) writes of a conference between Abaqa and his son Arghun in Dhū al-Qa'dah 678/March 1280 and goes on to say that subsequent to this meeting, Abaqa spent the *winter* (i.e., the following winter of 679/1280–1) near Arrān and that "Malik Raẕī al-Dīn Bābā-yi Qazvīnī and Jalāl al-Dīn Khaṭṭī became martyrs in that winter." The "martyrdom" of "al-Bābā Raẕī al-Mughulī, the *walī* of Mawṣil" is also mentioned and dated specifically to 679 in Ṣafadī (1931–, 10:61). The contemporary historian Bar Hebraeus (see previous footnote) puts Raẕī al-Dīn's decapitation on Thursday 8 August 1591 Seleucid/1280, which agrees with the two mentioned sources at least as far as the year is concerned, and says (again in agreement with Rashīd al-Dīn) that Raẕī al-Dīn's confederate Jalāl al-Dīn was executed at the same time. By contrast, Ibn al-Fuwaṭī [pseud.] puts these events among the happenings of 676/1277–8, evidently wrongly.

[25] Jājarmī 1959–71, 2:506–8, 761–4.

[26] Mustawfī [1960] 1983, 733; also (clearly following Mustawfī) Khvānd Amīr [1954] 1983, 3:117.

[27] Rāzī 1961, 3:159–60. Raẕī al-Dīn is also quoted by another Safavid author, Taqī al-Dīn Muḥammad Kāshī in his hitherto unpublished *Khulāṣat al-ash'ār va zubdat al-afkār*. In the manuscript copy of this work described by Aloys Spenger (1854, 1:17, no. 61), the date of Raẕī al-Dīn's death is apparently given as 909, which is more than 200 years too late.

Raẕī al-Dīn's son, 'Imād al-Dīn Ismā'īl, was a poet whose verse, in Mustawfī's view, "is better than that of his father," and who "died in Sulṭānīyah at the beginning of the reign of Sulṭān Abū Sa'īd Bahādur Khān," that is to say, around the year 716/1316.[28] Elsewhere, the same authority quotes two short poems of his.[29] In his biographical dictionary, *Talkhīs majma' al-ādāb fī mu'jam al-alqāb*, Ibn al-Fuwaṭī says that 'Imād al-Dīn Ismā'īl came from a famous family, mentions his father and his two uncles, Imām al-Dīn and Iftikhār al-Dīn, and adds that "I saw al-Ṣāḥib 'Imād al-Dīn Ismā'īl at the encampment (*mukhayyam*) of al-Ṣāḥib al-Wazīr Sa'd al-Dīn Muḥammad ibn 'Alī al-Sāwī, [alias: al-Sāvajī] at Ūjān and Arrān. He composed some fine poetry in Persian praising al-Ṣāḥib Sa'd al-Dīn in the year 705 [1305–6]" and he proceeds to quote, in Persian, the first verse of the *qaṣīdah* which Ismā'īl presented on that occasion.[30]

But this Ismā'īl is the author of an extant Persian *dīvān* of which an apparently unique copy, dated 14 Muḥarram 848/3 May 1444, is contained in the Paris manuscript supplément persan 795, fols. 497–536. It has been described briefly by Blochet,[31] though evidently without realizing that its author is identical with the 'Imād al-Dīn Ismā'īl mentioned by Mustawfī; otherwise, this *dīvān* seems to have escaped the attention of students of Persian literature.

Concerning the identity of the author no doubt is possible. In his otherwise rather uninformative prose introduction, the poet gives himself the names "Abū al-Faẕā'il Ismā'īl ibn Bābā ibn Abī al-Naṣr al-Iftikhārī al-Bakrī al-Qazvīnī," but also in the poems he refers by name to his father and his senior uncle[32] and calls himself "Ibn Bābā"[33]; moreover, the many historical allusions in the poems show that they belong to the end of the 13th and the very beginning of the 14th century. Thus, this author's identity with the poet mentioned in the biographical sources must be upheld, despite the somewhat disconcerting fact that the three poems of Ismā'īl's that are known from hitherto published sources (namely the two *qiṭ'ah*s cited by Mustawfī and the *qaṣīdah*

[28] Mustawfī [1960] 1983, 742.

[29] Ibid., 799–800.

[30] Ibn al-Fuwaṭī 1962–7, 2:683–4, no. 987. Ibn al-Fuwaṭī gives our poet's names as "'Imād al-Dīn Abū Muḥammad Ismā'īl ibn Raẕī al-Dīn Bābā ibn Nuṣrat al-Dīn Muḥammad al-Iftikhārī al-Qazwīnī"; although it is just about possible that our poet's grandfather bore the *laqab* Nuṣrat al-Dīn, the *kunyah* Abū Naṣr and the *ism* Muḥammad, it is perhaps more likely that here, as so often, Ibn al-Fuwaṭī has garbled the names; read perhaps: . . . ibn Abī Naṣr ibn Muḥammad . . .

[31] Blochet 1905–34, 3:434–7, no. 1969. The manuscript contains various other *dīvān*s, all listed by Blochet; in the margins of Ismā'īl's *dīvān* are poems by Nāṣir Bukhārā'ī.

[32] Fol. 510v, ult.: *dāram sharaf bi nisbat-i Bābā u Iftikhār*.

[33] Fol. 534r.

the first verse of which is quoted by Ibn al-Fuwaṭī) cannot be found in the manuscript. It is evident that this, like so many other so-called *dīvān*s, represents only a selection of the poet's *oeuvre*.

The poems in this collection are almost entirely panegyrics in praise of various dignitaries during the reign of Öljeytü (r. 703–17/1304–17); one ode actually mentions this ruler by name,[34] but it seems doubtful whether it was really intended to be presented to him. The poems are not arranged alphabetically, nor are there any superscriptions, but the name of the person to whom each poem is dedicated is generally indicated clearly enough in the verses themselves. The *qaṣīdah*s, *qiṭ'ah*s and strophic poems addressed to any particular person are in general grouped together roughly according to the rank of the patron. Thus, at the beginning, there are several poems to the Mongol generals Esen Qutlugh and Ṭūqmān, both known from historical sources. These are followed by a good number of poems to Öljeytü's two famous ministers: four to Rashīd al-Dīn Faẕl Allāh, and twelve to his colleague and rival Sa'd al-Dīn Muḥammad Sāvajī, who, as we have seen, is mentioned also by Ibn al-Fuwaṭī as our poet's special patron. As is known, after a long struggle for power between the two ministers, Sa'd al-Dīn was deposed and executed on 10 Shawwāl 711/19 February 1312, and succeeded as co-minister by Tāj al-Dīn 'Alī Shāh, who also appears in this *dīvān* as the addressee of two poems. Soon, he too came into conflict with Rashīd, who, largely as a result of Tāj al-Dīn's machinations, was disgraced and executed in 718/1318. But this is perhaps after the time of our poet who seems in any case to have nothing to say about the sorry end of his two patrons. Indeed, in one of his odes to Sa'd al-Dīn, the poet announces his withdrawal from the court and from the affairs of the world, after "long service," and introduces his "brother" (about whom we seem to have no other information) as his successor in service to the minister.[35]

Two poems address one "'Izz al-Dawlah va al-Dīn," in one of which he is given the title *dastūr*, perhaps the 'Izz al-Dīn Ṭāhir, who, according to Rashīd al-Dīn, was the "*vazīr* of Khurāsān" at the time of Abaqa.[36] Three poems, among them a long *tarjī'band*, address one "*Quṭb-i millat va dīn pādshāh*," whom Blochet identified (probably wrongly) with the well-known scholar Quṭb al-Dīn Shīrāzī. One poem mentions Shams al-Dīn Qāẕī, presumably the qāẕī of Qazvīn, whom we have already encountered in connection with the

[34] Fol. 501r.

[35] The *qaṣīdah* is on fol. 518v and ends with the verse: *bugẕāshtam īn khidmat-i dīrīn bi barādar • ū rā bi Khudā u bi Khudāvand sipurdam.*

[36] Rashīd al-Dīn Faẕl Allāh 1994, 2:1061.

events of 653/1255. For the identity of the other persons named in the poems, I have for the moment no suggestions.[37] The panegyrics are followed by a few *ghazal*s and a handful of *rubā'ī*s.

An evaluation of the literary merits of these poems must be left to native Iranian critics, but I have no doubt that they represent an interesting new source for the political history of Ilkhanid Iran. As a sample of the work of this long-forgotten poet, we append the text of a *qiṭ'ah*,[38] the only one, as far as can be seen, addressed not to one, but to both of the rival ministers (here called, for the sake of the metre, *Rashīd-i millat* and *Sa'd-i duval*, respectively).[39] After wishing them both a long life and never faltering good fortune, and excusing himself at some length for venturing, as a mere "nightingale," to offer his humble advice to these exalted individuals, the poet finally comes to the point in his very last line: "May you eternally remain in agreement with one another; may the door of strife and hypocrisy remain closed between you." As we know, the two ministers chose not to heed their poet's counsel.[40]

[37] I intend to return to this poet and his *dīvān* in the forthcoming volume VI of my continuation of Storey's *Persian literature*.

[38] Fols. 518r–v. The orthography of the manuscript is maintained, but I have added the diacritical signs for the "Persian" letters (p, ch, g), which are not distinguished in the manuscript, and a few vowel signs.

[39] Kambiz Eslami has pointed out to me that Shams al-Dīn Kāshānī too has praised both of these ministers at the end of his versified *Tārīkh-i mubārak-i Ghāzānī* (Paris manuscript supplément persan 1443), referring to Murtaẓavī 1991, 625.

[40] I am grateful to A. H. Morton for his useful comments on an earlier draft of this paper.

APPENDIX A

دو دادگر که ز ایزد خطابشان این باد
که باد تا بقیامتْ زمان زمان شما
زهی دو جان مکارم که چشمهء حیوان
خجل شود ز سر کلك درفشان شما
رشید ملّت و سعد دول که دور فلك
نیاورید و نیارد دگر بسان شما
کفاف اهل جهان در زمانه دانی چیست
فضالهء که فتد از سربنان شما
ز احتراق هبوط و زوال ایمن باد
همیشه طالع مسعود اختران شما
ز روی لطف یکی چند لفظ من شنوید
که هستم ازدل وجان خاصْ مدحْ خوان شما
روا بوَد که چو من بلبلی شکر گفتار
صغیر کم کُنَد از شاخ گُلستان شما
بر آستان شما سالها ثنا گفتم
که آسمان جلالست آستان شما
از آن مُلازمت و مدحْ گفتنم هرگز
خلاف قرض نشد حاصلی بجان شما
ازین سپس من و تحصیل اگر خلاص بوَد
ز بار قرض باقبال کامران شما
و گر چه من ز شما بهرهء ندارم لیك
جهان بکام شما باد و دوستان شما
درین میانه دو جا لفظ شایگان گفتم
گرفت اگر نکند طبع خرده دان شما
باتّفاق بمانید جاودان با هم
در خلاف و ریا بسته در میان شما

BIBLIOGRAPHY

‘AWFĪ, MUḤAMMAD. 1903–6. *Kitāb-i Lubāb al-albāb*. Ed. Edward G. Browne, Muḥammad Qazvīnī. 2 vols. Leiden : E. J. Brill ; London : Luzac & Co.

BAR HEBRAEUS. 1663. *Tārīkh mukhtaṣar al-duwal = Historia compendiosa dynastiarum*. Ed. & tr. Edward Pococke. Oxford : Henricus Hall.

—— 1890. *Kthābhā d-makhtbhānūth zabhnē L-mār(y) Grīghōrīōs = Chronicon syriacum e codd. mss. emendatum ac punctis vocalibus adnotationibusque locupletatum*. Ed. Paul Bedjan. Paris : Maisonneuve.

BLOCHET, E. 1905–34. *Catalogue des manuscrits persans de la Bibliothèque nationale*. 4 vols. Paris : Imprimerie nationale (v. 1–2) : Réunion des bibliothèques nationales (v. 3) : Bibliothèque nationales (v. 4).

IBN AL-ATHĪR. 1851–76. *Ibn al-Athiri Chronicon quod perfectissimum inscribitur*. Ed. Carolus Johannes Tornberg. 12 (text) + 2 (index) vols. Leiden : E. J. Brill.

IBN AL-FUWAṬĪ. [1962–7]. *al-Juz’ al-rābi‘ min Talkhīṣ majma‘ al-ādāb fī mu‘jam al-alqāb*. Ed. Muṣṭafá Jawād. 4 vols. Damascus : Wizārat al-Thaqāfah wa-al-Irshād al-Qawmī.

IBN AL-FUWAṬĪ [PSEUD.]. 1932. *al-Ḥawādith al-jāmi‘ah wa-al-tajārib al-nāfi‘ah fī al-mi’ah al-sābi‘ah*. Ed. Muṣṭafá Jawād. Baghdād : al-Maktabah al-‘Arabīyah, 1351.

IBN AL-ṬIQṬAQĀ, MUḤAMMAD IBN ‘ALĪ. 1895. *Al-Fakhrî*. Ed. Hartwig Derenbourg. Paris : É. Bouillon.

IBN KHALLIKAN. [1968–72]. *Wafayāt al-a‘yān wa-anbā’ abnā’ al-zamān*. Ed. Iḥsān ‘Abbās. 8 vols. Beirut : Dār Ṣādir.

JĀJARMĪ, MUḤAMMAD IBN BADR. 1959–71. *Mu’nis al-aḥrār fī daqā’iq al-ash‘ār*. Ed. Mīr Ṣāliḥ Ṭabībī. 2 vols. Tehran : Chāp-i Ittiḥād (v. 1) : Anjuman-i Ās̱ār-i Millī (v. 2), Bahman 1337–50 Sh.

KÂTIB ÇELEBI. 1835–58. *Kashf al-ẓunūn ‘an asāmī al-kutub wa-al-funūn*. Ed. & tr. Gustav Flügel. 7 vols. Leipzig and London : Oriental Translation Fund of Great Britain and Ireland.

KHVĀND AMĪR. [1954] 1983. *Tārīkh-i Ḥabīb al-siyar fī akhbār-i afrād-i bashar*. Ed. Muḥammad Dabīr Siyāqī, introd. Jalāl al-Dīn Humā’ī. 4 vols. Reprint, Tehran : Kitābfurūshī-i Khayyām, 1362 Sh.

MURTAẒAVĪ, MANŪCHIHR. 1991. *Masā’il-i ‘aṣr-i Īlkhānān*. 2nd ed. Tehran : Āgāh, 1370 Sh.

MUSTAWFĪ, ḤAMD ALLĀH. 1910–3. *Kitāb-i Tārīkh-i guzīdah*. Ed. Edward G. Browne. 2 vols. Leiden : E. J. Brill ; London : Luzac & Co.

—— [1960] 1983. *Tārīkh-i guzīdah*. Ed. ‘Abd al-Ḥusayn Navā’ī. Reprint, Tehran : Amīr Kabīr, 1362 Sh.

RASHĪD AL-DĪN FAẒL ALLĀH. 1994. *Jāmi‘ al-tavārīkh*. Ed. Muḥammad Rawshan, Muṣṭafá Mūsavī. 4 vols. Tehran : Alburz, 1373 Sh.

RĀVANDĪ, MUḤAMMAD IBN ‘ALĪ. 1921. *Kitāb-i Rāḥat al-ṣudūr va āyat al-surūr dar tārīkh-i Āl-i Saljūq*. Ed. Muḥammad Iqbāl. Leiden : E. J. Brill ; London : Luzac & Co.

RĀZĪ, AMĪN IBN AḤMAD. 1961. *Haft iqlīm*. Ed. Javād Fāẓil. 3 vols. Tehran : Kitābfurūshī-i Adabīyah, 1340 Sh.

ṢAFADĪ, KHALĪL IBN AYBAK. 1931–. *Kitāb al-Wāfī bi-al-wafayāt*. Ed. Helmut Ritter et al. 24 vols. to date (vols. 20 and 23 not published yet). Leipzig : Deutsche Morgenländische Gesellschaft, in Kommission bei F.A. Brockhaus ; İstanbul: Maṭba'at al-Dawlah.

—— 1911. *Nakt al-himyān fī nukat al-'umyān*. Ed. Aḥmad Zakī. Cairo : al-Maṭba'ah al-Jamālīyah.

SPRENGER, ALOYS. 1854. *A catalogue of the Arabic, Persian and Hindústány manuscripts of the libraries of the King of Oudh*. Calcutta : J. Thomas.

SUBKĪ, TĀJ AL-DĪN 'ABD AL-WAHHĀB. 1964–76. *Tabaqāt al-Shāfi'īyah al-kubrá*. Ed. Maḥmūd Muḥammad al-Ṭanāḥī, 'Abd al-Fattāḥ Muḥammad al-Ḥilw. 10 vols. Cairo : 'Īsá al-Bābī al-Ḥalabī.

Tash'īthā dh-mār(y) Ya(h)bhallāhā paṭrīy-arkhā wa-dh-rabban Ṣaumā = Histoire de Mar Jab-Alaha, Patriarche, et de raban Sauma. 1895. 2nd ed. Ed. Paul Bedjan. Paris, Leipzig : Otto Harrassowitz.

Ibrāhīm Sulṭān's Military Career

Priscilla P. Soucek

IBRĀHĪM SULṬĀN IBN SHĀHRUKH IBN TĪMŪR (796–838/1394–1435) is remembered primarily for his two decades as ruler of Shīrāz (817–38/1414–35), during which time he collaborated with Sharaf al-Dīn 'Alī Yazdī (d. 858/1454) in compiling his grandfather's biography in the *Ẓafarnāmah* and gained renown as a calligrapher of the Koran—actions which reflect his pious and scholarly temperament. When his life is examined in more detail, however, it becomes evident that military experience helped to shape his outlook, and that his prowess on the battlefield was memorialized by contemporary authors and recorded in manuscript illustration.

Before turning to Ibrāhīm's military training and experience with warfare, the basic outlines of his biography must be established. The Timurid period is richly documented with both historical and literary texts which taken together not only provide the outlines of Ibrāhīm's biography but also give insight into the cultural attitudes of the period. The best source of information on his early years is Sharaf al-Dīn 'Alī Yazdī's *Ẓafarnāmah*, a work compiled with Ibrāhīm's participation between 822/1419–20 and 828/1424–5.[1] For his later years, the major Timurid chronicles, Ḥāfiẓ-i Abrū's *Zubdat al-tavārīkh* and 'Abd al-Razzāq Samarqandī's *Maṭla'-i sa'dayn va majma'-i baḥrayn* offer the fullest treatment.[2] Additional details are found in the other standard sources for this period such as Faṣīḥ Khvāfī's *Mujmal-i Faṣīḥī*, Tāj al-Salmānī's *Shams al-ḥusn*, and Khvānd Amīr's *Ḥabīb al-siyar*.[3]

In addition to these sources concerning the wider Timurid world, others which reflect the cultural climate in Fārs, especially in Shīrāz where Ibrāhīm Sulṭān lived for nearly half of his life, provide insight into the way the region's largely Persian inhabitants reacted to the imposition of Timurid rule. Documenting this region's cultural legacy has been a life-long concern of Iraj Afshar, who has been instrumental in the publication of several texts which provide information relevant to the subject under consideration. These include not

[1] See Yazdī 1957 and 1972.

[2] See Ḥāfiẓ-i Abrū 1993; Samarqandī 1946–9.

[3] See Faṣīḥ Khvāfī 1960–2; Tāj al-Salmānī 1956 and 1988; Khvānd Amīr [1954] 1983 and 1994.

only his edition of *Anīs al-nās* and his collaboration with H. Modarressi in the editing of *Jāmiʻ al-tavārīkh-i Ḥasanī*,[4] but also shorter pieces which have appeared in composite volumes or scholarly journals of which he was the editor. Among them are excerpts from a *majmūʻah* (collection) associated with Sharaf al-Dīn ʻAlī Yazdī, which documents aspects of the cultural and artistic life of Fārs, and of which several copies are known.[5] Also important is a still unpublished text known as the *Risālah-i Muʻammā* or *Ḥulal-i muṭarraz*, written for Ibrāhīm Sulṭān by Sharaf al-Dīn ʻAlī Yazdī, which survives in several manuscript copies. The one used here is MS Or. 3509 in the British Library, London.[6]

As befits a descendant of Tīmūr, Ibrāhīm, Shāhrukh's second son, was born in an encampment on 28 Shawwāl 796/26 August 1394 in the middle of the "Five Year Campaign" (794–8/1392–6).[7] His mother, Ṭūṭī Khatūn or Ṭūṭī Āgha, was of Narin Mongol stock, but as was customary among the Timurids, Ibrāhīm's care was entrusted to a kind of surrogate family consisting of Tīmūr's second-ranking wife, Tūmān Āghā bint Amīr Mūsá Taychi'ut in conjunction with a guardian or *atābeg*, Amīr ʻUsmān ibn ʻAbbās Bahādur Qipchaq and a wet-nurse, Sādiqīn Āghā, who was both ʻUs̱mān's wife and related to Tīmūr.[8] Although Ibrāhīm's link to ʻUs̱mān was terminated by Tīmūr's execution of that *amīr* on suspicion of treachery in 797/1395,[9] Sādiqīn Āghā continued to participate in life at the Timurid court after her husband's demise.[10] Bonds established in his early years probably also led to Ibrahīm's later close friendship with ʻUs̱mān's sons Sulṭān Bāyazīd and particularly with Sayyidī Aḥmad, who became his *muhrdār* (seal-bearer), a position reserved for the most trusted of attendants.[11] Ibrāhīm evidently also remained close to his mother, Ṭūṭī Khātūn, as she would later accompany him to Shīrāz and supervise the care of his own children.[12]

Ibrāhīm's childhood within Tīmūr's extended family was affected by the locus of his grandfather's military activity. At the termination of the "Five Year Campaign" in 798/1396, Tīmūr's household returned to Samarqand where

[4] See Shujāʻ 1971; Yazdī (Tāj al-Dīn Ḥasan) 1987. [On the *Anīs al-nās*, see also C.-H. de Fouchécour's article in the present volume. Ed.]

[5] See Afshar 1978, 84–6; Raʻnā Ḥusaynī 1986.; see also footnote no. 72.

[6] See Rieu 1895, 126–7; Ṣafā 1984–, 4:118.

[7] Thackston 1989, 245–6; Shāmī 1937–56, 1:156–7, 2:117; Yazdī 1957, 1:504–11.

[8] Yazdī 1957, 1:515–6; Barthold 1956–62, 2:44; Woods 1990, 18, 43.

[9] Yazdī 1957, 1:544–5; Faṣīḥ Khvāfī 1960–2, 3:138.

[10] Yazdī 1957, 2:270.

[11] Ando 1990, 99–101, 163–4; Ḥāfiẓ-i Abrū 1993, 1:214.

[12] Ḥāfiẓ-i Abrū 1993, 1:596; Woods 1990, 45.

most remained during his Indian invasion; Ibrāhīm was among those welcoming the conqueror on his return in the spring of 801/1399.[13] Ibrāhīm and his "foster-mother" Tūmān Āghā also stayed in Samarqand when Tīmūr embarked on his "Seven Year Campaign" to the west in the following fall (802/1399), but by the spring of 803/1401 Tīmūr sent word that Tūmān Āghā was to bring "the children," including Ibrāhīm Sulṭān, to join the rest of the family at his encampment; their joyous reunion at Ūjān, near Sulṭānīyah, in early fall of 804/1401, was marked by feasting and the presentation of gifts.[14] At the conclusion of his Anatolian campaign in the spring of 805/1403, Tīmūr requested that Ibrāhīm, his elder brother Ulugh Beg, and their cousins Muḥammad Jahāngīr and Sa'd Vaqqāṣ, sons of Muḥammad Sulṭān ibn Jahāngīr, ride to meet him. This reunion, which occurred near Erzurum, was especially wrenching for the latter youths because Tīmūr was accompanied by the two-hundred horsemen in the funeral cortege of his grandson, their father, Muḥammad Sulṭān ibn Jahāngīr, who had died some weeks earlier.[15]

Tīmūr's male descendants were incorporated into military expeditions at an early age, but they remained under the tutelage of senior *amīr*s for several years thereafter. According to Yazdī, Ibrāhīm's *amīr*s participated in a brief and successful siege of the citadel at Fīrūzkūh in Dhū al-Qa'dah 806/May 1404. Afterwards, however, Ibrāhīm was among the young princes sent back to Samarqand under the protection of Tīmūr's wives rather than remaining with Tīmūr and the army.[16]

The year 807/10 July 1404–28 June 1405 was pivotal in Ibrāhīm's life. In the fall, shortly after his tenth birthday, he, his brother Ulugh Beg, and four of their cousins were the focus of attention at lavish celebrations on the occasion of their marriages in the Timurid encampment at Kān-i Gil on the outskirts of Samarqand.[17] Although some of these marriages may not have been consummated immediately because of the tender age of the parties involved, the new status of Ibrāhīm and Ulugh Beg was underscored in Tīmūr's preparations for an invasion of China, which began shortly after the wedding festivities. Each prince was also assigned to rule territory which the Timurid army hoped to occupy. Ulugh Beg's domain of Moghulistan from Tashkent to the border of China was partly under nominal Timurid control, but Ibrāhīm's assigned area,

[13] Yazdī 1957, 2:268–9.
[14] Ibid., 2:270.
[15] Ibid., 2:361.
[16] Ibid., 2:407–9.
[17] Ibid., 2:434–43.

a series of towns from Andīgān to Kāshghar and Khutan, stretched far beyond earlier Timurid conquests.[18]

It was apparently Tīmūr's plan that these two princes were to accompany his army and claim their new territories as they were conquered. For this expedition both princes were placed in the army's central corp near to Tīmūr himself, and each was accompanied by a seasoned *amīr* from Tīmūr's inner circle. The pairing of Ulugh Beg with his guardian, Amīr Shāh Malik, is predictable,[19] but the combination of Ibrāhīm Sulṭān with Amīr Shaykh Nūr al-Dīn is surprising, for they are not otherwise linked in historical sources;[20] this may help to explain why he alone of Tīmūr's *amīrs* is depicted in the illustrated version of Yazdī's *Ẓafarnāmah* prepared at Ibrāhīm's court.[21] Ibrāhīm and Shaykh Nūr al-Dīn must have been together frequently in the next few months, for the Timurid army normally camped in battle order.[22]

By the middle of Rajab 807/January 1405, Tīmūr's party had reached Utrār where preparations for the campaign continued, but in early Sha'bān/February Tīmūr was suddenly taken ill and died on 17 Sha'bān/19 February. Despite his youth, Ibrāhīm Sulṭān played a prominent role in the events which followed. The initial impulse of the *amīrs* at Utrar was to keep Tīmūr's death a secret and to continue the campaign as if nothing had happened; to that end, they decided to have Ibrāhīm take Tīmūr's place at the head of the army until Khalīl Sulṭān could join them and continue to lead them toward China.[23]

After dispatching Tīmūr's body to Samarqand for burial, which was soon followed by a second party with Ulugh Beg, several younger princes and Tīmūr's wives, Ibrāhīm Sulṭān and the *amīrs* set out as if on campaign, with drums beating and banners flying. Ibrāhīm's impersonation of Tīmūr was carried to the point that he even slept in Tīmūr's tent, with the conqueror's horsetail standard at the door.[24]

The copy of Yazdī's *Ẓafarnāmah* prepared at Ibrāhīm's court has a double-page painting depicting an event which followed Tīmūr's death. Its right side shows a bearded prince protected by the royal umbrella and its left contains an army's vanguard of musicians and flag-bearers.[25] Although Yazdī's chronicle of the events following Tīmūr's death is detailed, the focus of his narrative

[18] Ibid., 2:449.
[19] Ando 1992, 67, 103, 106–7.
[20] Ibid., 67, 110–3.
[21] Yazdī 1957, 2:488–9; Barthold 1956–62, 2:54, 57; Sims 1990–1, 201, 203, figs. 13, 16.
[22] Yazdī 1957, 2:452.
[23] Ibid., 2:477–8.
[24] Ibid., 2:480–1.
[25] Sims 1990–1, 210–1, figs. 36–7.

shifts repeatedly, so that the right and left sides of this painting are situated in two unrelated incidents.

This raises the question of which incident is depicted. The passage which borders the painting's right half records a conversation between Tīmūr's *amīr*s in which they pledge to observe his deathbed wishes and insure that his grandson Pīr Muḥammad ibn Jahāngīr accede to the throne, linking their plan with Tīmūr's well-known preference for descendants of his son Jahāngīr.[26] The second passage, flanking the painting's left half, describes Ibrāhīm Sulṭān's march at the head of Tīmūr's army with drums beating and banners flying.[27]

A comparison of these passages demonstrates that the painting depicts Ibrāhīm Sulṭān leading the Timurid army. However, two problems, one textual and the other pictorial, have led scholars to conclude that the person at the head of Tīmūr's army is not Ibrāhīm Sulṭān but rather Shāhrukh.[28] The two published versions of Yazdī's text, neither of which is a critical edition, contain Shāhrukh's name in a place where the logic of the narrative requires the name of Jahāngīr.[29] Furthermore, this painting's princely rider has a beard and moustache more appropriate for Shāhrukh than for the eleven-year-old Ibrāhīm Sulṭān.[30]

These two pieces of evidence may, however, be less convincing than they first appear. According to E. Sims, the princely rider's face has been repainted so that its beard and moustache may be later additions.[31] Also, the name of Shāhrukh found in published versions of Yazdī's text may be an interpolation. Shāhrukh's name does not seem to have been present in the manuscript on which the French Orientalist Pétis de la Croix based his summary translation.[32] If some copies of Yazdī's text were altered by inserting the name of Shāhrukh where it did not belong, such a change would parallel the alteration of other 15th-century chronicles to flatter him. The best known case is that of Mu'īn al-Dīn Naṭanzī who produced two versions of his *Muntakhab al-tavārīkh*. Another example is Maḥmūd Kutubī's *Tārīkh-i Āl-i Muẓaffar* which exaggerates Shāhrukh's role in the Timurid conquest of Fārs.[33]

Pending an examination of various manuscripts of Yazdī's text and a close study of this double-page painting, now divided between two collections,

[26] Yazdī 1957, 2:479.
[27] Ibid., 2:480, lines 12–20.
[28] Sims 1990–1, 210–1.
[29] Yazdī 1957, 2:479, line 11; Yazdī 1972, fol. 477r, line 9.
[30] Sims 1990–1, fig. 36.
[31] Ibid., 211.
[32] Yazdī 1722, 4:241–2 and 1722b, 2:393.
[33] Woods 1987, 89–93; Kutubī, 1985, 135.

it is reasonable to conclude that the double-page painting was intended to celebrate Ibrāhīm Sulṭān's march at the head of Tīmūr's army, an event which must have made a deep impression on him. Yazdī interprets it as a proof of the special affection which Tīmūr held for him, and as a prefiguration of his later rise to a position of power and glory.[34] Ibrāhīm Sulṭān's impersonation of Tīmūr was, however, of short duration. Within a couple of days, news that various claimants for Tīmūr's throne were hurrying toward Samarqand caused the *amīrs* to abandon this enactment; reversing course, they too, with Ibrāhīm Sulṭān in tow, headed toward the capital, even overtaking the party with Ulugh Beg and Tīmūr's wives.[35]

After reaching Samarqand and being denied entry by the *amīrs* in charge of that city's defense, Shāh Malik and Shaykh Nūr al-Dīn proceeded with Ulugh Beg and Ibrāhīm Sulṭān to Bukhārā, where they awaited clarification of the situation. There, the two princes and their *amīrs* resided in the citadel, each taking responsibility for one-half of the structure and one of its gates. When they realized that Khalīl Sulṭān had gained control of Samarqand, these *amīrs* began plotting his removal.[36] Soon, however, during Shāh Malik's absence, supporters of Khalīl Sulṭān gained the upper hand in Bukhārā as well, forcing Shaykh Nūr al-Dīn and the two princes to flee; the brothers eventually joined their father, Shāhrukh, at his encampment on the banks of the Murghab river.[37]

For the next few years, Ibrāhīm Sulṭān seems to have remained in Harāt, where he gained experience in civil administration by serving as his father's deputy under the supervision of a senior *amīr* in both 810/1407–8 and 811/1408–9.[38] The capture of Khalīl Sulṭān in the spring of 811/1408 allowed Shahrukh to enter Samarqand and install Ulugh Beg and his *amīrs* as its rulers. By the fall of 812/1409 Ibrāhīm Sulṭān himself was entrusted with the governorship of Balkh and its hinterland in place of Pīr Muḥammad ibn Muḥammad Sulṭān, who had recently been assassinated by his own *vazīr*.[39]

Despite his nominal independence, Ibrāhīm Sulṭān continued to rely on his father's senior commanders for assistance in a military crisis. During 815/1412–3, a threatened invasion of Ibrāhīm's domain by the ruler of neighboring Badakhshān was thwarted by several *amīrs* dispatched from Harāt. The rebel leader fled and his troops disbanded, which allowed the Timurid *amīrs*

34 Yazdī 1957, 2:470–1.
35 Ibid., 2:480–1, 484, 488–9.
36 Ibid., 2:488–9, 502, 504–5.
37 Ḥāfiẓ-i Abrū 1993, 1:20–2; Tāj al-Salmānī 1956, 41–4 and 1988, 32–5.
38 Ḥāfiẓ-i Abrū 1993, 1:196, 277.
39 Ibid., 1:319–20.

to install a more subservient local ruler.[40] The next military challenge facing Ibrāhīm Sulṭān, which arose in 818/1415, shortly after his installation as ruler of Shīrāz, would not be so easily resolved.

During the years which followed Tīmūr's death, western Iran was beset by various conflicts; rival Timurid governors raided or invaded each other's territories; the Qaraqoyunlu Turkmans encroached on the Timurid domain; and dissident *amīr*s, who were resisting Shāhrukh's attempts to control them, sought refuge in the area. By the fall of 816/1413 Shāhrukh marshaled his army and set out to deal with the region's problems. Although his initial goal was to curb Turkman power, he soon realized that the rebellion of his nephew, Iskandar Sulṭān ibn 'Umar Shaykh, was of more immediate concern. After seizing control of both Shīrāz and Iṣfahān, Iskandar declared *de facto* independence by minting coins in his own name. His apparent objective was to reconstitute Tīmūr's empire with himself as its ruler.[41]

The collapse of Iskandar Sulṭān's rebellion began in the summer of 817/1414, with Shāhrukh's siege of Iṣfahān, during which the ranks of Iskandar Sulṭān's supporters dwindled, especially after a pitched battle near the city. Finally, in Jumādá I 817/July 1414, Iskandar attempted to flee but was captured and blinded.[42] During the siege of Iṣfahān, and against the background of a revolt by its *kulū*s, or neighborhood leaders, Iskandar Sulṭān's deputies in Shīrāz too shifted their allegiance to Shāhrukh.[43] After three *amīr*s had been appointed governor of that city in rapid succession, Shāhrukh finally entrusted Shīrāz to Ibrāhīm Sulṭān, who had been managing the Timurid army's equipment and baggage. Shāhrukh then left for Harāt, arriving there on 12 Rajab 817/28 September 1414.[44]

The defeat of Iskandar Sulṭān at Iṣfahān did not, however, end the region's turmoil. By the next spring a new revolt was underway in Shīrāz. The uprising was initially sparked by the now blinded Iskandar Sulṭān in concert with his younger brother Bāyqarā, the ruler of Hamadān, with whom he resided. When their brother Rustam, the governor of Iṣfahān, learned of their plan to attack Shīrāz, he reacted by sending troops to intercept them. Although Iskandar was captured and subsequently executed, Bāyqarā continued toward Shīrāz, gathering support as he advanced. Ibrāhīm Sulṭān marshaled his troops and marched out to confront the invaders, but most of his *amīr*s defected to the

[40] Ibid., 1:467–70, Faṣīh Khvāfī 1960–2, 2:210.
[41] Ḥāfiẓ-i Abrū 1993, 1:494–504.
[42] Ibid., 1:530–7, 540–8.
[43] Yazdī (Tāj al-Dīn Ḥasan) 1987, 39–40.
[44] Ibid., 41; Ḥāfiẓ-i Abrū 1993, 1:537–40, 558–63.

rebel band, leaving him no choice but to return quickly to Shīrāz, where he took money and jewels from his treasury and then rode with his mother, Ṭūṭī Āghā, to Abarqūh.[45]

When the local dignitaries realized that Ibrāhīm had fled and that Bāyqarā was at the city gates with his troops, they welcomed him as the city's new ruler. In inciting his brother to rebel, Iskandar Sulṭān is said to have claimed that "all of my *amīr*s are in Shīrāz, and they will join you."[46] Bāyqarā also evidently found supporters among the local populace. Despite Ḥāfiẓ-i Abrū's characterization of his partisans as "ruffians" *(awbāsh)* and the "dregs of society" (*khasāyis al-nās*), the rapid collapse of Ibrāhīm Sulṭān's support among both the *amīr*s and the citizenry of Shīrāz underscores the region's resistance to external control.[47]

Shāhrukh responded to Ibrāhīm Sulṭān's defeat in Shīrāz as he had done to the crisis in Badakhshān, by sending senior *amīr*s to his rescue; this time, however, he himself came to join them. His senior commander, Jalāl al-Dīn Fīrūz Shāh, was immediately dispatched to Abarqūh with several *qushūn* (regiments) of reinforcements for Ibrāhīm Sulṭān, and word went out to various regional commanders to mobilize their troops and converge on Shīrāz. Within a few months, Jalāl al-Dīn, Ibrāhīm Sulṭān, and Rustam ibn 'Umar Shaykh had joined forces and reached Shīrāz, where Bāyqarā responded by preparing for a siege. However, faced with a massive Timurid army gathering that city, Bāyqarā realized that resistance was futile and began to plead for clemency. By early Ramaḍān 818/November 1417 this rebellion, begun in Rabī' I 818/ June 1415, had collapsed.[48]

Although the swift and unequivocal reaction of Shāhrukh and his *amīr*s to this crisis is indicative of their concern, terms granted to the rebels were surprisingly lenient. On the fifth of Ramaḍān, Bāyqarā came humbly before Shāhrukh and was granted a new post, albeit in the hinterland of Qandahār. Ḥasan Yazdī claims that all of Iskandar Sulṭān's *amīr*s were killed[49] but Ḥāfiẓ-i Abrū puts the number of those executed, "in the public interest" (*banā bar maṣlaḥat-i 'āmm*), at "two or three."[50] Shāhrukh tried to ensure the loyalty of the remaining rebels by granting them land exempt from rent or taxation (*suyūrghālāt va in'āmāt*).[51] Having bought stability with concessions, Shāhrukh

[45] Ḥāfiẓ-i Abrū 1993,1:591–6.
[46] Yazdī (Tāj al-Dīn Ḥasan) 1987, 41.
[47] Ḥāfiẓ-i Abrū 1993, 1:596.
[48] Ibid., 1:597–600, 2:601–5.
[49] Yazdī (Tāj al-Dīn Ḥasan) 1987, 42.
[50] Ḥāfiẓ-i Abrū 1993, 2:605.
[51] Ibid.

once more entrusted Shīrāz to Ibrāhīm Sulṭān and set out to visit local shrines on his way back to Harāt.[52]

Whatever its cost to the Timurid coffers, this peace was to endure until Ibrāhīm's death in Shawwāl 838/May 1435.[53] Despite the generally calm conditions in Shīrāz itself, Ibrāhīm Sulṭān became a seasoned commander during his period of governorship. His military campaigns were of two kinds, attacks on the neighboring regions of Luristān and Khūzistān, which were controlled by local rulers nominally subordinate to Shāhrukh in 825/1422, 828/1424 and 832/1429, and participation in Shāhrukh's campaigns against the Turkmans in north-west Iran during 823–4/1420–1 and 832–3/1429–30.

Of these, it was the battles against the Turkmans which were to prove the greatest challenge. The first campaign, of 823–4/1420–1, a response to Qarā Yūsuf's seizure of several important centers from Sulṭānīyah to Qazvīn, was deprived of its objective by Qarā Yūsuf's sudden death.[54] This left the Turkman army leaderless, and the Timurids were able to seize Tabrīz and to roam the countryside virtually at will. With his cavalry from Fārs, Ibrāhīm Sulṭān first besieged Marāghah and then, after spending the winter in Qarā Bāgh, joined forces with Shāh Malik. Their joint force of 20,000 attacked Nakhjavān and pursued a band of Turkman *amīrs*.[55] Finally, in mid-summer 824/1421 the Timurids encountered a substantial Turkman army near Akhlāṭ commanded by Qarā Yūsuf's sons Iskandar and Isfand.[56]

In the ensuing conflict near Akhlāṭ, which lasted several days, Ibrāhīm Sulṭān, his cousin Rustam ibn 'Umar Shaykh and their troops were situated in the Timurid army's right wing. A detailed description of this event, in the *Kitāb-i Diyārbakrīyah*, stresses their valor in battle and the fact that their stiff resistance caused the Turkman left wing to retreat. In Timurid sources the bravery of Rustam is particularly praised. Their actions forced Iskandar ibn Qarā Yūsuf to shift his tactics and focus his attack on the Timurid army's center led by Shāhrukh. First breaking its vanguard, the Turkmans then wreaked havoc in the army's core despite the presence of elephant-mounted archers, nearly seizing Shāhrukh's wives who had recently arrived from Harāt.[57] Eventually, however, the Timurids managed to drive back the attackers and proclaim a victory.

[52] Ibid., 2:606–10.

[53] Samarqandī 1946–9, 2 pt. 1:180–2, 184–6; Faṣīh Khvāfī 1960–2, 3:222–3.

[54] Ḥāfiẓ-i Abrū 1993, 2:710–25; Samarqandī 1946–9, 2 pt. 1:223–30; Faṣīh Khvāfī 1960–2, 3:241–3.

[55] Ḥāfiẓ-i Abrū 1993, 2:727, 752, 757.

[56] Ibid., 2:777.

[57] Ṭihrānī [1962–4] 1977, 1:83–8; Ḥāfiẓ-i Abrū 1993, 2:777–94; Khvānd Amīr [1954] 1983, 3:611–2.

After installing a new governor in Tabrīz, Shāhrukh disbanded his army in Ramaḍān 824/August–September 1421 and headed for Harāt.[58] Ibrāhīm Sulṭān was welcomed in Shīrāz as a victor by both the town's notables and the populace at large (according to the author of *Anīs al-nās*, some students—probably from local *madrasah*s—took the opportunity to complain about their straitened circumstances).[59] Ḥāfiẓ-i Abrū adds that the ruler of Khūzistān omitted to pay his respects, and consequently Ibrāhīm Sulṭān set out almost immediately on an invasion of that region.[60]

By 832/1429, after Iskandar ibn Qarā Yūsuf had managed to gain control over Tabrīz and to once more evict the Timurid garrison from Sulṭānīyah, Shāhrukh launched a second campaign. As the Timurid army left Harāt in Rajab 832/April 1429, Bāysunghur ibn Shāhrukh was assigned to its vanguard along with some of Shāhrukh's most trusted *amīrs*, such as Shaykh Luqman Barlās and 'Alīkā Kūkultāsh. Contingents from Shīrāz, Iṣfahān, Yazd, Abarqūh, and Kirmān all joined the main army at Ray in Ramaḍān 832/June 1429, but it is the one from Fārs led by Ibrāhīm Sulṭān which is singled out for praise by 'Abd al-Razzāq Samarqandī. Just before the Timurid army arrived, the Turkman garrison abandoned Sulṭānīyah, so that once again Shahrukh's forces advanced unhindered through Tabrīz and Khūy until they encountered the Qaraqoyunlu army near Salmās on 17 Dhū al-Ḥijjah 832/17 September 1429.[61]

During the ensuing battle of at least two days, Ibrāhīm Sulṭān and the army of Fars displayed exemplary bravery. They had been placed at the vanguard of the Timurid army's center near Bāysunghur's contingent, and Ibrāhīm personally led the charge. His ferocity in attacking Jahānshāh ibn Qarā Yūsuf caused Iskandar ibn Qarā Yūsuf to come to his brother's rescue. The pressure from Ibrāhīm Sulṭān and his warriors from Fārs along with the rest of Timurid army was eventually sufficient to force the Turkman army into a retreat led by Iskandar himself. After the battle, the Timurid army celebrated with prayers in a special mosque-tent.[62]

Shāhrukh's army is said to have had 100,000 horsemen, most of whom must have participated in the battle near Salmās, but it was Ibrāhīm Sulṭān's success in forcing the retreat of Iskandar ibn Qarā Yūsuf which came to epitomize the Timurid victory. Ibrāhīm Sulṭān's retinue included his mentor and

[58] Ḥāfiẓ-i Abrū 1993, 2:795–8.
[59] Ibid., 2:805–6; Shujā' 1971, 262.
[60] Ḥāfiẓ-i Abrū 1993, 2:805–6.
[61] Samarqandī 1946–9, 2 pt. 2:320–4.
[62] Ibid., 2:324–31; Khvānd Amīr [1954] 1983, 3:618–20.

advisor Sharaf al-Dīn ʻAlī Yazdī, who composed two quatrains about the prince's prowess which are quoted by both ʻAbd al-Razzāq Samarqandī and Khvānd Amīr. Both quatrains make liberal use of Ibrāhīm Sulṭān's *kunyah* "Abū al-Fatḥ" (The Victorious One), and the second concludes with a chronogram for the battle's date, 832.

Zi āʼīn-i s̱abāt-i Shāh Abū al-Fatḥ bi-jang
Khūn-shud zi ḥasad bi-rūz-i hayjā dil-i sang
Īn ḥāl zi kūhhā-yi Salmās bi-purs
Ka-z rāh-i ṣadā sharḥ dahand az dil-i tang

Iskandar-i Turkamān chū ʻiṣyān varzīd
Dārā-yi jahān sizā-yi ū vājib dīd
Az tīgh-i Abū al-Faṭh chū bi-grīkht zi jang
Tārīkh shud az qadr-i Abū al-Faṭh padīd

Translation

The firm resolve of Abū al-Fatḥ in combat
Flushed the [foe's] stone-heart with envy, on battle-day.
Inquire about this from the hills of Salmās,
Their reverberation evokes [his] anguish.

When Iskandar the Turkman a rebellion raised,
The age's Dara deemed his punishment meet.
His flight in battle from the spear of Abū al-Fatḥ
Was commemorated in: "the Might of Abū al-Fatḥ appeared."[63]

ʻAbd al-Razzāq Samarqandī's citation of these verses has led to speculation that they were intended for a chronicle of Ibrāhīm Sulṭān's life, which Sharaf al-Dīn mentions in the *Ẓafarnāmah*, but which was never written.[64] These two quatrains are, however, part of a longer narrative about the Turkman campaign. Sharaf al-Dīn himself includes them in the introduction to his treatise on verbal puzzles, *Risālah-i Muʻammā* or *Ḥulal-i muṭarraz*.[65] He mentions how he had the singular honor of accompanying Ibrāhīm Sulṭān "day by day and stage," which he describes as a rare privilege for a historian, in order to record Ibrāhīm's accomplishments.[66] He also includes eight couplets which he had composed about Ibrāhīm Sulṭān for the already completed *Tārīkh-i Humāyun*. The couplets in question compare Ibrāhīm Sulṭān to the Biblical

[63] Samarqandī 1946–9, 2 pt. 2:331; Khvānd Amīr [1954] 1983, 3:619–20. My translation.
[64] Yazdī 1957, 1:16–7 and 1972, xliv.
[65] *Risālah-i Muʻammā*, British Library, London, MS Or. 3509, fol. 7v.
[66] Ibid., fols. 7r–8v.

Patriarch Abraham. They also appear in the dedicatory preface of his *Ẓafarnāmah*.[67] Yazdī further comments that he has written the treatise on riddles at Ibrāhīm Sulṭān's request immediately after his own return to Shīrāz from the Āẕarbāyjān campaign, that is, in 832/1429.[68] Sharaf al-Dīn's treatise must have been known in Harāt because 'Abd al-Raḥmān Jāmī composed a similar work entitled *Hilyat al-ḥulal* in 856/1452–3.[69]

The stress placed on Ibrāhīm Sulṭān's role in the Timurid victory at Salmās by Samarqandī and Khvānd Amīr underscores its fame in the period, a prominence further enhanced by Yazdī's description of this campaign in his *Ḥulal-i muṭarraz*. It is therefore appropriate that a depiction of this incident was included in the opening pages of a copy of Firdawsī's *Shāhnāmah* prepared for him, now in the Bodleian Library, Oxford. Although it has long been assumed that this painting depicts Ibrāhīm Sulṭān in battle, the specific event recorded had never been identified (Figs. 1–2).[70]

A comparison of this painting's composition with textual descriptions of the battle at Salmās reveals their parallels. The two-page illustration shows the clash of two armies, each divided into three sections—the center, right and left wings—typical for the armies of this period. Each page has two zones of action, a foreground where the armies are engaged in combat, and a central area which shows the confrontation of two royal warriors. The prince depicted on fol. 7v advances looking straight ahead, preceded by three footmen and followed by a company of horsemen. The painting on fol. 6r shows a prince who glances apprehensively over his shoulder and who is preceded by a solitary footman. A group of horsemen, just behind the prince, are turned so that they face the viewer, as if uncertain whether to advance or to retreat. Taken together, these pages seem to depict the confrontation between Ibrāhīm Sulṭān and Iskandar ibn Qarā Yūsuf Turkman which led to Iskandar's flight and the rout of his army.

Even though the painting from the Bodleian manuscript is not physically connected to a description of Ibrāhīm Sulṭān's triumph at Salmās, it is most probable that this theme would have been recognized by its royal patron. The popularity of Sharaf al-Dīn's verses would have aided others in understanding its message. The painting could even be said to illustrate the final couplet of his second quatrain:

[67] Ibid., fol., 8v; Yazdī 1957, 1:16.

[68] *Risālah-i Mu'ammā*, fols. 9r–v.

[69] Ṣafā 1984–, 4:118. In fact, Jāmī and Yazdī had met each other in Harāt around 850/1446, see 'Abd al-Vāsi' Niẓāmī 1992, 106–7.

[70] *Shāhnāmah*, Bodleian Library, Oxford, MS Add. 176, fols. 6r, 7v; cf. Sims 1992, 45–8.

His flight in battle from the spear of Abū al-Fatḥ
Was commemorated in: "the Might of Abū al-Fatḥ appeared."

It is of interest that Sharaf al-Dīn describes himself as the "composer of this sketch" (*nigārandah-i īn taṣvīr*) in his discussion of the Āẕarbāyjān campaign, which suggests that he intended his remarks to provide a mental "image" of the events in question.[71] This hint of Sharaf al-Dīn's involvement in the illustrative process suggests that he may have had some connection with the work of Ibrāhīm Sulṭān's *kitābkhānah*. His more general participation in the creation of luxury manuscripts is corroborated by verses which he composed to decorate the bindings of particularly beautiful manuscripts. A group of such verses are among the portions of a *majmū'ah* from Timurid Shīrāz published by Iraj Afshar.[72]

The historical specificity and compositional accuracy of this battle painting offers a striking contrast to the generic scenes used to illustrate several battles in a copy of Yazdī's *Ẓafarnāmah* also linked to Ibrāhīm Sulṭān's patronage,[73] and suggests that the painter of the Bodleian *Shāhnāmah* frontispiece must have been aided in his task by an eye-witness to the event. Although none of the *Shāhnāmah* paintings is signed, the manuscript's illuminated dedication page bears a minute inscription "*dhahhabahu Naṣīr al-Sulṭānī*."[74] A *manshūr* (decree) contained in the *majmū'ah* mentioned above records the appointment of this same Naṣīr al-Dīn Muḥammad the illuminator (*muẕahhib*) as the *kalāntar* (supervisor) of Ibrāhīm Sulṭān's *kitābkhānah*. This *manshūr*, which extols Naṣīr al-Dīn's skill as a scribe, illuminator and painter, also requests that he supervise the work of other scribes, illuminators, and painters.[75] It is thus probable that the battle scene from Ibrāhīm Sulṭān's *Shāhnāmah* is the result of a collaboration between Sharaf al-Dīn 'Alī Yazdī and Naṣīr al-Dīn Muḥammad or one of the other painters active in Ibrāhīm's workshop. This creation of the visual record of a specific event gives

[71] *Risālah-i Mu'ammā*, fol. 7r.

[72] There are four manuscript copies of this *majmū'ah*: two in Tehran (in the former Kitābkhānah-i Majlis-i Sinā and in the Kitābkhānah-'i Markazī-i Dānishgāh-i Tihrān), one in Cambridge, England (Cambridge University Library), and one in İstanbul (Topkapı Palace Library), see Dānish'pizhūh 1972, 763–4 and 1961, 1371–7, no. 2576; Bayānī 1961, 240–1; Karatay 1961, 233, no. 676; Browne 1932, 107–9. For the printed text of the poems by Yazdī, see Afshar 1978, 84–6.

[73] Sims 1991, figs. 8–9, 14, 25–6.

[74] *Shāhnāmah*, fols. 16v–7r.

[75] See Ra'nā Ḥusaynī 1986, 71–2.

credence to Ibn 'Arabshāh's claim of having seen a pictorial synopsis of Tīmūr's campaigns on the walls of Samarqand palaces.[76]

Ibrāhīm Sulṭān's triumph at Salmās also represents the culminating episode of his military career. Tīmūr's sons and his older grandsons had often distinguished themselves on the battlefield by the age of seventeen or eighteen. By comparison, Ibrāhīm Sulṭān appears to have developed his military expertise more gradually. Texts of the period permit us to follow his military adventures: the siege at Fīrūzkūh in 806/1404, the Chinese expedition in 807/1405, the debacle in Shīrāz in 818/1415, his own campaigns during 825/1422, 828/1424 and 832/1428, and finally his triumphs of 832–3/1429–30 in northwestern Iran against the Turkmans. It is, however, the combination of Sharaf al-Dīn 'Alī Yazdī's verses and the painting in the Bodleian Library *Shāhnāmah* which leaves the most vivid impression of Abu al-Fatḥ Ibrāhīm Sulṭān ibn Shāhrukh ibn Tīmūr in his moment of glory.

This celebration of Ibrāhīm Sulṭān's military prowess in image and verse should not be viewed as mere flattery. As the citizens of 9th/15th-century Shīrāz were well aware, both the city's internal stability and its external security depended on the military fortitude of its ruler. Although modern evaluations of the Timurids often stress their cultural patronage, skill in the martial arts conferred high prestige in their own time. Even though he did not lead armies on far-flung conquests, Ibrāhīm Sulṭān's military accomplishments served to enhance the stability of the empire his grandfather had created.

[76] Ibn 'Arabshāh 1986, 465.

Fig. 1. Iskandar ibn Qarā Yūsuf in battle. Circa 833/1430. *Shāhnāmah*, Bodleian Library, Oxford, MS Add. 176, fol. 6r. 10.4 x 7.4 cm. By permission of the Bodleian Library

Fig. 2. Ibrāhīm Sulṭān directing the Salmās battle. Circa 833/1430. *Shāhnāmah*, Bodleian Library, Oxford, MS Add. 176, fol. 7v. 10.5 x 7.3 cm. By permission of the Bodleian Library

BIBLIOGRAPHY

'ABD AL-VĀSI' NIẒĀMĪ. 1992. *Maqāmāt-i Jāmī : gūshah'hā'ī az tārīkh-i farhangī va ijtimā'ī-i Khurāsān dar 'aṣr-i Tīmūriyān*. Ed. Najīb Māyil Haravī. Tehran : Nashr-i Nay.

AFSHAR, IRAJ. 1978. Ṣaḥḥāfī az nigāh-i farhang va tārīkh. In *Ṣaḥḥāfī-i sunnatī : majmū'ah-'i pānzdah guftār va kitābshināsī dar bārah-'i varrāqī, ṣaḥḥāfī, vaṣṣālī, mujalladgarī az yādgārhā-yi hunar-i Īrānī va Islāmī*. Ed. Iraj Afshar. Tehran : Kitābkhānah-'i Markazī va Markaz-i Asnād-i Dānishgāh-i Tihrān, 1357 Sh.: 77–94.

ANDO, SHIRO. 1992. *Timuridische Emire nach dem Mu'izz al-ansāb : Untersuchung zur Stammesaristokratie Zentralasiens im 14. und 15. Jahrhundert*. Berlin : K. Schwarz.

BARTOLD, A. A. 1956–62. *Four studies on the history of Central Asia*. Tr. V. and T. Minorsky. 3 vols. Leiden : E. J. Brill.

BAYĀNĪ, MAHDĪ. 1961. Majmū'ah-'i munsha'āt. *Rāhnamā-yi kitāb* 4, no. 3 (Khurdād 1340 Sh.): 239–44.

BROWNE, EDWARD G. 1932. *A descriptive catalogue of the Oriental MSS. belonging to the late E. G. Browne*. Completed & ed. Reynold A. Nicholson. Cambridge, [England] : [Cambridge] University Press.

DĀNISH'PIZHŪH, MUḤAMMAD TAQĪ. 1961. *Fihrist-i Kitābkhānah-'i Markazī-i Dānishgāh-i Tihrān*. Vol. 9, Tehran : Dānishgāh-i Tihrān, 1340 Sh.

—— 1972. Anīs al-nās. *Rāhnamā-yi kitāb* 14, nos. 9–12 (Āẕar-Isfand 1350 Sh.): 763–6.

FAṢĪḤ KHVĀFĪ. 1960–2. *Mujmal-i Faṣīḥī*. Ed. Maḥmūd Farrukh. 3 vols. Mashhad : Kitābfurūshī-i Bāstān, 1339–40 Sh.

ḤĀFIẒ-I ABRŪ. 1993. *Zubdat al-tavārīkh*. Ed. Kamāl Ḥājj Sayyid Javādī. 2 vols. Tehran : Vizārat-i Farhang va Irshād-i Islāmī : Nashr-i Nay, 1372 Sh.

IBN 'ARABSHĀH. 1986. *'Ajā'ib al-maqdūr fī nawā'ib Tīmūr*. Ed. Aḥmad Fāyiz al-Ḥimṣī. Beirut : Mu'assasat al-Risālah.

KARATAY, FEHMI EDHEM. 1961. *Topkapı Sarayı Müzesi Kütüphanesi Farsça yazmalar kataloğu : no. 1–940*. İstanbul : Kütüphane.

KHVĀND AMĪR. [1954] 1983. *Tārīkh-i Ḥabīb al-siyar fī akhbār-i afrād-i bashar*. Ed. Muḥammad Dabīr Siyāqī, introd. Jalāl al-Dīn Humā'ī. 4 vols. Reprint, Tehran : Kitābfurūshī-i Khayyām, 1362 Sh.

—— 1994. *Habibu's-siyar : tome three*. Tr. & ed. W. M. Thackston. 2 vols. Cambridge, Massachusetts : The Department of Near Eastern Languages and Civilizations, Harvard University.

KUTUBĪ, MAḤMŪD. 1985. *Tārīkh-i Āl-i Muẓaffar*. 2nd ed. Ed. 'Abd al-Ḥusayn Navā'ī. Tehran : Amīr Kabīr, 1364 Sh.

RA'NĀ ḤUSAYNĪ, KARĀMAT, ed. 1986. Manshūr-i kalāntarī-i Khvājah Naṣīr Muẕahhib. *Farhang-i Īrān zamīn* 27 (1365 Sh.): 69–72.

RIEU, CHARLES. 1895. *Supplement to the catalogue of the Persian manuscripts in the British Museum*. London : The Trustees of the British Museum.

ṢAFĀ, ẔABĪḤ ALLĀH. 1984–. *Tārīkh-i adabīyāt dar Īrān*. New ed. 5 vols. in 8 to date. Tehran : Firdawsī, 1363 Sh.–

SAMARQANDĪ, 'ABD AL-RAZZĀQ. 1946–9. *Maṭla'-i sa'dayn va majma'-i baḥrayn*. Ed. Muḥammad Shafī'. 2 vols. in 3. Lahore : Chāpkhānah-i Gīlānī, 1365–8.

SHĀMĪ, NIẒĀM AL-DĪN. 1937–56. *Tārīkh-i futūḥāt-i Amīr Tīmūr Kūrkān ma'rūf bih Ẓafarnāmah*. Ed. Felix Tauer. Prague : Archiv Orientální.

SIMS, ELEANOR. 1990–1. Ibrāhīm-Sulṭān's illustrated Ẓafar-nāmeh of 839/1436. *Islamic art* 4: 175–217.

—— 1992. Illustrated manuscripts of Firdausī's Shāhnāma commissioned by princes of the House of Tīmūr. *Ars orientalis* 22: 43–68.

TĀJ AL-SALMĀNĪ. 1956. *Šams al-ḥusn : beine Chronik vom Tode Timurs bis zum Jahre 1409*. Ed. Hans Robert Roemer. Wiesbaden : F. Steiner.

—— 1988. *Tarihnâme*. Tr. İsmail Aka. Ankara : Türk Tarih Kurumu Yayınları.

THACKSTON, W. M., tr. 1989. *A century of princes : sources on Timurid history and art*. Cambridge, Massachusetts : The Aga Khan Program for Islamic Architecture.

ṬIHRĀNĪ, ABŪ BAKR. [1962–4] 1977. *Kitāb-i Diyārbakrīyah : tārīkh-i Ḥasan Bayk Āq'qūyunlū va aslāf-i ū va anchah bidān muta'alliq ast az tavārīkh-i Qarāqūyunlū va Chaghātāy*. Ed. Necati Lugal, Faruk Sümer. 2 vols. in 1. Reprint with a Persian introd. by F. Sümer, Tehran : Ṭahūrī.

WOODS, JOHN E. 1987. The rise of Tīmūrid historiography. *Journal of Near Eastern studies* 46, no. 2 (April): 81–108.

—— 1990. *The Timurid dynasty*. Bloomington, Ind. : Indiana University, Research Institute for Inner Asian Studies.

YAZDĪ, SHARAF AL-DĪN 'ALĪ. 1723. *Histoire de Timur Bec, connu sous le nom du grand Tamerlan, empereur des Mongols et Tartares*. Tr. Pétis de la Croix. 4 vols. Delf : Reinier Boitet.

—— 1723b. *The history of Timur-Beg, known by the name of Tamerlain the Great, Emperor of the Moguls and Tartars : being an historical journal of his conquests in Asia and Europe*. Anon. English trans. from French trans. of Pétis de la Croix. 2 vols. London : Printed for J. Darby, E. Bell, W. Taylor, W. and J. Innys, J. Osborne, and T. Payne.

—— 1957. *Ẓafarnāmah : tārīkh-i 'umūmī-i mufaṣṣal-i Īrān dar dawrah-'i Tīmūriyān*. Ed. Muḥammad 'Abbāsī. 2 vols. Tehran : Amīr Kabīr, 1336 Sh.

—— 1972. *Ẓafarnāmah*. Ed. A. Urunbaev. Tashkent : Idārah-'i Intishārāt-i Fann.

YAZDĪ, TĀJ AL-DĪN ḤASAN. 1987. *Jāmi' al-tavārīkh-i Ḥasanī : bakhsh-i Tīmūriyān pas az Tīmūr*. Ed. Ḥusayn Mudarrisī Ṭabāṭabā'ī, Iraj Afshar. Karachi, Pakistan : Mu'assasah-'i Taḥqīqāt-i 'Ulūm-i Āsiyā-yi Miyānah va Gharbī, Dānishgāh-i Karāchī.

“The Good Companion” (*‘Anīs al-Nās*) : a Manual for the Honest Man in Shīrāz in the 9th/15th Century

*C.-H. de Fouchécour**

THE WORK UNDER DISCUSSION, *ANĪS AL-NĀS*, “SEEMS to have been forgotten, as had its author,” its eminent editor, Iraj Afshar, has remarked.[1] It was written in twenty chapters around 830/1426–7 by a man named Shujā‘, who dedicated it to the noted Timurid patron of arts and grandson of Tīmūr, Abū al-Fatḥ Ibrāhīm Sulṭān ibn Shāhrukh, who was the governor in Shīrāz of the provinces of Fārs, Kirmān and Luristān during the period between 817/1414 and 838/1435.[2] A manuscript copy of *Anīs al-nās* exists today which was made for the library of Ibrāhīm Sulṭān and which seems to date from the author's time.[3] It lacks part of chapter 19, all of chapter 20 and, presumably, a colophon, and must have been transferred to the library of Shāhrukh, Ibrāhīm Sulṭān's father, after Ibrāhīm Sulṭān's untimely death in 838/1435, as it bears on two pages the stamp of the library of Shāhrukh. Offered for sale to the Kitābkhānah-'i Millī in late 1320 Sh./early 1942, it immediately attracted the interest of the ever-attentive bibliophile Muḥammad Qazvīnī, who was then on the library's council and who highly recommended its immediate procurement.[4] Qazvīnī based his recommendation on the new information that he said the book presented “in passing” on “Āl Muẓaffar, Āl Īnjū, and on Ḥāfiẓ himself.”[5] The manuscript is now in the Kitābkhānah-'i

* Kambiz Eslami made invaluable comments and suggestions on several points in the article for which I am most grateful.

[1] Shujā‘ 1971, 11.

[2] [On Ibrāhim Sulṭān's military career, see Priscilla P. Soucek's article in the present volume. Ed.]

[3] According to Muḥammad Qazvīnī, the text of this manuscript is “almost undoubtedly” in the author's hand, see Qazvīnī 1984, 9:20, 39; Iraj Afshar, however, disagrees with Qazvīnī, attributing only the marginal additions and corrections to Shujā‘, see Shujā‘ 1971, introd., 15.

[4] Shujā‘ 1971, introd., 12.

[5] Qazvīnī 1984, 9:21; Qazvīnī adds that the book's style of composition and subject matter—which he characterizes as faded copies of *Qābūs'nāmah* and *Kalīlah va Dimnah*—are of “no importance whatsoever,” see ibid. In issuing that verdict Qazvīnī was of course relying on his fine sense of literary and historical tradition.

Majlis-i Shūrā-yi Islāmī (MS 6550), although it is not clear when it was transferred from the Kitābkhānah-'i Millī, if in fact Kitābkhānah-'i Millī followed Qazvīnī's recommendation and actually purchased it.[6] Using this manuscript, Iraj Afshar prepared a critical edition of *Anīs al-nās* in 1349 Sh./1970, which was published a year later in Tehran.[7]

The interest of the *Anīs al-nās* is multiple. Shujā' wrote each of the twenty chapters of his book while having before his eyes, opened at the corresponding chapters, the famous *Qābūs'nāmah* of the Prince of Gurgān and Ṭabaristān, Kaykāvūs ibn Iskandar, which had been written around 475/1082, i.e., almost three and a half centuries before Shujā' composed his book. The two works are books of *adab*; in other words, they discuss the behavior of man in society, and in doing so they treat the subject with a studied literary approach. One was a model for the other, but more than three turbulent centuries created a considerable historical distance between them. For those who consider tradition important, this unilateral contact presents a great interest.[8] But before bringing out the most striking divergence between the two works, that of the distribution of their chapters, a brief historical note is called for.

Shujā' himself, like Kaykāvūs before him, speaks of famous men of his time. Tīmūr, for instance, is a figure whose conquests are mentioned. Shujā' even refers the reader to a book on that very subject called *Kitāb-i Fatḥnāmah-'i Sulṭānī*, which was being compiled at the time under Ibrahīm Sulṭān's supervision and which later turned out to be the famous Timurid chronicle *Ẓafarnāmah* by Sharaf al-Dīn Yazdī.[9] Another important personage is Ibrāhīm Sulṭān himself who, as mentioned before, was the dedicatee of *Anīs al-nās*. His role as both a military leader and a patron of arts was highly regarded and

[6] Iraj Afshar notes that in 1331 Sh./1952–3 the manuscript "was offered" to the Minister of Culture, Mahdī Āẕar, who then asked Mujtabá Mīnūvī to give an appraisal of it, see Shujā' 1971, introd., 12.

[7] There is another manuscript copy of *Anīs al-nās* which was not recognized as such until the publication of Mr. Afshar's edition, see Dānish'pizhūh 1972. This is item no. 3982 in Kitābkhānah-'i Markazī-i Dānishgāh-i Tihrān and was initially identified as a *Risālah dar akhlāq va siyāsat* by Muḥammad Taqī Dānish'pizhūh when he was cataloging the manuscripts of the Kitābkhānah, see Dānish'pizhūh 1961b, 2976–8. Like the Majlis manuscript, this copy too lacks many folios. It begins from the middle of chapter 5 and ends at about the middle of chapter 18.

[8] See de Fouchécour, 1994.

[9] Shujā' 1971, 387; Qazvīnī 1984, 9:39, footnote no. 1. Relying on information found in two other sources (Dānish'pizhūh 1961, 1377 and Bayānī 1961, 240), M. T. Dānish'pizhūh considers this *Fatḥnāmah* a different work and attributes it to Sharaf al-Dīn's brother, Qavām al-Dīn Muḥammad, see Dānish'pizhūh 1961b, 2976, footnote no. 1. For a further discussion about the composition of *Ẓafarnāmah*, see Ando 1995.

praised in Ḥāfiẓ-i Abrū's *Zubdat al-tavārīkh*,[10] Dawlatshāh Samarqandī's *Taẕkirat al-shu'arā'*,[11] Khvandamīr's *Ḥabīb al-siyar*,[12] and, of course, Yazdī's *Ẓafarnāmah*,[13] among others. Ibrāhīm Sulṭān had earned that reputation. In 812/1409 he was appointed ruler of Balkh by his father, Shāhrukh. That appointment was followed by the governorship of the region of Fārs, a post he held until his death in 838/1435.

Nevertheless, the events discussed in *Anīs al-nās* pertain, for the most part, to princes who ruled in Shīrāz before the Timurids. These events, however, were not too distant and had strongly marked people's minds. More importantly, Shujā' brings out names tied to great historical and cultural ruptures. The earliest rupture referred to is in connection with Musta'ṣim Billāh, the last Abbasid caliph of Baghdād, whom Hülegü put to death in 656/1258.[14] Abū Isḥaq, the last Injuid ruler of Shīrāz, whom the Mozaffarid Mubāriz al-Dīn Muḥammad defeated in 757/1356 and executed the following year, is of special interest, because it was to his family that our author belonged.[15] In order to emphasize Abū Isḥaq's clemency, Shujā' attributes to him the anecdote which Kaykāvūs had told of the caliph Mu'āwīyah.[16] Closer to the time of Shujā' is Shāh Manṣūr, the last Mozaffarid ruler of Shīrāz, who died while fighting Tīmūr in 795/1393.[17] One exception to this list is Shāh-i Shujā' (r. 759–86/1357–84), a brilliant Mozaffarid and great patron of Ḥāfiẓ Shīrāzī, a royal figure with a positive image in *Anīs al-nās*, especially because of his generosity and fairness.[18] Shujā' recounts how Shāh-i Shujā' punished his own father Mubāriz al-Dīn Muḥammad, for his cruelty, by blinding him.[19]

As for Shujā', the author of *Anīs al-nās*, he was related to the Injuids, not to the Mozaffarids, more precisely to Abū Isḥaq, because the latter "was the son of the paternal uncle of the grandfather of the present author (i.e., Shujā')"[20]; his grandfather was thus the first cousin of Abū Isḥaq, ruler of Shīrāz from 743/1343 to 754/1353. We do not know any other name of Shujā', which he himself uses only once in the book.[21] As mentioned before, the last folios of

[10] See Ḥāfiẓ-i Abrū 1993, 1:559–60.
[11] See Dawlatshāh Samarqandī 1987, 287–8.
[12] See Khvāndamīr 1954, 3:537ff., 581, 594–5, etc.
[13] See Yazdī 1957, 1:15–6.
[14] Shujā' 1971, 233–4.
[15] Ibid, 303, 365.
[16] Ibid, 303–4; cf. 'Unṣur al-Ma'ālī 1992, 153–4 and 1951, 141–2.
[17] Shujā' 1971, 363.
[18] Ibid., 279–82.
[19] Ibid., 360–1.
[20] Ibid., 303.
[21] Ibid., 1971, 5.

both known manuscripts of *Anīs al-nās* are lost; they may have contained more specific information about our author. Sa'īd Nafīsī has referred to him as "Shujā'-i Shīrāzī."[22] But was he really from Shīrāz? He went there to seek princely help, but he does not seem to have had a good opinion of the *Shīrāzī*s.[23] More specifically, he displays a particular aversion toward two local *shaykh*s for their stupidity, incompetence, lasciviousness, ingratitude, arrogance, and greed.[24] These two are Mawlānā Nūr Samarqandī, a companion of Sayyid Shams al-Dīn Muḥammad Sayyid Sharīf (not to be confused with the celebrated and multifaceted scholar 'Alī ibn Muḥammad al-Jurjānī, also called Sayyid al-Sharīf, who lived for several years in Shīrāz and died there in 816/1413),[25] and Mawlānā Muḥammad Kurd, a former teacher of the Fazārīyah school in Shīrāz.[26] Shujā' ridicules them with a vengeance and in beautiful prose. But Shujā' is proud to be an Iranian, because, in his view, "the Iranians (*'ajamī*) are superior to non-Iranians, for one can adapt this type of people to one's own temperament."[27]

Shujā', furthermore, reckons himself among the poor of his time and he recounts what sort of experience it was to have to ask a rich person for help.[28] The experience which seems to have especially affected him was a misfortune whose origin is not fully explained but which forced Shujā' to flee "from the people of this day and age."[29] He runs into a trying confrontation with the chief of police (*ra'īs*) of the miserable village of Gūkān (in the district of Jahrum, to the south of Shīrāz), in the worst season, summer. No succor, no book, no conversation, just the babble of stupid peasants, a prison—until the moment he is told that writing a book for the prince of Shīrāz would save him.[30] And that he decides to do. He produces descriptions whose obviously literary style is beautiful; but certain concrete allusions are too emphatic to let literary dexterity obscure the underlying reality of an event that has been lived. Repeatedly, foolishness and fools are the target of Shujā''s criticism. He also complains that he suffered the loss of hope; solitude, which he makes the object of eloquent praise, is his only remedy.[31]

[22] Nafīsī 1965–6, 1:260.

[23] Shujā' was not alone; another contemporary of his, Sharaf al-Dīn 'Alī Yazdī (d. 858/1454), felt the same way, see Ṣafā 1984–, 4:302.

[24] This list of negative traits continues, see Shujā' 1971, 256–66, 326–9.

[25] See Tritton 1983.

[26] Shujā' 1971, 256–66, 326–9.

[27] Ibid., 266.

[28] Ibid., 321.

[29] Ibid., 5.

[30] Ibid., 4–11.

[31] Ibid., 26–7.

The dedicatee of the work is thus a prince. The dedication is made to immortalize his name and to earn a reward for the author. But Shujā‘'s goal is mainly to write a book of ethics (*akhlāq*)[32]—ethics associated with a certain milieu in Shīrāz in the 9th/15th century. His book is therefore not a mirror for princes, and that is an important difference between *Anīs al-nās* and the work of Kaykāvūs ibn Iskandar, the *Qābūs'nāmah*. For what readers was the book really intended?

In the chapter where he discusses marriage, Shujā‘ is more explicit on the manner in which he divides society. He prefers the middle class (*awsaṭ al-nās*)[33]; and it is for them that he enumerates the rules which should guide a man in the choice of a spouse. The upper class (to whom the normal rules of marriage do not apply) consist of the *mulūk va arbāb va iḥtishām*, princes, lords and high officials, their goal being to have many children.[34] The lower class (*mardum-i bāzārī*) know nothing else but to utter vulgarities and resort to blows, and are characterized by foolishness (*safāhat*).[35] Finally, another division of society, also quite common, was to distinguish between people of bad extraction (*bad aṣl*), whom Shujā‘ simply views as vile (*la'īm*) creatures, imbeciles (*safīh)*, and those who combined good extraction (*aṣīl*) with virtue (*hunar, hunarmand*).[36]

Such is this "good companion," this favorite of people, *Anīs al-nās*, whom Shujā‘ wishes to create and for whom he writes: a man who is neither truly powerful nor vulgar, a "well-born" man, in whom virtue finds a fertile ground, a comportment of respectable origin, a man whose parents themselves are "well-born." Shujā‘ writes for a social milieu from which he himself has come; he is not a courtier and scorns those whom he considers rustic, so he addresses himself to those at his level of society.

In order to better grasp the plan which guided Shujā‘ in the composition of his work, it is necessary to compare it to the plan which guided his model, the *Qābūs'nāmah* of Kaykāvūs ibn Iskandar.[37]

Kaykāvūs wrote for his son Gīlān Shāh; his intention was that of the educator of a prince, but his great originality was to write a princes' mirror whose frame he broke so that the prince could lose his position and be exposed to all the situations of an honest man of his time. Chapters 1 through 7

[32] Ibid., 11.
[33] Ibid., 224.
[34] Ibid.
[35] Ibid., 225.
[36] Ibid., 20–1.
[37] See also de Fouchécour 1986.

of the *Qābūs'nāmah* propose a personal moral life to every wise and noble man; the "Counsels of Anūshirvān" (*Dar yād kardan-i pandhā-yi Nūshīn'ravān*) (chapter 8) sums up the lessons of the previous chapters as if they were to be memorized.[38] Chapters 9 through 30 discuss the *ādāb*, rules of conduct to be observed in diverse circumstances of life in society; they are meant, basically, for a master of the house who has to regulate his life at home. Crafts and honorable functions, as well as the arts pertaining to them, are the subject of chapters 31 through 43; we see there the culmination of the princely function, around which everything else is organized. The *Qābūs'nāmah* is thus secretly inspired by the Aristotelian division of three spheres of life: individual, domestic, and communal. Nevertheless, chapter 44 (*Dar āyyin-i javānmardpīshagī* [or *juvānmardpīshagī*]) eschews all these divisions and introduces a cross section hierarchy based on the notion of *javānmardī*, the noble and generous conduct in relation to which all humans are organized. Such was the aim in the scheme of Kaykāvūs, the human ideal which he was proposing.

Almost four centuries later, Shujā' takes up Kaykāvūs's book, but with a different purpose in mind. His book starts with a lighter version of the *Qābūs'nāmah*'s chapter 8, the "Counsels of Anūshirvān." Except for three, all the chapters of the *Anīs al-nās* are fashioned after chapters 9 through 30 of the *Qābūs'nāmah*, which deal precisely with *ādāb*. As for chapter 5, it corresponds to chapter 32 of the *Qābūs'nāmah*, on commerce, a trade taken into account by an author who speaks to the middle class of his society. Chapter 18 corresponds to chapter 38 of the *Qābūs'nāmah*, on the boon companion (*nadīm*), who is conceived of by Shuja' as the boon companion of any important master of a household, not of the prince alone. Finally, chapter 20 of the *Anīs al-nās* (*Dar bāb-i ādāb-i 'avāqib-i aḥvāl andīshidan*) evidently must have discussed the importance of reflecting on the consequences of situations of life; Kaykāvūs did not reserve a chapter for this topic, and it is a great pity that this portion of both known manuscripts of the *Anīs al-nās* is lost; *aḥvāl*, the circumstances of life, are not actions (*a'māl*); Shujā' must thus have left the framework of morals in this chapter, and one would have loved to know what kind of *aḥvāl* had attracted his attention.

The following list shows the corresponding chapters of the two works:

[38] Ibid., 38–58, 188

Anīs al-nās	*Qābūs'nāmah*
1. *Dar naṣāyiḥ-i ḥukamā farzandān rā*	8. *Dar yād kardan-i pandhā-yi Nūshīn'ravān*
2. *Dar bāb-i ādāb-i dūst guzīdan va sharṭ-i ān*	28. *Dar āyīn-i dūst giriftan*
3. *Dar bāb-i ādāb-i zīstan bā dushman va sharṭ-i ān*	29. *Dar andīshah kardan az dushman*
4. *Dar bāb-i ādāb-i jam' kardan-i amvāl va sharṭ-i ān*	21. *Dar jam' kardan-i māl*
5. *Dar bāb-i ādāb-i tijārat va sharṭ-i ān*	32. *Dar bāzargānī kardan*
6. *Dar bāb-i ādāb-i 'ishq varzīdan va sharṭ-i ān*	14. *Dar 'ishq varzīdan* 15. *Andar tamattu' kardan*
7. *Dar bāb-i ādāb-i sharāb khvurdan va sharṭ-i ān*	11. *Dar āyīn-i sharāb khvurdan*
8. *Dar bāb-i ādāb-i muṭāyibah va muḥāvirah va nard va shaṭranj*	13. *Andar mizāḥ kardan va nard va Shaṭrānj bākhtan*
9. *Dar bāb-i ādāb-i tajammul va khānah kharīdan va sharṭ-i ān*	24. *Dar kharīdan-i ẓiyā' va 'uqār*
10. *Dar bāb-i ādāb-i zan khvāstan va sharṭ-i ān*	26. *Andar āyīn-i zan khvāstan*
11. *Dar bāb-i ādāb-i tarbiyat-i farzand*	27. *Dar ḥaqq-i farzand va ḥaqq shinākhtan*
12. *Dar bāb-i ādāb-i bardah kharīdan va sharṭ-i ān*	23. *Dar bardah kharīdan*
13. *Dar bāb-i ādāb-i mihmānī va sharṭ-i ān*	12. *Dar mihmān kardan va mihmān shudan*
14. *Dar bāb-i ādāb-i amānat nigāh dāshtan va sharṭ-i ān*	22. *Dar amānat nigāh dāshtan*
15. *Dar bāb-i ādāb-i 'afv va 'uqūbat va ḥājat khvāstan va sharṭ-i ān*	30. *Dar 'uqūbat kardan va ḥājat khvāstan va ravā kardan*
16. *Dar bāb-i ādāb-i shinākhtan-i aspān va sharṭ-i ān*	25. *Andar kharīdan-i [asb]*
17. *Dar jang va muḥārabat va ṣudā' va taqallub va taḥammul*	20. *Andar kārzār kardan*
18. *Dar bāb-i ādāb-i nadīmī va mulāzamat va sharṭ-i ān*	38. *Dar ādāb-i nadīmī-i pādshāh*
19. *Dar pīrī va javānī va sharṭ-i ān*	9. *Dar pīrī va javānī*
20. *Dar bāb-i ādāb-i 'avāqib-i aḥvāl andīshīdan*	—

Reading the parallel chapters in *Anīs al-nās* and *Qābūs'nāmah* makes it possible to measure quickly the degree to which Shujā' follows the older model or distances himself from it. He rarely copies Kaykāvūs' text but rather rewrites it, in the style of his time and often simplifying it, while developing those topics which are dear to him. He adorns his text with poetic passages, essentially *maṣnavī*s, *qiṭ'ah*s, *maṣal*s, and *ghazal*s; he likes to versify stories (*ḥikāyāt*). A comparison shows that Shujā' is more of a moralist than Kaykāvūs, occasionally more spiritual, as his interpretation of a Koranic verse (33/72) shows.[39]

Shujā' thus worked with the *Qābūs'nāmah* opened in front of him, but his audience was no longer that of Kaykāvūs, nor was the plan of the *Anīs al-nās* that of the *Qābūs'nāmah*. Between these two men, many masters had left their mark. The greatest of them was Sa'dī Shīrāzī, because he had effected a major transformation in Persian literature in the 7th/13th century. But the plan which had guided Sa'dī's *Būstān* and *Gulistān* was not that chosen by Shujā' either. Sa'dī's works are in the first place mirrors for princes (e.g., chapters 1 and 2 of *Būstān*); we can see in them the opposition between the two lifestyles of a prince and a *darvīsh* being pushed to the limit (chapters 1 and 2 of the *Gulistān*). Chapter 7 in both works is devoted to education; all the other ten chapters discuss the qualities and virtues which Sa'dī considered cardinal. Whereas Kaykāvūs viewed the conduct of *javānmardī* as the most fundamental in every man, the soul's readiness to live in the action of permanent grace toward God seems to be dearest to the thought of Sa'dī (chapter 8 of *Būstān*).

If we follow the progression of the chapters of the *Anīs al-nās* beyond the already mentioned chapter 1, we see that Shujā' begins by addressing the most fundamental topic which the famous work *Kalīlah va Dimnah* had discussed for generations: friendship and enmity (chapters 2 and 3). Shujā' thus takes up the greatest theme of all moral and political thought of Persian literature: since the life of men in society is at the same time most essential and most difficult, it is important first of all to discern the fact of alliances and oppositions and, on the individual level, the reality of friends and enemies. This reality is viewed with the aim of guiding people's behavior; the intention pushed Shujā', Kaykāvūs and many others to answer the question, how should one deal with friends and enemies? The other chapters of the *Anīs al-nās* take up, in a random manner, a number of chapters of the *Qābūs'nāmah*, which concern the life of a well-intentioned man. But the way in which they do so deserves special attention. Before dwelling on this, one should ask whether Shujā' was not animated by a dominant idea, as we have seen in the case of

[39] Ibid., 291.

Kaykāvūs and Sa'dī. Absorbed by his model *Qābūs'nāmah*, and having followed it in his overall plan, Shujā' seems bound to break up his topics, which were arranged solely according to the goal of the work: to educate an honest man.

As mentioned earlier, Shujā' re-writes the chapters of the *Qābūs'nāmah* while modifying them so as to adapt them to the cultural norms of his time and to correspond to the moral expectations of his milieu. Chapter 6, on the practise of love, seems to us to be especially elaborate in this respect.[40] We know that spiritual contemplation was introduced into Persian literature in the 5th/11th century, and that the Persian language placed itself at the service of this contemplation. In Shīrāz, the author who knew how most intensely to interconnect literature and spirituality was of course Ḥāfiẓ, who lived two generations before Shujā'. Shujā' names him twice and quotes him three times, something he does only exceptionally. The place where he quotes Ḥāfiẓ without naming him is the same chapter 6, at the precise moment when he wants to re-affirm through poetical statement what is the nature of perfect love.[41] He follows chapters 14 and 15 of the *Qābūs'nāmah*; he copies the beginning of chapter 14 from the *Qābūs'nāmah* and quickly departs from it, only to return to it and again to depart, and so forth.[42] Like all the chapters, this one is neatly divided into a series of *ādāb* and *sharā'iṭ*, and each *adab* and *sharṭ* is centered on one particular subject. It should be noted here that all the chapters of the book consist of a mixture of prose and poetry, the poems most often confirming poetically and helping the prose lessons to be retained more easily, somewhat the same way that Sa'dī used poems in the *Gulistān*. But the role reserved for poetry in chapter 6 is especially important. Stories and anecdotes, sometimes even elaborated thoughts are developed in verse form. The style and quality of Shujā''s own versified compositions are not usually high, perhaps just mediocre. Furthermore, quotations are acknowledged somewhat less seldom in this chapter than in the other ones.[43]

[40] See de Fouchécour, 1995.

[41] Shujā' 1971, 154; Ḥāfiẓ 1994, 521. The two cases where Shujā' does name Ḥāfiẓ pertain to the virtue of contentment (*qanā'at*) (122; Ḥāfiẓ 1994, 225), and to a meeting, which Shujā' believes true, between Ḥāfiẓ and Tīmūr (317; the famous *ghazal*: *agar ān Turk-i Shīrāzī . . .*).

[42] Another chapter where this repetitive borrowing occurs is chapter 4 (Gathering wealth), which is modeled after chapter 21 of the *Qābūs'nāmah* (On the acquisition of wealth). We see Shujā' come, leave, and return to the *Qābūs'nāmah* five times.

[43] The most notable exception, however, is a quotation from Niẓāmī Ganjavī in chapter 18 (404–6), where the last distich of a *ḥikāyat* from *Makhzan al-asrār* has been omitted so as to avoid mentioning the poet's name, cf. Niẓāmī Ganjavī 1984–5, 212–4.

Although the name of Ḥāfiẓ is missing from a quotation from him in chapter 6, this chapter is the fruit of a profound assimilation of Ḥāfiẓian thought as it was understood almost forty years after the poet's death in 792/1390. Chapter 6 of the *Anīs al-nās* may well have been regarded as a mandatory introduction for any reader of the *Dīvān* of Ḥāfiẓ, where the triple relationship of the Lover (*'āshiq*), the Beloved (*maḥbūb*), and Love (*'ishq*) is quite evident. As in Ḥāfiẓ, the love intended here is never expressly directed toward God, but toward the Beloved,[44] and it is clearly distinguished from friendship, which Shujā' regards as a reciprocal relationship, a condition not necessarily present in love.[45] We know that Ḥāfiẓ never used the word *shahvat* (carnal desire); for him the amorous path is essentially that of the Glance toward the Face. It is quite remarkable to see that Shujā' seizes one of the most fundamental Ḥāfiẓian notions, "the play of the Glance" (*naẓarbāzī*), and makes it the key to his exposition of what is essential in love: Love is kindled through the Glance; the play of the Glance is equivalent to the practice of pure love.[46] The greatest quality which Shujā' recognizes in the Lover is that of being able to do without anything (*istighnā'*)[47] because, for him as for Ḥāfiẓ, Love is above both the Beloved and His games of pride and coquetry (*nāz*).[48] Finally, Love is for Shujā' (and Ḥāfiẓ) the effect of a continuous assiduity in amorous enterprise; Shujā' calls it *uns* or *unsī* (specifically, "intimacy"),[49] something which gives more meaning to the word *anīs* (intimate, familiar) in the book's title, implying the idea of long intimacy. Toward the end of the chapter, Shujā' follows Kaykāvūs by saying that love of a man for a woman should be consummated; up until that point he had excluded the sphere of carnal love, which he does not seem to consider, any more than Ḥāfiẓ, the proper field for the development of spiritual love.

No chapter of the *Anīs al-nās* contains as many quotations, whether identified as such or not, as chapter 6. Shujā' is aware of venturing on a terrain which was very sensitive in his time; he must thus seek proof by having recourse to the names or words of great personages. These are, in chronological order: Ḥallāj (d. 309/922),[50] 'Abd Allāh Anṣārī (d. 481/1088),[51] Abū Muḥammad Rūzbihān Shīrāzī (d. 606/1209),[52] 'Aṭṭār Nīshābūrī (d. ca. 617/

[44] Shujā' 1971, 176.
[45] Ibid., 157.
[46] Ibid., 156.
[47] Ibid., 171.
[48] Ibid., 164.
[49] Ibid. 145.
[50] Ibid., 146, 159.
[51] Ibid., 157.
[52] Ibid., 184.

1220), who is not named,[53] Jalāl al-Dīn Rūmī (d. 672/1273), again, not named,[54] Sa'dī Shīrāzī (d. ca. 691/1292),[55] and Awḥadī Marāghah'ī (d. 738/1338).[56]

Chapter 6 is the most elaborate chapter of the *Anīs al-nās*. Shujā', as we have seen, discusses love in it. Chapter 2, on friendship and the choice of a friend, comes next in importance. It constitutes a rich collection of *ādāb*, of rules to follow in this matter; we have counted 19, the last discussing *javānmardī*, this noble human conduct, and Shujā' enumerates the conditions towards its realization.[57] One would need a greater number of pages than those of a short article to describe the contents of the chapters of the *Anīs al-nās*. As it is, we have to content ourselves with indicating some of the quite original pages of the work. On authentic friendship,[58] on the merchant who has succeeded and is establishing himself,[59] on what distinguishes a human (*banī'ādam*) from a true man (*insān*),[60] on the sessions during which the participants drink wine and on the desirable moderation in the consumption of wine,[61] on the choice of a spouse in the time of Shujā',[62] on the participation in the life of the neighborhood where one lives,[63] on the education of a son of middle class parents in the 9th/15th century,[64] on the choice of a good horse (an interesting chapter on hippology),[65] and on the words to say and not to say in society .[66]

Shujā''s borrowings from Persian literature are an essential component of his work, so integrated in its tissue that eliminating them would disintegrate the text. We just spoke of the brief quotations from Anṣārī, Rūzbihān and Sa'dī, and of a longer one (a *ghazal*) from Awḥadī, all of which Shujā' has duly acknowledged. But Shujā' does not particularly like to credit the authors from whom he borrows, except when their names strengthen his

[53] Ibid., 161–4 and 172–5; the quotations (which have some omissions and minor differences) are from *Manṭiq al-ṭayr*, see 'Aṭṭār Nīshābūrī 1978, 172–3 and 189–91, respectively.

[54] Shujā' 1971, 184–7; the quotation (with some minor differences) is from *Maṣnavī-i ma'navī*, see Jalāl al-Dīn Rūmī 1974, 171–3.

[55] Shujā' 1971, 145. Shujā' quotes only one *bayt* of a *ghazal*; see Sa'dī 1977, 578–9 for the complete text.

[56] Shujā' 1971, 177.

[57] Ibid., 52.

[58] Ibid., 30–3.

[59] Ibid., 85–90.

[60] Ibid., 94–7.

[61] Ibid., 92–8.

[62] Ibid., 218–27.

[63] Ibid., 214–7.

[64] Ibid., 228–48.

[65] Ibid., 330–54.

[66] Ibid., 397–401.

argument. We have already seen that he concealed the name of Niẓāmī.[67] Even more startling is his silence on the name of Kaykāvūs, even though his work is almost entirely, chapter after chapter, based on the *Qābūs'nāmah*. Two stories of historic nature are copied from the *Qābūs'nāmah*, but the personages are actualized (the caliph Mu'āwīyah becomes Abū Isḥāq the Injuid; the grandfather of Kaykāvūs becomes the Mozaffarid Muḥammad).[68] Two other authors from whom Shujā' borrows extensively without ever naming them are 'Aṭṭār and Rūmī. From 'Aṭṭār, he copies, besides the two aforementioned stories, three other *ḥikāyat*s taken again from the *Manṭiq al-ṭayr*[69] (like 'Aṭṭār, Shujā' sometimes spells Ayyās instead of Ayyāz). From Jalāl al-Dīn Rūmī he copies two *bayt*s from the *Dīvān-i Shams*[70] and the famous "history" on the artistic competition between Greeks and Chinese.[71] The large number of stories called *Kalīlah va Dimnah* is another source of inspiration for Shujā'.[72]

This brief listing of Shujā''s literary borrowings should suffice to show the importance of his approach. One could no doubt say much about Shuja''s debt to Sa'dī. But there is little to be said about the subject of unacknowledged borrowing: origins matter little in the intertextual game played in the mind. Hasn't Montaigne similarly exploited the work of Philippe of Commynes?

Two other important topics deserve mention. The first concerns the lexical aspect of Shujā''s work; one can approach it from two angles: that of words particular for his time, of a mostly technical nature; and that of terms which Shujā' explains, sometimes by linking them with their counterparts, as for example *naẓarbāzī* (chapter 6), *minnat*,[73] *ḥasad* and *ghabṭah*,[74] *'ujb* and *kibr*,[75] *insānīyat*,[76] *makkā*,[77] *mukārī*,[78] *jadd* and *ḥirṣ*,[79] *khirad* and *hunar*,[80] and *raqīb*.[81]

[67] See footnote no. 43.

[68] Shuja' 1971, 303–4, 360–1.

[69] Ibid., 132–3, 172–5, 202–4; cf. 'Aṭṭār Nīshābūrī 1978, 204–5, 189–91, 59–60, 161–4, respectively.

[70] Shujā' 1971, 96; cf. Jalāl al-Dīn Rūmī 1977, 1:255, lines 4639–40.

[71] See footnote no. 54.

[72] Shujā' 1971, 63–9, 373–83; cf. Naṣr Allāh Munshī 1972, 238–59, 86–8, respectively.

[73] Shujā' 1971, 31, lines 10ff.

[74] Ibid., 79, lines 19–20.

[75] Ibid., 91, lines 3–4.

[76] Ibid., 94–7.

[77] Ibid., 129, line 14.

[78] Ibid., 131, line 12.

[79] Ibid., 132, line 12.

[80] Ibid., 132, lines 12–7.

[81] Ibid., 169, line 4.

The second topic concerns Shujā‘'s *Tasannun* (Sunnism). He quotes both the Commander of the Believers ‘Alī [82] and ‘Umar ibn al-Khaṭṭāb.[83] He rebukes with irony Abū Ḥanīfah and Shāfi‘ī for not having spoken of love.[84] Toward the end of chapter 8, where discussion revolves around playing chess and backgammon, a reference is made to a "School of the Imam" (*maẕhab-i Imām*),[85] which may seem a rather ambiguous description. A closer examination of the sentence in which the reference is made shows that the sentence may have been altered. The sentence presently appears as follows:

> *Līkan az ādāb-i nard va shaṭranj ān-kih īn shughl rā ‘ādat-i khvīsh nasāzand va tā tavanand bih giraw na-bāzand, har chand bih maẕhab-i Imām nard va shaṭranj-i bī'giraw ḥarām.*

Translation

> *But [one] of the rules of [playing] chess and backgammon is that [one] should not make a habit of [playing] this game, and should try, as much as possible, not to play for stake, although in the School of the Imam it [is] prohibited to play chess and backgammon for stake.*

Contrary to the suggestion implied in the sentence, the logic of the subordinate clause following the subordinating conjunction *har chand* requires that the verb used there be opposite of the one used in the independent clause. That is to say, a negative auxiliary verb (such as *na-bāshad* or *na-buvad*) should have followed the word *ḥarām*. We know that in the Shāfi‘ite rite playing chess and backgammon was perceived as permissible.[86] We also know that at the time Shāfi‘ism was the dominant *maẕhab* in Shīrāz.[87] Considering all these factors, it would be safe to assume that the Imām referred to in the sentence is Imām Shāfi‘ī, and that Shujā‘'s original statement was altered by someone who was not in agreement with the Shāfi‘ite views on playing chess and backgammon, which incidentally gives more credence to the idea that the manuscript was not written by Shujā‘ himself.[88] Shujā‘'s recourse to Islamic law

[82] Ibid., 144, 207, 241.

[83] Ibid., 195.

[84] Ibid., 150.

[85] Ibid., 210.

[86] Nāṣir-i Khusraw attests to this in two of his poems, see Nāṣir-i Khusraw 1989, 202, 505.

[87] See Mustawfī 1958, 138.

[88] See footnote no. 3. Iraj Afshar does not mention any physical changes in the sentence, which suggests the alteration is most probably the work of the scribe of the book rather than a later change.

takes place only four other times. Once with respect to the consumption of wine, which was no doubt a major question in his time. Relying on *al-Kashshāf 'an al-asrār al-tanzīl* by the Mutazili scholar of the 5th–6th/11th–12th century, Abū al-Qāsim Maḥmūd ibn 'Umar al-Zamakhsharī, Shujā' interprets four famous verses of the Koran (16/69, 2/216, 4/46, 5/92) in which wine drinking is reproached.[89] Another instance occurs when the relationship between children and their parents is discussed.[90] In yet another passage, entrusted deposit (*amānat*) becomes the focus of a spiritual interpretation.[91] And finally the law of retaliation (*qiṣāṣ*) and its limitations are brought up, again with recourse to the *Kashshāf* of Zamakhsharī.[92] Shujā''s affinity to his spiritual milieu is thus unmistakable.

With these few pages dedicated to Iraj Afshar, the learned editor to whom we owe so many important texts, I wish to express my gratitude to him for having devoted a whole life to the literary wealth of Iran, so much of which had lain buried or forgotten for centuries in the country's libraries. Thanks to the exemplary edition prepared by Iraj Afshar, Shujā''s turn has come to take his place in the limelight of the great tradition of authors who wrote works on the *akhlāq*. By stressing the domain of "application" (*'amalī*), Aristotle made possible the well-known classification of the Stoics, for whom the egg of knowledge is composed of the shell of Logic, the white of Physics, and the yolk of Ethics. *Anīs al-nas* represents this tradition as it had evolved in Iran by the 9th/15th century.

[89] For the importance of *al-Kashshāf* during the period under discussion (especially during the time of Ḥāfiẓ), see Khurramshāhī 1994, 21–2; and Mu'īn 1990, 1:117–20.

[90] Shujā' 1971, 243–4 (referring to the Koran 19/46); 244–5 (Koran 31/13).

[91] Shujā' 1971, 291 (referring to the Koran 33/72, a better suited quotation than the one used in the *Qābūs'nāmah*, i.e., 4/61).

[92] Shujā' 1971, 359–60 (referring to the Koran 2/173–5).

BIBLIOGRAPHY

ANDO, SHIRO. 1995. Die timuridische Historiographie II : Šaraf al-Dīn ʻAlī Yazdī. *Studia Iranica* 24, no. 2: 219–46.

ʻAṬṬĀR NĪSHĀBŪRĪ. 1978. *Manṭiq al-ṭayr : maqāmāt al-ṭuyūr*. 3rd ed. Ed. Ṣādiq Gawharīn. Tehran : Bungāh-i Tarjumah va Nashr-i Kitāb, 2536 Shāhanshāhī.

DĀNISH'PIZHŪH, MUḤAMMAD TAQĪ. 1961. *Fihrist-i Kitābkhānah-'i Markazī-i Dānishgāh-i Tihrān*. Vol. 9, Tehran : Dānishgāh-i Tihrān, 1340 Sh.

—— 1961b. *Fihrist-i Kitābkhānah-'i Markazī-i Dānishgāh-i Tihrān*. Vol. 12, Tehran : Dānishgāh-i Tihrān, 1340 Sh.

—— 1972. Anīs al-nās. *Rāhnamā-yi kitāb* 14, nos. 9–12 (Āẕar–Isfand 1350 Sh.): 763–6.

DE FOUCHÉCOUR, C.-H. 1986. *Moralia : les notions morales dans la littérature persane du 3e/9e au 7e/13e siècle*. Paris : Editions Recherche sur les civilisations.

—— 1994. Le poète persan entre tradition et liberté aux temps médiévaux. *Kārnāmah*, no. 1: 5–19.

—— 1995. Nazar-bâzi : les jeux du regard selon un interprète de Hâfez. *Kārnāmah*, nos. 2–3: 3–10.

ḤĀFIẒ. 1994. *Ḥāfiẓ*. Ed. Sāyah. Tehran : Tūs, Chashm va Charāgh, 1373 Sh.

JALĀL AL-DĪN RŪMĪ. 1974. *Dawrah-i kāmil-i Maṣnavī-i maʻnavī*. 3rd ed. Ed. Reynold A. Nicholson. Tehran : Amīr Kabīr, 1353 Sh.

—— 1977. *Kullīyāt-i Shams, yā, Dīvān-i kabīr : mushtamil bar qasāʻid va ghazalīyat va muqaṭṭaat-i Fārsī va ʻArabī va tarjīʻāt va mulammaʻāt*. 2nd ed. Ed. Badīʻ al-Zamān Furūzānfar. Tehran : Amīr Kabīr, Bahman 2535 Shāhanshāhī.

KHURRAMSHĀHĪ, BAHĀ' AL-DĪN. 1994. *Ḥāfiẓ*. Tehran : Ṭarḥ-i Naw, 1373 Sh.

MUʻĪN, MUḤAMMAD. 1990. *Ḥāfiẓ-i shīrīn sukhan*. 2nd ed. Ed. Mahdukht Muʻīn. 2 vols. Tehran : Muʻīn, 1369 Sh.

MUSTAWFĪ, ḤAMD ALLĀH. 1958. *Nuzhat al-qulūb*. Ed. Muḥammad Dabīr Siyāqī. Tehran : Ṭahūrī, Isfand 1336 Sh.

NAṢR ALLĀH MUNSHI. 1972. *Tarjumah-'i Kalīlah va Dimnah*. 3rd ed. Ed. Mujtabá Mīnuvī. Tehran : Dānishgāh-i Ṭihrān, 1351 Sh.

NĀṢIR-I KHUSRAW. 1989. *Dīvān-i ashʻār*. 2nd ed. Introd. [Ḥasan] Taqī'zādah ; ed. Mujtabá Mīnuvī, ʻAlī Akbar Dihkhudā. Tehran : Dunyā-yi Kitāb, 1368 Sh.

NIẒĀMĪ GANJAVĪ. 1984–5. *Makhzan al-asrār*. Ed. Bihrūz Ṣarvatiyān. Tehran : Tūs, zamistān 1363 Sh.

QAZVĪNĪ, MUḤAMMAD. 1984. *Yāddāshthā-yi Qazvīnī*. 3rd ed. Ed. Iraj Afshar. 10 vols. in 5. Tehran : ʻIlmī, 1363 Sh.

ṢAFĀ, ẒABĪḤ ALLĀH. 1984–. *Tārīkh-i adabīyāt dar Īrān*. New ed. 5 vols. in 8 to date. Tehran : Firdawsī, 1363 Sh.–

SAʻDĪ. 1977. *Kullīyāt-i Saʻdī : Gulistān, Būstān, ghazalīyāt, qaṣāʼid, qiṭaʻāt va rasāʼil, az rū-yi qadīmtarīn nuskhah'hā-yi mawjūd*. 2nd ed. Ed. Muḥammad ʻAlī Furughī, Bahā al-Dīn Khurramshāhī. Tehran : Amīr Kabīr, 2536 Shāhanshāhī.

SHUJĀʻ. 1971. *Anīs al-nās : ta'līf-i sāl-i 830 Hijrī*. Ed. Iraj Afshar. Tehran : Bungāh-i Tarjumah va Nashr-i Kitāb, 1350 Sh.

TRITTON, A. S. 1983. al-Djurdjānī, 'Alī B. Muḥammad. *Encyclopaedia of Islam*. New ed. Vol. 2. Leiden : E. J. Brill: 602b–3a.
'UNṢUR AL-MA'ĀLĪ, KAYKĀVŪS IBN ISKANDAR. 1951. *A mirror for princes : the Qābūs Nāma*. Tr. Reuben Levy. New York : E. P. Dutton.
—— 1992. *Qābūs'nāmah*. 6th ed. Ed. Ghulām Ḥusayn Yūsufī. Tehran : Shirkat-i Intishārāt-i 'Ilmī va Farhangī, 1371 Sh.

Manṣūr Muṣavvir, "the Pride of the Painters" and His Son Shāh Muẓaffar, "the Rarity of the Age"

Kambiz Eslami

IN HIS HISTORY OF MUSLIM RULERS OF Moghulistan, the *Tārīkh-i Rashīdī*, the 10th/16th-century Chaghatayid author Muḥammad Ḥaydar Dūghlāt, better known as Mīrzā Ḥaydar, devotes a brief section to the identification and evaluation of prominent Persian painters of the 9th/15th to mid-10th/16th centuries.[1] He begins his account by naming a certain *Ustād* Manṣūr and his son, Shāh Muẓaffar, who evidently were both at one time or another court painters of the later Timurids. The information that Mīrzā Ḥaydar provides about this father and son duo seems to have been one of the very few near-contemporary accounts available to and used (sometimes erroneously) by students of Persian painting. I shall attempt here to supplement the information about Manṣūr by presenting some hitherto overlooked documents which I hope will help establish a more accurate and justifiable outline of the career of Manṣūr and Shāh Muẓaffar. Before that, however, it would be useful to recount what has been written about Manṣūr and his son, and furthermore to offer new speculations in light of the recorded and reliable data.

Besides being too brief, Mīrzā Ḥaydar's description of artists in the *Tārīkh-i Rashīdī*, which is actually a chronological and rating account, suffers from the rather unfortunate (yet not too uncommon) fact that it does not give precise dates of the activities of the artists. As far as our two painters are concerned, we learn that Manṣūr was most active during the time of Sulṭān Abū Sa'īd,[2] Tīmūr's great-grandson, who ruled over Transoxiana and Khurāsān from 855/1451 and 863/1459, respectively, until his downfall in 873/1469 at the hands of the Aqqoyunlu Sulṭān Ūzūn Ḥasan (r. 857–82/1453–78). Manṣūr's son, Shāh Muẓaffar, who died at the early age of twenty-four,[3] must have been a contemporary of the master Timurid/Safavid painter Kamāl al-Dīn Bihzād

[1] Muḥammad Ḥaydar Dūghlāt 1996, 164–6 and 1996b, 130–1.
[2] Idem 1996, 164 and 1996b, 130.
[3] Idem 1996, 165 and 1996b, 130.

(ca. 872–942/ca. 1467–1535/6),[4] if not even slightly senior, because his name is mentioned before that of Bihzād, and because, we are told, both of them were *protégés* (*tarbiyat yāftagān*) of ʻAlīshīr Navāʼī (844–906/1441–1501), the lifetime companion and *amīr* of Sulṭān Ḥusayn Bāyqarāʼ (r. 873–911/ 1469–1506).[5] From this we may safely assume that Shāh Muẓaffar too was born around 872/1467, and therefore died ca. 896/1491. A drawing in the famous Bahrām Mīrzā album in the Topkapı Palace Library in İstanbul is attributed to Shāh Muẓaffar by an *ʻunvān* (heading) which distinctly calls him *naqqāsh-i Khurāsānī* (Khurāsānī painter).[6] Even if we question the attribution, we can still give credence to the *nisbah* of Khurāsānī, which means Manṣūr could have come from Khurasan as well.[7] It is then possible that Manṣūr was already an accomplished artist in the culturally thriving Harāt during the fifth decade of the 9th/15th century, and that he joined Abū Saʻīd's atelier upon, or shortly after, the latter's conquest of Khurāsān in 863/1459. If we suppose that in 867/1463 (i.e., between 863/1459 and 873/1469, the year in which Abū Saʻīd was killed by Yādgār Muḥammad) Manṣūr was a man of forty years old, he then must have been born in 827/1424 in Harāt, which was at that time (and remained so for the next twenty-three years) under the reign of Tīmūr's son Shāhrukh, who was a less skillful military and political leader but certainly a more benevolent patron of the arts than his father. As we shall see later, Manṣur could also have participated in the activities of the ateliers of the

[4] Bihzād's exact date of birth has not been established with certainty. Scholars have proposed dates as early as ca. 844/1440 (Rice 1975, 222) or as late as ca. 872/1467 (Soudavar 1992, 86, 123, footnote no. 47, referring to Būdāq Munshī Qazvīnī's *Javahir al-akhbār*, MS Dorn 288 in the Saint Petersburg State University Library, fol. 111r). The fact that Būdāq Qazvīnī (b. 916–7/1510–2)—the only known and reliable contemporary source mentioning anything about Bihzād's age at the time of his death—suggests the early 870s as his birthdate argues for its use here.

[5] Muḥammad Ḥaydar Dūghlāt 1996, 165 and 1996b, 130.

[6] Topkapı Palace Library, İstanbul, Hazine 2154, fol. 40v; for a reproduction, see Binyon, Wilkinson, Gray [1933] 1971, pl. xcv. Relying primarily on stylistic grounds, Abolala Soudavar has rejected the attribution, suggesting that the drawing displays Jalayirid or early Turkman traits and should not be considered an original work by Shāh Muẓaffar, see Soudavar 1992, 95, 122–3, footnote nos. 37–8. It has also been maintained (Lentz and Lowry 1989, 313; Adle 1990, 230, 255) that the *ʻunvāns* added to the paintings of this *muraqqaʻ* are the work of Dūst Muḥammd, the Harāt-born Safavid calligrapher and painter, who oversaw the compilation of the *muraqqaʻ*, and who wrote the now famous introduction on the calligraphers, painters and illuminators of the past to it. It is thus rather suprising that in his introduction Dūst Muḥammd does not even mention the name of his fellow Khurāsānī painter Shāh Muẓaffar, whom he allegedly describes in the *ʻunvān* as "the rarity of the age" (*nādir al-ʻaṣrī*)—a phrase used in the captions only for one other painter, Bihzād, see Dūst Muḥammad 1993; Roxburgh 1996, 2:869, 942.

[7] As we shall see later, Manṣūr may have originally come from Shīrāz, and moved back and forth between Shīrāz and Harāt.

Qaraqoyunlu Sulṭān Pīr Būdāq ibn Jahānshāh and Sulṭān Ḥusayn Bāyqarā', and could have worked in different capacities in those rulers' libraries.

In issuing his verdicts on the merits of the painters' works, Mīrzā Ḥaydar draws candid comparisons between them. He calls Manṣūr an *ustād* "than whom there was none better" during the time of Sulṭān Abū Sa'īd. Aside from his son Shāh Muẓaffar, no one else had Manṣūr's "fine, thin brush." Still, it was "somewhat dry."[8] His "hunting [scenes]" (*girift va gīr*)[9] were extremely effective, although again Shāh Muẓaffar surpassed him in that many times over. Shāh Muẓaffar himself painted with extreme subtlety, grace, and maturity (*nāzukī, malāḥat va pukhtagī*). He left behind seven or eight finished paintings, some pen-and-ink drawings (*qalam siyāhī*), and at least a pupil, Darvīsh Muḥammad, who later became Mīrzā Ḥaydar's own painting teacher.[10] A little further on, Mīrzā Ḥaydar even goes so far as to ranking the painters: in first place was Khvājah 'Abd al-Ḥayy, second was Shāh Muẓaffar, and third was Bihzād.[11]

Shāh Muẓaffar is also mentioned by the 10th/16th-century Mughal Emperor Ẓahīr al-Dīn Muḥammad Bābur in his memoirs *Bāburnāmah*. He describes him as having "painted delicately" and having done "swift and delicate floral work."[12] Bābur reiterates the fruitful relationship that existed between Mīr 'Alīshīr and the two painters, Shāh Muẓaffar and Bihzād, saying that it was through Mīr 'Alīshīr's good offices "that master Bihzad . . . and Shah-Muzaffar became so famous for painting."[13] Whether there was a good relationship between the two painters themselves is not known. Some sort of rivalry must have existed between the two; after all, they were both regarded

[8] *Khushktar* is evidently the word used in the two manuscripts on which W. Thackston has based his translation, see Muḥammad Ḥaydar Dūghlāt 1996, 164. According to T. W. Arnold, the word used in the manuscripts from which he translated his text is *khunuktar* (Binyon, Wilkinson, Gray [1933] 1971, 189), which does not really make sense in this context. It is likely that the scribes of the manuscripts (or perhaps Arnold) misread *khushktar*. In fact, Arnold seems to have combined two separate sentences and come up with a rather far-fetched translation. In the Persian text edited by Thackston these sentences are: *Ammā chīzī khushktar-ast. Girift va gīr rā bi-ghāyat muḥkam sākhtah* (Muḥammad Ḥaydar Dūghlāt 1996, 164). Arnold's translation reads: "But he [=Manṣūr] was somewhat more refreshing (as an artist) in that his strokes were firmer" (Binyon, Wilkinson, Gray [1933] 1971, 189).

[9] Thackston has translated *girift va gīr* as "animal combat scenses" (Muḥammad Ḥaydar Dūghlāt 1996, 164 and 1996b, 130); for a comment on Arnold's translation of this sentence, see footnote no. 8.

[10] Muḥammad Ḥaydar Dūghlāt 1996, 166 and 1996b, 131. Fakhrī Harātī, the 10th/16th-century translator of Mīr 'Alīshīr's *Majālis al-nafā'is*, says that Darvīsh Muḥammad was a student of Bihzād, see Mīr 'Alīshīr Navā'ī [1945] 1984, 154.

[11] Muḥammad Ḥaydar Dūghlāt 1996, 165 and 1996b, 130.

[12] Bābur 1996, 226.

[13] Ibid., 214.

as masters of their craft,[14] and both must have felt proud to have been brought up by such leading artists of the period as Manṣūr and Mīrak. It is even possible that the competition between the two was perhaps so strong that those sources sympathetic toward Bihzād (e.g., Khvānd Amīr, Vāṣifī, Būdāq Qazvīni, and Qāẕī Aḥmad) reacted to the whole situation by choosing to ignor Shāh Muẓaffar and remaining completely silent about him (and his father).

It was with the exhibition of miniatures at Burlington House in January–March 1931 and with the publication, two years later, of its detailed catalog, *Persian miniature painting*, by L. Binyon, J. V. S. Wilkinson, and B. Gray, that Manṣūr and Shāh Muẓaffar were introduced to western audiences. Among the items exhibited at Burlington House was the Bahrām Mīrzā album, mentioned earlier, which included (as it does now) two drawings attributed to Shāh Muẓaffar. One of the drawings depicts the prophet Muḥammad on his *mi'rāj* (ascension) to heaven,[15] while the other one shows an angel offering a certain Sayf al-Mulūk on a horse what seems to be a plate of fruits (Fig. 1).[16] The catalog of the exhibition also provided a translation of both Mīrzā Ḥaydar's and Bārbur's texts pertaining to our painters.[17]

[14] The last sentence in Mīrzā Ḥaydar's evaluation of Shāh Muẓaffar can be read in two different ways: *Ustādān-i īn ṣanā'at ū rā bi-ghāyat 'azīz mīdārand* (The masters of this art consider him very dear), or *Ustādān īn ṣanā'at-i u rā bi-ghāyat 'azīz mīdārand* (The masters [of this art] consider this art of him [=pen-and-ink drawing] very dear), see Muḥammad Haydar Dūghlāt 1996, 165.

[15] See footnote no. 6.

[16] Topkapı Palace Library, İstanbul, Hazine 2154, fol. 86r. In his study of album-making under the Timurids and Safavids, David Roxburgh has provided the most detailed examination of the drawing yet, speculating that the character named Sayf al-Mulūk may be referring to 'Alī ibn Abī Ṭālib, see Roxburgh 1996, 2:909. A more probable explanation can be found in a classic folk tale known by the same name as that of the main character. Below is a very brief summary of the story from the only version of it available to me (*Seyfilmülâuk hikâyesi*, 1959). The Ghaznavid Sulṭān Maḥmūd was fortunate to have a *vazīr* like Khvājah Aḥmad ibn Ḥasan Maymandī, who was always ready to tell strange and amusing stories. Khvājah had heard of the story of Sayf al-Mulūk, but was eager to learn more, so he sent his men everywhere to see if they could find more details about the story. One of the men goes to India, where he stumbles upon a storyteller who happens to be the only man alive who knows the complete story of Sayf al-Mulūk. According to the storyteller, Solomon—here a prophet, advocating conversion to Islam—grants the wishes of an heirless Egyptian ruler named 'Āṣim ibn Ṣafwān and his childless *wazīr* Nu'mān to have children, on the condition that they accept Islam and spread the word of Islam in their land. Both sides keep their promises. The king and his *wazīr* each become a father to a son, whom they name Sayf al-Mulūk and Sa'īd, respectively. On his twentieth birthday, Sayf al-Mulūk receives presents from Solomon, including a ring and a picture of a beautiful girl. He falls in love with the girl and leaves the kingdom to look for her, eventually finding her after much hardship. The drawing attributed to Shāh Muẓaffar may depict the point when presents from Solomon are delivered to Sayf al-Mulūk.

[17] Binyon, Wilkinson, Gray [1933] 1971, 189–91.

The first critical attempt to identify potential finished miniatures of Shāh Muẓaffar was made in 1961 by Basil Gray in his *Persian painting*, where he tried to explain the "old-fashioned" nature of a series of miniatures that some scholars[18] had considered to be works of Bihzād by attributing them to an earlier group of painters, including Shāh Muẓaffar.[19] The miniature which Gray selected to attribute to Shāh Muẓaffar and to reproduce belongs to a manuscript of Mīr ʻAlīshīr's *Khamsah* which was copied in Harāt in 890/1485, the year in which Mīr ʻAlīshīr actually finished the composition of one its pieces, *Sadd-i Iskandarī*.[20] In "Shaykh ʻIrāqī overcome at parting"[21] the most original of the volume's paintings, as he put it, Gray saw a composition fundamentally different from that of Bihzād's. Whereas Bihzād generally preferred to let "internal rhythms" dictate his "formal" patterns, the painter of "Shaykh ʻIrāqī" has put aside the subtle manifestations of individual emotions to emphasize his group scene.[22]

Shāh Muẓaffar and Manṣūr became subjects of discussion in yet another study by Gray—this time about 8th/14th-century Persian painting.[23] Here—still using Mīrzā Ḥaydar's work as his supporting source—he associated the era of Manṣūr's activities not with the Timurid Sulṭān Abū Saʻīd but rather with the Ilkhanid Abū Saʻīd (r. 717–36/1317–35), and suggested a Jalayirid painting from the same Hazine 2154 album as a possible work of Shāh Muẓaffar.[24]

A new context for understanding the disposition of Manṣūr's and Shāh Muẓaffar's works was provided by Abolala Soudavar in his 1992 publication,

[18] E.g., Stchoukine and Robinson, see Robinson 1958, 64, 66.

[19] See Gray [1961] 1977, 117–21.

[20] The *Khamsah* manuscript is now divided between the Bodleian Library in Oxford (*Ḥayrat al-abrār*, *Farhād u Shīrīn*, *Sabʻah-'i sayyārah*, *Sadd-i Iskandarī*) and the John Rylands Library in Manchester (*Laylā u Majnūn*), and contains twelve other paintings, see Robinson 1958, 64–7 and 1980, 116–7, and works cited there; Soudavar 1992, 97, 123, footnote no. 40; Suleiman, 1970; and Bahari 1996, 156–65. As we shall see later, another scholar has also attributed another painting from this manuscript ("A camp scene" from *Laylā u Majnūn*) to Shāh Muẓaffar.

[21] In *Ḥayrat al-abrār*, Bodleian Library, Oxford, MS Elliot 287, fol. 34r.

[22] Gray [1961] 1977, 121. Gray attempted to support that view by quoting Mīrzā Ḥaydar as saying that Shāh Muẓaffar was "a master of group pictures" (ibid.). I have not been able to find that quotation in *Tārīkh-i Rashīdī*, as Gray does not give a precise reference. The closest mention would be where the Chaghatayid author says that "during his lifetime [Shāh Muẓaffar] finished seven or eight scenes (Muḥammad Ḥaydar Dūghlāt 1996, 130), or, according to Arnold's translation (which is probably what Gray had in mind), "during his lifetime [Shāh Muẓaffar] completed eight group pictures" (Binyon, Wilkinson, Gray [1933] 1971, 189–90).

[23] See Gray 1979.

[24] Ibid., 108–10, and pl. xxvi.; Topkapı Palace Library, İstanbul, Hazine 2154, fol. 42v.

Art of the Persian courts. The book, which contains selections from Soudavar's own collection—the Art and History Trust Collection—offers a new perspective on Shāh Muẓaffar's *oeuvre*, while attributing, for the first time in many years, a painting from that collection to Manṣūr. In the "Coronation of Sulṭān Ḥusayn Mīrzā Bāyqarā'," a painting from an unknown manuscript, Soudavar found evidence of Manṣūr's style and technique as reported by Mīrzā Ḥaydar and Bābur.[25] Soudavar's attribution is further fortified by his argument that the painting is contemporaneous with the actual coronation of Sulṭān Ḥusayn Bāyqarā' (873/1469), and that Manṣūr was the only painter at the court at the time whose status was high enough for him to be asked to paint the ceremony.

Manṣūr probably also supervised the painting of "The harem of Sulṭān Ḥusayn Mīrzā Bāyqarā'," which Soudavar attributes to his son Shāh Muẓaffar.[26] The painting, from a *dīvān* of Amīr Khusraw Dihlavī, is dated 886/1481, and can very well represent the work of a very young Shāh Muẓaffar. Soudavar furthermore traces the development of the young artist by convincingly attributing to him five other illustrations which meet the criteria posed by constraints of quantity, date, and style.[27] All five illustrations were most likely created within a span of less than five years, from ca. 888/1483 until 891/1486, and have in common such elements as similar facial features and generally youthful ambiance. One of the illustrations ("A camp scene") is from the same *Khamsah* of 'Alīshīr Navā'ī (dated 890/1485), mentioned earlier[28]; one ("Shīrīn receiving Khusraw in her palace") is from a *Khamsah* of Amīr Khusraw Dihlavī[29]; one ("The two wrestlers") is from a *Gulistān* of Sa'dī (dated 891/1486)[30]; two ("Humāy and Humāyūn entertained" and "Humāyūn hunting") from a *Humāy u Humāyūn* of Khvājū-yi Kirmānī (ca.

[25] Soudavar 1992, 86–8.

[26] Ibid., 90.

[27] Zeren Tanindi had noted similarities among some of these illustrations in her study (1979), but did not attribute any one to any particular artist.

[28] *Laylā u Masjnūn*, John Rylands Library, Manchester, MS Turk 3, fol. 16v. Robinson (1958, 67 and 1980, 116) suggests that the only other painting in *Laylā u Majnūn* ("Majnūn visited by camel-rider"), and "The portrait of a princess shown to Bahrām Gūr" in Bodleian Library's *Sab'ah-i sayyārah* are probably also by the same painter who painted "A camp scene."

[29] *Khamsah*, Chester Beatty Library, Dublin, MS 163, fol. 54v.

[30] *Gulistān*, Art and History Trust Collection, Houston, Texas, MS 36, fol. 21r (Soudavar 1992, 101–5). This fine copy of *Gulistān* was most likely made for 'Alīshīr Navā'ī, and was in the library of several Mughal emperors, some of whom wrote inscriptions on its second page. Soudavar has identified Jahāngīr's (r. 1014–37/1605–27) note which says the volume's paintings are all by *Ustādzādah* (lit. son of *ustād*), whom Soudavar identifies as Shāh Muẓaffar because Manṣūr was the only painter of his time to be known as *ustād*. Jahāngīr had initially added the name of this *Ustādzādah*, but now only "Shāh M" is visble to the naked eye, see Soudavar 1992, 98.

888/1483).[31] The painting "Humāyūn hunting" (Fig. 2) is the most lively of them all, one which displays force and human vitality in a most colorful manner, one which the young Shāh Muẓaffar must have particularly enjoyed creating. It has all the elements that Bābur and Mīrzā Ḥaydar recounted when they compared Shāh Muẓaffar's work with that of his father Manṣūr: an extremely effective hunting scene, delicate flowers, graceful movements, and skillful execution. It is as if Mīrzā Ḥaydar and Bābur were looking at this very painting when they were describing Shāh Muẓaffar's style. It is also tempting to think that at the same time they were perhaps looking at a similar scene by Manṣūr.

In actuality, there is a superb painting of ca. 840s/1440s which shows seven horsemen vigorously in pursuit of some fleeing animals (including a leopard, rabbits, foxes, and deer) on a field covered with tufts of grass and four bare trees, and which is inscribed in the lower left-hand corner with the name of the artist who painted it, Darvīsh Manṣūr (Fig. 3).[32] There is really no need to doubt the attribution, and we can safely regard the painting as one of Manṣūr's earlier works. Traces of Bāysunghur atelier style in it can indicate that Manṣūr was perhaps trained by a master of that school. The painting is in one of the "Saray" albums in the Diez collection of the Oriental Division of the State Library at Berlin—albums which are believed to have originally belonged to the larger group of albums including Hazine 2153, 2154, and 2160. There are two drawings in the published catalog of the Diez "Saray" albums that show close similarities to the "Hunting scene," and thus can be attributed to Manṣūr as well. One is a drawing of a leopard, a peacock, and a horseman about to strike a foot soldier with his sword.[33] The other drawing—which İpşiroğlu dates to the late 14th century—depicts an unusually curved tree on whose leafy end branches some birds are sitting and two are mating, while a sitting fox fills the empty gap between the curved tree and the trunk of another tree.[34] Both drawings reaffirm Manṣūr's early fascination with animals, especially birds (more on this later), and the ease and skill with which

[31] *Humāy u Humāyūn*, Topkapı Palace Library, İstanbul, MS Revan 1045, fols. 42v, 23r.

[32] Staatsbibliothek zu Berlin - Preußischer Kulturbesitz - Orientabteilung, Diez A, Fol. 70, Bl. 1.; for a color reproduction, see İpşiroğlu 1964, pl. xxviii. See also Kühnel (1959, 77), who identified Darvīsh Manṣūr with our painter for the first time.

[33] Staatsbibliothek zu Berlin - Preußischer Kulturbesitz - Orientabteilung, Diez A, Fol. 72, Bl. 12, Nr. 1.; for a reproduction see, İpşiroğlu 1964, pl. xlviii.

[34] Staatsbibliothek zu Berlin - Preußischer Kulturbesitz - Orientabteilung, Diez A, Fol. 73, Bl. 50, Nr. 4.; İpşiroğlu 1964, 102; for a reproduction, see ibid., pl. xxxviii. The smudged inscription on the bottom right-hand corner of the drawing that identifies the painter as one *Ustād* Shams al-Dīn *Naqqāsh* can be dismissed as it seems to be of a much later date.

he could portray their demeanor and subtle movements.[35] The provenance of these works clearly demonstrates that they are closely related to the two drawings attributed to Shāh Muẓaffar in Hazine 2154, and to the Hazine 2153 and 2160 paintings and drawings commonly thought to be works of Muḥammad Siyāh Qalam, who is probably none other than Shāh Muẓaffar's pupil, Darvīsh Muḥammad.[36] It would not be too far-fetched then to argue that the albums represent—among other things—the interests and efforts of their original compiler or compilers to keep the works of a father, his son, and the latter's pupil together.

• • •

Among the Timurid sources published in Iran during the past few decades is a collection of letters and decrees, a manuscript copy of which came into the possession of the Iranian bibliophile and scholar Rukn al-Dīn Humāyūnfarrukh in the summer of 1335 Sh./1956. The *majmū'ah*, which lacked several leaves from the beginning, was entitled *Mansha' al-inshā'*, and was collected by a certain Abū al-Qāsim Shihāb al-Dīn Aḥmad Khvāfī known as Munshī. The manuscript, which is believed to be in Shihāb al-Dīn's hand, is dated mid-Jumādá I 938/late December 1531, and was dedicated to a Khvājah Amīr Beg, whom Humāyūnfarrukh identifies as Amīr Beg Ẓahīr al-Dīn Muḥammad al-Kajjānī Tabrīzī, the then acting *amīr* of Khurāsān.[37] The letters, decrees, and book notices that are included in this collection are by Shihāb al Dīn's teacher and mentor, Niẓām al-Dīn (or, according to Khvānd Amīr, Kamāl al-Dīn) 'Abd al-Vāsi' Niẓāmī (d. 909/1503–4), who worked in the Epistolary Office (*Dīvān-i Tarassul*) of the Timurid Sulṭān Abū Sa'īd, Yadgār Muḥammad, and Sulṭān Ḥusayn Bayqarā', and who was famous for his dexterity in writing ornate and flowery texts—no doubt a prerequisite for someone in his position. *Mansha' al-inshā'*, even in its incomplete state, displayed that characteristic quite well. It was also the same style of writing that Humāyūnfarrukh noticed in another manuscript that he acquired from an auction several years later. This other manuscript, also entitled *Mansha' al-inshā'*, was in a different handwriting from that of the first manuscript, but was quite

[35] Manṣūr could have worked at the Shīrāz court of the Qaraqoyunlu Sulṭān Pīr Būdāq ibn Jahānshāh, and have participated in the production of the illustrations of the Gulistān Palace copy of *Kalīlah va Dimnah*. For a reproduction of most of the illustrations of this manuscript, see Vladislav 1958.

[36] See Robinson 1981, 63. Solomonic stories also provide further connection between some of Muḥammad Siyāh Qalam's paintings (Topkapı Palace Library, İstanbul, Hazine 2153, fols. 164v–5r, reproduced in color in İpşiroğlu 1984, pls. 56a–b) and Shāh Muẓaffar's "Sayf al-Mulūk" drawing, see footnote no. 16; and Hasse 1981, 52–3.

[37] 'Abd al-Vāsi' Niẓāmī 1979–, 1:32. For a reproduction of the manuscript's colophon, see Humāyūnfarrukh 1966, 49.

similar in the types of document it contained. Further examination revealed that Humāyūnfarrukh had in fact obtained a copy of the missing leaves from his first copy of the *Mansha' al-inshā'*. Internal evidence from the new manuscript led Humāyūnfarrukh to believe that sometime in the late 10th/16th century, a man named Vā'iẓī Kāshifī (not to be confused with the author of *Anvār-i suhaylī*) obtained the complete manuscript of the *Mansha' al-inshā'* and decided to claim it as his own work. He began copying the work, replacing Shihāb al-Dīn Aḥmad's name with that of his own, and deleting the name of the *amīr* to whom Shihāb al-Dīn had dedicated his book. Judging from the poor quality of his transcription, it is clear that he must have gotten tired of copying the book he obviously found difficult to understand and transcribe, and quit half way through. He most probably also destroyed the original leaves of the manuscript from which he had transcribed. It was this portion of the book that Humāyūnfarrukh published in Tehran in 1979 as the first of a two-volume book-set, whose second volume—a facsimile of the part of the book believed to be in the compiler's hand—was promised to follow, but never did. Throughout all this, Humāyūnfarrukh seems to have been under the impression that his copy of *Mansha' al-inshā'* was the only copy of the book.

However, the Egyptian National Library (the Dār al-Kutub) holds another manuscript copy of *Mansha' al-inshā*, but here the name Malik Aḥmad al-Kashshāfī (or Kāshifī) appears as the compiler of the book.[38] There is a date (910 [1504–5]) on the last page of the manuscript, which, unlike the Humāyūnfarrukh copy, is not part of the colophon, and may be a later addition. This copy has fewer errors of transcription, and is different from Humāyūnfarrukh copy as far as the order of contents is concerned. Also, it seems that documents in the former are more complete than in the latter, but a final verdict on that must await the full publication of Humāyūnfarrukh's edition.

Mansha' al-inshā is an obscure yet extremely important source for the study of the social, political, and cultural milieu of Khurāsān during the time of the later Timurids. Among the documents preserved in it is a foreword by 'Abd al-Vāsi' to a treatise—now apparently lost—written by a "Mawlānā Manṣūr Muṣavvir," who cannot be anyone else but our painter Manṣūr.[39] The treatise, called *Hamāmah'nāmah* (Book of pigeons), contained what was probably a long time's worth of knowledge about pigeons, and, more importantly,

[38] *Mansha' al-inshā'*, Egyptian National Library, Cairo, MS 129 Adab-i Farsī, fols. 2v, 147v; *Fihris al-makhṭūṭāt al-Fārisīyah* 1966–7, 2:194–5. I am most indebted to Bernard O'Kane who sent me a copy of this manuscript.

[39] *Mansha' al-inshā'*, Egyptian National Library, Cairo, MS 129 Adab-i Farsī, fols. 11v–12r; 'Abd al-Vāsi' Nizāmī 1979–, 1:43–4.

was illustrated with paintings by Manṣūr himself of various types of this bird known at the time.[40]

'Abd al-Vāsi' begins the foreword[41] with the praise of God, and then goes on to list two incidents whereby pigeons earned their angelic reputation and man's love for them. The listing is important because it sets the stage for 'Abd al-Vāsi' to offer a counter-view of the prevalent religious strictures on pigeon-keeping. The first incident occurred after the landing of Noah's Ark on the summit of Mount Jūdī, when Noah sent a pigeon to see if the earth was dry or still flooded. "As the pigeon approached the land and stepped into the water, the feathers on its feet fell out because of the bitterness of the water, and the portion of its legs touching the torturous waters became bloody and red. When it returned and described the events, Noah prayed to God that the pigeon be loved by man." The other incident mentioned relates to the prophet Muḥammad and to the time when he emigrated to Medina. The polytheists were chasing him, and he sought refuge in a cave, "at whose opening a pigeon immediately laid an egg and sat on it, so that the polytheists thought that there was no one in the cave and therefore passed by it." Prophet Muḥammed "petted the bird with his blessed hand and prayed to God that good and prosperity fall upon it, and that it might be loved and respected by man."

The ban imposed by religious scholars on pigeon-flying could not have been easily dismissed, so 'Abd al-Vāsi' tries to explain the ban as something brought about by the actions of "the rude youth and prying individuals," who "would go on the rooftops which command views of the women's quarters of the houses of Moslems, and begin, without any fears, throwing pebbles and stones at people's houses and their neighbors." Having conveyed the inherent goodness of the bird, 'Abd al-Vāsi' then moves on to introduce Manṣūr's work:

> Since with the passage of time and with much practice and experience, the compiler (creator) of these paintings, Manṣūr Muṣavvir (*may Gad forgive his sins*) had gained complete knowledge of the characteristics of various types of pigeons, and since he could distinguish the good types from the bad types, his agreeable friends and companions kept requesting from his humble self to write a treatise containing characteristics and features of that [bird], so that those happy individuals who are interested

[40] It is a curious coincidence that the famous Mughal illuminator and painter Manṣūr (10th–11th/16th-17th centuries) too was more than anything else a painter of nature subjects, particularly birds, see Titley, 1984, 193–4.

[41] For the text of the *khuṭbah*, reproduced from the Dār al-Kutub copy, see Appendix A.

> in it for enjoyment, would easily find the truth about it, and need not spend a great deal of time to gain experience for it. And *God facilitated such a task*, and the writing of the treatise was completed, and it was called *Hamāmah'nāmah*.

It is difficult to date this document, but a speculation can be offered. Shihāb al-Dīn (or Malik Aḥmad) does not seem to follow any particular chronological order in compiling 'Abd al-Vāsi''s writing samples, which can be dated anywhere from the time when he worked for Abū Sa'īd Gūrkānī until the time when he was employed by Sulṭān Ḥusayn Bāyqarā'. What is certain, however, is that Manṣūr could not have compiled *Hamāmah'nāmah* at an early age. References to the "passage of time" and "much . . . experience" on the part of Manṣūr can signify that he embarked on this project at a very mature age, perhaps in his fifties. If we suppose that he was born around 827/1424—as we suggested earlier—he then could have been working on *Hamāmah'nāmah* when Sulṭān Ḥusayn Bāyqarā' was already ruling over Khurāsān in mid-870s/early 1470s. This conjecture is further strengthened by the fact that Sulṭān Ḥusayn Bāyqarā' is recorded to have had quite an affinity for pigeons.[42] Could the ever-hedonistic Sulṭān not also have persuaded Manṣūr to take on the task of writing and illustrating a book about his favorite bird? If we accept this proposition, then we can argue that Mughal kings Akbar and Jahāngīr were probably following an established pattern when they were asking their court painter Manṣūr Jahāngīr Shāhī to paint live animals for them.

There is still another, equally significant, document in *Mansha' al-inshā'* that pertains to Manṣūr, and that is a decree (*manshūr*) appointing him as the head of the artists of the royal atelier in Harāt.[43] We know of several such decrees, including one from Ibrāhīm Sulṭān ibn Shāhrukh (796–838/1394–1435), naming Naṣīr al-Dīn Muḥammad the illuminator (*muẕahhib*) as the administrator of his atelier,[44] one from Shāh Ismā'īl (r. 907–30/1501–24)—or Shāh Ṭahmāsb (r. 930–84/1524–76)—naming Bihzād to a similar position, but with authority at a state level, in 928/1522,[45] one from Shāh Ṭahmāsb to *Ustād* Ḥasan Muẕahhib Baghdādī,[46] and one from Shāh 'Abbās I (r. 995–

[42] Bābur 1993, 3:340.

[43] *Mansha' al-inshā'*, Egyptian National Library, Cairo, MS 129 Adab-i Farsī, fols. 76v–7v (the latter portion of the text is repeated on fols. 78r–v, with the word *zā'id* in between some of its lines); 'Abd al-Vāsi' Nizāmī 1979–, 1:250–3.

[44] See Ra'nā Ḥusaynī 1986, 70–2.

[45] See Bahari 1996, 184–6.

[46] See Qāẓī Aḥmad Qumī 1987, 145–7.

1038/1587–1629) to Āqā Riẕā Muṣavvir.[47] The ruler granting this position to Manṣūr is not named in the *manshūr*, but—as we shall see soon—he could very well be Sulṭān Abū Sa'īd.

The decree[48] begins with an often inscrutable introduction in praise of God, which includes quite a number of oblique metaphors and similes, and which takes up about a third of the text of the *manshūr*. From the very beginning, the abundance of terms pertaining to visual artistic creation leaves no doubt that the *manshūr* deals with the art of creating paintings and drawings.

The author of the decree claims that patronizing the arts (*ra'āyat-i jānib-i hunar*) is an old tradition and should be part of the responsibilities of all intellectuals (*aṣḥab-i baṣar*). It has been one of the mandatory tasks of any eminent sulṭān. Therefore, since "Mawlānā Nāṣir al-Dīn Manṣūr Muṣavvir," the pride of the painters (*iftikhār al-muṣavvirīn*), has proven his ability in creating extraordinary and fine paintings/drawings (*taṣvīr-i naqshbandī-i khāmah-i litāfat'nigār-i gharā'ib'āsār*) over others, and since he is unparalleled in the art of painting and linear calligraphy (*taḥrīr*), it became necessary for the author of the *manshūr* to patronize him "in the best manner possible" as if he were Mānī (*Mānī'vār*). This *manshūr* was then written so that other painters would follow Manṣūr's way of painting (*qalam-i ū dastūr-i hunar . . . gardad*). Because Manṣūr has achieved the highest ranks in the field of painting, other masters and artists present at the court are by virtue of this *manshūr* obliged to follow Manṣūr's commands. He in turn should carefully examine works of those individuals and decide on their ability and talent as artists, and delegate work to them accordingly. With his expert knowledge (*dīdah-i baṣīrat*), he must identify what is good or bad in their work, and differentiate them so.

Court guards should be considerate of Manṣūr and should not prevent him (unduly?) from coming to or leaving the court, as they do with other

[47] The exact nature of this decree is not known as only part of it exists, see ibid., 151–2. *Mansh' al-inshā'*also contains a *farmān* from Sulṭān Ḥusayn Bāyqarā' appointing an individual to the post of librarian of his library. According to Humāyūnfarrukh, the name of the librarian in his copy is erased (the Dār al-Kutub copy, fols. 63v–4r, has *fulān* (lit. so-and-so) in place of the name); it may have initially referred to Mīrak, Bihzād's teacher and foster parent, of whom we know from Qāẕī Aḥmad (1987, 134) that he was Sulṭān Ḥusayn's librarian for some time, see 'Abd al-Vāsi' Niẕāmī 1979–, 1:204–5.

[48] For the text of the decree, reproduced from the Dār al-Kutub copy, see Appendix B. Prior to its publication in *Mansha' al-inshā'* ('Abd al-Vāsi' Niẕāmī 1979–), the text of the *manshūr* was published by Dr. Humāyūnfarrukh in an article in the Persian journal *Vaḥīd* (Humāyūnfarrukh 1969, 839–40, 994–6). While taken from the same manuscript, the two versions differ in certain instances, which may well be the result of different readings at different times. The *manshūr* seems hopelessly incomprehensible in some places, and contains errors of transcription.

individuals. They should consider him the greatest and best painter of the court—higher and better than other artists and employees. Manṣūr in turn should not deviate from his submission to the will of the Sulṭān, and should continue to serve him with the greatest sincerity. This way, Manṣūr's honesty (*yak rangī*) will earn him a place among the rare individuals of the age.

The Sulṭān's children, *amīr*s, *vazīr*s, servants, retinue, tribesmen, etc. should be thoughtful of Manṣūr's rights and feelings (*ra'āyat-i ū rā vājib dārand va murāqibat-i ū rā vājib shināsand*). Consuls and falconers should not ask him for tolls for his four-legged animals; and under no circumstances should sheriffs inconvenience his relatives. In fact, they should not bother complaining [about Manṣūr or his relatives].

Humāyūnfarrukh dates this decree to before 888/1483, which he says is the year when 'Abd al-Vāsi' was removed from his post in the Epistolary Office and was replaced by Khvānd Amīr.[49] He furthermore suggests that the decree is from Sulṭān Ḥusayn Bāyqarā', and that Bihzād was a product of Manṣūr's school.[50] However, as mentioned earlier, Mīrzā Ḥaydar associates Manṣūr with the court of Abū Sa'īd, which means as far as Manṣūr's main forte was concerned, his relationships with other rulers (be they Pīr Būdāq or Sulṭān Ḥusayn) were not as important in the eyes of the Chaghatayid author. If Manṣūr had in fact been appointed to the highest rank of artists during the reign of Sulṭān Ḥusayn, it would have been highly unlikely that Mīrzā Ḥaydar would still associate him with the Abū Sa'īd period.

There is still more reason to believe that the *manshūr* is from Abū Sa'īd. The Dār al-Kutub copy of the text begins with two explanatory lines to the effect that the *manshūr* was composed by 'Abd al-Vāsi' at the direction (*ishārat*) of Mawlānā 'Abd al-Ḥayy Munshī, who apparently was not happy with a previous *nishān* (proclamation) written for Manṣūr.[51]

> *Jahat-i Manṣūr Muṣavvir nishānī nivishtah būdand va arbāb-i qalam dar taḥsīn-i ān mubālighah va iṭrār az ḥadd mī'guẓarānīdand. Bi-ishārat-i Mawlānā 'Abd al-Ḥayy Munshī dar hamān majlis badīhah bayn al-suṭūr nivishtah.*

[49] Humāyūnfarrukh 1969, 996. Humāyūnfarrukh's claim that Khvānd Amīr took over the job of composing royal letters and decrees after the removal of 'Abd al-Vāsi' rests on his assertion that Khvānd Amīr wrote the decree about Bihzād's directorship of the royal library for "Sulṭān Ḥusayn Bāyqarā'" on 27 Jumādá I 889/22 June 1484, which is thirty-nine years earlier than the date mentioned in the Paris manuscript of the decree. In 889 Khvānd Amīr could not have been more than eight or nine years old.

[50] Ibid.

[51] *Mansha' al-inshā'*, Egyptian National Library, Cairo, MS 129 Adab-i Farsī, fol. 76v.

Translation:

> A proclamation had been written for Manṣūr Muṣavvir, and [in a gathering] writers exaggerated in praising it. In that same gathering, at the direction of Mawlānā ‘Abd al-Ḥayy, [‘Abd al-Vāsi‘] wrote [this text] extemporaneously.

Mawlānā ‘Abd al-Ḥayy was the chief *munshī* of Sulṭān Abū Sa‘īd, who "became world-famous" by conducting the Sulṭān's correspondence. According to Qaẓī Aḥmad, the only other rulers he served in that capacity were the Aqqoyunlus, including Ūzūn Ḥasan and Ya‘qūb Beg.[52] No known contemporary source has associated ‘Abd al-Ḥayy with the court of Sulṭān Ḥusayn Bayqarā'. He then could not have asked ‘Abd al-Vāsi‘—obviously one of his pupils—to compose a decree on behalf of Sulṭān Ḥusayn.[53]

Finally, we consider a couple of documents which may provide us with samples of Manṣūr's writing. They come in another collection of letters and decrees of the period called *Farā'id-i Ghiyāṣī*, which was collected and categorized in ten sections by Jalāl al-Dīn Yūsuf Ahl, a descendant of the famous 6th/12th-century Ṣūfī, Shaykh Aḥmad Jām. From examining the documents in the six manuscripts that were used for the (incomplete) critical edition of the *Farā'id-i Ghiyāṣī*, it would appear that Yūsuf Ahl initially wanted to collect documents pertaining to the notables of his own family, but after he finished the first version of his compilation in 837/1433-4, the scope of his project expanded to include works of other dignitaries as well. We know for certain that he added more samples to his work as late as 860/1455-6, which seems to be the date of one of his letters to ‘Abd al-Raḥmān Jāmī included in one of the manuscript copies of the book.[54] It is quite possible, however, that he—or his

[52] Khvānd Amīr [1954] 1983, 108 and 1994, 2:409; Qāẓī Aḥmad Qumī 1987, 43 and 1959, 84.

[53] It is interesting to see how free the higher-ranked royal *munshīs* were in composing decrees, and how excluded the Sulṭān became in the latter part of the process.

[54] Yūsuf Ahl 1977–, 1:28, pref. The manuscripts on which Dr. Heshmat Moayyad has based his edition are: (1). Universitätsbibliothek Tübingen copy, possibly copied by Yūsuf Ahl himself, last five chapters only, 293 documents. (2). Ayasofya Kütüphanesi copy, 861/1457, selections from all ten chapters, 134 documents. (3). Kütüphane-i Esat Efendi copy, 10th/16th century (seems older than 5 and 4), first five chapters only, 305 documents. (4). Bibliothèque nationale copy, 10th/16th century (seems to have been copied from 3), 247 documents. (5). Kitābkhānah-'i Markazī-i Dānishgāh-i Tihrān copy, 10th/16th century, all ten chapters, 452 documents (not all). (6). Tübingen (?) copy, 130 documents. An apparently Turkish version of the *Farā'id-i Ghiyāṣī*, dated Rabī' I 881/July 1476 and containing all ten chapters, exists in the Keir Collection, which seems to have escaped the attention of the editor of the book, see Robinson 1978, 22. I have been unable to examine this copy for the present article.

offspring—continued to add to the *Farā'id-i Ghiyāṣī* well into the 870s/1470s, as suggested by the existence of more documents in later manuscripts. This also corresponds well with Khvānd Amīr's assertion, which puts Yūsuf Ahl in the category of scholars of Ṣulṭān Abū Sa'īd's time.[55]

Farā'id-i Ghiyāṣī contains two documents written by a man named Manṣūr. One is a letter addressed to a certain qāẓī named Sarāj al-Dīn al-Iṣfahānī, and another is a reply to a sulṭān who had apparently sent this Manṣūr a *manshūr*.[56] Manṣūr's full name is cited as Manṣūr ibn Muḥammad al-Shīrāzī, but an epithet (*laqab*) of Nāṣir al-Dīn is added to the same name at the beginning of the book, where a list of the authors of the book's documents is given.[57] The reply itself[58] begins with the glorification of an unnamed ruler whose *manshūr* has taken the author, this "lowest slave," (*bandah-'i kamtarīn*) from obscurity (*khumūl*) to renown (*qabūl*), and has turned his hardship (*ẕillat*) into relief (*'izzat*). He tells us that he is treating the "heavenly gift" of the sulṭān like a crown on his head, and that the contents of the *manshūr* have in a sense revived him (here he refers to the myth of Alexander, who unsuccessfully looked for the fountain of life). The kindness that the sulṭān has shown him in the *manshūr* has moved him in turn to give thanks and blessings. He prays that the ruler's treatment of and kind sentiments for men of science and learning (*arbāb-i 'ilm va faẓl*), as well as for the righteous (*ahl-i ṣalāh*), will produce more greatness for the sovereign. He also says that he has always been looking forward to being invited to the court of the ruler, and that he would welcome the opportunity to pay his homage to the ruler. He prays that God will allow him to achieve his wish, and that He will protect the ruler.

The combination of the document's nature and its author's name makes an identification of Manṣūr ibn Muḥammad al-Shīrāzī with our painter Manṣūr Muṣavvir quite plausible.[59] Assuming that the letter is written by Manṣūr Muṣavvir and addressed to Sulṭān Abū Sa'īd, we can speculate as to the date

[55] Khvānd Amīr [1954] 1983, 4:102, 104, and 1994, 2:407.

[56] Yūsuf Ahl 1977–, 2: 379–80; 1:216–8.

[57] The *laqab* in the Esat Efendi and Bibliothèque nationale manuscripts is cited as Jalāl al-Dīn and Shihāb al-Dīn, respectively, see ibid., 1:17, 218; but the more reliable Ayasofya and two other manuscripts give Nāṣir al-Dīn as the *laqab* for Manṣūr ibn Muḥammad al-Shīrāzī.

[58] For the text of this reply, see Appendix C. I am most grateful to Professor Heshmat Moayyad who gave me permission to reproduce the text here.

[59] Manṣūr's authorship of these letters should be taken into consideration with the understanding that Yūsuf Ahl generally edited the documents in his book for maximum orنateness, see Yūsuf Ahl 1977–, 1:28, pref. Also, there is a "model" reply-to-rulers letter in yet another collection of letters of the period that is similar to Manṣūr's letter, and could have been used by him, see Shihāb al-Munshī 1978, 15–6.

of the letter and of the *manshūr* that prompted it. The fact that Manṣūr says he wanted to go to the court may indicate that he was physically absent from the current residence of Sulṭān Abū Sa'īd. It is possible that Abū Sa'īd appointed Manṣūr while he was working at the court of Pīr Būdāq in Shīrāz during the early 860s/late 1450s. By then Manṣūr had probably built a reputation for himself as a masterly painter, news and evidence of which could easily have reached the Timurid Sulṭān. On the other hand, the tone of the *manshūr* does not conform with the chaotic pre-863/1458 situation in Khurāsān. But perhaps that is reading too much into Manṣūr's statement, and we can simply assume that he was only looking forward to working at the court, and that Abū Sa'īd named him head artist of his Harāt atelier at some time during the last few and relatively calm years of his reign.

Fig. 1. Sayf al-Mulūk. Attributed to Shāh Muẓaffar. Circa 884/1479. Topkapı Palace Library, İstanbul, Hazine 2154, fol. 86r. 26 x 21 cm. By permission of the Topkapı Palace Library

Fig. 2. Humāyūn hunting. Attributed to Shāh Muẓaffar. Circa 888/1483. *Humāy u Humāyūn*, Topkapı Palace Library, İstanbul, MS Revan 1045, fol. 23r. 28.5 x 19 cm. By permission of the Topkapı Palace Library

Fig. 3. Hunting scene. Attributed to Manṣūr. Circa 840s/1440s. Staatsbibliothek zu Berlin - Preußischer Kulturbesitz - Orientabteilung, Diez A, Fol. 70, Bl. 1. 37.5 x 23.4 cm. By permission of the Staatsbibliothek zu Berlin

APPENDIX A

'Abd al-Vāsi' Niẓāmī's Preface to *Ḥamāmah'nāmah* (*Mansha' al-inshā'*, Egyptian National Library, Cairo, MS 129 Adab-i Farsī, fols. 11v-2r).

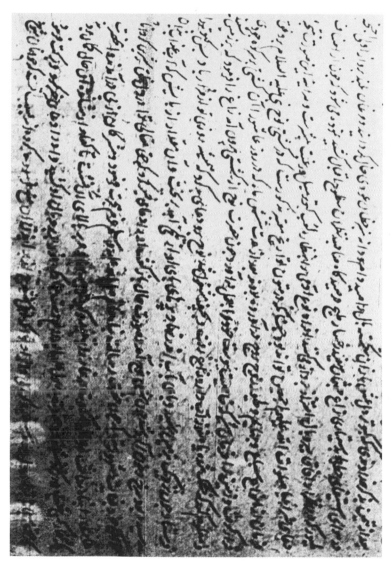

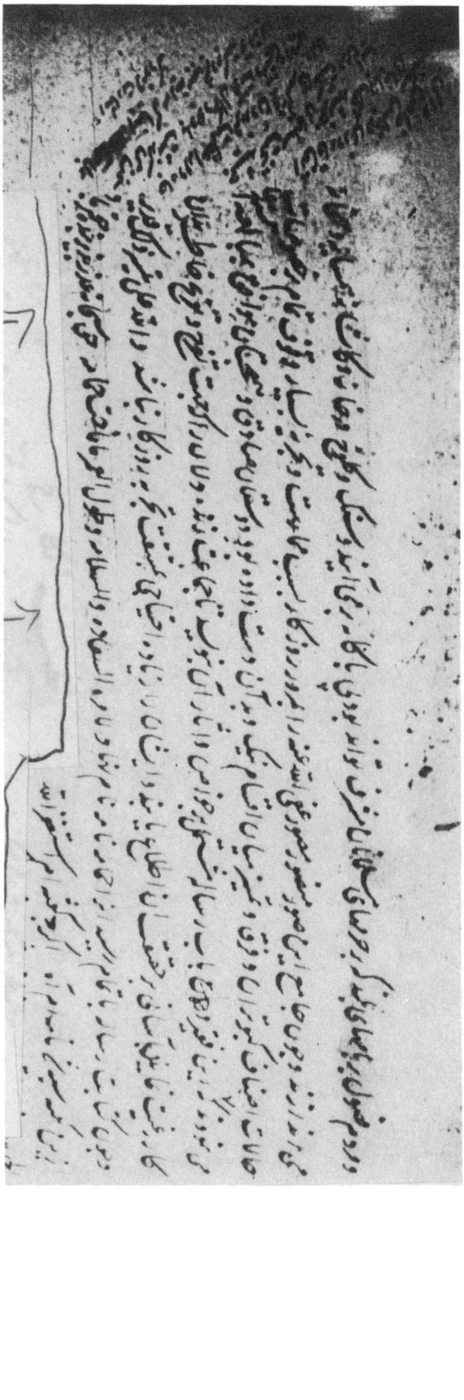

APPENDIX B

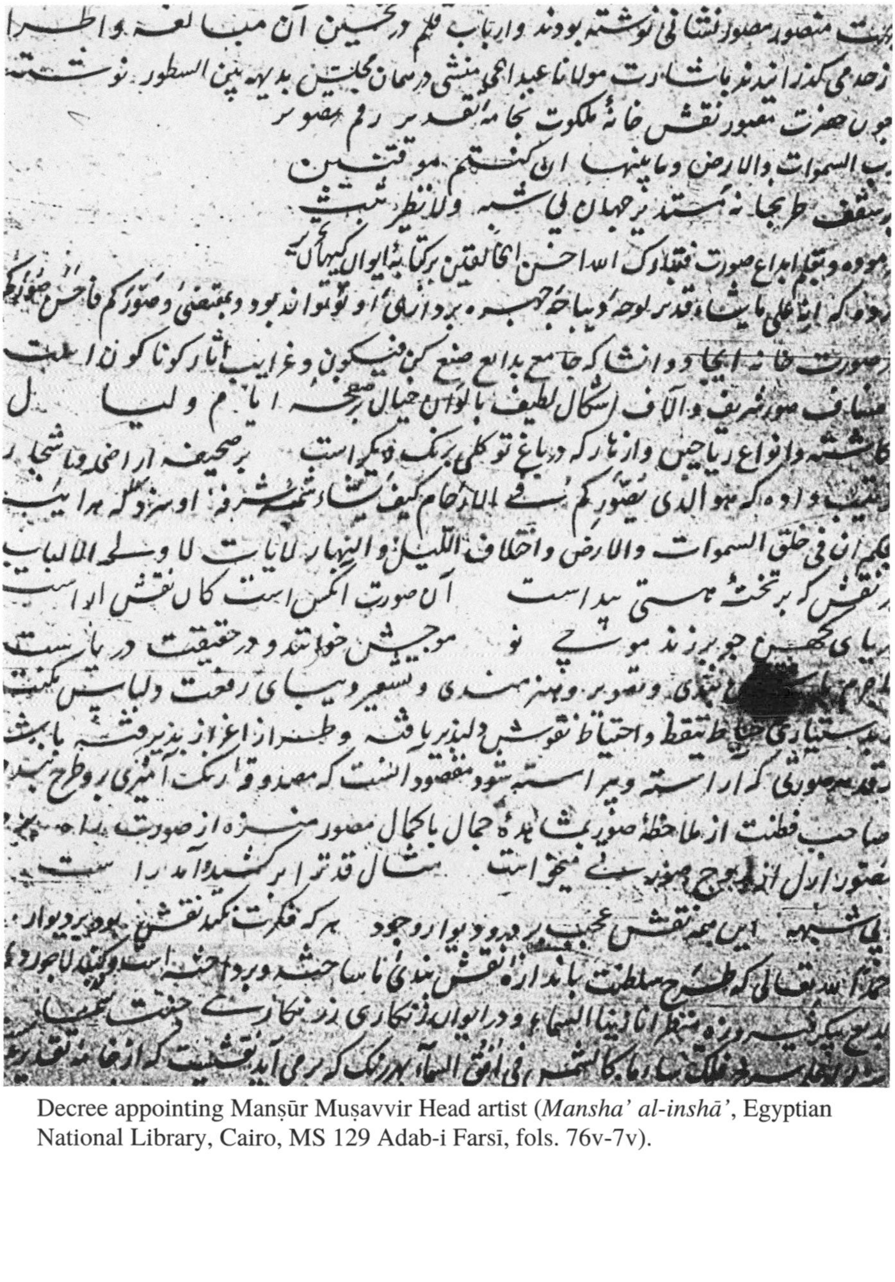

Decree appointing Manṣūr Muṣavvir Head artist (*Mansha' al-inshā'*, Egyptian National Library, Cairo, MS 129 Adab-i Farsī, fols. 76v-7v).

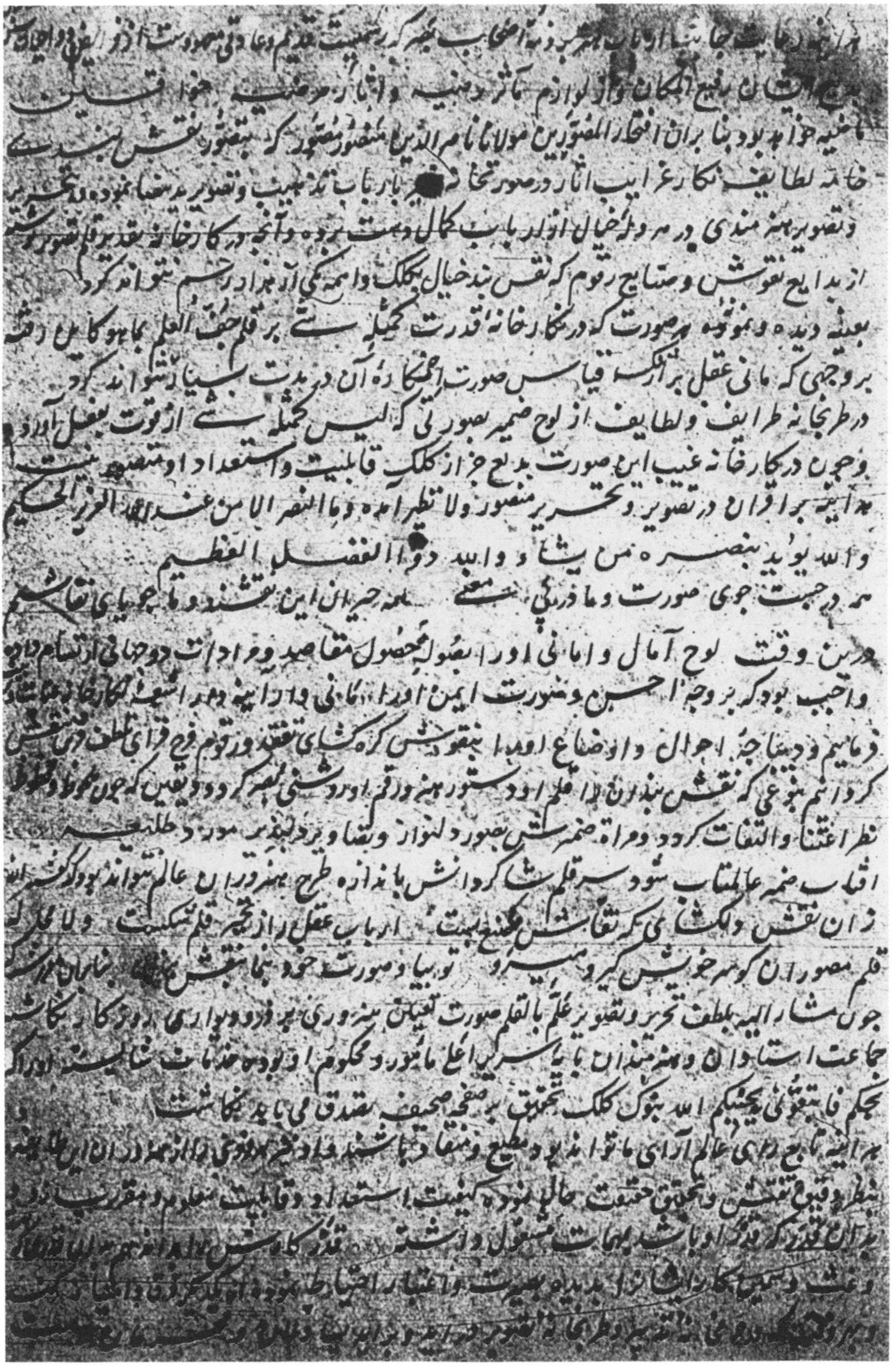

وما النصر الا من عند الله العزیز الحکیم

والله یؤید بنصره من یشاء والله ذو الفضل العظیم

Decree appointing Manṣūr Muṣavvir Head artist (partial repeat) (*Mansha' al-inshā'*, Egyptian National Library, Cairo, MS 129 Adab-i Farsī, fols. 78r-v).

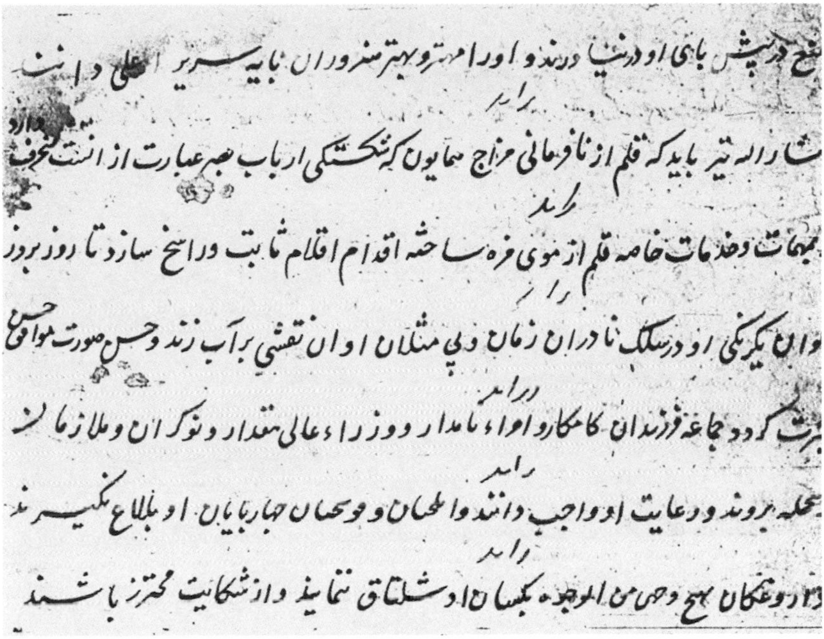

نخ در پیش پای او در نیا درنده و او را مهتر و بهتر سروران تا به سریر اعلی دانند
برابر
شاء الله تیر باید که قلم از نافرمانی مزاج همایون که شکستگی ارباب بصر عبارت از آنست نکشد
گزند
مهمات و خدمات خاصه قلم از موی مژه ساخته اقدام اقلام ثابت و راسخ سازد تا روز بروز
راز
و این یکی رو در سلک نادران زمان و بی مثالان او آن نقشی بر آب زند و حسن صورت موافق حسن
در آید
برت گرد و جماعه فرزندان کامکار و امراء نامدار و وزراء عالی مقدار و نوکران و ملازمان
رانید
بحله برونند و رعایت او واجب دانند و احسان و مهمان جهارپایان او بلاغ بگیرند
رانید
دار و عکان بهیچ وجه من الوجوه بکسان او دستلاق ننمایند و از شکایت محترز باشند

APPENDIX C

من انشاء الفاضل[1] منصور بن محمد[2] الشیرازی
فی جواب احدی السلاطین[3]

منشور حیات جاودانی　　　توقیع مطالب و امانی

منشور حیات بخش و توقیع سعادت رسان و مثال عدیم المثال واجب الاتباع و الامتثال و طغرای ملك آرای جهانگشای وشمامهء گلزار قدسی و گلدستهء حدائق فردوسی اعنی نگاشتهء خامهء گوهربار درر نثار و رقم زدهء کلك زرنگار سحر آثار منشیان حضرت سلطنت شعار فلك اقتدار جمشید آثار، مخدوم سلاطین کام کار، مستخدم خواقین رفیع مقدار، (ع): (که باد تا ابد از عمر و جاه برخوردار)[4]، خسرو زمین و زمان، جهاندار دولت قرین صاحب قران،

بیت

طراز کسوت کشور گشائی　　نگین خاتم فرمان روائی

دارای ممالك هفت اقلیم[5]، پادشاه اسلام خلد الله سبحانه فی دوام خلافته ملکه[6] و سلطانه، که غبار موکب معلایش سرمهء دیدهء روشنان افلاك باد، و فتراك دولت پاینده اش معتصم ساکنان مرکز خاك، نعل سمندش حلقهء گوش تاجداران، و خم کمندش طوق گردن کشان و شهریاران، بندهء کمترین را از کنج خمول به اوج قبول و از حضیض ذلت به ذروهء عزت رسانید، وآن تحفهء غیبی را چون تاج

۱. نسخهء پاریس: من انشاء الفاضل العلامة شهاب الدین الملة و الدین . . .

۲. نسخهء اسعد افندی: محمد شاه الشیرازی.

۳. نسخهء اسعد افندی: جواباً لبعض السلاطین انارالله برهانه؛ نسخهء پاریس: الی واحد من السلاطین.

٤. نسخهء توبینگن درون پرانتز را ندارد.

۵. نسخهء اسعد افندی: اقلام.

٦. نسخهء اسعد افندی: و ملکه.

برسر نهاد و چون دل در برگرفت، و آن موهبت قدسی را به لب جان بوسید و بردیدهء روان مالید.

شعر

آنچه اسکندر میان[7] تیرگی جست و نیافت
در سواد خط آن منشور مضمر یافتم
ز اشتیاق دست[8] گوهر بارش آن منشور[9] را
گاه برلب گاه بردل گاه برسر یافتم

اصناف مرحمت و بنده نوازی که در مطاوی مثال مطاع واجب الاتباع مندرج بودبه ادعیهء عرش فرسای و اثنیهء آفاق پیمای مقابل گردانید، ومراسم ضراعات و لوازم عبودیات[10] اقامه[11] نموده در طی مناجات سحرگاهی از حضرت الهی مسألت کرد که هر تربیتی و عاطفتی که دربارهء ارباب علم و فضل و اهل صلاح فرمایند سلطنت تازه و عظمت بی اندازه کرامت کناد، و اولیای دولتش را تا قیام ساعت وساعت قیام به هر ساعت ملکی در طاعت آید، و به هر ماهی شاهی مسخر گردد، و به هر روزی مملکتی روزی شود، واعدای حضرتش را در هر زمانی زیانی[12] و در هر حالی زوالی[13] مقدر گردد، و هر صبحی نجحی به شامی ناکامی مبدل گشته هر دمی در دامی گرفتار آیند.

پیوسته برمرقبهء ارادت غیبی مترصد و مترقب است که از مهب *لاتیأسوا من روح الله* نسیمی نعیمی و رجائی رخائی، که متضمن احراز سعادت بساط بوس باشد، متنسم گردد و دیدهء رمد

۷. نسخهء اسعد افندی و پاریس: درون.

۸. نسخهء اسعد افندی: درر.

۹. نسخهء پاریس: مکتوب.

۱۰. نسخهء توبینگن در اینجا پایان یافته است. نسخهء اسعد افندی: عبودیت.

۱۱. نسخهء پاریس: باقامه.

۱۲. نسخهء پاریس *زیانی* را ندارد.

۱۳. نسخهء پاریس: روانی.

دیده را به اکتحال خاك سلطنت آستان[۱۴] منور گرداند.

بیت

یارب این آرزوی من چه خوش است

تــو بــدیـــن آرزو مــرا بــرســـان

دراز نفسی از حدگذشت[۱۵]، (اختصار بردعا اولی است)[۱۶]

بیت

یارب پناه دولت و دینش تو کرده ای

اندر پناه خویش بدار ایــن پنــاه را

---

۱۴. نسخهء پاریس: آشیان.

۱۵. نسخهء پاربس: زیادت ابرام نمیدهد دراز . . .

۱۶. نسخهء اسعد افندی درون پرانتز را ندارد.

BIBLIOGRAPHY

'ABD AL-VĀSI' NIẒĀMĪ, NIẒĀM AL-DĪN. 1979–. *Mansha' al-inshā'*. Compiled by Abū al-Qāsim Shihāb al-Dīn Aḥmad Khvāfī. Ed. Rukn al-Dīn Humāyūnfarrukh. 1 vol. to date. Tehran : Dānishgāh-i Millī Īrān, Isfand 1357 Sh.–

ADLE, C. 1990. Antopsia, in absentia : Sur la date de l'introduction et de la constitution de l'album de Bahrâm Mirzâ par Dust-Moḥammad en 951/1544. *Studia Iranica* 19, no. 2: 219–56.

BĀBUR, ẒAHĪR AL-DĪN MUḤAMMAD. 1993. *Bâburnâma : Chaghatay Turkish text with Abdul-Rahim Khankhanan's Persian translation.* 3 vols. Turkish transcription, Persian ed. and English tr. by W. M. Thackston, Jr. Cambridge, Massachusetts : The Department of Near Eastern Languages and Civilizations, Harvard University.

—— 1996. *The Baburnama : memoirs of Babur, prince and emperor.* Tr., ed., and annotated by W. M. Thackston. Wshington, DC : Freer Gallery of Art : Arthur M. Sackler Gallery, Smithsonian Institution ; New York : Oxford University Press.

BAHARI, EBADOLLAH. 1996. *Bihzad, master of Persian painting*. London and New York : I.B. Tauris.

BINYON, L., WILKINSON, V. S., and GRAY, B. [1933] 1971. *Persian miniature painting : including a critical and descriptive catalogue of the miniatures exhibited at Burlington House, January–March, 1931*. Reprint, New York : Dover Publications.

DŪST MUḤAMMAD. 1993. Dībāchah. In *Kitāb'ārāyi dar tamaddun-i Islāmī : majmū'ah-i rasā'il dar zamīnah-'i khvushnivīsī, murakkab'sāzī, kāghazgarī, tahzīb, va tajlīd : bih inẓimām-i farhang-i vāzhgān-i niẓām-i kitāb'ārāyi*. Ed. Najīb Māyil Hiravī. Mashhad : Bunyād-i Pizhūhishhā-yi Islāmī, Āstān-i Quds-i Raẓavī, 1372 Sh.

Fihris al-makhṭūṭāt al-Fārisīyah allatī taqtanīhā Dār al-Kutub ḥattá 'ām 1963 M. 1966–7. Cairo : Maṭba'at Dār al-Kutub.

GRAY, BASIL. [1961] 1977. *Persian painting*. Reprint, New York : Rizzoli.

—— 1979. History of miniature painting : the fourtheenth century. In *The arts of the book in Central Asia : 14th–16th centuries*. Ed. Basil Gray. Boulder, Colorado : Shambhala : UNESCO: 93–120.

HAASE, CLAUS. 1981. On the attribution of some paintings in H. 2153 to the time of Timur. *Islamic art* 1: 50–5.

HUMĀYŪNFARRUKH, RUKN AL-DĪN. 1966. Dastah gulī taqdīm bi-dūstdārān-i kitāb. *Hunar va mardum* 49 (Ābān 1345 Sh.): 41–60.

—— 1969. Hunar-i dawrah-'i Tīmūrī va Kamal al-Dīn Bihzād. *Vaḥīd* 6, no. 10: 833–40 (pt. 1; Mihr 1348 Sh.); 11: 994–1011 (pt. 2; Ābān 1348 Sh.).

İPŞİROĞLU, M.Ş. 1964. *Saray-Alben : Diez'sche Klebebände aus den Berliner Sammlungen.* Wiesbaden : Franz Steiner Verlag GmbH.

—— 1984. *Siyah Qalem.* Roma : Salerno Editrice.

KHVĀND AMĪR. [1954] 1983. *Tārīkh-i Ḥabīb al-siyar fī akhbār-i afrād-i bashar.* Ed. Muḥammad Dabīr Siyāqī, introd. Jalāl al-Dīn Humā'ī. 4 vols. Reprint, Tehran : Kitābfurūshī-i Khayyām, 1362 Sh.

—— 1994. *Habibu's-siyar : tome three*. Tr. & ed. W. M. Thackston. 2 vols. Cambridge, Massachusetts : The Department of Near Eastern Languages and Civilizations, Harvard University.

KÜHNEL, ERNST. 1959. Malernamen in den Berliner "Saray"-Alben. *Kunst des Orients* 3: 66–77.

LENTZ, THOMAS W., LOWRY, GLENN D. 1989. *Timur and the princely vision : Persian art and culture in the fifteenth century*. Los Angeles : Los Angeles County Museum of Art.

MĪR 'ALĪSHĪR NAVĀ'Ī. [1945] 1984. *Tazkirah-'i Majālis al-nafā'is*. Ed. 'Alī Aṣghar Ḥikmat. Reprint, Tehran : Kitābfurūshī-i Manūchihrī, 1363 Sh.

MUḤAMMAD ḤAYDAR DŪGHLĀT. 1996. *Tārīkh-i Rashīdī : tārīkh-i khvānīn-i Mughūlistān*. Persian text ed. W. M. Thackston. Cambridge, Massachusetts : The Department of Near Eastern Languages and Civilizations, Harvard University.

—— 1996b. *Mirza Haydar Dughlat's Tarikh-i-Rashidi : a history of the Khans of Moghulistan*. Tr & ann. W. M. Thackston. Cambridge, Massachusetts : The Department of Near Eastern Languages and Civilizations, Harvard University.

QĀẒĪ AḤMAD QUMĪ. 1959. Calligraphers and painters : a treatise by Qādī Aḥmad, son of Mīr-Munshī, circa A.H. 1015/A.D. 1606. Tr. V. Minorsky. Introd. B.N. Zakhoder, tr. from the Russian by T. Minorsky. Washington : Freer Gallery of Art.

—— 1987. *Gulistān-i hunar*. 3rd ed. Ed. Aḥmad Suhaylī Khvānsārī. Tehran : Kitābfurūshī-i Manūchihrī, 1366 Sh.

RICE, DAVID TALBOT. 1975. *Islamic art*. Revised ed. New York : Thames and Hudson.

ROBINSON, B.W. 1958. *A descriptive catalogue of the Persian paintings in the Bodleian Library*. Oxford : Oxford University Press at the Clarendon Press.

—— 1980. *Persian paintings in the John Rylands Library : a descriptive catalogue*. London : Sotheby Parke Bernet.

—— 1981. Siyah Qalam. *Islamic art* 1: 62–5.

ROXBURGH, DAVID J. 1996. *Our works point to us : album making, collection, and art (1427–1565) under the Timurids and Safavids*. 2 vols. Ph.D. diss. University of Pennsylvania.

Seyfilmülûk hikâyesi. 1959. İstanbul : İstanbul Maarif Kitaphanesi ve Matbaası.

SHIHĀB AL-MUNSHĪ. 1978. Humāyūn'nāmah. Compiled by Muḥammad ibn 'Alī ibn Jamāl al-Islām al-mulaqqab bih Shihāb Munshī. Ed. Rukn al-Dīn Humāyūnfarrukh. Tehran : Dānishgāh-i Millī Īrān, Isfand 2536 Shāhanshāhī.

SOUDAVAR, ABOLALA. 1992. *Art of the Persian courts : selections from the Art and History Trust Collection*. New York : Rizzoli.

SULEIMAN, HAMID. 1970. *Miniatures to poems of Alisher Navoi*. Tashkent : Fan.

TANINDI, ZEREN. 1979. *A fifteenth century manuscript of Humāy u Humāyūn*. *Persica* 8: 129–32.

TITLEY, NORA M. 1984. *Persian miniature painting and its influence on the art of Turkey and India : the British Library collections*. Austin : University of Texas Press.

VLADISLAV, JAN. 1958. *Persian fables*. Pictures selected and photographed by W. and B. Forman from the collections of Persian miniatures in the Teheran Imperial Library. London : Spring Books.

YŪSUF AHL. 1977–. *Farā'id-i Ghiyāṣī*. Ed. Hishmat Mu'ayyad. 2 vols. to date. Tehran : Bunyād-i Farhang-i Īrān, 2536 Shāhanshāhī–

The Nuncios of Pope Sixtus IV (1471–84) in Iran

Angelo Michele Piemontese

THE BLOSSOMING OF DIPLOMATIC RELATIONS between Iran and Italy under Ḥasan Beg Bahādur Khān Āq'qūyūnlū, commonly called Sulṭān Ūzūn Ḥasan (r. 857–82/1453–78), constituted a grand-scale enterprise attested by an exchange of missions of unprecedented level and frequency between 1471/875–6 and 1475/879–80. Historians have as a rule focused on relations between Iran and Venice. It is worthwhile, however, to gather the available data in order to shed light on the history of relations which the Aqqoyunlu diplomacy established above all with Rome and also maintained with other Italian states.[1] The functions, routes, and identity of the ambassadors from all quarters pose multiple questions with respect to the correlation of the events. I shall attempt here to identify the nuncios sent to Iran by Pope Sixtus IV (1471–84).

Pope Calistus III (1455–8) initiated a policy to fight the Ottoman enemy at sea and support in this manner the eastern ally who fought him on land. The same policy was followed by Pius II (1458–64), who succeeded Calistus III, but it later languished under the latter's successor, Paulus II (1464–71).[2] Since his election as Pope in 1471, Sixtus IV, who was a Franciscan named Francesco della Rovere and a Ligurian from Savona, had demonstrated the tenacity and breadth of his diplomatic initiative toward strengthening the alliance with Iran, resuming, once again, the strategy introduced by Calistus III.

A wave of jubilation greeted the return, on 23 January 1473, of Oliviero Carafa, cardinal of Naples, with the fleet of the naval league under his command from a successful attack on İzmir in Rabī' I 877/August 1472. It was an encouraging victory for the Pope, who had organized the league and the papal fleet.[3] However, the planned celebration of the triumph of the king of Iran over his Ottoman rival, which was candidly anticipated in Rome, was thwarted by the stinging defeat which Fatiḥ Meḥmed II inflicted on Ūzūn Ḥasan in the battle of Başkent in Rabī' I 878/August 1473. Within a year, however, hopes for a redressment of the situation were revived.

[1] Pou y Martí 1949.
[2] Di Fonzo 1986.
[3] Guglielmotti 1886, 2:348–60, 367–72; Piemontese 1991.

If we glance back at the inception of the pontificate of Sixtus IV,[4] we see a joyous event. Several ambassadors presented themselves to the new Pope: "Azimaomet" (Ḥājjī Muḥammad), ambassador from Iran, and, "two other nuncios, one from 'Osson Cassan' (Ūzūn Ḥasan), the other from the king of 'Zorziania' (Georgia)."[5] In Rome, "the three ambassadors from Ūzūn Ḥasan" (*tribus oratoribus Somcassani*) together met with Sixtus IV, who named as nuncio to Iran "a Franciscan friar, a very intelligent person." At the same time, Caterrino Zeno was also selected as Venice's ambassador to Iran.[6] On 20 August 1471, Sixtus IV remitted a gratification of 400 Venitian *florins* to "the three ambassadors of Ūzūn Ḥasan,"[7] and in October, the five ambassadors left in Venitian galleys via Alexandria for Cyprus and Caramania.[8]

The name of the Franciscan whom Sixtus IV sent as nuncio to "Ūzūn Ḥasan the lord reigning by the Black Sea" (*Osson Cassianum dominum Imperatorem apud mare ponticum*), and who left with the other four ambassadors, was Antonio Mazzoni.[9] He can be identified as a confidential go-between for Francesco della Rovere, now Pope, and Cardinal Bessarion (1403–72), a humanist originally from Trébizonde (Trabzon). From 1450 until 1455, Mazzoni was the envoy of the papal state to Bologna, and since 1458 a friend of della Rovere and protector of the Franciscan Order.[10] Antonio Mazzoni should not, however, be confused with Antonio de Mazono (or Massonio, or Manzoni[11]), also a confidant of both della Rovere and Bessarion, whom Sixtus IV later appointed Bishop of Paphos in Cyprus on 17 November 1473.[12]

There is in a parchment codex kept at the Archivio di Stato, Milan, a copy of a list of phrases used by the Roman curia to address Ūzūn Ḥasan, his family, and Rome's Christian partners and correspondents in Lebanon, Russia,

[4] He was elected on 9 August 1471, soon after the death of Paul II on 26 July. Before that, from 1464 until 1469, he was the general intendant of the Franciscan Order.

[5] Halecki 1964, 249. These two nuncios had first arrived at Venice with the ambassador from the king of Poland, Casimir IV (1447–92).

[6] *Asnād-i marbūṭ bih ravābiṭ-i tārīkhī-i Īrān va Jumhūrī-i Viniz az dawrah-'i Īlkhānān tā 'aṣr-i Ṣafavī* 1973, 15 (Persian section), 17–8 (Italian section).

[7] Archivio segreto vaticano, vol. 487, fol. 97v, 20 August 1471; Rome, Archivio di Stato, reg. 845, Mandati, Primus Bullarium Sixti IV, fol. 3.

[8] Cornet 1856, 30–1.

[9] Archivio segreto vaticano, vol. 42, Sixti IV Capitulor. 1471–82, lib. 7, fol. 313ff., receipt of Dominicus Petri de Venetiis, 1 October 1471, fol. 6. See also Gaspare da Verona and Canensius 1904, 190. "*Apud mare ponticum*" refers to Trabzon, the homland of its last princess, Despina Theodora Komnenos (Despina Khātūn), wife of Ūzūn Ḥasan.

[10] Coccia 1973.

[11] Hackett 1901, 568.

[12] Pou y Martí 1949, 89, 209, docs. 205, 518.

and Armenia.[13] The list, entitled *Ad Regem Persarum nomine Pontificis* (To the King of the Persians in the name of the Pope), was given to "Grifo Belga" (Gryphon, of Flemish origin) by Sixtus IV at the time of the embassy's departure for Iran.

Gryphon, who was a theologian, an Arabist, and a very learned Franciscan, had spent the past twenty-five years at Mount Lebanon, Beirut, as the representative of Rome among the Maronites. In 1475, while traveling with his inseparable colleague François of Barcelona, he was seized by a sudden illness and was forced to leave the ship in Cyprus. He died on July 18 in Famagusta.[14] Five years earlier, Gryphon had met Anselme Adorno (1424–83) and his son Jean in Beirut. The father and son were on their pilgrimage to the Holy Land—a journey approved by Charles the Bold, Duke of Burgundy (r. 1467–77).[15] Since 1459 the Pope had invited Burgundy to join the alliance with Iran. In September 1473 Charles the Bold sent the same Anselme Adorno on a diplomatic mission to Iran, via Germany and Poland, and in the company of Ludovicus Bononiensis. The latter was another Franciscan—apparently Ludovico Severi of Bologna—who between 1455 and 1479 served as Rome's roving nuncio to Ethiopia, Iran, Armenia, and other countries, and who, in 1461, passed through Flanders during his diplomatic mission to Burgundy.[16] Adorno stopped in Poland in April 1474, but Ludovicus made it all the way to Iran, reaching Tabrīz in May 1475.

A remarkable personality among these 15th-century ambassadors, Ludovicus Bononiensis was far from being "an impostor and a charlatan," as certain historians would contend.[17] One of the items that Ludovicus brought back with him from Iran was a notarized act, which has escaped the attention of his biographers.[18] The act concerns a letter from Ūzūn Ḥasan, which the Franciscan must have delivered to Sixtus IV before the galley carrying the five ambassadors weighed anchor for Cyprus. Ūzūn Ḥasan addressed the letter to Paulus II in Ramaḍan 875/February–March 1471 from Qarā'āghāch, the heart of Aqqoyunlu power. Ludovicus had reached Qarā'āghāch while accompanied by the Genoese nobleman Antonio Squarzafico and Stefano, a Genoese citizen originally from the Ligurian town of San Remo. The letter

[13] For a facsimile of the list, see Vilāyatī 1996, 238; for the text and an English translation of it, see Appendix B. The parchment codex contains copies of diplomatic documents and address lists for the period between 1453 and 1496.

[14] Lammens 1899, 102–4; Wadding 1933, 146–8.

[15] Adorne 1978, 202–4, 346–7.

[16] Landwehr von Pragenau 1901; Bughetti 1938; Severi 1976; Walsh 1977; and Richard 1977, 271–8.

[17] Bryer 1980; Setton 1978–84, 2:222–3.

[18] For the text and English translation of this letter, see Appendix A.

was translated into Latin on 25 July 1471 at Caffa, Theodosia, a Genoese colony, in the office of Girolamo Panissari, a Genoese Dominican and the city's last bishop.[19] The Latin text of the letter is similar to the Italian version of a *Fatḥnāmah* from Ūzūn Ḥasan which was brought to Venice in February 1474.[20]

In this letter Ūzūn Ḥasan announces his great victories, during the campaigns of 871–4/1467–9, over the Qaraqoyunlu Jahānshāh and the Timurid Sulṭān Abū Sa'īd. He mentions his conquest of "Babillonia" (Baghdād), and the new extent of his realm, which had now become an Aqqoyunlu empire, and whose limits are described as reaching India (east) and Cathay (north) in Asia, and Ethiopia in Africa (south). There remained, in the west, between Iran and Europe, the Ottoman obstacle. Ūzūn Ḥasan had fulfilled his part of the prior deal to build a kingdom so great that it would be able, in alliance with Rome, to threaten and attack this rival. He confirmed the pacts and asked his ally to respect his obligations. *Itaque prout promisisti, tu ita perfice*, reads the text. In other words, the Pope should keep his promise; he should strengthen the old friendship; and he should send his nuncio (*homo tuus*). Bartolomeo Platina (1421–81), a biographer of the popes and a librarian at the Vatican, relates that this friendship was initiiated by Calistus III, when in 1457 he sent, with rich presents, Ludovicus Bononiensis as nuncio to "Ūzun Ḥasan the prince of Persians and of Armenia" (*Ad Usuncassanum Persarum & Armeniae principem*).[21]

Sixtus IV confirmed Rome's confidence in the nuncio Ludovicus, and on 19 February 1472 renewed the bull issued in 1461 by Pius II in his behalf. He declared in a safe-conduct dated 12 April 1472: "we appoint our worthy brother Ludovicus the Patriarch of Antioch as our personal nuncio in various parts of the world to conduct many great and arduous negotiations, and to attend to very urgent matters." At the beginning of the following December, Sixtus IV sent to Iran, as papal nuncio, Marianus of Ragusa, a Franciscan whom other documents seem to call Marino de Catharo. His colleague, Antonius de Catharo, joined him while on his way to Hungary.[22]

Marino de Catharo does not seem to be identical with Marino Saxo whose mission was simultaneous with that entrusted to Brother Gryphon. Sixtus IV had appointed Marino Saxo as ambassador to Ūzūn Ḥasan because Saxo knew him and had visited him on previous occasions. According to the diary kept

[19] Vigna 1879, 703–13; Vigna (Raimondo) 1887, 175–82.
[20] Malipiero 1843, 67–8.
[21] Platina 1933, 345.
[22] Pou y Martí 1949, 60, 84, 155–6, 217–9, docs. 137, 190, 375, 377, 538.

by Cicco Simonetta, the secretary of state of the Duke of Milan, Saxo met the Duke at his residence at Pavia on 13 July 1475. Saxo had the task of persuading the Duke, Galeazzo Maria Sforza (1444–76), to send with him an ambassador from Milan to Iran in order to encourage Ūzūn Ḥasan to start an offensive against the Ottomans.

As it is evident from Simonetta's diary, Saxo had arrived at Pavia on June 6th: "An ambassador from Ussun Cassano Assambech [i.e. Ūzūn Ḥasan] has arrived here tonight around 11 o'clock. He has a brief from the Pope exhorting the Duke to be a pleasant and good host. The ambassador in question voyaged by sea, landed at Venice, and then proceeded to Naples and finally to Rome, from where he has come here. He has six horses at his disposal."[23] In an earlier brief dated 16 April 1475, and addressed to the Commune of Florence, Sixtus IV had commended "the ambassador of the great and powerful prince Assambech," who had just informed him about Ūzūn Ḥasan's "preparations and the determination" to attack "our common enemies, the Turks."[24] This unnamed ambassador may have also been sent to Stephen the Great, *voivod* (prince) of Moldavia (1457–1504), who in a letter dated 28 November 1474 informed Sixtus IV that Ūzūn Ḥasan had just communicated to him, through certain "oratores," his plan of offensive against the Ottomans. We know that one of Ūzūn Ḥasan's ambassadors to the court of Stephen was a Jewish physician from Trabzon named Isḥāq Beg, who did in fact carry a similar letter to the Moldvian king.[25] Stephen charged Paolo Ogniben, a Venitian envoy returning from Iran, to transmit his letter to the Pope. On 6 March 1475, the Venetian senate authorized Ogniben to go to Rome.[26]

Jan Długosz (1415–80), a canon from Krakow who was also a diplomat, an historian, and a confidant of Casimir IV, relates that in 1475, evidently toward February–March, the same Isḥāq Beg (whom he describes as *Isaac, genere Graecus de Trapesunda, sed secta Mahumetu* "Isaac, originally a Greek from Trabzon but professing the Muslim religion"), arrived "with twelve horses" in Lithuania at the court of Casimir IV. Passing through Krakow, Isḥāq was on a mission to Hungary, to Sixtus IV at the Vatican, and to Venice, among other places.[27] According to a letter dated 23 June 1475 from Francesco

[23] Simonetta 1962–, 169, 180, 277. Saxo's full itinerary was Venice, Naples, Rome, Florence, and then Pavia.

[24] Müller 1879, 220, doc. clxxx.

[25] The Romanian historian Constantin Esarcu, who originally discovered the letter, proposes the year 1474 as the date when this particular letter was carried by Isḥāq Beg to the king, while another scholar, P. Cancel, suggestes an earlier date of 1472, see Bageacu 1991, 20, 26. For the Latin and Persian versions of the letter, see ibid., 18–20.

[26] Barbaro and Contarini 1973, 311–2.

[27] Długosz 1711–2, 2: col. 530–1; idem 1863–87, 5:626.

Maletta, the ambassador of Milan to Naples, "an ambassador from Ussun-Chassan" was on board a Venetian ship *en route* to Venice.[28] But it was all too late. In the morning of 6 June 1475, the Ottoman admiral Gedik Aḥmed Paşa conquered Caffa.

According to Venitian documents, roundly contradicted by Długosz's testimony, Isḥāq Beg was "a Jewish doctor of Spanish origin." Without citing any evidence, the editor of the Venetian documents seems to imply that in October 1472, while on a mission to Rome at the court of Sixtus IV, Isḥāq Beg converted to Christianity.[29] This is an error reproduced also by some art historians.[30] No historical source, Roman or otherwise, confirms the conversion of a Jew or a Muslim so prominent as the ambassador of the king of Iran. A slim anonymous Italian poem, composed during the siege of Croya (Aqchahisar, Albania, 1477) and preserved in a unique manuscript, recounts the 1472 naval campaign of Cardinal Oliviero Carafa. It includes the story of several conversions: a "pagan" ambassador from "Usoncasan" was baptized at Rhodes, then another ambassador sent by him to Sixtus IV "became a Christian in Rome" together with his servants.[31] No mention is made of this story in a Latin poem of 1807 verses finished in Rome on 5 December 1477 by the papal protonotary Robert Flemming (d. 1483), who was a nephew of Richard Flemming, Bishop of Lincoln and founder of Lincoln College, Oxford. Printed in order to be distributed throughout Christendom, this poem consisted of a defence of Sixtus IV, whose conduct was being criticized by some of his adversaries.[32]

Ludovicus Bononiensis took a different route. On 27 November 1477, the Pope charged the nuncio to Iran to present himself to Sigismund, the Duke of Austria. On 31 December, Sixtus IV gave him a new safe-conduct. Ludovicus was going to set out "with his companions and servants, up to the number of twelve."[33]

[28] *Monumenta Hungariae historica. Magyar Diplomacziai Emlèkek Mátyàs király Korábóe 1458–1490* 1877.

[29] Berchet 1865, 8–9.

[30] Aronberg Lavin 1967, 3–17.

[31] Medin 1927–8, 808, 813.

[32] Pacifici 1921; Campana 1948, 88–98.

[33] Pou y Martí 1949, 510, 513, docs. 1021, 1030.

APPENDIX A

LITTERAE UZUNCASSAN AD PAULUM PAPAM II

Roma, Biblioteca Vallicelliana, MS. B 19, fols. 179v–81
[I. Rogatio, fols. 179v–80]

In nomine Domini amen. Haec transductio, sive translatio in lingua latina eiusdem litterae Domini Uzuncassan, qui nominatur Assambech, quae est scripta lingua Arabica, ac directa vobis Beatissimo Domino nostro pape Paulo, et quae transivit delata per Reverendum D. Fratrem Ludovicum de Bononia, ac praesentata nobis Hieronymo Panizario Sacrae Theologiae Magistro ac Episcopo Caffensi, translatata in lingua latina ad instantiam et requisitionem dicti Domini Fratris Ludovici per interpretes communitatis Caffae, ac mediante quodam Armeno nomine Colli de Soltania civitate Persarum, peritissimo in lingua arabica, scribente in lingua latina Joanne de Vesima Notario et Cancellario curiae nostrae. Et qui Joannes bisterque interpretari fecit dictam litteram ne in dicta translatione aut traductione aliquis error incideret, sed ad litteram prout iacet in lingua illa Arabica in lingua latina tenor verus apparet. Vobis igitur Beatissimo Domino nostro pateat evidenter, et sic notum sit prout nos supradicti Hieronymus Panizarius Episcopus Caffensis vidimus tenuimus palpavimus dictam litteram, scriptam in lingua Arabica, et illam nobis praesentibus per interpretes communitatis Caffae exponi fecimus et declarari per illa vocabula clariora, per quae substantia dictae litterae clarius intelligeret. Et ne aliqua suspicio haberi posset, intelligere disposuimus de veritate iniuncta et intelligenda, propterea accersiri fecimus Nobilem Antonium Secquarzaficum civem nostrum et Stephanum de Sancto Romulo civem Januensem, qui interfuerunt cum dicto Domino Fratre Ludovico dationi dictae litterae; et dictus Antonius Interpres, qui fuit inter praefatum Dominum Uzuncassam, et dictum Fratrem Ludovicum, qui duo iuraverunt ad Sacra Dei Evangelia dictam litteram scriptam in Arabico processisse de curia praefati Domini Uzuncassam, et illam dari vidisse in manibus dicti Domini Fratris Ludovici, ac audivisse illam legi tam coram praefato Domino Uzuncassam, quam coram dicto Domino Fratre Ludovico; et qui testes testificati sunt super veritate dictae litterae, itaque omnis est a nobis ablata suspicio, attento maxime, quod dictus Antonius est homo optimae famae, et filius nobilis Ioannis Secquarzafici uniusmodi ex dictionibus civibus civitatis Caffae, et dictus Stephanus est etiam civis Januae cognitus ab omnibus et homo optimae et dignae famae; propter quod dictam litteram approbamus confirmamus, et veram esse testamur. Illam itaque sic translatam in latino in claram formam iussimus scribi, et ad veritatem premissorum eam fecimus nostri Sigilli Impressione muniri. Caffae Anno MCCCCLXXI. Die. XXV. Julij cuius litterae tenor est talis.

[II. Texte, fols. 180r–v]

In nomine justi Dei. Haec sunt verba Assambech fortis hominis: tibi mano omnium magnorum, et cunctorum magnorum maiori, magnitudo cuius multiplicatur in successores multos, qui es ditior in civitatibus et castris super omnes Dominos mundi, qui cum sis magnanimus semper augere desideras statum tuum, et multiplicare divitias tuas semper studes. Sub te enim militant Reges, Duces, et Barones, super quos tu omnium maior militas cum sis locumtenens Christi Papa Paule. Quomodo os meum te laudare potest? Tu exsuperas omnes laudes Christianorum, tu sis Princeps in Dei nomine, tibi enim notifico ad causae nostrae processerunt, ut ibi, et haec est veritas substantia, prout nunc tibi scribo super illis pactis, promissionibus, et ordinationibus factis prius eo tempore quo homo tuus ad me cum veritate venit. Ego firmus sto, et maneo. Verum quidem illa pacta facta fuerunt tempore quo inimicus noster Jamsa maiorem obsesserat Babilloniam maximam, huiusmodi exercitum, qui post captam Babilloniam super me venit cum maxima multitudine, et cum amicus meus fueris, tua benedictione mediante, ipsum inimicum meum superavi et vici. Post haec filius eius Arsandach nomine, qui patre maiorem exercitum habebat, et ipse super me venit cum exercitu maximo, fregi rupi et trucidavi, et idem tua mediante benedictione. Homo non potest ire contra voluntatem Dei. Non enim potestate mea, aut viribus meis superavi illos, sed virtute Dei qui secundum eorum malam dispositionem, illos male disposuit. Unam omnes illos a maiore ad minorem trucidavi: ipsos malos Deus pessime perdidit. Tertio supervenit Soltamnossait qui erat magnus Rex Persarum cum centum septuaginta millibus hominum, exceptis centum et septuaginta millibus currum cum gubernatoribus ipsorum. In nomine Domini illos CLXX. cum curribus, et Rectoribus curruum perdidi, Duces et Barones trucidavi, omnium Dominorum capita ad suas Regiones misi, et cum ipsi male dispositi forent propterea illos Deus pessime perdidit. Et gratias ago Deo meo, quoniam omnes illos perdidi et superavi. Et si rogares quot Regna, patrias quot ceperim, sic respondere possum, caput tot Regnorum est India, finis locus Cathay, latus unum est Asia: et alius Ethiopia. De omnibus est laudandus Deus. Omnes civitates fortissimas, et castra cepi, propter causas istas tardus fui ad complendum ordinata et promissa per me. Sed si mihi largitur vitam Deus, promissa complebo. Super quibus promissionibus sto, et firmissimus maneo. Super illis igitur verbis prioribus et pactis praemissis dormio semper et vigilo, illa verba nunquam expellens a me, desiderans explere promissa, quae sunt ordinata cum amicitia tua. Nihil igitur disponere debeo, quam quod promisi amicitiae, quod fiet praesto cum benedictione tua magna. Nihil enim mihi obstabit cum qua tua benedictione, nihil est aliud, quam ad te obviam venire. In Deum igitur iuro, et bis in ipsum iuro Deum, quod firmus sum super promissionem quam feci. Itaque prout promisisti, tu ita perfice. Erit igitur Deus in auditorium nostrum. Literae tuae rogo non deficiant ad me cum homine tuo. Litera haec scripta est more nostro Turco Anno a Maemeto citra octingentesimo septuagesimo quinto de mense Lamadi, circa finem in loco nominato Chracagiam.

Ego Molona Eroch suprascripta verba audiuj ab ore Domini Assambech
Assam Beg Filius Othman
Danda Assam, Ber Candi, Pirm Acmot, Baia Mac Begnim

[III. Completio, fol. 181]

Ego Joannes de Vesima quondam Constantini publicus Imperiali auctoritate notarius, et Cancellarius praefati Domini Hieronymi Panizarij Sacrae Theologiae Magistri ac Dei et Aspostolicae sedis gratia Episcopi Caffensis omnibus supradictis interfui: Et de mandato praefati Domini Episcopi translatam dictam litteram de dicta lingua arabica in lingua latina quantumcumque melius potui et prout mei ingenij parvi facultas tradidi. Nam pro certo melius sonat in lingua illa arabica iuxta relationem interpretum, quem sonet in lingua latina. In qua quidem littera sunt multae litterae Aureae. Et primae litterae aureae quae sunt in principio sic sonant: *In nomine iusti Dei*. Secundae litterae quae sunt partim de incausto, et partim de colore croceo, quae litterae croceae faciunt quoddam signum quadratum[34] cum quaedam cauda longa supposita litteris nigris sic sonant in latino: *haec sunt verba Assambech fortis hominis*. Tertiae litterae aureae, quae subsequuntur, sic sonant: *In Dei nomine*. Aliae litterae aureae quae sequuntur sic sonant: *Homo non potest ire contra voluntatem Dei*. Aliae litterae aureae quae sequuntur sic sonant: *In Dei nomine*. Aliae litterae aureae in medio lineae positae sic sonant: *Gratias ago creatori meo, quia illos omnes perdidi et superavi*. Aliae litterae aureae quae sequuuntur sic sonant: *de omnibus est laudandus Deus*. Et in fine litterae est subscriptio Cancellarij in litteris nigris quae sonant prout quia. Sunt insuper quaedam signa quinque. Signum unum rotundum maius caeteris in quo signo sunt verba prout superius continetur. Duo alia signa, quae sunt in fine litterae in angulo a parte posteriori, sonant prout superius continetur. Et alia duo signa sunt etiam a parte posteriori non in angulo sed quasi in medio litterae, et sonant etiam prout superius continetur. Et ad veritatem premissorum manu propria scripsi, et signum meum Notarij apposui consuetum.

[34] This is what the notary calls the *tamgha*, for which see for instance Rabino 1950, 120, pl. ix.

TRANSLATION*

LETTER OF ŪZŪN ḤASAN TO POPE PAUL II
Rome, Biblioteca Vallicelliana, MS. B 19, fols. 179v–81

[I. Entreaty, fols. 179v–80]

In the name of the Lord, Amen. This is a transference, or translation into the Latin tongue of the same letter of the Lord Ūzūn Ḥasan, who is called Assambech, which was written in the Arabic tongue, and directed to you Our Most Blessed Lord Pope Paul, and which arrived by the conveyance of the Reverend Lord Brother Ludovicus of Bologna, and was presented to us by Hieronymus Panizarius Professor of Holy Theology and Bishop of Caffa, translated into the Latin tongue at the insistence and request of the said Lord Brother Ludovicus through the translators of the community of Caffa, and with the mediation of a certain Armenian by the name of Qulī[35] from Sulṭānīyah, a city of Persians, most knowledgeable in the Arabic tongue, and with Giovanni of Vesima,[36] the Secretary and Chancellor of our court, writing it in Latin. And this Giovanni had the said letter translated two and three times so as to avoid the incursion of any error in the said translation or transference, but the true tenor, to the letter, appears in the Latin tongue just as it does in the Arabic tongue. And so to you, our Blessed Lord, may it be absolutely clear, and may it be noted, that just as I, the aforementioned, so did Hieronymus Panizarius Bishop of Caffa: we looked at, held, tested (lit. palpated) the said letter, written in the Arabic tongue, and while we were present we had the letter set out and made clear by the translators of the community of Caffa through clearer words, through which the substance of the said letter might more clearly be understood. And lest any suspicion might possibly be entertained, we arranged to understand concerning the truth of the things enjoined and needing to be understood, and for that reason we caused to be summoned the Nobleman Antonius Secquarzaficus our fellow citizen, and Stephen of Saint Romulus, a citizen of Janua, who were present at the giving of the said letter to the said Master Brother Ludovicus; and [we summoned] the said translator Antonius,

*[I am grateful to Mark Becker of Princeton University for providing the English translations of the Latin documents included in Professor Piemontese's article. Ed.]

[35] An Armenian interpreter who translated several letters from Ūzūn Ḥasan at Caffa between 1471 and 1474. He is called *Coia Colli* (Khvājah Qulī) (Iorga 1914, 352) and also *Coratolli* (*Monumenta Hungariae historica. Acta Estera* 1877).

[36] In the text Vicina and then Secina. Vesima: a portion of the "Riviera" to the west of Genoa, see Ferro 1988, 1:42. For Giovanni of Vesima, a 15th-century notary, see Polonio 1977, 163, 239, 309.

who was in the entourage of the above mentioned Lord Ūzūn Ḥasan, and the said Brother Ludovicus, who both swore by the Holy Gospels of the Lord that the said letter, written in Arabic, originated from the court of the said Lord Ūzūn Ḥasan, and that they saw the letter given into the hands of the said Lord Brother Ludovicus, and that they heard it read in the presence of the above mentioned Lord Ūzūn Ḥasan, as well as the said Lord Brother Ludovicus; and these witnesses testified to the veracity of the said letter, and therefore all suspicion is removed from me, since it was diligently determined that the said Antonius is a man of the best reputation, and the noble Giovanni son of Secquarzaficus is of the same sort, according to the accounts of the citizens of the state of Caffa, and the said Stephen is also a citizen of Janua known by all and a man of the highest and deserved reputation; on account of which the said letter we approve and confirm, and we testify that it is genuine. And so the letter, thus translated into the Latin tongue we ordered to be transcribed into a lucid form, and to the truth of these statements we ordered the letter to be corroborated with the Impression of our Seal. Given at Caffa, in the year 1471, the 25th of July, of which the tenor is as follows:

[II. Text, fols. 180r–v] [37]

In the name of the just God. These are the words of the great man Ūzūn Ḥasan: to you great of all the great, and greater than all the great, whose greatness is multiplied in many successors, you who are richer in states and castles (*castris*) beyond all of the Lords of the world, who, because you are great spirited, desire always to increase your status, and are always eager to multiply your riches. For under you fight Kings, Dukes and Barons, above whom you fight greater than all since you are the deputy (*locumtenens*) of Christ, Pope Paul. How is my mouth able to praise you? You surpass all the praises of Christians, may you be First in the name of God, truly to you I make known to [where] our causes have proceeded, just as then, and this is the truth and substance, in the same way now I write to you concerning those agreements, promises, and arrangements made previously, at the time when your man came to me with the truth.[38] I stand firm, and so remain. But indeed those

[37] This portion of the document has already been published, see Baronio 1592–1677, 11:32–3, 10:510–1. The Ms. Vallicelliana, B 29, *Collectio Literarum Summorum Pontificum, Regum et Principum*, is a parchment collection of copies of letters from popes, kings, and princes, Rome, 15th century, 33 x 23.5 cm.

[38] [The sentence is gramatically awkward, with no object for *ad*; I have supplied "where." Tr.]

agreements were made at the time when our enemy Jamsa[39] had besieged greater Baghdād greatest,[40] an army of this sort, which, after Baghdād was captured, came upon me with the greatest multitude, and since you were my friend, with your mediating benediction, my very enemy I overcame and conquered. After that his son, Ḥasan ʻAlī[41] by name, who had a greater army than his father, even came himself upon me with the greatest army, [which] I shattered, I broke, and I slaughtered, again with your mediating benediction. A man is not able to go against the will of God. Truly I conquered them not by my own power, nor by my strength, but by the virtue of God, who, in accordance with their bad disposition, disposed them badly. Together I slaughtered all of them, from the greater to the lesser: those bad men God most foully destroyed. Thirdly came upon me Soltamnossait,[42] who was great king of the Persians with 170,000 men, not to mention 170,000 chariots with their drivers. In the name of the Lord those 170,000 with their chariots and drivers of the chariots I destroyed, the Dukes and Barons I slaughtered, I sent the heads of all of the Lords to their own regions, and since they were badly disposed therefore God most foully destroyed them. And I give thanks to my God, since I destroyed all those men and overcame them. And if you were to ask how many Kingdoms, how many countries I captured, I am able to respond thus, the chief of the many Kingdoms is India, the last place is Cathay; one side is Asia, and the other is Ethiopia. For all these things must God be praised. I captured all the most highly fortified states and castles, for which reason I was slow to complete what I arranged and promised. But if God grants me life, I will fulfill my promises. Concerning which promises I stand, and I remain most firm. Over those former words, therefore, and promised agreements always I sleep and wake, never driving those words away from me, desiring to fulfill my promises, which were arranged with your friendship. Therefore I ought not arrange anything, other than what I promised to your friendship, which will come about immediately with your great blessing. For with that great blessing of yours nothing will stand in my way; there is nothing else than to come to meet you. To God therefore I swear, and a second time to the same God I swear, that I am firm on the promise that I made. And

[39] Jahānshāh Qaraqoyunlu. After having taken Baghdād in 870/1466, he was defeated at Mush in 872/1467. On the events and known personages mentioned from here on, see Woods 1976, index and 106, 109–12, 127–9, 135–6, 158, 216.

[40] [*Babillonia* is modified by both "greater" (*maiorem*) and "greatest" (*maximam*). Tr.]

[41] Ḥasan ʻAlī, the son of Jahānshāh, who was defeated at Marand in Ṣafar 873/August 1468 and a few months later in Shawwāl 873/April 1469 near Hamadān.

[42] Timurid ruler Abū Saʻīd who was defeated and executed in 873/1469.

so just as you promised, do you thus accomplish. Therefore God will be in our audience. I ask that your letter not fail to reach me with your messenger. This letter was written according to our custom in the Turkish year of Moḥammad, eight hundred and seventy-fifth, toward the end of the month of Lamadus,[43] in the place named Qarā'āghāch.[44]

I, Molona Eroch, heard the above-written words from the mouth of Lord Ūzūn Ḥasan[45]
Assam Beg Filius Othman
Danda Assam, Ber Candi, Pirm Acmot, Baia Mac Begnim[46]

[III. Supplement, fol. 181]

I, Giovanni of Vesima, formerly public Secretary by Imperial authority, son of the late Constantinus, and Chancellor of the aforementioned Lord Hieronymus Panizarius Professor of Holy Theology and by the grace of God and the Apostolic See Bishop of Caffa, was present at all of the aforementioned events. And on the instruction of the aforementioned Lord Bishop I translated the said letter translated from the said Arabic tongue into the Latin tongue as well as I could and according to the capacity of my small intellect. For certainly, the letter sounds better in that Arabic tongue, according to the report of the translators, than it sounds in the Latin tongue. In this letter there

[43] I.e. toward the end of Ramaḍān 875/20–2 March 1471. An alternative restitution would be Jumādá I or II/ 22–4 November, 21–3 December 1470.

[44] Qarā'āghāch (plane-trees), at the foot of the "Sulṭān" mountain to the north of the middle course of the Araxes in the Qarābāgh range. It was the southern region of medieval Arrān, near Shirvān and Gurjistān (Georgia). A pleasant wintering place and a wooded strategic location, Qarā'āghāch had been a possession of the Mongol Ilkhanids and of the Timurids; subsequently integrated by the Aqqoyunlu in Aẕarbāyjān, it served as the family capital of the Aqqoyunlu clan until springtime festival of *Nawrūz*. Sulṭān Ya'qūb Āq'qūyūnlū died there on 11 Ṣafar 896/24 December 1490, see Khunjī 1957, 87–9, 92, 108, 111.

[45] This chancellor who undersigned the message dictated by Ūzūn Ḥasan may be Mawlānā Shaykh Aḥmad, who was at that time in charge of the Sulṭān's private correspondence, see Ṭihrānī [1962–4] 1977, 2:488.

[46] These names are entered in the little circles, as legends on the stamps (described in detail by the notary, part III) of the personages who had endorsed the letter. They are perhaps "Danda Assam": Dana Khalīl, brother of Queen Saljūqshāh and tutor of Prince Maqṣūd; "Ber Candi": Qāẓī 'Alā' al-Dīn 'Alī Bayhaqī, the army judge; "Pirm Acmot": Pīr Aḥmad, perhaps Pīr Aḥmad Beg Qarāmānī, who, supported by the Ottomans, does not seem to have been Ūzūn Ḥasan's ally; "Baia Mac Begnim": *mahd-i 'ulyā begum*, the queen Saljūqshāh Begum, Ūzūn Ḥasan's wife, cf. Khunjī 1957, 25 and 108.

are, indeed, many golden letters. And the first golden letters which are in the beginning read thus: *In the name of the just God.* And the second letters which are partly in ink and partly in saffron color, which saffron letters make a certain squared-sign with a certain long tail placed underneath in black letters, read thus in Latin: *These are the words of the great man Assambech.* And the third golden letters, which follow underneath, read thus: *In the name of God.* Other golden letters which follow read thus: *A man is not able to go against the will of God.* Other golden letters which follow read thus: *In the name of God.* Other golden letters placed in the middle of the line read thus: *I give thanks to my creator, because all of those men I destroyed and overcame.* Other golden letters which follow read thus: *For all these things must God be praised.* And at the end of the letter is the signature of the Chancellor in black letters which reads the same.[47] There are in addition a certain five signs. One round sign is larger than the others in which sign are words just as are contained above. Two other signs, which are at the end of the letter in the corner across from the last part (*a parte posteriori*), read just as is contained above. And two other signs are also across from the last part (*a parte posteriori*), not in the corner but as it were in the middle of the letter, and also read just as is contained above. And to the truth of the aforementioned I have written in my own hand, and I have affixed my usual sign of Notary.

[47] [The meaning of the words *prout quia*, which I have translated "the same," is doubtful. Tr.]

APPENDIX B

Milano, Archivio di Stato, Archivio Ducale, Registro Ducale 214, fol. 73, p. 145

Ad Regem Persarum nomine Pontificis
Magno ac Potenti Asambech alias Uxoncassan.
Uxori eiudsem
Dilecte in christo filiae magnae et potenti Principesse Despine Theodore.
Filiis Uxoncassan
Magno et Potenti principi Horgul Mahhamed filio Asambech.
Magno et potenti Principi Soltan Chalil filio Asambech.
Magno et potenti principi Lalibech filio Asambech.
Domino Caramano
Magno ac potenti principi Cassambech magno caramano.
Praestanti uiro Barandurbegh magni et potentis principis Assambech magno secretario.
Dilecto in christo filio Aseuazadur magni ac potentis Principis Assambech capitaneo.
Dilecto in christo filio Cozamirat thesaurario ac Camerario magni ac potentis principis Asambech.
Venerabili fratri Dauid Patriarchae maronitarum in monte libano.
Dilecto filio Petro de fontanella ordinis minorum in monte libano.
Dilecto in christo filio Mangher armeno capitaneo in abaruner catholico.
Dilecto in christo filio Rabam cassis s. episcopo armeno in carpeto.
Dilecto in christo filio Nobili uiro Johanni Duci Russiae.

TRANSLATION

Milan, Archivio di Stato, Archivio Ducale, Registro Ducale 214, fol. 73, p. 145

To the king of the Persians in the name of the pope.
To the great and powerful Assambech alias Uxoncassan [Ūzūn Ḥasan].
To the wife of the same.
To the beloved daughter in Christ, the great and powerful princess, Despine Theodore.
To the sons of Ūzūn Ḥasan.
To the great and powerful prince, Ūghūrlū Muḥammed, son of Ūzūn Ḥasan.
To the great and powerful prince, Sulṭān Khalīl, son of Ūzūn Ḥasan.

To the great and powerful prince Lalibech,[48] son of Ūzūn Ḥasan.
To the Lord Caramanus.
To the great and powerful prince Qāsim Beg Qarāmānī, great Caramanus.
To the outstanding man Bāyundur Beg, great secretary of the great and powerful prince Ūzūn Ḥasan.
To the beloved son in Christ, Astuacatur, captain of the great and powerful prince Assambech.
To the beloved son in Christ, Khvājah Mir'āt, treasurer and chamberlain of the great and powerful prince Ūzūn Ḥasan.
To the venerable Brother David, patriarch of the Maronites in Mount Lebanon.
To the beloved son in Christ, Pietro de Fontanella of the order of minors in Mount Lebanon.
To the beloved son in Christ, Mangher, Armenian captain in catholic Abaruner.[49]
To the beloved son in Christ, Rabam, *qassīs* (the priest) Holy Armenian Bishop in Carpeto.
To the beloved son in Christ, noble Ivan, Duke of Russia.[50]

[48] This unknown nickname could apply to Prince Maqṣūd.
[49] Aparaner or Aparan was an important village in the province of Emjak in Armenia.
[50] Ivan III, Duke of Russia (1462–1505).

BIBLIOGRAPHY

ADORNE, JEAN. 1978. *Itinéraire d'Anselme Adorno en Terre sainte : 1470–1471.* Ed. Jacques Heers, Georgette de Groër. Paris : Éditions du Centre national de la recherche scientifique.

ARONBERG LAVIN, MARILYN. 1967. The altar of Corpus Domini in Urbino : Paolo Uccello, Joos van Gent, Piero della Francesca. *The art bulletin* 49, no. 1 (March): 1–24.

Asnād-i marbūṭ bih ravābiṭ-i tārīkhī-i Īrān va Jumhūrī-i Vinīz az dawrah-'i Īlkhānān tā 'aṣr-i Ṣafavī : fihrist-i namāyishgāh. 1973. Tehran : Kitābkhānah-'i Markazī va Markaz-i Asnād-i Dānishgāh-i Tihrān, 1352 Sh.

BAGEACU, VIOREL. 1991. Irtibāṭ-i Ūzūn Ḥasan va Ishtifin Kabīr farmānravā-yi Muldavī. In *Yāftah'hā-yi Īrānshināsī dar Rūmānī : majmū'ah-i maqālāt.* Tehran : Nashr-i Tārīkh-i Īrān, zamistān 1370 Sh.

BARBARO, GIOSOFAT and CONTARINI, AMBROGIO. 1973. *I Viaggi in Persia degli ambasciatori veneti Barbaro e Contarini.* Ed. L. Lockhart, R. Morozzo della Rocca, M. F. Tiepolo. Rome : Istituto poligrafico dello Stato, Libreria.

BERCHET, GUGLIELMO 1865. *La repubblica di Venezia e la Persia.* Torino : G. B. Paravia e comp.

BRYER, ANTHONY. 1980. Ludovico da Bologna and the Georgian and Anatolian embassy of 1460–1461. In *The empire of Trebizond and the Pontos.* London : Variorum Reprints: chapter X: 178–98.

BUGHETTI 1938. Nuovi documenti intorno a Fra Lodovico da Bologna, O.F.M. Missionario e Nunzio Apostolico in Oriente, (1460–1461). *Studi francescani* 35: 128–46.

CAMPANA, AUGUSTO. 1948. Roma di Sisto IV. Le Lucubraciunculae Tiburtinae di Robert Flemmyng. *Strenna dei romanisti* 9: 88–98.

COCCIA, ANTONIO. 1973. Vita e opere del Bessarione. *Miscellanea francescana* 73, fasc. 3–4 (Luglio-Dicembre): 265–93.

CORNET, ENRICO, ed. 1856. *Le guerre dei Veneti nell'Asia 1470–1474 : Documenti cavati dall'Archivio ai frari in Venezia.* Vienna : Libreria Tendler & comp.

DI FONZO, LORENZO. 1986. Sisto IV : Carriera scolastica e integrazioni bibliografiche, (1414–84). *Miscellanea francescana* 86, fasc. 2–4 (Aprile–Dicembre): 1–491.

DŁUGOSZ, JAN. 1711–2. *Ioannis Długossi seu Longini Historia Polonica.* 2 vols. Lipsiae : Sumptibus Ioannis Ludovici Gleditschii & Mauritii Georgii Weidemanni.

—— 1863–87. *Opera omnia.* Ed. Ignatius Żegota Pauli. 14 vols. Cracoviae : Czas.

FERRO, GAETANO. 1988. *La Liguria e Genova al tempo di Colombo.* 2 vols. Rome : Istituto poligrafico e Zecca dello Stato, Libreria dello Stato.

GASPARE DA VERONA and CANENSIUS, MICHAEL. 1904. *Le vite di Paolo II.* Ed. Giuseppe Zippel. Castello : S. Lapi.

GUGLIELMOTTI, ALBERTO. 1886. *Storia della marina pontificia nel medioevo dal 728 al 1499.* 2 vols. Rome : Tipografia Vaticana.

HACKETT, J. 1901. *A history of the Orthodox church of Cyprus from the coming of the apostles Paul and Barnabas to the commencement of the British occupation (A.D. 45–A.D. 1878) : together with some account of the Latin and other churches existing in the island.* London : Methuen & Co.

HALECKI, OSCAR. 1964. Sixte IV et la chrétienté orientale. In *Mélanges Eugène Tisserant.* 2: 241–64.

IORGA, N. 1914. Venise dans la Mer Noire. III. *Bulletin de la Section historique, Académie roumaine* 2: 335–70.

KHUNJĪ, FAẔL ALLĀH IBN RŪZBIHĀN. 1957. *Persia in A.D. 1478–1490 : an abridged translation of Faḍlullāh b. Rūzbihān Khunjī's Tārīkh-i 'ālam-ārā-yi Amīnī.* Tr. V. Minorsky. London : The Royal Asiatic Society of Great Britain and Ireland.

LAMMENS, H. 1899. Frère Gryphon et le Liban au XVe siècle. *Revue de l'Orient chrétien* 4: 68–104.

LANDWEHR VON PRAGENAU, MORIZ. 1901. Ludwig von Bologna, Patriarch von Antiochien. *Mittheilungen des Instituts für Österreichische Geschichtsforschung* 22: 288–96.

MALIPIERO, DOMENICO. 1843. Annali veneti. Ed. Francesco Longo. *Archivio storico italiano*, 7/1: 1–586; 7/2: 589–720.

MEDIN, ANTONIO. 1927–8. Per l'origine della voce "sancassan" : Le gesta di Husun [sic] Hasan in un cantare del sec. XV. *Atti del Reale Istituto veneto di scienze, lettere, ed arti* 87: 799–814.

Monumenta Hungariae historica. Magyar Diplomacziai Emlèkek Mátyàs király Korábóe 1458-1490. 1877. Budapest : Magyar Tudományos Akadémia: II, doc. 186, 266–7.

Monumenta Hungariae historica. Acta Estera. 1877. Budapest : Magyar Tudományos Akadémia: V, 259–60; VII, 293–5.

MÜLLER, JOSEPH, ed. 1879. *Documenti sulle relazioni delle città toscane coll'Oriente cristiano e coi Turchi fino all'anno MDXXXI.* Florence : M. Cellini.

PACIFICI, VINCENZO. 1921. *Un carme biografico di Sisto IV del 1477.* Tivoli : Società tiburtina di storia e d'arte, Villa d'Este.

PIEMONTESE, ANGELO MICHELE. 1991. La représentation de Uzun Hasan sur scène à Rome (2 mars 1473). *Turcica* 21–3: 191–203.

PLATINA. 1933. *Platynae historici Liber de vita Christi ac omnium pontificum (aa. 1–1474).* Ed. Giacinto Gaida. Città di Castello : S. Lapi.

POLONIO, VALERIA. 1977. L'amministrazione della res publica genovese fra Tre e Quattrocento. *Atti della Società ligure di storia patria*, n.s. 17.

POU Y MARTÍ, JOSÉ MARíA, ed. 1949. *Bullarium Franciscanum continens constitutiones, epistolas, diplomata Romanorum pontificum.* Vol. 3. Florentin : Ad Claras Aquas (Quarracchi).

RABINO, H. L. 1950. Coins of the Jalā'ir, Ḳara Ḳoyūnlū, Mus͟ha'sha', and ĀḲ Ḳoyūnlū dynasties. *The numismatic chronicle and journal of the Royal Numismatic Society.* 6th ser., 10: 94–139, pls. vii–x.

RICHARD, JEAN. 1977. *La papauté et les missions d'Orient au Moyen Age (XIIIe–XVe siècle).* Rome : École française de Rome.

SETTON, KENNETH M. 1978–84. *The Papacy and the Levant, (1204–1571).* 4 vols. Philadelphia : American Philosophical Society.

SEVERI, ANGELO BARGELLESI. 1976. Nuovi documenti su fr. Lodovico da Bologna al secolo Lodovico Severi, Nunzio Apostolico in Oriente (1455–1457). *Archivum franciscanum historicum* 69: 3–22.

SIMONETTA, CICCO. 1962–. *I diari di Cicco Simonetta*. Ed. Alfio Rosario Natale. 1 vol. to date. Milan : Antonino Giuffrè.

ṬIHRĀNĪ, ABŪ BAKR. [1962–4] 1977. *Kitāb-i Diyārbakrīyah : tārīkh-i Ḥasan Bayk Āq'qūyunlū va aslāf-i ū va ānchah bidān muta'alliq ast az tavārīkh-i Qarāqūyunlū va Chaghātāy*. Ed. Necati Lugal, Faruk Sümer. 2 vols. in 1. Reprint with a Persian introd. by F. Sümer, Tehran : Ṭahūrī.

VIGNA, AMEDEO. 1879. Codice diplomatico delle Colonie Tauro-Liguri, durante la Signoria dell' Ufficio di S. Giorgio (mcccclìii mcccclxxv). *Atti della Società ligure di storia patria* 7/2: 9–491.

VIGNA, RAIMONDO. 1887. *I vescovi domenicani liguri*. Genoa.

VILĀYATĪ, 'ALĪ AKBAR. 1996. *Tārīkh-i ravābiṭ-i khārijī-i Īrān dar 'ahd-i Shāh Ismā'īl Ṣafavī*. Tehran : Daftar-i Muṭāla'āt-i Siyāsī va Bayn al-Milalī, 1375 Sh.

WADDING, LUKE. 1933. *Annales Minorum seu trium ordinum a S. Francisco institutorum*. Ed. J. M. Fonseca ab Ebora, P. Bonaventurae Marrani. Vol. 14. Florentin : Ad Claras Aquas (Quarracchi).

WALSH, RICHARD J. 1977. Charles the Bold and the crusade : politics and propaganda. *Journal of medieval history* 3, no.1 (March): 53–86.

WOODS, JOHN. 1976. *The Aqqoyunlu : clan, confederation, empire : a study in 15th/ 9th century Turko-Iranian politics*. Minneapolis and Chicago : Bibliotheca Islamica.

Yeomanly Arrogance and Righteous Rule : Fazl Allāh ibn Rūzbihān Khunjī and the Mamluks of Egypt

Ulrich W. Haarmann

1

THE HISTORY OF THE MAMLUK SULṬĀNS OF EGYPT and Syria has received unprecedented scholarly attention during the past thirty years.[1] Numerous historical texts, as well as archival documents of the time, written in Arabic, have been discovered, edited, and occasionally even translated into a European language so that a larger readership of historians can profit from their content. Also, the copious contemporary Western travel literature—mainly pilgrim reports—is beginning to be exploited systematically (albeit less conspicuously) as an important supplementary source for the history of Egypt and the Levant in the later Middle Ages.[2] One category of sources on this particular chapter of Middle Eastern history, however, has been suffering glaring neglect so far: reports written by non-Egyptian, non-Syrian Muslim visitors to the Mamluk kingdom. The majority of these travellers were *Maghāribah* who on their way from the west to the Holy Places of the Ḥijāz were bound to come through Egypt and, in particular, through its shining capital city Cairo.[3]

[1] Examples of this development are: (1) the publication of the *Mamluk Studies Review* which is exclusively devoted to the history of Mamluk Egypt and Syria, by Bruce Craig and others at the University of Chicago; (2) the organization of specifically Mamluk research symposia, first in Washington DC in 1981 (for its proceedings see the journal *Muqarnas* 2 (1984)), and then in Homburg in 1994; (3) the appearance of Mamluk "tertiary" literature, i.e., survey articles on the state-of-the-art in Mamluk studies, see Humphreys 1991, chaps. 5, 7 and 10; Garcin 1995, lxxxvi–xcvi; Haarmann 1995; and (4), last but not least, the republication of Mamluk classics, notably of the numerous studies on the Mamluk institution by David Ayalon in the London based Variorum Reprints, see Ayalon 1977, 1979, 1988 and 1994.

[2] Shaun Marmon of Princeton University was one of the first scholars to go through the various central and south European pilgrimage reports of the 14th, 15th, and early 16th centuries in her research on non-military servitude in Mamluk Egypt, Syria and Arabia, see Marmon 1995.

[3] One such travelogue with largely untapped first-hand information on the Mamluk sultanate at the turn of the 13th–14th century is al-Qāsim ibn Yūsuf al-Tujībī al-Sabtī's *Mustafād al-riḥlah wa-al-ightirāb*, see Tujībī 1975; the text is being analyzed in a Kiel M.A. thesis by Bettina Zantana.

We know much less still about Eastern Muslim travellers to the Mamluk domains. They were, so it seems, not as numerous and certainly not as prolific as their Moroccan and Spanish counterparts. And they did not necessarily write in Arabic. Therefore, their work was neglected by many an expert on the history of late medieval Egypt on linguistic grounds.

It is the great merit of Iraj Afshar, who is being honored in this volume, to have led us to one particularly important representative of this group of learned Iranian visitors to the Mamluk lands, the famous Shāfiʻī jurist and theologian Faẕl Allāh ibn Rūzbihān Khunjī Iṣfahānī (860–925/1456–1519)[4] of Shīrāzī background. Khunjī not only twice visited the Ḥijāz but also stayed in Cairo for several months between his two sojourns in Mecca and Medina.

Khunjī has left us several works containing information on his stay in the Mamluk kingdom. One text should be cited first: his Arabic epistle *Hidāyat al-taṣdīq ilá ḥikāyat al-ḥarīq* dealing with the big fire in the precinct of Medina in Ramaḍān 886/October 1481. For the only known copy of this *risālah*, believed to be in Khunjī's own handwriting, has been discovered, studied, and published in facsimile by Iraj Afshar.[5] It is of considerable historical and literary importance. For one thing, it is one of the two extant Arabic works by Khunjī, the other being *Ibṭāl nahj al-bāṭil wa-ihmāl kashf al-ʻāṭil*.[6] It furthermore gives important autobiographical information on Khunjī's activities in Mamluk Egypt and in the Ḥijāz, a province under Mamluk suzerainty at that time. And, like Khunjī's Persian *Mihmān'nāmah-'i Bukhārā*,[7] this epistle clearly reveals its author as a highly sensitive individual who presents his musings both in dialogues and inner monologues.

[4] These dates represent our current state of knowledge, see Khunjī 1992, postscriptum, 110. Our author is not the only scholar from Khunj to have visited the Mamluk kingdom and to have found his way into the voluminous prosopography of the 9th/15th-century notables compiled by Sakhāwī, see Sakhāwī 1934–6, 9:7, no. 27, on Muḥammad Shams al-Dīn ibn Muḥammad ibn Aḥmad ibn ʻAbd al-ʻAzīz ibn ʻAbd al-Salām al-Khunjī al-Shīrāzī al-Shāfiʻī (born in 866/1460–1), a promising scholar whom Sakhāwī had met and taught in Mecca.

[5] See Khunjī 1969b. The manuscript used for this reproduction belongs to the Malik Library, Tehran, MS 611. Mr. Afshar's introduction was later re-published, with some changes, in Afshar 1975. For the edited and printed text of *Hidāyah*, see Khunjī 1969; for a Persian translation of the portion of chapter 3 of *Hidāyah* which describes the fire and events following it, see Khunjī 1994–5, 109–15.

[6] See Khunjī 1962, 31; the text of *Ibṭāl* is included in Muḥammad Ḥasan al-Muẓaffar's refutation of it, *Dalā'il al-ṣidq*, see Muẓaffar 1976.

[7] See Khunjī 1962 and 1976.

Much research has been devoted to Khunjī over the past forty years, ever since Vladimir Minorsky published his famous summary translation of Khunjī's Aqqoyunlu chronicle *Tārīkh-i 'ālam'ārā-yi Amīnī* in 1957.[8] In the second place, Iranian scholars such as Muḥammad Amīn Khunjī,[9] Manūchihr Sutūdah,[10] Muḥammad 'Alī Muvaḥḥid,[11] Javād Ṭabāṭabā'ī[12] and Rasūl Ja'fariyān deserve to be named. The latter published in 1993 a newly discovered work by Khunjī called *Wasīlat al-khādim ilá al-makhdūm*. Ja'fariyān has classified this theological work, which is in Persian and recounts the virtues of the Twelve Imams, as yet another work belonging to the body of literature composed by the "Twelver Sunnis."[13] In his introduction, Ja'fariyān also provided more information on the recent discovery of an incomplete manuscript copy of Khunjī's long thought lost, *Badī' al-zamān fī qiṣṣat Ḥayy ibn Yaqẓān*.[14] Russian or—for that matter—Soviet fellow-countrymen of the great V. Minorsky, have also taken up his concern for our author.[15] For a brief period in the early seventies, research on Khunjī seems to have been some kind of a preserve for the Freiburg historical school directed by Hans Robert Roemer, a close friend

[8] See Idem 1957 and 1992. In a letter sent to Iraj Afshar shortly before the publication of his translation, Minorsky referred to *Tārīkh-i 'ālam'ārā-yi Amīnī* as an orphan pearl (*durr-i yatīm*), a history unlike any other history (*bi-tārīkhhā-yi dīgar shabīh nīst*), adding that he had spent many years working on it (*chand sāl sar-i ān guzarāndam*), see Khunjī (Muhammad Amīn) 1956, 176; and Afshar 1997, 42.

[9] See Khunjī (Muḥammad Amīn) 1956.

[10] Editor of *Mihmān'nāmah-'i Bukhārā*, who prefaced his edition with an informative introduction, see Khunjī 1962.

[11] Editor of Khunjī's *Sulūk al-mulūk*, see Khunjī 1984. See also footnote no. 17.

[12] Author of a critical (sometimes contentious) study of Iranian political ideas which, drawing from *Sulūk al-mulūk* and *Mihmān'nāmah-'i Bukhāra*, argued that Khunjī's political thought represented a declining intellectual system, one which resisted or failed to comprehend the transformations that were taking place in Europe, see Ṭabāṭabā'ī 1989. A similar conclusion is reached by Ḥusayn Īzadī in a recent article, see Īzadī 1991–2.

[13] Khunjī 1993, 19–43. The manuscript that Mr. Ja'fariyān has used for his 1993 edition is now housed in Kitābkhānah-'i 'Umūmī-i Ḥaẓrat-i Āyat Allāh al-'Uẓmá Najafī Mar'ashī in Qum, see Ḥusaynī and Mar'ashī 1975–, 16:66. Since then, two other manuscript copies of this text (one in Kitābkhānah-'i Gharb in Hamadān, see Maqṣūd Hamadānī 1977, 453) have been identified, which Mr. Ja'fariyān is planning to use for a new edition of the work. (Information on the Gharb manuscript was kindly provided by Professor Hossein Modarressi).

[14] Khunjī 1993, 11–2. This manuscript of *Badī'* is also kept in Kitābkhānah-'i Mar'ashī in Qum, see Ḥusaynī and Mar'ashī 1975–, 19:379–81.

[15] It may suffice here to mention the names of A. N. Boldyrev, M. A. Salié, S. K. Ibragimov, and R. P. Dzhalilova. The last-named translated selections from *Mihmān'nāmah-'i Bukhārā* into Russian, see Khunjī 1976. Also, V. Minorsky's English summary translation of *Tārīkh-i 'ālam'ārā-yi Amīnī* was the basis of a Russian translation by T. A. Minorsky, see Khunjī 1987.

of our celebrated septuagenarian.[16] Of British vintage is Ann K. S. Lambton's analysis of Khunjī's increasingly pragmatic political thinking after his first Uzbek protector Shaybān Khān had succumbed to Shāh Ismā'īl in 916/1510.[17] And then, last but not least, we now have the long awaited critical edition, and enhanced summary translation, of the *Tārīkh-i 'ālam'ārā-yi Amīnī* by John Woods.[18] Woods is a student of the late Martin Dickson of Princeton University who did more than anybody else for the inclusion of non-Arab, i.e., Persian and Turkish, source materials into the study of late medieval and early modern Middle Eastern history in the United States.

2

In the context of his first and second *Ḥajj*, undertaken presumably in the years 877–9/1473–4 and 886–7/1481–2 respectively, Khunjī spent several months on Mamluk territory. Apparently during his first trip,[19] he visited Palestine, specifically Jerusalem and Hebron. In Jerusalem he attended the funeral of his Ṣūfī master Jamāl al-Dīn Ardistānī, a well-known and highly prolific adept of the Suhrawardīyah *ṭarīqah*.[20] In Cairo, where his mother died during his second visit, Khunjī sought the proximity of the leading scholars of the time. In disciplines as far afield as *ḥadīth*, legal dogmatics and Arabic syntactic stylistics (*'ilm al-ma'ānī*),[21] Khunjī was to excel, as we learn from his main Egyptian

[16] One should name Erika Glassen who gave a sensitive profile of Khunjī's personality in her two contributions (Glassen 1972 and 1979); Ursula Ott, who translated selections from *Mihmān'nāmah-'i Bukhārā* into German (Khunjī 1974); and Ulrich W. Haarmann, now of the University of Kiel, with his two contributions (Haarmann 1974 and 1979). Also, Monika Gronke (now of the University of Cologne) is conducting research on Khunjī's *oeuvre*.

[17] See Lambton 1981, 49–71. The gist of this article is to be found also in Lambton 1981b, chap. 11, 178–200. In both publications, Khunjī's political thinking, as elaborated in his *Sulūk al-mulūk*, is discussed. On *Sulūk al-mulūk*, mention was already made of Javād Ṭabāṭabā'ī's article (see footnote no. 12). Introductions to the two critical editions of *Sulūk al-mulūk* by their respective editors, Muḥammad Niẓām al-Dīn / Muḥammad Ghaws̱ and Muḥammad 'Alī Muvaḥḥid (Khunjī 1966 and 1984), contain useful information. The text edited by Muvaḥḥid, however, is more reliable. *Sulūk al-mulūk* has been translated into English by Muhammad Aslam (Khunjī 1974b) who has also written an article on Khunjī, see Aslam 1965.

[18] See Khunjī 1992. In his monograph on the Aqqoyunlu, John Woods made ample use of Khunjī's *Tārīkh-i 'ālam'ārā-yi Amīnī*, see Woods 1976, esp. 21–2.

[19] Not the second, as Sakhāwī implies, see the comment by Minorsky in Khunjī 1992, annex vi, 108.

[20] For further references to Ardistānī, see Haarmann 1974, 342–4.

[21] This, and not "semantics", is the contents of the *'ilm al-ma'ānī*; correspondingly, the translation of Sakhāwī's *tarjama* of Khunjī (Khunjī 1992, annex vi, 107) should be corrected.

teacher, the well-known polymath and historian Shams al-Dīn al-Sakhāwī (d. 902/1497), who proudly devoted a lengthy biography to his erudite Iranian student in his grand dictionary of 9th/15th century celebrities *al-Ḍaw' al-lāmi'* [22] and included him also into another major work of his.[23] The quality of Khunjī's Arabic, both his prose, poetry and *saj'*, as documented in the *Hidāyah* is remarkable. It corroborates Sakhāwī's judgment who attributed Khunjī's honorable appointment at the court of Sulṭān Ya'qūb Āq'qūyūnlū (r. 883–96/1478–90) to his eloquence (*balāghah*) and exquisite style (*ḥusn ishāratihī*).[24]

Khunjī's visit to Egypt in 886/1481 was long enough to afford him an opportunity even to meet Sulṭān al-Malik al-Ashraf Qāyitbay (r. 872–901/1468–96), who was known for his piety and thus—all the dark and even brutal sides of his rule notwithstanding—[25] seems to have been generally looked upon as a fit company for a righteous Muslim. Qāyitbāy had worked long and hard to acquire this reputation. Having come to Egypt from Circassia in the distant Caucasus, early in his career he had admirably mastered Arabic and knew sections of the Koran by heart. "His general conduct was highly laudable; he passed most of the night praying and reading the Koran."[26] Qāyitbāy spent a substantial part of his wealth on the entertainment of religious scholars.[27] It must have been during one of these prayer and reading sessions that our author gained access to him. Khunjī mentions this conversation in the subchapter on the night patrol (*'āss*, pl. *'asas*) in his manual of statecraft, *Sulūk al-mulūk*, a work written in 920/1514 in Bukhara at the court—and at the behest—of the Uzbek ruler 'Ubayd Allāh Khān. Functioning night-guards were, in Khunjī's conviction, an essential requisite of proper Islamic governance. The institution of the night-police had been established by the caliph 'Umar I,[28] yet had, in subsequent centuries, gradually fallen into neglect in the Muslim world. All the more, Khunjī was elated to find this regulation perfectly implemented in Qāyitbāy's Cairo. The first person admitted to the ruler each morning was the high functionary who—as the Sulṭān's deputy—super-

[22] See Sakhāwī 1934–6, 6:171, no. 580. For English and Persian translations of the text in *al-Ḍaw' al-lāmi'*, see Khunjī 1992, annex vi, 107–8 and 1962, 21, respectively.

[23] See Woods' footnote in Khunjī 1992, annex vi, 108.

[24] Sakhāwī 1934–6, 6:171, no. 580.

[25] On Qāyitbāy's sultanate, see Petry 1993, 15–118.

[26] Khunjī 1984, 214.

[27] Petry 1993, 31.

[28] Khunjī 1984, 211–2.

vised the security of the capital in nocturnal patrols and had to report on any incidents that had occurred.[29]

For a brief moment Khunjī even became an agent in Mamluk politics. The context was the fire, mentioned above, that destroyed some of the buildings in al-Rawḍa al-Nabawīyah in Medina. The event itself[30] (including earlier fires), the transmission of the dramatic news to Egypt, and Qāyitbāy's reaction (he ordered the swift repair of the damage,[31] a task that was to last seven months)[32] are described in detail in Khunjī's *Hidāyah*, a text which also contains brief terminological studies on the notion of *ḥarīq* as mentioned in Prophetic *ḥadīth*, as well as an epilogue with several dirges (*marāthī*) that were composed after the event.

Khunjī's—marginal, to be true—involvement in the event began in early spring of 887/1482 when a close friend of his (*aqrab aṣdiqā'ī wa-aḥabb aḥibbā'ī*),[33] a certain Sayyidī al-Khwājā Shams al-Dīn ibn al-Zamin, informed him of the catastrophe which had taken place in Medina a few months earlier.[34] Ibn al-Zamin had just left the citadel where Sulṭān Qāyitbāy had charged him with the necessary reconstruction work. For a long time this "smart [bedouin] Arab" (*min duhāt al-'arab*) had tried to extricate himself from this hazardous assignment not only "for fear of the Sulṭān's changing moods and because of his overall unreliability,"[35] but also because the sum apportioned for the reconstruction of the mosque by the naive and, at the same time, notoriously covetous Sulṭān was far below the estimated minimum cost, so that in the end he himself might have been held responsible for the deficit.

Making his undecided[36] friend aware of the grave repercussions a negative response would have on his status and security, and also appealing to his optimism, Khunjī eventually talked the man into complying with the Sulṭān's command. In return, Khunjī agreed to accompany Ibn al-Zamin on his risky mission to the Ḥijāz—a price that, in hindsight, was gladly paid by Khunjī

[29] Ibid., 214.

[30] As a good traditionist, he enumerates the names (and documents the probity) of all the *shaykh*s of Medina who informed him of the fire, see Khunjī 1969, 96–7.

[31] Ibid., 101.

[32] Ibid., 106.

[33] Ibid., 101.

[34] This encounter took place in the mosque of Bardī Beg, close to the Bāb al-Naṣr in the north of the Fatimid city of Cairo, see ibid., 100–1.

[35] Ibid., 102.

[36] The term *istikhārah*, "request for the exoneration from a difficult choice," quite tellingly is used twice in Khunjī's masterly description of the inner fight his friend went through under the impact of Qāyitbāy's request, see ibid.

since this visit to Medina (and Mecca) gave him a chance to meet and study with Sakhāwī, whom he had unsuccessfully sought in Cairo.

Sakhāwī has left us a detailed biography of this Muḥammad ibn ʿUmar ibn al-Zamin (824–97/1420–92). He reportedly began his career as a merchant travelling as far afield as Anatolia and Europe until Qāyitbāy, immediately after his accession to the throne in 872/1468, put him in charge of the buildings of Mecca. In 879/1474 Medina was added to Ibn al-Zamin's areas of responsibility. He was therefore the logical candidate to supervise the restoration of the dome and the minaret of the mosque in that city eight years later, his advanced age notwithstanding. The respect Ibn al-Zamin paid to foreigners, especially foreign scholars like Khunjī, is expressly mentioned and praised by Sakhāwī.[37]

On 28 Rabīʿ I 887/17 May 1482, the restoration team left Cairo, arriving in Medina four weeks later.[38] We are informed in detail about the repair measures, progressing steadily from building to building, and also about the sometimes difficult choices to be made between the exact reconstruction of a monument in such a sensitive location and the urge to change and improve the former architecture.[39] After seven months, the job was completed, also much to the delight of the Sharīf of Mecca and Medina, Muḥammad ibn Abī al-Barakāt al-Ḥasanī, who visited the construction site and personally joined the workmen, transporting soil and stones himself. He thus set an example for other citizens of Medina who from then on helped to bring the work to a speedy end and no doubt also contributed to keeping the costs of repair within range, much to the relief, we can safely assume, of the apprehensive superintendent, Ibn al-Zamin.

Khunjī stayed in Medina for some more months in 887/1482 to continue his studies and then returned to his home country. Five years after the fire, in Shaʿbān 892/July–August 1487, he entered the services of Sulṭān Yaʿqūb Āq'qūyūnlū. By 897/1492 this news had also reached Sakhāwī, who recorded it in the chapter devoted to Khunjī in his prosopography.

[37] Sakhāwī 1934–6, 8:260–2, no. 703. On Ibn al-Zamin's building activities in Egypt, Syria, and Arabia, see Burgoyne 1987, 572–3, and Meinecke 1992, 1:195, 197; 2:400, no. 24, 404–5, no. 50, 410, no. 74, 411, no. 80, 415, no. 101, 421–2, no. 127, and 436, no. 196.

[38] Khunjī 1969, 103.

[39] Ibid., 104–6.

3

Only on one very specific occasion, Khunjī's strong, and at times enthusiastic, pro-Mamluk sentiment was put to the test—at least in retrospect. In Ramaḍān 885/November 1480, i.e., only a few months before Khunjī's second arrival in Egypt, Qāyitbāy's chief minister, the great *dawādār* Yashbak min Mahdī al-Ẓāhirī (Jaqmaq al-Ṣaghīr), having suppressed seditious bedouins in the Syrian desert at Qāyitbāy's command, invaded Aqqoyunlu territory on his own authority.[40] Yashbak was not unknown to the Aqqoyunlu generals; seven years earlier, in 877/1473, he had frustrated Sulṭān Ūzūn Ḥasan's attempt to invade into Mamluk Syria.[41] This time Yashbak (incidentally one of the most fascinating individuals of late Mamluk history, a man equally renowned for his bold resolve[42] and his profound interest in cultural matters)[43] was not successful at all. His attack ended in complete disaster. Having crossed the Euphrates, Yashbak and his generals laid siege to al-Ruhā (Urfa, Edessa), but were soon[44] routed by Sulṭān Ya'qūb's numerically superior army that was led by the generals Bāyandur, Sulaymān Beg Bījan, and Khalīl Beg Baktāsh. Yashbak was captured and, apparently at Bāyandur's personal order, most cruelly and ignominiously put to death.[45]

40 A succinct description of this campaign is given in Woods 1976, 142–3, 276–7. The most detailed printed Arabic account is found in Ibn Iyās' *Badā'i' al-zuhūr fī waqā'i' al-duhūr*, see Ibn Iyās 1960–84, 3:165ff., 170–2. A detailed study on Mamluk-Turkman relations still remains to be written.

41 A previous undertaking of Yashbak in Syria against the rebellious Dulghadır prince Shāh Suwār (875–7/1471–2) has been described by the bilingual (Arabic and Turkish) scholar and *littérateur* Shams al-Dīn Muḥammad ibn Maḥmūd al-Ḥalabī, known as Ibn Ajā (d. 881/1476); his text, *Riḥlat (*or *Tārīkh) al-Amīr Yashbak,* has been edited twice: see Ibn Ajā [1974] and 1986, 65–177.

42 His brutality was legendary; he became known as the scourge of the bedouins of Upper Egypt, see Holt 1986, 196.

43 Sakhāwī grudgingly concedes outstanding cultural excellence to this leading Mamluk, see Sakhāwī 1934–6, 10:272–4, no. 1077 especially p. 273 ("he made an unprecedented career for a member of his race" [*wa-rtaqā li-mā lam yaṣil ilayhi fī waqtinā ghayruhū min abnā' jinsihī*]) and p. 274 ("he acquired indescribable quantities of precious books, purchasing them or having them copied" [*shirā'an wa-stiktāban*]); a full set of al-Ṣafadī's twenty-nine volume prosopography *Kitāb al-Wāfī bi-al-wafayāt*, copied for Yashbak's private library, now serves as the key text for modern editions. This brilliant side of a fascinating, profoundly enigmatic, personality has been described by Barbara Flemming, see Flemming 1969. She rightly insisted, as early as 1969, on the need for a comprehensive study of the life and the work of this unusual general. Yashbak wrote both in Arabic—we know of a book entitled *Shajarat al-nasab al-sharīf al-nabawī*—and in Turkish. His Turkish poems are preserved in the *Dīvān* of Sultan Qānṣawh al-Ghawrī, see the reference in Yalçın 1993, 124–5 (cited in the context of Ghawrī's Turkish *marṣiye* on Yashbak).

44 Actually, "in less than an hour," see Ibn Iyās 1960–84, 3:171.

45 Details of Yashbak's short captivity and gruesome execution at the hands of a black slave with the Turkish name of Uzdamur are recorded in ibid., 3:172.

Since the young Sulṭān Ya'qūb, however, needed Mamluk benevolence in his struggle with inner opponents in the so-called third Aqqoyunlu civil war and since also the Mamluks needed a quiet front in the north-east, a speedy rapprochement took place. The Aqqoyunlu ruler did everything to assuage Qāyitbāy's wrath over the execution of his best general, sending tokens of reconciliation to Cairo. A formal apology for the killing of Yashbak was sent to Qāyitbāy. The Mamluk captives who had been detained in Tabrīz, the capital of the Aqqoyunlu, were set free and sent home, donned in robes of honor. Yashbak's death could not be undone, nor Yashbak's invasion and the wanton siege of al-Ruhā in the sacred month of Ramaḍān.[46] But subtle diplomacy managed to bring the enemies of yesterday together more swiftly than some of their common adversaries, notably the Ottomans, could have imagined.

When Khunjī came to Cairo in 886/1481, this new, albeit tenuous, partnership between the Aqqoyunlu and the Mamluks had already begun. Also, the Aqqoyunlu prisoners held captive in Egypt ever since 877/1473 had by then left Cairo, and Qayitbāy had even permitted, for the first time since Ūzūn Ḥasan's death in 882/1478, the Iraqi pilgrimage convoy to join the *Ḥajj* ceremonial in the Ḥijāz.

In his discussion of Yashbak's attack on Aqqoyunlu territory as presented in his chronicle of Sulṭān Ya'qūb's rule, the *Tārīkh-i 'ālam'ārā-yi Amīnī* (a work written only in 907/1501 or even later,[47] i.e., from a safe distance of many years after the events), Khunjī voices the highly volatile sentiments held against the Mamluks at the court of Tabrīz during these crucial years and months. He personally seems to have felt the same way. Reconciling these oscillating and contradictory judgments must have been one of his goals in *Tārīkh-i 'ālam'ārā-yi Amīnī*. On the one hand, admiration for Mamluk Egypt as a bulwark of Islam and gratitude to the Mamluks as guardians of Islam in times of affliction, and, on the other, irritation over the insubordination and aggression of Qāyitbāy's yeoman Yashbak, as well as pride over the military feat of the Aqqoyunlu army at al-Ruhā had to be brought in congruence.

The chapter on Yashbak's campaign[48] appropriately begins with a eulogy of Egypt, the heartland of Islam (*bayẓat al-Islām*), as is stated in a

[46] Khunjī 1992, 190–1.

[47] Ibid., introd., 5.

[48] Ibid., 187–99. These passages were the subject of a seminar at the University of Kiel in the winter term 1994–5, in which Doris Kröll and Hasan Safavi participated with much enthusiasm.

familiar saying of this period.[49] Egypt is the most blessed country on earth, on whose cheek the attirer of nature (*mashshāṭah-'i ṣun'*) has drawn a blue (*nīl*) line (= the river Nile) to avert the evil-eye of the envious. He extols the religious fervor of the Egyptians (the mosques are so full that anyone who leaves the sanctuary if only for a moment will find his place taken by another fervent believer) and attributes the country's legendary wealth and prosperity to this ubiquitous profound piety. In comparison to other rulers, those of Egypt have always been famed for their support of the cause of Islam.[50] Indeed, it was the Mamluks who, as successors to the Ayyubids, salvaged Syria, Egypt, and the territories further west from destruction at the hands of the vile Mongol aggressors.[51] All subsequent attempts by the Ilkhans of Iran to invade Syria and Egypt were triumphantly warded off by the strong and valiant Egyptian armies who even managed to impede the mighty Tīmūr from conquering Egypt.[52]

This made the invasion into the Aqqoyunlu lands by Yashbak, who is derogatorily named Bāsh Beg, all the more shocking.[53] He was tempted to exploit the crisis in the Aqqoyunlu domains after the death of Ūzūn Ḥasan. Treacherously, he turned to al-Ruhā (during Ramaḍān) shooting deadly Greek fire on those trapped in the beleaguered city. This despicable slave without a name (*bī'nām*)[54] and therefore without any personal legitimacy[55] (a vitriolic allusion to the slave-status and the unknown genealogy of the Mamluks) faced, together with his powerful companions from among the Syrian governors, the awe-inspiring resistance of the Aqqoyunlu armies now set in march. Whereas the Muslim warriors of Egypt had never in the past allowed their dun colored

[49] Ibid., 191. Further in the book (p. 386), Egypt is described as *qubbat* (dome of) *al-Islām*. The notion of Egypt as the core of Sunnī Islam was widespread in the 15th century. The contemporary work *al-Faḍā'il al-bāhirah fī maḥāsin Miṣr wa-al-Qāhirah* by Abū Ḥāmid al-Qudsī contains rich material to substantiate the prestige adduced to Egypt and Cairo in this period, see Qudsī 1969, especially p. 82.

[50] Khunjī 1992, 191.

[51] The historical details are not always correctly given. For instance, Khunjī makes the Circassian (not the Qipchaq Turkish) Mamluks succeed the Ayyubids in the rule over Egypt (ibid., 187); he declares Hülegü's son (instead of Ket-Buqa) the commander of the Mongol force that met the Mamluks led by al-Malik al-Ashraf (instead of al-Malik al-Muẓaffar Quṭuz) at 'Ayn Jālūt (ibid., 188). This list could be continued.

[52] Ibid., 189.

[53] Ibid.

[54] Ibid., 190.

[55] In vain, he would claim comradeship (*khvāja'tāshī*) and equality with his adversaries with all their noble pedigrees, see ibid.; on the term *khvāja'tāshī* (Arabic, *khushdāshīyah*) and its historical significance see Ayalon 1951, 29–31.

Arab steeds (*samand-i mukāvaḥah*) to race on the battlefield without an explicit ruling based on the Law (*bī'fatvā-yi Sharī'at*),[56] this time everything was different. This vain and haughty general imitated instead the wicked pre-Islamic tradition of Egyptian rulership, the *ẓulm* of the Pharaohs.[57] But due punishment ensued. Bāyandur won the day. The ever-victorious Mamluk army was shamefully defeated, and, in addition to Yashbak, its leaders were taken prisoner: notably Qānṣawh al-Yaḥyāwī, the military governor (*dārūghah*) of Damascus,[58] and Ūzdamur, viceroy of Aleppo, together with officers of the two highest Mamluk ranks.[59] Yashbak alone was executed; the others were taken to Tabrīz, only to be released with all honors within a short time, in conformity with the maxim, that the victor should, in gratitude for his victory, grant pardon in return to his defeated opponent.[60] An old dream of the Chinghizids and other rulers of Iran (*'ajam*), namely a crushing triumph over the Mamluks, had finally come true, heralding other shining victories in the future.

4

When Khunjī wrote his *Sulūk al-mulūk* in 920/1514, i.e., more than a dozen years after the *Tārīkh-i 'ālam'ārā-yi Amīnī*, he had long since been forced to leave Āẕarbāyjān for the inhospitable north. Shāh Ismā'īl had mounted the throne of Tabrīz, effacing the last vestiges of Aqqoyunlu power in northwest Iran, and had even begun the forced wholesale conversion of the population of the Safavid domains to Shī'ism. Khunjī had escaped to Bukhārā via Khurāsān, only to hear of the victory of the anathematized chief of the Red-heads (*ṭāqiyah-yi surkh*) over his Uzbek protector Shaybān Khān in 916/1510. Of course, a few years later the tide began to turn. The Ottomans vanquished Ismā'īl, and the Uzbeks, his hosts, regained strength when they forced Bābur, Ismā'īl's short-time ally and lieutenant in Bukhārā and Samarqand, out of Central Asia.[61] However, in 920/1514, three years before the Ottomans were to annihilate the Mamluk sultanate, it was the unimpaired fame of the Mamluks

[56] Khunjī 1992, 191.

[57] On this, see the numerous Koranic references (notably 43/51, 20/78) to Pharaoh and his crimes, as quoted in ibid., 192–3.

[58] Ibid., 196.

[59] Khunjī knew the Mamluk hierarchy well; he speaks of the *muqaddamū alf*, the highest generals, as *umarā-yi hazār*, and of the amīrs of forty with their bands (*ṭablkhānah*) as *arbāb-i ṭabl*, see ibid., 197.

[60] Ibid., 198.

[61] On these events, see Haarmann 1974, 336–9.

as paragons of right belief and prime defenders of Sunnī Islam against the damnable *rawāfiḍ* which seems to have been dominant in Khunjī's mind. He evidently considered the Mamluks (whose country he knew and liked) to be the prime fighters for the right path of Islam, more even than the Ottomans and Uzbeks. As lords of the Islamic heartland, they were the object of his admiration. Yashbak's blunder of 885/1480, for which he paid such a high price, was long since forgotten. Egypt and its capital city, more than any other place, were the unquestioned *Dār al-Islām-i Miṣr-i mu'aẓẓamah*, the prestigious seat of Islam.[62] Egypt had by now become unattainable for him and could thus innocuously be furnished with the most glorious attributes. There was no danger that reality might harshly disprove this nostalgic view of his beloved former host country.

This process of idealizing Mamluk Egypt can best be studied in Khunjī's presentation of the shadow caliphate of Cairo. In at least one passage of the *Tārīkh-i 'ālam'ārā-yi Amīnī* of the year 1501 or thereabout, he clearly describes the Mamluk sulṭāns as the successors to the caliphs of Baghdād in their function as guardians of the Holy Cities of the Ḥijāz.[63] A few pages later, however, he qualifies "the armies of Muslim Egypt," i.e., the Mamluks, as soldiers "who regard themselves as the regiments of the Abbasid caliph."[64] Historical truth was diametrically different from this statement, much as Khunjī must have disliked this state of affairs. The Egyptian caliphs were puppets in the hands of the Mamluks, not vice versa. Writing the *Sulūk al-mulūk* in his Uzbek exile, the Khunjī of the year 920/1514 became even less judicious. In this, his latest, work the venerable Abbasid caliphs[65] are presented as the sovereign helmsmen of effective power in Egypt who enjoy the loyal assistance of their plenipotentiaries, the Mamluk sulṭāns (*khulafā'-i 'Abbāsī dar diyār-i Miṣr bi-khilāfat istiqlāl dārand va salāṭīn-i Miṣr vukalā-yi īshānand*).[66] After the revolutionary changes in Iran, which had affected him personally so profoundly, he seems to have felt more desperately than ever the need for such a symbol of legitimacy, political stability and religious unity.

And another factor, a geographical one, may have been conducive to this idealizing attitude towards the caliphate of Cairo. The farther away one was from Egypt, the higher the respect was which these Abbasid figurehead ca-

[62] Khunjī 1984, 214.
[63] Khunjī 1992, 188.
[64] Ibid., 191.
[65] A recent bibliography on the growing literature on the Abbasid caliphate of Cairo is to be found in Garcin 1995, lxxxvii.
[66] Khunjī 1984, 365.

liphs enjoyed (and were allowed to enjoy by their Mamluk masters). In India and in the Yemen, coins were struck in the name of the Cairo caliphs who in the Egyptian capital itself had long since been shorn of any effective power and functioned as no more than some sort of a fifth supreme *qāẓī*, representing a fifth, neutral *madhhab*. And Transoxiana, where Khunjī languished in exile, was also very far away indeed from that blessed and felicitous heartland of Islam on the banks of the Nile.[67] It was, however, the right location for such an exaggerated view on the caliphate. Nostalgia, despair, and utopian dreams have always been bad counsel to the sober minds of narrators of contemporary history.

[67] Other examples of his enthusiastic, albeit conventional, praise of Egypt can be found in Khunjī 1992, 187: Egypt is "the chosen country on earth" (*intikhāb-i mamālik-i dunyā*) or "the quintessence of the inhabited world" (*khulāṣah-'i rub'-i maskūn*).

BIBLIOGRAPHY

AFSHAR, IRAJ. 1975. Hidāyat al-taṣdīq ilá ḥikāyat al-ḥarīq : risālah'ī nāshinākhtah az Faẕl Allāh Khunjī. In *Majmū'ah-i kamīnah*. Tehran : Farhang-i Īrān Zamīn, 1354 Sh.: 300–4.

—— 1997. Fārsī'nivīsī-i mustashriqān (1). *Faṣlnāmah-i gulistān* 1, no. 2 (summer): 37–50.

ASLAM, MUHAMMAD. 1965. Faḍl-ullah bin Rūzbihān al-Iṣfahānī. *Journal of the Asiatic Society of Pakistan* 10, no. 2 (December): 121–34.

AYALON, DAVID. 1951. *L'esclavage du Mamelouk*. Jerusalem : Israel Oriental Society.

—— 1977. *Studies on the Mamlūks of Egypt, (1250–1517)*. London : Variorum Reprints.

—— 1979. *The Mamlūk military society*. London : Variorum Reprints.

—— 1988. *Outsiders in the lands of Islam : Mamluks, Mongols, and eunuchs*. London : Variorum Reprints.

—— 1994. *Islam and the abode of war : military slaves and Islamic adversaries*. Aldershot, Great Britain and Brookfield, Vt. : Variorum Reprints.

BURGOYNE, MICHAEL. 1987. *Mamluk Jerusalem : an architectural study*. With additional research by D. S. Richards. London : Published on behalf of the British School of Archaeology in Jerusalem by the World of Islam Festival Trust.

GARCIN, JEAN-CLAUDE. 1995–. *Etats, sociétés et cultures du monde musulman médiéval x-xve siècle*. 1 vol. to date. Paris : Presses universitaires de France.

GLASSEN, ERIKA. 1972. Šāh Ismā'īl I. und die Theologen seiner Zeit. *Der Islam* 48: 254–68.

—— 1979. Krisenbewußtsein und Heilserwartung in der islamischen Welt zu Beginn der Neuzeit. In *Die islamische Welt zwischen Mittelalter und Neuzeit : Festschrift für Hans Robert Roemer zum 65. Geburtstag*. Beirut and Wiesbaden : In Kommission bei F. Steiner: 175–9.

FLEMMING, BARBARA. 1969. Šerīf, Ġavrī und die 'Perser'. *Der Islam* 45: 81–93.

HAARMANN, ULRICH W. 1974. Staat und Religion in Transoxanien im frühen 16. Jahrhundert. *Zeitschrift der Deutschen Morgenländischen Gesellschaft* 124: 332–69.

—— 1979. K͟hundjī, Faḍl Allāh b. Rūzbihān. *Encyclopaedia of Islam*. New ed. Vol. 5. Leiden : E. J. Brill: columns 53b–5b.

—— 1995. Mamluk studies—a western perspective. *al-Majallah al-'Arabīyah lil-'ulūm al-insānīyah* 51 (rabī'): 329–47.

HOLT, P. M. 1986. *The Age of the Crusades : the Near East from the eleventh century to 1517*. London and New York : Longman.

HUMPHREYS, R. STEPHEN. 1991. *Islamic history : a framework for inquiry*. Rev. ed. Princeton : Princeton University Press.

ḤUSAYNĪ, AḤMAD and MAR'ASHĪ, MAḤMŪD. 1975–. *Fihrist-i nuskhah'hā-yi khaṭṭī-i Kitābkhānah-'i 'Umūmī-i Ḥaẓrat-i Āyat Allāh al-'Uẓmá Najafī Mar'ashī*. 27 (text) + 2 (index) vols. to date. Qum : Kitābkhānah, 1354 Sh.–

IBN AJĀ, MUḤAMMAD IBN MAḤMŪD. [1974]. *Tārīkh al-Amīr Yashbak al-Ẓāhirī*. Ed. ʻAbd al-Qādir Aḥmad Ṭulaymāt. Cairo : Dār al-Fikr al-ʻArabī.

—— 1986. *al-ʻIrāk bayna al-Mamālīk wa-al-ʻUthmānīyīn al-Atrāk : maʻa Riḥlat al-Amīr Yashbak min Mahdī al-Dawādār*. Ed. Muḥammad Aḥmad Duhmān. Damascus : Dār al-Fikr.

IBN IYĀS. 1960–84. *Badāʼiʻ al-zuhūr fī waqāʼiʻ al-duhūr*. 2nd ed. Ed. Muḥammad Mustafá. 6 vols. Cairo : ʻĪsá al-Bābī al-Ḥalabī ; Wiesbaden : In Kommission bei F. Steiner.

ĪZADĪ, ḤUSAYN. 1991–2. Andīshah-i siyāsī-i Faẕl Allāh ibn Rūzbihān Khunjī. *Kayhān-i andīshah* 39 (Āẕar/Day 1370 Sh.): 128–45.

KHUNJĪ, FAẔL ALLĀH IBN RŪZBIHĀN. 1957. *Persia in A.D. 1478–1490 : an abridged translation of Faḍlullāh b. Rūzbihān Khunjī's Tārīkh-i ʻālam-ārā-yi Amīnī*. Tr. V. Minorsky. London : The Royal Asiatic Society of Great Britain and Ireland.

—— 1962. *Mihmān'nāmah-'i Bukhārā : tārīkh-i pādshāhī-i Muḥammad Shaybānī*. Ed. Manūchihr Sutūdah. Tehran : Bungāh-i Tarjumah va Nashr-i Kitāb, 1341 Sh..

—— 1966. *Kitāb-i Sulūk al-muluk : dastūr-i ḥukūmat-i Islāmī*. Ed. Muḥammad Niẓam al-Dīn, Muḥammad Ghawṣ. Ḥaydarābād, Dakan : Vizārat-i Farhang-i Dawlat-i Hind.

—— 1969. Hidāyat al-taṣdīq ilá ḥikāyat al-ḥarīq. Ed. Muḥammad Taqī Dānish'pizhūh. In *Yādnāmah-'i Īrānī-i Mīnūrskī : shāmil-i maqālāt-i taḥqīqī marbūṭ bi-muṭālaʻāt-i Īrānī*. Ed. Mujtabá Mīnuvī, Iraj Afshar. Tehran : Dānishgāh-i Tihrān: 77–113.

—— 1969b. Risālah-'i nāshinākhtah'ī az Faẕl Allāh Khunjī. Introd. Iraj Afshar. In *Yādnāmah-'i Īrānī-i Mīnūrskī : shāmil-i maqālāt-i taḥqīqī marbūṭ bi-muṭālaʻāt-i Īrānī*. Ed. Mujtabá Mīnuvī, Iraj Afshar. Tehran : Dānishgāh-i Tihrān: 3–35.

—— 1974. *Transoxanien und Turkestan zu Beginn des 16. Jahrhunderts : Das Mihmān-nāma-yi Buḫārā des Faḍlallāh b. Rūzbihān Ḫunǧī*. Tr. Ursula Ott. Freiburg : K. Schwarz.

—— 1974b. *Muslim conduct of state : based upon the Suluk-ul-muluk of Fadl-Ullah ibn Ruzbihan Isfahani*. Tr. Muhammad Aslam. Islāmābād : University of Islamabad Press.

—— 1976. *Mihmān'nāmah-'i Bukhārā*. Ed. R. P. Dzhalilova, A. K. Arends. Moscow : Idārah-'i Intishārāt-i Dānish, Shuʻbah-'i Adabīyāt-i Khāvar.

—— 1984. *Sulūk al-mulūk*. Ed. Muḥammad ʻAlī Muvaḥḥid. Tehran : Khvārazmī, Isfand 1362 Sh.

—— 1987. *Tarikh-i alam-ara-ii Amini*. Tr. T. A. Minorsky, ed. Z. M. Buniiatov, O. A. Efendiev. Baku : Elm.

—— 1992. *Tārīkh-i ʻālam-ārā-yi Amīnī : with the abridged English translation by Vladimir Minorsky [entitled] Persia in A.D. 1478–1490*. Ed. John E. Woods. London : Royal Asiatic Society.

—— 1993. *Wasīlat al-khādim ilá al-makhdūm : dar sharḥ-i ṣalavāt-i Chahārdah Maʻṣūm*. Ed. Rasūl Jaʻfariyān. Qum : Kitābkhānah-'i ʻUmūmī-i Āyat Allāh al-ʻUẓmá Marʻashī Najafī, 1372 Sh.

—— 1994–5. Guzārish-i ātish'sūzī-i Masjid-i Nabavī dar sāl-i 866 va banā-yi mujaddad-i ān az zabān-i yak shāhid-i ʻaynī : tarjumah-'i risālah-'i Hidāyat al-taṣdīq ilá ḥikāyat al-ḥarīq az Faẕl Allāh ibn Rūzbihān Khunjī, m. 927. Tr. & introd. Rasūl Jaʻfariyān. *Mīqāt-i ḥajj* 10 (zamistān 1373 Sh.): 106–16.

KHUNJĪ, MUḤAMMAD AMĪN. 1956. Faẕl Allāh ibn Rūzbihān Khunjī. *Farhang-i Īrān Zamīn* 4 (1335 Sh.): 173–84.

LAMBTON, ANN K. S. 1981. Changing concepts of authority in the late ninth/fifteenth and early tenth/sixteenth centuries. In *Islam and power*. Ed. Alexander S. Cudsi, Ali E. Hillal Dessouki. Baltimore and London : The Johns Hopkins University Press: 49–71.

—— 1981b. The Imām/Sultan : Faḍl Allāh b. Rūzbihān Khunjī. In *State and government in medieval Islam : an introduction to the study of Islamic political theory : the jurists*. Oxford and New York : Oxford University Press: 178–200.

MAQSŪD HAMADĀNĪ, JAVĀD. 1977. *Fihrist-i nuskhah'hā-yi khaṭṭī-i Kitābkhānah-'i Gharb, Madrasah-'i Ākhūnd-Hamadān.* Tehran : Chāpkhānah-i Āẕīn, 2536 Shāhanshāhī.

MARMON, SHAUN. 1995. *Eunuchs and sacred boundaries in Islamic society*. New York : Oxford University Press.

MEINECKE, MICHAEL. 1992. *Die mamlukische Architektur in Ägypten und Syrien, (648/1250 bis 923/1517)*. 2 vols. Glückstadt : Verlag J. J. Augustin.

MUẒAFFAR, MUḤAMMAD ḤASAN. 1976. *Dalā'il al-ṣidq : munāqashah 'ilmīyah mawḍū'īyah ma'a Ibn Rūzbihān fī raddihi 'alá al-Ḥillī fī masā'il al-khilāfīyah bayna al-Shī'ah al-Imāmīyah wa-jumhūr al-Sunnah.* Cairo : Dār al-Mu'allim.

PETRY, CARL F. 1993. *Twilight of majesty : the reigns of the Mamlūk Sultans al-Ashraf Qāytbāy and Qānṣūh al-Ghawrī in Egypt*. Seattle and London : University of Washington Press.

QUDSĪ, ABŪ ḤĀMID. 1969. *al-Faḍā'il al-bāhirah fī maḥāsin Miṣr wa-al-Qāhirah.* Ed. Muṣṭafá al-Saqqā, Kāmil al-Muhandis. Cairo : Wizārat al-Thaqāfah, Markaz Taḥqīq al-Turāth.

SAKHĀWĪ, MUḤAMMAD IBN 'ABD AL-RAḤMĀN. 1934–6. *al-Ḍaw' al-lāmi' li-ahl al-qarn al-tāsi'*. 12 vols. Cairo : Maktabat al-Qudsī, 1353–5.

ṬABĀṬABĀ'Ī, JAVĀD. 1989. Faẕl Allāh ibn Rūzbihān Khunjī va tajdīd-i īdi'ūlūzhī-i khilāfat. In *Darāmadī falsafī bar tārīkh-i andīshah-i siyāsī dar Īrān.* 2nd ed. Tehran : Daftar-i Muṭāla'āt-i Siyāsī va Bayn al-Milalī, 1368: 183–200.

TUJĪBĪ, AL-QĀSIM IBN YŪSUF. 1975. *Mustafād al-riḥlah wa-al-ightirāb*. Ed. 'Abd al-Ḥafīẓ Manṣūr. Tripoli and Tunis : al-Dār al-'Arabīyah lil-Kitāb.

WOODS, JOHN. 1976. *The Aqqoyunlu : clan, confederation, empire : a study in 15th/9th century Turko-Iranian politics*. Minneapolis and Chicago : Bibliotheca Islamica.

YALÇIN, MEHMET. 1993. *Dîvan-ı Qânṣûh al-Ġûrî : a critical edition of Turkish poetry commissioned by Sulṭan Qânṣûh al-Ġûrî (1501–1516)*. Ph.D. diss. Harvard University.

A Chinese Dish from the Lost Endowment of Princess Sulṭānum (925–69/1519–62)

Abolala Soudavar

INTRODUCTION

DESPITE ITS OWN LONG-ESTABLISHED TRADITION OF ceramic production, Iran valued throughout the middle ages the refined techniques of Chinese porcelain, the highest quality of which was referred to as *chīnī-i Faghfūrī*. *Faghfūr* was the Arabicized version of *Baghpūr*, literally meaning Son of God in Middle Persian, and equivalent to the appellation Son of Heaven that the Chinese used for their emperors.[1] Thus, the phrase *chīnī-i Faghfūrī* referred to porcelain from the imperial kilns of China and, by itself, indicated that porcelain imports in Iran predated the Mongol invasions. Otherwise, these porcelains would have been referred to as *Qā'ānī* rather than *Faghfūrī*, as *Qā'ān* was the title used for the Yuan emperors (1271–1368) in the Persian lands.

Persian merchants had settled in China prior to the Mongol invasions of the 13th century and some, such as the fleet-owner of Persian descent, P'u Shou-kêng, had achieved great wealth and power.[2] Persian traders so dominated the trade between China and the Middle East that Persian became the *lingua franca* along both the Silk Road and the maritime trade routes from the Persian Gulf to the Sea of China. As both China and Iran came under Mongol rule, many more took advantage of the *pax mongolica* and settled and prospered in China;[3] a prosperity that inevitably became the solicitation target of religious institutions in the Persian motherland. Thus, when the Moroccan traveler Ibn Baṭūṭah visited the port of Zaytūn—modern day Ch'üan-chou (Quanzhou)—in mid-8th/14th century, he encountered a certain Shaykh Burhān al-Dīn who gathered donations for the Ṣūfī congregation of the Shrine of Abū Isḥāq Kāzirūnī in Kāzirūn, Iran.[4]

Much like today's Chinese expatriates who have facilitated trade with China by adapting export production to local markets, Persian merchants reoriented the production of the Chinese kilns—which had suffered from a

[1] Pelliot 1959–73, 1:652.
[2] Medley 1975, 32.
[3] Bailey 1996, 7; Chen Da-Sheng 1992, 191–3.
[4] Soudavar 1992, 78–80; Ibn Baṭūṭah 1853–8, 4:89, 271.

crumbling market due to the Mongol invasions—towards the Persian lands. New products emerged from these kilns, larger in size than traditional Chinese vessels and more adapted to the Middle Eastern food servings, with a pattern of decoration that made use of the concentric and geometrical designs of Islamic wares in order to fill their larger surfaces. And cobalt blue—mainly imported from the province of Kirmān in Iran—was gradually used for underglaze painting over the admired white porcelain.[5] The result was the creation of the blue-and-white porcelain that was initially considered "extremely vulgar" by the educated Chinese elite, but was subsequently embraced as the most elegant type of porcelain.[6]

THE ALLURE OF CHINESE PORCELAIN AT THE PERSIAN COURTS

Perhaps the earliest recorded evidence of Chinese porcelain specifically crafted for the Persian market is a reference included in a will-letter of the celebrated Ilkhanid *vazīr*, Rashīd al-Dīn Fa̤zl Allāh (d. 718/1318), reproduced in one hundred copies and distributed throughout the Ilkhanid empire. There, the *vazīr* listed his vast holdings and enumerated some of his most valuable objects. In a section pertaining to the hospital that he had built within the Rab'-i Rashīdī complex at Tabrīz, he boasted to have commissioned "one thousand elaborately designed jars (*khumrah*) for syrups" from China, "bearing his epithets (*alqāb*)" and inscribed with the syrup name, and also, lidded boxes (*qūṭī*) for drug mixtures.[7] Chinese porcelain jars were luxurious and expensive items that only individuals like the immensely rich Rashīd al-Dīn could afford to buy in such quantities. Thus, in a 14th-century painting of an illustrated copy of the *Shāhnāmah*, the porcelain holdings of Rashīd al-Dīn were used as an indicator of his identity: Rashīd al-Dīn—who was trained as a physician—is portrayed in an apothecary surrounding with porcelain jars.[8] But, since Rashīd

[5] Medley 1975, 32–4.

[6] Ibid., 32; Pope 1981, 44.

[7] Rashīd al-Dīn Fa̤zl Allāh 1980, 214.

[8] The painting in question is in an album in the Topkapı Palace Library in İstanbul (Hazine 2153, fol. 112v). It actually depicts (and is entitled) the poet Daqīqī being stabbed to death by his servant, see Soudavar 1996, 150–3, Atasoy 1970, 41–2, and, for a color reproduction, Gray 1979, 99, pl. xxi. But as argued elsewhere (Soudavar 1996), it is a Jalayirid painting that was made for insertion in the celebrated—and presently dispersed—Ilkhanid *Shāhnāmah* of Abū Sa'īd Bahādur Khān (r. 717–36/1317–35), or a later Jalayirid copy of it. Every painting of this *Shāhnāmah* project was meant to illustrate not only an episode of the *Shāhnāmah* but also an event in the Mongol history, and thus in this painting the death of Daqīqī was to evoke the death of Rashīd al-Dīn as both authors were killed before they could finish their works.

al-Dīn was executed in 718/1318 and his building activity at the Rab' was mostly in the first decade of the 7th/14th century, and since the production of blue-and-white started ca. 1320,[9] the depicted jars are not blue-and-white but seem to be of the Longquan type celadon.

For the *vazīrs* who rose to power and accumulated much wealth under Turco-Mongol rulers, possession of Chinese porcelain was *de rigueur*. Invariably though, they were arrested while in office, and saw their possessions confiscated for the benefit of the Sulṭān. Such is the case of the powerful *vazīr* Majd al-Dīn Muḥammad who amassed great riches and dislodged his former protector, 'Alīshīr Navā'ī (844–906/1441–1501), as the second most powerful man of the kingdom, but soon fell in disgrace. Upon seeing the confiscated riches of his *vazīr*, which included Chinese porcelain of the highest quality, the Timurid Sulṭān Ḥusayn Bāyqarā' (r. 873–911/1469–1506) exclaimed: "it was our expectation from Majd al-Dīn Muḥammad that should he have come across such valuable pieces he should have presented them to us."[10]

Timurid princes cherished blue-and-white ceramics, and Ulugh Beg (r. 850–3/1447–9) reputedly built a *chīnī'khānah* (porcelain house) to house his collection of Chinese porcelain.[11] The Safavids (907–1105/1501–1694) continued the tradition set by their predecessors and collected both Yuan and Ming blue-and-white. The only surviving Safavid collection of blue-and-white is the one endowed by Shāh 'Abbās I (r. 995–1038/1587–1629) to the Ardabīl Shrine where a special *chīnī'khānah* was created for its display.[12] So famous has become this endowment that a blue-and-white dish with a blurred endowment inscription, displayed in the "Romance of the Taj Mahal" exhibition at the Los Angeles County Museum of Art in 1989, and at the time of publication of this article on loan to the Brooklyn Museum, was presumed to have come from the Ardabīl Shrine collection.[13] As we shall see, it was actually part of an earlier collection gathered by the great aunt of Shāh 'Abbās I, the princess Mahīn Bānū, better known as Sulṭānum (925–69/1519–62), and endowed to the Shrine of the Eighth Shī'ite Imām Riẓā at Mashhad.

[9] An attempt to reattribute Yuan wares to the Sung period (Kessler 1993, 134–43) has been discredited among others by S. G. Valenstein (1994, 71–4), citing kiln-site archeological evidence reported in recent Chinese publications.

[10] Khvānd Amīr 1938, 415.

[11] Lentz and Lowry 1989, 229; Bābur 1996, 86.

[12] Pope 1981, pl. 4. The collection is now at the Mūzih-i Millī-i Īrān (formerly Mūzih-i Īrān-i Bāstān) in Tehran.

[13] Pal et al. 1989, 166–9.

PRINCESS SULṬĀNUM

The blue-and-white vessel in question is a very large Ming dish (43 cm. wide) of ca. 828–33/1425–30 (Fig. 1), most probably imported into Persian lands under the Timurids (771–913/1370–1507). Three inscriptions are carved on it. The first reads (Fig. 2):

Shāh Jahān ibn Jahāngīr Shāh; 16, 1053

Translation

Shāh Jahān son of Jahāngīr Shāh; 16, 1053

It is written in a fine *nasta'līq* script and gives the name of its owner, the Mughal emperor Shāh Jahān (r. 1037–68/1628–57), and the date it entered into his possession, the year 1053/1644, equivalent to his 16th regnal year. This inscription is on the outer edge of the foot-ring and visible when the dish rests on a table or a tray, while the other two are not. The second inscription is an inventory mark under the foot-ring that reads *251 tūlah* and records the weight of the dish at the time of acquisition as 2.91 kg. (Fig. 2).[14] The third inscription is carved in the form of a seal type roundel on the bottom of the dish. Strong signs of abrasion indicate that there was an unsuccessful attempt to erase it. As the initial carving was deep, the inscription (Fig. 3) can still be deciphered as follows:

Vaqf-i 'atabah-'i Raẕavīyah • 'an Mahīn Bānū-yi Ṣafavīyah

Translation

Endowed to the Raẕavī Shrine • By Mahīn Bānū, the Safavid [Princess]

The inscription is in the form of rhyming couplets that Persian rulers and dignitaries used on their seals and coinage. The Raẕavī Shrine refers to the

[14] A *tūlah* is an Indian weight measure that was used for precious items, especially herbs (see, for instance, Abū al-Faẕl ibn Mubārak 1989, 1:85); it weights 2.5 *miṡqāl* (*miṡqāl* = 4.64 g.), see Dihkhudā 1969. A similar inscription found at the bottom of a small Hung-chin (Hongzhi) bowl that once belonged to the Mughal emperor Jahāngīr Shāh (r. 1014–37/1605–27) reads: *28 tūlah, 2 māshah*, see Pope 1981, pl. 6J. Pope thought these inscriptions to indicate the day and the month of acquisition (ibid., 56–7), while they clearly indicate the bowl's weight with a precision of a 1/12th fraction of a *tūlah* known as *māshah*, see Dihkhudā 1973.

shrine of the Eighth Imām Riẕā, who is buried at Mashhad, and Mahīn Bānū Sulṭānum, who was the full sister of Shāh Ṭahmāsb (r. 930–84/1524–76).[15]

Sulṭānum is known from historical sources as a learned princess who had received instructions in fine arts, and was taught calligraphy by the scribe Dūst Muḥammad, the head of the royal library-atelier in mid-10th/16th century.[16] Specimens of her calligraphy are included in the Bahrām Mīrzā album in the Topkapı Palace Library in İstanbul.[17] She was much respected by Ṭahmāsb, and accompanied him on hunting trips, and even watched official ceremonies on horseback at his side, at a time when it was customary for royal brides and princesses to sit on a palanquin and watch from afar.[18]

When the Mughal emperor Humāyūn (r. 937–47/1530–40, 962–3/1555–6) sought asylum in Iran and help from Ṭahmāsb in 951/1544, the Shāh demanded that he convert to Shī'ism. As Humayūn refused, Ṭahmāsb grew angry and threatened to kill him. The critical situation was diffused by the intervention of Sulṭānum who persuaded her brother to assist Humāyūn in his efforts to recapture his lost throne.[19] Her role as advisor to the king became legendary and in a letter addressed to Shāh 'Abbās, one of his generals deplored the lack of wise advisors—like Sulṭānum—in the monarch's retinue.[20] Rumors about her intimate relationship with Humāyūn's trusted lieutenant, Bayram Khān, had spread in Safavid circles, even though Ṭahmāsb jealously watched over his sister and dissuaded all potential suitors by his violent reactions to any hint of amorous intent or marriage proposal.[21] As Ṭahmāsb slipped into religious bigotry, he promised the hand of his sister to the Disappeared Twelfth Imām, the Mahdī, for whose expected return a white horse was saddled every evening at the gates of the royal encampment.[22] Thus, Sulṭānum remained an unmarried woman, and consequently she endowed her considerable wealth to various shrines and pious institutions in her own lifetime. More particularly, in confirmation of the second inscription on our dish, the Safavid chronicler Qāẓī Aḥmad Qumī related that Sulṭānum endowed "her jewelry and chinaware (*chini'ālāt*)" to the Shrine of the Eighth Imām at Mashhad.[23]

[15] Ḥasan Beg Rūmlū 1979, 536.

[16] Būdāq Munshī Qazvīnī, *Javāhir al-akhbār*, State Public Library, Saint Petersburg, MS Dorn 288, dated 984/1576, fol. 110r; cf. Adle 1993, 287.

[17] Hazine 2154, fol. 7r; see also Soudavar 1992, 172, and Roxburgh 1996, 2:816, 1128–9.

[18] Gulbadan Begam [1902] 1972, 169–70, 69 (Persian section), and 1996, 114.

[19] Riazul Islam 1970, 29–37; Soudavar 1992, 172–3.

[20] Navā'ī 1987, 2:21.

[21] Soudavar 1992, 172–3.

[22] Membre 1993, 25.

[23] Qāẓī Aḥmad Qumī 1980–4, 1:431.

FROM MASHHAD TO AGRA

The Sulṭānum dish was certainly acquired by Shāh Jahān in Agra where he stayed from late Shawwāl 1052/mid January 1643 to 26 Dhū al-Qa'dah 1054/ 24 January 1645.[24] However, two questions are pertinent in respect to its transition from Mashhad to Agra: how was this dish removed from the Shrine, and why did Shāh Jahān purchase or accept a previously endowed plate in his treasury, a clear violation of the Islamic law, the *sharī'ah*?[25]

The answer to the first question is that it must have been removed from the Shrine during the period between Sulṭānum's death in 969/1562 and 1053/ 1644, the year of its acquisition by Shāh Jahān, or, more precisely, at the time of the conquest of Mashhad by the Uzbek Prince 'Abd al-Mu'min (d. 1006/ 1598) in 998/1590. Two years earlier, 'Abd al-Mu'min had accompanied his father 'Abd Allāh Khān II (r. 991–1006/1583–98) in the conquest of Harāt, and had massacred the Qizilbāsh garrison stationed there. At Mashhad, as a last ditch effort, the defeated Qizilbāsh garrison retreated within the confines of the Shrine where massacres were traditionally avoided, even by Sunnī Uzbeks. To no avail. 'Abd al-Mu'min's troops not only massacred all the Qizilbāshs and the workers of the Shrine, but looted every gold and silver object, jewel studded lamps, carpets, valuable Korans and "Chinese vessels," and subsequently traded them "for the price of cheap ceramic shards" among themselves.[26] The Uzbeks were finally driven out of Mashhad in 1007/1598. In the meantime, the looted Chinese vessels were most probably sent to Transoxiana, from where the Mughal emperors managed to acquire some, along with numerous calligraphy specimens of the celebrated calligrapher Mīr 'Alī (active first half of 10th/16th century), as well as some of the finest illustrated manuscripts (Mīr 'Alī himself was taken from Harāt to Bukhārā around 935/1529).

The answer to the second question is more problematic. Instead of trying to completely erase the endowment engraving, it seems that a few key letters within specific words (such as the "*q*" in *vaqf* and the "*f*" in *Ṣafavīyah*) were initially erased to modify their meaning. However, the result was far from

[24] Beach and Koch 1997, 11.

[25] Exceptionally, relying on the concept of *tabdīl bih aḥsan* (exchange for a better [item]) a religious scholar could allow an endowed property to be exchanged for something more useful when the usefulness of the original property was diminished, see Salīmī'fard 1991, 41–2. In our case, however, it is highly unlikely that a Safavid religious scholar would have granted permission for the "exchange" of a porcelain dish endowed by the sister of Shāh Ṭahmāsb. Furthermore, had there been a "legal exchange," the abrasion of the endowment roundel would have been unnecessary.

[26] Iskandar Munshī 1970, 1:412–3.

successful and any Mughal superintendent would have recognized the endowment nature of the inscription. The fact that the Shāh Jahān inscriptions are on the foot-ring and not on the bottom of the plate,[27] perhaps indicates that a covering attachment—be it a wooden base, a metal plate, or an extra layer of ceramic—had been added to the bottom (inside the foot-ring) to conceal its provenance; and it may well be that the otherwise unexplained clusters of small holes on the bottom of the dish (Fig. 3) were drilled for attachment of such a cover.[28]

[27] The ownership inscription of endowed vessels were carved on the outside of the footring so that subsequent alterations would be visible at all times (see, for instance, the carvings on the Ardabīl vessels, Pope 1981, pl. 6). For items of the royal treasury, however, one would think that a concealed engraving would be more proper. In the case of the two Rockefeller plates at the Asia Society in New York, the Shāh Jahān ownership inscription of one of them (1975.150) is carved on the bottom, while for the other (1975.151) it is on the outside of the foot-ring (Pal et al. 1989, 167–9).

[28] It was not possible to weigh the dish before the publication of this article. Should the dish be weighed in the future, and should its weight be lower than the inscribed 2.9 kg.—and assuming that the Shāh Jahāh measures were correct—one may then ascribe the difference to the weight of a missing bottom cover.

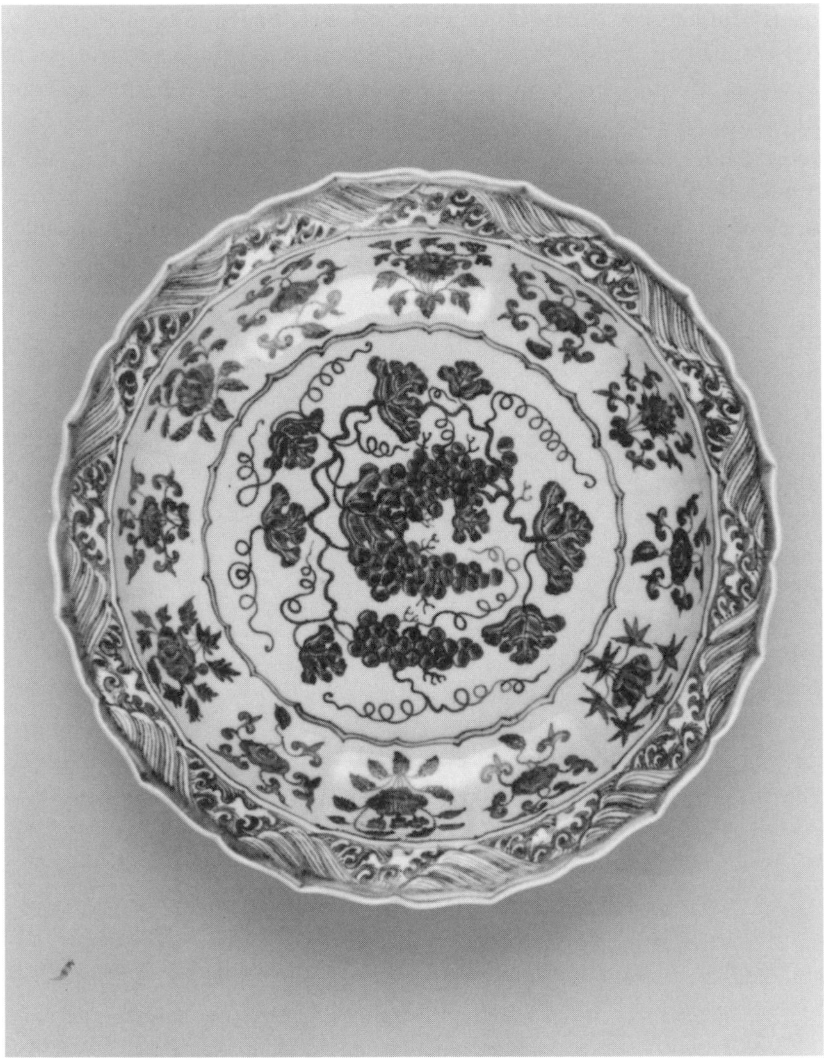

Fig. 1. Large dish with grape design. China, Xuande period (1426-35). Porcelain, underglaze cobalt blue decoration. No. L.1991.4. Anonymous loan. Brooklyn Museum of Art. Diam: 17 in. Height: 3 in. By permission of the Brooklyn Museum of Art

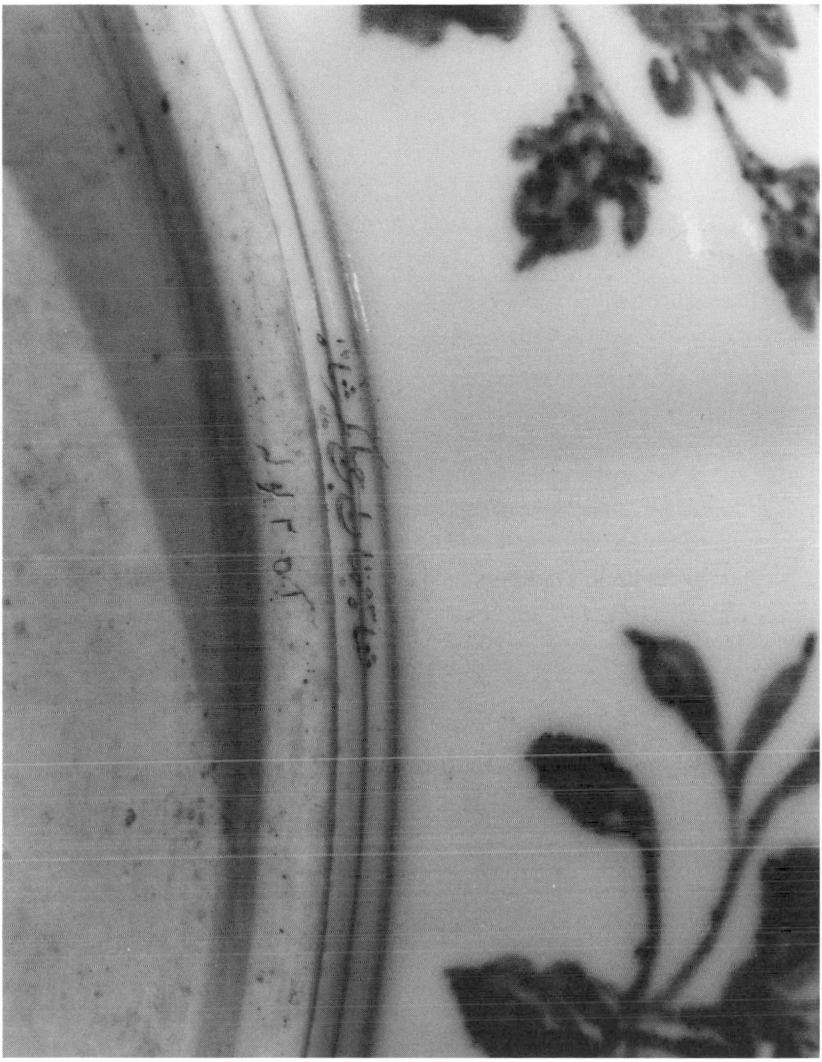

Fig. 2. Detail of the large dish. Ownership engraving of Shāh Jahān. By permission of the Brooklyn Museum of Art

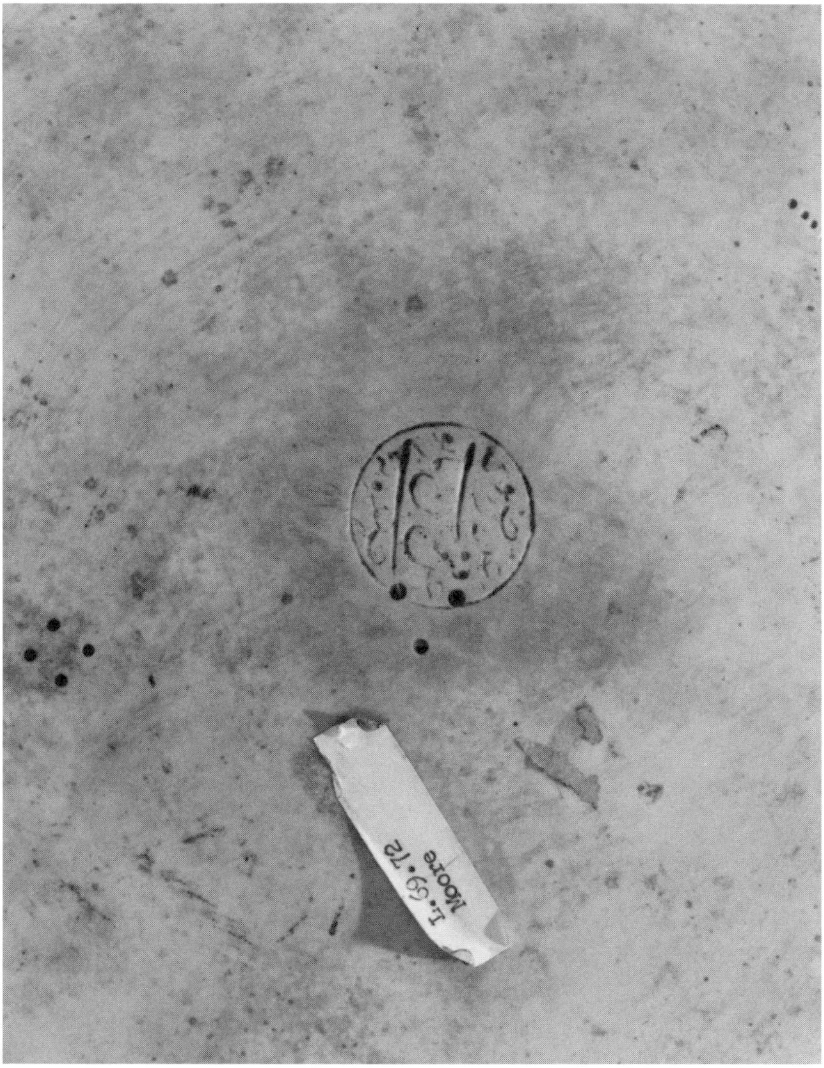

Fig. 3. Detail of the large dish. Endowment engraving of Princees Solṭānum. By permission of the Brooklyn Museum of Art

BIBLIOGRAPHY

ABŪ AL-FAẒL IBN MUBĀRAK. 1989. *The Ā'īn-i Akbarī*. Tr. H. Blochmann, H. S. Jarrett, ed. D. C. Phillott, Jadu-nath Sarker. 3 vols. in 2. Delhi : Low Price Publications.

ADLE, C. 1993. Les artistes nommés Dust-Moḥammad au XVIe siècle. *Studia Iranica* 22, no. 2: 219–96.

ATASOY, NURHAN. 1970. Four Istanbul albums and some fragments from fourteenth-century Shah-namehs. *Ars Orientalis* 8: 19–48.

BĀBUR, ẒAHĪR AL-DĪN MUḤAMMAD. 1996. *The Baburnama : memoirs of Babur, prince and emperor*. Tr., ed., & annotated by Wheeler M. Thackston. Wshington, DC : Freer Gallery of Art : Arthur M. Sackler Gallery, Smithsonian Institution; New York : Oxford University Press.

BAILEY, G. A. 1996. The Stimulus : Chinese porcelain production and trade with Iran. In *Tamerlane's tableware : a new approach to Chinoiserie ceramics of fifteenth- and sixteenth- century Iran*. Ed. Lisa Golombek, Robert B. Mason, Gauvin A. Bailey. Costa Mesa, CA : Mazda Publishers in association with Royal Ontario Museum.

BEACH, MILO CLEVELAND and KOCH, EBBA. 1997. *King of the world : the Padshahnama, an imperial Mughal manuscript from the Royal Library, Windsor Castle*. With new tr. by Wheeler Thackston. London : Azimuth Editions ; [Washington, DC] : Sackler Gallery.

CHEN DA-SHENG. 1992. Sources from Fujian on trade between China and Hurmuz in the fifteenth century. In *Timurid art and culture : Iran and Central Asia in the fifteenth century*. Ed. Lisa Golombek, Maria Subtelny. Leiden and New York : E. J. Brill.

DIHKHUDĀ, 'ALĪ AKBAR. 1969. *Lughat'nāmah*. Fascicle 148. Tehran : Sāzmān-i Lughat'nāmah, Isfand 1347 Sh.: 1140.

—— 1973. *Lughat'nāmah*. Fascicle 195. Tehran : Sāzmān-i Lughat'nāmah, 1352 Sh.: 68.

GRAY, BASIL, ed. 1979. *The arts of the book in Central Asia : 14th–16th centuries*. Boulder, Colorado : Shambhala : UNESCO.

GULBADAN BEGAM. [1902] 1974. *Humāyūn-nāma : (the history of Humāyūn)*. Tr., introd. & notes by Annette S. Beveridge. Reprint, Lahore : Sang-e-Meel Publications.

—— 1996. *Le Livre de Humâyûn*. Tr. Pierre Piffaretti, ed. Jean-Louis Bacqué-Grammont. Paris : Gallimard : UNESCO.

ḤASAN BEG RŪMLŪ. 1979. *Aḥsan al-tavārīkh*. Ed. 'Abd al-Ḥusayn Navā'ī. Tehran : Bābak, Isfand 1357 Sh.

IBN BAṬŪṬAH. 1853–8. *Voyages d'Ibn Battuta : texte arabe, accompagné d'une traduction*. Tr. C. Defrémery and B. R. Sanguinetti. 4 vols. Paris : Impr. nationale.

ISKANDAR MUNSHĪ. 1971. *Tārīkh-i 'ālam'ārā-yi 'Abbāsī*. 2nd ed. Ed. Iraj Afshar. 2 vols. Tehran : Amīr Kabīr ; Iṣfahān : Kitābfurūshī-i Ta'yīd, 1370 Sh.

KESSLER, ADAM T. 1993. *Empires beyond the Great Wall : the heritage of Genghis Khan*. Los Angeles : Natural History Museum of Los Angeles County.

KHVĀND AMĪR. 1938. *Dastūr al-vuzarā' : shāmil-i aḥvāl-i vuzarā-yi Islām tā inqirāẕ-i Tīmūriyān, 914*. Ed. Sa'īd Nafīsī. Tehran : Kitābfurūshī va Chāpkhānah-'i Iqbāl, 1317 Sh.

LENTZ, THOMAS W. and LOWRY, GLENN D. 1989. *Timur and the princely vision : Persian art and culture in the fifteenth century*. Los Angeles : Los Angeles County Museum of Art ; Washington, DC : Arthur M. Sackler Gallery.

MEDLEY, MARGARET. 1975. Islam, Chinese porcelain and Ardabīl. *Iran* 8: 31–7.

MEMBRÉ, MICHELE. 1993. *Mission to the Lord Sophy of Persia, (1539–1542)*. Tr., introd. & notes by A. H. Morton. London : School of Oriental and African Studies, University of London.

NAVĀ'Ī, 'ABD AL-ḤUSAYN, ed. 1987. *Shāh 'Abbās : majmū'ah-i asnād va mukātibāt-i tārīkhī hamrāh bā yāddāshthā-yi tafṣīlī*. 2nd ed. 3 vols. in 2. Tehran : Zarrīn, 1366 Sh.

PAL, PRATAPADITYA et al. 1989. *Romance of the Taj Mahal*. London : Thames and Hudson Ltd. ; Los Angeles : Los Angeles County Museum of Art.

PELLIOT, PAUL. 1959–73. *Notes on Marco Polo*. 3 vols. Paris : Impr. nationale.

POPE, JOHN ALEXANDER. 1981. *Chinese porcelains from the Ardebil shrine*. 2nd ed. London : [Published for] Sotheby Parke Bernet by Philip Wilson ; Totowa, NJ : Biblio Distribution Centre.

QĀẒĪ AḤMAD QUMĪ. 1980–4. *Khulāṣat al-tavārīkh*. Ed. Iḥsān Ishrāqī. 2 vols. Tehran : Dānishgāh-i Tihrān, 1359–63 Sh.

RASHĪD AL-DĪN FAẒL ALLĀH. 1980. *Savāniḥ al-afkār-i Rashīdī*. Ed. Muḥammad Taqī Dānish'pizhūh. Tehran : Kitābkhānah-'i Markazī va Markaz-i Asnād[-i Dānishgāh-i Tihrān], Isfand 1358 Sh.

RIAZUL ISLAM. 1970. *Indo-Persian relations : a study of the political and diplomatic relations between the Mughul Empire and Iran*. Teheran : Iranian Culture Foundation.

ROXBURGH, DAVID J. 1996. *"Our works point to us" : album making, collecting, and art (1427–1565) under the Timurids and Safavids*. 2 vols. Ph.D. diss. University of Pennsylvania.

SALĪMĪ'FARD, MUṢTAFÁ. 1991. *Nigāhī bih Vaqf va āṡār-i iqtiṣādī-ijtimā'ī-i ān*. Mashhad : Bunyād-i Pizhūhishhā-yi Islāmī, Āstān-i Quds-i Raẕavī, 1370 Sh.

SOUDAVAR, ABOLALA. 1992. *Art of the Persian courts : selections from the Art and History Trust Collection*. New York : Rizzoli.

—— 1996. *The Saga of Abu-Sa'id Bahādor Khān : the Abu-Sa'idnāmé*. In *The court of the Il-khans, 1290–1340*. Ed. Julian Raby, Teresa Fitzherbert. Oxford : Oxford University Press, 95–218.

VALENSTEIN, SUZANNE G. 1994. Concerning a reattribution of some Chinese ceramics. *Orientations* 25, no. 12 (December): 71–4.

Texts, Inscriptions, and the Ardabīl Carpets

Sheila S. Blair

IRAJ AFSHAR IS WELL-KNOWN TO ALL STUDENTS AND scholars of Iranian studies as a masterful historian who has edited and published a wide variety of medieval texts. One of his many interests is the use of specialized terminology, particularly that concerning art and architecture. A good example of his methodology is his recent study of the flat-woven carpets known as *zīlū*.[1] He began by collecting citations in written sources, including early geographies, histories, literary texts and dictionaries, and then matched that textual information with extant fragments which survive from the 10th/16th century. In homage to this historian and his method, I offer this short article on a related topic, Safavid pile carpets, particularly the matched pair known as the Ardabīl carpets, to show how texts and inscriptions can help us understand the meaning and use of works of art.

The two Ardabīl carpets are the most famous Safavid carpets. There is a well-preserved one acquired by the Victoria and Albert Museum, London in 1893 (inv. no. 272-1893), and a patched one presented by J. Paul Getty to the Los Angeles County Museum of Art in 1953 (inv. no. 53.50.2) (Fig. 1).[2] Neither carpet is complete. The London carpet is bigger (it now measures 10.5 by 5.3 meters, or 34.5 by 17.5 feet), than the Los Angeles carpet, which has been drastically shortened and lost its outer border (it now measures 7.3 by 4.1 meters, or 23.1 by 13.5 feet).[3]

[1] Afshar 1992.

[2] The basic publication of the Los Angeles carpet is Stead 1974; the most up-to-date information about the pair is summarized in Beattie 1986. More recent articles include Ittig 1993, Wearden 1995, and King 1996.

[3] Kambiz Eslami kindly brought my attention to an article in the newspaper *Iran Times* (vol. xxvii, no. 17 for Friday, July 11, 1997) about a third Ardabīl carpet. A similar story was published in the newspaper *Iṭṭilāʻāt* from July 2, 1997. According to the stories (whose details differ slightly), this carpet had been exported from Iran during the Persian Gulf War and bought by a British collector. Iranian authorities successfully reclaimed the carpet on the grounds that it had been exported illegally, and it is to go on display in the Carpet Museum (*Mūzih-i Farsh*) in Tehran. From the photographs in *Iran Times* and *Iṭṭilāʻāt*, the carpet has the same design as the matched pair of Ardabīl carpets in London and Los Angeles and approximately the same dimensions (52 square meters). Technical examination is necessary to verify its authenticity, for this third carpet is without provenance.

Both carpets show the same design. The field contains a central sunburst surrounded by sixteen pendants, with two mosque lamps hanging from the pendants on the longitudinal axis. Each corner of the field repeats a quarter of the central composition. Worked in ten colors—black, three blues, green, three reds, white, and yellow—these elements seem to float above a deep blue ground strewn with arabesques. A cartouche at one end of each carpet contains a poetic couplet, followed by the signature *'amal-i bandah-i dargāh Maqṣūd Kāshānī, sanah-i 946*, that is, "work of a servant of the court, Maqṣūd of Kashān, [in] the year 946," which corresponds to 1539–40.

Both carpets are knotted in wool on silk warps and wefts; three shoots of two-stranded silk follow each row of asymmetrical knots. The two carpets are said to differ, however, in knot count, texture, and pile length.[4] The London carpet has fewer knots per square centimeter (46 vs. 62, or 324 vs. 400 knots per square inch) and its pile is reportedly harsher, shorter, stronger and more densely packed than that of the Los Angeles one, which is described as silkier, softer and longer.

Since they were brought to the West, these huge medallion carpets have been the subject of a continuing stream of publications, many of which deal with their history and their common name, the Ardabīl carpets. Both carpets were acquired in the late 19th century from the London firm of Vincent Robinson and Co. The London firm, in turn, had supposedly acquired them from the Manchester firm of Ziegler and Co., which reported that the carpets had come from the shrine at Ardabīl in northwestern Iran. This was the shrine for the Ṣūfī Shaykh Ṣafī al-Dīn (d. 735/1334), the eponymous founder of the Safavid dynasty, rulers of Iran from 907/1501 to 1105/1694.

The attribution to Ardabīl was generally accepted, and 19th-century travellers' reports lent weight to this attribution. Most noteworthy was the evidence left by two English travelers who visited Ardabīl in 1843. In describing the shrine, William Richard Holmes mentioned the remnants of a once magnificent carpet bearing a date of manufacture of some 300 years earlier. It lay on the floor of the lofty antechamber to the principal tombs.[5] Holmes' published account was corroborated by notes left by his traveling companion, Keith Edward Abbott, the British council in Tabrīz. He specifically mentioned the date, writing that "In the apartment devoted to prayer there is a carpet bearing the date 946 of the Hejira woven in with the pattern—as it is now the

[4] Stead 1974, 17–8. This information needs to be confirmed by technical examinination of the two carpets side by side.

[5] Holmes account, (1845, 37–8), is cited in Weaver 1984, 49, footnote no. 17; Beattie 1987, 367b; Ittig 1993, 82–3, footnote no. 18; and King 1996, 91, footnote no. 14.

1259th year of that era the carpet must have been manufactured 313 lunar years ago."[6]

Despite the general acceptance of the name "Ardabīl carpets," however, doubts about their provenance quickly arose. It was recognized that dealers often put forward an attribution to a famous place to enhance the pedigree of their wares and thus increase their sale value. Scholars added dissenting voices based on other evidence. A. H. Morton, for example, pointed out that the carpets were not recognizable in an inventory compiled by the superintendent (*mutavallī*) of the Ardabīl shrine in 1172/1759.[7] Martin Weaver, following a detailed survey of the shrine in 1969 and 1970, noted that the London carpet was larger than most of the rooms at the shrine, such as the main prayer hall known as the *Dār al-Ḥuffāẓ* (8.9 by 5.8 meters) or the *chīnī'khānah* (porcelain house; 9.7 meters square).[8]

These questions raised sufficient doubts that alternative provenances for the two carpets were suggested. One was the shrine of Imām Riẕā at Mashhad in eastern Iran. It too had been restored in the Safavid period, and several rooms there were large enough to accommodate the two carpets. In her review of the carpets' history, May Beattie concluded that the question of provenance was intractable: since valuable historical information had been distorted and lost in the tangled web of the carpet trade, further speculation was fruitless.[9]

Two further analyses of the carpets by scholars at the Victoria and Albert Museum in the 1990s, however, suggested that the carpets themselves might add further information to the argument. Jennifer Wearden analyzed the design and repairs to the London carpet.[10] She identified the three steps in laying out the design. The designer first set out the central medallion, the corner medallions, and the two lamps. He then traced a swirling pattern of tightly

[6] Abbott's notes are in the Public Office in London (FO251/40), cited in Weaver 1984, 49; Ittig 1993, 83, footnote no. 19; and King 1996, 91, footnote no. 14.

[7] Beattie, Housego, and Morton 1977, 470–1; cf. *Ganjīnah-'i Shaykh Ṣafī* 1969, 76–7. King (1996, 91, footnote no. 16), showed, however, that the carpets were on the list as item B8 (i.e., *Qālīchah kih az qālīhā-yi buzurg-i mundaris baqi mandah, 4 pārchah = Rugs which are remnants of large, tattered carpets, 4 pieces*), but since they had been cut down to fit other rooms in the shrine, they were listed as four pieces of large carpets.

[8] Noted in Morton 1974–5, pt. 1, 31–2 and summarized in Weaver, 1984. Weaver did note that the only room at the shrine big enough to contain the carpets was the octagonal building known as the *Jannat Sarāy*, but argued that placing the carpets side by side there would have left four areas of floor uncovered on the four sides. This part of his argument was often over-looked and he was quoted as saying that no room at the Ardabil shrine was large enough to contain the carpets.

[9] Beattie 1986, 368a.

[10] Wearden 1995.

coiled leafy stems. These thin stems, executed in yellow green, bear a mixture of naturalistic and composite blossoms. On top of this, the designer placed a second pattern of swirling leafy stems. This second set of stems, which are thicker and less densely packed and executed in reddish brown, bears only palmette blossoms.

Wearden's technical examination also showed that the designer had made subtle adjustments when weaving the design so that the upper half of the carpet (the end with the inscription) was slightly different from the lower half (the end without the inscription). The mosque lamp in the upper half, for example, is slightly longer than that in the lower half. To judge from photographs, the oval pendants in the top half are also larger. This alteration in scale seems to have been intentional, probably done to create an optical illusion so that the two lamps and pendants would appear the same size when viewed from the bottom end. Masons used the same technique when building minarets: the bands at the top are usually wider and in higher relief than those at the bottom, so that they appear the same size to the viewer standing on the ground.

Wearden also identified seven areas where the London carpet had been repaired, using pieces from the second carpet in Los Angeles. The most significant repair was to the lower border where some 13 centimeters (5 inches) of the field was missing. Based on the areas of repairs, she estimated that the carpet had originally measured approximately 10.67 meters (or some 35 feet long) and therefore that the width was one-half the original length.

Donald King then matched Wearden's data on the design and repairs of the London carpet to the history of the shrine at Ardabīl, arguing that the well-known attribution to Ardabīl was correct.[11] He noted that the two carpets, when laid side by side, would have formed a square some 10.67 meters on a side and would have fit perfectly within the *Jannat Sarāy* at Ardabīl. To judge from the plan reproduced in Morton,[12] this domed hall measures over 16 meters in diameter and can comfortably accommodate the two carpets.[13]

King's attribution of the large medallion carpets to the hall known as the *Jannat Sarāy* with the shrine at Ardabīl is correct, and to the evidence of design and repairs to the carpets, we can add the evidence of the writing on them. The cartouche at the top end of each carpet contains the opening distich from a *ghazal* by the 8th/14th-century lyricist Ḥāfiẓ:

[11] King 1996.

[12] Morton 1974–5, pt. 1, 48.

[13] King (1997) also summarized his argument in a letter to the editors of *Hali*, accompanied by a new plan of the shrine in which he corrected the scale of the carpets as shown in the *Jannat Sarāy*.

Juz āstān-i tū'am dar jahān panāhī nīst
sar-i marā bi-juz īn dar ḥawālah'gāhī nīst[14]

Translation

Other than thy threshold I have no refuge in the world
My head has no resting place other than this doorway.

The inscription in the cartouche was meant to be read and appreciated by someone seated on the carpets, for the text is written facing upwards at the top. The cartouche provides direction to a design that might otherwise seem symmetrical and confirms Wearden's suggestion, made on the basis of the design, that the carpets were meant to be viewed from the lower side.

Furthermore, virtually every noun in the verse has, in addition to its meaning in the poem, an association with the shrine at Ardabīl and specifically the *Jannat Sarāy*. The distich opens with the noun *āstān*, literally threshold and the common Persian word for shrine.[15] The opening words of the couplet immediately situate the reader sitting on the carpet in his current context as visitor to a shrine. Such shrines often accorded sanctuary or asylum (*bast*). The first shrine to be so recognized was precisely the one in which the carpets lay: that of Shaykh Ṣafī at Ardabīl. Tīmūr granted this right as a boon to Khvājah 'Alī, Shaykh Ṣafī's grandson and chief Shaykh at the shrine, in 806/1404.[16]

The second line of the distich on the carpets relates not just generally to the shrine at Ardabīl but specifically to the *Jannat Sarāy*. To parallel the threshold (*āstān*) and refuge (*panāh*) mentioned in the first line, Ḥāfiẓ juxtaposed doorway (*dar*) and resting place (*ḥawālah'gāh*). The doorway is further specified by the adjective "this" (*īn*), so the person reading the poem while seated on the carpet in the *Jannat Sarāy* could immediately take the phrase "this doorway" as a direct reference to his actual situation in front of the main doorway leading from the *Jannat Sarāy* to the courtyard.

Similarly, the reader could interpret the resting place (*ḥawālah'gāh*) as an allusion to the room's function as the intended resting-place of Shāh Ṭahmāsb (r. 930–84/1524–76), the Safavid Shāh who substantially enlarged the shrine in the 10th/16th century. Morton first identified the *Jannat Sarāy* as Ṭahmāsb's tomb in his lengthy and thorough analysis of the shrine based on the description in the *Ṣarīh al-milk*, the list of properties owned by the shrine

[14] Ḥāfiẓ 1994, 155, no. 75.

[15] The shrine for Imām Riẓā at Mashhad, for example, is properly known as the Āstān-i Quds-i Raẓavī; see Mawlawī, Moṣṭafawī and Šakūrzāda 1987.

[16] Calmard 1989. For the description of Tīmūr's granting this boon, see Appendix II in Minorsky's translation of the *Tadhkirat al-muluk* (1943, 189–95).

drawn up on 1 Shawwāl 977/9 March 1570.[17] The term used there for the *Jannat Sarāy* is *maqṣūrah*, often used to describe part of a mosque, and indeed Morton found evidence that the *Jannat Sarāy* was later used as a mosque. On formal grounds, however, he rightly rejected the original designation of the *Jannat Sarāy* as a mosque, for the building is octagonal, and the center of the *qiblah* wall is filled not by a prayer niche but by a doorway. Rather, he argued, the octagonal shape suggested that the large room must have been designed for some ritual function special to dervishes or as a tomb. Had it been a tomb, its huge size suggested that it was meant for Ṭahmāsb.[18]

Robert Hillenbrand's architectural analysis of the *Jannat Sarāy* underscores its function as a tomb.[19] The single largest building on the site, it represented an unusually munificent effort on the part of the patron. Furthermore, it occupies a commanding position at one end of the great inner courtyard. The octagonal hall also fits within the tradition of domed octagonal mausolea in Iran, beginning with the monumental tomb of the Mongol Sulṭān Ūljāytū at Sulṭānīyah, in which a spacious two-story interior was opened with eight niches. At Ardabīl the architect worked to open the exterior as well, with deep external bays that invite entry into the building, and this idea of opening up the octagon became a trend in Safavid funerary architecture.

Though a tomb, the *Jannat Sarāy* was undoubtedly used for prayer as well, as shown by the noun opening the second line of Ḥāfiẓ's couplet on the carpets: *sar-i marā* (my head). Anyone praying on the carpets within the *Jannat Sarāy* would face the couplet and the doorway beyond, which opens to the southwest and the *qiblah*. While bowing in prayer, his forehead would touch the carpet, a realization of the reference in the verse to the resting place of his head.

Along with layout and design, the inscription, then, confirms that the Ardabīl carpets were made for use as prayer carpets. The designation of these carpets for a religious setting differentiates them from other contemporary carpets, such as a medallion carpet with hunting scenes in Milan.[20] Although smaller than the Ardabīl pair (it measures 5.7 by 3.65 meters) and different in style, the hunting carpet is equally splendid in technique, design and execution. The design shows a red medallion in the center filled with cranes and cloud bands. The medallion is surrounded by a lively hunting scene, in which

[17] Morton 1974–5, pt. 2, 42–3.

[18] Although he was actually buried at Mashhad.

[19] Hillenbrand 1986, 771.

[20] Milan, Poldi Pezzoli Museum, no. 154, see *Arts of Islam* 1976, 98, no. 58 and color plate no. 60.

figures wearing the distinctive Safavid turban fight lions, deer, and other animals set against a dark blue ground.

In addition to the figural motifs, the design makes the hunting carpet inappropriate for a religious setting. Like the Ardabīl carpets, the hunting carpet is designed so that each corner is a repeat of the other three. In this case, however, the carpet is not meant to be seen from one end but from the center, for the design is laid out in radiating tiers of animals, figures, and other motifs. The centrifugal design of the hunting carpet is emphasized by the cartouche in the center with the name of the designer, Ghiyās̱ al-Dīn Jāmī, and the date 949 [1542–3]. The location of the signature is not a sign of the artist's hubris, but of his humility, for the king would have sat enthroned in the center of the carpet, viewing the radiating tiers of decoration. The artist's signature would have been literally under the king's foot.

A similarly placed signature can be seen in a contemporary painting showing "The celebration of *'Īd*" (Fig. 2). The painting has been detached from a celebrated manuscript containing the collected poems of Ḥāfiẓ, probably made for Ṭahmāsb and then given to his brother Sām Mīrzā.[21] The two couplets inscribed in cartouches along the parapet of the palace describe the festivities of *'Īd-i Fiṭr*, the celebration marking the breaking of the fast during Ramaḍan. After sighting the new moon, participants are encouraged to look upon a beautiful face to ensure good luck in the month to come. In the poem, Ḥāfiẓ encourages viewers to behold the new moon in the king's face, a clever conceit praising the ruler.

The painting depicts the celebration. Three courtiers on the roof top await the new moon. Other courtiers below gaze upon the enthroned monarch, intended to represent the reigning Safavid Shāh Ṭahmāsb, whose name and titles were once inscribed above the door.[22] The artist signed his work in a cartouche at the base of the throne, *'amal-i Sulṭān Muḥammad 'Irāqī*, "the work of Sulṭān Muḥmammad of 'Irāq." The artist was lauded by Dūst Muḥammad, the Safavid court librarian and chronicler, as the master of his age and the

[21] Once in the Cartier collection, this magnificent manuscript has recently been cut up and the pages dispersed. This page in the Art and History Trust Collection is now on loan to the Sackler Gallery in Washington DC, see Soudavar 1992, 159–61, no. 59. Soudavar (1997, 54–60) and Soucek (1990, 58–69) give slightly different interpretations to the manuscript based on the various signatures, inscriptions and styles of painting.

[22] The inscription over the doorway now reads: *al-Hādī Abū al-Muẓaffar Sām Mīrzā* (the guide, the victorious Sām Mīrzā), but the title *Abū al-Muẓaffar* was reserved for Ṭahmāsb and the hastily written text was probably substituted for the original when the book was given to Sām Mīrzā.

foremost painter in Ṭahmāsb's studio.[23] The location of Sulṭān Muḥammad's signature shows his subservience to Ṭahmāsb: like Ghiyāṣ al-Dīn Jāmī's signature on the hunting carpet, Sulṭān Muḥammad's signature on the throne puts the artist's name literally under the ruler's feet. Ḥāfiẓ's poem was a clever encomium eulogizing his patron, the Muzaffarid ruler Shāh Shujā', and similarly Sulṭān Muḥammad's signature on the painting is a clever visual conceit connecting the painter with his patron, Shāh Ṭahmāsb.

Such witty allusions, both written and visual, clearly delighted the Safavid audience. Thus, an illustration to a manuscript of Ḥāfiẓ's poems made for Ṭahmāsb shows a carpet that resembles contemporary ones, for the design of the carpet in the painting, with an arabesque scroll sprouting peonies and other flowers, recalls that of the Ardabīl carpets. In the same vein, contemporary carpets were decorated with a couplet from Ḥāfiẓ that puns on their place and function. These examples show how fruitful it can be to match texts, inscriptions and objects. Objects, like texts, are valuable historical documents which can help us reconstruct political and social settings. And texts, in turn, can help us explain the function and meaning of objects. It is to the credit of Iraj Afshar that he appreciated both sides of the question.

[23] Dūst Muḥammad's celebrated account of past and present scribes and painters, written in 951/1544 as the preface to the album he prepared for Ṭahmāsb's brother Bahrām Mīrzā (İstanbul, Tokapı Palace Library, Hazine 2154) has been translated by Thackston (1989, 335–50).

Fig. 1. The Ardabil carpet. Iran, 946/1540. Wool and silk. No. 53.50.2. Gift of J. Paul Getty. Los Angeles County Museum of Art. 23 1/2 x 13 feet = 716.3 x 396.2 cm. By permission of the Los Angeles County Museum of Art

Fig. 2. The celebration of *'Īd*. By Sulṭān Muḥmammad. Circa 933/1527. Art and History Trust Collection, Houston, Texas. On loan to the Sackler Gallery, Washington, DC. 20 x 15 cm.

BIBLIOGRAPHY

AFSHAR, IRAJ. 1992. Zīlū. *Iranian studies* 25, nos. 1–2: 31–6.

Arts of Islam : Hayward Gallery, 8 April – 4 July 1976. 1976. London: Arts Council of Great Britain.

BEATTIE, M. 1987. Ardabīl carpets. *Encyclopaedia Iranica*. Vol. 2. London and New York : Routledge & Kegan Paul: 365b–8b.

BEATTIE, MAY, HOUSEGO, JENNY, and MORTON, A. H. 1977. Vase-technique carpets and Kirman. *Oriental art* 23, no. 4 (winter): 455–71.

CALMARD, J. 1989. Bast. *Encyclopaedia Iranica*. Vol. 3. London and New York : Routledge & Kegan Paul: 856a–8b.

Ganjīnah-'i Shaykh Ṣafī. 1969. Tabrīz : Kitābkhānah-'i Millī-i Tabrīz, 1348 Sh.

ḤĀFIẒ. 1994. *Ḥāfiẓ*. Ed. Sāyah. Tehran : Tūs, Chashm va Charagh, 1373 Sh.

HILLENBRAND, ROBERT. 1986. Safavid Architecture. In *Cambridge history of Iran*. Vol. 6. Ed. Peter Jackson, Laurence Lockhart. Cambridge [Cambridgeshire] : Cambridge University Press: 759–842.

HOLMES, WILLIAM RICHARD. 1845. *Sketches on the shores of the Caspian : descriptive and pictorial*. London : Richard Bentley.

ITTIG, ANNETTE. 1993. Historian's choice : the Victoria & Albert Museum's 'Ardabil' carpet. *Hali* 69 (June/July): 81–3.

KING, DONALD. 1996. The Ardabil puzzle unravelled. *Hali* 88 (September): 88–92.

—— 1997. Missing pieces. *Hali* 90 (January): 51.

MAWLAWĪ, 'A.-Ḥ., MOṢṬAFAWĪ, and ŠAKŪRZĀDA, E. 1987. Āstān-e Qods-e Rażawī. *Encyclopaedia Iranica*. Vol. 2. London and New York : Routledge & Kegan Paul: 826b–37a.

MINORSKY, V., tr. 1943. *Tadhkirat al-mulak : a manual of Ṣafavid administration (circa 1137/1725) : Persian text in facsimile (B.M. Or. 9496)*. London : E. J. W. Gibb Memorial : Luzac & Co.

MORTON, A. H. 1974–5. The Ardabīl shrine in the reign of Shāh Ṭahmāsp I. *Iran* 12: 31–64 and 13: 39–58.

SOUCEK, PRISCILLA. 1990. Sultan Muhammad Tabrizi : painter at the Safavid court. In *Persian masters : five centuries of painting*. Ed. Sheila R. Canby. Bombay : Marg Publications: 55–70.

SOUDAVAR, ABOLALA. 1992. *Art of the Persian courts : selections from the Art and History Trust Collection*. New York : Rizzoli.

—— 1997. "Tawṭi'ah-'i 'uẓmá" va Abū al-Muẓaffar Shāh Ṭahmāsb Ṣafavī. *Īrān'shināsī* 9, no. 1 (bahār 1376 Sh.): 51–79.

STEAD, REXFORD. 1974. *The Ardabil carpets*. Malibu : The J. Paul Getty Museum.

THACKSTON, W. M., tr. 1989. *A century of princes : sources on Timurid history and art*. Cambridge, Massachusetts : The Aga Khan Program for Islamic Architecture.

WEARDEN, JENNIFER. 1995. The Ardabil carpet : the early repairs. *Hali* 80 (April/May): 102–7.

WEAVER, MARTIN E. 1984. The Ardabīl puzzle. *The Textile Museum journal* 23: 43–51.

Iran's Ottoman Diplomacy During the Reign of Shāh Sulaymān I (1077–1105/1666–94)

Rudi Matthee *

THE PEACE OF ZUHĀB (OR QAṢR-I SHĪRĪN), CONCLUDED IN 1049/1639 between Safavid Iran and the Ottoman Empire, must be considered a watershed in Safavid military, commercial and diplomatic history. Concluding almost a century and a half of hostilities between two archenemies, the accord obviated the need for either state to be prepared for imminent war in Āẕarbāyjān and Mesopotamia. Although it would be a mistake to see the peace as the *beginning* of a weakened fighting spirit among the Iranians and the root cause of the ineffectiveness and disintegration of the Safavid war machine, it certainly contributed to a long-term process of diminishing military alertness. Less readily recognized are the commercial repercussions of the relaxation of tension following the agreement. Zuhāb contained a clause that enjoined both states to allow merchants to pass unhindered through each other's territory, and henceforth trade between Iran and the Levantine ports across Anatolia and Mesopotamia was conducted in greater security and without the frequent interruptions that had plagued caravan traffic during the height of the wars between the Safavids and Ottomans.[1] The peace, finally, proved to

*An earlier version of this paper was presented at the Third Conference of the European Society of Iranian Studies, Cambridge, U. K., September 1995. I would like to thank Drs. Paola Orsatti and Angelo Piemontese for checking my transcription of the Italian texts, and Drs. Maurizio Pistoso and Anna Vanzan for clarifying some problems with the translation.

[1] For various versions of the Turkish text of the treaty, see Vaḥīd Qazvīnī 1951, 50–4; Muhandis Bāshī 1969, 74–7; I'timād al-Salṭanah 1984–8, 2:940–3; Navā'ī 1981, 39–42; and Iskandar Munshī and Vālah Iṣfahānī 1938, 223–7. Persian versions are included in Navā'ī 1981, 35–8; Vaḥīd Māzandarānī 1971, 81–2; Muhandis Bāshī 1969, 77–81; Iskandar Munshī and Vālah Iṣfahānī 1938, 220–3; Feridun Beg 1858, 2:299–301. For various copies of the text of the treaty in manuscript form, see Dānish'pizhūh 1985. An English version of the Turkish and some relevant passages appear in Edmonds 1957, 125–7. A good discussion of the terms of the treaty can be found in Braun 1969, 22, 37–41. Further discussions concerning merchants (and Iranian pilgrims passing through Ottoman territory) were held during the visit of an Ottoman embassy to Iṣfahān in 1657/1067–8. In exchange for a twenty-year truce, the Ottomans were said to have been willing to agree to Safavid requests for the lightening of tolls imposed on Iranian pilgrims to Mecca, and for a provision that would allow descendants of Iranian merchants who died on Ottoman soil to inherit their goods and capital, see Algemeen Rijksarchief, The Hague, VOC 1229, J. Willemsz., Gamron, to Heren xvii, 30 November 1657, fol. 834.

be remarkably durable: it was to last until the 1720s, when the eclipse of Safavid authority impelled the Ottomans to join the Russians in occupying parts of northern Iran. Its legacy, in fact, endures until today, since the boundaries it stipulated were, with minor adjustments, reaffirmed in all subsequent border arrangements between Iran and the Ottoman Empire, and indeed, continue to demarcate the borders between modern Iran, Iraq and Turkey.[2]

The peace accord signed, both parties scrupulously adhered to its terms, confirming its status and verifying future peaceful intentions through diplomatic exchange. In the period from 1050/1640 to 1072/1662 the Ottomans and Safavids thus each sent four missions to each other's capitals.[3] In the following three decades, this exchange continued, albeit on a reduced level. Aside from the congratulatory Ottoman and Safavid missions of 1078/1667 and 1103/1691, respectively, the Ottomans only seem to have dispatched envoys to Iṣfahān in 1095–7/1684–5, years in which new crises threatened to disrupt the peace once again. The Iranians, in turn, do not seem to have reciprocated with a substantive embassy in this period.[4]

A paucity of published sources from within the Ottoman and Safavid state systems in the later 17th century makes it exceedingly difficult to draw definitive conclusions about the motivations of both states in their mutual pacifism. Pending another installment in Bekir Kütükoğlu's publications on Ottoman-Safavid relations in the 17th century, the Ottoman diplomatic record beyond 1021/1612 is limited to a few scattered letters and thus remains rather unclear.[5] As for Iran, the available court chronicles do not provide us with much information between 1074/1663–4, the last year covered in the *'Abbāsnāmah*, and 1105/1693, the first year narrated in the *Dastūr-i shahriyārān*.[6] The information contained in these and other Persian-language

[2] For the continuation of Ottoman-Safavid diplomatic relations in the 18th century, see Tucker 1996.

[3] Braun 1969, 42. The information in Braun's study is mostly based on Muḥammad Ṭāhir Vaḥīd Qazvīnī's *'Abbāsnāmah* (Vaḥīd Qazvīnī 1951); see also Ṣābitiyān 1964, 342–4.

[4] See I'timād al-Salṭanah 1984–8, 2:994–5; Riyāḥī 1989, 43–4. Diminished Iranian diplomatic activity following the cessation of Safavid-Ottoman hostilities is also reflected in the leveling off of contact with Russia in this period, see Matthee 1993. For the 1095–7/1684–5 Ottoman mission, see infra.

[5] Kütükoğlu has thus far published two studies of diplomatic relations between the two powers, the second of which (an expanded version of the first) goes up to 1612, see Kütükoğlu 1962 and 1993; see also Saray 1990, 45–7. In addition, a few letters written to Safavid rulers by Sulṭâns Meḥmed IV and Aḥmed II appear in Navā'ī 1981, 203–5, 250–7, and 271–7.

[6] See Naṣīrī 1994. Two letters sent to the Porte by Shāh Sulaymān and his grand *vazīr*, Muḥammad Ṭāhir Vaḥīd Qazvīnī, in the early 1690s, appear in Navā'ī 1981, 278, 280–1.

sources generally concerns the factual exchange of embassies and missions and fails to throw much light on their mandates and objectives. In the absence of Safavid archival repositories of Ottoman-Safavid diplomatic correspondence, we are therefore unable to probe Iranian objectives and intentions from within.

Even without explicit documentation, it is easy to see what motivated the Ottomans to abstain from further aggression and conquest in the east. Baghdād, the city over which the two powers had fought many wars and which had frequently changed hands in the course of time, had definitely fallen under Ottoman control in 1048/1638. Sulṭân İbrâhîm I (r. 1049–58/1640–8) is said to have shown himself content with the extent of Ottoman eastward expansion after the reconquest of the city. The Janissaries presumably lost interest in Iran after fighting a series of inglorious and unrewarding wars in Armenia. The Ottoman state, meanwhile, experienced a period of disarray following the execution of the grand *vezir*, Kemânkeş Ḳarâ Muṣṭafâ Paşa, in 1053/1644. For the next twelve years, İstanbul witnessed the rapid succession of no fewer than eighteen grand *vezir*s, four of whom were executed and eleven of whom were dismissed.[7] As importantly, the Ottomans in the same period were distracted by military developments on their western borders. In the 1640s their attention shifted toward the Mediterranean, where they became entangled in a prolonged conflict with Venice, known as the Candian Wars, over the isle of Crete.[8]

It is, at first glance, more difficult to understand what inspired Iran to refrain from any provocations that might have led to a resumption of war. Having lost Mesopotamia, including the holy cities of Shī'ism, the Safavids might reasonably be expected to have used every opportunity, and especially the Ottoman imbroglio over Crete, to regain these territories. What is known about long-term processes in the Safavid state nevertheless allows us to offer a tentative answer to that question. The most important of these processes was the decline of the Qizilbāsh, the traditional mainstay of Iran's fighting force. Contemporary sources relate how the Safavid grand *vazīr* Mīrzā Muḥammad Sārū Taqī (1044–55/1634–45) deliberately withheld funds from the military in an effort to undermine the Qizilbāsh. The results were soon visible in scenes of mass desertion by unpaid soldiers from the Iranian army fighting before Baghdād.[9] Planning new wars naturally did not fit into this strategy. Muḥammad

[7] Mantran 1989, 237.

[8] See Luft 1968, 120–2, which is mostly based on the works of Joseph Hammer-Purgstall and Johann Wilhelm Zinkeisen, in addition to the Persian court chronicles written under Shāh 'Abbas II.

[9] See Colenbrander 1899, 116.

Sārū Taqī had close links with the inner palace and especially with the eunuchs and the women of the harem. As both groups were themselves in the forefront of the anti-Qizilbāsh movement, their role cannot be discounted either. Indeed, there are suggestions that the *dargāh* may have constituted the core of the pacifist faction within the Safavid ruling elite. In 1038/1629, the year of Shāh Ṣafī's accession, the ruler's great-grandmother appeared in the royal council to hold pleas against renewed anti-Ottoman campaigning.[10] The Frenchman Chardin in the 1660s similarly attributed the unwarlike atmosphere in Iran to the eunuchs and women of the harem.[11] His compatriot Sanson a generation later echoed this with his claim that the palace eunuchs were averse to the destruction of Ottoman power.[12]

Iran's pacifist tendencies were temporarily interrupted during the reign of Shāh 'Abbās II (1052–77/1642–66). Significantly, however, this ruler set out and managed to recapture Qandahār from the Mughals, but refrained from making a bid on Baghdād. Peace as a principle was next adopted by Shāh Sulaymān I, who succeeded Shāh 'Abbās II in 1077/1666, precisely at the time when a great deal of international pressure began to be exerted on Iran to resume war with the Ottomans. The accord of Zuhāb had ended the "hot war" between the Safavids and the Ottomans. As it ushered in a "cold peace" between the two powers, it did not diminish the diplomatic wrangling of third parties bent on rekindling hostilities for their own purposes. Ever since the fall of Constantinople in 857/1453, Christian Europe, horrified by the Ottoman advance in the Balkans and the threat it was seen to pose to central Europe, had been engaged in efforts at anti-Ottoman coalition building. These efforts were alternatively led by the Papacy, Venice, and the ones who bore the brunt of Ottoman aggression, the Austrians, while over time the Poles and Russians were to play a prominent role as well. The only European nation not to join this common front was France, Austria's main rival and the other great continental power. Iran had been an object of Western attempts to isolate the Ottomans by encirclement from the days of the Aqqoyunlu ruler Ūzūn Ḥasan (r. 857–82/1453–78), when, following the loss of the Christian Black Sea enclave of Trébizonde (Trabzon), a number of missions were exchanged between Tabrīz, Rome and Venice.[13] The rise to power of the Safavids and the Ottoman expansion into Syria and Mesopotamia shortly thereafter had led to the fierce Ottoman-Safavid hostility that had made Iran an active participant

[10] Smidt 1930, 748.
[11] Chardin 1811, 5:325–6.
[12] Sanson, letter from Iṣfahān, 13 September 1691, in Kroell 1979, 50.
[13] Palombini 1968, 16–31; Piemontese 1991. [See also Angelo Michele Piemontese's article in the present volume, and the sources quoted therein. Ed.]

in this strategy. Though it never resulted in the formation of an actual anti-Ottoman alliance, the intensive diplomatic traffic through which the contacts between Iran and the European states were maintained continued until the end of Safavid rule.

Shāh Sulaymān is known to have rejected all European proposals for anti-Ottoman initiatives. His reaction to these are famously captured in a statement ascribed to him by Francesco Gemelli Careri. According to this Italian traveler, the Shāh, in response to pressure to resume war with the Ottomans, insisted that, since he had made peace with İstanbul, he could not renege on his word. In reply to the counter argument that, having concluded their wars with the Christian powers, the Turks would not hesitate to take up arms against Iran again, he let it be known that he would be content to be left with Iṣfahān.[14] This last statement may be apocryphal; at least it is not found in any eyewitness account. In time it would, however, become a metaphor for the lax and irresolute image of Shāh Sulaymān that has persisted until today.[15]

There is nothing to suggest that Shāh Sulaymān was an emblem of courage and resoluteness and that his lack of leadership did not seriously impair the speed and direction of decision-making at a court riven by factionalism. Gemelli Careri's verdict echoes the assessment of others, among them Engelbert Kaempfer, one of the few western travelers who was not only present at the Safavid Court at this time but also left an eyewitness account. The Shāh, Kaempfer insisted, from time to time proclaimed that he would rather leave minor challenges [to the peace] unanswered than undertake a revenge campaign the outcome of which would be uncertain.[16]

It nevertheless stands to reason that the Iranian decision to maintain amicable relations with the Ottomans was motivated by more than royal lethargy. Shāh Sulaymān's aversion to military confrontation, after all, was neither unconditional nor comprehensive. In 1084/1673, when a new war with the Ottomans seemed imminent, Iranian army commanders were present in all provinces bordering on Ottoman territory, reviewing the troops and the *matériel*, and assessing the governors' readiness to fight in case the Turks would declare war.[17] Villagers were recruited to strengthen the fortresses of Yerevan.[18]

[14] Gemelli Careri 1699–1700, 2:128.

[15] The story was repeated by Father Krusinski and in modern times taken up by Lockhart and others as an illustration of Shāh Sulaymān's spinelessness, see Krusinski [1740] 1973, 1:58; and Lockhart 1958, 30.

[16] Kaempfer 1977, 75. According to the same observer, this also explained the Shāh's lackadaisical attitude vis-à-vis the Uzbek raids in Khurāsān.

[17] Chardin to Cosimo III, Grand Duke of Tuscany, Tabrīz, 15 May 1673, in Kroell 1982, 318–9.

[18] Geĭdarov 1967, 172, referring to Zakariia͡ Aguletsi͡ 1938, 197.

In the course of Shāh Sulaymān's reign, the Safavid army also mounted various campaigns to put a halt to Uzbek incursions into Khurāsān and the revolt led by Bābā Sulaymān in Kurdistān. Several observers indeed adduce motives beyond mere pacifism for Iran's lack of bellicosity in its relations with the Ottomans. There is Gemelli Careri's claim that Sulaymān's pacifist sentiments had been instilled by his grand *vazīr*, Shaykh 'Alī Khān—who was rumored to harbor anti-Christian and secret Sunnī convictions—and by various counselors who apparently saw the Ottomans as a buffer against the Christian West. These courtiers, Gemelli Careri averred, were afraid that, once the Christian forces had overpowered the Ottoman state, they would take on Iran as well.[19]

Gemelli Careri's remarks about the forces behind Shāh Sulaymān's pacifism do not stand alone. His observation about Shaykh 'Alī Khān's suspected Sunnī leanings, for instance, merely echo the rumors that had surrounded this formidable magistrate from the moment of his appointment.[20] In the course of time, these rumors even made their way to Europe, where Shaykh 'Alī Khān's presumed secret adherence to Sunnī Islam was seen as his primary motivation for dissuading a spineless and effeminate Shāh from waging war on the Ottomans.[21]

While it is impossible to verify Shaykh 'Alī Khān's religious convictions, much less to assess the role they may have played in his perspective on foreign policy, irritation with European demands feeding on anti-Christian sentiments cannot be discounted as a motivating factor. However, more tangible motives are suggested as well in the contemporary sources. As a second incentive for the grand *vazīr*'s reluctance to foster war with the Ottomans, European observers noted the fact that Shaykh 'Alī Khān's landholdings were mostly located at the frontiers of Mesopotamia, that is, in the vicinity of Kirmānshāh, in Kurdistān, the homeland of the Zanganah tribe from which the grand *vazīr* hailed.[22] A third motive is proposed by Petrus Bedik (Petik'), a Catholic-Armenian missionary-cum diplomat, who stayed in Iran from 1670/1080–1 to 1673/1083–4 and again in 1675–6/1086–7, and who subsequently published an important yet little-known travel account. Bedik plausibly

[19] Gemelli Careri 1699–1700, 2:128.

[20] See Matthee 1994, and the sources quoted therein.

[21] See Pietro Ricciardi's *Che nelle emergenze presenti sia necessaria, anzi necessarissima una Missione in Persia per dar l'ultimo crollo al Turco commune nemico delli Christiani et apportar una grave confusione al Ré Francese unico collega del medesimo*, MS copied in Vienna in 1691 and now held in the private archive of the Dutch Royal Family, The Hague, Archive of Willem III, inventory no. A16, xii, fol. 18. The reference to Shaykh 'Alī Khān in this pamphlet is anachronistic, since he had died in 1101/1689.

[22] See Ezser 1973, 272.

attributes Shaykh ʿAlī Khān advocacy of a peaceful policy towards the Turks to his budgetary policies rather than to any religious urges.[23] Other sources elaborate on this by emphasizing the energy with which Shaykh ʿAlī Khān pursued a policy of cost reduction coupled with revenue enhancement.[24] However, as will be seen below, broader strategic concerns are likely to have been the ultimate determinant of Safavid policy vis-à-vis the Ottomans.

As was noted earlier, Shāh Sulaymān's accession was soon followed by a flurry of international diplomatic activity, most of it prompted by a successful Ottoman offensive against the Habsburgs and İstanbul's naval assault on Crete in late 1666, and centering on attempts to entice Iran into anti-Ottoman alliance. Some of the contacts concerned religious and especially missionary issues. Such, for instance, was the nature of most of the correspondence conducted between the Iranian Court and the Holy See.[25] In most cases, a combination of concerns underlay overtures to Iran. The Poles, for example, were motivated by questions of trade and diplomacy in soliciting Iran. In 1667 the treaty of Andrusovo between Poland and Russia had put an end to a prolonged period of war and hostile relations over the Ukraine between these two powers, opening up visions of shared action against the Ottomans. The treaty of Andrusovo, in addition, included a clause that allowed Russian merchants to travel through Poland on their way to western Europe, and Polish merchants to traverse Russia *en route* to Iran.[26] Following this, a Polish embassy led by Bogdan Gurdziecki (the Georgian) traveled to Iran in 1668/1078–9. It was his task to propose the creation of an anti-Ottoman alliance. This part of his mission may, however, have been subordinate to a more urgent task: to encourage the ratification of an agreement that had been concluded in 1667/1077–8 between the Russians and Iranian-Armenian merchants whereby the latter obtained trading privileges in exchange for a promise that the silk that they previously carried to the ports of the Levant would henceforth be transported via Russia. Gurdziecki was specifically commissioned to ensure that a part of this new commercial flow would be carried to Poland.[27] He was received in

[23] Bedik 1678, 250–1.

[24] For this, see Matthee 1994.

[25] See *A chronicle* 1939, 1:417ff.

[26] Troebst 1993, 193.

[27] See Żevakin 1940, 144–5; Józefowicz 1962, 333–4. We are otherwise informed about Bogdan Gurdziecki through the travelogue of the Dutch sail maker Jan Struys. Gurdziecki freed Struys from captivity in 1670 by buying him from an Iranian merchant. Having made himself impossible with his Polish compatriots, and having killed one of his companions, he did not dare to go back to Poland and stayed on in Iran until 1677/1088, see Struys 1676, 255–8, and Algemeen Rijksarchief, The Hague, VOC, Generale Missiven, Maetsuycker et al., Batavia, to Amsterdam, 5 July 1677, in Coolhaas 1971, 180.

audience by Shāh Sulaymān in February and March 1670/Shawwal–Dhū al-Qa'dah 1080, together with the Archbishop of Nakhichevan, Matt'eos Awanik', who had been enlisted to represent Louis XIV, Pope Clemens IX, the Duke of Tuscany and the Doge of Venice in seeking Iran's participation in an anti-Ottoman coalition.[28]

Moscow had long been part of the European effort to include Iran in an anti-Ottoman league.[29] Rivalry and enmity between Russia and Poland, however, had often prevented the Russians from marching in step with other Christian powers. This changed with the treaty of Andrusovo, which altered the balance of power in eastern Europe and turned the Tsar once again into a active participant in efforts to isolate the Porte. The dispatch of three full-fledged embassies to Iṣfahān in addition to nine ordinary missions in the following decade reflects this renewed interest.[30]

The next spate of diplomatic activities centering on the Ottoman threat took place in 1673–4/1083–5, years in which Safavid-Ottoman tension threatened to erupt into yet another war, and Russian, English and French envoys all vied for the Safavid Court's attention. The French and English delegations had converged on Iṣfahān to obtain or extend trading rights; as for the Russians, their mission combined commercial objectives with a political mandate. Having come to Iran with the report of the Polish victory at Khorzin against the Ottoman army, they intended to exhort the Shāh to join the recently formed Polish-Russian league and to march against Baghdād. The extent of these complications became evident when Gregori Lusikent visited Moscow in 1671/1081–2 as envoy of the Shāh and representative of the Armenian merchants of new Julfa. Part of his task was to demand Russian compensation for the goods stolen from Iranian merchants during the recent Sten'ka Razin rebellion. Official Iranian ire over this was matched by Russian irritation that the Shah had failed to arrest and extradite a delegation representing the same Sten'ka Razin when it visited Iṣfahān. Moscow's refusal to pay indemnification for the lost goods did little to improve relations, despite Lusikent's efforts to mend fences. How far Russia's stock had fallen in Iran was revealed in the cold reception the next Russian mission to Iṣfahan received. F. Voznictsyn, the head of the mission, was made to kneel before the Shāh, who also failed to

[28] See Kevorkian 1989, 15–6.

[29] For their efforts until 1639/1048–9, see Matthee 1993.

[30] Bushev 1976, 136. These were, embassies: A. Priklonskiĭ, 1671–2; B. E. Myshet͡skii, 1675–6; S. K. Chirikov; and, missions: I. Men'shov, 1670; F. Voznict͡syn, 1672; K. Khristoforov, 1673; G. Dolgov, 1674; Fedot'ev, 1674, N. Alekseev, 1676; K. Khristoforov, 1676; and N. Lorionov, 1676.

make the customary inquiry about the Tsar's health. Needless to say, Iran's participation in an anti-Ottoman coalition was not on the agenda.[31]

Polish losses in Podolia, coupled with a sudden deterioration in Ottoman-Safavid relations, prompted both the Russians and the Poles to continue their diplomatic overtures toward Iran in the next few years. By way of missions led by A. Priklonskiĭ and K. Khristoforov, the Russians exhorted the Shāh in 1672–3 to join the recently formed Polish-Russian league and to march against Baghdād.[32] Shāh Sulaymān rejected Khristoforov's suggestion to that effect, revealing his motives with the promise that he would attack Baghdād once Russia and Poland were actually engaged in a war against the Turks, and provided they were to assure him that they would not make peace without him. The obvious long-term frustration with European power politics reflected in these words was underscored by a remark made by Shaykh 'Alī Khān during the same talks. In response to a request for a more detailed answer to the proposal for an anti-Ottoman alliance, the grand *vazīr* , who appears to have been in the forefront of an anti-Russian faction at the court, is said to have retorted that the "Christian powers had at various times engaged the kings of Iran to join them in making war against the Turks, after which they had [always] made peace without their participation."[33]

Despite his ostensible refusal to resume hostilities with the Ottomans, Shāh Sulaymān in the fall of 1084/1673 headed to Qazvīn in a move that was seen by some as a preparation for a new war over Baghdād.[34] During his sojourn in Qazvīn the following year he received the Spanish cleric Pedro Cubero Sebastian, who carried with him a letter from Polish marshal and future king, Jan III Sobieski (r. 1674–96), written in June of 1673, in which the latter proposed the formation of joint military operations against the Porte.[35] In Ṣafar 1085/May 1675 there were reports that the Ottomans and the Safavids

[31] Bayburdyan 1996, 140–2.

[32] Algemeen Rijksarchief, The Hague, VOC 1302, F. de Haze, Gamron, to R. van Goens, Ceylon, 2 May 1673, fol. 731r; VOC 1285, F. de Haze, Gamron, to Heren XVII, 31 July 1673, fol. 381r; and Chardin 1811, 3:113–5, 203ff. The Abbé Carré notes the presence of a Polish embassy in Iṣfahān at the same time. Such an embassy is not mentioned by other eyewitness sources, such as Chardin and the Dutch, which only refer to a Russian delegation. The reference may be to Gurdziecki's brother, who seems to have gone to Iṣfahān to request permission for Bogdan to stay in Iran as a Muslim, see Algemeen Rijksarchief, The Hague, VOC, Generale Missiven, Maetsuycker et al., Batavia, to Amsterdam, 5 July 1677, in Coolhaas 1971, 180. In Jumādá I 1084/August 1673 an envoy from the Paşa of Baṣrah also arrived in Iṣfahān; his mission, however, was unrelated to the conflict, see Carré 1947, 2:809–10; and Chardin 1811, 3:134–5.

[33] Chardin 1811, 3:203.

[34] Algemeen Rijksarchief, The Hague, VOC 1291, Gamron to Heren XVII, 27 April 1674, fol. 596v.

[35] See Richard 1995, 1:97.

had clashed over the issue of tolls and customs at the border of the districts of Baghdād and Baṣrah. One month later, a potential *casus belli* presented itself with the arrival of envoys from Khūshāb, an autonomous part of Kurdistān that, feeling threatened by Ottoman designs to annex it, offered to become tributary to the Safavid state. After deliberations with his ministers, the Shāh declined the offer, and the ruler of Khūshāb was told to accommodate himself as best he could with the Porte.[36] The decision to defuse the mounting tension may have been informed by the reaction of the Ottomans who, meanwhile, had moved artillery and other military equipment from Alexandretta to Baghdād.[37] Ottoman intimidation similarly may have determined the outcome of a meeting which the Shāh held on Jumādá I 13th/August 5th with his officers to discuss a Russian request for the sending of 20,000 troops against the Ottomans that had been conveyed by a Russian envoy who had arrived the previous month. This too was rejected, the Shah's argument being that it would be better to dishonor a contract with the Russians than to break the peace with the Ottomans.[38]

None of the signals sent out by the Safavid Court prevented the Christian powers from continuing their attempts to draw Iran into an anti-Ottoman coalition. Their diplomatic initiatives culminated in the period from 1683/1094 to 1685/1096–7. In the former year the Ottoman armies unsuccessfully besieged Vienna and were defeated by the Polish forces. The antecedents to some of the missions generated by this latest round of war in Europe are, again, not limited to questions of military strategy. In 1682 Pope Innocent XI appointed the German Sebastian Knab O. P. as the new Archbishop of Nakhichevan in Armenia and sent him to Iran with a papal letter for the Safavid Shāh. On his way east, Knab stopped in Vienna, where he pleaded with the Austrian Emperor Leopold I (r. 1655–1705) for assistance in his project of founding a Dominican convent at Iṣfahān, while offering his services as the Emperor's representative at the Safavid Court. As an Ottoman attack on Hungary and Austria was no longer in doubt in the Spring of 1683/1094, the Emperor handed Knab a letter in which he requested the Shāh to organize a campaign against the Ottomans in order to relieve the beleaguered European powers. Before leaving Vienna, Knab also received another papal letter, written on June 19th and reflecting the state of the Ottoman advance, in which Pope Innocent exhorted the Shāh in the same manner. Arriving in Poland, Knab

[36] Chardin 1811, 9:232–3, 243; see also Kaempfer 1977, 75–6.

[37] Nointel to Colbert, Aleppo, 10 August 1674, in Bibliothèque nationale, Paris, Collection Clairambault 297, fols. 141–8.

[38] Chardin 1811, 9:337.

similarly received a letter from Jan III Sobieski, who in the midst of a campaign in full force found time to meet the traveling cleric.[39]

Having turned Polish emissary as well, Knab headed for Iran with instructions to inform the Shāh about the Turkish defeat—which had taken place on Ramaḍān 10th/August 12th at the Battle of Kahlenberg—as well as about the creation of a league between the Polish and the Austrian states and the crucial role the Pope had played in this, and the desirability of including Russia once peace had been arranged between the Poles and the Russians (in reality the Holy League between Poland, Austria and Venice only came into being in March 1684, while the inclusion of Russia occurred in 1686 following a Polish-Russian treaty). In light of this, he was to advise the Iranians of the opportuneness of concerted military action against the Ottomans.[40] Delayed in Russia, Knab only arrived in Iṣfahān in Dhū al–Qa'dah 1095/October 1684.

Knab was by no means the only envoy representing the Polish King at the Safavid Court at this point. Poland had kept up its dispatch of envoys to Iran by sending various envoys and couriers in 1087/1676—following the treaty of Zuravno, which made Poland cede the Ukraine to the Ottomans—and by dispatching a number of missions between 1682/1093–4 and 1684/1095–6.[41] Du Mans relates how Jan III Sobieski wrote eight letters to the Shāh in the course of his campaign between September and November 1683/Shawwāl and Dhū al-Ḥijjah 1094, from the various places in Hungary where he confronted the Ottoman army, such as Parkàny, Szecsen, and Esztergom (Gran).[42] These were relayed to Iṣfahān through a number of different couriers and envoys. One of these was Bogdan Gurdziecki, who once again was dispatched to Iṣfahān in February 1684/Rabī' I 1095. In the second half of the same year two more envoys named Adam Kantecki and Teodor Miranowicz also set out for Iran. Petrus Bedik, who in 1683 had been named ambassador

[39] Eszer 1973: 215–86.

[40] Ibid., 268–70.

[41] For the various Polish missions to Iran in this period, see Reychman and Zajączkowski 1968, 181–2; Żevakin 1940, 145–6; and Kaempfer 1977, 267. The reference to a Gurdziecki mission to Iran in 1676 in Reychman/Zajączkowski and Żevakin contradicts the information about his staying in Iran until 1677/1088, cf. footnote no. 26. The Polish envoy who arrived in Iṣfahān in Jumādá II 1087/August 1676 (at the same time that two Russian emissaries arrived as well) was most likely Piotr Żukowski. A courier rather than a full-fledged ambassador, Żukowski does not seem to have had any substantive message for the Shāh. It was said that, arriving without the usual and obligatory presents, he merely requested the finalization of some outstanding issues between the Shāh and the Polish representatives in Iran, see Algemeen Rijksarchief, The Hague, VOC, Generale Missiven, Maetsuycker et al., Batavia, to Amsterdam, 5 July 1677, in Coolhaas 1971, 179–80.

[42] Richard 1995, 1:296.

of the Christian League to Iran and who, on his way, passed through Warsaw to pick up letters from Jan Sobieski, would have been the next.[43] Bedik, however, was never to reach Iran, for he disappeared somewhere along the Polish-Russian border. His position as Polish envoy was taken by Count Constantin Salomon Siri Zgorski, an Armenian who had been made nobleman in Poland.[44]

Aside from the Polish missions and several missionaries, two more western delegations were present in Iṣfahān in this same period. The first represented the Russian Tsar and was headed by the Greek Konstantin Khristoforov (Constantin Christoforowicz), who had earlier been sent to the Porte. The other one was the embassy of Ludvig Fabritius, who in 1684/1095–6 visited Iran for a second time as the representative of the King of Sweden. Like most embassies coming from the north, the Fabritius mission combined trade issues with diplomatic objectives.

We are, through the writings of Kaempfer, the mission's secretary, and Fabritius himself, relatively well informed about the fate of the Swedish delegation.[45] Having entered the city on Rabīʿ II 3rd/March 30th, ten days after the Iranian New Year, *Nawrūz*, the emissaries had to wait a full four months before being officially received by the Shāh on Shaʿbān 27th/July 30th.[46] Plausible as Fabritius's explanation sounds, the delegation might have had to wait as long for a first audience even in "normal" circumstances. It was customary practice for Safavid rulers to make foreign delegations wait for long periods of time before receiving them in audience, usually collectively and on the occasion of a holiday such as *Nawrūz*, when a lavish banquet would be organized for the entire Court and its foreign guests. Chardin explains that letting foreign envoys wait for long periods of time was deliberate Safavid policy designed to enhance the impression of the Court's magnificence and importance.[47] During his audience with Shāh Sulaymān, Fabritius handed over his

[43] A papal blessing in 1684 turned this league into the so-called Holy League.

[44] See Chowaniec 1926, 150–60; and Kevorkian 1989, 33–4. In 1675/1086 Shāh Sulaymān had dispatched Bedik as his envoy to Russia. See ibid., 25. Zgorski had earlier been sent to İstanbul as representative of the Polish king. He became the founder of the Jesuit mission in Shamākhī in northern Iran; see Avril 1692, 261–2.

[45] A thorough study of Fabritius and his three missions to Iran is now available; see Troebst forthcoming. Thanks to Stefan Troebst for sending me an advance draft of this study.

[46] The reason Fabritius gives for this long initial delay is that Shāh Sulaymān, having recently lost his favored wife, was advised by his astrologers to abstain from taking on any state affairs lest more bad luck would befall him, see letter Ludvig Fabritius to Steno Bjelke, 3 July 1684, in Meier-Lemgo 1965, 276; see also Kaempfer 1977, 78–9, 252.

[47] Chardin 1811, 5:491.

requests in the form of four points. Among these was a suggestion made to the Shāh by the Swedish King Charles XI to join the European anti-Ottoman alliance, with the news that the Swedes had already called up 12,000 soldiers to assist Iran.[48]

If it was customary for foreign emissaries to be received in audience at great intervals, generally during major holidays, it was similarly not unusual for them to have to wait interminably before receiving the Shāh's final answer together with permission to leave. In March 1685/Rabīʿ II 1096 Knab—who himself was only received in audience during that month's *Nawrūz* celebration—wrote a letter to Emperor Leopold I in which he mentioned that the Polish, Swedish and Russian envoys were still waiting for a reply to the letters that they had submitted six months earlier. He added that the only sign of readiness for war among the Safavids was the presence of an army in parts of Georgia, which, decimated by the plague the year before, had been recalled.[49]

The patience of the various foreign delegates would be tested for another year, for it was only in the summer of 1098/1686, more than two years after arriving in the Safavid capital, that Fabritius (presumably with the Russian and Polish envoys) finally received permission to depart. The Court's procrastination in expediting the matter only seems to amplify the widely accepted notion that the European powers courted an Iranian ruler who, in response, showed a glaring lack of interest in any proposals urging him to rise from his inertia. The nature of the Shāh's final message to the various envoys, however, suggests otherwise. To be sure, the results were meager indeed: in the end, the Safavid Court rejected any suggestion for joint action. Fabritius relates how the Shāh informed him that he would be happy to oblige the Swedish King in all his wishes except for any proposal to resume hostilities with the Ottomans. "My forebears," Fabritius had Shāh Sulaymān continue, "made peace, and I have confirmed and formalized this for eternity. Cursed be the one who will first draw the sword again . . . We let ourselves be prompted by the Christian powers to greatly distract the Turks, but then the Christian powers made peace without so much as mentioning us once."[50]

Further details about the final audience granted to the various envoys reveal the full scope of Safavid political concerns and strategic considerations. According to Sanson, the German envoy [Knab] during his audience

[48] In his published travelogue Kaempfer states that King Charles "promised" to commit 12,000 troops (Kaempfer 1977, 266). In the protocol of the secret audience the Latin term *transmisit* (sent), is used instead. For the difference in wording and its significance, see Haberland 1993, 410–25.

[49] Knab to Leopold I, 26 March and 29 April 1685, in Eszer 1974, 263–70.

[50] Fabritius 1955, 99–100.

mentioned the advantages for Iran of joining the anti-Ottoman league. To this the Shāh is said to have responded that he did not see any greater advantage in joining than in living in peace with his neighbors. To the Polish envoy, who insisted that the time had come for the Safavids to take back Baghdād, Baṣrah and Erzurum, the Safavid ruler showed his familiarity with current developments in Europe by responding that those cities were no more important to Iran than Kamieniecz was to the Poles (who had lost this city to the Ottomans in 1672). He added that once Poland had recaptured Kamieniecz, it would be up to the Iranian to take possession of the three Ottoman cities.[51] Sulaymān's message for the Russian envoy was equally trenchant and even more revealing. It would, the Russians argued, be easy for Iran to defeat the Ottomans given their current predicament. "May the Sulṭân be humiliated," the Shāh replied, "but may he not perish . . . It is not in our interest to have a Grand Sulṭân who is too weak. His territory functions as a barrier between our empire and the Christian powers." Shaykh 'Alī Khān is said to have completed this homily with a graphic metaphor by declaring that it was dangerous to open up a plugged-up beehive as one might be stung by the bees, and to have shown satisfaction at the fact that Iran was tranquil whereas its most redoubtable enemy was engaged in war with the Christians. By joining an anti-Ottoman league, he concluded, Iran might provoke an attack by a Sunnī coalition of Tatars, Uzbeks and Mughals.[52]

Leaving the issue of Shāh Sulaymān's personal leadership aside, we might conclude that, rather than sheer inertia, strategic and geopolitical considerations informed the Court in its inaction. There is no doubt that by the 1680s Safavid officials were fully cognizant of the lamentable state of the Iranian army. This, as well as a careful calculation of the relative strength of potential allies and foes must have convinced the ruling elite that it would be unwise to upset the fragile peace with the Ottomans. Their experience with the Europeans, who had long sought to lure Iran into an anti-Ottoman alliance without ever following up on any of their promises for military assistance, no doubt further strengthened the Iranians in their determination to maintain neutrality in the conflict between the Ottomans and the Christian powers. A final concern, little appreciated by westerners, was the possibility that Iran's immediate neighbors might come together in an anti-Safavid coalition. The specter of a Sunnī league directed against Shī'ite Iran was hardly far-fetched, for the Ottomans, Mughals and Uzbeks had at various times suggested the formation

[51] This is a reference to the Polish loss of the stronghold of Kamieniecz, situated across from Khotin on the Dniestr in Podolia (today in Ukraine), to the Ottomans in 1672.

[52] Sanson 1694, 140–4.

of such a league, and only Mughal-Uzbek mutual suspicion and different interests and priorities had, at times, prevented the implementation of that idea.[53]

A survey of a broader array of available sources only confirms that the image of a meek and supine Safavid Court unwilling to stand up to its archenemy invoked in the various narratives does not adequately reflect reality. For one, Knab, writing in April 1685, claimed that the Porte had sent an envoy to Iṣfahān with the aim of bringing several families subject to the Sulṭân but living in Iran back under its authority. According to Knab, the envoy had been told that no one wishing to live in Iran would be evicted by force.[54] A more activist policy is also reflected in the Safavid reaction to the information coming out of Europe. In his letters King Sobieski informed the Safavid ruler about his victories and, in general, about the progress of the anti-Ottoman struggle. Du Mans, who was in a position to know since he translated the Court's foreign correspondence (and who, being French, may be trusted to have encouraged the Shāh not to resume war with the Ottomans), asserted that the Polish King in his writings enjoined Sulaymān to organize a campaign against Baghdād and other spots along the Tigris that had formerly belonged to Iran, swearing that peace with the Ottomans could never come to pass until the restitution to Iran of its former possessions.[55] Shāh Sulaymān, in turn, was apparently inspired to take back Baghdād after reading the accounts of the liberation of Vienna. Spies sent to Turkey confirmed the Ottoman defeat.[56] At the same time, Sulṭân Meḥmed IV is said to have responded to the disquieting news that the Polish King had sent an ambassador to Iṣfahān by dispatching his own mission to Iran (which may have been different from the one noted by Knab). The rich gifts the mission brought with it were designed to change the Safavid Court's mind and apparently achieved their goal.[57] Rumor also had it that the Ottomans had mollified Iran and secured a continued peaceful relationship with the Safavids by paying them money and by easing restrictions on the pilgrim traffic to Mecca, the latter being a perennial source of conflict between the two states.[58] The Ottomans may even have pleaded for Safavid assistance against the Christian powers, a request to which Shāh Sulaymān reportedly reacted by saying that "when Babylon had been restored to him, he might be induced to assist him, but that otherwise, when the war with the

[53] Farooqi 1989, 10–56; and Burton 1997, 27, 65, 79, 144, 341, 346–7.

[54] Knab to Leopold I, 29 April 1685, in Eszer 1974, 270.

[55] Richard 1995, 1:296; see also Levi-Weiss 1925, 72.

[56] Chowaniec 1926, 156.

[57] See Richard 1995, 1:121–2, quoting Beregani 1698, 1:421–2.

[58] See Eszer 1973, 267. For the issue of the pilgrim traffic, see Tucker 1996.

Christians was over, his objective would be to get back that fortress which belonged to his domain of old."[59]

Written in the same vein but more spectacular in content are several anonymous reports and letters kept in the Casanatense Library and Lincei Academy in Rome, Italy. The Casanatense Library holds a narrative of an alleged diplomatic initiative by Shāh Sulaymān which is entitled "True report of the war which the King of Iran has declared on Meḥmed IV, the Grand Turk, in the month of June 1684, with the campaign of that King's army to lay siege to Baghdād." This narrative appears in Appendix A. The Lincei Academy holds a series of letters exchanged between Shāh Sulaymān and various rulers in Europe as well as the King of Abyssinia (Ethiopia). There is thus a letter from the Safavid Shāh to King Sobieski from Poland that confirms the receipt of the previously sent letters, and expresses appreciation for the candor and friendship shown in these, while returning the compliments and the expression of friendship.[60] Under the heading "Reports from Constantinople and other places," the same library contains a purported correspondence between the Ottoman Sulṭân Meḥmed IV and Shāh Sulaymān, in which the former scolds the latter for being a thief for having moved against Baghdād and a traitor for having joined in a league with the Christian powers, threatening military revenge. The latter, in turn, responds by informing the Ottoman Sulṭân that he has indeed moved his troops against Baghdād, has sacked the area around the city, and has brought many of the area's inhabitants under his rule, adding that the Christian powers had never caused him grief in the same way as the Ottoman Sulṭân. Both of these letters appear in Appendix B. A third pair of letters in the same library represents an ostensible exchange of letters between Shāh Sulayman and the Ethiopian King Prete Ianni (Prester John), in which the former informs the latter that he has moved against Baghdād. With the letter Shāh Sulaymān sent twelve horses "with stirrups made of the finest gold which were looted from that infamous and lascivious tyrant." The ruler of Ethiopia,

[59] Quoted in Setton, 1991, 281, without a reference.

[60] *Lettera scritta da Izach Soleman Ré di Persia alla Maesta del Re di Polonia, con una nova relatione di vittorie, e d'altri acquisti di città, e prede d'animali, e prigioni fatti da Morlacchi nel paese de Turchi, e da Cosacchi contro i Tartari.* Venetia, 1684; and *Interpretatione della lettera scritta da Izach Soleman Ré di Persia alla Maesta di Giovanni III, Ré di Polonia.* Accademia di Lincei, Rome, 173 A10 (24).

in turn, invites the Safavid monarch to join in a common struggle against the Turks, while sending four elephants to Iran via Livorno with a Dutch ship.[61]

The presence of the mythical Prester John as a participant in the latter correspondence as well as our knowledge of the actual events and developments in Iran at the time make it easy to unmask these tracts as examples of the *Turcica* genre. After the Ottoman seizure of Constantinople in 857/1453, an anti-Turkish literature had developed in Europe in which the line between fact and fiction was blurred. The polemical treatises, pamphlets and books, containing letters and reports, tended to reappear at times of armed conflict or when tensions between the Ottomans and the Christian powers were running high. First appearing in German, these so-called apocryphal letters of the Sulṭân in time made their way to Italy, Poland and Russia, where they surfaced in the various languages spoken in those regions.[62] The ones that describe the campaign of the Shāh against the Sulṭân apparently made their way to Iran as well, for a letter written by Raphaël du Mans from Iṣfahān in June of 1685/Sha'bān 1096 contains the following passage:

> We have here received various reports from France and from elsewhere in the Christian world. According to these, the King of Iran has organized a campaign to dethrone the Grand Sulṭân. They give details about their mutual encounter(s), attacks, and defensive moves.[63]

Du Mans's comment on this summarizes what has since come to be seen as the essence of Iran's foreign policy under Shāh Sulaymān: "It is nothing like that. The Persians are without power, without will, and can't even think about organizing a march."[64]

Western hopes for a comprehensive alliance against the Ottomans did not vanish in the 1680s. Thus in 1691 a tract dedicated to Emperor Leopold I and the Dutch Stadtholder William III (r. 1689–1702) called for the necessity,

[61] *Sincero raguaglio delle vittorie ottenute dal Prete Ianni contro li Turchi esposto in una lettera da lui inviata, con quattro elefanti carichi d'oro al Ré di Persia, confermato dalle relationi, che porta la nave Gran Cerva d'Oro Olandese, approdata in Livorno per mezo d'un mercante, che ha dimorato per molti anni nel Gran Cairo. Con la fedele risposta del Ré di Persia al Prete Ianni, con l'avviso dell'assedio di Babilonia, di ricche spoglie riportate dal medemo Ré contro li Turchi, e di dodici superbissimi cavalli, con freni d'oro, e ricoperti di porpora, mandati al Prete Ianni*. Venetia, 1684. Accademia di Lincei, 173 A13 (8).

[62] See Waugh 1978.

[63] Raphaël du Mans, letter from Iṣfahān, 30 June 1685, in Richard 1995, 1:295.

[64] Ibid., my translation.

indeed the urgency, of sending a mission to the Shāh of Iran.[65] Yet the Safavid authorities continued to reject all proposals to incorporate Iran into an anti-Ottoman league. In 1690/1101 Shāh Sulaymān sent the Ḥusayn Khān Beg embassy to Moscow to congratulate Tsar Peter with his accession to the throne. Arriving in Moscow on 12 Rajab 1103/20 March 1692, the Safavid ruler's envoy officially informed the Romanov Tsar that Iran was not willing to join the anti-Ottoman league that the Russians had sought to forge for so long.[66] The Ottomans too at this time must have convinced themselves of Iran's peaceful intentions, for in 1689/1100–1 the Ottoman Sulṭân Süleyman II, writing to the Mughal Emperor Aurangzeb, no longer dwelled upon the customary Safavid threat to orthodox Islam and refrained, for the first time, from seeking to form an alliance against Iran.[67] Under Shāh Sulṭān Ḥusayn (r. 1105–35/1694–1722), Iran continued to maintain friendly relations with various European powers. In fact, until the end of Safavid rule, it remained one of the principles of Iran's foreign policy to keep a *cordon sanitaire* around the Ottoman state in place by maintaining friendly relations with Christian powers that continued to be enemies of the Ottomans. As the German traveler Schillinger observed at the turn of the 18th century: "It is one of his [i.e., Shāh Sulṭān Ḥusayn's] maxims of state to maintain everlasting friendship with the Muscovites, the Poles and the Germans in order to keep the Turks in check."[68] Geopolitical considerations, however, dictated that friendship should never extend beyond the exchange of embassies.

[65] Pietro Ricciardi's *Che nelle emergenze* (see footnote no. 21). As its title indicates, this tract was mostly composed with the aim of confusing the French King, called the sole ally of the Ottomans.

[66] Bushev 1976, 135, 139.

[67] Farooqi, 1989, 67.

[68] Schillinger 1707, 218.

APPENDIX A

VERA RELATIONE DELLA GUERRA, CHE HÀ DICHIARATO IL RÉ DI PERSIA À MEHEMETT IV GRAN TURCO NEL MESE DI GIUGNO 1684 CON LA MARCHIA DELL'ESERCITO DEL DETTO RÉ ALL'ASSEDIO DI BABILONIA

In Venetia & Todi per Gio. Domenico Faostini con lic. de Superiori, 1684.
Biblioteca Casanatense, Rome, Miscellanea 608/43

Subito, che il Ré di Persia intese la sconfitta del formidabile esercito Ottomano sotto Vienna d'Austria, considerando, che miglior congiura non haverebbe potuto havere per riacquistare la gran città di Babilonia, immediatamente spedi al Gran Turco in Costantinopoli un'ambasciata, colla quale espose alla porta, che il Gran Signore tenendo ingiustamente la detta Città, la debba restituire al Ré di Persia, come legitimo Padrone, altramente gl'haverebbe dichiarata la Guerra; e nell' istesso tempo diede ordine al suo Kabaf Kablan, cioè il Gran Maresciallo del Regno, che facesse ogni sforzo per unire un grand' Esercito di Cavalleria e Fanteria, e d'aggiungerli à quello, che continuamente tiene, che è di 50 m. Cavalli, oltre la guardia del Ré; & che s'incamminasse verso il Tauris; & poscia il Ré haverebbe seguitato con un' altra armata il detto maresciallo per portarsi sotto Babilonia, ed esser pronto ad assediarla, in caso che il Gran Turco no glie l'havesse voluta restituire, conforme di gia il Ré si persuadeva.

Di Costantinopoli si ha avviso, che sia arrivato nel mese di Giugno l'inviato del Ré di Persia colà, che ammesso all'audienza del Divano, ha domandato da parte del suo Ré la restitutione di Babilonia del [sic, should be *nel*] termine di due Settimane, altrimenti gl'haverebbe da parte del suo Ré intimata la Guerra. Passate le due Settimane, ritornò di nuovo all' Audienza per saperne la Volontà del Gran Signore di quel che gl'havea esposto alla passata audienza, & li fu risposto, che il Gran Signore accettava la Guerra, e che Babilonia Amuratte l'haveva acquistata con un fiume di sangue, e se il Ré la voleva, se l'andasse a pigliare, che ci haverebbe ritrovato buoni Difensori.

Il Soffi, dopo esser stato accertato della rotta data alli Principi Europei sotto Vienna alli Mussulmani, e del inseguito acquisto fatto per essi della Citta di Strigonia, & essendo ancora stato avvisato, che li detti Principi s'univano per progedire le incominciate Victorie, & in particolare della potente Armata Navale, che si preparava dalli Venetiani con l'unione d'altri Principi Europei, diede ordine al di lui Armadole, cioè il di lui primo Ministro di Stato, che dovesse ordinare à tutti gli Asas Bascy, cioè li Generali delle Militie a piedi, & a Cavallo, con ordine, che tutti li Balucchi Bascy, cioè tutti gli Ufficiali delle dette Militie, e che li Sardar, ò siano i Capitani, con li Veliy, che cosi chiamano li Tenenti, che per il giorno delli 15 Aprile si dovessero ritrovare con tutte le Militie, si a piedi, come a cavallo à Reuan, Città delle sue frontiere, quale precedentemente era stata munita d'ogni sorte di Vettovaglia per lo vitto, come anche d'ogni sorte di monitione da Guerra.

Comparvero tutti nel termine prefisso ne i contorni della detta Città di Reuan alli luoghi destinati sotto li padiglioni, pronti a i cenni del di loro Soltano, Quale alli 17 proveduto del Caznadar, ò sia Tesoriere del Regno, col di lui Daftardar, cioè il Maggiordomo, diede la rassegna à tutte le Soldatesche, e ciaschedun Soldato, per ordine Regio fu regalato del Caznadar, e gli Ufficiali, conforme si costuma di un Combaz, cioè d'un Giustacuore di Drappo d'oro, & essendo durata qualche giorno tal funtione, applaudita da tutta la militia, che gridava Afach, Afach Soffi, Babam, cioè Viva, Viva il Ré nostro Padre.

Ciò fatto, e ritrovata la Cavalleria numerosa di 40 mila, e l'Infanteria ascendente a 50 m. Fanti, ne diede il Soffi il supremo comando all'Asas Torpino Manfar col darli il bastone di comando, e la veste solita.

Ciò terminato, il detto Asas Manfar, conforme gl'ordini Regij, impose all'Asas Emir Ghintelboga, che precedesse con 20 Sardar, per Vanguardia, & havendo ciascheduno Sardar 500 cavalieri, onde la vanguardia di 10 m. cavalleri si pose in marchia via la riva del fiume Tigris, con ordine di occupare tutti li luoghi circonvicini a Bagdet e dopoi ordinò, che l'Asas Efiel Melchinenser seguitase con altri 10 m. cavalieri, e dopoi ordinò all'Asas Teofilo Abaldnoh, che seguisse con 20 m. fanti, e 30 pezzi di Cannone, e qualche mila carri di Vettonaglia, e dopo il detto Asas Manfer si pose in marchia con la rimanente infanteria guidata dall' Asas Salapio Zaratton, e dall' Asas Melebisella Caras, postovi nel mezzo il rimanente del Bagaglio con 40 pezzi di Canone, spallegiata da 10m. Cavalieri sotto la di lui condotta, havendo lasciato per la di lui retroguardia altri 10 m. cavalieri sotto la condotta dell'Asas Melchei Dauroni, e marchiando a lenti conat, cioè a camino breve di un giorno. Giunsero alli 18 di Maggio à vista di Bagdet, chiamata Babilonia, munita di 30 m. Turchi sotto il comando del Bassà Berhac, e nel riconoscere li posti è seguita qualche scaramuccia da una parte all'altra, restando bloccata detta piazza, e distesa la maggior parte della Cavalleria, & Infanteria dalla parte di Levante contro la porta bianca, che risguarda il cantone della Torre, chiamata Dgigalsadè allargandosi verso il Bastione detto delli Uccelli rimpetto alla ripa del fiume Tigris e quando siansi per aprirsi le trinciere non si sa, solo si dice, che li Persiani habbino occupati varij Castelli circonvicini, e che nel di loro Esercito vi siano esperti Topponieri, cioè Bombardieri, e che un Bassa parente di Mustafa vnire [sic] decapitato, per sfuggire simile incontro si sia ricovrato appresso il Soffi, che lo ricevè a Reuan con 2 m. Turchi, quali sono stati ripartiti nell' Esercito.

TRANSLATION

TRUE REPORT OF THE WAR WHICH THE KING OF IRAN HAS DECLARED ON MEḤMED IV, THE GRAND TURK, IN THE MONTH OF JUNE 1684, WITH THE CAMPAIGN OF THAT KING'S ARMY TO LAY SIEGE TO BAGHDĀD

Venice, 1684 [1095]

As soon as he learned of the routing of the formidable Turkish army at Vienna in Austria, the King of Iran, considering that he could not have had a better stratagem to regain the great city of Baghdād, immediately sent an embassy to the Grand Turk in Constantinople through which he let it be known to the Porte that the Grand Sulṭân, since he unjustly held the said city, should return it to the King of Iran as its legitimate master, and that otherwise the latter would declare war. At the same time he ordered Kabaf Kablan, the Grand Marshal of the realm,[69] to make every effort to assemble a large army consisting of cavalry and infantry, and to add this to the standing army of 50,000 cavalry troops, aside from the royal guard, and to march toward Tabrīz, and then the King would have followed the said marshal with another army in order to move to Baghdād and to be ready for a siege, in case the Grand Turk would not want to return it, as the King had already convinced himself he would not.

It is reported from Constantinople that in June the emissary of the King of Iran arrived there and that, received in audience at the Divân, he requested on behalf of his King the restitution of Baghdād within two weeks, [saying] that, otherwise, he would have to declare war on behalf of his King. When the two weeks had passed, he went to have another audience in order to learn what the Grand Sulṭân had decided with regard to what he had presented to him during the previous audience. He was told that the Grand Sulṭân accepted war, and that [Sulṭân] Murâd had conquered Baghdād in a river of blood, and that if the King wanted it he should go and take it, but that he would find it well defended.

The Shāh, having determined the truth of the Muslim rout by the European rulers at Vienna and their subsequent conquest of the city of Esztergom/

[69] "Kabaf Kablan" might be referring to the Qizilbāsh *amīr*, Kalb'alī Khān, who was in fact sent to the Ottoman court of Aḥmed II by Shāh Sulaymān in 1103/1691 to congratulate the Sulṭân with his accession, see I'timād al-Salṭanah 1984–8, 2:994–5.

Gran,[70] and having also been informed that the said rulers had united to continue their initial victories, and in particular [having been informed] about the powerful fleet which the Venetians were preparing in unison with other European rulers, ordered his *I'timād al-Dawlah*, that is, his prime minister of state, to give orders to all *asas bashi*s, that is, the commanders of the infantry and the cavalry, to order that all *baluchi bashi*s, that is, all officials of the said militias, and the *sardār*s, or the captains, with the *vālī*s, as the lieutenants are called, to come together on April 15th with all militias, both infantry and cavalry, at the frontier city of Yerevan, which beforehand had been supplied with all kinds of victuals as well as ammunition.[71]

They all appeared at the arranged time in the surroundings of the city of Yerevan at their designated locations in the army camps, ready for signs from their Sulṭān who, on the 17th, accompanied by the *Khazanah'dār*, or Treasurer of State, with his *Daftardār*, that is, the Maggiordomo, reviewed all troops, and at royal order and according to custom each soldier was given a *qumāsh*, that is, a doublet of goldthreaded cloth by the Treasurer and the officers; a procedure that took several days and that was applauded by all soldiers shouting "*Afuch, ufuch Soffi, babam*," that is, "Long live the King, my father."[72]

This done and the cavalry numbering 40,000 and the infantry of 50,000 being assembled, the King appointed Asas Torpino Manfar supreme commander by giving him the commanding baton and the usual robe [of honor].[73]

When this was finished, the said Asas Manfar, following royal orders, gave orders to Asas Emir Ghintelboga to take the lead with 20 *sardārs* as a vanguard, each *sardār* having 500 cavalry troops, after which the vanguard of 10,000 cavalry set out on a march alongside the river Tigris, with the order to occupy all places around Baghdād; he subsequently ordered Asas Efiel Melchinenser to follow with another 10,000 cavalry troops, after which he gave orders to Asas Teofilo Abaldach, who followed with 20,000 infantry troops, 30 pieces of cannon, and some thousand carts of victuals, after which

[70] Gran or Esztergom, situated on the Danube in Hungary close to the present Slovak border, was the scene of the next Ottoman defeat and was reconquered in late September 1683/Shawwāl 1094.

[71] The terms *sardār*, army commander, and *vālī*, provincial governor, reflect real positions in the Safavid hierarchy. The terms *asas bashi* and *baluchi bashi* may refer to the positions of *'asas bâşı* (head of guards) and *bölük bâşı* (captain of the Janissaries) in the Ottoman army.

[72] "Afach" might be a corruption of *'āfiyat* or *'āfiyat bāsh* (may you be healthy).

[73] "Asas Torpino Manfar" is perhaps identical with the real Safavid *sardār* of the time Manṣūr Khān, who was appointed governor of Kirmān in 1076/1665–6, see Mashīzī 1990, 323.

the said Asas Manfer set on a march with the remaining infantry led by Asas Salapio Zaratton and Asas Melebisella Caras, with the remainder of the bagage placed in the middle with 40 pieces of cannon, carried by 10,000 cavalry troops under his command, having left a rearguard of another 10,000 cavalry troops led by Asas Melchei Dauroni; and they marched in slow "conat"(?), that is, in day-long marches. On the 18th, they arrived within sight of Baghdād, called Babilonia, which was supplied with 30,000 Turks under the command of Paşa Berhac, and while the sites were reconnoitered a skirmish between the parties followed, but the said fortress remained blocked, and the greatest part of the cavalry and infantry was spread out on the east side against the white gate, which defends the tower area called Dgigalsade (*Jigalzadah*?), extending toward the bastion called that of the birds opposite the bank of the river Tigris; it is not known when the Persians are going to mount an attack opening up the trenches; it is only said that they took various surrounding castles, and that there are skilled cannonmasters in their army, and that a paşa related to Muṣṭafâ [fearing] that he might be decapitated, had escaped this fate by taking refuge with the Shāh, who received him at Yerevan with 2,000 Turks, who have been integrated into the [Persian] army.[74]

[74] Asas Emir Ghintelboga, Asas Efiel Melchinenser, Asas Teofilo Abaldach, Asas Salapio Zaratton, Asas Melebisella Caras, and Asas Melchei Dauroni, mentioned in this paragraph, cannot be identified in any Persian sources, and all seem to be fictitious Ottoman names.

APPENDIX B

AVVISI DI COSTANTINOPOLI ET ALTRI LUOGHI, CON LA MOSTRA DELLE GALERE DELLA SER.MA REPUBBLICA DI VENETIA, & OBBEDIENZA D'ALCUNE ISOLE, E POPOLI A DETTA REPUBBLICA. CON LE LETTERE SCRITTE DAL GRAN TURCO AL RÉ DI PERSIA, E LA RISPOSTA, CHE DÀ IL RÉ DI PERSIA AL GRAN TURCO & ALTRE LETTERE TROVATE NELL'HAVER PRESO UNA PEOTTA[75] CON FINTE INSEGNE DE CRISTIANI & C

Venetia, 1684. Accademia di Lincci, Rome, 173 A10 (25)

MEHMET IV GRAN TURCO À IZACH SOLEMAN RÉ DI PERSIA

Mi vien detto, che con un grosso Essercito hai passato l'Eufrate e sei gionto a Letta; di poi entrato ne confini de Babilonia hai meso a fuoco, & a sacco ogni cosa; e non contento di questo ristretto assieme tutto l'Esercito, con grandissimo impeto vuoi passare pi oltre, dividendo alli soldati oltra il bottino delle robbe da loro fatto, le possessioni, le ville, le castella, & e le citta, di sorte, che io stupisco nel pensare in che modo tu vogli mostrar un'animo non gia di Vincitore, ma di ladrone, & anco esserti collegato con li Christiani nostri nemici. Ma con tutto questo sappi, che noi ci mettiamo all'ordine fatta una bellissima scelta di soldati di tutta la Grecia, di venirti a trovare & provarci con esso teco, ancor che ci paia & in vero sia poco onore a un grandissimo, e potentissimo Monarca fare a gara, e contendendo con un Ladrone, e non osservante della nostra Legge Maomettana.

Il Grand Turco
Belgrado li 25 Aprile 1684

IZACH SOLEMAN À MEHEMET RÉ DE TURCHI

Essendo io accampato a piedi del Monte Tauro, poco di poi inviarò l'essercito con quella maggior sollecitudine verso Babilonia o dove mi sara piu comodo; e per questo poco tempo ho sacchegiato un gran tratto di paese, di sorte, che molte di quelle genti per paura si sono rese alla nostra obedienza. Per tanto

[75] Anna Vanzan tells me that a *peotta* (or *peota*), or *peata*, as it is called today, is a Venetian boat, mainly used for carrying goods. A kind of *peotta* was used to take dignitaries to visit the islands in the lagoon and to watch the region's spectacles. Noble families also used the *peotta* to take part in races and processions on the canals.

molto mi maraviglio, che facendo noi per Ius, e ragione di guerra tante, e si memorabil cose, tu habbi ardire di biasmarci, e dir mal di noi, ma non ci curiamo d'essere ne biasmati, ne lodati dal nemico (e che anco ti facci maraviglia, che habbiamo fatto lega con li Christiani, i quali mai ci hanno dato fastidio, come hai fatto tu) ma solamente cerchiamo di haver vittorie.

Dal Padiglione, li 10 maggio 1684. Il Re di Persia.

TRANSLATION

REPORTS FROM CONSTANTINOPLE AND OTHER PLACES, WITH THE DISPLAY OF GALLEYS OF THE REPUBLIC OF VENICE, AND THE OBEDIENCE OF VARIOUS ISLES AND PEOPLES TO THE REPUBLIC, AND WITH LETTERS WRITTEN BY THE GRAND TURK TO THE KING OF IRAN AND THE RESPONSE BY THE LATTER TO THE FORMER, AND OTHER LETTERS FOUND DURING THE TAKING OF A VESSEL WITH FAKE CHRISTIAN FLAGS

Venice, 1684.

MEḤMED IV TO SHĀH SULAYMĀN, KING OF IRAN

I have been told that you have crossed the Euphrates with a large army and that, having reached Letta[?] and entered the area surrounding Baghdād, you have burned and pillaged everything, and that, not content with this, having assembled the entire army, you intend to go further in your extraordinary impetuosity, dividing among the soldiers, beyond the spoils that they have already obtained, property, villas, fortresses and cities, in such a manner that I marvel at the spirit which you demonstrate, which is not that of a victor but that of a thief, and also that you have made common cause with our enemies the Christians. You should know in all of this, however, that we are assembling a most beautiful selection of soldiers from all over Greece to confront you, although in truth it seems to us that there would be little honor for a great and mighty monarch to engage in competition with a thief and someone who does not observe our Muslim law.

The Grand Turk
Belgrade, 25 April 1684

SHĀH SULAYMĀN TO MEḤMED, KING OF THE TURKS

As I am campaigning at the foot of mount Taurus, shortly I will send the army with great promptness to Baghdād or wherever it will suit me; and in this brief period of time I have pillaged a great tract of land in such a way that many people from there have submitted to us out of fear. I am therefore astonished that, while we are, by right and reason, engaged in so many wars and memorable affairs, you have the audacity to curse me and speak ill of me; however, we care neither about enemy insults nor enemy praise (even if you are wondering at our ties with the Christians who, unlike you, have never given us grief); we only seek to be victorious.

From the army camp, 10 May 1684, The King of Iran.

BIBLIOGRAPHY

AVRIL, PHILIPPE. 1692. *Voyage en divers états d'Europe et d'Asie, entrepris pour découvrir un nouveau chemin à la Chine : contenant plusieurs remarques curieuses de physique, de geographie, d'hydrographie & d'histoire : avec une description de la grande Tartarie, & des differens peuples qui l'habitent*. Paris : Claude Barbin, Jean Boudot, George & Louis Josse.

BAYBURDYAN, VAHAN. 1996. *Naqsh-i Arāmanah-'i Īrānī dar tijārat-i bayn al-milalī tā pāyān-i sadah-i 71 mīlādī*. Tr. Idīk Bāghdāsāriyān (Girimānīk). Tehran : [s.n.], 1375 Sh.

BEDIK, PETRUS. 1678. *Cehil Sutun, seu explicatio utriusque celeberrimi, ac pretiosissimi theatri quadraginta columnarum in Perside orientis, cum adjecta fusiori narratione de religione, moribus*. Vienna : Leopoldi Voigt.

BEREGANI, NICOLÀ. 1698. *Historia delle guerre d'Europa dalla comparsa dell'armi ottomane nell'Hungheria l'anno 1683*. 2 vols. Venice : Bonifacio Ciera.

BRAUN, HELLMUT. 1969. *Das Erbe Schah 'Abbās I. Iran und seine Könige, 1629–1694*. Ph.D. diss. University of Hamburg.

BURTON, AUDREY. 1997. *The Bukharans : a dynastic, diplomatic, and commericial history, 1550–1702*. New York : St. Martin's Press.

BUSHEV, P. P. 1976. Puteshestvie iranskogo posol'stva Mokhammeda Khoseĭn Khan-Beka v Moskvu v 1690–1692 gg. *Strany i narody Vostoka* 18: 135–72.

CARRÉ, BARTHÉLEMY. 1947–8. *The travels of the Abbé Carré in India and the Near East, 1672 to 1674*. Tr. Lady Fawcett. Ed. Charles Fawcett, Richard Burn. 3 vols. London : Hakluyt Society.

CHARDIN, JEAN. 1811. *Voyages du Chevalier Chardin, en Perse, et autres lieux de l'Orient*. Ed. L. Langlès. 10 vols. and atlas. Paris : Le Normant, imprimeur-libraire.

CHOWANIEC, CZESŁAW. 1926. Z dziejów polityki Jana III na Bliskim Wschodzie, 1683–1686. *Kwartalnik historyczny* 40: 150–60.

A chronicle of the Carmelites in Persia and the Papal missions of the XVIIth and XVIIIth centuries. 1939. 2 vols. London : Eyre & Spottiswoode.

COLENBRANDER, H. T., ed. 1899. *Dagh-register gehouden int Casteel Batavia vant passerende daer ter plaetse als over geheel Nederlandts-India : anno 1636*. The Hague : Martinus Nijhoff.

COOLHAAS, W. PH., ed. 1971. *Generale missiven van gouverneurs-generaal en raden aan Heren XVII der Verenigde Oostindische Compagnie*. Vol. 4. The Hague : Martinus Nijhoff.

DĀNISH'PIZHŪH, MUḤAMMAD TAQĪ. 1985. Paymān'nāmah'hā-yi Īrān. In *Nāmvārah-'i Duktur Maḥmūd Afshār*. Ed. Iraj Afshar, Karīm Iṣfahāniyān. Vol. 1. Tehran : Mawqūfāt-i Duktur Maḥmūd Afshār Yazdī, 1364 Sh.: 127–38.

ESZER, AMBROSIUS. 1973. Sebastianus Knab O.P. Erzbischof von Naxiḳewan, (1682–1690) : Neue Forschungen zu seinem Leben. *Archivum fratrum praedicatorum* 43: 215–86.

——— 1974. Zu einigen bisher ungeloesten Problemen um Sebastianus Knab O.P. *Archivum fratrum praedicatorum* 44: 263–70.

FABRITIUS, LUDVIG. 1955. Kurtze Relation von meine drei gethane Reisen. Appendix to S. Konovalov's "Ludvig Fabritius's account of the Razin rebellion." *Oxford Slavonic papers* 6: 95–101.

FAROOQI, NAIMUR REHMAN. 1989. *Mughal-Ottoman relations : a study of political & diplomatic relations between Mughal India and the Ottoman Empire, 1556–1748*. Delhi : Idarah-i Adabiyat-i Delli.

FERIDUN BEG. 1858. *Münşeât üs-salâtin*. 2 vols. İstanbul : Dar üt-Tıbaat ül-Âmire, 1274–5.

GEĬDAROV, M. KH. 1967. *Remeslennoe proizvodstvo v gorodakh Azerbaĭdzhana v XVII v.* Baku : Izd-vo Akademii nauk Azerbaĭdzhanskoĭ SSR.

GEMELLI CARERI, FRANCESCO. 1699–1700. *Giro del mondo*. 6 vols. Naples : Guiseppe Roselli.

HABERLAND, DETLEF. 1993. Das "Sechste Buch" der Amoenitates exoticae : Überlegungen zu einer kritischen Ausgabe der Briefe Engelbert Kaempfers. In *Engelbert Kaemper, Werk und Wirkung : Vorträge der Symposien in Lemgo (19.-22.9.1990) und in Tokyo (15.-18.12.1990)*. Ed. Detlef Haberland. Stuttgart : Franz Steiner: 410–24.

ISKANDAR MUNSHĪ and VĀLAH IṢFAHĀNĪ. 1938. *Ẕayl-i Tārīkh-i 'alam'ārā-yi 'Abbāsī*. Ed. Suhaylī Khvānsārī. Tehran : Kitābfurushī-i Islāmīyah, 1317 Sh.

I'TIMĀD AL-SALṬANAH, MUḤAMMAD ḤASAN KHĀN. 1984–8. *Tārīkh-i muntaẓam i Nāṣirī*. Ed. Muḥammad Ismā'il Rıẓvanı. 3 vols. Tehran : Dunyā-yi Kitāb, 1363–7 Sh.

JÓZEFOWICZ, ZOFIA. 1962. Z dziejów stosunków polsko-perskich. *Przegląd orientalistyczny*, no. 4: 329–38.

KAEMPFER, ENGELBERT. 1977. *Am Hofe des persischen Grosskönigs, 1684–1685*. Tr. & ed. Walter Hinz. Tübingen, Basel : Erdmann.

KEVORKIAN, RAYMOND H. 1989. Diplomatie et mouvement de libération arménien de la guerre de Candie au siège de Vienne (1683). *Moyen Orient & Océan Indien = Middle East & Indian Ocean* 6: 1–44.

KROELL, ANNE, ed. 1979. *Nouvelles d'Ispahan, 1665–1695*. Paris : Société d'histoire de l'Orient.

——— 1982. Douze lettres de Jean Chardin. *Journal asiatique* 270, nos. 3–4: 295–338.

KRUSINSKI, JUDASZ TADEUSZ. [1740] 1973. *The history of the late revolutions of Persia*. Tr. Father Du Cerceau. 2 vols in 1. Reprint, New York : Arno Press.

KÜTÜKOĞLU, BEKIR. 1962. *Osmanlı-İran siyâsî münâsebetleri, (1578–1590)*. 1 vol. published only. İstanbul : İstanbul Üniversitesi Edebiyat Fakültesi Yayınları.

——— 1993. *Osmanlı-İran siyâsî münâsebetleri, (1578–1612)*. İstanbul : İstanbul Fetih Cemiyeti.

LEVI-WEISS, DORES. 1925. Le relazioni fra Venezia e la Turchia dal 1670 al 1684 e la formazione della sacra lega : capitolo III. *Archivio veneto-tridentino* 8: 40–100.

LOCKHART, LAURENCE. 1958. *The fall of the Ṣafavī Dynasty and the Afghan occupation of Persia*. Cambridge : [Cambridge] University Press.

LUFT, PAUL. 1968. *Iran unter Schah 'Abbās II., (1642–1666)*. Ph.D. diss. University of Göttingen.

MANTRAN, ROBERT. 1989. L'Etat ottoman au XVIIe siècle : stabilisation ou déclin? In *Histoire de l'Empire Ottoman*. Ed. Robert Mantran. Paris : Fayard: 227–64.

MASHĪZĪ, MĪR MUḤAMMAD SA'ĪD. 1990. *Tazkirah-i Ṣafavīyah-i Kirmān*. Ed. Bāstānī Pārīzī. Tehran : Nashr-i 'Ilm, 1369 Sh.

MATTHEE, RUDI. 1993. Anti-Osmaanse allianties en Kaukasische belangen : diplomatieke betrekkingen tussen Safavidisch Iran en Moscovitisch Rusland, (1550–1639). *Sharqiyyât* 5: 1–21.

——— 1994. Administrative stability and change in late-17th-century Iran : the case of Shaykh 'Ali Khan Zanganah, (1669–89). *International journal of Middle East studies* 26, no. 1 (February): 77–98.

MEIER-LEMGO, KARL, ed. 1965. *Die Briefe Engelbert Kaempfers*. Wiesbaden : Franz Steiner.

MUHANDIS BĀSHĪ, JA'FAR KHĀN. 1969. *Risālah-'i Taḥqīqāt-i sarḥadīyah*. Ed. Muḥammad Mushīrī. Tehran : Bunyād-i Farhang-i Īrān, 1348 Sh.

NAṢĪRĪ, MUḤAMMAD IBRĀHĪM. 1994. *Dastūr-i shahriyārān : sālhā-yi 1105 tā 1110 H. Q. pādshāhī-i Shāh Sulṭān Ḥusayn Ṣafavī*. Ed. Muḥammad Nādir Naṣīrī Muqaddam. Tehran : Mawqūfāt-i Duktur Maḥmūd Afshār Yazdī, 1373 Sh.

NAVĀ'Ī, 'ABD AL-ḤUSAYN, ed. 1981. *Asnād va mukātibāt-i siyāsī-i Īrān : az sāl-i 1038 tā 1105 H. Q. : hamrāh bā yāddāshthā-yi tafṣīlī*. Tehran : Bunyād-i Farhang-i Īrān, 1360 Sh.

PALOMBINI, BARBARA VON. 1968. *Bündniswerben abendländischer Mächte um Persien, 1453–1600*. Wiesbaden : Franz Steiner.

PIEMONTESE, ANGELO MICHELE. 1991. La représentation de Uzun Hasan sur scène à Rome, (2 mars 1473). *Turcica* 21–3: 191–203.

REYCHMAN, J. and ZAJĄCZKOWSKI, A. 1968. *Handbook of Ottoman-Turkish Diplomacy*. Rev. & expanded tr. Andrew S. Ehrenkreutz. Ed. Tibor Halasi-Kun. The Hague and Paris : Mouton.

RICHARD, FRANCIS. 1995. *Raphaël du Mans missionnaire en Perse au XVIIe s*. 2 vols. Paris : Société d'histoire de l'Orient : L'Harmattan.

RIYĀḤĪ, MUḤAMMAD AMĪN. 1989. *Sifāratnāmah'hā-yi Īrān : guzārishhā-yi musāfirat va ma'mūrīyat-i safīrān-i 'Usmānī dar Īrān*. Tehran : Tūs, 1368 Sh.

ṢĀBITIYĀN, Z̤., ed. 1964. *Asnād va nāmah'hā-yi tārīkhī-i dawrah-'i Ṣafavīyah*. Tehran : Kitābkhānah-'i Ibn Sīnā, 1343 Sh.

SANSON. 1694. *Estat present du royaume de Perse*. Paris : La veuve de Jacques Langlois, et Jacques Langlois.

SARAY, MEHMET. 1990. *Türk-İran münâsebetlerinde Şiiliğin rolü*. Ankara : Türk Kültürünü Araştırma Enstitüsü.

SCHILLINGER, FRANZ CASPAR. 1707. *Persianische und ost-indianische Reise*. Nuremberg : Johann Christoph Lochners.

SETTON, KENNET M. 1991. *Venice, Austria, and the Turks in the seventeenth century*. Philadelphia : American Philosophical Society.

SMIDT, JAN. 1930. Reisverhaal van Jan Smidt, 26 Juli 1628–14 Juni 1630. In *Bronnen tot de geschiedenis der Oostindische Compagnie in Perzië, 1611–1638*. Ed. H. Dunlop. The Hague : Martinus Nijhoff.

STRUYS, J. J. 1676. *Drie aanmerkelijke en seer rampspoedige reysen, door Italien, Griekenlandt, Lijflandt, Moscovien, Tartarijen, Meden, Persien, Oost-Indien, Japan en verscheyden andere gewesten.* Amsterdam : Jacob van Meurs, Johannes van Someren.

TROEBST, STEFAN. 1993. Isfahan-Moskau-Amsterdam : Zur Entstehungsgeschichte des moskauischen Transitprivilegs für die Armenische Handelskompanie in Persien, (1666–1676). *Jahrbücher für Geschichte Osteuropas* 41, no. 2: 180–209.

—— Forthcoming. Die Kaspi-Volga-Ostsee-Route in der Handelskontrollpolitik Karls XI. die schwedischen Persien-Missionen unter Ludvig Fabritius, 1679–1700. *Forschungen zur osteuropäischen Geschichte* 53 (1997)

TUCKER, ERNEST. 1996. The peace negotiations of 1736 : a conceptual turning point in Ottoman-Safavid relations. *Turkish Studies Association bulletin* 20, no. 1 (spring): 16–37.

VAḤID MĀZANDARĀNĪ, GHULĀM ʻALĪ, ed. 1971. *Majmūʻah-ʼi ʻahdnāmah'hā-yi tarīkhī-i Īrān : az ʻahd-i hakhāmanishī tā ʻaṣr-i Pahlavī, 559 qabl az Mīlād-1942 (1320 Shamsī).* Tehran : Vizarat-i Umūr-i Khārijah-ʼi Shāhanshāhī.

VAḤĪD QAZVĪNĪ, MUḤAMMAD ṬĀHIR. 1951. *ʻAbbāsnāmah yā sharḥ-i zindagānī-i 22 sālah-i Shāh ʻAbbās Sānī (1052–1073).* Ed. Ibrāhīm Dihgān. Arāk : Kitābfurūshī-i Dāvūdī, Isfand 1329 Sh.

WAUGH, DANIEL CLARKE. 1978. *The great Turkes defiance : on the history of the apocryphal correspondence of the Ottoman Sultan in its Muscovite and Russian variants.* Columbus : Slavica Publishers.

ZAKARIIA AGULETSI. 1938. *Dnevnik Zakariia Aguletsi.* Ed. S. V. Ter-Avetisyan. Yerevan : Armfan-i hratarakchʻutʻyun.

ŻEVAKIN, E. S. 1940. Persidskiĭ vopros v russko-evropeĭskikh otnosheniiakh XVII v. *Istoricheskie zapiski* 8: 129–62.

Three Safavid Documents in the Record Office of Denmark

Faridun Vahman

THERE ARE THREE SAFAVID DOCUMENTS IN THE Record Office of Denmark (Rigsarkiv), two belonging to Shāh Ṣafī I (r. 1038–52/1629–42), and one to Shāh Sulaymān I (r. 1077–1105/1666–94). The two from Shāh Ṣafī are addressed to Duke Frederick III (1609–70) of Holsten Gottorp (now a part of Germany). Although they are identical in their contents, they are different in their style of hand-writing and in composition.

On 22 October 1635 the Duke of Holsten sent a large delegation consisting of 100 men to Iran, hoping to sign a trade treaty with Shāh Ṣafī. In August 1637/Rabī' I–II 1047, after suffering great hardship, the delegation headed by Otto Brüggermann (1600–40) and Philip Cruse (1597–1676) arrived in Iṣfahān by way of Russia and the Caspian Sea. During five months of sojourn in Iṣfahān, they were received on several occasions by the Shāh and accompanied him in hunting. Eventually, they left Iran with precious presents from Shāh Ṣafī to the Duke of Holsten and arrived back to Gottorp in April 1639.

The two documents of the Danish Record Office describe this visit and indicate that Shāh Ṣafī sent his ambassador, Imām Qulī Beg Qājār (Īshak Āqāsī), to Denmark with the Danish delegation. Using the traditional diplomatic language of time, Shāh Ṣafī expressed the hope that the relations between the two Royal Houses would continue as before and that other ambassadors would be exchanged in the future. It is not clear why there are two versions of the same letter. It may be surmised that one of the letters was used as a copy of the original in case of loss (Figs. 1–2; for a translation of document no. 1, see Appendix A).

No trade treaty was concluded and Otto Brüggermann was soon executed because of his failure in this mission and because of promising military help to Iran. But the secretary of the Danish delegation, Adam Olearius (1603–71), recorded the events of the journey in detail, leaving for posterity his unique description of this undertaking. His book *Offt begehrte Beschreibung der newen orientalischen Reise*, has since been translated into many languages.[1]

• • •

On 6 December 1691/15 Rabīʿ I 1103 an official delegation from Iran arrived to the court of the Danish king Christian V (1670–99). The objective of the mission was to demand compensation for the confiscated merchandise belonging to Iranian merchants which was seized by a Danish ship in Indian Ocean. Four years earlier in 1687, the Danish ship "Antonietta" had captured the vessel "Walendis" and had taken it to the Danish colony of Trankebar on the southeastern coast of India. At that time the Danish East Asiatic Company (Østasiatisk kompagni) was active in India and used Trankebar as a base for its activities. These activities often involved military clashes between well-armed Danish ships and the Bengali navy. It was in such clashes that the "Walendis" had been captured and its merchandise, partly belonging to Indians and partly to Armenian Iranians of Julfā, had been seized.

The Iranian ambassador and his company were received by the king on 11 December 1691/20 Rabīʿ I 1103, at which time they presented their credentials and a letter from Shāh Sulaymān addressed to the former king Christian IV, who had died forty-three years earlier in 1648. Despite this diplomatic blunder, and despite the fact that the Iranians refused to take off their turbans, even at the audience ceremony, the meeting ended pleasantly. The king promised to see to the matter and to inform the ambassador of the result. Nevertheless, the outcome of the investigations was not favorable for the Iranians. In a letter dated 30 December 1691 and addressed to the Danish king, the East Asiatic Company argued that since the Bengalis had been in war with the Danish merchant vessels and had inflected great losses against them, it was best for the Iranians to seek compensation from the Bengali court.[2]

Despite this outcome, the exquisitely embroidered purse in which the Iranian ambassador had carried his credentials was kept and is now at the

[1] Originally printed in Schleaswig by J. zur Glocken in 1647. English translation: *The voyages & travels of the ambassadors sent by Frederick Duke of Holstein, to the great Duke of Muskovy, and the King of Persia*, tr. John Davies, London : Printed for Thomas Dring and John Starkey, 1662. Persian translations: *Safarnāmah-'i Ādām Uli'āriyūs : bakhsh-i Īrān*, tr. and notes Aḥmad Bihpūr, Tehran : Sāzmān-i Intishārātī va Farhangī-i Ibtikār, 1363 Sh. [1984]; *Safarnāmah-'i Ādām Ūli'āriyūs*, tr. Ḥusayn Kurdbachchah, 2 vols., Tehran : Shirkat-i Kitāb barā-yi Hamah, 1369 Sh. [1990]; See also ʻAbd al-Ḥusayn Navā'ī, *Īrān va jahān*. 2 vols. to date, Tehran : Mu'assasah-'i Nashr-i Humā, 1364–9 Sh. [1985–90], 1:314–20.

[2] See also ʻAbd al-Riẓā Hūshang Mahdavī, *Tārīkh-i ravābiṭ-i khārijī-i Īrān*, Tehran : Amīr Kabīr, Isfand 1349 Sh. [1971], 76–7.

Danish Museum of Decorative Art (Danske kunstindustrimuseum), while the letter of Shāh Sulaymān with the comprehensive inventory of the disputed merchandise and the names of the Armenian merchants is kept at the Record Office of Denmark.

In his letter Sulaymān ensures the ruler of his respect and informs him of the total value of the merchandise, in all 9,000 *tūmān*s, partly in cash and the remainder in merchandise. After listing the names of the Armenian merchants (12 in total) who had suffered the loss, he argues that the merchants are usually not involved in disputes between states, particularly when the Danish Royal House, like all other European kings had an amicable relation with the Safavid dynasty. He also reminds the king of Denmark that in a similar incident a few year back, the Danes had returned the properties of the Iranians amounting to 1000 *tūmān*s, and that certainly this confiscation of merchandise had been done without the king's knowledge. At the end he also expresses the hope that in the future the Danes would not attack the Armenian merchants who profess the same Christian religion.

The list of the merchandise is a scroll of 20 cm. width and 80 cm. length. On the top, the total value of the merchandise (9,000 *tūmān*s) and its equivalent in Indian *rupee*s (192,140 *rupee*s) are given. This is followed by the detailed list of the merchandise and the names of the owners. The list containing sugar, fabric, jam, and lac provides a useful picture of the kind of goods imported from India at the time of the Safavids (Figs. 3–4; for a translation, see Appendices B and C)

APPENDIX A*

FIRĀDRĪK BEG [FREDERICK], *VĀLĪ* [KING] OF QŪLISTĀN [HOLSTEN], THE GLORIOUS, THE POWERFUL, THE GREAT

To Your Excellency, the ruler of glory, the greatness of dignity, the bravery of justice. Reputable for fairness and bravery, dignity and glory, with lion-like heroism, the select among the just kings of Christianity, the chief of all the glorious monarchs of the faith of Jesus, the great and elevated king [Firādrīk Beg, *Vālī* of Qūlistān, the glorious, the powerful, the great]: may your destiny be happy and heavenly; all friendly, best regards and glorious, affectionate admirations are [herewith] offered, due to the ultimate friendship which has continuously existed between this sublime dynasty and the exalted kings of *Farang* [Europe]. All [our] efforts and concerns are to help the prosperity and to safeguard the grandeur and to enhance the glory of that sublime and *khurshīd kulāh* king [i.e., a king who is so elevated that the sun becomes his hat]. May the affairs of the two worlds be as such to satisfy you.

Now, I bring to Your good attention that the desire for friendship requires that at this moment the honorable Plusūs Kurūpūs [Philip Cruse] and Ūtā Burūkhmān [Otto Brüggermann], whom you had sent to this deserved direction with kind letters, have presented themselves to [this] glorious audience, and what was required of these intelligent ambassadors in this mission they have performed in the best manner possible, which increased affection and friendship; they [also] related the oral messages confided to them, which were welcomed and strengthened the foundation of kindness and friendship. In return, our glorious Majesty is dispatching towards that [i.e., your] direction, and along with the aforementioned ambassadors, Imām Qulī Bayk Qājār, Īshak Aqāsī, in order to [further] establish the foundation of friendship and unity, and delegated to him certain matters that at the time of his audience [with Your Excellency] he would present and mention them.

It is the manner of friendship to always conduct this good method of relationship, and to continuously exchange friendly-titled letters and intelligent ambassadors, which contributes to the cause of unity and friendship. [It is hoped that His Excellency would] permit the said ambassador to return soon and inform our (*īn-ṭaraf*) officials of whatever important affairs that you may have here without any hesitation, so that royal attention be devoted to their accomplishment.

No more verbosity. In the long run, may all affairs end in happiness.

* [I am very grateful to Farhad Eslami for translating the documents in this article, and also to Professor Hossein Modarressi for clarifying some problems in the text of the documents. Ed.]

APPENDIX B

KIRISTĪ'ARN [CHRISTIAN], THE FOURTH

Greetings, respects, glorification, and honors are presented at the opening of the gate of friendship and founding the construction of recognition to the great and dignified King of Zhūyitah [Jutland, a peninsula west of Denmark], Iskāniyah [Scandinavia, the Northern Kingdom], Finiyah [Finlandia], Islandiyah [Island], Nurvizhiyah [Norway], and other States of Dīnmirgh [Denmark], [Kiristī'arn the Fourth]. All of [our] exalted resolutions and the utmost of [our] shining intentions are devoted to their highest degree to [wish] that the affairs of grandeur and dignity of that occupant of the throne of kingdom and glory are in order and the matters of [his] glory and fortune are stable.

Now, [herewith] it will be brought to Your friendly attention that at this time it was presented to this throne of kingdom that some 9,000 *tūmān*s which were partly in cash and mostly in merchandise [of] Ūhān [Johanes], Ya'qūbkhān [Jacob], Grīgūr [Gregor] son of Mārkūs [Marcus], Āvīd, Khājīk, Zakaryā, Ārābīd, Āghā Pīrī, Uvānis [Ovanes], Grīgūr [Gregor] son of Khāchidūz, Sarkiz [Sarkis], and Siqmūn [Simon], some their own belongings and some belonging to the Armenians of [the district of] Julfā in the capital of Iṣfahān, who were their clients, were put in a vessel, which had the mark of the Farangān [European] Valindīs [Walendis], and were navigating the sea in way of trade. Around the Kālī Qal'ah on the border of Sīlān [Ceylon], some of Your Excellency's subjects confronted them and captured them, along with the belongings of some Indians, because a dispute between them [i.e., your subjects] and the Indian Ruler, and confiscated and held [the property] in the Qal'ah of Tirankibār [Trankebar], which belongs to Your Excellency.

Since the merchants are not involved in disputes between kings and states, and that this glorious dynasty [i.e., the Safavids] has never had a dispute with the occupants of the throne of that [i.e., your] side, and that all justice-loving kings of Europe has endless friendship with this just, benevolent dynasty, and as a result, two or three years ago, when 1,000 *tūmān*s of properties belonging to the same Christians which were fallen into the hands of Your Excellency's subjects in the same manner, were returned to them, therefore, the current confiscation of the aforementioned merchandise must have been without Your Excellency's knowledge.

It is worthy of [your] rule of justice that Your Excellency's subjects be ordered to return the said cash and merchandise to the said Christians, and that [they] no longer violate the rights of these individuals, with whom Your

Excellency shares a common religious faith. This way [Your Excellency] continues to adhere to the policies of friendship and cordiality, and always add clarity and purity to the pleasant spring of mutual friendship and sincerity by informing [us] of your desires, wants, and wishes.

APPENDIX C

KIRISTĪ'ARN [CHRISTIAN], THE FOURTH

As mentioned in His Majesty's auspicious letter, what the Armenians of [the district of] Julfā in the capital of Iṣfahān had put from among their own and their clients' merchandise in a vessel which had the mark of Valindīs [Walendis], and which was captured by the subjects of the great and dignified King of Zhūyitah, Iskāniyah, Finiyah, Islandiyah, Nurvizhiyah and other states of Dīnmirgh, Kiristī'arn, The Fourth [is the following]: The total cash and merchandise amounts to 192,140 *rupee*s, in the currency of India, and 9,000 *tūmān*s, in the Iranian currency:

[Total] Cash:	1,500 *rupee*s (in the chest)
[Total] Merchandise:	Fabric: 527 *bastah*s (package)
	Sugar: 623 *qiṭ'ah*s (piece)
	Jam: 112 *dabbah*s (jars)
	Lac: 25 boxes *bastah*s (package)
	Chest full of clothes and merchandise (in addition to the cash *rupee*s mentioned before): 14 *'adl*s (bolt)
	Miscellaneous items: 16 *būqchah*s (packs)

Ūhān son of Biqūs had brought to the aforementioned ship 66,000 *rupee*s (which equals 3,150 *tūmān*s) of the assets of his client Uvānīs:

Cash:	773 *rupee*s (in the chest)
Merchandise:	Fabric: 203 *bastah*s
	Sugar: 6 *qiṭ'ah*s
	Jam: 50 *dabbah*s
	Miscellaneous items: 4 *būqchah*s
	Chest full of clothes and merchandise (in addition to the cash *rupee*s mentioned before): 1 *'adl*

Grīgūr son of Mārkūs had brought to the aforementioned ship 11,000 *rupee*s (which equals 525 *tūmān*s) of the assets of his client Kasbir [Casper]:

[Merchandise]:	Fabric: 44 *bastah*s Jam: 8 *dabbah*s Miscellaneous items: 2 *būqchah*s

Khājīk son of Uvānīs had brought to the aforementioned ship 8,650 *rupee*s (which equals 413 *tūmān*s) of the assets of his client Vāsil son of Mānās:

[Merchandise]:	Fabric: 30 *bastah*s Jam: 2 *dabbah*s Miscellaneous items: 1 *būqchah*

Ārābīd son of Ya'qūb had brought to the aforementioned ship 9,980 *rupee*s (which equals 476 *tūmān*s) of the assets of his clients Fūkār son of Bīdrus and Makirdīj [?]:

[Merchandise]:	Fabric: 47 *bastah*s Jam: 8 *dabbah*s Miscellaneous items: 2 *buqchah*s

Uvānīs son of Mūsīs had brought to the aforementioned ship 7,330 *rupee*s (which equals 350 *tūmān*s) of his own assets:

[Merchandise]:	Fabric: 27 *bastah*s

Siqmūn had brought to the aforementioned ship 321,500 *rupee*s (which equals 1,356 *tūmān*s) of his own assets as well as those entrusted to him by some group [of individuals]:

Cash:	527 *rupee*s (in the chest)
Merchandise:	Fabric: 5 *bastah*s Sugar: 275 *qiṭ'ah*s Miscellaneous items: 1 *būqchah* Chest full of clothes and merchandise ([this is] other than the [chest of] *rupee*s mentioned before): 13 *'adl*s

Ya'qūbkhān son of Zādūr had brought to the aforementioned ship 39,320 *rupee*s (which equals 1,786 *tūmān*s) of the assets of his client Zādūr son of Biqūs:

Cash:	200 *rupee*s
Merchandise:	Fabric: 113 *bastah*s
	Sugar: 4 *qiṭ'ah*s
	Jam: 36 *dabbah*s
	Miscellaneous items: 5 *būqchah*s

Āvīd son of Zādūr had brought to the aforementioned ship 2,490 *rupee*s (which equals 119 *tūmān*s) of the assets of his client Zakaryā:

Merchandise:	Fabric: 10 *bastah*s

Zakaryā son of Rāpul [?] had brought to the aforementioned ship 7,040 *rupee*s (which equals 336 *tūmān*s) of the assets of his clients Uvānīs Kallah Gūsh and Sulṭān Kal:

[Merchandise]:	Fabric: 28 *bastah*s
	Jam: 8 *dabbah*s
	Miscellaneous items: 1 *būqchah*

Āghā Pīrī son of Uvdīk [?] had brought to the aforementioned ship 4,400 *rupee*s (which equals 210 *tūmān*s) of the assets of Grīgūr son of Mirkiz [i.e., Mārkūs]:

[Merchandise]:	Fabric: 20 *bastah*s
	Lac: 12 1/2 *bastah*s

Sarkiz had brought to the aforementioned ship 980 *rupee*s (which equals 49 *tūmān*s) of his own assets:

[Merchandise]:	Sugar: 125 *qiṭ'ah*s

Grīgūr son of Khāchidūr [i.e., Khāchidūz] had brought to the aforementioned ship 2,800 *rupee*s (which equals 140 *tūmān*s) of his own assets:

[Merchandise]:	Sugar: 213 *qiṭ'ah*s
	Lac: 12 1/2 *bastah*s

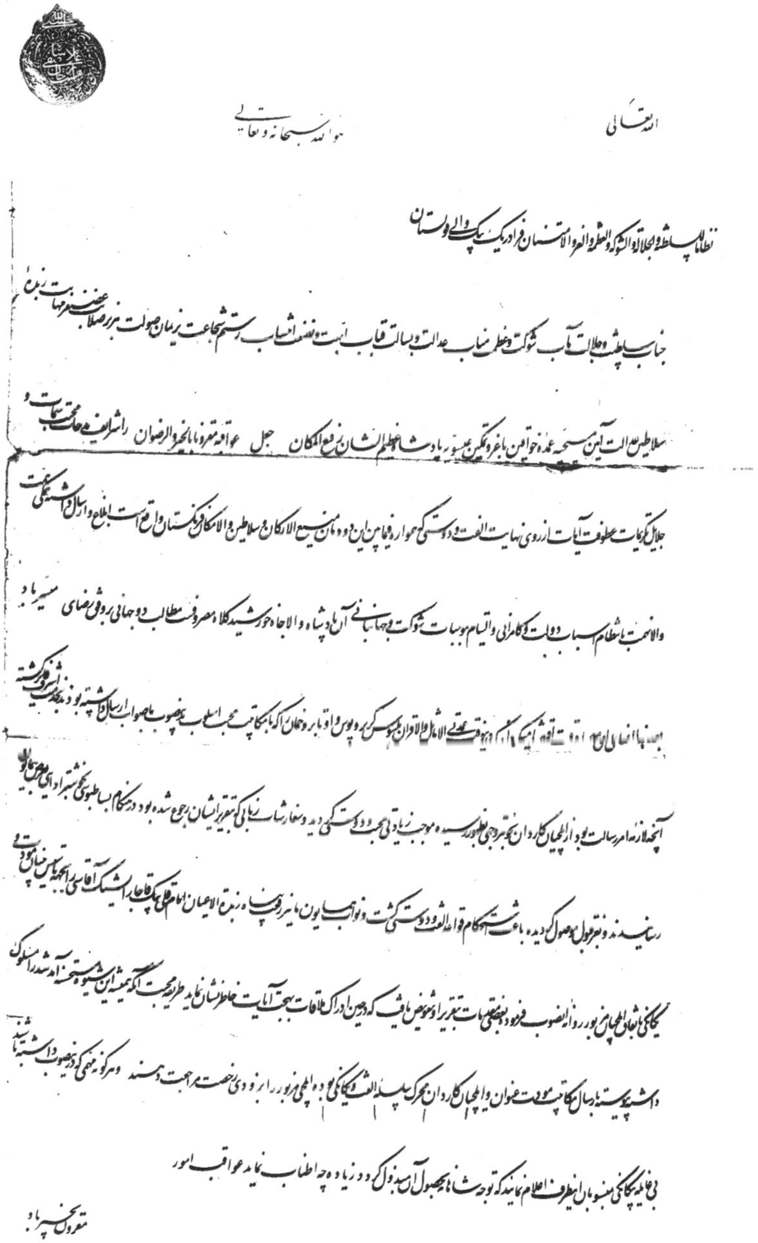

Fig. 1. Shāh Ṣafī's letter to Duke Frederick III, King of Holsten (Version A). 1637? Record Office of Denmark (Rigsarkiv)

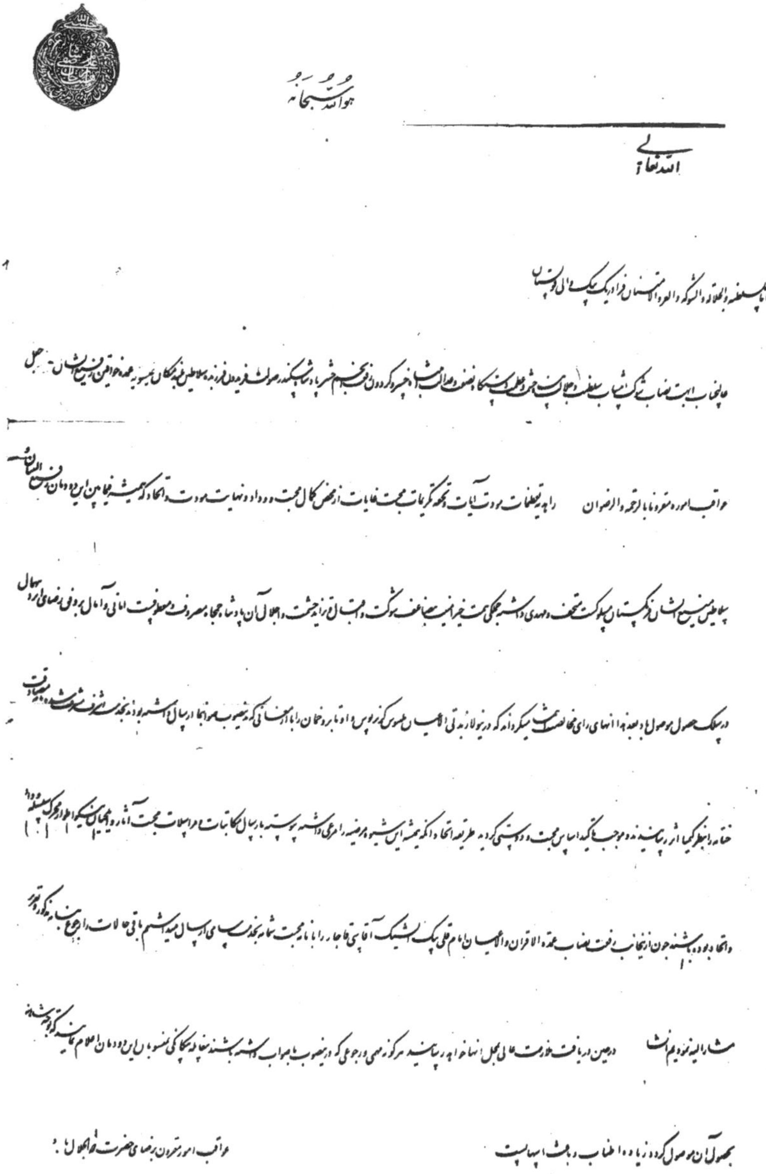

Fig. 2. Shāh Ṣafī's letter to Duke Frederick III, King of Holsten (Version B). 1637? Record Office of Denmark (Rigsarkiv)

Fig. 3. Shāh Sulaymān's letter to King Christian V. 1691? Record Office of Denmark (Rigsarkiv)

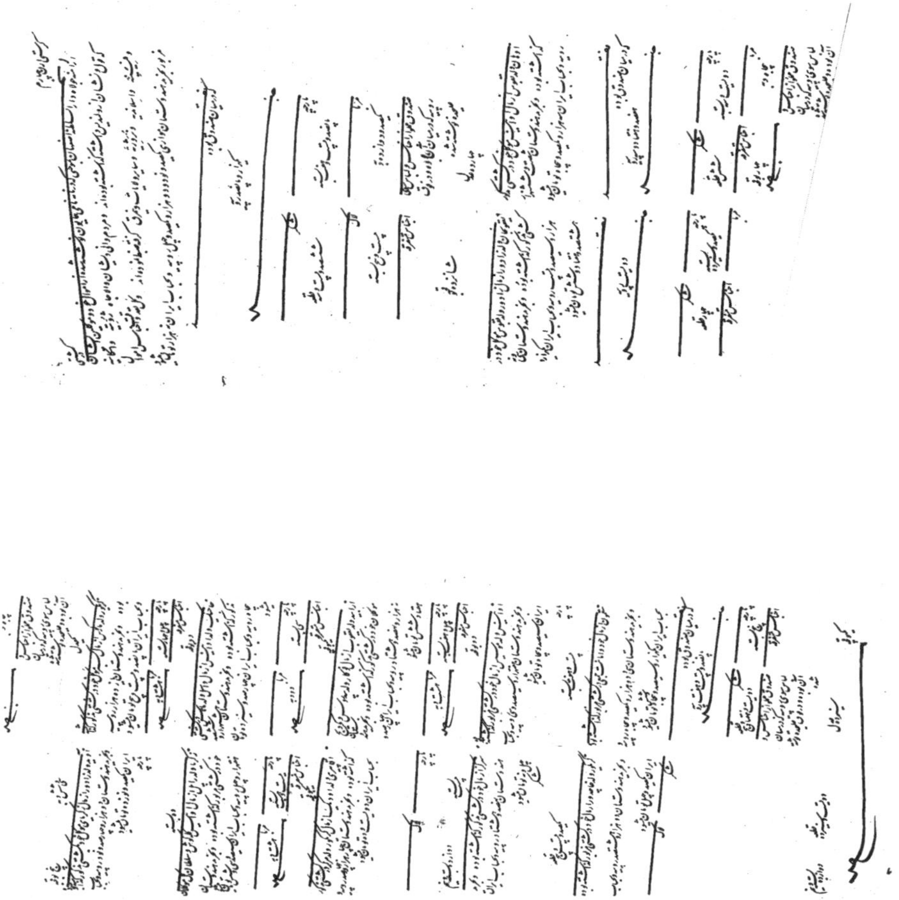

Fig. 4. List of merchandise attached to Shāh Sulaymān's letter. 20 x 80 cm.

Culinary Arts in the Safavid Period

M. R. Ghanoonparvar

ACCORDING TO IRANIAN LEGEND, COOKING IS AN ART imparted by Ahrīman (the Zoroastrian spirit of evil) to a mythological king, Āzhīdahāk, or Ẕahhāk. At a time when people were eating only vegetables, Ahrīman appears in the guise of a cook to the king, preparing the flesh of animals to give the king the strength to shed blood. Eventually, through the machination of Ahrīman, two snakes grow from Ẕahhāk's shoulders. Ahrīman again appears, this time in the guise of a physician, who prescribes as the only remedy to calm the snakes daily feedings of a dish prepared of the brains of two young men. In time, two cooks evolve a plan to save one of the men each day by substituting the brain of a sheep and mixing it with the brain of the other sacrificed young man. Hence, the art of cooking developed from this time, in particular to make the flesh of slaughtered animals more palatable for human consumption.[1]

Despite this gruesome beginning, however, much attention has been paid to this human activity of the preparation and cooking of food; some have even elevated it to the level of an art or science. Whether or not the inauspicious legend of Ahrīman and Ẕahhāk has any bearing on the art of cooking, there seems to be a "curse" of sorts, accompanying it in that, unlike other arts in which the artist finds a window to immortality, as it were, through the aesthetic appeal of such arts to the higher senses of sight and sound, cooking is essentially a mundane art form, primarily serving the physical survival of human beings and appealing to the "baser" senses of taste and smell. Unlike a poet or a painter, whose work may survive to immortalize him, the culinary artist's creation, when at its best, is certain to be consumed and to vanish. In one sense, the work of a culinary artist may belong to the category of what has been called the "'self-consuming' artifact," such as dominoes arranged in intricate patterns to be set in motion, the climax to which is the ultimate collapse of the arrangement.[2] But even the general non-utilitarian nature of such arts excludes cooking, placing it in a lower aesthetic category. For an imaginative cook who has mastered his craft and approaches the status of a creative artist,

[1] Firdawsī 1988–, 1:48–51.

[2] See a very interesting study by Stanley Fish, 1972.

then, there remains the dilemma of how, in addition to practicing his art, he may fulfill his yearning for immortality through his creation. It is perhaps partly to resolve this dilemma that such an artist may seek help from another medium, namely writing, in an attempt to leave behind a testament to and a record of his artistic creations and talent.

Two such records from the Safavid period (907–1105/1501–1694) were edited by Iraj Afshar and published in 1360 Sh./1981 in one volume, entitled *Kārnāmah va Māddat al-ḥayāh*[3] which deserve attention and which will be the primary focus of this essay. The first text, the *Kārnāmah : dar bāb-i ṭabbākhī va ṣan'at-i ān,* is authored by Ḥājjī Muḥammad 'Alī Bāvarchī Baghdādī who wrote it as a gift to a nobleman named Mīrzā'ī during the time of Shāh Ismā'īl (r. 907–30/1501–24). The second text, the *Māddah al-ḥayāh : risālah dar 'ilm-i tabbākhī,* is authored by Nūr Allāh, a chef to Shāh 'Abbās I (r. 995–1038/1587–1629) who may have even been a descendant of Muḥammad 'Alī Bāvarchī.[4]

These two Safavid texts are significant in that they are apparently the first texts of their kind, that is, primarily written as cookbooks. Earlier texts do exist in which the subject of cooking is addressed; however, the authors of such texts generally utilized the culinary arts as a vehicle for other purposes, such as explaining the medicinal attributes of certain foods or even as a medium for writing satire and parodies. An example of the latter category is the 15th-century *Dīvān* of Abū Isḥāq Aṭ'amah.[5] Abū Isḥāq's work is important in terms of culinary art, particularly in that it records the names of various dishes and even ingredients. However, the *Dīvān* is primarily a work of satire, Sufi allegories, and parodies of the works of the great masters and the poet's contemporaries—on the whole, a literary work. In fact, Abū Isḥāq himself stated that since the great masters had exhausted every avenue in the realm of poetry, he looked to culinary art as a new domain.[6] He also said that the great masters had built the "house of poetry," but it neither had a toilet nor a kitchen; 'Ubayd Zākānī, the 14-century poet and satirist known for his obscene verses, provided the toilet, and he, the kitchen. However, this kitchen was the source of food for thought rather than for the body. Even the choice of verse over

[3] Afshar 1981–; the cover title of the book is different: *Āshpazī-i dawrah-'i Ṣafavī.* The text of the book includes a detailed introduction about the history of Persian cooking, as well as a bibliography of various Arabic and Persian cookbook manuscripts. A second volume to include two other texts (one from the 9th century, and another from the 13th century) has been completed but not yet published, see ibid., introd. 25–6, and Afshar 1983.

[4] Afshar 1981–, introd. 30.

[5] See Aṭ'amah [195–] and Mīrzāyif 1971.

[6] Aṭ'amah [195–], 4–5.

prose, for the most part, suggests that the author of the *Dīvān* did not intend his work to be used as a cooking manual, but primarily as literature.[7]

On the other hand, these Safavid texts, as mentioned, are essentially cookbooks rather than literary texts, the authors of these texts being professional chefs and not literary artists. Both are conscious of cooking as an art, and the act of writing the recipes to them serves primarily as a medium to record their culinary abilities, not as an exercise in literary production, as was obviously the case with Abū Isḥāq.

The first text, *Kārnāmah*, which is dated 927/1520–21, includes an introduction and twenty-two chapters on various categories of foods. The author claims that this is the first text of its kind, on "cooking and its craft" (*ṭabbakhī va ṣan'at-i ān*).[8] The recipes include measurements for the ingredients, often detailed directions for the preparation of foods, including the types of utensils and pots to be used, as well as instructions for decorating and serving the finished dishes. Rice and a variety of other grains (wheat and barley), legumes (chick peas, split peas, fava beans, mung beans), other vegetables (spinach, leeks, coriander, eggplants, squashes, onions, cabbage, beets), nuts (pistachios, almonds, walnuts), meats (lamb, chicken, beef, game birds, venison), herbs (mint, dill weed), and spices (saffron, cinnamon, ginger) are among the common ingredients used in the recipes. Although these ingredients and their combinations in various dishes are not very different from those used commonly in Iran today—in fact, many of the recipes have not changed significantly—the frequency and rather large amounts of meat used in various dishes, as suggested by the authors, mark a substantial difference. Obviously, one should keep in mind that the recipes represent the types of food and food preparation particular to affluent, aristocratic households which not only explains the generous use of such comparative luxuries as saffron but the huge quantities (e.g., 1 *man* [probably the equivalent of six kilos] flour, 1 *man* meat, 1/2 *man* onions, etc.) as well. In any case, it does not seem likely that the average Iranian household at this time was able to prepare such elaborate and comparatively expensive food, despite the author's claim in his introduction that he has written the book "for the benefit of the nobility as well as the public" (*khāṣṣ va 'āmm*).[9]

As a culinary artist rather than merely a recorder of recipes known to him, Bāvarchī is aware of creativity in his work when he claims to have invented a number of the recipes in *Kārnāmah*, and promising to record other

[7] For a discussion of this text, see Javādī n.d.
[8] Afshar 1981–, 37.
[9] Ibid., 36.

inventions in the future. Nevertheless, his rather conservative approach even in regards to his innovations suggests that he holds sacred certain conventions regarding foods. In other words, he is not one to throw things together just to see what will happen. His inventions remain within the well-established categories and may actually be viewed as variations or imitations of one form or another. Parenthetically, this practice common in other arts, such as literature—in which the pre-20th-century poet's achievements, for example, were measured in terms of imitation of the works of the masters and adherence to conventional literary forms within which the artist or poet was able to display his creativity and innovations—seems to have also been common among these culinary artists, who stayed within conventional culinary genres even when they engaged in creating new dishes.

In practical terms, the *Kārnāmah* was probably written as a manual for would-be chefs and apprentice cooks. Nevertheless, by today's standards, this collection of Safavid recipes can be used with only slight modifications. Each of the chapters of *Kārnāmah* deals with one category of food, including one chapter on *kamāj*es (pies); five chapters on *āsh*es, *shūrbā*s, and *harīsah*s (varieties of pottages and soups); five chapters on various rice dishes; and chapters on *qilyah*s (stews), *kabāb*s, and confections. The text reads very much like a manual, with detailed instructions and explanations where necessary. Most recipes include serving instructions and provide useful hints to the reader on how to achieve the best results in preparing a particular dish. Bāvarchī avoids excessive digression in presenting the recipes, a cumbersome practice used frequently by Nūr Allāh, the author of *Māddah al-ḥayāh*, who devotes many pages to the praise of the king and other nobilities. In the case of *Kārnāmah*, the author's interest in the art of cooking is apparent; he uses writing as a medium to exhibit his cooking talents.

The second text, *Māddah al-ḥayāh*, written seventy-six years after *Kārnāmah*, is in many respects different from the earlier text. Whereas Bāvarchī begins his work with a pertinent introduction to foods and food preparation, then informs the reader of the circumstances which prompted him to write the book, and finally provides a table of contents at the end of this introduction, Nūr Allāh, on the other hand, adheres to contemporary writing conventions, beginning his introduction with an elaborate mixture of prose and verse in praise of the Almighty, the Prophets, the Imāms, and the Shāh. Like the *Kārnāmah*, Nūr Allāh's text is also a gift which he has prepared to present to his patron. In regards to food preparation itself, the introduction to this latter text contains very little; in fact, it is doubtful that Nūr Allāh actually intended his book to be used by the average person for the purpose of cooking. He states in his introduction that given the famous saying, "*Vaṣf al-ʿaysh niṣf al-ʿaysh*" (describing pleasure is worth half the pleasure), he determined to compose "a treatise on the science or craft (*ʿilm*) of cooking, to benefit those who seek or have some knowledge of this craft."[10] In other words, unlike the author of *Kārnāmah*, Nūr Allāh was most likely not writing his book for the consumption of the general public; and secondly, the book may well have been written for the pleasure gained from the descriptions of foods, rather than as an actual guide to cooking. In this respect, not only has he had to resort to writing as a medium to record his craft, but he is also at least partially entrapped by the medium in the final analysis, for the end result, as suggested by the author, is reading about the art of cooking rather than practicing it. Perhaps conscious of his work as a manual to be read, Nūr Allāh calls on the spirits of past master chefs to aid him in his endeavor and states, in an indignant tone, that he hopes "the envious and those with evil intentions" will be powerless against him,[11] which seems to suggest that there was some rivalry among different chefs at the court of Shāh ʿAbbās I, some of whom did not wish Nūr Allāh well, and that in writing his manual, Nūr Allāh is trying to gain the favor of his patron.

In the same vein, following the prefatory remarks, Nūr Allāh devotes a few words in a separate section to the characteristics of an *ustād*, or master chef. He states: "An *ustād* is he who would by no means neglect his task from beginning to end and would never entrust it to someone else."[12] Furthermore, he must be devoid of pride and known for his faith and trustworthiness. On a more practical level, Nūr Allāh observes that an *ustād* "must keep himself clean, both outwardly and inwardly. He must keep cooking utensils clean, and he must especially wash the meat, for the taste of food . . . is the result of piety and cleanliness." Nūr Allāh also advises the *ustād* to be patient and good-tempered with his subordinates and to avoid obscenities.[13]

As a guide to cooking, *Māddah al-ḥayāh* is not as useful as *Kārnāmah*. For instance, Nūr Allāh does not consistently provide measurements or even step-by-step directions, at times merely naming the recipe and stating that a particular dish is well-known and requires no detailed description. On one occasion, he even states that to describe two particular recipes "would be troublesome for both the reader and the writer" (*mawjib-i dard-i sar-i khvānandah va nivīsandah mī'shavad*).[14] Nevertheless, in terms of anecdotes and information on favorite dishes of the court, or even references to other

[10] Ibid., 190.
[11] Ibid., 191.
[12] Ibid., 194.
[13] Ibid.
[14] Ibid., 202.

famous contemporary cooks, *Māddah al-ḥayāh* is clearly a more interesting text. There are, for instance, several recipes which Nūr Allāh claims were invented by various Safavid kings, including a venison recipe by Shāh 'Abbās I.[15] Such examples provide the opportunity for him to embellish his text with verses about the Shāh or in praise of morality.

Another feature of *Māddah al-ḥayāh* is Nūr Allāh's obsession with the use of Arabic phrases and words. An interesting example is his rather consistent use of the Arabic preposition *ma'a* for the Persian *bā*, which makes his prose even more archaic and unnatural today. In this respect, too, *Kārnāmah* is a more useful text for cooking than is *Māddah al-ḥayāh.*

In sum, a comparison between these two Safavid cooking manuals reveals that the author of the earlier text is more conscious of and even prides himself on his craft as a chef, the book serving as a manual or a record of his artistic talents in a form available to him which might gain him a degree of artistic recognition, even immortality; whereas the author of the second text, although still attempting to write a cooking manual, becomes involved in the medium of writing to some degree, perhaps hoping for material gain or status by trying his hand in another art, that of panegyric literature.

[15] Ibid., 205.

BIBLIOGRAPHY

AFSHAR, IRAJ, ed. 1981– *Kārnāmah va Māddat al-ḥayāh : matn-i dū risālah dar āshpazī az dawrah-'i Ṣafavī : 'aṣr-i salṭanat-i Shāh Isma'īl Avval va Shāh 'Abbās Avval*. 1 vol. to date. Tehran : Surūsh, 1360 Sh.–

—— 1983. Jild-i duvvum-i Āshpazī va sarnivisht-i Ṣaydanah. *Āyandah* 9, no. 6 (Shahrīvar 1362 Sh.), 482.

AṬ'AMAH, ABŪ ISḤĀQ. [195-] *Dīvān-i Mawlānā Busḥāq Ḥallāj Shīrāzī mashhūr bih Shaykh Aṭ'amah*. Shīrāz : Kitābfurūshī-i Ma'rifat, [133- Sh.]

FIRDAWSĪ. 1988–. *Shāhnāmah*. Ed. Jalāl Khāliqī Muṭlaq. Introd. Iḥsān Yārshāṭir. 5 vols. to date. New York : Bibliotheca Persica ; Costa Mesa, California : Mazda Publishers.

FISH, STANLEY E. 1972. *Self-consuming artifacts : the experience of seventeenth-century literature*. Berkeley : University of California Press.

JAVADI, HASAN. n.d. *The life and works of Bushaq : a fifteenth century poet of the culinary arts*. Unpublished paper.

MĪRZĀYIF, 'ABD AL-GHANĪ. 1971. *Abū Isḥāq va fa''ālīyat-i adabī-i ū*. Doshanbeh : Nashrīyāt-i Dānish.

New Facts on Nādir Shāh's Campaign in India

Willem Floor

CONTEMPORARY SOURCES ON NĀDIR SHĀH'S INDIAN campaign are few. Documents from the Dutch East India Company (Vereenigde Oost-Indische Compagnie) [VOC] dealing with this subject are therefore especially valuable. In my discussion of Nādir Shāh's decision to invade India, I draw on information contained in the Company's archives, and I offer a translation of some of the documents. None of these sources has so far been used or published in its entirety.[1]

NĀDIR'S DECISION TO INVADE INDIA

It is a generally accepted fact that Nādir Shāh decided to invade India during the siege of Qandahār in 1150/1737–8.[2] However, data from contemporary Dutch sources suggest that he had contemplated such an action well before that year.

Already on 5 February 1734/1 Ramaḍān 1146, the Dutch agent in Iṣfahān, Mattheus van Leypsigh, reported that it was rumored that after his suppression of Muḥammad Khān Balūch's revolt, Nādir Shāh had intended to subjugate the Balūch and take Qandahār, and that he had also intended "to pay a visit to the country of the Great Mughal."[3] A similar sentiment was voiced when van Leypsigh reported on 8 May 1734/4 Dhū al-Ḥijjah 1146 that "it would seem that Tamas Chan [Ṭahmāsb Qulī Khān] wants to attack Qandahār, of which it is now said that the Indians [Mughals] have a hold on it, [and] after which he will go to Kābul from that [town]."[4]

These statements can, of course, be relegated to the realm of rumors and may have had no grounds whatsoever. However, the Dutch were wary of unreliable and unfounded rumors, and if they reported them at all, they com-

[1] Two of the translated letters (see Appendices C and D) were also known in abridged form and were available to James Fraser, who reproduced them in his book, see Fraser [1742] 1973, 143–51 and 1984, 97–102.

[2] See Lockhart 1938, 115–9, 123.

[3] Algemeen Rijksarchief, The Hague, VOC 2323, 5 February 1734, fol. 960. On Muḥammad Khān Balūch's revolt, see Floor 1983, 63–93.

[4] Algemeen Rijksarchief, The Hague, VOC, 8 May 1734, fol. 1102.

mented on their spurious nature. In these two instances, van Leypsigh reported the rumors, furthermore indicating that there might be some truth in them. This may also explain van Leypsigh's remark to Ṭahmāsp Qulī Khān Jalāyir, governor of Iṣfahān, on 27 November 1734/1 Rajab 1147, when the latter transmitted Nādir Shāh's order to the Dutch to supply him with ships. Van Leypsigh's response to the Shāh's order was that if the Shāh intended to use the ships against the Mughals, the Masqaṭ Arabs, or the Turks, he would never receive them.[5] The VOC director in Bandar 'Abbās even confirmed this in an official letter to Ṭahmāsp Qulī Khān Jalāyir, saying that the Dutch did not discount the possibility of an Iranian action against India.[6]

Nādir Shāh's information about India must have been quite up-to-date, since an Iranian ambassador, 'Alī Mardān Khān Faylī, had already been sent to the Mughal court in 1142/1730.[7] At that time, an alleged pretender to the Mughal throne was also staying in Iṣfahān. It is not known, however, whether Nādir had contacts with this person.[8] He had, however, contacts with a former *vazīr* of Muḥammad Shāh, the Great Mughal, while the presence of the sizable Banyan community also provided him with a source of information on India. In fact, Nādir Shāh used to refer to India as the "Banyan caravansarai."[9]

India figured prominently in Nādir Shāh's scheme of the world. One of his biographers, Muḥammad Kāẓim, wrote that on the occasion of the crowning of 'Abbās III, the infant son of the deposed Ṭahmāsb II, in Rabī' I 1145/ September 1732, Nādir swore in the presence of those present: "I will throw reins around the necks of the Ottoman Sulṭân, of Ḥusayn Shāh Afghān, of Muḥammad Shāh of India, and of Abū al-Fayẓ Khān, the ruler of Tūrān, and will make them serve this magnificent court."[10] As a first step, however, he sent, for a second time, an embassy to India led by Muḥammad 'Alī Khān, who died in Thatta (Sind) on his return voyage.[11] When the costly goods belonging to Muḥammad 'Alī Khān, with an estimated value of 60,000 *tūmāns*, were not released by the authorities in Sind, Nādir became so enraged that he

[5] Ibid., VOC 2357, 5 December 1734, fol. 116.

[6] Ibid., VOC 2357, 27 December 1734, fol. 463. The director took this possibility very seriously as is borne out by the fact that he informed his colleague in Surat about it on 20 January 1735/25 Sha'bān 1147, see ibid., VOC 2357, 24 August 1735, fol. 229.

[7] Riazul Islam 1970, 139ff.

[8] Algemeen Rijksarchief, The Hague, VOC 2163, 30 March 1730, fol. 218.

[9] Ibid., VOC 2477, 13 April 1739, fol. 457.

[10] Muḥammad Kāẓim 1985, 1:234.

[11] See Riazul Islam 1970, 141 for details on this embassy. According to Algemeen Rijksarchief, The Hague, VOC 2322, fol. 335 vs (12 September 1732 and appendix of 28 September 1732) Muḥammad 'Alī Khān had instructions to demand, *inter alia*, 500,000 *tūmāns* of debt incurred by Shāh Humāyūn during his refuge in Iran in the 1530s.

almost sent a fleet to India to take revenge for this insult. Instead, he sent two envoys, Ṣafī Khān and Muḥammad Sa'īd Beg, to fetch the goods. The two left in December 1735/Sha'bān 1148 from Bandar 'Abbās with a Dutch ship and returned on 22 February 1736/9 Shawwāl 1148.[12] Reports from van Leypsigh and the Dutch trading office in Kirmān indicate that, following the return of the last envoys, Nādir was quite eager to send more emissaries to India: Ḥasan 'Alī Khān (the Mu'ayyir Bāshī) was supposed to be sent in March 1736/Dhū al-Qa'dah 1148; next 'Alī Mardān Khān Faylī was expected to go;[13] then, in November 1736/Jumādá II–Rajab 1149, Mīrzā Taqī Khān was supposedly selected to leave for India to demand the payment of 300,000 *tūmāns*; it was even reported that, in case of a refusal, Nādir himself would go and collect the money.[14]

All these facts clearly indicate that Nādir Shāh had his sights set on India well before 1150/1737. Prior to his invasion of India, Nādir also had contacts with Indian magnates. In fact, on 1 April 1736/19 Dhū al-Qa'dah 1148, an Iranian physician, who was in the service of the *vazīr* of the Great Mughal, arrived in Iṣfahān as his master's envoy.[15] Also, in December 1736/Rajab–Sha'bān 1149, Nādir received the son (probably Maḥabbat Khān) of 'Abd Allāh Khān, the Balūch chief of Kalāt, who had come to Iṣfahān to offer his assistance against Ḥusayn Khān of Qandahār. According to Dutch reports, the Kābul Afghans too offered their support, because Ḥusayn Khān had plundered their lands. Nādir must have considered these envoys to be of great importance, for he accompanied them as far as Qumshah.[16] In that very month, van Leypsigh reported that Mīrzā Taqī Khān Shīrāzī asked the Dutch to sell ships to Nādir Shāh, who needed them to attack the rebellious Arabs of the Persian Gulf, the Masqaṭ Arabs, and India.[17]

According to van Leypsigh's report, Nādir Shāh seriously considered invading India as soon as he began the siege of Qandahār in June 1737/Ṣafar–Rabī I 1150. He wanted "to pluck some of its golden feathers," the report informs us.[18] He sent an ambassador, Muḥammad Khān Turkumān, to the Mughal court to once again claim Shāh Humāyūn's debt to Iran, an excuse

[12] Algemeen Rijksarchief, The Hague, VOC 2356, 22 December 1735, fol. 717; 30 August 1735, fol. 2202; 8 August 1736, fol. 2356.

[13] Ibid., VOC 2416, 16 March 1736, fols. 2396, 2543.

[14] Ibid., VOC 2417, 10 December 1736, fol. 3978.

[15] Ibid., VOC 2416, 11 April 1736, fol. 2433.

[16] Ibid., VOC 2417, 26 December 1736, fol. 3934; See Lockhart 1938, 113 on Nādir's campaign against other sons of 'Abd Allāh Khān.

[17] Algemeen Rijksarchief, The Hague, VOC 2417, 26 December 1736, fol. 3917.

[18] Ibid., VOC 2448, 11 June 1737, fol. 1341.

that was interpreted by the Dutch as Nādir's "unreasonable lust" for conquering India.[19] The Dutch also reported that around this time Nādir began approaching the Iranians in the service of the Great Mughal to ask for financial support. On the other hand, Muḥammad Shāh himself had begun sending large presents to Nādir. In fact, in early 1150/1737, he was said to have offered 20 *lakh* of *rupee*s to Nādir to leave him in peace.[20] At that time, Nādir Shāh was also regularly receiving presents from a certain "Mila Goda Jaar Chan Zemiendaar of Godabaad," who can only be Miyān Khudāyār Khān, *zamīndār* of Khūdābād, the Kalhurā chief of Sind.[21] These contacts are borne out by various Iranian and Indian sources. Their significance, however, has so far not been fully appreciated by historians. The *Ma'āṣir al-umarā'* records that Nādir wrote to Khudāyār Khān to allow his troops to pass through Sind to invade India.[22] A similar intention is referred to in the *Tuḥfat al-kirām*.[23] The *Jahāngusha-yi Nādirī* and the *Nādirnāmah* state that Khudāyār Khān had been sending petitions to Nādir when he was staying at Delhi.[24] The reason for these contacts between Nādir and Khudāyār Khān may have been their earlier relations. Still, the passing of Nādir's ambassador, Muḥammad Khān Turkuman, through Sind to Delhi, and, even more, the death in Moltan of Muḥammad Khān's deputy, a certain Mīrzā Muḥammad Riẓā, may also have played a role.[25] However, the Dutch reported that one of Nādir Shāh's generals, Khān Jān, had suffered a defeat against Mughal troops commanded by "Godajaar Chan Lettie," the Kalhurā chief.[26] By writing the petitions or sending presents, the latter may have wanted to appease Nādir, who was furious over this defeat. According to a rumor reported by van Leypsigh, Nādir wanted to send an army commanded by four generals to India.[27] Although Hanway

[19] Ibid., VOC 2448, 11 June 1737, fols. 1341, 1372; on this embassy, see Riazul Islam 1970, 143.

[20] Algemeen Rijksarchief, The Hague, VOC 2448, 11 June 1737, fols. 1372–3; VOC 2476, 15 May 1738, fol. 888.

[21] Ibid., VOC 2448, 7 March 1738, fol. 2352.

[22] Shāhnavāz Khān Awrangābādī 1979, 1:818.

[23] 'Alī Shīr Qāni' Tattavī 1971, 448.

[24] Mahdī Khān Astarābādī 1962, 339; *Nādirnāmah* 1964, 90.

[25] Algemeen Rijksarchief, The Hague, VOC 2248, fol. 1434; see also Riazul Islam 1970, 143, footnote no. 6.

[26] Algemeen Rijksarchief, The Hague, VOC 2448, 26 October 1737, fol. 1434; this probably refers to the campaign by Pīr Muḥammad and Khān Jān in Makrān and Balūchistān in 1148–9/1736–7, see Lockhart 1938, 117; the appellation "Leti" is also mentioned in Shāhnavāz Khān Awrangābādī 1979, 1:817 and in *A genuine history* 1741, 21, where it has been misspelt as "Fitte," despite the fact that the Dutch original has "Littie." See footnote no. 30 for full information on the Dutch source.

[27] Algemeen Rijksarchief, The Hague, VOC 2448, 4 November 1737, fol. 447.

was right when he stated that Nādir Shāh did not need the help of a fifth column to take India, this nevertheless is by itself no argument to reject the existence of regular relations, if not collusion, between Nādir Shāh and some leading Indian magnates before the invasion, as has been suggested by many sources.[28]

CASUS BELLI?

Another issue that deserves attention is the absence of a reply from Muḥammad Shāh to the letter that Muḥammad Khān Turkumān had brought from Nādir. According to Shaykh ʻAlī Ḥazīn, the Mughal court was unable to decide what to reply. Muḥammad Bakhsh Āshūb, however, included in his *Tārīkh-i shahādat* the draft of a reply by Muḥammad Shāh which stated that a nobleman would be appointed as ambassador as requested by Nādir Shāh.[29]

In the Dutch archives the undated translation of an undated letter, allegedly from Muḥammad Shāh to Nādir Shāh, has been preserved that may be another draft of a reply, or the reply itself, as Dutch sources explicitly state.[30] From internal evidence it is clear that the letter was written prior to Nādir Shāh's invasion of India and before the siege of Qandahār. Also, it was probably written in reply to a mission which took place before the one undertaken by Muḥammad Khān Turkumān and which is only mentioned by Shaykh ʻAlī Ḥazīn.[31] The distinguished Qizilbāsh to whom Muḥammad Shāh refers in this letter was Muḥammad Aslān Khān Ustājlū, about whom I have been unable to find any information.[32] As is clear from the letter (parts of which are reproduced here), its contents constituted a sufficient *casus belli* for Nādir Shāh.

The letter, which also has been printed in its entirety in an English translation of an unpublished Dutch report written in 1741 about Nādir's invasion, is allegedly in reply to a letter written by Nādir Shāh just after his conquest of Kābul. Nādir demanded in this letter that the frontier between Iran and India

[28] For a discussion of these sources, see Riazul Islam 1970, 146, footnote no. 3; and Lockhart 1938, 124.

[29] On this issue, see Riazul Islam 1970, 144

[30] For the text of this letter, see Algemeen Rijksarchief, The Hague, VOC 2399, fols. 214–20. It is also reproduced in VOC 2584, fols. 1880–2090, in a manuscript report entitled *Verhandeling Concerneerende de invasie van den Persiaansen Koning Nadircha in het Mogolse Ryk geduurende de Jaren 1738 en 1739, Zijne huyshouding in de Hoofdstad Dhilly. Mitsgaders desselfs depart na Persien; ter ordre van den E.E. Agtb. Heere Joan Albert Sichterman Directeur der Bengaalse Directie uyt de successieve aangekomene geschreevene Nouvelles enz. g'excerpeert*. An English translation of this report was published in 1741 as *A genuine history*, see *A genuine history* 1741.

[31] Riazul Islam 1970, 143, footnote no. 2.

[32] *A genuine history* 1741, 16.

be henceforth the river Indus. In his reply to this *'arẓdast* or request—as he calls Nādir's letter—Muḥammad Shāh refers to a letter with a totally different content from that indicated in the report. Muḥammad Shāh refers *inter alia* to Nādir's "intentions against Candahar, to besiege that Castle, and to expel the Governor from thence." Muḥammad Shāh had also asked the Indian viceroys of Kābul and Multan that they should not allow fleeing Afghans to escape into India territory, which makes it clear that Nādir had not as yet taken Qandahār.[33] Muḥammad Shāh then continues to vilify Nādir, calling him faithless and perfidious, one who has dared to aspire to a throne that is not his, not knowing that it is not every stone that produces a glittering sapphire. "Thou art not yet so far advanced as to be entitled to send Ambassadors, or write Letters to the Type of Heaven, according to the Custom of Kings." After having informed Nādir that Iran is a gift to the Safavids from the Mughal court; that he, Muḥammad Shāh, has hundreds of thousands of soldiers at his command, whom he lists, he concludes: "They shall after this march into Persia, release Thamas Mirza from his confinement, and replace him on the royal throne of Persia . . . If then, leaving thy presumption, thou considerest thy safety and welfare, and turnest thy self to repentance and amendment before thou art punished according to thy deserts, for which purpose this mighty army is appointed, perhaps the servants of my court may blot out the records of thine offences with the pen of grace; if not, look to thyself, and none else."[34]

Other letters and documents in the same volume of correspondence sent from Batavia to Amsterdam are not dated but they can be dated as no later than November 1737/Sha'bān 1150. If this letter was indeed written in late 1736 or early 1737, it explains another Dutch report, dated October 1737/ Rajab 1150, in which the Great Mughal was said to have given *his* Afghans permission to help their brothers in Iran.[35]

[33] See Lockhart 1938, 122, according to whom this refers to the situation in 1737, before Nādir's conquest of Qandahār.

[34] Ibid., 19–23; for the Dutch original, see Algemeen Rijksarchief, The Hague, VOC 2399, fols. 214–20.

[35] Algemeen Rijksarchief, The Hague, VOC 2448, 26 October 1737, fol. 1434. For the Muḥammad Shāh letter, see ibid., VOC 2399, fols. 214–20, although the Dutch report, referred to in footnote no. 30, wrongly suggests that the letter was sent at a later date as implied by the chronological arrangement of its material.

INVASION OF MAKRAN AND GWADAR

The above information leaves little doubt about Nādir Shāh's intentions to invade India prior to 1737/1150. When Nādir finally began his invasion in Rabī' I 1150/June–July 1737, he simultaneously ordered Mīrzā Taqī Khān Shīrāzī to prepare an army of 30,000 men and 14 large ships for a campaign against Sind. Muḥammad Taqī Khān asked the Dutch for a ship to transport supplies and troops to Divil (near modern Karachi). Since he promised to land the infantry near Cape Jashk, the Dutch felt they could not refuse his request and therefore complied with it.[36] When Nādir was pursuing the ruler of Sind, Khudāyār Khān, in Muḥarram 1153/March 1740, he ordered Muḥammad Taqī Khān to try to capture the latter unawares. By that time, Muḥammad Taqī Khān had claimed the conquest of Kij-Makran and Gwadar. He informed the Dutch that on his arrival in Makran many chiefs, hung with chains, had submitted themselves to him. They included "Sjeeg Kassum, former Walie of Makroen [Shaykh Qāsim, *vālī* of Makran], Amier Godadaet [*Amīr* Khudādād], Amier Hassat Dolla [*Amīr* Asad Allāh], Amier Hoetie [*Amīr* Hūtī?], Amier Baraemie [*Amīr* Bahramī?], as well as all the Baluch grandees." He then moved to Gwadar, where at three *manzil*s (stages) from the port "Sjeeg Noer Mhamed [Shaykh Nūr Muḥammad], son of the murdered Sjeeg Ballaed [Shaykh Bilār]" and his chiefs came to him.[37] Muḥammad Taqī Khān entered Gwadar on 11 Shawwāl 1152/11 January 1740, where he took possession of all sailing vessels and *dinghi*s (rowing vessels). He intended to stay in Gwadar until 1 Dhū al-Qa'dah 1152/30 January 1740 to destroy the remaining enemies and appoint a new governor.[38] However, despite his claim that he had subjugated the Balūch, Muḥammad Taqi Khān was defeated in Dhū al-Ḥijjah 1152/February 1740 by Balūch tribes led by Malik Dīnār. Two months later Muḥammad Taqī Khān was back in Bandar 'Abbās, having achieved virtually nothing.[39]

[36] Algemeen Rijksarchief, The Hague, VOC 2477, 12 April 1739, fol. 462; VOC 2510, 22 October 1739, fol. 1353; 11 November 1739, fol. 414; 25 December 1739, fol. 119.

[37] Ibid., VOC 2511, fol. 898; fols. 1284–8. Shaykh Bilār, was the uncle of "Sheh Kasem," the last Buledai chief. Shaykh Bilār had forsaken the Zikri faith for Islam and was then opposed by Malik Dīnār, chief of the Gikchi tribe and defeated by him with the help of other Zikris. Shaykh Qāsim asked for help from Nādir Shāh, who then sent Mīrzā Taqī Khān to him. On this episode, see *Baluchistan through the ages*, 1980, 1:584; on the tenets of the Zikri faith see ibid., 2:570–5. I have been unable to identify the other local chiefs mentioned in this letter.

[38] Ibid.

[39] Lockhart 1938, 184; on Malik Dīnār, see footnote no. 37.

APPENDIX A[40]

COURT NEWS, 27 DECEMBER 1738 [15 RAMAḌĀN 1151]

Sixteen days ago the Great Mughal gave leave to Nesamel Moulk [Niẓām al-Mulk][41] to depart in the company of the Amarou Chandoran [*Amīr al-Umarā'* Khān Dawrān][42] and Commer Goedichan [Qamar al-Dīn Khān][43] as well as of Mahmetchan Bhenges [Muḥammad Khān Bangash][44] and many others. Six days ago the court gave leave to depart to three of four viceroys to join the king's army which has taken up positions six miles from here.[45] This army is two miles wide and 15 miles long, and is increased daily by new arrivals. If this army were trained after the European model it could conquer the whole world. However, there is no order; each commander does as he pleases.

It is said that the army will move in four columns on the 19th or 21st of this month to take up position seven miles further away. The army columns will maintain a distance of 10 miles between one another to improve their supply situation.

The fifth of next month the army will set out, without taking up [fixed] positions, and proceed eight miles every day, till it has joined the army at Lahoor [Lahore], which is 175 miles from here.

Today news arrived here that Thamas Coeliechan [Ṭahmāsb Qulī Khān, i.e., Nādir Shāh] has arrived in person 200 miles above Lahore with an army of 50,000 men. His vanguard is commanded by his son, who has reinforced the bridge over the river Attock, which is at a distance of 100 miles from Lahore, with 25,000 soldiers.

40 Translation of a letter preserved in Algemeen Rijksarchief, The Hague, VOC 2427, fols. 545–50. Proper names are identified, transliterated, or translated in square brackets when they are encountered for the first time. After that, they replace the original form and appear without the square brackets.

41 Niẓām al-Mulk was the leader of the so-called Tūrānī party at court.

42 Khān Dawrān Khān, the leader of the so-called Hindūstān party at court.

43 Qamar al-Dīn Khān was the chancellor or *vazīr al-mamālik* of Muḥammad Shāh, the Mughal emperor.

44 Muḥammad Khān Bangash, an Afghan soldier of fortune, nawab of Farrukhābād.

45 According to another letter from Delhi, Muḥammad Shāh "the day before yesterday ordered Niẓām al-Mulk, Khān Dawrān Khān and Qamar al-Dīn Khān to take to the field. They are now camped five miles outside the city and have to depart on 11 Ramaḍān. The Great Mughal has given [them] 1,5 *kurūr* of *rupee*s and three elephants. Many magnates and heathen Rajputs are preparing themselves to depart. They have 1200 pieces of cannon commanded by three generals, 500 battle-trained elephants, 100,000 horsemen and 200,000 foot soldiers," Algemeen Rijksarchief, The Hague, VOC 2427, by Voulton, 17 December 1739, fol. 551.

According to other news, it is said that one of his [i.e., Nādir's] sons has arrived with an army of 50,000 men at Chandola Gousseratte [?] 40 miles from Lahore. However, this is uncertain. Meanwhile, another of his sons has gone towards Maur touranie[46] with an army of 30,000 men.

Yesterday, the emperor sent orders to Niẓām al-Mulk to depart. He replied that His Majesty also needs to take the field by his side to form a second army. If this [army] is formed it will be a considerable [one]; however, nothing has been decided yet. Meanwhile, two armies are coming to reinforce our royal army. The first one amounts to 30,000 horsemen, not counting the match-lock men, who usually are three times their number. They are commanded by Niẓām al-Mulk's son. The other, [commanded] by the *ghenieme* [rebels] of Sam Ragia,[47] is 50,000 horsemen strong, and march 20 to 25 miles per day. The royal army, however, only moves at a speed of five to seven miles, because it is burdened with tents and supplies.

The heathen Ragia Sewaag Jetsing [Rajah Sawai Jai Singh],[48] who lives 15 days from here, is approaching with an army of 50 to 60,000 horsemen. Also coming is Sadaatchan [Sa'ādat Khān Burhān al-Mulk],[49] who is 18 days' journey from here with 60,000 horsemen, having been summoned by the emperor with great urgency. The Ragia of Nervare is with 60,000 horsemen at a distance of eight miles, and the Ragia of Attes[50] with 10,000 horsemen six days' journey from here. This does not include a large number of others, who have to gather here this month with groups of 2000, 1000, and 500 horsemen. It is likely that this army will amount to 5 *lakh* (500,000 horsemen) and that it will have a countless number of match-lock men. If the army can defend itself, then Nādir Shāh has to be very lucky to defeat it. However, one has reason to fear that if the army of the Great Mughal does not put up an orderly defense, Nādir Shāh will not have too much trouble in doing so.

It is said that Nādir Shāh is a man of great equity, both towards the soldiers and to others. However, with regard to the provincial governors and the heathens, he despoils them totally, not leaving them a penny's worth. Further, he is very strict with the rebels, not sparing one of them. However, he gives his protection to all who seek it. Many people look forward to Nādir Shāh's

46 This may refer to Taraori, at 10 miles from Karnal. It may also refer to the campaign of Riẕā Qulī Mīrzā, Nādir Shāh's eldest son and viceroy, in Transoxiania or Moorish Tartary.

47 The Ganim [*ghenieme*] or Marathas under their leader Baji Rao I [Sam Ragia] were collaborating with the Mughal emperor.

48 Sawai Jai Singh or Jai Singh II, Sawai of Amber, an important Sikh leader.

49 Sa'ādat Khān, Subahdar of Oudh.

50 The Ragia [Rajah] of Nervare may be identified as the Rajah of Mewar (Udaipur), one of the Rajput princes. The Rajah of Attes [?] is unknown to me.

coming, because the emperor is so weak in governing that nothing is really done. His soldiers are badly paid, because the heathen clerks steal everything and therefore are as rich as the generals. It is believed here that the troubles will be over in three to four months. The governor of Lahore, a brother-in-law of Qamar Qulī Khān, has taken the field against Nādir Shāh with 70,000 horsemen.

APPENDIX B[51]

LETTER FROM LAHORE DATED 11 RAMAḌĀN [1151] [23 DECEMBER 1738]

My dear brother, Muḥammad Semman, May God preserve you.
I am healthy and wish day and night that you also may continue that way. I have received your letter of 5 Schabaan [Sha'bān] [1151] [18 November 1738], in which you reported that the general Ṭahmāsb Qulī Khān has come to subjugate the empire of Hindoostaan [Hindūstān], and that you therefore were very worried. Also, that if he would take the town of Jellaalabaadh [Jalālābād], he certainly would try to seize also the town of Peschoor [Peshawar], because that is why he has come to Jalālābād. The King of Dhilly [Delhi] has sent his army and therefore this problem should be resolved with God's blessing.

The aforementioned general has put to flight Nasir Chan [Nāṣir Khān], who held the Gijber [Khyber] and Gerba [?] mountains against him. This happened, because they [i.e., the Persians] had made peace with some Patthanen [Pathans] who guided his army along another route. He engaged Nāṣir Khān on 13 Sha'bān [1151] [26 November 1738], and totally defeated his troops. Some say that they have killed Nāṣir Khān, while others maintain that he has been taken prisoner, and still others have it that he has fled. I also hear that the Pathans have taken him to the town of Attek [Attock]. The army of Ṭahmāsb Qulī Khān has arrived in the aforementioned town of Peshawar. They plundered it for 12 hours. The people of that area have fled to Lahore, taking with them as much of their possessions as possible. The remainder has been plundered by the enemy. The king's son has arrived in Lahore, while the Iranian army has reached the river Attock. Nāṣir Khān's son, *foijsdaar* [*fawjdār*] [military commander] of Attock, has permitted his men to flee. The inhabitants of the provinces of Gojeraat [Gujarat], Moraadabaad [Murādābād], Ammabaadh [Aḥmadābād] also have fled and come towards Lahore. I hope that God will punish nobody that way. However, such is the state of affairs currently. His Eminence, Sekkeria Chan [Ẕakariyā Khān],[52] does not allow anybody to leave his province. Some Mughals who had deserted were apprehended at the river Goondwaal [?] and returned to the aforementioned city. His Excellency has all routes guarded to prevent anybody from leaving. The inhabitants have hired wagons and camels to use, if need be. On 7 Ramaḍān [1151] [19 December 1738] the aforementioned viceroy of Lahore received a letter addressed

[51] Algemeen Rijksarchief, The Hague, VOC 2427, fol. 550.
[52] Ẕakariyā Khān, the Subahdar of Lahore.

both to His Excellency and to the merchants from Schjehaan-abaad [Jahānābād], in which it was reported that the lords Niẓām al-Mulk, Khān Dawrān Khān, Qamar al-Dīn Khān, and Muḥammad Khān Bangash, as well as all their subordinates, were about to march, and had arrived at a place called Badelli [Badli Sari]. The inhabitants of Lahore were very happy with this news, because if these [lords] arrive soon, the assaults of the Alianen ['Alaviyān i.e., Persians] will be prevented. The lord Nawab Ẕakariyā Khān has left with 3,000 horsemen on 3 Ramaḍān [1151] [16 December 1738]. He wants to muster one *lakh* of soldiers within four days. His Excellency has ordered all *fawjdār*s per "*perwanan*" [order] to join him. I believe that a major battle will take place, for the general has a large army with him. May God grant king Mohamad Scha [Muḥammad Shāh] all that is good.

Everything is very expensive here, viz.

9 "*ceer*"s [*sīr*][53] of wheat for one *ropij*;
7 *sīr*s of rice for one *ropij*;
19 *sīr*s of peas for one *ropij*;
1.25 *sīr*s of ghee for one *ropij*;
3.5 *sīr*s of oil for one *ropij*;
1.25 *sīr*s of Japanese copper for one *ropij*;

The Mughals pay here for each golden Mhoor (*muhr*) 13 *rupees* and 10 *annas*.[54] For one *rupee* one buys here one *rupee* and 10 *annas* of silver. Nobody wants to buy silk, *atlas*,[55] *soesjes*[56] or linen. Those who have lent money to merchants demand it back, a reason why there are many disputes among them.

53 One *man* equals 40 *sīr*. One *man*, probably the *man-i Akbarī* is meant here, weighed 25.155 kg. Thus, one *sīr* equals 628 grams.

54 The golden *muhr* weighed 169 grains of gold and was equal to 10, later 13, *rupee*s.

55 *Atlas* is a silken fabric.

56 *Soesjes* are cotton fabrics.

APPENDIX C[57]

LETTER FROM DELHI, RECEIVED 15 FEBRUARY 1739 [6 DHŪ AL-QA'DAH 1151]

I, who hope the best for you and live in the hope of enjoying your favor, cannot but inform you about the situation of Jahānābād, or Delhi, as I do herewith. It has now been eight months since Nādir Shāh started his invasion, advancing from the Iranian empire to Qandahār and then onwards to Kābul, the most distant frontier of the Hindūstān empire. On his arrival there he seized that town and from there he sent an ambassador to the Great Mughal. Since his arrival the pavilion[58] of the emperor Muḥammad Shāh has been pitched to meet the enemy outside the city in the Moslem month of Rabulauwel [Rabī' al-Awwal] (or according to our calendar the month of June). Because of disputes among the courtiers, nothing has been undertaken as yet, let alone that an army take the field. However, the emperor has remitted by draft a considerable sum to the Nabab Nāṣir Khān, the governor of Peshawar, to keep the Pathans, the original inhabitants, under control. In this way 40 *lakh*s of *rupee*s have been remitted in three separate installments. He [i.e., Nāṣir Khān] has used this to raise a considerable army and has prepared himself for battle, while expecting further necessary support from a mighty army from Delhi. However, by the month of Redjep [Rajab] (or October) nothing of that nature materialized. Meanwhile, Nādir Shāh had fully satisfied the lords and inhabitants of the Kābul province. He had subjugated them, in particular the Pathans, who are the major warriors of those parts. He also had negotiated with the aforementioned Nāṣir Khān. Nobody in Delhi intervened on behalf of the said governor to assist him, despite the fact that he gave battle and was totally defeated. The Pathans led the victor by a secret route to Peshawar, and he seized the town. The governor was forced to flee, but was overtaken by these Pathans, who delivered him into the enemy's hands. It was in Sha'bān (or November) that Nādir Shāh made his entry into Peshawar. After he had detained the said governor, Nāṣir Khān, for some time, the latter not only was set free, but was even elevated to the rank of minister. After this news became

[57] Algemeen Rijksarchief, The Hague, VOC 2485, translation of a Persian letter from Mhamet Feysallac, who resides at court, to Pieter Laurens Phoonsen, director of the Surat factory, dated 5 Shawwāl/16 January 1739, fols. 861–4. As mentioned earlier, this letter was also known in abridged form and was available to James Fraser, who reproduced it in his book, see Fraser [1742] 1973, 143–8 and 1984, 97–100.

[58] I have translated pavillion for *voor thente*, although the Dutch text gives a literal translation of the word *pīsh'khānah*, which means "the tents and other equipment sent ahead to the place where the prince or commanding general decides to halt or encamp."

known here on the first of Ramaḍān (or December) the *Amīr al-Umarā'*, the first Baxie [*Mīr Bakhshī*][59] or general, Khān Dawrān Bahādur, the Nabab Assof Jaabhadur Nesam ulmolk [Āṣif Jāh Bahādur Niẓām al-Mulk], and the Wasier Ulmamalek [*Vazīr al-Mamālik*] Qamar al-Dīn Khān were allowed to depart. They received from the royal treasury one *caroor* [*korur*] or hundred times 100,000 *rupees*, while they were [allowed] to keep their Jagiers [*jagir*] or land assignments, in addition to receiving 700 pieces of cannon and 3,000 falconnets [small cannon]. They were joined by several *emirs* [*amīrs*], who with much pomp left Delhi, and pitched their tents outside the city at Badli Sari, where they continue to recruit additional troops. The Nabab Sa'ādat Khān Burhān al-Mulk, governor of Ood [Oudh], who too had already been summoned to join the march of the royal army, and had crossed the river Genga [Ganges] on his way to Delhi, has, on reception of [new] instructions that he should return to his government, made a turnabout and has marched home. There has never been any friendship between Niẓām al-Mulk, Qamar al-Dīn Khan, and Khān Dawrān Bahādur, so that between the two of them nothing effective can be decided upon. The emperor has, therefore, no other choice to satisfy Khān Dawrān Bahādur, but to order Niẓām al-Mulk and Qamar al-Dīn Khān to take the field, while Khān Dawrān Khān remains with the emperor at court. Because of this the two first mentioned have not been willing to march. Meanwhile, information has been received that the Iranian [i.e., Nādir Shāh], at the advice of Nāṣir Khān, has adopted Indian dress and abandoned Iranian dress, and has sat down on the ceremonial royal throne at Peshawar according to the custom of these parts. He also ordered his army to cross the river Attock and march to Lahore. On receiving this news, the emperor, Muḥammad Shāh, lost heart entirely. He asked the chiefs of the barges [*platboomde vaartuigen*] there [i.e., Delhi] how many days it would take them to reach Pattena [Patna] and Casjibenarres [Benares]. When Niẓām al-Mulk and Qamar al-Dīn Khān learnt about this they presented a petition to His Majesty, with the following contents: "Though his slaves, they will not march, unless His Majesty in person accompanies the royal army. Therefore, it is required that he appear there." A few days of exchange of correspondence followed, and, after much deliberation, it was decided that Sa'ādat Khān would have to go to court to stay with

[59] The *Mīr Bakhshī* was the paymaster-general of the army.

His Majesty, if the army should actually march.[60] To that end, a certain courtier, named Morithchan [Murād Khān], has been sent to this lord. The latter, however, was, on his return to Oudh, attacked by robbers, who plundered his baggage. After much difficulty the messenger was able to appear in person before this lord and informed him about the emperor's order. However, His Excellency had been afflicted with such illness that he could not move, let alone obey the emperor's order. The emperor having learnt this sent him his own personal physician to cure this lord. Meanwhile, a petition was sent to the emperor, as well as three letters to the three aforementioned lords, by the Souba [Subah] of Lahore, Ẕakariyā Khān, who reported that the army of Nādir Shāh, or Ṭahmāsp Qulī Khān, was nearby and very powerful. Further, that the local chiefs of the province had joined forces with him. However, he had only readied a small force to oppose the enemy. He therefore requested immediate assistance from His Majesty, or else everything would be lost. For Emmenabaad [Imīnābād] (an important town in the province of Lahore) which had been manned by the *fawjdār* Calenderchan [Qalandar Khān], who had 10,000 horsemen, had fallen. This had been brought about by a certain Amierbeekchan [*Amīr* Beg Khān], an adherent of Nāṣir Khān, who had taken service with Nādir Shāh. He had recruited a great number of Pathans with his own money, had attacked at night and had taken Imīnābād. He immediately declared the city to be part of Nādir Shāh's domain. On hearing this rumor, the Navab Ẕakariyā Khān, who had set up camp 10 *coss*[61] from Lahore with 20,000 horsemen, immediately returned to the city. Finally, the royal army marched on 9 Shawwāl (or January) and arrived the next day at Sonpit, where it encamped. Nādir Shāh himself is still in Peshawar, and we have to wait to see what will happen. Grain is dear here, while God's rod appears to be ready to mete out punishment. The subordinate *mansepdhaar*s [*mansabdār*s or functionaries] do not receive their monthly pay at all, which not only includes the royal servants, but even those of the *ammerauw* [*omara* or magnates]. Therefore, the soldiers are listless, while the civilians are afraid. I have written you all that I know, and I shall also do so concerning further developments. I still

[60] A letter from Patna has the following additional information. The *amīr*s, on learning that Muḥammad Shāh wanted to flee, returned to Delhi to prevent this. "They now only want to take the field if Muḥammad Shāh accompanies them. He is said to have refused to do so. Only Nawab Sa'ādat Khān has moved, but only eight miles, and now demands money from Muḥammad Shāh to pay his troops." Algemeen Rijksarchief, The Hague, VOC 2427, summary letter from B. Aukema, chief of Patna factory to A. Sichterman, director in Bengal, 27 January 1739, fol. 549.

[61] A *coss* is a measure of length. The *jaribi coss* measures 4,000 yards, while the *rasmi coss* measures 2,000 to 2,500 yards.

expect the Great Mughal to win, because the respect for the emperor depends on this. As a result of his negligence the conflicts among the great lords have increased. The emperor, undoubtedly, will join the royal army, because it is necessary. All the heathen lords are to join as well; whether they actually do so will be known in three or four days.

APPENDIX D[62]

LETTER FROM DELHI, DATED 20 SHAWWĀL (31 JANUARY 1739)

In my previous letter, dated 15 Shawwāl [1151] [26 January 1739], I wrote you about the situation in Delhi and that Nādir Shāh had advanced from Iran as far as the river Attock. Also about the preparations by the *amīr*s or great lords Āṣif Jāh Niẓām al-Mulk, the imperial chancellor, and *Mīr Bakhshī* or paymaster-general Khān Dawrān Bahādur to oppose Nādir Shāh. Before receiving the news about Lahore, I had no doubt that that the [previous] letter would be delivered and that you would read its contents. However, now on the 18th of this month, news has been received from Lahore that the Nawab Ẕakariyā Khān has fled and that Nādir Shāh has taken possession of that city and proclaimed his rule. He has promised that nobody will be harmed. He has sent an army of 30,000 men composed of Georgians and other horsemen, under the command of three of his *amīr*s, against the advancing lords of Muḥammad Shāh, while he himself remains in the castle of Lahore. This news has caused consternation in Delhi and has led to a topsy-turvy situation. The emperor summoned the crown prince on Friday the 19th, who appeared with much pomp and was received in a friendly manner. He was granted additional land assignments. Next, the emperor left the castle at 10 a.m.; the vanguard of his troops was commanded by the crown prince. They went as far as the royal pleasure garden, where they camped in closed tents, and on the following day proceeded from there with all haste to the royal army, to attack the Iranian army. His Majesty has already informed his great lords to expect and receive him. A very dark cloud hangs over the head of the emperor of Hindūstān. May heaven reward the conclusion [of all this] with a good success. Everybody here is looking for means to save themselves and their family and many flee to Senegger [Srinagar], which is in the jurisdiction of the heathen lord Jessingsawaay [Sawai Jai Singh]. May God assist us. Until now neither old *mansabdār*s (chief of a certain number of soldiers) nor new ones have received any pay from the emperor. All the soldiers are very dissatisfied about this. Sa'ādat Khān has still not appeared here, although it is said that he has arrived at the river Ganges. Time will tell.

With regard to the Nawab of Lahore, Ẕakariyā Khān, you should know that in response to a letter from Nāṣir Khān, former governor of Peshawar,

[62] Algemeen Rijksarchief, The Hague, VOC 2485, translation of a Persian letter from and to the same persons as in Appendix C, received 16 February 1739, fol. 865. As mentioned earlier, this letter was also known in abridged form and was available to James Fraser, who reproduced it in his book, see Fraser [1742] 1973, 149–51 and 1984, 101–2.

and currently minister to Nādir Shāh, Ẕakariyā Khān sent a certain Keetsaatchan [?], a confidant of his, to the victorious Iranian. He was taken by Nāṣir Khān to pay his respects to Nādir Shāh, who received him warmly and granted him two robes of honor. After having submitted his [i.e., master's] message and having received the required reply he returned to Lahore accompanied by an envoy. Ẕakariyā Khān received the latter in the audience hall, and publicly responded to the proposals with firm and scathing words, whereupon he arrested the envoy. Ẕakariyā Khān then left the city with his troops and approached Nādir Shāh's army. He then engaged the latter, ordering the cannon that he had brought with him to start firing. However, before the latter could be charged many of Nādir Shāh's horsemen attacked, sabre in hand, and caused a massacre. This forced Ẕakariyā Khān to withdraw, which allowed Nādir Shāh's troops to occupy the city. A certain Jachan [probably Jān Khān] entered the palace and the Iranian soldiers the castle, where they proclaimed their king's rule. It has been impossible to find out how this could happen so fast. It is rumored that Nādir Shāh personally is in Lahore, but that he has sent his troops onwards against the royal army. I conclude with expressing hope to receive a favorable reply to my communications so as to be able to continue in reporting what will befall further.

APPENDIX E[63]

LETTER FROM DELHI

[He refers to his previous letters and reports that] Ẕakariyā Khān has been taken prisoner. Nādir Shāh has taken Lahore with all [its] ammunition serviceable for battle against its former owner. The conqueror has marched to the hamlet Serhind, which he easily seized. There he has put his army in battle formation. The emperor, Muḥammad Shāh, has advanced with his might close to Karnaal. This is an advantageous position, where he is preparing himself to receive the Iranian. However, the latter has taken up position at a distance of 10 *coss*. Now and then the two armies probe each other with small marauding groups, without any clashes taking place so far. The most important issue is that in the royal army famine has broken out, because of a lack of provisions, both for man and beast. This has caused an epidemic and consequently much mortality, which increases daily, according to rumors. This is made worse by the unwillingness of the soldiers [to fight], because they still have not received their pay. The Nawab Sa'ādat Khān arrived here on the 9th Siket [18 February 1739], and continued his journey towards the royal army with a small suite on the following day. After his arrival there it was decided to do battle with the enemy on the arrival of the new moon (according to our calendar on 9 March). As I have written before, the number of inhabitants here decreases daily, because they seek a more secure haven, fearing the unpredictability of the royal army. His Majesty has appointed Lutfullachan bhadur [Luṭf 'Alī Khān Bahādur] as *naib* [*nā'ib* or deputy] and Sidie Fallaakchan [Sayyid Fallak Khān] as *fawjdār* during his absence. These gentlemen are doing their best to guard this city against marauding robbers in these troubled times, just as each inhabitant guards his own house.

From this it is clear that the Mughal throne is getting more and more unstable, despite the fact that one should not believe this too strongly. Experience, however, shows that bad times are more frequent than good ones.

[63] Ibid., VOC 2485, Mhamed Feysalla to Pieter Laurens Phoonsen, 14 Siket or 23 February 1739, (received 13 March 1739), fol. 869.

APPENDIX F[64]

THE DELHI MASSACRE

Until 17 Jelhet [29 March 1739] the Iranians have behaved like animals. Sa'ādat Khān did not fail to show and hand over all state treasures to Nādir Shāh.[65] He did the same for those belonging to Niẓām al-Mulk, Qamar al-Dīn Khān, and other *amīr*s as well as those belonging to wealthy inhabitants. Nādir Shāh had their valuable possessions taken to his army outside the city, a total of 3,000 donkey loads. Muḥammad Shāh is still detained in the castle. When Nādir Shāh arrived with his army of 50,000 men they occupied all the houses of both poor and rich and committed all kind of insolent acts. Niẓām al-Mulk and Qamar al-Dīn Khān therefore called on Sa'ādat Khān to appeal to Nādir Shāh to put an end to the violence. However, Sa'ādat Khān ordered them out. That evening it was said that Sa'ādat Khān had committed suicide by taking poison and that Nādir Shāh had ordered his troops to leave the city. The two great lords also received permission to return to their homes. However, this [news] had disastrous consequences. A group of bloodthirsty people spread the story that Nādir Shāh had been killed by Muḥammad Shāh. The population attacked the Iranians, who had to defend themselves. The result was an enormous massacre, during which at least 100,000 people were killed.[66] Nādir Shāh had given orders to kill anybody who defended himself. As a result, it seemed as if it was raining blood, for the channels were streaming with it. As many as 10,000 women and children were imprisoned. Niẓām al-Mulk and

[64] This is a summary of the information contained in a letter filed as: Algemeen Rijksarchief, The Hague, VOC 2475, Mhamet Feysella to Phoonsen, received 18 April 1739, fols. 881–4.

[65] Sa'ādat Khān was appointed by Nādir Shāh as his chief minister or *vazīr*. He arrived in Delhi on the 28th to reassure the population that they had nothing to fear. Thus, his fellow Indians were confirmed in the belief that he was a traitor. Algemeen Rijksarchief, The Hague, VOC 2475, Extract Sourats Dagregister [summary of Surat Diary], Tuesday, 28 February 1739, fol. 872; letters from Delhi to Mr. Phoonsen, the VOC Surat director, received on 28 March 1739, fol. 874 .

[66] Another version of these events is as follows: Nādir Shāh arrived in Delhi on 14 Jelhet [25 March 1739] and took lodging in the "daregiekoe"[?] or the royal palace. He remained there for three days. A great many people, who had nothing to eat, were gathering there. The Iranian soldiers pushed and beat them back. This led to fights and people attacking the soldiers. As a result of the ensuing repression as many as 50,000 died. There was also a lot of rapine and plunder. The roads are infested with robbers. The troops of Jessay [Saway Jai Singh] have reached Delhi, and all heathen princes are moving against the Persian. Algemeen Rijksarchief, The Hague, VOC 2475, the Agra broker Beherridas to Phoonsen, 14 Jelhet (received 10 April 1739), fols. 877–8. See Lockhart, 149 on the extent of the massacre and on the dates, which are slightly different.

Qamar al-Dīn Khān went bareheaded, their hands tied with their turbans, to Nādir Shāh and begged him on their knees to spare the inhabitants, and to take his revenge on them, because they were the cause of the revolt. Nādir Shāh then ordered his troops to stop the killing, who obeyed immediately. He did so, however, on condition that the two great lords would give him 10 *korur* of *rupee*s before he returned the throne and left Delhi, which they had promised to do.[67] As a result all those imprisoned were set free, but not those women who had to suffer the will of these butchers. The robbing and plundering still continues, but not the killing. The 100,000 *korur* were paid in gold, jewelry and silverware. The city is now also suffering from famine. After Nādir Shāh had inspected the treasures he ordered all furniture to be taken from the houses of the well-to-do; even the pack animals of Niẓām al-Mulk and Qamar al-Dīn Khān were not spared.[68] Nādir Shāh also sent an escort of 4,000 horsemen to Oudh to fetch the treasures of Sa'ādat Khān.

[67] Nādir Shāh's rule was publicly proclaimed on 27 Seket [8 March 1739], Algemeen Rijksarchief, The Hague, VOC 2475, letter from Delhi (received 28 March 1739), fol. 874; see also fol. 878 [Wednesday 15 April 1739] where it is mentioned that his rule was also proclaimed in Aḥmadābād, but no real effort was made to effectuate it. In fact, the proclamation had only been made in a few city quarters; coins were struck in Nādir Shāh's name. These are mentioned for Qāsimbāzār and even for Patna. Algemeen Rijksarchief, The Hague, VOC 2469, Christoffel Ring, deputy Cassembazaar to J.A. Sichterman, director at Hougly, 2 April 1739, fol. 763; In the latter town only 101 "monster siccas" [sample coins] and 51 golden muhrs were struck. Algemeen Rijksarchief, The Hague, VOC 2469, A. Prent and Jan Thielen in Cariemabaad [Karīmābād] to Ringh, Cassembazaar, 4 April 1739, fol. 770, see also fols. 773–4.

[68] Nādir Shāh ordered 30,000 camels to be sent to Delhi to carry his booty. Algemeen Rijksarchief, The Hague, VOC 2455, extract Spahans dagverhaal [summary of Iṣfahān diary], 20 June 1739, fol. 287v.

BIBLIOGRAPHY

'ALĪ SHĪR QĀNI' TATTAVĪ. 1971. *Tuḥfat al-kirām*. Ed. Ḥusām al-Dīn Rāshidī. Ḥaydarābād : Sindī Adabī Būrd.

Balochistan through the ages : (district gazetteers). 1980. 2nd ed. 2 vols. Quetta : Nisa Traders.

FLOOR, WILLEM. 1983. The revolt of Shaikh Ahmad Madani in Laristan and the Garmsirat, (1730–1733). *Studia Iranica* 12, no. 1: 63–93.

FRASER, JAMES. [1742] 1973. *The history of Nadir Shah*. Reprint, Helhi : Mohan Publications.

—— 1984. *Tārīkh-i Nādir Shāh Afshār*. Tr. Abū al-Qāsim Khān Nāṣir al-Mulk. Reissue of the 1321/ 1904 ed. Tehran : Pasārgād, 1363 Sh.

A genuine history of Nadir-Cha, present Shah or emperor of Persia, formerly call'd Thamas Kouli-Kan. : with a particular account of his conquest of the Mogul's country : together with several letters between Nadir-Cha and the Great Mogul, and from Nadir-Cha to his son. 1741. London: J. Watts, B. Dod.

LOCKHART, LAURENCE. 1938. *Nadir Shah : a critical study based mainly upon contemporary sources*. London : Lazco & Co.

MAHDĪ KHĀN ASTARĀBĀDĪ. 1962. *Jahāngushā-yi Nadirī*. Ed. 'Abd Allāh Anvār. Tehran : Anjuman-i Āṣar-i Millī, 1341 Sh.

MUḤAMMAD KĀẒIM. 1985. *'Ālam'ārā-yi Nādirī*. Ed. Muḥammad Amīn Riyāḥī. 3 vols. Tehran : Kitābfurūshī-i Zavvār, 1364 Sh.

Nādirnāmah. 1964. In *Manshūr al-vaṣīyat va dastūr al-ḥukūmat*. Ed. Ḥusām al-Dīn Rāshidī. Ḥaydarābād : Sindī Adabī Būrd: append. 4, 89–96.

RIAZUL ISLAM. 1970. *Indo Persian relations : a study of the political and diplomatic relations between the Mughul Empire and Iran*. Teheran : Iranian Culture Foundation.

SHĀHNAVAZ KHAN AWRANGABĀDĪ. 1979. *The Maāthir-ul-umarā : being biographies of the Muḥammadan and Hindu officers of the Timurid sovereigns of India from 1500 to about 1780 A.D.* Tr. H. Beveridge. Revised, annotated, and completed by Baini Prashad. 2 vols. in 3. Patna : Janaki Prakashan.

The Visit of Three Qajar Princes to England (May–September 1836/Ṣafar–Jumādá I 1252)

Roger M. Savory *

THE HISTORICAL BACKGROUND

IT HAD BEEN THE PRACTICE OF THE SECOND Qajar monarch, Fatḥ ʻAlī Shāh (r. 1212–50/1797–1834), to appoint his principal sons to provincial governorships, on condition that they paid an annual sum to the throne, and these Qajar princes acted like sovereigns in their provinces.[1] On 13 Shawwāl 1213/20 March 1799 Fatḥ ʻAlī Shāh designated his son ʻAbbās Mīrzā to succeed him, but ʻAbbās Mīrzā died in 1249/1833. In Ṣafar 1250/June 1834, a little over four months before his own death, Fatḥ ʻAlī Shāh designated ʻAbbās Mīrzā's son, Muḥammad Mīrzā, as his heir-apparent, and

> the appointment of Muḥammad Mīrzā as *walī ʻahd* was recognized by the British and Russian governments in an exchange of notes expressing their mutual desire to act together over the matter of his succession and in the maintenance of the internal tranquillity, independence and integrity of Persia.[2]

However, this nomination was not accepted by ʻAbbās Mīrzā's brothers ʻAlī Mīrzā Ẓill al-Sulṭān, Ḥasan ʻAlī Mīrzā, and Ḥusayn ʻAlī Mīrzā Farmānfarmā. Since Fatḥ ʻAlī Shāh had begotten between 120 and 150 sons, it is perhaps not surprising that the succession should have been disputed. Ẓill al-Sulṭān proclaimed himself Shāh at Tehran, with the title of ʻAlī Shāh, and Ḥusayn ʻAlī Mīrzā followed suit in Fārs, adopting the title Ḥusayn Shāh.[3]

---

* This paper is a revised and expanded version of a paper entitled "A Qajar Prince's Sojourn in England in 1836: Najaf Qoli Mīrzā's Memoirs," presented to the Conference on 19th Century Persian Travel Memoirs, University of Texas at Austin, April 8 and 9, 1994.

[1] Najaf Qulī Mīrzā [1839] 1971, 1:viii–ix.
[2] Lambton 1978, 392b.
[3] Fraser [1838] 1973, 1:8.

Ḥusayn 'Alī Mīrzā had been appointed governor of Fārs in 1213/1798–9 with the title Farmānfarmā, and held that position until his death in 1251/1835–6.[4]

With the encouragement of the British envoy, Sir John Campbell, and of the Russian representative in Iran, Muḥammad Mīrzā, the heir-apparent, marched on Tehran at the head of a force commanded by Sir Henry Lindsay Bethune.[5] Ẓill al-Sulṭān surrendered, and was present at his nephew's coronation[6] as Muḥammad Shāh on 14 Ramaḍān 1250/14 January 1835.[7] With one dangerous rival out of the way, Muḥammad Shāh, again at the initiative of Sir John Campbell,[8] despatched a force against Ḥusayn 'Alī Mīrzā Farmānfarmā at the end of Shawwāl 1250/end of February 1835. That half of the force which was under the command of Sir Henry Lindsay Bethune confronted the Farmānfarmā's army outside Iṣfahān[9] and defeated it, largely due to the superiority of the royal artillery. The royal army entered Shīrāz, and the Farmānfarmā, his brother Ḥasan 'Alī, and other Qajar princes were captured. Ḥasan 'Alī was blinded, and the other princes were sent to a prison at Ardabīl, but the Farmānfarmā died *en route* of cholera.[10] Three of the Farmānfarmā's sons: Riẓā Qulī Mīrzā, Najaf Qulī Mīrzā, and Tīmūr Mīrzā, escaped from

[4] Riẓā Qulī Mīrzā 1982, 734. Fraser does not think highly of Ḥusayn 'Alī Mīrzā, whom he describes as a "man of weak intellect and irresolute mind"; Ẓill al-Sulṭān, he says, was formidable only from being governor of the *ark* (*arg*: citadel) of Tehran, in which were deposited the treasures of the sovereign. Ḥasan 'Alī Mīrzā, he says, was a "man of more ability and strength of mind," and had a "reputation for liberality and courage," see Fraser, [1838] 1973, 1:7–8. The editor of Najaf Qulī Mīrzā's *Safarnāmah* gives what is probably a fairer assessment of Ḥusayn 'Alī Mīrzā: "Unlike many of his brothers", he says, "he was not fearless or adventurous, but he was a man of integrity (*salīm al-nafs*). If he had not been incited by his brother Ḥasan 'Alī Mīrzā Shujā' al-Salṭanah, and by 'Abd Allāh Khān Amīn al-Dawlah, the *vazīr-i a'ẓam* of Fatḥ 'Alī Shāh, and if his younger brother Ẓill al-Sulṭan had not ascended the throne in Tehran, perhaps he would not have had ambitions to be king himself, and his family would not have suffered difficulties and homelessness," see Riẓā Qulī Mīrzā 1982, 734–5.

[5] Henry Lindsay, afterwards Sir Henry Lindsay Bethune (1787–1851), first went to Iran in 1810 as a member of Sir John Malcolm's mission. After 1821 he became an instructor to the Persian army. He returned to Iran in 1834–5, but his third mission to Iran in 1836 was "repudiated by the shah," see Fasā'ī 1972, 234, footnote no. 13. According to Fasā'ī, the "encouragement" included a subvention of 70,000 *tūmāns*, see ibid., 232.

[6] Sykes 1915, 2:427.

[7] Fasā'ī 1972, 233.

[8] Lambton 1978, 393a.

[9] Near "Ḳumis͟ha" (ibid.); near "Izadkhvāst" (Fasā'ī 1972, 233, 235); near "a village on the low road between seventy and eighty miles distant from Ispahan" (Fraser, [1838] 1973, 1:13).

[10] Fraser [1838] 1973, 1:31–2. According to Aṣghar Farmānfarmā'ī Qājār, he died in Rabī' I 1251 [June–July 1835], see Riẓā Qulī Mīrzā 1982, 735.

Shīrāz and made their way via Baṣrah and Najaf to Baghdād.[11] They had decided to accept their father's advice that further resistance was futile, and would only signal his own death; he counseled them either to retire to Najaf or Karbalā, "and there lead holy and religious lives, praying for me and for yourselves," or to go to England, and there implore the assistance of the British government.[12] They chose the second option, and it is with the sojourn of the three princes in England between May and September 1836/Ṣafar–Jumādá I 1252, and their relations with the British government that this paper is concerned.[13]

THE SOURCES

The primary sources for the study of this episode in the Anglo-Persian relations are two close versions of a single travel account by two of the princes. The longer version called *Rumūz al-siyāḥah* is written by Najaf Qulī Mīrzā, while the shorter version, which is the text published by Aṣghar Farmānfarmā'ī Qājār, and which is also known as *Ẕikr-i vaqāyi'-i vafāt-i Khāqān*, is the work of Riẕā Qulī Mīrzā.[14] According to Iraj Afshar, the six known manuscript copies of these versions are: (1) a copy in the Kitābkhānah-'i Millī, Tehran, dated 1256/1840; (2) a copy in the Kitābkhānah-i Markazī-i Dānishgāh-i Tihrān, dated 1277/1860–1; (3) a manuscript "possibly copied from the original manuscript,"[15] dated 1311/ 1893–4, and used for Farmānfarmā'ī's edition; (4) a copy in the Kitābkhānah-'i Majlis-i Shūrā, Tehran, dated 1320/ 1902–3; (5) a copy in the India Office Library in London, Or. 12,083, dated 1265/1848–9, also used for Farmānfarmā'ī's edition[16]; (6) a manuscript belonging to the grand-daughter of Najaf Qulī Mīrzā's son, Nawẕar Mīrzā, who

[11] Two younger brothers (Shāhrukh Mīrzā and Iskandar Mīrzā) probably went with them, see ibid., 742.

[12] Fraser [1838] 1973, 1:39–40.

[13] Denis Wright has also studied this episode, using, among other sources, the unpublished material in the India Office Library and Records, the Public Record Office at Kew, and especially the Royal Archives in Windsor Castle, where the diary of the young princess Victoria who met the princes in July 1836 and recorded her impressions of them in it, is kept, see Wright 1985, 87–101.

[14] See Iraj Afshar's introd. to Riẕā Qulī Mīrzā 1982 (no pagination). The authorship of the travelogue(s) does not seem to interest Farmānfarmā'ī greatly (he did use both versions for his edition), because despite the obvious change of narrator in each version, he still refers to Najaf Qulī Mīrzā as the author of both the *Safarnāmah* and the *Rumūz al-siyāḥah*, see ibid., 746.

[15] Farmānfarmā'ī's introd. to Riẕā Qulī Mīrzā 1982 (no pagination).

[16] Dr. M. I. Waley, Curator for Persian and Turkish of the Oriental and India Office collections in the British Library, tells me that this copy is in fact titled *Rumūz al-siyāḥah*, and is "definitely by Najaf Qulī Mīrzā" (personal communication).

brought this manuscript with him to Iran in 1265/1848–9, also used for Farmānfarmā'ī's edition.[17] Furthermore, there is the work entitled *Journal of a residence in England, and of a journey from and to Syria, of Their Royal Highnesses Reeza Koolee Meerza, Najaf Koolee Meerza, and Taymoor Meerza, of Persia*, "originally written in Persian by H. R. H. Najaf Koolee Meerza . . . and translated, with explanatory notes, by Assaad Y. Kayat . . . printed for private circulation only,"[18] which seems to be a translation of *Rumūz al-siyāḥah*, or selections from it.

AS'AD YA'QŪB KHAYYĀT

As'ad Ya'qūb Khayyāt (b. 1811), a Syrian of Greek descent, was chief dragoman or interpreter to Mr. Farren, the British consul-general at Damascus. He was "an excellent linguist, who, though still young, could speak English, French, and Italian, besides Greek, Latin, Arabic, and some other oriental languages."[19] Khayyāt himself claims a knowledge of Arabic, Persian, Turkish, and occidental languages.[20] He was therefore admirably well equipped to act as interpreter for the three princes on their journey from Baghdād to England. Khayyāt was keenly aware of the special nature of the journey: "to have Asiatic travelers, men of distinction, who write their views on all they have observed, is a singular phenomenon,"[21] and he points out that the princes were "the first members of the Persian Royal Family that ever visited England."[22]

As to the translation, Khayyāt says that he obtained a copy of this work (i.e., the *Rumūz al-siyāḥah*) from the princes after their return to Baghdād in 1837, "and executed the translation."[23] He endeavored, he says, "simply to render the Persian text into English, with the closest adherence to the original that could be tolerated consistently with an exhibition of the meaning of the Author." He goes on to say:

> I have naturally supposed that greater interest would be excited in the work, the more perfectly it should be clothed in its oriental dress. In numerous cases where a metaphor, or word, would have in English but a

[17] According to Farmānfarmā'ī, Nawẕar Mīrzā was the son of Riẓā Qulī Mīrzā not Najaf Qulī Mīrzā, see ibid.

[18] See Najaf Qulī Mīrzā [1839] 1971.

[19] Fraser [1838] 1973, 1:58.

[20] Najaf Qulī Mīrzā [1839], 1:xv.

[21] Ibid., 1:vii.

[22] Ibid., 1:x. At the age of only 36, Khayyāt published an autobiography in which he recounted his experience with the princes, see Kayat 1847, 101ff.

[23] Najaf Qulī Mīrzā [1839], 1:xv.

> remote or no allusion to the thing intended, I have still chosen to retain the word or phrase, for the purpose of showing the Persian actual style of writing and genius of the language. The Author has also in some cases used flights of language which, in the present refined state of the English, may be considered as deficient in taste. I however have not ventured to modify them, for the above-mentioned reason, but have chosen rather to annex some explanatory notes, which I hope will lead to their meaning.[24]

On the whole, Khayyāt makes good his promise to adhere closely to the Persian text, but, as will be seen, there is a number of instances where he either omits or glosses over material which he probably considered to be politically sensitive.

Khayyāt "exceedingly regrets" that about twenty pages of the Persian manuscript were taken from him by Bedouin as he made his way from Baghdād to Damascus in 1837. When the marauding Bedouin searched his saddle-bags and discovered only books and papers, they told him that he was fool to carry "such a load of useless papers and books, which could be neither eaten nor drunk." Khayyāt told them that some of the papers were pages from the Koran, hoping thereby to dissuade them from stealing them. Unfortunately, the Bedouin said that the "*mulla*" attached to their tribe "had been long seeking for a copy", and took about twenty sheets "in mistake for the Korân."[25] The missing portion of the manuscript apparently recounted the arduous journey of the princes after their flight from Shīrāz until their arrival in Damascus, where Khayyāt joined them and remained with them during the rest of their journey to England.

THE CHARACTER OF THE ROYAL PRINCES

The father of the three princes, Ḥusayn 'Alī Mīrzā Farmānfarmā, was one of five elder sons of Fatḥ 'Alī Shāh who were all born in the same year, 1203/1788–9.[26] The three princes differed greatly in character. The assessment of them made by Khayyāt in general tallies with that made by James Fraser, who was appointed by the British government as their *mihmāndār* or personal escort upon their arrival in London, and who traveled with them on their return journey as far as Constantinople. Khayyāt says that the eldest brother, Riẓā Qulī Mīrzā Nāyib al-Iyālah, was "a man of superior talent and wisdom"; he was the vicegerent of his father. The second brother, Najaf Qulī Mīrzā Vālī, was a "well-known Persian and Arabic scholar, an excellent poet . . . exceedingly

[24] Ibid., 1:xvi.
[25] Ibid., 1:123–4
[26] Riẓā Qulī Mīrzā 1982, 734.

fond of literature." Tīmūr Mīrzā Ḥusām al-Dawlah was "a celebrated warrior, horseman and hunter." He had been governor of Būshihr and Dashtistān for many years, and had met a number of English people in the course of his duties there.[27] Fraser adds some details about the personal appearance and manner of the princes: Riẓā Qulī Mīrzā, the eldest son of Farmānfarmā, was "tall, and of a very pleasing countenance; a man of very amiable dispositions, gentlemanly feelings and manners;" he had a "great deal of innate dignity of character." He was thirty-two years of age. Najaf Qulī Mīrzā was "a small and slender person: his light hair, blue eyes, and peculiar features announce his Georgian blood" (his mother was a Georgian); he was extremely short-sighted, and was of a shy disposition. At the time of the death of Fatḥ 'Alī Shah, he was governor of Bihbahān and Kuhgīlūyah. His manners, says Fraser, were "less gentle than those of his elder brother, and want the open frankness of those of the younger;" his "ungainly exterior covers more talent and learning than is possessed by either of the others." In Fraser's opinion, Najaf Qulī Mīrzā was the leader of the three. He was "shrewd and intelligent, well versed in the learning and accomplishments of his own country, a keen observer, an acute reasoner, with a decidedly intriguing and diplomatic turn, and a general force of character which has given great weight to his opinion with his brothers." Riẓā Qulī Mīrzā, says Fraser, "never comes to any decision on matters of consequence without consulting" Najaf Qulī Mīrzā. Indeed, Najaf Qulī Mīrzā "is always set forward as the negotiator, where such is required." Fraser's opinion is borne out by the fact that it was Najaf Qulī Mīrzā who was delegated to negotiate with Lord Palmerston, the British Foreign Secretary, after the arrival of princes in London. Both Najaf Qulī Mīrzā and Tīmūr Mīrzā could be convivial. Although Najaf Qulī Mīrzā was ascetic in manner, Fraser remarks that "judging from his unrestrained enjoyment of the good things of this world at times, his philosophy does not appear to have produced a very regulating effect on his conduct." He might appear "taciturn and morose" to strangers, but in private he loved jokes and bon-môts "to season a good glass of wine." Tīmūr Mīrzā, as befitted his dashing nature, enjoyed wine and women. Born of the same mother as Riẓā Qulī Mīrzā, he was tall, slender, and muscular; "horses, dogs, hawks, guns, swords and pistols are his passion."[28]

[27] Najaf Qulī Mīrzā [1839], 1:x.

[28] Fraser [1838] 1973, 1:19–23. Tīmūr Mīrzā was the author of the *Bāznāmah-i Nāṣirī* (Book of faconry), which has been translated by D. C. Phillott, see [Tīmūr Mīrzā] 1908. According to Storey ([1953] 1972, 1153, quoting Riẓā Qulī Khān Hidāyat's *Tārīkh-i Rawẓat al-ṣafā-yi Nāṣirī*), the three princes were respectively the first, third, and fifth of the seventeen sons of Farmānfarmā (Farmānfarmā'ī says "nineteen," see Riẓā Qulī Mīrzā 1982, 737).

RELATIONS BETWEEN THE PRINCES AND THE BRITISH GOVERNMENT

The three princes landed at Falmouth in Cornwall on 6 Ṣafar 1252/23 May 1836,[29] after a long and fatiguing journey from Damascus via Beirut, Alexandria, Malta, Gibraltar, and Cadiz, a journey during which the princes had ample opportunity to express the well-known Persian antipathy to travel by sea. From Falmouth the princes proceeded by coach to Bath, an important coaching junction for the West Country during the 19th century. There they were visited by Sir John Henry Willock, who addressed them in fluent Persian. At first the princes were astonished at finding someone in a foreign country who was able to speak Persian, but soon learned that Willock had spent eighteen years in the service of ʻAbbās Mīrzā as an instructor to the cavalry, and had actually met the princes fourteen years previously in Shīrāz in the company of the British ambassador.[30]

From Bath the princes wrote letters to King William IV (r. 1830–7), to Lord Palmerston, the British Foreign Secretary, and to Lord Glenelg, who had recently (April 1835) been appointed Colonial Secretary in Lord Melbourne's second ministry.[31] The letters informed the king and his ministers of the princes's arrival in England. Khayyāt was dispatched to London with the letters on 26 May, and the princes were "left alone, and we could not speak the language of the people, neither they ours." Crowds gathered outside York House hoping to catch a glimpse of the princes. "Some fine English young men of excellent manners" visited them every evening to learn Persian, "so we became schoolmasters of Persian, and pupils of English. We endeavored to take and give lessons by signs with our fingers, which caused much laughter." Nevertheless, time hung heavily on their hands as they anxiously awaited the reply of the British government, and on some days they had nothing to do but look out of the window and gaze at the beautiful women—on one occasion said to number 5,000—gathered outside. Eventually some of the women plucked up courage to enter York House. "All lady visitors were asked to write down their names…in this way we had about a thousand visitors of these most illustrious houris."[32] Finally, on 2 June 1836, the long-awaited reply from London arrived in the form of a letter from Khayyāt, but "some hints" contained in his letter caused the princes's concern. This concern was

[29] Najaf Qulī Mīrzā [1839], 1:246.

[30] Ibid., 1:257; Riẓā Qulī Mīrzā 1982, 339–40. See also Savory 1985, 80.

[31] Stephen and Lee 1921–2, 8:380b. Charles Grant was raised to the peerage on 8 May 1835 with the title of Baron Glenelg.

[32] Najaf Qulī Mīrzā [1839], 1:260–2; Riẓā Qulī Mīrzā 1982, 345–8.

increased the following day when the princes were visited by "Blane Sahib," a former "*balyos*"[33] of Būshihr. Blane's replies to the princes's questions "were almost like those which Khvaja Assaad gave us in his letter," and "this also gave us additional reason to be unhappy and full of anxiety."[34] I mentioned above that Khayyāt does not always fulfill his promise to adhere closely to the Persian text in his translation, and his versions of the correspondence between the princes and officials of the British government are a notable instance of this. An examination of the Persian text of the letters, given in full in the *Safarnāmah*, will make it clear why the princes, at this early stage in their sojourn in England, were already "full of anxiety."

The arrival of the princes in England placed the British government in a dilemma. The fundamental problem, from the point of view of the British government, was that the British, along with the Russians, had formally recognized Muḥammad Shāh as the legitimate successor of Fatḥ 'Alī Shāh. Muḥammad Shāh was thus an ally of Britain, and the princes were technically in rebellion against his authority. On the other hand, the British thought it must accord courtesy and hospitality to princes

> with whom many of our countrymen, British officers and travellers, had lived in amicable intercourse; whose protection and good-will they had profited by; and who had made a journey of many thousand miles, and encountered many dangers, to solicit a return of these good offices; and who were, moreover, the first natives of central Asia of any considerable rank who had ever given such a proof of confidence in Great Britain.[35]

What were the princes asking the British government to do on their behalf? According to Khayyāt, the Farmānfarmā had persuaded his sons "not to go to war" against Muḥammad Shāh, but "to solicit His Britannic Majesty's friendly mediation with Mohammed Shah."[36] Fraser is much more explicit. The princes did hope, he says, that Great Britain would be able to secure their possession of, "and, in fact, a sort of sovereignty in," the province of Fārs.[37]

As noted above, the princes, after their arrival in England, first despatched letters to the King, the Foreign Secretary, and the Colonial Secretary. The gist of their letter to the King is as follows:

[33] *Bâlyoz*, a Turkish term originally denoting the Venetian ambassador to the Porte. It was later used to denote European diplomatic or consular officials in general, see Lockhart 1979.

[34] Najaf Qulī Mīrzā [1839], 1:262–3; Riẕā Qulī Mīrzā 1982, 349.

[35] Fraser [1838] 1973, 1:62.

[36] Najaf Qulī Mīrzā [1839], 1:xi.

[37] Fraser [1838] 1973, 1:67.

> After the death of Fatḥ ʻAlī Shāh, and the disorders in the affairs of Iran, news of which will of course have reached your ears, I did not consider it expedient to remain in that country, but conceived the desire to be honored by an audience with Your Majesty. Now, more than a year later, God be praised we reached Bath on Wednesday 8 Ṣafar 1252/25 May 1836. We have paused here for a few days, and have sent our interpreter Khvājah Asʻad on ahead to seek an audience with you and to beg you to issue the necessary orders without delay.[38]

The contents of the letter to Lord Palmerston, the Foreign Secretary, are as follows:

> Our never-failing good fortune and innate virtues (*saʻādat-i azalī va maḥāsin-i fiṭrī*) dictated that we seek the honor of an audience with the British government, and we made this our goal. Today, the 8th Ṣafar 1252/25 May 1836, we have arrived in Bath, and have decided to stay here for a few days to recover from our difficult and exhausting journey. We have sent ahead our chief interpreter (*bāsh tarjumān*) to obtain permission for us to have an audience with His Majesty, in whatever manner and at whatever place the government shall decide. Since Your Excellency the Foreign Secretary is responsible for making arrangements of this sort, we ask you to use your good offices to look to our affairs. God willing we shall meet shortly.[39]

The third letter was written to the Colonial Secretary, Lord Glenelg:

> Now that fate and a desire to be received in audience by the King of England and Emperor of India has brought us to these shores, we hope that a detailed account of our affairs will be heard. Having traveled over land and sea we have arrived at Bath, and have decided to stay here a few days to recover from the rigors of the journey. We have despatched Khvājah Asʻad, our chief interpreter, with a letter requesting an audience with the King at whatever time and place he shall decide. Since Your Excellency's friendship toward Iran and India is well known, we are confident that Your Excellency will be well disposed toward us and will extend his hospitality to us. Since we will meet shortly, we will conclude at this point.[40]

These three letters, Khayyāt says, were penned by Najaf Qulī Mīrzā.[41]

[38] Riẓā Qulī Mīrzā 1982, 340–1.
[39] Ibid., 1:341–2.
[40] Ibid., 1:342–3.
[41] Najaf Qulī Mīrzā [1839], 1:258.

On 16 Ṣafar 1252/2 June 1836 the princes received the letter from Khayyāt, referred to above, which caused them so much anxiety. According to the English version

> We received a letter from Khoojah Assaad, saying that the government was informed of our arrival, and that nothing was yet decided with regard to our affairs and our reception, and that he hoped to be with us soon; some other hints were also given in his letter. Indeed, the letter of Khoojah Assaad gave us much to think about, and required a good deal of reflection. Having come so far from our homes, and encountered a hundred thousand difficulties and suffering, this made us unhappy, and through the whole night we were troubled with painful reflections and had scarcely any sleep.[42]

The Persian text is much more explicit:

> The ministers are pleased at your arrival, but are perplexed (*mutaḥayyir*)[43] about how to display the degree of friendship and to arrange the formalities of becoming mutually acquainted (*marāsim-i ta'āruf*) which are due to persons of your station. God willing I shall soon return [to Bath]. All the ministers and members of the Cabinet are perplexed and pensive (*mutafakkir*) about your affairs, on account of the alliance with Muḥammad Shāh, and they are deliberating how to steer a middle course between friendship and support. I meditated deeply on the contents of this letter. If, after enduring such hardships to reach England, our visit should prove fruitless, how were we to return, and where were we to go?"[44]

It will be recalled that the following day, 3 June 1836, "Blane Sahib" called on the princes, and his message, which was even more discouraging, made the princes additionally unhappy:

> We questioned him about our situation. He answered us in the same way. In view of the special relationship (*khuṣūsīyyāt*) [of the British government] with the government of Muḥammad Shāh, it was difficult for our goal to be achieved and for matters to be settled in a manner compatible with our rank and dignity. This conversation disturbed us even more, and we consulted with one another. It was Blane's opinion that we would not receive a reply to our letters. Our talk with Blane induced in us a degree of despair and consternation that is impossible to describe.[45]

[42] Najaf Qulī Mīrzā [1839], 1:262–3.

[43] I have translated *mutaḥayyir* as "perplexed"; it could be rendered "at their wit's end," but this seemed too strong in the context.

[44] Riẓā Qulī Mīrzā 1982, 348–9.

[45] Ibid., 349.

Blane's gloomy prognostications were not justified. No sooner had he left than Khayyāt returned from London, bearing a reply from Lord Palmerston. Palmerston said he was delighted by the news of their arrival, and that he hoped that they would come to London and allow him to call on them, when they could tell him everything they wanted him to do:

> I (*īnjānib* [i.e., Riẕā Qulī Mīrzā]),[46] because of the special relationship [between the British government] and Muḥammad Shāh, thought it possible that I would not be treated as befitted my station, and so I refused to go [to London]. Instead, I wrote a letter and sent it with my brother Vālī [i.e., Najaf Qulī Mīrzā] and Khayyāt on 18 Ṣafar 1252/4 June 1836. My thinking was that, if Najaf Qulī Mīrzā became convinced of the friendship and support of the British government, I would go to London; otherwise, I would not go to London, and would seek help from some other government.[47]

On arrival in London, Najaf Qulī was called on by Sir John McNeill, a surgeon and diplomat who from 1824 to 1835 "was attached to the East India Company's legation in Persia, at first in medical charge, and latterly as political assistant to the envoy." On 30 June 1835 he was appointed secretary to the mission sent by the British government to Tehran to congratulate Muḥammad Shāh on his accession; this appointment led to his being decorated with the Order of the Lion and the Sun, First Class. On 9 February 1836, he was appointed minister plenipotentiary, and on 25 May 1836, two days after the royal princes landed at Falmouth, he was appointed envoy and minister plenipotentiary to Muḥammad Shāh.[48] McNeill spoke Persian extremely well, and there is no hint in the *Safarnāmah* that the princes distrusted him because of his accreditation to the British Legation in Tehran. As soon as McNeill heard of Najaf Qulī Mīrzā's arrival in London, he went to call on him. He answered all Najaf Qulī Mīrzā's purposes and matters of concern, and promised to devote all his efforts toward setting his affairs in order.[49]

On 19 Ṣafar 1252/5 June 1836 Najaf Qulī Mīrzā placed Riẕā Qulī Mīrzā's letter inside a letter of his own and sent both by the hand of Khayyāt to Lord Palmerston. When Palmerston read the contents, and learned that the princes

[46] This passage is one of several that make it clear that Riẕā Qulī Mīrzā must be the author of the *Safarnāmah*.

[47] Riẕā Qulī Mīrzā 1982, 349–50.

[48] Stephen and Lee 1921–2, 12:693. McNeill was of course instrumental in the fall, in 1251/1835, of Muḥammad Shāh's progressive *vazīr*, Mīrzā Abū al-Qāsim Qā'im Maqām Farāhānī, see Ādamīyat 1973, 5–27.

[49] Riẕā Qulī Mīrzā 1982, 352.

"intended no sedition in Iran, he was very pleased, and promised to visit Najaf Qulī Mīrzā the following day and listen to the prince's requests."[50]

> The [next] day, 20 [Ṣafar 1252/6 June 1836], a group of officials and members of the nobility called on the esteemed brother [i.e., Najaf Qulī Mīrzā] in the morning, and in the afternoon Lord Palmerston himself called. After an exchange of compliments, the two engaged in a conversation which is too long to write down in full.[51] The gist of it was: "You are princes of the blood royal and the 'cream of the crop' (*zubdah-yi malikzādagān*), and our concern for your nation and government exceeds that for our own government. If your intention is reconciliation with our government, we are at your disposal (*qadam i shumā bar chashm*), and we will do our utmost to bring your affairs to a satisfactory conclusion with the Shāh of Iran. I personally will leave no stone unturned to help. But if your intentions are not peaceful, we will not countenance discord and turmoil in Iran." My brother made adequate replies to the minister, and their meeting concluded by his saying that: "We wish to avoid enmity and conflict with the government of Muḥammad Shāh, but the British government will not be negligent in furthering our affairs and supporting us." It was decided that a person of distinction, of ambassadorial rank, be at his [i.e., Najaf Qulī Mīrzā's] service night and day.[52] Any request [we] may have should be referred to him, and we will reply to and send an answer to his letter. The meeting between my brother Vālī and Lord Palmerston the Foreign Secretary concluded at this point.[53]

The personal escort appointed by the British government was James Baillie Fraser, who had been asked to take charge of the princes on 31 May 1836 and had obtained suites at Mivart's Hotel in Brook Street for the three princes, three servants and the interpreter.[54] For several days, (21 3 Ṣafar 1252/7–9 June 1836), Najaf Qulī Mīrzā was visited by a variety of ministers, members of the nobility and eminent personages. One of these was Sir Gore Ouseley who, twenty years previously, in the reign of Fatḥ 'Alī Shāh, had been a British envoy to Iran and had been received by the Farmānfarmā in Shīrāz; when Sir Gore visited Najaf Qulī Mīrzā's suite, he at once recognized and remembered the names of the Farmānfarmā's former servants.[55]

50 Ibid. Najaf Qulī Mīrzā ([1839], 1:262–3) incorrectly states that Najaf Qulī Mīrzā stayed in McNeill's house.

51 Khayyāt, however, gives a fuller version of this interview.

52 Najaf Qulī Mīrzā ([1839], 1:265) says "A Mohammadan shall be appointed to attend you daily." Khayyāt cannot really have thought that this was likely.

53 Riẓā Qulī Mīrzā 1982, 353.

54 Fraser [1838] 1973, 1:69.

55 Riẓā Qulī Mīrzā 1982, 355.

On 25 Ṣafar 1252/11 June 1836 Lord Palmerston, having consulted the Cabinet, sent a letter to Riẕā Qulī Mīrzā in Bath telling him that he and Tīmūr Mīrzā were the king's guests, and should come to London forthwith; on 28 Ṣafar/14 June the two princes left Bath for London.[56] On 6 Rabī‘ I 1252/21 June 1836, Lord Palmerston called on the princes:

> He came on the part of the government to learn all our plans and views, as he was to inform all the other vizirs of it; he asked us to put everything down in writing: this, I believe, he requested, so that we may always be held responsible by our own written pledge that nothing new should occur.[57]

Once again, there are nuances in Riẕā Qulī Mīrzā's account which are missing in Khayyāt's translation:

> Lord Palmerston said: "I am authorized by the government to listen to your propositions and to get a written statement of them from you." I said: "I have several times set down our petition in writing in summarized form, and have sent messages. However, if you wish, I am ready to tell you our petition orally and to make a more detailed written statement for the government." An extended conversation ensued on all matters. Finally, he explained that the British government had decided to satisfy us in every way and to act as intermediary with Muḥammad Shāh. I replied: "That is all very well, but Muḥammad Shāh is an absolute monarch, and if he does not respond favorably to your mediation on our behalf in accordance with our wishes, what will you do next, and what course shall we pursue then?" Lord Palmerston, after thinking deeply, said: "I do not have the authority to answer that question. I shall have to refer it to *Kānṣīl* [i.e., Council, Cabinet]. Do write down a detailed account of our conversation today; it will then be discussed in Cabinet and an answer sent to you." We wrote down our propositions in full as requested, and they were translated by Mīrzā Ibrāhīm Shīrāzī, who had lived in London for twelve years; the propositions were then dispatched to the government. As he was leaving, Lord Palmerston invited us to be his guests at his home the following Sunday, and we accepted.[58]

It is obvious that the British government exercised extreme caution in their handling of this delicate situation. However, Lord Palmerston was now

[56] Riẕā Qulī Mīrzā (1982, 371) says 26 Ṣafar, but since Khayyāt only delivered Palmerston's letter to them on the 26th (ibid., 370) it is unlikely that the princes left Bath the same day.

[57] Najaf Qulī Mīrzā [1839], 1:291.

[58] Riẕā Qulī Mīrzā 1982, 386–7.

satisfied, and, as a result, the princes began to receive invitations from members of the government, including the Prime Minister Lord Melbourne, and from members of the royal family. In addition, London's social hostesses vied with one another in issuing invitations to the princes to attend social engagements. The princes placed great trust in Fraser's judgment as to which social invitations they should accept. Riẕā Qulī Mīrzā said to Fraser:

> Our honour is in your keeping. We are strangers, you must be our guide and guard. Where you tell me to go, I will go. Where you think I should not go, I will not visit; and remember, I go nowhere without you.[59]

The main concern of the princes was that they should not become a public gazing-stock, a "*khirs-e-Dushmunzearee*," that is, a monster to attract public notice.[60]

Despite all the kindness shown to them in England, it was only natural that the princes should occasionally become melancholy when they worried about the safety of their families.[61] It was therefore with the greatest relief that they heard in July 1836 that their "wives and families had been liberated by the Shah, without hurt or detriment." Some family members had entered the service of Muḥammad Shah; others had reached Baghdād in safety.[62] Then, on 18 Rabī' II 1252/2 August 1836, Lord Palmerston called on the princes, and brought the welcome news that their affairs had nearly reached a successful resolution (*maṭālib-i shumā maqrūn bi-ṣavāb ast*), and that they were free to leave whenever they wished.[63] Fraser, he said, would accompany them as far as Baghdād. He concluded by saying that the King wished to meet them in private audience.[64] Khayyāt adds a comment which does not appear in the Persian text:

> In truth, Lord Palmerston was in every respect very kind and polite, a striking proof of the friendship and union of the two empires.[65]

59 Fraser [1838] 1973, 1:128.

60 Ibid., 1:127. I have been unable to verify this expression.

61 Ibid., 1:150–1.

62 Ibid., 1:168–9.

63 Riẕā Qulī Mīrzā 1982, 477; Najaf Qulī Mīrzā ([1839], 2:88) says that Fraser would accompany them as far as Constantinople.

64 Najaf Qulī Mīrzā [1839], 2:88.

65 Ibid.

The promised audience with King William IV took place on 3 August 1836, according to Fraser. The King said to the princes:

> You are my sons, and to the best of my ability and power I shall strive to order your affairs and to set your minds at rest; we shall not be negligent in any way.[66]

The princes thought that the King was "a most gracious, excellent king; exceedingly kind and affable."[67] They estimated that he was "about eighty years old."[68] The princes had some decided opinions on the Stuarts. The House of Stuart, they correctly state, had ceased more than a century ago[69]; Charles I "was a sanguinary and arbitrary prince. He wished to subvert the Constitution, to dispense with Parliament, and to reign despotically. The English, however, put an end to his career by decapitating him. James II attempted, like his grandfather, to reign despotically, but he was obliged to abdicate."[70]

The princes were eager to leave London without delay. Since the end of the social season, their ennui had increased.[71] There were some final contretemps: Riz̤ā Qulī Mīrzā refused to attend the prorogation of Parliament on 20 August, because he could not be seated in a place compatible with his rank. The fact that some ladies were given preference to him in seating particularly rankled, although the princes did acknowledge that English ladies were superior to Persian ladies "in education and usefulness and intellect."[72] Two of the princes's servants "defected," and elected to stay in England: Taqī the cook, because he had taken a liking to English beer; and the tailor because he found English women to his liking.[73] Finally, on 3 September 1836/21 Jumādá I

[66] Riz̤ā Qulī Mīrzā 1982, 479; Fraser [1838] 1973, 1:301. As usual, the chronology is confusing. Riz̤ā Qulī Mīrzā (1982, 478) says Wednesday 21 Rabīʿ II 1252/5 August 1836. The 21st of Rabīʿ II 1252 was actually a Friday.

[67] Najaf Qulī Mīrzā [1839], 2:91. The Persian text uses the word *mutavāz̤iʿ* (modest).

[68] Ibid. William IV was in fact seventy years of age on 3 August 1836, having been born on 21 August 1765. Even if the princes were thinking in terms of lunar years, William would still have been only about seventy-three.

[69] In 1714.

[70] Najaf Qulī Mīrzā [1839], 2:91–2. The last sentence is Khayyāt's own; Riz̤ā Qulī Mīrzā (1982, 480) says that the dynasty died out after Charles II.

[71] Fraser [1838] 1973, 1:282.

[72] Ibid., 1:306–8.

[73] Ibid., 1:310–1.

1252, the princes left London for Dover, and crossed the Channel to Calais, with the faithful Fraser in attendance.

When the time drew near for Fraser and the princes to part company, both parties rose above the petty irritations and the occasional friction which had been an inevitable part of their daily contact over several months. On their journey from Baghdād to England, the princes had made a large part of the journey by sea. The aversion of all Iranians to sea travel had been powerfully reinforced by rough weather in the course of this voyage, and the princes had demanded that as much of their return journey as possible should be by land. November 1836 therefore found them in Rumania, where Riẓā Qulī Mīrzā fell seriously ill of a fever. Fraser himself contracted the fever, but managed to throw it off after three days. He wrote:

> It was only now, in this extremity of danger, that the restlessness of my own mind, and the sinking of my own heart, rendered me sensible of how much I truly loved the prince—how much, in spite of all petty causes of vexation, his mild and amicable manners and real goodness of heart had won upon my own affections.[74]

When they arrived at Constantinople, the Persian agent, Muḥammad Āqā, tried to stir up trouble by complaining to the Porte about the hospitality shown by the Ottoman government to "rebels and enemies of the Shah."[75] As if this were not enough, the plague raged at Constantinople and, in the absence of proper sanitary precautions, 1,200 people a day died. Tīmūr Mīrza was ill for a time. These misfortunes made the princes reflect that:

> We see that the English government has always been our real friends, and you, Saheb Fraser, our true and sincere adviser. As for those infidel Turks, men without faith or fear, what have they to do with us?[76]

According to Fraser,

[74] Ibid., 2:178. Fraser had initially formed a bad impression of the Persian character, see Wright, 1994, 127–8. Wright says: "Fraser never overcame his early dislike of the Persian character," (1994, 128) but this passage suggests that close contact with the princes had caused him to think again.

[75] Fraser [1838] 1973, 2:221–2.

[76] Ibid., 2:246.

England and the English people had risen in their estimation every step they had made away from it."[77]

It would be interesting to explore the British government archives for more information on Cabinet discussions on the delicate problem posed by the princes's appeal to the British government for assistance, but this must be the subject of another paper.

[77] Ibid., 2:253–4. The fate of the three princes after their departure from Constantinople is as follows. The Ottoman authorities finally gave the princes permission to leave Constantinople on 14 February 1837 [8 Dhū al-Qa'dah 1252] (Fraser [1838] 1973, 2:257), and they traveled to Baghdād, where they were reunited with their families, and took up residence under official British protection (Riẕā Qulī Mīrzā 1982, 740). Each prince had been granted a pension of 2,000 British pounds by the British government (ibid.). Fraser had been instrumental in securing this stipend for the princes. He had argued that "in the present aspect of Eastern affairs these men are worth any pecuniary sacrifice to this country," and in Russian hands would provide a pretext for "introducing her troops into Persia" (Wright 1992, 132). In Baghdād, the three princes found two other Qajar princes who were living on an allowance (*muqarrarī*) from the Ottoman government: Allāhvirdī Mīrzā and Sulaymān Mīrzā, who were both sons of Fatḥ 'Alī Shāh, and therefore uncles of the princes (Riẕā Qulī Mīrzā 1982, 740). Muḥammad Shāh made repeated attempts to persuade the three princes to return to Iran, and promised to restore to them all their lands. The princes, however, distrusted the Shāh, and refused to return to Iran during Muḥammad Shāh's lifetime. (Farmānfarmā'ī quotes the British traveler Edward L. Mitford, who was in Baghdād in 1840, as saying that the princes were right in thinking that their lives would be in danger if they returned to Iran, see ibid., 741; Lambton (1978, 393) mistakenly states that the three princes "returned in 1836 to the Ottoman Empire and spent the rest of their lives there in exile."). After his accession in 1264/1848, Nāṣir al-Dīn Shāh renewed the attempt to lure the princes back to Iran, and Riẕā Qulī Mīrzā, having made over to his second son Nawẕar Mīrzā all his personal estates in Fārs, sent him to Iran in 1265/1848–9 to see which way the wind was blowing. Nawẕar Mīrzā was granted asylum by Sultan Mīrzā Ḥusām al-Salṭanah, a paternal uncle of Nāṣir al-Dīn Shāh, and eventually was able to reclaim all his father's lands in Fārs. Finally, in 1279/1862–3, Riẕā Qulī Mīrzā responded favourably to another invitation from Nāṣir al-Dīn Shāh, and, with the consent of the British government, returned to Iran with his brother Tīmūr Mīrzā, but died *en route* at Qal'ah Ḥājjī Karīm near Kirmān Shāh, and his body was sent to Najaf for burial. Tīmūr Mīrzā continued his journey to Mashhad, and was subsequently received in audience at Niyāvarān by Nāṣir al-Dīn Shāh, to whom he donated most or all of the jewels belonging to his deceased brother Riẕā Qulī Mīrzā. Tīmūr's love of hunting, especially falconry, which was also a passion of Nāṣir al-Dīn Shāh, won him the favour of the Shāh, who made him a *muqarrab-i khāṣṣ*, and allotted him a pension of 12,000 *tūmān*s a year, at a time when the average pension was 2–3,000 *tūmān*s a year. Farmānfarmā'ī quotes Dūst 'Alī Khān Mu'ayyir al-Mamālik as saying that Tīmūr Mīrzā died during the first third of the latter's reign, i.e., between 1848 and 1864 (Riẕā Qulī Mīrzā 1982, 746). This cannot be correct, because Tīmūr Mīrzā did not return to Iran until 1862–3, and apparently lived to a ripe old age (ibid.). In regard to the fate of Najaf Qulī Mīrzā, Farmānfarmā'ī says that nothing is known about him. He conjectures that he probably died in Iraq, and certainly several years prior to the death of Riẕā Qulī Mīrzā which, as we know, occurred in 1279/1862–3. He further conjectures that Najaf Qulī Mīrzā had no offspring, at least no male offspring. Had he had any, he says, it is highly probable that they would have returned to Iran, as did the children of Riẕā Qulī Mīrzā, who settled in Fārs (ibid., 741–6).

BIBLIOGRAPHY

ĀDAMĪYAT, FARĪDUN. 1973. *Maqālāt-i tārīkhī*. Tehran : Shabgīr, 1352 Sh.

FASĀ'Ī, ḤASAN. 1972. *History of Persia under Qājār rule*. Tr. Heribert Busse. New York & London : Columbia Unviersity Press.

FRASER, JAMES BAILLIE. [1838] 1973. *Narrative of the residence of the Persian Princes in London in 1835 and 1836, with an account of their journey from Persia and subsequent adventures*. 2 vols. in 1. Reprint, New York : Arno Press.

KAYAT, ASSAAD Y. 1847. *A voice from Lebanon, with the life and travels of Assaad Y. Kayat*. London : Madden & Co.

LAMBTON, A. K. S. 1978. Ḳādjār. *Encyclopaedia of Islam*. New ed. Vol. 4. Leiden : E. J. Brill: 387b–99a.

LOCKHART, L. 1979. Bālyōs. *Encyclopaedia of Islam*. New ed. Vol. 1. Leiden : E. J. Brill: 1008a.

NAJAF QULĪ MĪRZĀ [1839] 1971. *Journal of a residence in England, and of a journey from and to Syria, of Their Royal Highnesses Reeza Koolee Meerza, Najaf Koolee Meerza, and Taymoor Meerza, of Persia*. 2 vols. in 1. Reprint, Farnborough, England : Gregg International Publishers.

RIẒĀ QULĪ MĪRZĀ. 1982. *Safarnāmah-i Riẓā Qulī Mīrzā Nāyib al-Iyālah, navah-i Fatḥ 'Alī Shāh*. 2nd ed. Ed. Aṣghar Farmānfarma'i Qājār. Tehran : Asāṭīr, 1361 Sh.

SAVORY, ROGER. 1985. Muslim perceptions of the West : Iran. In *As others see us : mutual perceptions, East and West*. Ed. Bernard Lewis, Edmund Leites, Margaret Case. New York : International Society for the Comparative Study of Civilizations: 73–89.

STEPHEN, LESLIE and LEE, SIDNEY, eds. 1921–2. *Dictionary of national biography*. 22 vols. London : Oxford University Press.

STOREY, C. A. [1953] 1972. *Persian literature : a bio-bibliographical survey*. Vol. 1, pt. 2. Reprint, London : Luzac & Co.

SYKES, P. M. 1915. *A history of Persia*. 2 vols. London : Macmillan and Co.

[TĪMŪR MĪRZĀ]. 1908. *The Bāz-nāma-yi Nāṣirī : a Persian treatise on falconry*. Tr. D. C. Phillott. London : Bernard Quaritch.

WRIGHT, DENIS. 1985. *The Persians amongst the English : episodes in Anglo-Persian history*. London : I. B. Tauris & Co.

—— 1994. James Baillie Fraser : traveller, writer and artist, 1783–1856. *Iran* 32: 125–34.

Armenian Social Democrats, the Democrat Party of Iran, and *Īrān-i Naw* : a Secret Camaraderie

Janet Afary *

INTRODUCTION

CHRONICLERS OF THE CONSTITUTIONAL REVOLUTION have often hailed the courage and fearless commitment of the Armenian revolutionaries who participated in the restoration of the Constitutional order in 1327/1909. What is often lost in these accounts, however, is the contribution of Armenian social democrats to the debates over revolutionary and democratic ideas in the Second Constitutional Period of 1327–9/1909–11. As historians in the West have become more committed to documenting the multicultural nature of their societies and social movements, so should we pay more attention to the fact that the democratic order of the Constitutional Revolution stemmed in part from the multicultural and multiethnic leadership of the revolutionary movement which included religious dissidents, non-Persians, and non-Muslims.

Iraj Afshar, who has contributed so much to our understanding of the Constitutional Revolution, published in 1980 a new documentary collection entitled *Awrāq-i tāzah'yāb-i Mashrūṭīyat marbūṭ bih sālhā-yi 1325–1330 Qamarī* [1] which is of considerable importance for gaining an understanding of the above issues. This volume stands out in particular for illuminating the origins of the Democrat Party (*Firqah-'i Dimūkrāt-i Īrān*) (1327–9/1909–11), Iran's first modern political party, and the intellectual and organizational contribution of several Armenian-Iranian social democrats to the Party. Afshar's facsimile publication in this volume of close to one hundred pages of private correspondence conducted in French between two Armenian-Iranian social democrats, Vram Pilossian and Tigran Ter Hacobian (T. Darvish), and Majlis deputy and leader of the Democrat Party, Sayyid Ḥasan Taqī'zādah, shows that there was a close affinity of ideas between the Muslim and Armenian

* I am grateful to Kambiz Eslami for his many suggestions and helpful editing of this article.

[1] Afshar 1980; the cover title of the book is slightly different: *Awrāq-i tāzah'yāb-i Mashrūṭīyat va naqsh-i Taqī'zādah.*

social democrats who created the Party. The correspondence indicates that the idea of forming the Party took shape in Tabrīz during the siege of that city in the late 1326–early 1327/winter and spring 1909.[2] The letters also point to the intimate camaraderie of Ter Hacobian and Pilossian with the two celebrated Transcaucasian Muslim social democrats, Ḥaydar Khān ʻAmū Ughlū and Mehmet Emin Resulzade, who also worked within the Democrat Party. Moreover, Resulzade and Ter Hacobian helped shape the journal *Īrān-i naw* which remains one of the most sophisticated socialist newspapers of 20th century Iran.

THE TABRĪZ SOCIAL DEMOCRATS, THE ORIGINS OF THE DEMOCRAT PARTY, AND *ĪRĀN-I NAW*

On 23 Jumādá I 1326/23 June 1908, the Majlis was closed by a royalist coup led by the Russian officer of the Cossack Brigade, Colonel Liakhoff. Many leading Constitutionalists of Tehran went into exile, and the revolutionary center moved to Tabrīz. The Āẕarbāyjān Provincial Council (*Anjuman-i Iyālatī-i Āẕarbāyjān*, also known as *Anjuman-i Tabrīz*), the social democratic Secret Center (*Markaz-i Ghaybī*), and the rank-and-file *mujāhidīn* fighters would soon form the revolutionary army of Tabrīz whose military leadership was held by the former horse-dealer and outlaw Sattar Khān and his colleague the stone mason Bāqir Khan. A number of Transcaucasian revolutionaries (Muslims, Armenians, Georgians), as well as many Iranian-Armenians, joined the resistance as well.

On 19 Ramaḍān 1326/16 October 1908, a group of thirty mostly Armenian social democrats, who held leadership positions in the resistance army of Tabrīz, organized a conference in that city where they discussed the future direction of the movement. Two different political strategies were discussed during this conference. The majority believed that socialists should struggle for the establishment of liberal democracy and for the achievement of radical social and economic progress for the poor and the working class of Āẕarbāyjān and ultimately Iran. The minority argued that social democrats must temporarily abandon their more radical agenda, and instead fully enter the democratic movement, forming alliances with the leadership of the Constitutional movement.[3] After the meeting Vasu Khachaturian and Arshavir Chalangarian on behalf of the majority, and Tigran Ter Hacobian who represented the

[2] Pilossian to Taqī'zādah, 19 August 1909, in Afshar 1980, 239–40. See also Chaquèri 1988, 1–51.

[3] Afary 1994, 30–6.

minority wing of the conference, each sent copies of the minutes of the meeting to the leading Russian Marxist Georgi Plekhanov.[4]

The correspondence between Taqī'zādah, Pilossian, and Ter Hacobian shows that following the victory of the Constitutionalists and the reconquest of Tehran in Jumādá II 1327/July 1909, the minority wing of the Tabrīz social democrats defied the majority and followed through on precisely the policies they had presented at the October 1908 conference. They became close colleagues of the Majlis deputy Ḥasan Taqī'zādah, who had arrived in Tabrīz in mid Dhū al-Ḥijjah 1326/late December 1908, and explored with him the possibility of organizing Iran's first modern political party.

Taqī'zādah returned to Tehran on 21 Rajab 1327/8 August 1909 after its reconquest by the revolutionary army, and became the foremost member of the provisional government which began preparations for elections to the Second Majlis. During the same period, Taqī'zādah campaigned for the formation of the Democrat Party which he and his colleagues from Tabrīz had discussed. Gradually, branches of the Democrat Party were formed in a number of cities, including Tabrīz, Urūmīyah, Mashhad, Rasht, Kirmānshāh, Iṣfahān, Qazvīn, and Hamadān. Many of the local branches published their own newspapers, but the most important newspaper of the Party was *Īrān-i naw* which was published in Tehran between 1327/1909 and 1329/1911.[5]

Īrān-i naw had a circulation of two to three thousand and was the most sophisticated daily paper of Tehran during the Second Constitutional Period. The paper was founded in Rajab 1327/August 1909 (hence the phrase "*Rajab 1327*" incorporated in its caption title) and began publication on 7 Sha'bān 1327/24 August 1909. It became the official organ of the Central Committee of the Democrat Party on 21 Shawwāl 1328/26 October 1910. Edward G. Browne would thus praise *Īrān-i naw* for its contribution to the Constitutional Revolution:

> *Iran-i-Now* had the most extraordinary adventures in defending its Liberal policy and during the period of its publication was frequently the object of vehement attacks on the part of the journals which opposed it, so that most of its time was spent in polemics and it became both the

[4] See Chaquèri 1979, 44–9 and Ravāsānī 1989, 101–17. Ravāsānī and Iṭṭiḥādīyah, who has made extensive use of these documents in her study of the development of political parties during the Constitutional Revolution, have assumed that Ter Hacobian was a member of the Dashnak Armenian nationalist party. But Taqī'zādah, as we shall see later, argues otherwise, see Ravāsānī 1989, 104 and Iṭṭiḥādīyah 1982, 244.

[5] Ṣadr Hāshimī [1948–53] 1984–5, 1:345–48. For a list of the newspapers of this period see Gharavī Nūrī 1973, 76–103. See also Iṭṭiḥādīyah 1982, 218 and Kuhin 1981–3, 2:537–60.

> agent and victim of important political events . . . Since the *Iran-i-Now* was in opposition, that is to say was the partisan and organ of the minority (i.e., the Democrats), it was always liable to repression or suppression, and was the constant object of the anger, vengeance and recriminations of the supporters of the Government.[6]

The paper, which introduced European-style journalism to the country, broke new ground in its social criticism. Its targets included class society, prejudice towards women, anti-Semitism, and other forms of ethnic and religious prejudice. In addition, the journal made significant literary contributions. Some of the earliest poems of Malik al-Shu'arā' Bahār and Lāhūtī Kirmānshāhī, two leading poets of the early 20th century, were first published in *Īrān-i naw*.[7] The works of several major European writers, among them Alexandre Dumas and Leo Tolstoy, were made accessible to the Iranian public through Persian translations. Edward G. Browne's *The Persian Revolution of 1905–1909* was translated and published in serialized form in *Īrān-i naw* soon after its publication in Britain. Browne's lectures in Europe in behalf of the Constitutionalists were also extensively reported in *Īrān-i naw*.

Of special importance was the regular coverage of the debates in the Parliament under the title *Akhbār-i Dār al-Shura-yi Millī* (News of the National House of Consultation). These reports provided readers with a perspective different from that of the official *Rūznāmah-i Majlis* (Majlis Newspaper) which sided with the conservative Moderate Party (*Ijtimā'iyūn I'tidāliyūn*). *Īrān-i naw* printed letters and commentaries on social issues of the time. It discussed—often in articles written by women—the need for greater freedom for and education of women, the many grievances of workers and artisans, and, to a lesser extent, the oppression of the peasantry. In addition, it reported on major labor and socialist movements on the international scene. Reports on China, India, Russia, and North Africa, as well as news of labor movements, socialist organizations, and especially women's suffragists in Western Europe were published with much sympathy. The editorials were highly critical of the imperialist policies of the European powers in the Middle East, Asia, and Africa. The harshest criticisms were reserved for the tsarist government, which had occupied the northern provinces of Āẕarbāyjān, Gīlān, and Qazvīn, while a strong bond of solidarity was drawn between the revolutionary movements in Russia and Iran.

[6] Browne [1914] 1983, 52–3.
[7] Kubíčková 1968, 366–7.

The nominal editor of *Īrān-i naw* in its first year was Muḥammad Shabastarī, also known as Abū al-Ẕiyā', a former editor of the paper *Mujāhid* in Tabrīz.[8] The principal financial backer of the paper, as well as its managing editor, was a wealthy Armenian named Joseph Basil, who also financed the Dashnak Armenian paper *Ārāvud* (Morning).[9] The editorial board included Muslims and Armenians from both Iran and Transcaucasia. The actual editor, Mehmet Emin Resulzade (1884–1954), a Muslim social democrat from Baku, came to Gīlān in 1327/1909 on behalf of the Organization of Social Democrats (*Firqah-'i Ijtimā'iyūn 'Āmiyūn*). A month after the reinstitution of the constitutional government, he helped to establish *Īrān-i naw* in Tehran. Resulzade had been involved in the 1905 Russian revolution, had joined the Russian Social Democratic Workers Party, and had assumed the editorship of the socialist paper *Tekâmül* (December 1906–March 1907) in Baku. Even before his arrival in Iran in 1327/1909, Resulzade was known as an accomplished journalist, poet, and playwright. Though he knew little Persian at first, and for the first three months worked through a translator, Resulzade regularly contributed to the paper, and some of his articles appeared under the pen name *Nīsh* (Sting).[10]

Many of the more ground-breaking theoretical articles in *Īrān-i naw* did not have Resulzade's signature. Edward G. Browne has argued that the more significant articles were written by Amīr Ḥājibī, also known as Ghulām Riẕā. He identifies Ḥājibī as a Georgian who assumed the identity of a Muslim, wrote his articles in French, and had them translated into Persian.[11] The correspondence between Taqī'zādah and Ter Hacobian confirms, however, that it was Ter Hacobian, an Iranian-Armenian and not a Georgian, who, under the pen name T. Darvīsh, submitted many of the more important theoretical essays that were published in the paper, particularly after autumn of 1328/1910.[12] These articles were originally written in French and then translated into Per-

[8] It was difficult to remove Abū al-Ẕiyā' as editor after the paper became the official organ of the Democtar Party. There was much arguing over money before he agreed to relinquish his position, see Afshar 1980, 328–9.

[9] Ṣadr Hāshimī [1948–53] 1984–5, 1:110–1.

[10] After Resulzade was expelled from Iran by the government, his biography appreared in *Īrān-i naw* 3, no. 55, 30 May 1911. See also Bennigsen and Wimbush 1979, 204; and Ādamīyat 1975, 96–7.

[11] Browne [1914] 1983, 52.

[12] Ter Hacobian to Taqī'zādah, 1 November 1910, in Afshar 1980, 318. Most of the columns and editorials in *Īrān-i naw* do not have a signature. It is, therefore, difficult to determine which were written by Resulzade. Many of the more substantial essays, however, have Ter Hacobian's pen name.

sian. Ter Hacobian, who had studied political science in Switzerland, was a key theoretician of the minority wing of the Tabrīz social democrats. It was he who had written to Plekhanov in the fall of 1908 and argued for a "democratic," rather than a "social democratic" ideology for the future party.

Both Pilossian and Ter Hacobian corresponded in French with Taqī'zādah because, as members of ethnic minorities, they were beginners in the Persian language, a deficiency they deplored and were trying to remedy.[13] Our information about both men and their other Armenian colleagues is limited, but a closer look at their letters to Taqī'zādah, as well as some of Ter Hacobian's writings, shows the extent to which these two Armenian social democrats helped shape the Democrat Party and its organ *Īrān-i naw*.

THE LETTERS OF PILOSSIAN TO TAQĪ'ZĀDAH : A NEW FORM OF ORGANIZATION IN IRAN

Pilossian, who signed his letters and articles under the pen names *Baḥr* (Sea) or *Dihātī* (Peasant), was active in forming committees of the Democrat Party in Tabrīz.[14] Seven letters from Pilossian to Taqī'zādah have survived and appear in *Awrāq*. In these letters, written between 19 August 1909/2 Sha'bān 1327 and 19 October 1910/14 Shawwāl 1328, Pilossian proposed new ways of developing the Party nationally and giving it specifically Iranian characteristics. He warned Taqī'zādah that membership should not be limited to Āẕarbayjānīs, adding "you must find members among the Persians as well, so that the Party will not have a provincial character."[15] He also suggested that an appropriate Persian substitute for the word Democrat be found, asking "do you have a Persian or Arabic word that would mean 'democrat'? I am afraid this European word would keep away those who always have a repugnance for foreign words. Furthermore, they may equally confuse it with 'social democrats'. In any case, I do not give much weight to a name, as long as our compatriots do not find it inappropriate."[16]

When Taqī'zādah wrote to him of the growth of the Party in Tehran in January 1910/Dhū al-Ḥijjah 1327–Muḥarram 1328, Pilossian rejoiced at the development, replying that it was indeed a tremendous achievement "to have in an Oriental country 390 people under the flag of a democrat party,

[13] Ter Hacobian to Taqī'zādah, 1 November 1910, in Afshar 1980, 317–8.

[14] Pilossian to Taqī'zādah, 19 August 1909, in Afshar 1980, 240.

[15] Pilossian to Taqī'zādah, 3 February 1910, in Afshar 1980, 260.

[16] Ibid. The name *Āmiyūn*, roughly meaning "of the people" was suggested instead and was used intermittently in party documents, but the organization was primarily known to all as the *Firqah-'i Dimūkrāt-i Īrān*. The name "Social Democrat" would presumably have discouraged liberal politicians (whom the the Democratic Party was courting) from joining.

especially when this party is organized on a European model."[17] The letters indicate that the Armenian social democrats were involved not only in the organizational work of the Party, but also in establishing its ideological direction.[18] Pilossian wrote the internal regulations of the Party in French and told Taqī'zādah that he was sending them to Tehran for adoption by the Central Committee.[19]

In his letter of 19 August 1909/2 Sha'bān 1327, Pilossian sent a list of possible candidates which the joint committee of Armenian and Muslim social democrats in Tabrīz had drafted, and suggested that they be asked to run for elections to the Second Majlis: "We must strive to create within the second parliament an organized democratic majority. People are tired of the revolution and its upheavals. They want peace. If the Constitutionalists are not organized both inside and outside the Parliament, peace will never arrive."[20]

A month later, Pilossian would anxiously inquire about the work of the Democrat Party and Majlis elections: "Internal disorders on the one hand, and the presence of foreign soldiers on the other hand, threaten the integrity and independence of the country. We must have energetic and truly patriotic men in the Second Majlis, because if the Second Majlis does not satisfy people, and does not put an end to the anarchy in the provinces, our very independence will be in danger."[21] Seasoned Party members were not to be engaged in military campaigns in the provinces because they were needed in Tehran. When the famous Transcaucasian Muslim social democrat Ḥaydar Khān 'Amū Ughlū accepted an assignment to fight the Shāhsavan brigand Raḥīm Khān in the town of Karaj, north of Tehran, Pilossian wrote to Taqī'zādah that Ḥaydar Khān's "presence in Tehran is indispensable for the progress of the Democrat Party [and] we have begged him not to go. Please do everything necessary to keep him in Tehran because he is a good organizer and a good propagandist."[22]

Despite their relatively moderate politics compared to other socialists of the time, Pilossian and his colleagues were concerned about the growing power of the anti-constitutionalist forces and felt that such challenges to the new order should be dealt with swiftly and severely. When a "reactionary" aristocrat,

[17] Pilossian to Taqī'zādah, 26 January 1910, in Afshar 1980, 247–8.

[18] Pilossian to Taqī'zādah, 19 August 1909, in Afshar 1980, 239–40.

[19] Ibid., 238–42, and Afshar 1980, appendix, 366 (11–23). The internal regulations reprinted in facsimile in *Awrāq* appear to be in Ter Hacobian's handwriting and not Pilossian's. It is, of course, quite possible that the two collaborated on composing the document.

[20] Pilossian to Taqī'zādah, 19 August 1909, in Afshar 1980, 240.

[21] Pilossian to Taqī'zādah, 19 September 1909, in Afshar 1980, 244.

[22] Pilossian to Taqī'zādah, 26 January 1910, in Afshar 1980, 250.

Ḥabīb Allāh Muvaqqar al-Salṭanah, who had been expelled from the country along with the former Shāh, Muḥammad 'Alī Mīrzā, returned to foment trouble, he was executed in Muḥarram 1328/January 1910 and Pilossian wrote with Jacobin enthusiasm: "We read in the newspapers of the latest news in Tehran regarding the arrest of certain reactionaries and the hanging of Movakkeres-Saltanéh. Well done. If such measures had been taken a few months earlier the reactionaries and the mullahs would not have become so arrogant as they are now. One must be merciless towards these people. Without this [harshness] we shall never have peace."[23]

Despite the growth of the Tabrīz branch of the Democrat Party, Pilossian and his colleagues did not hesitate to abide by the decisions of the Central Committee in Tehran:

> For a very long time we have been organizing a section of the Democrat Party in Tabriz and we will probably have the pleasure of including you in the Committee. We shall place ourselves under the internal disposition of the Central Committee and we shall conform to the instructions we receive for the Tabriz section of the organization. You have done very well in organizing the Tehran Central Committee. Because the people of Tehran are more educated than those of Tabriz, it is not logical to place the former under the orders of the latter.[24]

The ideological solidarity between Armenian and Muslim social democrats was impressive. Taqī'zādah pointed out that the Dashnaks in Tehran provided jobs for members of their organization, and that Armenians such as Ter Hacobian, who were not affiliated with the Dashnak Party, often remained unemployed. Nevertheless, Ter Hacobian and Pilossian were committed to the Democrat Party and competed with the Dashnaks in recruiting young Armenian social democrats to their organization.[25] Pilossian and his Armenian colleagues in Tabrīz also felt that the Democrat Party should consult with them before recruiting any Armenians or Georgians. "You should never enter into relations with either the Armenians or the Georgians without asking for our advice; just as we do not know the Persians very well , in the same way you do not know the Armenians."[26]

Pilossian encouraged Taqī'zādah to maintain absolute secrecy in the work of the provisional Central Committee of the Party in Tehran. The Armenian

[23] Pilossian to Taqī'zādah, 3 February 1910, in Afshar 1980, 257.

[24] Ibid., 251–2.

[25] See the draft letter by Taqī'zādah dated 28 Ramaḍān 1328/3 October 1910 (Afshar 1980, 223) which shows that Ter Hacobian was not a Dashnak, certainly not by this time.

[26] Pilossian to Taqī'zādah, 3 February 1910, in Afshar 1980, 254.

social democrats also kept their connection to Taqī'zādah and the Democrat Party secret because the involvement of non-Muslims in the leadership of the Party could give the conservative Moderate Party, as well as the anti-constitutionalists, ample ammunition against the Democrats.[27]

Despite their strong loyalty to Taqī'zādah and the Central Committee, the Armenian social democrats recognized the importance of their own contribution to the Democrat Party. When the Party began to expand in Tehran, Taqī'zādah did not keep regular contact with his Tabrīz comrades, despite their urgings. Pilossian's anxiety is clear in his letters. He believed that this lack of communication would deprive the Muslim intellectuals in Tehran of the regular guidance and help of their Armenian colleagues in Tabrīz and would ultimately hurt the Party irrevocably.[28]

THE LETTERS AND ESSAYS OF TIGRAN TER HACOBIAN

A second set of four letters in *Awrāq* was written by Ter Hacobian to Taqī'zādah between 21 January 1910/9 Muḥarram 1328 and 1 November 1910/27 Shawwāl 1328. From Tabrīz, Ter Hacobian reported to the Central Committee of the Democrat Party in Tehran on the progress of the Tabrīz chapter and contributed articles to *Īrān-i naw*.[29] After Taqī'zādah was forced to leave Tehran in Rajab 1328/July 1910, Ter Hacobian moved from Tabrīz to Tehran where he joined the editorial board and also became a consultant to the Central Committee.

Taqī'zādah's absence severely disrupted the work of the Democrat Party. Upon his arrival in Tehran, Ter Hacobian wrote of the complete chaos and disorganization in the Democrat Party, including the parliamentary faction. "Almost everything is lost," he wrote to Taqī'zādah, "your return to Tehran is absolutely necessary."[30] Contemporaneously, Ter Hacobian suggested a total reconstruction of the Party and began to recruit working-class members. He organized a labor union for telephone workers, recruited pharmacy workers, and worked within the Iranian-Armenian community. Had it not been for his insufficient knowledge of the Persian language, Ter Hacobian claimed in his letters, he could have easily recruited 400 to 500 new members into the Party. Meanwhile he continued to support the activities of the literary center where the meetings of the Party were taking place, and encouraged the formation of other cultural and political clubs among Persian intellectuals.[31]

[27] Ibid., 253.
[28] Pilossian to Taqī'zādah, 9 May 1910, in Afshar 1980, 267–8.
[29] Ter Hacobian to Taqī'zādah, 23 May 1910, in Afshar 1980, 321–2.
[30] Ter Hacobian to Taqī'zādah, 1 November 1910, in Afshar 1980, 319.
[31] Ibid., 311–20.

In late Dhū al-Qa'dah 1328/November 1910, the Bakhtiyārī-Democrat coalition government was near collapse, and the nation was threatened with more aggressive political maneuvers from Britain and Russia. In the pages of *Īrān-i naw* Ter Hacobian called for the formation of a National Salvation Committee (*Kumītah-'i Najāt-i Millī*). This was to be a coalition of the various left and liberal political parties and heads of tribes, one which Ter Hacobian had hoped would restrain the more conservative Moderate Party.[32] A few months later, however, the new regent Abū al-Qāsim Khān Nāṣir al-Mulk successfully adopted a similar tactic, except that in his plan a broad conservative majority was created to oppose the Democrats and support the Moderate Party.

A New Concept Of Nationality for the Democrat Party

Two central themes appear in Ter Hacobian's writings: (1) His belief that a new concept of nationality transcending ethnic and religious affiliations should be developed; (2) his abhorrence of political terrorism and critique of social democrats who had succumbed to terrorism in their efforts to remove the conservative opposition.

The first theme, the construction of a new concept of nationality, was also a great concern of several other social democrats of this period such as Taqī'zādah and Resulzade, and would be reflected in the program of the Democrat Party. The subject of political rights for non-Muslims (Jews, Armenians, Zoroastrians), as well as Muslims who did not belong to the Shī'ite Ithná 'Asharī branch of Islam, was a highly controversial one during both the First and Second Constitutional Periods. In the spring of 1325/1907, a heated debate developed over article 8 of the proposed Supplementary Constitutional Laws (*Mutammim-i Qānūn-i Asāsī*). This article, which was originally adopted from the Belgian Constitution of 1831, had been proposed by a seven-member commission which included Taqī'zādah.[33] It stated, "The people of the Persian Empire are to enjoy equal rights before the Law."[34] "The People" were defined as male and middle class members of society who were not religious dissidents such as Bahā'īs or Azalī-Bābīs. Partly in response to that article, Shaykh Faẕl Allāh Nūrī, the staunchly anti-constitutionalist *mujtahid*, who had referred to the Supplementary Laws as *Ẕalālat'nāmah* (Book of Deviance),[35] proposed article 2, which stated that no legal enactment of the

[32] Ibid.; *Īrān-i naw*, 7 November 1910, 1.
[33] Ādamīyat 1976–[1992], 1:408, 417–8.
[34] Browne [1910] 1995, 374.
[35] Malik'zādah 1984, 4:873.

Majlis could "be at variance with the sacred principles of Islam."[36] He also called for the establishment of a committee of *'ulamā* to monitor all deliberations in the Majlis.[37] After much heated debate and discussion, both article 2 and article 8 were ratified and incorporated into the Supplementary Constitutional Laws.

Taqī'zādah and his colleagues took pride in ratifying article 8 and felt that even in its modified form, the Supplementary Constitutional Laws had made a breakthrough by recognizing the equal rights of *dhimmi*s (recognized non-Muslims) in Iranian society. In his lecture to a British audience at the Central Asian Society in November 1908, Taqī'zādah, who was in London to appeal to the European community for the restoration of the constitutional order, began by speaking of article 8 as one of the most important achievements of the First Majlis, if not the most important one:

> One thing established by the Constitution was religious equality . . . a real religious equality, and not a theoretical one. Before that non-Mussulmans had been treated as not on the same plane in the matter of liberty of observance as the followers of the Prophet . . . The clerical element in Persia was against the framing of a fundamental law of religious liberty, but the reformers succeeded in getting it through, and obtaining recognition of the great principle that in the eyes of the law and the Administration there should be no difference between Christian or Muhammadan, Zoroastrian or Jew.[38]

After the restoration of the constitutional order in Tehran in Jumādá II 1327/ July 1909, Ter Hacobian, Resulzade, and Taqī'zādah further developed this new concept of nationality in their writings, as well as in their activities. Ter Hacobian felt that the issue was not only a matter of equal protection for non-Muslims and Muslims before the law, but also implied a new concept of nationality in which ethnic and religious affiliations were altogether irrelevant:

> We must create a new [concept] of nationality which will be Iranian. It would be the same to us if people speak different languages or worship different gods. In our view, there should be no differentiation among ethnic groups (*les nations*). We shall recognize only one nation—the Iranian nation, the Persian citizen.[39]

[36] Browne [1910] 1995, 372–3.
[37] Ādamīyat 1976–[92], 1:412–6.
[38] Browne 1909, 10. Mansour Bonakdarian brought this article to my attention.
[39] Pilossian to Taqī'zādah, 21 January 1910, in Afshar 1980, 304.

Resulzade continued this line of thought in his political treatise *Tanqīd-i Firqah-'i I'tidāliyūn yā Ijtimā'iyūn-i I'tidāliyūn* (Critique of the Moderate Party or Social Moderates) in which he developed a scathing critique of the ethnic prejudices of the Moderate Party.[40] The most provocative section of the treatise was its commentary on the role of religion and on the attitudes of the Moderate Party toward members of non-Muslim ethnicities. The Moderates had called for the unity of all Iranians, claiming they were all "Muslims and followers of one religion and one ideology." This argument showed that the Moderate Party "did not recognize a single person other than Muslims as citizens of Iran." Their attitude was thus similar to that of the tsarist government which accused the revolutionaries of being "fooled by the Jews, sold out to the foreigners, and enemies of the nation." The truth, however, was that "the history of the Iranian revolution, which still continues, shows that [many] *Fidā'īs* [who helped restore the constitutional order] came from among the ranks of these same non-Muslims."[41]

These views were also reflected in the program of the Democrat Party which was presented to the Majlis and published in *Īrān-i naw* on 19 Rabī' I 1329/20 March 1911. The program called for "equality of all people of the nation before the government and the law without distinction of race, religion, or nationality," as well as "complete separation of political power from religious power."[42]

The Democrats' commitment to equal civil rights especially troubled the conservative Moderate Party and gave the opponents of Taqī'zādah the opportunity to remove him from the Majlis. In the spring of 1328/1910, a case was brought up in the Majlis which involved two Ismā'īlī Iranian victims, men who were both Muslim and Shī'ite but did not belong to the dominant Ithná 'Asharī branch of Shī'ism. When the two Ismā'īlī men returned to their village near Nayshābūr from a pilgrimage to Mecca, they were killed as a result of a religious edict (*fatwá*) issued by a local cleric, Shaykh Bāqir, and upheld by the leading *mujtahid* of Mashhad. Taqī'zādah called attention to the matter in the Majlis and asked that the police arrest and prosecute Shaykh Bāqir who apparently had killed the men himself and confiscated their property. When Shaykh Bāqir was arrested by the Armenian chief of police Yephrem Khan, the *'ulamā* were outraged. Those who had waited for an opportunity to force out the leader of the Democrat Party, including some of the

[40] Resulzade 1982. The treatise was originally published in Tehran in 1328/1910.

[41] Resulzade 1982, 75–6.

[42] *Īrān-i naw*, 20 March 1911, 1. For a more detailed discussion of the Democrat Party and its agenda, see Afary 1996.

Najaf *'ulamā*, saw this as their chance. Taqī'zādah was accused of conduct that was "in conflict with the Muslim characteristics of the nation and the holy *sharī'ah* laws."[43] The condemnation by the *'ulamā* was not openly debated in the Majlis since this would have brought to surface the unconstitutional nature of their conduct. Instead, on 24 Jumādá II 1328/2 July 1910, Taqī'zādah was quietly asked to take a three-month leave of absence from the Majlis.[44]

In Tabrīz, Pilossian was outraged by this treatment of Taqī'zādah and the pressure by Sayyid 'Abd Allāh Bihbahānī and other members of the *'ulamā* to force Taqī'zādah out of the Majlis. He complained to Taqī'zādah that had they been informed sooner and been kept abreast of the events in Tehran, they could have helped him by organizing demonstrations in his support. Through public protestations in Tabrīz, Pilossian argued, they could have warned the Majlis that it had no right to expel a delegate of the province of Āẕarbāyjān without the express approval of that community.[45] But Taqī'zādah had not informed his colleagues and no such demonstration in his support took place. Instead, some members of the Democrat Party, who were angry with the unconstitutional treatment of their leader, resorted to political terrorism, thereby further alienating the progressive community that had placed much of its hope in the Democrat Party.

Ter Hacobian's Critique of Political Terrorism

On 8 Rajab 1328/16 July 1910, Sayyid 'Abd Allāh Bihbahānī was gunned down in his home by four members of the *mujāhidīn* who were associated with Haydar Khān and the Democrats. Bihbahānī, the leading constitutionalist *mujtahid*, who with his son led the Moderate Party, had been blamed for the censure of Taqī'zādah in the Majlis. The murder of the seventy-year-old cleric, one of the two ranking *'ulamā* who had been the initial leaders of the Constitutional Revolution, created mass outrage. The bazaars closed in protest, and both Ḥaydar Khān and Taqī'zādah, who was then still in Tehran, were implicated.[46] This incident led to the exile of Taqī'zādah from Iran and subsequent terrorist actions by supporters of the Moderate Party against members of the Democrat Party. The assassination of Bihbahānī and the subsequent killings of supporters of both the Democrat and the Moderate Parties seriously demoralized the public. It seemed that their many sacrifices for the reestablishment of the parliament and the constitution had proved futile. Rather

[43] Afshar 1980, 230–1, 207–17; see also, Taqī'zādah 1993, 152–5, 348–9.

[44] Afshar 1980, 226. See also the report in the *Times* (London), 4 July 1910, 6.

[45] Pilossian to Taqī'zādah, 9 May 1910, in Afshar 1980, 267–8.

[46] Malik'zādah 1984, 6:1336–7; Kasravī 1971–2, 130–1.

than solving conflicts in a democratic fashion, as all had hoped, the contending political parties now resorted to assassination and terrorism.

Of particular significance in this period are a series of eight essays in *Īrān-i naw* in which Ter Hacobian analyzed the question of political terrorism and declared it detrimental to the progressive cause. He tried to demonstrate why political terrorism was destructive and presented the contemporary social democratic analysis that progressive changes in social conditions of a society resulted only from fundamental changes in economic structures and not from the removal of individual leaders through terrorism.

Ter Hacobian began by explaining the point of view of the adherents of political terrorism. Those who tried to justify terrorism as a viable means for social change considered it a powerful tool through which the state machinery could be crushed. The proponents of this ideology argued that when the authorities faced individual acts of terrorism they became concerned for their personal safety. This, in turn, led the government to adopt a more moderate course of action and lessened the prevalent political oppression of the people. The advocates of political terrorism argued that their actions "awakened the populace," so that when citizens realized that the aim of the rebels was to help the poor and oppressed, they became politically conscious. They were further strengthened by the knowledge that the revolutionaries were not weak, but were strong and capable men who could hurt the regime.[47]

Ter Hacobian then presented his rebuttal, and in the process gave a short synopsis of his social democratic views as well. He contended that socialism rejected political terrorism as a viable course of action. Individual leaders were not the cause of deteriorating social conditions, economic structures were. With the gradual development of means of production according to "scientific means," a new, freer, and more developed social formation came into being. Each new stage of production gave birth to new social classes which in turn determined the political character of society. With each progressive stage of culture, from the hunter gatherer society, to agriculture, and finally to capitalist society, the "influence of religion" on the people also diminished.

The Iranian Revolution was itself a result of growing capitalist relations of production which necessitated an end to the reign of the *khān*, the landlords, and the monarch, Ter Hacobian wrote. The revolution, however, had developed only half-way and unless there was a corresponding change in the means of production, it could proceed no further. Ultimately, once new social

[47] Ter Hacobian, "Terror," *Īrān-i naw*, 18 December 1910, 1–2.

classes began to grow stronger, and the new society gained an independent life of its own, the old government and the old ways of life would disappear.[48]

The murder of an influential figure would not alter a system of government or challenge oppressed social forces to make a revolution. We cannot allow "revolution and terror" to become synonymous, he contended. Revolution was the act of a whole society which had acquired the necessary material, intellectual, and spiritual forces to take "the role of the midwife" in giving birth to a new society. Terrorism was a "futile one-shot act," which stemmed from the illusion that society could be transformed in one stroke and through an individual's will.[49]

"Every dictator and every absolute monarch represents a certain class," Ter Hacobian argued. "Napoleon represented the French bourgeoisie, Pugachev represented the Russian peasantry, while Nādir Shāh represented the *khān*s of Iran." Just as no building could stand without proper foundations, so no government could remain in power without its class foundations. The supporters of political terrorism made a grave mistake when they compared the government to a machine, using the analogy that if one removed a few nuts and bolts the whole system would collapse. The political machinery of the government needed an internal social revolution before its life could be ended. If indeed terrorism had such magical powers, Ter Hacobian argued, then no system of government would exist for long. There were always many who were discontented, and if indeed the political terrorism of a few instigated the movement of the whole, then the continuing fight between the ruling classes and the forces of opposition would result in a series of unstable governments.[50]

"History shows that the result of acts of terror is not revolution but an unleashing of counter-revolution."[51] Drawing upon the example of the Russian Revolution, Ter Hacobian presented a chart which listed the number of imprisoned revolutionaries and acts of political terrorism carried out in the first decade of the 20th century in Russia. The chart showed that in the aftermath of the Russian Revolution, when many acts of terrorism were committed, there was a significant increase in the level of government repression as well. Thus in 1909 alone, 240,000 revolutionaries were imprisoned in addition to the thousands who were killed or sent to exile in Siberia. Terrorism neither disturbed the government nor succeeded in changing the foundations

48 Ter Hacobian, "Terror: 3," *Īrān-i naw*, 21 December 1910, 1.
49 Ter Hacobian, "Terror: 4," *Īrān-i naw*, 29 December 1910, 1–2.
50 Ibid.
51 Ter Hacobian, "Terror: 6," *Īrān-i naw*, 31 December 1910, 2.

of power. Rather, as the case of Russia demonstrated, after each act of terrorism "repression gains more, the inhumane acts of the government increase."[52]

In fact, terrorism had had yet another disastrous effect, Ter Hacobian warned. Revolutionaries, terrorist, and murderers became the same in the minds of people. Political terrorism resulted in the loss of respect for revolutionary ideas among the people and took away from revolutionary organizations the one foundation they could count on, namely, the people's support and sympathy which was of utmost significance for any revolution.[53]

The political salvation and security of Iran depended upon its adherence to democracy. Terrorism not only did not improve the situation of the country, it created a further excuse for foreign enemies to enter the country on the pretext of ending internal disorder. The autocrats did not fear the hand grenades of a terrorist, but they trembled at the thought of an educated and orderly nation aware of its power and its rights.[54]

The detailed discussion of terrorism in *Īrān-i naw* points to the significant political disagreements within the Democrat Party In the months following the assassination of Bihbahānī and others. Ter Hacobian's strong criticism of political terror and his emphasis on the way it alienated the masses from the revolutionaries was significant. Clearly Ḥaydar Khān 'Amū Ughlū was among the targets of this criticism. A new ideological rift had emerged within Iranian socialism and would continue to exist throughout the 20th century. This was not a division between those who opted for alliance with liberal politicians and those who wanted to push for a more radical agenda including workers' rights. It was an ideological division between those who saw political terrorism as a viable means towards reaching the end of a new social order, and others who rejected it, but nevertheless adhered to a quasi mechanical concept of Marxism in which economic structures determined ideological superstructures and modernization progressively eliminated the influences of cultural and religious beliefs.

CONCLUSION

The Democrat Party and its organ *Īrān-i naw* began a new era of social democratic politics and journalism in the 20th century Iran. As the writings of Pilossian and Ter Hacobian have demonstrated, Armenian social democrats were involved at every stage of the formation of the Party and made important

[52] Ter Hacobian, "Terror: 7," *Īrān-i naw*, 3 January 1911, 2.
[53] Ter Hacobian, "Terror: 7 [8]," *Īrān-i naw*, 4 January 1910, 1–2.
[54] Ibid.

organizational and intellectual contributions to it. They oversaw the development of the Tabrīz branch of the party and made many suggestions about the composition and activities of the Central Committee in Tehran. They proposed new delegates for the Second Majlis and contributed to the by-laws and program of the Democrat Party. They brought new recruits to the Party, especially from within the Armenian community, organized labor unions, and became involved in the political and cultural clubs of the Democrats. They also provided Taqī'zādah, Resulzade, and other Muslim social democrats with constant support and advice. Ter Hocobian was an outspoken critic of political terrorism and showed that it could lead to a strengthening of the conservative opposition and alienation of the ordinary people. The Armenian social democrats and their Muslim colleagues saw their intellectual cooperation as a possible model for a future Iranian society. They were committed to a new concept of nationality, one in which prejudicial attitudes towards non-Muslims were replaced by social integration and solidarity. They also envisioned a multiethnic social democratic Iranian society in which Muslims and non-Muslims lived in harmony and worked towards a secular progressive society.

Because nearly everyone in the Democrat Party kept the involvement of Armenian social democrats secret, fearing an outburst by the conservative opposition against the Party, this important dimension of the Constitutional Revolution was nearly lost to us. Taqī'zādah himself, as well as leading historians of the Constitutional Revolution such as Kasravī and Malikzādah who mentioned the role of Armenian social democrats, also downplayed its importance, sometimes in a misguided effort to legitimize the Revolution. With his effort to bring to light neglected or forgotten aspects of the Constitutional Revolution, Iraj Afshar has once again made us aware of the multidimensionality of that revolution, and its important contribution to the origins of democracy in Iran.

BIBLIOGRAPHY

ĀDAMĪYAT, FARĪDŪN. 1975. *Fikr-i dimūkrāsī-i ijtimā'ī dar Nahẓat-i Mashrūṭīyat-i Īrān*. Tehran : Payām, 1354 Sh.

—— 1976–[92]. *Īdi'ūlūzhī-i Nahẓat-i Mashrūṭīyat-i Īrān*. 2 vols. Tehran : Payām (v. 1) : Rawshangarān (v. 2), 2535 Shāhanshāhī–[1371 Sh.]

AFARY, JANET. 1994. Social democracy and the Iranian Constitutional Revolution of 1906–11. In *A century of revolution : social movements in Iran*. Ed. John Foran. Minneapolis : University of Minnesota Press: 21–43.

—— 1996. *The Iranian Constitutional Revolution, 1906–1911 : grassroots democracy, social democracy, and the origins of feminism*. New York : Columbia University Press.

AFSHAR, IRAJ, ed. 1980. *Awrāq-i tāzah'yāb-i Mashrūṭīyat marbūṭ bih sālhā-yi 1325–1330 Qamarī*. Tehran : Jāvīdān, 1359 Sh.

BENNIGSEN, ALEXANDRE and WIMBUSH, S. ENDERS. 1979. *Muslim national communism in the Soviet Union : a revolutionary strategy for the colonial world*. Chicago : University of Chicago Press.

BROWNE, EDWARD G. 1909. *The Persian Constitutionalists*. London : Central Asian Society.

—— [1914] 1983. *The press and poetry of modern Persia : partly based on the manuscript work of Mírzá Muḥammad 'Alí Khán 'Tarbiyat' of Tabríz*. Reprint with new pref. by Amin Banani, Los Angeles : Kalimát Press.

—— [1910] 1995. *The Persian Revolution of 1905–1909*. Reprint with new introd., correspondence, and reviews, ed. Abbas Amanat. Washington, DC : Mage Publishers.

CHAQUÈRI, COSROE, ed. 1979. *La Social-démocratie en Iran : articles et documents*. Florence : Edition Mazdak.

—— 1988. The role and impact of Armenian intellectuals in Iranian politics, 1905–1911. *Armenian review* 41, no. 2–162 (summer): 1–51.

GHARAVĪ NŪRĪ, 'ALĪ. 1973. *Ḥizb-i Dimūkrāt-i Īrān dar dawrah-'i duvvum-i Majlis-i Shūrā-yi Millī*. Tehran : 'A. Gharavī Nūrī, 1352 Sh.

ITTIḤĀDĪYAH, MANṢŪRAH. 1982. *Paydāyish va taḥavvul-i aḥzāb-i siyāsī-i Mashrūṭīyat : dawrah-i avval va duvvum-i Majlis-i Shūrā-yi Millī*. Tehran : Nashr-i Gustarah, 1361 Sh.

KASRAVĪ, AḤMAD. 1971–2. *Tārīkh-i hijdah sālah-i Āẓarbāyjān*. 5th ed. Tehran : Amīr Kabīr, Day 1350 Sh.

KUBÍČKOVÁ, VERA. 1968. Persian literature of the 20th century. In *History of Iranian literature*. Ed. Jan Rypka. Dordrecht, Holland : D. Reidel Publishing Co.: 353–418.

KUHIN, GU'IL. 1981–3. *Tārīkh-i sānsūr dar maṭbū'āt-i Īrān*. 2 vols. Tehran : Āgāh, 1360–2 Sh.

RAVĀSĀNĪ, SHĀPŪR. 1989. *Nahẓat-i Mīrzā Kūchak Khān Jangalī va avvalīn jumhūrī-i shūrāyī dar Īrān*. 2nd ed. Tehran : Nashr-i Sham', 1368 Sh.

RESULZADE, MEHMET EMIN. 1982. Tanqīd-i Firqah-'i I'tidāliyūn yā Ijtimā'iyūn-I'tidāliyūn. In *Marāmnāmah'hā va niẓām'nāmah'hā-yi aḥzāb-i siyāsī-i Īrān dar dawrah-'i duvvum-i Majlis-i Shūrā-yi Millī*. Ed. Manṣūrah Ittiḥādīyah (Niẓām Māfī). Tehran : Nashr-i Tārīkh-i Īrān, 1361 Sh.: 59–86.

ṢADR HĀSHIMĪ, MUḤAMMAD. [1948–53] 1984–5. *Tārīkh-i jarā'id va majallāt-i Īrān*. 4 vols. Reprint, Iṣfahān : Kamāl, 1363–4 Sh.

TAQĪ'ZĀDAH, ḤASAN. 1993. *Zindagī-i ṭūfānī*. 2nd ed. Ed. Iraj Afshar. Tehran : 'Ilmī, 1372 Sh.

An Illustrated *Maṣnavī-i Ma'navī*

B.W. Robinson

QAJAR PAINTING FOUND ITS MOST PRESTIGIOUS outlets in oil painting, lacquer, and enamel; the Timurid and Safavid tradition of the manuscript *de luxe* had faded in the 18th century and was almost extinct. Apart from some fine Korans, one can only recall the *Dīvān of Khāqān* (Fatḥ 'Alī Shāh) in the Royal Library at Windsor,[1] three presentation copies of Fatḥ 'Alī Khān Ṣabā's *Shāhanshāhnāmah*,[2] the Viṣāl or Dāvarī *Shāhnāmah*,[3] and, of course, the monumental "Arabian nights" in the Gulistān Palace Library, Tehran.[4] So when a good Qajar illustrated manuscript turns up, it is worth recording, even if it does not quite aspire to "royal" quality. Such a manuscript is the subject of this article, which is intended simply to introduce and record it.[5] It is a copy of the *Maṣnavī-i ma'navī* of Jalāl al-Dīn Rūmī, and was acquired some twenty-five years ago by the late Mr. Massoudi from a member of the family of Mas'ūd Mīrzā Ẓill al-Sulṭān (1266–1336/1850–1918), the eldest son of Nāṣir al-Dīn Shāh (r. 1264–1313/1848–96). This prince was appointed governor of Fārs in 1279/1863, and of Iṣfahān in 1283/1867,[6] and became notorious for cutting down the magnificent trees along the Chahār Bāgh to sell, and for destroying or dismantling several of the surviving Safavid

[1] Holmes 1893, no. 152; Robinson 1967, 78–9.

[2] They are (1) Oxford, Bodleian Library, MS Elliot 327, presented by Fatḥ 'Alī Shāh to Sir Gore Ouseley (Robinson 1952, 175–9); (2) London, India Office Library, Ethé 901, presented by Fatḥ 'Alī Shāh to the East India Company (Robinson 1976, 244–9); (3) Vienna, Nationalbibliothek, Flügel 639, presented by Fatḥ 'Alī Shāh to the Emperor Franz I (Duda 1983, 13–5). There is also a very similar copy in the Majlis Library, Tehran, MS 15234 (Ibn Yūsuf Shīrāzī 1939–42/3, 482–3).

[3] An heirloom in the Viṣāl family of Shīrāz till it was purchased by the Empress Farah; it is now housed in Mūzih-'i Riẓā 'Abbāsī, Tehran, MS 599. Sixty-eight miniatures, the great majority by the celebrated Shīrāz painter Luṭf 'Alī, but a few by Dāvarī and Farhang, sons of the poet Viṣāl; they are dated between 1270/1853–4 and 1280/1863–4; see Sharīfzādah 1991, 247–69, Nūrānī Viṣāl 1991, and Sharīfzādah 1993.

[4] MS 556. See Ātābāy 1976, in which 80 of the miniatures are reproduced in color.

[5] Mr. Karīm'zādah Tabrīzī has briefly described three of the paintings of this manuscript in the third volume of his monumental work which, I am happy to acknowledge, is an invaluable companion to the study of Persian painting; see Karīm'zādah Tabrīzī 1985–, 3:1437. It should also be noted here that this manuscript was sold at Christie's on 24 April 1990.

[6] Bāmdād 1968–75, 4:81.

palaces.[7] Unlike many private collectors, Mr. Massoudi was always anxious that his treasures should be shared and enjoyed as widely as possible, and I am indebted to his daughter Maryam for permission to publish and for giving me every facility for studying and photographing it. She thus carries on her father's generous and enlightened practice of making his collection readily available to all lovers of Persian art. His house and collections were plundered by a mob during the 1979 Revolution, but a number of items were recovered by his daughter after his death.

Jalāl al-Dīn Rūmī in the considered opinion of the late Professor Edward G. Browne "is without doubt the most eminent Sufi poet whom Persia has produced, while the mystical *Mathnawi* deserves to rank amongst the greatest poems of all time."[8] The *Maṣnavī*, a poem of 26,660 couplets, is confidently described by its author as "the roots of the roots of the roots of the religion, and the discovery of the mysteries of reunion and sure knowledge" (with a good deal more in the same vein).[9] Browne is rather more specific and slightly less flattering: "It contains a great number of rambling anecdotes of the most various character, some sublime and dignified, others grotesque and even (to our ideas) disgusting, interspersed with mystical and theosophical digressions, often of a most abstruse character, in sharp contrast with the narrative portions which, though presenting some peculiarities of diction, are as a rule couched in very simple and plain language."[10]

Other works of moral or philosophical character interspersed with anecdotes, such as the *Būstān* and *Gulistān* of Sa'dī and the *Makhzan al-asrār* of Niẓāmī, are frequently encountered in illustrated copies, but the *Maṣnavī* hardly ever, though there are two in the British Library (Add. 27263[11] and Or. 7693[12]), one with only two miniatures in the National Museum, New Delhi,[13] and one in the Metropolitan Museum of Art.[14] The present copy is, therefore, of no little interest, as it contains 56 miniatures. It is dated 1279–80/1862–4, and the fact that four of the miniatures are signed by Yaḥyá, son of the celebrated Ṣanī' al-Mulk, sets the seal on its importance.

[7] Ibid., 4:98–9; D'Allemagne 1911, 4:79–80.
[8] Browne [1902–24] 1928, 2:515.
[9] Jalāl al-Dīn al-Rūmī 1881, pref., i.
[10] Browne [1902–24] 1928, 2:520.
[11] Rieu 1879, 2:584–6; Titley 1977, 68, no. 201.
[12] Meredith-Owens 1968, 68.
[13] Author's notes.
[14] Smith Cochran 1914, 95–98.

The manuscript measures 27 x 17 cm., written surface 18 x 10.5 cm. The binding, of red leather with sunk medallions, is impressed with a stamp giving the binder's name as Ḥasan ibn Muḥammad al-Ḥusaynī with the date 1278/1861–2. The text, in a small neat *nasta'līq*, is in four columns of 21 lines to the page, and the pages are numbered as pages not folios, starting afresh with each of the six parts (*mujallad*). Marginal annotations appear throughout. Each part begins with an illuminated heading of fine quality. The total number of pages is 704, i.e., 352 folios. The colophons give the dates 1279/1862–3 and 1280/1863–4, but no copyist's name.

The following list of the miniatures gives the number, the page reference in the manuscript and the reference in the excellent Tehran lithographed edition of 1307/1890, prefixed by T.[15] The miniatures do not spread into the side margins, and are thus all 10.5 cm. wide; their slightly varying height is given in lines of text, each line corresponding approximately to 0.95 cm.

1. Bk. I, p. 13, T p. 11, 7 lines deep
   The caliph, wearing a Qajar crown, questioning Laylā and Majnūn. Carpet of rich scrollwork design.
2. Bk. I, p. 28; T p. 24; 10 lines deep.
   The lion in philosophical discussion with other animals.
3. Bk. I, p. 48; T p. 42; 8 lines deep.
   The merchant and the parrots.
4. Bk. I, p. 51; T p. 45; 9 lines deep.
   The merchant, his family, and the dead parrot.
5. Bk. II, p. 14; T p. 116; 6 lines deep.
   A villager feels a lion in the darkness, thinking it was an ox; the dead ox lies beside him.
6. Bk. II, p. 65; T p. 157; 9 lines deep. (Fig. 1).
   A drunken youth interrogated by two night watchmen in the street.
7. Bk. II, p. 71; T p. 162; 8 lines deep.
   The caliph Mu'āviyah, who had forgotten prayer time, visited in bed by the Devil (*Iblīs*), represented as an old man wearing a pointed and tasselled cap.
8. Bk. II, p. 93; T p. 181; 8 lines deep.
   The Prophet and his wife Āyishah discussing repentance.
9. Bk. III, p. 16; T p. 206; 8 lines deep.
   Majnūn caressing a dog that lived in Laylā's village.
10. Bk. III, p. 21; T p. 209; 7 lines deep.
    A jackal of unusual color appears as a peacock among the other jackals.
11. Bk. III, p. 26; T p. 214; 8 lines deep.
    Imrān lying with the mother of Moses (who becomes pregnant) under the bed on which her husband is asleep.

[15] For full bibliographic information on this edition, see Jalāl al-Dīn al-Rūmī 1890.

12. Bk. III, p. 28; T p. 216; 8 lines deep.
    Women arriving at the house of Imrān to see Moses.
13. Bk. III, p. 42; T p. 232; 9 lines deep. (Fig. 2).
    School scene: pupils with their master, whom they had deceived by a trick. The instruments of the bastinado lie ready. Signed, "*raqam-i Yaḥyá.*"
14. Bk. III, p. 53; T p. 241; 8 lines deep.
    David seated with the Sage Luqmān.
15. Bk. III, p. 61; T p. 249; 10 lines deep.
    Daqūqī leading his seven followers in prayer on the sea-shore. Two ships in the sea have not been painted in.
16. Bk. III, p. 78; T p. 277; 8 lines deep.
    The hare, the elephant, and the moon's reflection (the story as in *Kalīlah va Dimnah*).
17. Bk. III, p. 91; T p. 277; 8 lines deep.
    Youth riding a camel, in converse with four men. The story is of a merchant who falsely accuses the young man of killing his servant.
18. Bk. III, p. 106; T p. 291; 8 lines deep. (Fig. 3).
    The Blessed Virgin Mary, asleep by a stream, approached by the archangel Gabriel. She is represented in dishabille, whilst he is dressed like a Qajar prince, with wings.
19. Bk. III, p. 125; T p. 308; 7 lines deep.
    The half-naked ascetic Ṣadr-i Jahān falling in love with a young prince on a throne.
20. Bk. III, p. 127; T p. 315; 8 lines deep.
    Ṣadr-i Jahān falls fainting before a youth from Bukhārā, riding a white horse.
21. Bk. III, p. 129; T p. 316; 7 lines deep.
    Ṣadr-i Jahān comforted by the young prince, who changes his foolishness into good sense.
22. Bk. III, p. 130; T p. 317; 7 lines deep.
    Ṣadr-i Jahān and the young prince in converse by a throne.
23. Bk. IV, p. 2; T p. 324; 9 lines deep.
    A young lover fleeing from the night-watch. Signed, "*Yaḥyá.*"
24. Bk. IV, p. 3; T p. 324; 9 lines deep. (Fig. 4).
    The young lover finds his beloved by a stream in a garden. Signed, "*reqam-i Yaḥyá.*"
25. Bk. IV, p. 5; T p. 326; 8 lines deep. (Fig. 5).
    Lovers embracing in a garden.
26. Bk. IV, p. 11; T p. 331; 7 lines deep.
    The lover apologizing to his beloved for his sin of deception.
27. Bk. IV, p. 18; T p. 338; 9 lines deep.
    Solomon receiving presents sent by Bilqīs, Queen of Sheba. Weapons displayed on tables, and loaded mules in the background.
28. Bk. IV, p. 20l; T p. 340; 8 lines deep.
    The perfume-seller and his customer.

29. Bk. IV, p. 27; T p. 347; 9 lines deep.
    Solomon and Bilqīs enthroned, attended by three demons.
30. Bk. IV, p. 30; T p. 349; 8 lines deep.
    Muḥammad's nurse Ḥalīmah with an old man, watching idols falling from their pedestal.
31. Bk. IV, p. 42; T p. 360; 9 lines deep.
    Solomon in a ruined city.
32. Bk. IV, p. 69; T p. 386; 9 lines deep.
    Moses before Pharaoh, defying his magic.
33. Bk. IV, p. 76; T p. 393; 9 lines deep.
    Pharaoh enthroned with his wife Āsiyah, who educated Moses.
34. Bk. IV, p. 95; T p. 411; 8 lines deep.
    'Azīz and his sons in a landscape.
35. Bk. IV, p. 103; T p. 419; 9 lines deep.
    Young couple copulating in a garden, watched by the husband in a tree.
36. Bk. IV, p. 109; T p. 424; 8 lines deep.
    The archangel Gabriel, with multiple wings, appearing to the Prophet .
37. Bk. V, p. 12; T p. 439; 8 lines deep.
    Abraham and the peacock.
38. Bk. V, p. 35; T p. 462; 8 lines deep.
    Pair of lovers seated on a carpeted terrace, with a view of distant mountains. A fine violet carpet with Victorian scrollwork.
39. Bk. V, p. 39; T p. 466; 8 lines deep.
    Negro maid watching her mistress committing bestiality with an ass on a couch.
40. Bk. V, p. 48; T p. 474; 8 lines deep.
    The angel Azrael humbling himself in the dust.
41. Bk. V, p. 53; T p. 479; 8 lines deep.
    Ayāz removing his fur coat from a chest.
42. Bk. V, p. 58; T p. 484; 7 lines deep.
    A youth and a girl meeting on a terrace. Signed, "*Yaḥyá*."
43. Bk. V, p. 59; T p. 485; 8 lines deep.
    Two men in the house of Ayāz, one of them lifting the fur coat from the chest (cf. no. 41).
44. Bk. V, p. 66; T p. 491; 8 lines deep.
    Women in a bath-house; one of them has fainted.
45. Bk. V, p. 69; T p. 494; 7 lines deep. (Fig. 6).
    The lion and the fox in the forest, the latter informing the former about the ass.
46. Bk. V, p. 73; T p. 499; 8 lines deep.
    Bearded man performing sodomy on a youth who holds a dagger.
47. Bk. V, p. 95; T p. 521; 8 lines deep.
    Majnūn visited by three relatives in the desert.
48. Bk. V, p. 108; T p. 533; 8 lines deep.
    A father giving his daughter advice, both seated on a carpeted terrace.

49. Bk. V, p. 113; T p. 538; 8 lines deep. (Fig. 7).
    The champion (*pahlavān*) from Mūṣil, sword in hand, embracing the maid (who was intended for the caliph), having slain a lion that had entered the encampment. Marginal note in *shikastah*, dated 1281/1865.
50. Bk. V, p. 115; T p. 540; 8 lines deep.
    The maid enjoying copulation with the champion, after scorning the performance of the caliph.
51. Bk. V, p. 119; T p. 544; 8 lines deep.
    Ayāz prostrating himself before Sulṭān Maḥmūd, who is enthroned and attended by four courtiers.
52. Bk. VI, p. 18; T p. 565; 9 lines deep.
    Scene on a moonlit terrace: a youth in gold brocade coat asleep, having removed his cap, is contemplated by his mistress, with arms akimbo. He had fallen asleep waiting for her.
53. Bk. VI, p. 21; T p. 568; 9 lines deep.
    The Prophet and his favorite wife Āyishah encountering a blind man in the street.
54. Bk. VI, p. 54; T p. 598; 8 lines deep.
    A man aiming an arrow, against a background of a brown hillside and ruined building.
55. Bk. VI, p. 81; T p. 629; 8 lines deep. (Fig. 8).
    Moses as the Good Shepherd, carrying a sheep that had gone astray.
56. Bk. VI, p. 104; T p. 667; 8 lines deep.
    Barren landscape, with an angel lifting eyes and hands to heaven (from a story of the prophet Hud). Bk. VI, p. 107. End of text; pp. 108–15 are covered with verses in *shikastah*.

The painter Yaḥyá was the youngest of the three sons of Abū al-Ḥasan Khān Ghaffārī Ṣanī‘ al-Mulk; all three sons became painters, the other two being Asad Allāh Khān and Sayf Allāh.[16] Yaḥyá apparently bore a striking resemblance to his father, and at the instance of Nāṣir al-Dīn Shāh he was awarded the name of Abū al-Ḥasan III (Ṣanī‘ al-Mulk was actually Abū al-Ḥasan II). Influenced no doubt by his family environment, he soon took up painting and displayed fine talent in both water-color and oils. Yaḥyá Ẕokā’ records and reproduces two of his works: (1) his most famous work, an oil-painting of the old Arg Square (*Maydān-i Arg*), showing the pool and the Pearl Cannon (*Tūp-i Marvārīd*), a European (*Farangī*) couple, two veiled women with a veiled little girl, and several horse-drawn carriages; this picture is signed, "*raqam-i khānaẕād Mīrzā Abū al-Ḥasan Khān pisar-i Ṣanī‘ al-Mulk fī sanah 1303*"[17]; (2) another well-known work, an oil-painting of the private saloon of the Shāh (*uṭāq-i mubārakah-i Birilyān*), signed "*ḥasb al-amr-i*

[16] See Karīm'zādah Tabrīzī 1985–, 1:21–2; Suhaylī Khvansārī, 1976; Ẕokā' 1963; and Sāsānī 1948.

[17] Ẕokā' 1970, 28.

bandagān-i a'láḥaẓrat-i Shāhanshāhī arvāḥ al-'ālamīn fadāh, Uṭāq-i Mubārakah-i Birilyān bi-dast-i khānah'zād Abū al-Ḥasan Khān tashakkul yāft, 1305 [1887–8]."[18]; Muḥammad 'Alī Karīm'zādah Tabrīzī also records a water-color portrait of Ḥājjī Mīrzā 'Abd al-Muṭallib, Yaḥyá's maternal uncle and a portrait of an unidentified Qajar notable, signed, "*Khānah'zād Abū al-Ḥasan Ṣāiṣ, 'a. 1294* [1877]."[19]

In Rajab 1307/March 1890, it appears that Yaḥyá was under something of a cloud following the suicide, at his house, of his cousin, the painter Abū Turāb Ghaffārī, older brother of Kamāl al-Mulk.[20] Yaḥyá is known to have been alive during the period 1313–24/1896–1906,[21] but the exact year of his death does not seem to have been recorded.[22]

As will have been seen, four of the miniatures in our manuscript bear the signature of Yaḥyá (nos. 13, 23–4, 42), and it is probable, though not absolutely certain, that he was also responsible for the others. Illustrators of contemporary lithographed books usually only signed a small proportion of the illustrations in any given volume. The miniatures are all stylistically consistent, though the animal pictures (nos. 2, 10, 16, 45) may appear to differ from the rest. However that is only due to their subject-matter; the lion in nos. 2 and 45 could certainly be by the same hand as that in no. 49.

In view of the fact that Yaḥyá was alive during the period 1896–1906, the miniatures in this manuscript must represent an early stage of his career, when he was closely following his father's style as exemplified in the great 'Arabian nights' manuscript. Yaḥyá's miniatures are indeed very close to these latter, though falling somewhat behind them in quality. His work is sometimes marred by infelicities of drawing, as for instance the night-watchman's hands in no. 6, of the bodily proportions of the archangel Gabriel in no. 18, and of the youth in no. 42. However he can achieve a convincingly romantic atmosphere (nos. 24–5) and considerable dramatic vigor (no. 49), and his women are nearly always charming. It would be interesting to see miniatures from his later years; they might well be up to his father's standard. Meanwhile this manuscript bears witness to his early skill as a miniature painter, though hitherto he has been known only as a portraitist and painter in oils.

[18] Ibid., 238.

[19] Karīm'zādah Tabrīzī 1985–, 1:22; 3:1438. [Mr. Y. Ẕokā' has kindly provided a list of other known works of Yaḥyá, see Appendix A. Ed.]

[20] Ibid., 1:22; I'timād al-Salṭanah 1971, 686.

[21] See Appendix A, item no. 16.

[22] In his biographical account of Kamāl al-Mulk, the famous Iranian statesman and scholar, Ẕukā' al-Mulk Furūghī, revealed that Yaḥyá had been dependent on alcohol, opium and the like, adding "he did not accomplish much (*bi-jā'ī narasīd*)," see Ghanī 1980–4, 9:784.

APPENDIX A

The following list of Mīrzā Yaḥyá's known works was kindly supplied by Mr. Yaḥyá Ẕokā' of Tehran who has done extensive research on the painter. All the paintings on this list bear Yaḥyá's signature; we have, however, transcribed only those that are relatively elaborate [Ed.]

1. Portrait of Mustawfī al-Mamālik, not dated, probably around 1290/1873. Initially in the Gulistān Palace (Kākh-i Gulistān), this painting was transferred to the Niyāvarān Palace before the 1979 Revolution. Present whereabouts unknown.

2. A water-color painting of two young men, Majd al-Dawlah and Ja'far Qulī Khān Jalāl al-Mulk, in the Gulistān Palace (no. 8135), signed "*raqam-i khānahzād Abū al-Ḥasan Khān, 1290* [1873–4]."

3. A water-color portrait of an unidentified man in Qajar costume, wearing a *sardārī* and a cap, in the Gulistān Palace (no. 8036), signed "*Khānahzād Abū al-Ḥasan Ṣāiṣ Ghaffārī, 1291* [1874–5]."

4. An oil canvas depicting a rustic cottage with cows, horses and fowl, in the Gulistān Palace (no. F/332), dated 1293/1876.

5. A portrait of his father Ṣanī' al-Mulk, signed "*Yādgār-i Abū al-Ḥasan Ṣāliṣ, ṣūrat-i marḥūm Ṣanī' al-Mulk ast, az rū-yi kār-i ān marḥūm kashīdah shud, 1293* [1876]."[23]

6. A copy of Raphael's *The Fire in the Borgo*, in the Mūzih-i Millī-i Īrān (formerly Mūzih-i Īrān-i Bāstān), dated 1296/1878–9.

7. Large oil canvas depicting a coffee-house with its crowd of patrons, and servers and entertainers, with a two-storied house within the confines of a garden in the background and bare rocky hills in the distance, in the Gulistān Palace, and signed "*Khānahzād Abū al-Ḥasan, sanah 1297* [1879–80]."

8. A landscape depicting a summer resort, in the Gulistān Palace, dated 1297 [1879–80].

9. An oil painting containing portraits of Sardār-i Mākū' and his sons in the Ethnology Museum (Muzih-i Mardumshināsī) of Tehran, and signed "*raqam-i khānahzād-i Shāhanshāh Mīrzā Abū al-Ḥasan Khān, sanah 1304* [1886–7]."

10. A landscape painting of Niyāvarān, in the Gulistān Palace, dated 1305/1887–8.

11. A landscape painting of Dushān Tappah, in the Gulistān Palace, dated 1305/1887–8.

12. An oil painting showing an orchard and a field of summer vegetables (*jālīz*), signed "*bar ḥasb-i amr-i qadar qudrat-i a'láḥaẓrat-i Shāhanshāh ruḥi va ruḥ al-'ālamīn fadāh, khānahzād Abū al-Ḥasan Ṣāiṣ Ghaffārī, 1305* [1887–8]." Similar to item no. 1, this painting too was transferred to the Niyāvarān Palace before the 1979 Revolution. Its present whereabouts is also unknown.

[23] For a reproduction of this painting, see Suhaylī Khvansārī 1989, 9.

13. A head and shoulder (*nīmtanah*) portrait of Nāṣir al-Dīn Shāh, in the Gulistān Palace (no. 70), undated.

14. An official oil painting portrait of Nāṣir al-Dīn Shāh, depicting him with a *jiqqa* on top of his head, and a bejeweled sword in his hand, in the Gulistān Palace, undated.

15. A small water-color painting depicting a rural landscape, in the Gulistān Palace, undated.

16. His last known painting is an undated portrait of Muẓaffar al-Dīn Shāh (r. 1313–24/1896–1906) in the old Majlis building.

Fig. 1. A drunken youth. By Yaḥyá, Abū al-Ḥasan III. Circa 1279/1862–3. 10.5 x 8.5 cm. Present whereabouts unknown

Fig. 2. School scene. By Yaḥyá, Abū al-Ḥasan III. Circa 1279/1862–3. 10.5 x 8.5 cm. Present whereabouts unknown

Fig. 3. The blessed Virgin Mary. By Yaḥyá, Abū al-Ḥasan III. Circa 1279/1862–3. 10.5 x 7.6 cm. Present whereabouts unknown

Fig. 4. Young lovers. By Yaḥyá, Abū al-Ḥasan III. Circa 1279/1862–3. 10.5 x 8.5 cm. Present whereabouts unknown

Fig. 5. Lovers embracing in a garden. By Yaḥyá, Abū al-Ḥasan III. Circa 1279/ 1862–3. 10.5 x 7.6 cm. Present whereabouts unknown

Fig. 6. The lion and the fox in the forest. By Yaḥyá, Abū al-Ḥasan III. Circa 1279/ 1862–3. 10.5 x 6.6 cm. Present whereabouts unknown

Fig. 7. The champion (*pahlavān*) from Mūṣil. By Yaḥyá, Abū al-Ḥasan III. Circa 1279/1862–3. 10.5 x 7.6 cm. Present whereabouts unknown

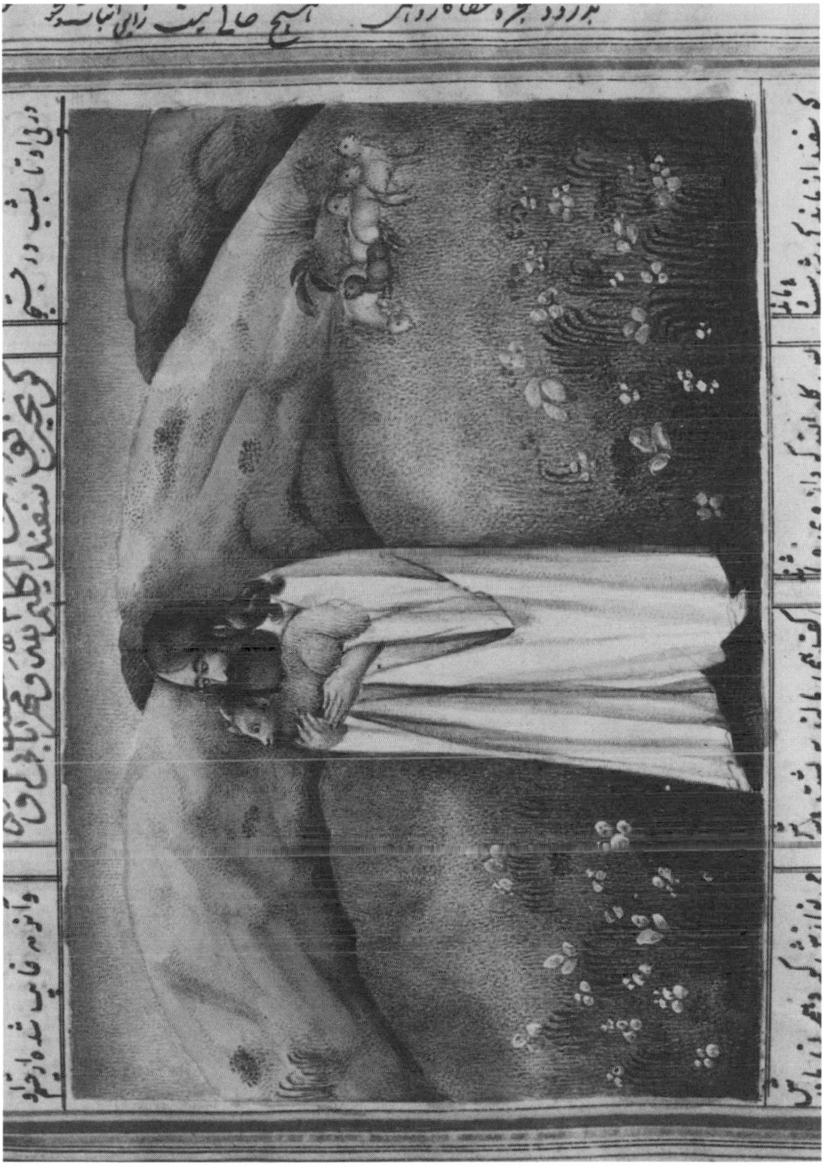

Fig. 8. Moses as the good shepherd. By Yaḥyá, Abū al-Ḥasan III. Circa 1279/1862–3. 10.5 x 7.6 cm. Present whereabouts unknown

BIBLIOGRAPHY

ĀTĀBĀY, BADRĪ. 1976. *Fihrist-i dīvān'hā-yi khaṭṭī-i Kitābkhānah-i Salṭanatī va kitāb-i Hazār va yak shab.* Tehran : Kitābkhānah, 2535 Shāhanshāhī.

BĀMDĀD, MAHDĪ. 1968–75. *Sharḥ-i ḥāl-i rijāl-i Īrān dar qurūn-i 12 va 13 va 14 Hijrī.* 6 vols. Tehran : Kitābfurūshī-i Zavvār, 1347 Sh.–Bahman 1353 Sh.

BROWNE, EDWARD G. [1902–24] 1928. *A literary history of Persia*, 4 vols. Reprint, Cambridge, [England] : The University Press.

D'ALLEMAGNE, HENRY-RENÉ. 1911. *Du Khorassan au pays des Backhtiaris : trois mois de voyage en Perse.* 4 vols. Paris : Hachette et cie.

DUDA, DOROTHEA. 1983. *Islamische Handschriften I : persische Handschriften.* 2 vols. Vienna : Verlag der Österreichischen Akademie der Wissenschaften.

GHANĪ, QĀSIM. 1980–4. *Yāddashthā-yi Duktur Qāsim Ghanī.* Ed. Sīrūs Ghanī. 12 vols. London : S. Ghanī.

HOLMES, R. R. 1893. *Specimens of royal, fine, and historical book-binding selected from the Royal Library, Windsor Castle.* London : W. Griggs & Sons.

IBN YŪSUF SHĪRĀZĪ. 1939–42/3. *Fihrist-i Kitābkhānah-'i Majlis-i Shūrā-yi Millī.* Vol. 2. Tehran : Majlis, 1318–21 Sh.

I'TIMĀD AL-SALṬANAH. 1971. *Rūznāmah-'i khāṭirāt-i I'timād al-Salṭanah.* 2nd ed. Ed. Iraj Afshar. Tehran : Amīr Kabīr, 1350 Sh.

JALĀL AL-DĪN RŪMĪ. 1881. *The Mesnevī.* Tr. J. W. Redhouse. London : Trübner & Co.

—— 1890. *Maṡnavī-i ma'navī.* Ed. Āqā Mīrzā Maḥmūd Khvānsārī. Tehran : Āqā Mīrzā Ḥabīb Allāh, 1307.

KARĪM'ZĀDAH TABRĪZĪ, MUḤAMMAD'ALĪ. 1985– *Aḥvāl va āṡār-i naqqāshān-i qadīm-i Īrān va barkhī az mashāhīr-i nigārgar-i Hind va 'Uṣmānī.* 3 vols. to date. London : M.'A. Karīm'zādah Tabrīzī.

MEREDITH-OWENS, G.M. 1968. *Handlist of Persian manuscripts, 1895–1966.* London : The Trustees of the British Museum.

NŪRĀNĪ VIṢĀL. 1991. Shāhnāmah-i Dāvarī, az nafāyis-i Mūzih-i Riẓā 'Abbāsī. *Mūzih'hā* 11 (pā'īz 1370 Sh.): 6–11.

RIEU, CHARLES. 1879. *Catalogue of the Persian manuscripts in the British Museum.* 3 vols., London : The Trustees of the British Museum.

ROBINSON, B. W. 1958. *A descriptive catalogue of the Persian paintings in the Bodleian Library.* Oxford : Oxford University Press.

—— 1967. *Persian miniature painting from collections in the British Isles.* London : Victoria and Albert Museum.

—— 1976. *Persian paintings in the India Office Library.* London : Sotheby Parke Bernet.

SĀSĀNĪ, KHĀN MALIK. 1948. Buzurgtarīn naqqāsh-i 'aṣr-i Qājārīyah. *Iṭṭilā'āt-i māhiyānah* 2 (Urdībihisht 1327 Sh.): 29–32.

SHARĪFZĀDAH, 'ABD AL-MAJĪD. 1991. *Nāmvarnāmah.* Tehran : Mu'āvinat-i Pizhūhishī[-i Sāzmān-i Mīrāṡ-i Farhangī-i Kishvar] bā hamkārī-i Idārah-'i Kull-i Mūzih'hā-yi Tihrān, 1370 Sh.

—— 1993. Sukhanī dīgar dar bārah-'i 'Shāhnāmah-'i Dāvarī'. *Mūzih'hā* 13–4 (bahār va tābistān 1372 Sh.): 53–63.

SMITH COCHRAN, ALEXANDER. 1914. *A catalogue of the collection of Persian manuscripts including also some Turkish and Arabic presented to the Metropolitan Museum of Art, New York*. New York : Columbia University Press.

SUHAYLĪ KHVĀNSĀRĪ, AḤMAD. 1976. Panj Abū al-Ḥasan-i naqqāsh dar yak qarn. *Hunar va mardum* 169–70 (Ābān/Āẕar 2535 Shāhanshāhī): 61–5.

—— 1989. *Kamāl-i hunar : aḥvāl va āṣār-i Muḥammad Ghaffārī Kamāl al-Mulk*. Tehran : Muḥammad 'Alī 'Ilmī : Surush, 1368 Sh.

TITLEY, NORAH M. 1977. *Miniatures from Persian manuscripts : a catalogue and subject index of paintings from Persia, India, and Turkey in the British Library and the British Museum*. London : British Museum Publications.

ẔOKĀ', YAḤYÁ. 1963. Mīrzā Abū al-Ḥasan Khān Ṣanī' al-Mulk Ghaffārī. *Hunar va mardum* 10 (Murdād 1342 Sh.): 14–27; 11 (Sharīvar 1342 Sh.): 16–33.

—— 1970. *Tārīkhchah-'i sākhtimānhā-yi Arg-i salṭanatī-i Tihrān va rāhnumā-yi Kākh-i Gulistān*. Tehran : Anjuman-i Āṣār-i Millī, 1349 Sh.

Albert Hotz and His Photographs of Iran : an Introduction to the Leiden Collection

Jan Just Witkam

ALBERTUS PAULUS HERMANUS HOTZ (1855–1930) came from a well-to-do Dutch family of industrialists. His father was co-owner of a large iron-casting plant in The Hague. But that was by no means the only occupation of the family. In 1874 J.C.P. Hotz, the father, founded the Persian Trading Association (Vennootschap Perzische Handelsvereeniging J.C.P. Hotz & Zoon) a consortium which brought together Dutch venture capital necessary for setting up trade with Iran. Instigated by the Dutch consul-general in Būshihr, Mr. Keun van Hoogerwoerd, he was convinced that the Dutch should not miss the business opportunities which were being seized by other nationals. That same year, at the age of only 19, Albert Hotz traveled to Iran to start commercial activities on behalf of the association. His stay in Iran lasted only a year, for the death of his father in 1875 forced him return to the Netherlands. When he returned to Iran a year later, Hotz opened two offices of the association in Baṣrah and Iṣfahān, followed by offices in Būshihr, Shīrāz and Ṣ ulṭānābād, the head office being in London. Besides being one of the participants in the Imperial Bank of Persia, he was also active in the carpet trade and tried to develop transport on the Kārūn river, to name but two of his additional operations.[1] In 1895 the entire enterprise came to a standstill again, which brought Hotz into dire financial straits. After a short period of renewed activities, it all ended in 1903.

In 1893 Hotz had married Lucy Helen Woods, the daughter of Henry Woods Pasha, a British marine officer, who had become *aide-de-camp* to the Ottoman Sulṭân Abdülhamid II (r. 1876–1909), in İstanbul. They had three children.[2] Hotz established himself in London, but his aversion to the English atrocities in the Boer war in South Africa (1899–1902) made him decide to move back to Holland in 1902. From 1909 until 1921, with interruptions, he became consul-general of the Netherlands in Beirut. Later he moved to Cologny, Switzerland, where he died in 1930.

[1] For the Hotzes' role in the activities of the bank, see Jones 1986, 61–5. For their involvement in a dispute with an Iranian merchant over some trade bills, see Floor 1983.

During the later years of his life, at least from 1913 onwards, perhaps even earlier, he kept extensive diaries which still have value as a source for our knowledge of day-to-day life of the epoch in Beirut, London, and Switzerland, and for our knowledge of Hotz's personal history. Volumes for 1913, 1915, 1916, 1917, 1919, and 1925 are preserved and kept in the Western Manuscripts Department of the Leiden University Library (Afdeling Westerse Handschriften, Bibliotheek der Rijksuniversiteit Leiden) (inv. no. BPL 2736–41).

Hotz's wide Persian interests became evident from his exhibit in the Colonial Exhibition of Amsterdam (Internationale Koloniale en Uitvoerhandel Tentoonstelling) in 1883. From the catalog which he produced for the exhibit for this widely publicized event (which, for the first time, gave the Dutch public a full taste of the exotic), it becomes clear that he had a great number of Persian products and commodities to offer for export, from animal hides, to minerals, oil samples from Dālakī, all sorts of artifacts, carpets, and brass work, to ibex horns and, of course, opium.[3] As for the latter commodity, Hotz had specific ideas. During this time the Dutch East Indies government had a monopoly on the opium trade in Indonesia, and Hotz, with the idea of expanding his activities, must have had visions of Dutch embassies and consulates in the Far East serving as sale points for his Persian-made opium. But nothing ever came of this. Among Hotz's boxes of documentation there is one labeled "Opium" which contains a number of smaller tracts on the opium question, mainly in the Far East.

Hotz made another *faux pas*. In the early 1890s he drilled for oil at Dālakī in southern Iran, but as results failed to materialize as quickly as he had hoped, he folded this activity. His drilling towers were probably the very first structures of this type that were erected in Iran. Pictures of these, too, are preserved in his collection of photographs.

Nothing, so far, distinguished Hotz from any of his contemporaries, fellow-industrialists, and colleagues of international commerce who undertook any activity that could be made profitable. What did distinguish him, however, was his avid collecting of all sorts of information and documentation about Iran. He did this, no doubt, for the benefit of his firm and his own commercial and industrial activities, but there was more to it. He became an enthusiastic photographer and a passionate book collector. Not only did he leave a substantial collection of photographs that he had taken himself, but he also

[2] Hotz's grandson, Mr. Ch. Haccius, is at the time of publication of this articles living in Dublin.

[3] See [Hotz] 1883.

bought photographs from other, commercial photographers in Iran. Most of these are now in Leiden, and all together the Hotz photograph collection in the Leiden University Library consists of 1159 photographs. One must realize that preserving pictures of a country was at that time only possible by collecting photographs. It is true that long before the invention of photography in 1839, there had been travelogues illustrated with engravings and drawings, but sufficiently realistic information on the geographical, cultural, and ethnological features of any country came within reach of a wide public only with the spread of photography. Many commercial photographers set up businesses to cater to the needs of monarchs, administrators, tourists, and businessmen such as Hotz. Hotz was in many more ways different from the ordinary entrepreneur of his time. Although he had had no formal academic education, he wrote, in the course of the years, a number of memoirs and books on the history of the relations between Iran and the Netherlands. A publication of source materials about the activities of the Dutch East India Company (Nederlandsche Oost-Indische compagnie) was prepared by him. He did not complete it, however, and his friend Hendrik Dunlop published the first volume after Hotz's death.[4]

Hotz's splendid collection of atlases and geographical works is still available in the library of the Royal Geographical Society in London. His private library, consisting of over 10,000 volumes, can be best characterized as an impressive reference tool of a gifted amateur in the geography of the Middle East with an emphasis on Iran. Comprising most of his photographs, some Arabic manuscripts, and a large documentation system, it is now kept in the Leiden University Library.

All of these materials were bestowed on the Leiden University by Hotz's widow in 1935. By 1936 a two-volume catalog of the entire collection was published.[5] The catalog did not, however, contain any description of the photographs and documentation system. The collection of books was incorporated in the Leiden University collections, and the volumes still bear shelf marks with the name of their former owner. They have been integrated in the central library's catalog ever since 1935.

The photographic collection was not entered in the library's catalog, and this omission almost caused it to be forgotten, though not lost. The same is true of the boxes of documentation. For some time they were placed, together with all of the books, in a special Hotz Room in the University Library, but in the early 1960s they were, for reasons of security, placed out of sight in the

[4] See Dunlop 1930–.
[5] See *Bibliotheek A. Hotz* 1935–6.

library's closed stacks. As they never had been given reference numbers, they could not be ordered by the Library's readers. This policy was changed in 1983, when the new University Library of Leiden University was about to be opened, and the old building had to be completely vacated. An unsuitable and incongruous structure, the old building, a converted chapel with countless extensions and additions and full of unexpected corners and attics, had been used as a library for slightly less than four centuries. When a building is emptied, many forgotten things come to light again. That is a story in itself. But, the Hotz photographs and the documentation boxes were among such rediscovered materials, well kept and untouched by readers.

The 1159 photographs are preserved in fifteen albums and five portfolios, consecutively numbered with two digits as albums 1–13, 15–6 and portfolios 14, 17–20. Each photograph has now been given an individual number of three digits, which is used in combination with the album number. Thereby each photograph in the collection has its unique reference. Ten albums (albums 1–10) contain some 657 photographs which Albert Hotz took during his long trip through Iran, from south to north, to the Caucasus and Russia, between 1890 and 1891. Hotz also made photographs of Iranian antiquities in Persepolis and other places. The following short survey of the contents of the collection is derived from the work by Vuurman and Marten.[6]

> *Album 1* contains 71 photographs taken by Hotz during his trip through Iran. They were, like most photographs in the other albums, printed as platinotypes by the firm of J. Thomson in London. The album contains pictures from Bandar ʻAbbās, Būshihr, Khārg Island, Baṣrah, Baghdād, Muḥammarah, Bandar-i Nāṣirī, Ahvāz, Shūshtar, Dālakī, Shīrāz and Kāzirūn. Many duplicates of these are kept in albums 4, 5, 7, 9, and 10.
>
> *Album 2* contains 72 photographs of the middle part of the journey. It contains pictures from Shīrāz, Persepolis, Pāsārgād, Iṣfahān, and Ṣulṭānābād. Doubles of these are kept in a number of other albums. Offices and personnel of Hotz's firm are depicted and identified with captions and legends.
>
> *Album 3* contains 72 photographs from the final part of the journey. It contains pictures of several hotels, guesthouses, offices, etc. from Ṣulṭānābād, Tehran, Tabrīz, Erevan, Tiflis, Rostov, and İstanbul.
>
> *Album 4* contains 67 photographs taken in 1891 which mainly concern "road construction in Persia." The photographs were taken along the middle part of Hotz's journey. Aspects of public transport such as coaches, post offices, post horses, caravansarais, tollhouses, bridges, river boats, and so forth are shown. This album too contains several duplicates.

[6] Vuurman and Marten 1995.

Album 5 contains 23 photographs (21 in platinotype and 2 in albumen prints) of offices and personnel of Messrs. J.C.P. Hotz & Co. and of the Imperial Bank of Persia. Locations in Tehran, Iṣfahān, Shīrāz, Tabrīz, Baghdād, and Baṣrah are shown.

Album 6 contains 66 photographs, all made in platinotype. They are all duplicates which also appear in albums 7–10.

Album 7 contains 22 photographs (platinotype prints) illustrating carpet-weaving. There are photographs from Ṣulṭānābād, Iṣfahān, and "Meshed-i Madar-i Sulayman." Among others, people active in different stages of wool-producing, weaving, and knitting are shown.

Album 8 contains 44 photographs in albumen print, which were already produced in other albums as platinotype prints. On the whole, both the album and the photographs are in a bad state of preservation.

Album 9 is titled "A collection of Photographs taken in Persia, Turkey, and the Caucasus, during a seven months' journey in 1891." Platinotype prints by J. Thomson. (Vol. I). It contains 111 photographs of Strait of Hurmuz (1), Būshihr (13), Khārg Island (5). Baṣrah, Euphrates and Tigris (11), Baghdād (5), Bandar-i Nāṣirī (8), River Kārūn and Ahvāz (4), Shūshtar (10), Dālakī (4), Kāzirūn (8), Shīrāz (27), Persepolis (10), Pāsārgād (3), and Iṣfahān (2).

Album 10 is the sequel to album 9. It too is titled "A collection of Photographs taken in Persia, Turkey, and the Caucasus, during a seven months' journey in 1891." Platinotype prints by J. Thomson. (Vol. II). It contains 110 photographs of Iṣfahān (25), Ṣulṭānābād (9), "Enshidan" (3), Ibrāhīmābād (2), Qum (3), Tehran (5), Tabrīz (2), Erevan (2), Tiflis (11), and İstanbul (9). There are, in addition, 39 photographs taken *en route*. There is some emphasis on the carpet industry and on the Armenians of Julfā near Iṣfahān.

Album 11 contains 72 collodium prints of photographs taken by Ernst Hoeltzer (1835–1911), dating from the 1890s with pictures mainly from Iṣfahān, Julfā, Kāshān, Qum, and Tehran. It contains town views, notables, artisans, and craftsmen. Hotz apparently purchased these from Hoeltzer, who lived for a long time in Iṣfahān, where he had married an Armenian woman.

Album 12 contains 69 collodium prints of photographs by Hoeltzer, and 6 others which cannot be identified. The Hoeltzer photographs mainly concern Iṣfahān (25). There are also pictures of Farīdan (9), Julfā (8), "Rhorood" (5), and Kāshān. Quite a number of the Hoelzer photographs have been identified and described by Iraj Afshar in his *Ganjīnah-'i 'aks'hā-yi Īrān*.[7] Album 13 contains 72 photographs (albumen prints) made around 1890 by the French photographer Antoine Sevruguin, who was active as a commercial photographer in Tehran from about 1880 onward. They were apparently purchased by Hotz. The prints contain the usual Sevruguin negative registration numbers. The album contains views

[7] See Afshar 1992, 77–8, 86.

of Kāzirūn, Shīrāz, Baghdād, Takht-i Rustam, Būshihr, Iṣfahān, Baṣrah, Kirmān, 'Alī'ābād, and Rasht.

Portfolio 14 contains 41 loose photographs, pasted on cardboard. There are 19 photographs, both platinotype and albumen prints, from Iran. Their technical quality and state of preservation are bad. The remaining 22 photographs were taken in Europe.

Album 15 contains 74 photographs by Antoine Sevruguin. Many show scenes of daily life, women in traditional attire, scenes from Kurdistān, dancers, music ensembles, weaving, families, people on horseback, street vendors, and a dentist.

Album 16 is the sequel to album 15, and its 28 photographs by Sevruguin are numbered consecutively 75–102. They were mostly taken in Iṣfahān, Tehran, and Baghdād.

Portfolio 17 contains 26 photographs in different formats, pasted on cardboard. They are both platinotype and albumen prints from negatives of several photographs in Europe, Russia, and Iran. Some can be identified as works of Hotz, Hoeltzer, Jules Lind, and Sevruguin, while there are some from a Russian photographer.

Portfolio 18 contains 18 photographs of groups of pupils and teachers of the Osmaniye Mohamedan College and the Syrian Protestant College, both in Beirut. Some photographers are identified as works of Sarrafian and Guiragossian.

Portfolio 19 contains 46 photographs of a great variety of subjects: 6 show Hotz's stand and Ziegler's stand at the Amsterdam exhibition of 1883, 12 are from the Dutch East-Indies, 10 are from Russia, and 12 are from Egypt. Some photographers are identified as works of Joseph Fietta, A. Scavo Fils, Pascal Sébah.

Portfolio 20 contains 57 photographs of as great a variety as portfolio 19: École de droit in Beirut, Odessa, Shaṭṭ al-'Arab, Moscow, Beirut, Smyrna, Damascus. Some photographers are identified as works of A. Scavo Fils of Beirut, S. Antonopulo of Odessa, David Gazala of Baghdād, Joseph Fietta of Saint Petersburg, Bonfils.

There are more photographs in the Hotz collection. These were found in the boxes with the documentation materials, and have not yet been identified or described. As they may be relevant to the documentation, they have been left where they were found, for the time being.

Some of the Hotz materials have gone to institutions other than Leiden University Library, but the Leiden collection is by far the largest. Main repositories of Hotz photographs outside the Leiden library must be mentioned:

Amsterdam, Royal Institute of the Tropics (Koninklijk Instituut voor de Tropen). Collection of 230 platinotype prints of Hotz's photographs (1213/1–238). These can be identified with numerous Hotz photographs in the Leiden albums, notably albums 9 and 10.

Edinburgh University Library. Collection of 35 photographs by Hotz from Iran (Phot. I 11.57).

Leiden, Department of Art History and Cabinet of Prints (Prentenkabinet der Rijksuniversiteit Leiden). Collection of 37 platinotype prints from Hotz's travels in 1891. These are duplicates of several of the Leiden albums, notably in albums 9 and 10.

Leiden, Museum of Ethnography (Rijksmuseum voor Volkenkunde). Collection of 199 albumen prints (1959–2160), and an album of 22 platinotype prints on carpet-making, of 1891. Similar to the Leiden album 7.

London, Royal Geographical Society. An unknown number of Hotz's own photographs of his travel through Iran, Turkey, and the Caucasus in 1890 and 1891. Probably similar to the ones in the Leiden albums, notably albums 9 and 10.

Rotterdam, Museum of Ethnography (Museum voor Volkenkunde Rotterdam). Collection of 67 albumen prints (F4021–96/98) and two albums (FA0049/1–2) with contents similar to Leiden albums 9 and 10.

Only recently has the photograph collection been cataloged. A catalog database was created using the SquareNote program, which is written by Lucy Linch and David Cook. It functions mainly by the catchwords which one attaches to the objects described. The captions which Hotz wrote on the leaves on which the photographs are pasted served, in the English translation, as a starting point for the descriptions. Very general categories, such as persons, buildings, crafts, Islamic punishments and so on were added to the items in the database. As complete as possible an index of geographical names was entered as well. All photographs have been given individual numbers. This is only the first step towards the study of the photographic collection; the database allows for all sorts of future extensions and expansions.[8] But much more needs to be done, including the enhancement of the descriptions of the pictures. A selection of the photographs has already been published by Vuurman and Martens.[9]

In addition, it is important to try to establish a firm link between the photographic collection and the other documentation materials collected by Hotz. Only this makes the integrated research of documentation, the personal history of the collector, and the photographic collection possible. It is fortunate that the different materials have always been kept together. In time the results will be evident.

[8] Two assistant students from the Utrecht University, Ms. Dorothée Tutuarima and Mr. Guido van Dongen, have performed the task of cataloging the photographs.

[9] See Vuurman and Martens 1995.

Hotz's documentation system deserves some attention here. It consists of about eighty boxes in which a great number of smaller publications are contained. These are arranged according to subject, as is clear from the labels on the back. Hotz must have been a compulsive collector of all sorts of ephemeral materials, both concerning Iran and concerning other issues which interested him. It is this sort of material which usually does not survive, since libraries and archives often do not collect them in an organized way. And even if they do, such materials are often very difficult to find in formalized library catalogs. The Hotz documentation collection contains all sorts of smaller publications and pamphlets. These are preserved according to a roughly designed subject division in some eighty boxes and portfolios. A selection of the subject headings, with indication of the number of boxes or portfolios, is as follows:

> Other than Iran
> Educational institutions in Beirut (1), International Geographical Congress, London 1895 (1), International Orientalist Congresses (1), Islam (1), Jordan (1), Marine (1), Opium (1), Palestine (2), Shipping (1), Syria (2), Turkey (1).
>
> Concerning Iran
> Ancient history (1), Antiquities (2), Arts and craftsmanship (1), Avesta (2), Bibliography (1), Chronology (1), Consular reports: Iṣfahān, Shīrāz, Kirmān, Sīstān; Baṣrah, Baghdād, İstanbul; Rasht, Mashhad, Kirmanshah; Miscellaneous (4), Description of the country (3), General subjects (1), Geography (medieval and Arabic geographers) (1), Geology, botany, and zoology (1), History (5), Pre-Islamic history (4), Pre-Islamic language (3), Language and script (1), Literature (2), Islamic manners and customs (1), Maps of Turkey and Iran (1), Newspapers in European languages (1), Roads (2), Tapestry (1) Trade (2), Travels (5).

The contents of these boxes has yet to be fully analyzed. Simple browsing gives the impression that the boxes contain materials that shed more light on the subject matter of the photographs. A reverse effect can also be seen. Several smaller publications reflecting the history of photography in Iran and the Middle East can be found in the boxes. One notable example of this is the discovery of a copy of Bonfils's list of photographs available for sale. Few people have preserved such precious documents, but Hotz did. As already said, it is only by an integrated research of the Hotz photographs, the documentation materials which he collected, and biographical and autobiographical materials, that quality results can be achieved. In Hotz' case, it is only by a fortunate coincidence that this is possible at all.

Fig. 1. The Persian Section of the Colonial Exhibition of Amsterdam, 1883. Bibliotheek der Rijksuniversiteit Leiden

Fig. 2. An oil-drill rig at Dālakī, southern Iran. Bibliotheek der Rijksuniversiteit Leiden

Fig. 3. Albert Hotz and his wife Lucy Helen Woods. Bibliotheek der Rijksuniversiteit Leiden

BIBLIOGRAPHY

AFSHAR, IRAJ. 1992. *Ganjīnah-'i 'aks'hā-yi Īrān, hamrāh-i tārīkhchah-'i vurūd-i 'akkāsī bih Īrān*. Tehran : Nashr-i Farhang-i Īrān.

Bibliotheek A. Hotz : uitheemsche landen, in het bijzonder Perzië en het oosten, aardrijkskunde - geschiedenis - literature - art. 1935–6. 2 vols. Leiden : Universiteits-bibliotheek.

DUNLOP, HENDRIK, ed. 1930–. *Bronnen tot de geschiedenis der Oostindische Compagnie in Perzië*. 1 volume published only. The Hague : Martinus Nijhoff.

ENGELBERTS, THERESIA H. E. 1995. *Een Pers uit een vreemd land : levensschets van Albertus Paulus Hermanus Hotz*. [The Hague] : n.p. (Privately published).

FLOOR, WILLEM. 1983. Hotz versus Muḥammad Shafī' : a case study in commercial litigation in Qājār Iran, 1888–1894. *International journal of Middle East studies* 15, no. 2 (May): 185–209.

[HOTZ, ALBERT]. 1883. *Description des Articles exposés à l'Exposition Internationale, Coloniale et d'Exportation Générale d'Amsterdam 1883*. [The Hague] : n.p.

JONES, GEOFFREY. 1986. *Banking and empire in Iran : The history of the British Bank of the Middle East*. Vol. 1. Research by Frances Bostock, Grigori Gerenstein, Judith Nichol. Cambridge [Cambridgeshire] : Cambridge University Press.

VUURMAN, CORIEN and MARTEN, THEO. 1995. *Perzië en Hotz : Beelden uit de fotocollectie-Hotz in de Leidse Universiteitsbibliotheek : Catalogus bij een tentoonstelling in de Leidse Universiteitsbibliotheek van 30 januari tot 4 maart 1995 (Ramadan tentoonstelling 1415)*. Leiden : Legatum Warnerianum, Bibliotheek der Rijksuniversiteit.

A Sketch of Translation and the Formation of New Persian Literature

Jerome W. Clinton

INTRODUCTION *

THE QUESTION I BEGIN WITH IS THAT OF HOW ISLAMIC literature evolved from a system in which Arabic was the sole medium to one in which the number of languages roughly equals the number of communities that profess Islam, and which embraces languages as diverse as French and Indonesian. The facts of this historical evolution are reasonably well known, but rarely explored as part of a united, coherent history. That is, the ways in which other languages and literatures—most notably Greek, Syriac, and Middle Persian—contributed to the growth and development of Arabic in the early Islamic period is increasingly well mapped.[1] But sequel to that process—the propagation of new literatures in Persian, Turkish, and other languages through the interaction of Arabic with the indigenous literary traditions of Asia and Africa—has not, although one specific case, the emergence of New Persian, has been the subject of a number of studies.[2] In particular, the role of translation in this process has been little studied despite its obvious centrality. While literary historians of the new traditions assert the importance of the influence of the languages that preceded it—Arabic, Persian, Turkish—they rarely pause either to examine that influence in detail or to discuss what was transmitted and how. In several studies, Gilbert Lazard has greatly advanced our understanding of the formation of the New Persian language and of the character of the earliest poetry, but the question of what specific debts the earliest poets

---

* An earlier draft of this paper was prepared for a meeting of the Middle East Literary Seminar held at Princeton in the spring of 1991, and was one half of a joint presentation with Walter Andrews of the University of Washington under the rubric *Translation and the invention of new literatures : Persian and Ottoman.* I should like to thank Professor Andrews for helping me to clarify my thoughts on this topic.

[1] Martin Sprengling addresses the larger question of foreign contributions to Arabic in an article entitled *Persian into Arabic*, see Sprengling 1939–40. There are brief but informative chapters on the contributions of Greek, Persian and Syriac to Arabic generally, but with some attention to literature more narrowly conceived, by L. E. Goodman, C. E. Bosworth, and R. Y. Ebied respectively, in the book *Arabic literature to the end of the Umayyad period*, see Beeston, et al. 1983, 460–82, 483–96, 497–501.

[2] See, for example, Lazard 1964, 1975, and 1993.

owed to their predecessors still remains open. There are several reasons this may be so. The most important is surely that the relative paucity of texts from both sides of the divide make such studies problematic.[3] It is tempting to settle for such generalities as the new literature "growing up" in a milieu dominated by Arabic learning and literature. Beyond that, since literary history, particularly in its initial phase, is the offspring of modern nationalism, it does not lend itself to the careful chronicling of a nation's cultural debts.[4] Furthermore, few poetic texts survive either from the Middle Persian period, or from the early Islamic period roughly the early 3rd/9th through 5th/early 10th centuries, when the Samanids and Ghaznavids ruled in Khurāsān and Central Asia. However, while the scantiness of our sources precludes the kind of detailed and nuanced account I would like to give, and which may be possible for subsequent literatures, enough survives to suggest the general outlines of the process.

In what follows, I wish to do several things: first, to sketch briefly the general features of the growth of Persian, or New Persian, literature, giving particular attention to the role that translation played in its development; second, to examine what contemporary attitudes were toward translation; and, finally, to suggest how the particular dynamics of the growth of New Persian anticipate the growth of subsequent new literatures. Since Persian was the first language to challenge the literary hegemony of Arabic, and also contributed directly to the development of subsequent Islamic literary languages, such a study may provide insights into the role of translation in Islamic literary history generally. First, however, I should like to clarify some of the assumptions underlying this study.

By translation here I mean the transfer both of literary technique and of content from one language to another. That is, this transfer may either be of such formal features as genre, prosody, rhetorical figures and terminology, or of such specific content as themes, *topoi*, myths, and narratives, or, of course, of both. At one pole of this universe is the rendering from one language into another of a specific text by a specific poet as a conscious act of literary fealty. At the other is the anonymous and unmarked appropriation of another poet's work. In the passage from Arabic into Persian, we encounter few examples of translation that belong to either of these poles, and many that fall into the

[3] Ehsan Yarshater has studied the situation for Middle Persian in his article *The development of Iranian literatures*, see Yarshater 1988. For the early Islamic period, see Lazard 1964.

[4] I have discussed the way in which the author of the premier literary history of Persian, Ẕabīḥ Allāh Ṣafā, deals with this question in *Nuktah'ī chand dar bārah-'i vaẓ'-i kunūnī-i tārīkh-i adabī dar Īrān*, see Clinton 1994.

middle ground where translation is partial and acknowledgment of the original tacit and indirect. In any case, translation invariably includes a measure of adaptation of the linguistic and cultural content of one language to another not the total replacement of one tradition by another, but a synthesis of two, or more.[5]

We tend to think of translation as principally a matter of thematic content, but often what is most influential in shaping a new tradition, or reshaping an old one, is the importation of new forms. When successful, translated forms quickly gain acceptance as indigenous creations. The *ghazal* in the Islamic world and the sonnet in the Christian are parallel examples of such successful inventions from the pre-modern period. They originated in Persian and Italian respectively, but traveled by translation to all the languages of their respective traditions. The short story, novel and free verse are European forms that now virtually define modernity in world literature. Thematic content can travel independent of form, or bring its form with it, and so the Arabic love poems of Majnūn for his beloved Laylī become Niẓāmī's great Persian romantic narrative of *Laylī u Majnūn,* which, begets new *Laylī u Majnūn*s in Turkish, Urdu and other languages.

To complete this gloss, we need to include mention of translation, into a new language, of works from the native tradition that were written either in another language or dialect of that tradition that has ceased to be widely understood. Here the translation of the national epic material of Iran from Middle Persian into New Persian, first into prose and then into poetry, is an obvious illustration of how crucial this can be. Nor is it a routine event. There are many examples of breaks within a tradition brought about by its absence. Anglo-Saxon literature was virtually unknown to the poets and writers of the English Renaissance, and, looking closer to home, Ottoman Turkish literature is still largely a closed book to modern Turks. New Persian literature would have taken on a very different character had works like the *Shāhnāmah* and *Vīs u Rāmīn* suffered a similar fate, and, again, translation was the agency by which this lacunae was prevented.

To return to my original assertion that translation must logically have been the central agency in the propagation of new Islamic literatures, I ground it in my observation that the first generation of poets and writers in any new tradition or radical redirection in an established tradition are bilingual, and

[5] Dick Davis has referred to this synthesis by the agency of translation as "literary syncretism" in an unpublished paper of the same name read for the first time to the departmental seminar of the Department of Judaic and Near Eastern Studies, Ohio State University, in October 1991. I am grateful for his generous permission to cite his work here.

that an essential element of their role as founders of the new tradition is translation from an adjacent literary tradition, whether richer, better established or more powerful politically. This is obviously true for the modern period when each of the world's languages in turn has "modernized" itself by appropriating and adapting the forms and substance of European literature. I believe it holds true for earlier historical periods as well.[6]

Certainly, the relevance of translation for understanding Islamic literary history is easily demonstrated. The example of Ibn al-Muqaffa' provides a clear and many layered illustration of this. His most famous work, *Kalīlah wa-Dimnah,* is an Arabic translation of a Middle Persian translation of the Sanskrit *Pancha Tantra,* a treatise on ethics and government cast in the form of beast fables. Its popularity in the Sasanian court made it an obvious candidate for rendering into Arabic at a time when the caliphate court was absorbed in learning the skills of empire from its Iranian predecessors. Ibn al-Muqaffa's Arabic version quickly became an exemplary text of classical Arabic prose, a position it still holds. Its status within the Arabic tradition, in turn, is surely one reason Rūdakī chose to translate, or retranslate, *Kalīlah wa-Dimnah* into New Persian a century and a half later at the beginning of the Persian renaissance, although the desire to recover a part of the Middle Persian tradition may have been another.[7]

TRANSLATION AND THE FORMATION OF NEW PERSIAN LITERATURE

Although little of it has survived, we know from indirect sources that Sasanian culture was a rich, varied and cosmopolitan literary culture. Its principal vehicles were literary dialects of Middle Persian. In the first two centuries after the Islamic invasions of the mid-17th century, the colloquial form of Middle Persian, Dari, which had long been the *lingua franca* of western Iran, gained prominence in central Asia as well, and even displaced another Middle Persian language, Soghdian, as the principal spoken language of the area. From at least the second century on, there were attempts to write Dari in Arabic characters, and to translate or write Pahlavi lyrics and stories in it, to make of

[6] I have at times been contradicted when I made this observation, since, as I have already suggested, there seems to be an innate resistance to acknowledging outside influences on one's national literature. But while I make no claim to familiarity with all traditions in all periods, no one has yet offered me a counter example that withstands careful scrutiny.

[7] Brockelman 1978.

Dari, in short, a new literary language.[8] Initially, the differences between Dari and Pahlavi were slight. Lazard described them as essentially those of different levels of usage. However, with the passage of time, changes in grammar, pronunciation and vocabulary made Dari a separate dialect from Pahlavi. Literary Dari came to be known as Persian (Fārsī/Pārsī), or, in modern scholarly parlance, New Persian.[9]

The fortunes of New Persian followed the political fortunes of the Iranian aristocracy. The famous story recorded in the *Tārīkh-i Sīstān* of how Ya'qūb Lays̱ coerced the performance of eulogy in Persian, provides a vivid illustration of how the fortunes of a language and politics are linked.[10] A less coercive but equally significant illustration is the policy of the Tahirids and Samanids of supporting indigenous Iranian literary culture as a means of securing the acceptance of their rule over Khurāsān and Central Asia. Their immediate predecessors had made themselves unpopular by their exclusive sponsorship of Arab letters. As local Iranian dynasties came to govern in Eastern Iran and Central Asia in the second and third centuries of Islam, Persian came into increasing usage as a literary language.[11]

[8] Lazard 1975. The fourth volume of *The Cambridge History of Iran*, in which Lazard's article appeared, contains a bibliography of the most important studies of this period, except those by L. Richter-Bernburg (1974) and L. P. Elwell-Sutton (1975 and 1976), which became available after its appearance.

[9] Lazard (1993) clarifies the use, in the 10th–11th centuries, of the terms *Darī* or *Pārsī-i Darī* for New Persian.

[10] The anecdote is worth citing at length. The History of Sīstān (*Tārīkh-i Sīstān)* is an anonymous Persian chronicle whose inital portion dates from the 5th/11th century. It records a moment when the Saffarid ruler Ya'qūb Lays̱ defeated his enemy, the Kharijite 'Ammār, in 251/865, a victory of major importance about which poets recited victory odes in Arabic. After one of these recitations Ya'qub lost patience. "When this poem was recited, he was not educated (*'ālim*) and did not understand. Muḥammad ibn Vaṣīf was present. He was the clerk of the chancery and knew *adab* well, but at that time there was no written literature in *Pārsī*. So Ya'qub said "Why should they recite what I cannot understand?" Muḥammad Vaṣīf then began to compose poetry in Persian. He recited/composed the first Persian poetry in *'Ajam* [i.e., eastern Iran], and before him no one had composed poetry since while the Persians were there literature (*sukhan*) was recited or sung to the *rūd* like a *khosravānī* (a sung lyric in Dari). And when they were driven out of *'Ajam*, and the Arabs came, their poetry was in Arabic and for everyone learning and poetry was in Arabic. In *'Ajam*, there was no one before Ya'qub who was great enough that poems would be recited for him, except for Ḥamzah ibn 'Abd Allāh al-Shārī, but he was educated and knew Arabic, and poets recited to him in Arabic...Muḥammad ibn Vaṣīf recited this poem:

O, *Amīr* for whom the *amīrs* of the world, both great and small • Are slaves and servants and clients and dog handlers and pages / The Eternal Script conferred a tablet of sovereignty on • The generous Prince Abū Yūsuf Ya'qūb ibn Lays̱." (*Tārīkh-i Sīstān* [1935] 1987, 209–10).

[11] Clinton 1988; Bosworth 1983, 494–6.

At the beginning of its development, the budding New Persian literary language had essentially two linguistic sources to draw on directly, Arabic and Middle Persian. Arabic contained not only the literary material of Arabic—pre-Islamic, Umayyad and early Abbasid poetry—but also a large body of translations from Middle Persian, including texts like *Kalīlah wa-Dimnah,* that had their ultimate origins in Sanskrit or other, non-Iranian languages. One of the principal contributions of Iranian Muslim poets and writers was to translate the bulk of Middle Persian literature into Arabic.[12] This Arabic material was available principally in manuscripts and codices, although poetic texts, at least, must often have been transmitted orally as well as in writing. The Middle Persian material, both poetry and prose, was available both in written and oral form, although, again, the division between written and oral transmission was probably not always that sharply drawn, and the rapid disappearance of Middle Persian manuscripts and codices in the centuries after the establishment of New Persian as a viable literary medium make it difficult to know just what materials were available to Iranian poets and writers at this time.[13]

As a result of the different roles assigned to them as vehicles for Islamic culture, prose and poetry followed different paths in the development of New Persian literature. Prose, as a vehicle for the transmission of learning, met serious opposition from those who felt that the world of Islamic learning should not be divided.[14] There seems to have been no objection to the production of poetic works in New Persian. Poetry, as a form of discourse that had the distortion or misrepresentation of truth as its essence, was not considered a vehicle for the recording or transmission of learning.[15] This privileging of prose over poetry as a vehicle for the transmission of religious culture in the Islamic period reflects both Koranic attitudes toward poets and poetry, and the biases of pre-Islamic, that is, Sasanian, scribes.[16] Since the fortunes of prose have been described by L. Richter-Bernburg in the work cited above, I will concern myself with poetry here.

[12] Lazard remarks upon the importance of Arabic translations of Middle Persian literary texts as a source for the regeneration of Persian literature in the Islamic period, see Lazard 1975. For an earlier and broader account, see Sprengling 1939–40.

[13] Before the invention of cheap paper made from wood chips in the 19th century, writing was principally a means of recording compositions, not an aid to the compositional process itself.

[14] Richter-Bernburg 1974 and Boyce 1957.

[15] The belief that poetry was an essentially untruthful medium was deeply grounded in Arabic-Islamic learned literature, cf. Ajami 1988.

[16] On the functions of scribes (*dabīrs*) in the pre-Islamic period, see Tafażżoli 1993 and Muḥammadī 1995, 99–125; on the contempt of the literate *dabīr* for the illiterate poet, see Boyce 1957.

In the rapid and remarkable evolution of Persian poetry during the Samanid and Ghaznavid periods, the contributions of Arabic and Middle Persian materials rarely overlapped. Briefly stated, Arabic provided the principal lyric genre, the *qaṣīdah*, the poetic register, and both the nomenclature and some essential features of metrics and rhyme. Middle Persian served as a repository for the stories and themes of narrative poetry. Middle Persian poetry may also have been the source of courtly *topoi* as well as the short lyric forms, the quatrain and *ghazal* that gained enormous popularity in Persian after the 11th century.[17]

While Arabic poetry itself found its way into New Persian, Arabic poems did not. The agency of transmission was almost exclusively the translation of individual lines, metaphors and images, not of poems or of larger conceits.[18] The poetry of Manūchihrī Dāmghānī (d. ca. 432/1040) provides a striking illustration of the internal dynamic by which New Persian shaped and limited the Arabic elements it incorporated. Manūchihrī was a consummate master of the Persianate *qaṣīdah* and the inventor of the first major prosodic departure from the *qaṣīdah* form, the *musammaṭ*, or strophe poem.[19] He was, in short, a poet of exceptional originality as well as great technical skill. One of the ways he showed this was by making his familiarity with and mastery of Arabic poetry a defining feature of his work. In this, he was unique among his fellows. However, it was a stylistic innovation that, unlike his invention of the *musammaṭ,* no one imitated.[20] Manūchihrī's attempts to find a home for the Arabic *qaṣīdah* in Persian were a failure. Moreover, among all his imitations of Arabic, there is no poem that we can comfortably call a translation of a specific poem by a specific poet.

[17] For the role of indigenous Persian prosody in New Persian see Elwell-Sutton 1976, and, more recently, Vaḥīdiyān Kāmyār 1991, 1991b, and 1988; see also Reinert 1973, where some of the formal and thematic transformations of Persianate poetics is discussed.

[18] Shafī'ī Kadkanī's *Ṣuvar-i khiyāl dar shi'r-i Fārsī* contains a lengthy appendix that gives examples of such borrowings, see Shafī'ī Kadkanī 1987, 659–75.

[19] See Clinton 1972.

[20] I have found no early criticism of Manuchihrī for his "Arabism." Shams-i Qays (1956, 437) singles out a *qaṣīdah* of his as an example of a poem in which the poet has marred his work by using Arabic words not in common use among Iranians, but does not offer this a a general criticism of his poetry. It is worth noting that in the same passage, Shams-i Qays objects equally to the use of uncommon Middle Persian (*Pahlavī*) words without, however, providing an example.

CONTEMPORARY ATTITUDES TOWARD TRANSLATION

Despite the vigorous translation activity throughout this early period, there are no extended discussions of the technique or esthetics of translation either in works of prosody or elsewhere. There are, however, a number of brief but suggestive comments by both prosodists and poets.[21] For reasons that will emerge shortly, I would like to begin with the former. Three Persian works of prosody survive from the 5th–6th/11th–early 13th centuries, and all three have something to say about our subject. The earliest of these, from the late 5th/11th century, is Muḥammad ibn ʻUmar al-Rādūyānī's *Tarjumān al-balāghah* in which sections 64 and 65 concern "Translation" and "Translation of the Sayings and Proverbs [particularly those of the Prophet Muhammad]."[22] Rādūyānī considers translation a form of eloquence, and the best translations are, he says, "those which convey the whole subject (*ma'nī*), and in words (*lafẓ*) that are eloquent and concise."[23] He illustrates this point with examples of translations in which he identifies some of the authors of the originals, but none of the translators, indicating, I believe, that the translations are his own. It was indeed commonplace among the poets and *litterateurs* of that time and region to translate between the two languages.

The second author, Rashīd al-Dīn Muḥammad Vaṭvāṭ (d. 573/1177–8), was himself a poet of some distinction, and he tells in his introduction that he undertook his work on prosody, the *Ḥadā'iq al-siḥr fī daqa'iq al-shi'r*, because he found Rādūyānī's work inadequate, and his examples poorly chosen. He includes one brief section on translation, of which he says only that in it the poet turns Arabic poetry into Persian and Persian into Arabic, and provides an illustration of each, and states that the translations are his own.[24] While Rashīd al-Dīn's explicit statement offers no increment to Rādūyānī's observations on translation, the implications of the justification he gives for

[21] For the names of those whose titles alone we know, see Elwell-Sutton 1975. The Arab prosodic tradition was far more developed than Persian, but Arabic writing prosodists did not concern themselves with translation either from or into other languages. It is worth noting that Kaykāvūs ibn Iskandar does not include skill at translation among the accomplishments that an aspiring poet should acquire in his chapter on poets in the *Qābūsnāmah*, although he does seem to assume some knowledge of Arabic, see Kaykāvūs ibn Iskandar 1992, 189–92 and 1951, 182–5. In the second discourse "On poets and poetry" in his *Chahār maqālah*, Niẓāmī ʻArūẓī mentions a mastery of *saraqāt* (literary theft) and *tarājim* (translation/interpretation, or, biographies) in the catalog of skills that a good poet must possess, but does not elaborate, see Niẓāmī ʻArūẓī 1969, 48. For the use of *tarājim (=tarjuman)* in this meaning, see Smyth 1994, 291–302, esp. 296.

[22] Rādūyānī 1949, 115–21.

[23] Ibid., 115.

[24] Vaṭvāṭ [1930] 1984, 69.

recasting the work of his predecessor suggest a high level of concern that he not be accused of plagiary. We shall see that implication made explicit in the last and most influential of these works of prosody, the *al-Mu'jam fī ma'ā'īr ash'ār al-'Ajam,* of Shams-i Qays written in 614/1217–8.[25]

The *Mu'jam* is principally a practical guide to Persian metrics, but in its conclusion (*khātimah*) Shams-i Qays turns to the varieties of rhetorical figure, metaphor, simile and allusion. He does not have a separate section on translation here but includes it in his chapter on the many categories of literary theft. The general term he uses is *intiḥāl*, which he defines as outright theft of another's poetry "without change or alteration in the words or themes."[26] But Shams-i Qays includes, and illustrates with examples, several other, subtler categories of plagiarism involving the appropriation of a conceit or image or turn of phrase. The author's attitude toward outright plagiarism is essentially our own, and, for the most part, he takes questions of primacy in matters of verbal invention very seriously indeed. However, at the end of this section, Shams-i Qays states that the masters of prosody have said "that if a poet hits upon a theme (*ma'nī*) and dresses it in disagreeable words and expresses it in unpleasant language, and then another [poet] takes that very theme and displays it in pleasing language and acceptable words (*lafẓ*), he takes priority, and that theme becomes his property."[27] In such a case, that is, the inventor can claim precedence, but he can no longer claim sole ownership.

Let me pause to emphasize the two elements necessary to license what would otherwise be condemned as theft: (1) the thematic content of the original is sound but it is badly expressed; (2) the translator has improved on the original's verbal texture. This argument in exactly this form has become in Shams-i Qays' time the conventional justification for any work that might be seen as derived from the work of another, including, specifically translation. Finally, Shams-i Qays does not mark translation as in any fundamental sense different from other kinds of plagiarism even though the theft is between languages not within a single one. Since all three prosodists only cite single *bayt*s as illustrations, they leave open the question of whether the convention articulated by Shams-i Qays applies to whole lyrics (*qaṣīdah*) and narratives as well.

[25] In 1973, in a short notice in *Rāhnamā-yi kitāb* (13:513–4), Iraj Afshar announced the recent acquisition of what turned out to be the oldest known copy of *al-Mu'jam* by the then Kitābkhānah-i Majlis-i Sinā. The manuscript, dated Jumādá I 739/November 1338, was later used by Sīrūs Shamīsā for a two-volume critical edition of the text, the first one of which was published in 1373 Sh./1994, see Shams-i Qays 1994–.

[26] Shams-i Qays 1994–, 1:397.

[27] Ibid., 1:403; for an English translation of the "Conclusion" section of *al-Mu'jam*, see Clinton 1989, 103–26.

Since translations of specific poems seem never to have been attempted, the question does not bear on them. Narratives were translated, however, and at least three narrative poets—Abū al-Qāsim Firdawsī (d. 411/1019–20), Fakhr al-Dīn Gurgānī (d. ca. 466/1073) and Niẓāmī Ganjavī (d. ca. 606/1209)—include their observations on the nature and degree of their indebtedness to earlier poets and writers in their works. And in so doing, they make clear that in his formulation Shams-i Qays is articulating a conventional understanding of the constraints on borrowing, whether through translation or re-translation, that antedates *al-Mu'jam* by at least two centuries. And, as we shall see, for poets the question of indebtedness overshadow that of whether his indebtedness is to a work in another language or to one in an earlier version of his own language.

The earliest comment on translation is to be found in Firdawsī's poetic recension of the *Shāhnāmah*. The actual nature and number of Firdawsī's sources is presently the subject of debate, with some arguing that they are more numerous and varied than the description provided by the poet himself.[28] However, for our purposes, his description is what is relevant; and, as he describes his task within the text itself, he essentially versified a prose recension of the text in New Persian that had been prepared some years earlier. Along the way, he includes a passage of roughly a thousand couplets that had been completed by another poet, Daqīqī (d. ca. 367/977) who was murdered by a slave before he could carry the task any further. Firdawsī deals with his relations to the prose text at several points, and to both that text and Daqīqī's verses in a famous passage that occurs roughly two thirds of the way through the whole work. The prose recension he describes as containing stories that were very ancient and precious, like a goblet of pearls, but in prose—that is, precious but poorly presented. No one was able to put these stories into verse, presumably because it was in Pahlavi, and this disturbed him. Then a poet—unspecified here but clearly Daqīqī—undertook the task. However, he died before he had completed more than a thousand verses. Firdawsī pays his predecessor due honor for opening the way, but this seems no more than conventional politeness since he has just said that he found his verses weak and deficient. Indeed, he recited them to the ruler as an example of how not to do the job.

[28] The arguments for Firdawsī's having employed oral as well as written sources have been marshaled most recently and persuasively by Davidson 1994. For a contrary view, see the review of her book by M. Umīdsālār 1995.

Nigah kardam īn naẓm-i sust āmadam
Basī bayt-i nātandurust āmadam
Man īn zān bi-guftam kih tā Shariyār
Bi-dānad sukhan guftan-i nā-bikār

Translation

When I looked at these verses they seemed feeble to me.
I found many *bayt*s that were unsound.
I recited them to the *shahryār*
so that he might recognize bad poetry.[29]

Roughly forty years later, Fakhr al-Dīn Gurgānī completed his translation of the Parthian romance, *Vīs u Rāmīn* at the court of the Seljuq governor of Iṣfahān. In the introductory portion of the poem, and in accordance with a convention already well established for narrative poems, the poet describes how and why he composed the poem in terms that echo Firdawsī.[30] He was first asked by his patron what he knew of the story of *Vīs u Rāmīn*, he says, and then requested to versify it in Persian. He responds to the initial question by saying that it is a famous and delightful story, but in Pahlavi, which few read now, and in prose, and very badly told. Gurgānī is at pains to emphasize both how attractive the original story is and how flat and unpoetic the Pahlavi rendering of it is. He then expatiates on how he will beautify it, adding rhyme, meter, and embedding fine sentiments and choice expressions in it, until it becomes, "as pretty as a treasure full of gems" (*zībā chū pur gūhar yakī ganj*).[31]

The texts from which Firdawsī and Gurgānī worked have been lost, and so we have no clear standpoint from which to evaluate their literary quality. However, in both cases, they were either in prose or perceived as being in prose. Pahlavi verse was written without line breaks and was, moreover, based on a system of accents and syllable-counting that would have appeared to be prose to anyone, like Gurgānī, who was trained in Perso-Islamic prosody. In both cases, to translate them into New Persian poetry was to make them more beautiful.[32] That is, by their translations, both poets fulfilled the two conditions necessary to give them legitimate claim to the work they had appropriated.

[29] Firdawsī 1994, 6:136. My translation.

[30] Fakhr al-Dīn Gurgānī 1970, 26–30 and 1972, 16–9.

[31] Idem 1970, 29 and 1972, 18.

[32] Shaul Shaked has reviewed the history of the "decipherment" of Middle Persian verse in his article *Specimens of Middle Persian verse*, see Shaked 1970.

The force of this convention for describing a poet's relation to his source was generalized beyond this specific context some years later by the third poet, Niẓāmī Ganjavī. In 593/1197, Niẓāmī completed a long narrative poem, *Haft paykar* (Seven beauties), whose protagonist is the half legendary Sasanian royal figure Bahrām Gūr. Firdawsī included an account of Bahrām's adventures in his work, albeit a very different one from that which Niẓāmī is about to tell. His particular dilemma is that he wishes to retell a story that is neither in an unfamiliar language, nor in prose, but in Persian verse by a highly esteemed poet. He does this in two separate passages, using different strategies in each. In the first, which comes in the introductory matter of the poem, he says, in essence, that he is simply presenting parts of the story that Firdawsī has not told.

Ānch azū nīm guftah bud guftam
Gawhar-i nīm suftah rā suftam
Va ānch dīdam kih rāst būd va durust
māndamash ham bar ān qarār-i nukhust [33]

Translation

That which was left by him half-said
I say; the half-pierced pearl *I* thread.
While that which I found right and true,
Just as before I've left to view.[34]

He goes on to say here that he has also ransacked other sources to find new material to include in his own poem.

This would seem to have been adequate justification since, indeed, he tells a very different story than Firdawsī. However, in a second, later passage he returns to the relation of his poem to Firdawsī's again, and this time articulates the familiar convention, but modified in such a way as assert his superiority to Firdawsī without suggesting that his illustrious predecessor was anything but a very fine poet. He begins by saying that while it is his general practice not to base his poems on tales that have already been told (i.e., given poetic form) sometimes there is no escaping the need to do so.

[33] Niẓāmī Ganjavī 1994, 7.

[34] I have used, here and below, the new English translation by Julie Scott Meisami, see Niẓāmī Ganjavī 1995, 11.

Līk chūn rāh-i ganj khānah yakīst
Tīrhā gar dū shud nishānah yakīst [35]

Translation

Yet since the path to treasure's one—
a single mark, thoug harrows twain—[36]

In such a case he solves the problem by improving on the original.

Chūn na-bāshad zi bāz-guft gurīz
Dānam angīkht az palās ḥarīr [37]

Translation

When repetition must be made,
I silk from sackcloth can create.[38]

This I read as general statement of how he improves on his source. In the next lines, he alludes specifically to Firdawsī, without either mentioning him by name, but in such a way as both to acknowledge Firdawsī's primacy and skill and assert his own superiority.

Dū muṭarriz bi-kimiyā-yi sukhan
Tāzah kardand naqdhā-yi kuhan
Ān zi mis nuqrah kard nuqrah-'i khāṣṣ
Vīn kunad nuqrah rā bi-zar khalāṣ
Mis chū dīdī kih nuqrah shud bi-iyār
Nuqrah gar zar shavad shigift madār [39]

Translation

The ancient coin has been made new,
through alchemy of speech, by two:
That one from brass pure silver drew:
I'll turn to gold that silver. You,
Who've seen brass equal silver, should
not marvel when silver turns to gold.[40]

[35] Idem 1994, 37.
[36] Idem 1995, 56.
[37] Idem 1994, 37.
[38] Idem 1995, 56.
[39] Idem 1994, 37.
[40] Idem 1995, 56.

Niẓāmī's boasting of his prowess (*fakhr*) is a familiar convention of the tradition, as is his comparison of himself to the magician, the goldsmith and the weaver. What is remarkable, again, is his elaborate articulation of his relationship to his illustrious predecessor.

CONCLUSIONS

The generation of a new literature is a remarkably complicated and multifaceted process. In the case of Persian, it includes translation first of Middle Persian language materials, poetry especially and often of non-Iranian origin, into Arabic—almost surely with the intent of preserving the Iranian cultural heritage. These Persian materials in Arabic are then recaptured for an exclusively Iranian milieu by a second translation into New Persian. The first stage was made possible by the wealth of Sasanian literature, the large number of bilingual Iranians, the absence of a pre-Islamic Arab imperial literary tradition, and the long-standing Muslim Arab admiration for things Sasanian. It may have been further aided by the Islamic rejection of poetry as serious, signifying discourse.

The second stage of this process included no parallel translation of distinctively Arabic materials into Persian to assure, for instance, that Iranians with limited Arabic would have access to the foundation documents of Arabic literary life—*Jāhilīyah* poetry, for instance. While it is tempting to attribute the neglect of Arabic to an extension of the sentiments of the Shu'ūbīyah, a desire, that is, to assert a separate and distinct cultural identity, other factors suggest a more complex explanation. There were, after all, a great many translations of individual *bayts* of Arabic poetry, and that suggests at least an admiration for Arabic poetry. Second, New Persian translations of the *Jāhilīyah* poems or the works of Abbasid masters would have been a striking anomaly, since there does not seem to be a developed tradition of translating lyric poems or the works of individual poets into either Arabic or Middle Persian. Finally, Arabic had no tradition of poetic narrative and did not invent one to accommodate the Middle Persian poetic narratives translated into it. In retranslating Middle Persian narrative poems from Arabic prose versions into New Persian, first as prose, then to verse, Iranian poets were restoring and continuing an indigenous tradition.

There is little to suggest that the Islamic tradition was in any sense inclined to develop an attitude toward literary translation comparable to that of the western European tradition. One, that is, in which translation takes on the aspect of a conscious act of literary fealty. That aside, the particular circumstances surrounding the invention of New Persian literature freighted the act of appropriating an earlier poet's work in such a way that, in fact, almost the opposite of that attitude prevailed. Poets were obliged to belittle their predecessors and assert their own superiority in order to escape the taint of plagiary. Whether this attitude was restricted to the specific context and to Persian exclusively, or whether it casts its shadow over the whole of Islamic literary evolution is a question that waits upon further studies.

BIBLIOGRAPHY

AJAMI, MANSOUR. 1988. *The Alchemy of glory : the dialectic of truthfulness and untruthfulness in medieval Arabic literary criticism.* Washington, DC : Three Continents Press.

BEESTON, A. F. L., et al. 1983. *Arabic literature to the end of the Umayyad period.* Cambridge [Cambridgeshire] and New York : Cambridge University Press.

BOSWORTH, C. E. 1983. The Persian impact on Arabic literature. In *Arabic literature to the end of the Umayyad period.* Cambridge [Cambridgeshire] and New York : Cambridge University Press: 483–96.

BOYCE, MARY. 1957. The Parthian Gōsān and Iranian minstrel tradition. *Journal of the Royal Asiatic Society of Great Britain and Ireland* pts. 1–2: 10–45.

—— 1983. Parthian writings and literature. In *Cambridge history of Iran.* Vol. 3., pt. 2. Ed. Ehsan Yarshater. Cambridge [Cambridgeshire] : Cambridge University Press: 1151–65.

—— 1983b. Manichaean Middle Persian writings. In *Cambridge history of Iran.* Vol. 3., pt. 2. Ed. Ehsan Yarshater. Cambridge [Cambridgeshire] : Cambridge University Press: 1196–204.

BROCKELMAN, C. 1978. Kalīla wa-Dimna. *Encyclopaedia of Islam.* New ed. Vol. 4. Leiden : E. J. Brill: 503a–6b.

CLINTON, JEROME W. 1972. *The Divan of Manūchihrī Dāmghānī : a critical study.* Minneapolis : Bibliotheca Islamica.

—— 1988. Court poetry at the beginning of the classical period. In *Persian literature.* Ed. Ehsan Yarshater. Albany, NY : Bibliotheca Persica: 75–95.

—— 1989. Shams-i Qays on the nature of poetry. *Edebiyât* n.s. 1, no. 2: 101–27.

—— 1994. Nuktah'ī chand dar bārah-'i vaẕ'-i kunūni-i tarikh-i adabī dar Īrān. *Īrān'nāmah* 12, no. 1 (zamistān 1372 Sh.): 35–50.

DAVIDSON, OLGA M. 1994. *Poet and hero in the Persian Book of kings.* Ithaca, NY : Cornell University Press.

ELWELL-SUTTON, L. P. 1975. The foundations of Persian prosody and metrics. *Iran* 13: 75–97.

—— 1976. *The Persian metres.* Cambridge [Cambridgeshire] and New York : Cambridge University Press.

FAKHR AL-DĪN GURGĀNĪ. 1970. *Vīs u Rāmīn.* Ed. Magali A. Todua, Alexander A. Gwakharia. Tehran : Bunyād-i Farhang-i Īrān, zamistān 1349 Sh.

—— 1972. *Vis and Ramin.* Tr. George Morrison. New York and London : Columbia University Press.

FIRDAWSĪ. 1994. *Shāhnāmah-'i Firdawsī : matn-i intiqādī az rū-yi chāp-i Muskaw.* Ed. Sa'īd Ḥamidiyān. 9 vols. in 4. Tehran : Nashr-i Qaṭrah, 1373 Sh.

KAYKĀVŪS IBN ISKANDAR. 1951. *A mirror for princes : the Qābūs Nāma.* Tr. Reuben Levy. New York : E. P. Dutton.

—— 1992. *Qābūsnāmah.* Ed. Ghulām Ḥusayn Yūsufī. 6th ed. Tehran : Shirkat-i Intishārāt-i 'Ilmī va Farhangī, 1371 Sh.

LAZARD, GILBERT. 1964. *Les premiers poètes persans, (IXe-Xe siècles) : fragments rassemblés, édités et traduits.* 2 vols. Tehran : Institut franco-iranien.

—— 1975. The Rise of the New Persian language. In *Cambridge history of Iran.* Vol. 4. Ed. R. N. Frye. London : Cambridge University Press: 595–632.

—— 1993. *The origins of literary Persian.* Bethesda, MD : Foundation for Iranian Studies.

MUḤAMMADĪ, MUḤAMMAD. 1995. *Farhang-i Īrānī pīsh az Islām va āṣār-i ān dar tamaddun-i Islāmī va adabīyāt-i 'Arabī.* 3rd rev. ed. Tehran : Tūs, 1374 Sh.

NIẒĀMĪ 'ARŪẒĪ. 1969. *Chahār maqālah.* Ed. Muḥammad Mu'īn. Tehran : Ibn Sīnā, 1348 Sh.

NIẒĀMĪ GANJAVĪ. 1994. *Haft paykar-i Niẓāmī Ganjavī : matn-i 'ilmī va intiqādī az rū-yi qadīmī'tarīn nuskhah'hā-yi khaṭṭī-i qarn-i hashtum bā ẕikr-i ikhtilāf-i nusakh va sharḥ-i abyāt va ma'nī-i lughāt va tarkībāt va kashf al-abyāt.* Ed. Barāt Zanjānī. Tehran : Dānishgāh-i Tihrān, 1373 Sh.

—— 1995. *Haft paykar : a medieval Persian romance.* Tr. Julie Scott Meisami. Oxford and New York : Oxford University Press.

RĀDŪYĀNĪ, MUḤAMMAD IBN 'UMAR. 1949. *Kitāb-i Tarjumān al-balāghah : bā fāksīmīlah-'i nuskhah-'i munḥaṣir bi-fard-i kitāb muvarrikhah-'i 507 Hijrī.* Ed. Ahmed Ateş. İstanbul : İstanbul Üniversitesi.

REINERT, BENEDIKT. 1973. Probleme der vormongolischen arabisch-persischen poesiegemeinschaft und ihr reflex in der poetik. In *Arabic poetry : theory and development.* Ed. G. E. Von Grunebaum. Wiesbaden : Otto Harrassowitz: 71–106.

RICHTER-BERNBURG, LUTZ. 1974. Linguistic Shu'ūbīya and early Neo-Persian prose. *Journal of the American Oriental Society* 94, no. 1 (January–March): 55–64.

SHAFĪ'Ī KADKANĪ, MUḤAMMAD RIẒĀ. 1987. *Ṣuvar-i khiyāl dar shi'r-i Fārsī : taḥqīq-i intiqādī dar taṭavvur-i īmāzhhā-yi shi'r-i Pārsī va sayr-i naẓarīyah-'i balāghat dar Islām va Īrān.* 3rd ed. Tehran : Āgāh, 1366 Sh.

SHAKED, SHAUL. 1970. Specimens of Middle Persian verse. In *W. B. Henning memorial volume.* Ed. Mary Boyce and Ilya Gershevitch. London : Lund Humphries: 395–405.

SHAMS-I QAYS. 1956. *al-Mu'jam fī ma'āyīr ash'ār al-'Ajam.* Ed. Muḥammad ibn 'Abd al-Vahhāb Qazvīnī, Mudarris Raẓavī. Tehran : Dānishgāh-i Tihrān, 1335 Sh.

—— 1994–. *al-Mu'jam fī ma'āyīr ash'ār al-'Ajam.* Ed. Sīrūs Shamīsā. 1 vol. to date. Tehran : Firdaws, 1373 Sh.–

SPRENGLING, MARTIN. 1939–40. Persian into Arabic. *American Journal of Semitic Languages and Literatures* 56: 175–224, 325–36 (pt. 1); 57:302–5 (pt. 2).

TAFAẒẒOLI, AḤMAD. 1993. Dabīr. *Encyclopaedia Iranica.* Vol. 6. Costa Mesa, CA : Mazda: 534b–7b.

TĀRĪKH-I SĪSTĀN. [1935] 1987. Ed. Malik al-Shu'arā' Bahār. Reprint, Tehran : Padīdah "Khāvar", 1366 Sh.

UMĪDSĀLĀR, MAḤMŪD. 1995. Review of *Poet and hero in the Persian Book of kings,* by Olga M. Davidson. *Majallah-'i Īrān'shināsī* 7, no. 2 (tābistān 1374 Sh.): 436–57.

VAḤĪDIYĀN KĀMYĀR, TAQĪ. 1988. *Vazn va qāfiyah-'i shi'r-i Fārsī.* Tehran : Markaz-i Nashr-i Dānishgāhī, 1367 Sh.

—— 1991. *Barrasī-i mansha'-i vazn-i shi'r-i Fārsī.* Mashhad : Āstān-i Quds-i Raẓavī, 1370 Sh.

—— 1991b. *Ḥarfhā-yi tāzah dar adab-i Fārsī.* Ahvāz : Jihād-i Dānishgāhī, 1370 Sh.

VAṬVĀṬ, RASHĪD AL-DĪN MUḤAMMAD. [1930] 1984. *Ḥadā'iq al-siḥr fī daqā'iq al-shi'r*. Ed. 'Abbās Iqbāl. Reprint, Tehran : Kitābkhānah-i Sanā'ī: Kitābkhānah-'i Ṭahūrī, Bahman 1362 Sh.

YARSHATER, EHSAN. 1988. The development of Iranian literatures. In *Persian literature*. Ed. Ehsan Yarshater. Albany, NY : Bibliotheca Persica: 3–37.

Un conte en persan local de Gīv (region de Bīrjand)

Gilbert Lazard

IL Y A PRESQUE CINQUANTE ANS, IRAJ AFSHAR ET MOI, suivant ensemble des cours à la Faculté des lettres de Téhéran, nous nous rencontrions souvent pour nous perfectionner mutuellement en français et en persan. Depuis, nous n'avons cessé d'échanger à intervalles des informations et des publications. Je lui dois aussi de m'avoir à l'occasion facilité des voyages d'enquête dialectologique dans la province iranienne. Il est donc juste que je lui offre dans ce volume, avec mon amical souvenir, un modeste fruit de ces voyages.[1]

Le texte ci-dessous a été recueilli, en octobre 1963, au cours d'une enquête sur des parlers persans d'Iran oriental, dans le village de Gīv, situé à quelques dizaines de kilomètres au sud de Bīrjand. Il a été conté par une femme d'une trentaine d'années, illettrée, qui n'avait jamais quitté le village. Le récit est visiblement tronqué et maladroit, la syntaxe souvent boiteuse: la conteuse, sans doute intimidée, a multiplié les hésitations et les faux départs. Mais c'est assurément un spécimen authentique du persan que les villageois parlent entre eux. Je l'ai seulement émondé des hésitations et des lapsus.

Outre les six voyelles du persan commun, le dialecte a un *ā* distinct de *a*. Il y a aussi un *ē*, qui, semble-t-il, ne se distingue de *e* qu'en syllabe ouverte inaccentuée non finale. *e* apparaît notamment là où le persan commun a *ow*, *ab*, *âv*, *âb*, ex.: *jele* = *jelow*, *le* = *lab*, *ge* = *gâv*, *e* = *âb*. Le consonantisme est le même qu'en persan commun. Les nasales finales sont articulées très faiblement et souvent amuïes.

[1] Le conte présenté ici est connu par d'autres versions recueillies dans diverses régions d'Iran et d'Asie centrale. Fażl Allāh Muhtadī (Ṣubḥī) (d. 1341 Sh./1962) a le premier rassemblé les différentes versions de cette histoire, et il en a publié deux (sous les titres *Chilgīs* et *Chilgazahmū*) dans le second volume de sa collection de contes populaires *Afsānah'hā* (Téhéran : s.n., [Isfand] 1325 Sh. [1947]: 100–20). Dans son avant-propos, Ṣubḥī mentionne des versions de ce conte provenant de Kāshān, Yazd, Qazvīn, Bukhārā, Samarqand, et du Tajikistan (100, 114). Une version plus longue, intitulée *Jāntīgh va chihilgīs*, est connue à Chanāqchī, village des environs de Sāvah, et figure dans le second volume de *Qiṣṣah'hā-yi Īrānī* d'Abū al-Qāsim Injavī Shīrāzī (Téhéran : Amīr Kabīr, 1353 Sh. [1974]: 193–204). Je remercie M. Kambiz Eslami qui m'a aimablement fourni ces renseignements.

Les noms font leur pluriel en *-o(n)*. L'*ezâfe* et l'article indéfini ont tous deux la forme *-e* (enclitique). La postposition correspondant à *-râ* est généralement *-a* après consonne, *-r* après voyelle. Les pronoms sont : *me*, *te*, *i/u*, *mâ*, *šemâ*, *ino/uno*. Il n'y a pas de forme correspondant aux enclitiques *-am*, *-at*, etc. du persan commun, mais les pronoms ci-dessus peuvent devenir enclitiques en fonction de possessifs, ex. *pedar-me* "mon père." Exemple de conjugaison: "faire" présent *mokonom*, *mokoni*, *mokone/mokoneš/mokonede*, *mokonem*, *mokonen*, *mokonan*. A la 3e personne du singulier, le type *mokoneš* s'emploie pour les personnes (= *u mikonad*), le type *mokonede* pour les choses, ex.: *pul nadâreš* (cet homme) "n'a pas d'argent," *pul nadârede* (cette bourse) "ne contient pas d'argent." Le suffixe *-e* peut aussi renvoyer à un objet (inanimé): *didom-e* "je l'ai vu." Verbe "être" enclitique: *-om*, *-i*, *-e/-â*, *-em*, *-en*, *-an*. La troisième personne du singulier comporte une composante déictique: *-e* (ou *haste*) réfère à un sujet proche, *-â* (ou *hastâ*) à un sujet lointain, cf. ci-dessous, § 4, 6, 7, 8, 13, 19.

TEXTE

[1] yak pâdešâe beda, i pâdešâ dumâd šeda-vo ayâle can sâl nadešta. yak darviše namâšom[2] biomada dar serâ i-o[3] bexânda-vo gofta ke: darviš, agar šemâ bexâne(n) ke mâ ayâle can sâl šeda nadârem-o[4] šemâ bexâne(n) ke mâ ayâle dešta bâšem, ana[5] i gaš[6] dega ke bien[7] har ci lâycq šemâ bedânem vâ[8] šomâ xendâd.[9] darviš biâmada, bâd a can vax ayâle xodâ vâ i dâda-vo biâmada gofta: aga merda bâšeš-am[10] u-r nega dâre(n), aga zenda bâšeš-am nega dâre(n).

[2] tâ de hafta i baca be denyâ âmada merda-vo i-r deštan-vo[11] darviš gofta ke baca-r ce kerden? goftan: mâ xo can ruz šeda u-r deštim,[12] niâmadin,[13] u-r beraftan dafn kerdan. u dam berafta vâ le ju[14] dida ke bale i baca-r xo daran-

[2] *namâšom* = *namâz-e šâm*.

[3] *dar serâ i* = *dar-e sarâ-ye in*.

[4] *nadârem*, etc.: le roi parle à la 1re personne du pluriel.

[5] *ana* = "voici."

[6] *gaš(t)* = "fois."

[7] *bien* = "venir": subj. 3pl.

[8] *vâ*: prép. "à" (avec "donner," etc.) et aussi "pour."

[9] *xendâd* = *xâhim dâd*.

[10] *bâšeš-am* = *bâšad-ham*.

[11] *deštan-vo*, *daran-vo*, etc.: j'interprète ainsi ce qui, en débit rapide, est réalisé *deštamo*, *daramo*, etc. On parle du roi à la 3e personne du pluriel.

[12] *mâ xo . . . u-r deštim* = *mâ ke . . . u-râ dâštim*.

[13] *niâmadin* = *nayâmade-id*.

[14] *le ju* = *lab-e ju*.

vo[15] i baca-r zenda kerda. zenda šeda baca-vo goftan: i darviš ce še[16] ke mâ i-r yak cize bedem? goftan: darviš xo farâr ke bera.[17]

[3] u dam i baca-r deštan-vo i mattabi[18] šeda-vo u dam ami pedar i vâ xo ceni ciz dešta ana ambâr dešta-vo xona dešta-vo gofta ke babâ[19] i baca ētiâte[20] daro-r[21] vâ nakone ke i bacaga[22] âšeq šu[23] ke agar bere[24] šagl-e doxtar parizâd-a bine-vo nabâdâ az piš mâ farâr kone vâ xo[25] bere.[26]

[4] i berafta yag ru be gardeš xed[27] ami nukar-e xo, gofta ke daro-r vâ ko. derâ-r vâ kerda-vo dida ke vokahâ[28] var i divâlo xo yak šaglahâ kandeyâ[29] ke dil i[30] ba qaš hamunja rafta-vo bemerda.

[5] bemerda-vo hami nukara xabar biârda vâ pâdešâ ke qable âlam agar mokošen agar mebaxšen ke be zur pesar šemâ am me[31] kali-r bestonda-vo dar-a vâ kerd, ana unja bemerda. pâdšâ gofta: beren u-r biâren, agar bemerdeš-am xo dega u-r jam xenke,[32] ana ce kâr konom? namâsti[33] ceni kâre mekerdi.

[6] beraftan i-r var pešt-e xo kerdan biârdan, bacaga zenda šeda-vo bedeš i unja.[34] lebâs var dešta-vo bedavida berafta bedavida berafta-vo berafta-vo berafta be yag dee rasida. be yag dee[35] rasida dida ke da[36] i de xo yak sarosedâe-â, yag goftošenide-â, gofta: bâbâ da i de-e šemâ ce xabar āvâl-a?[37]

[15] *i baca-r xo daran = in bacce-râ ke dârand.*
[16] *ce še = ce šod.*
[17] *farâr ke bera = farâr kard (be)raft.*
[18] *mattabi = maktabi.*
[19] *babâ = bâbâ.*
[20] *ētiâte* = "attention," forme sans doute analogue à *zude* (accentué sur la première syllabe) "vite."
[21] *daro-r = darhâ-râ.*
[22] *bacaga*: *baca* + suffixe diminutif *-a*.
[23] *šu = šavad.*
[24] *bere = beravad.*
[25] *vâ xo = barâ-ye xod.*
[26] *ke agar . . .*: la phrase est boiteuse, mais le sens est clair.
[27] *xe(d)*: prép. "avec"
[28] *vokahâ*: interjection.
[29] *kandeyâ*: probablement < *kanda-e* (article indéfini) + *-â* "il y a des images gravées."
[30] *dil i = del-e u (del-e in).*
[31] *am me < a(z) me = az man.*
[32] *jam xenke = jam' xâhid kard.*
[33] *namâsti = nemixâsti.*
[34] *bedeš i unja = bud u ânjâ.*
[35] *yag dee = yek deh-i.*
[36] *da*: prép. = *dar* "dans."
[37] *xabar āvâl = xabar-o ahvâl.*

[7] gofta: ana de de-e mâ yak cize vâdi[38] âmada ke âdamo-r boxore, guspand moxore, heyvo moxore. i bâr dega gofta ke cete[39] kase-â, cete cize-â? gofta: hâlâ mâ xo nandonem,[40] jerat xo nankonem[41] berem nāzik u. de nafar joel-am[42] unja be i rasidan, gofta: šemâ kojâ meren? goftan: mâ merem merem ke vâ xo arus vâdi konem. gofta: hamu darde ke šomâ dâren me-ham vâ hamu dard merom. biâmadan har se tâ ino goftan ke biâyn[43] šemâ-ham, hami de tâ-r-vo hamu yake ke ceni hamu darviš zenda kerda.

[8] diga hamu rafta-vo gofta: biâ tâ berem, me u har ce ke has, me u-r mekošom, refiqo me-r šemâ jamâvari konen. raftan raftan refiqon ino-r jamâvari kerdan-vo yag pâdešâe beda, goftan ke pâdešâ i ceni kase vâdi âmada, gofta me u cize ke bimāni hastâ[44] me u-r mokošom.

[9] bād u dam berafta, i-r beberdan be nazzik nahang, nahang-e bedeš nahang-e bedeš. hanceni ke be nahang rasideš gofteš: bien, gâve[45] hastâ ke, gâv-e câqe, ke i-re am mio[46] de šaqqa konen-vo yak šaqqe[47] biâren ke tu dehen u endâzom bemireš. beraftan beraftan, hanceni ke i fuš kešida i zeda var tu dehen i-o i-r bekošta. biomadan-vo u-r vâ kešidan.[48]

[10] pâdešâ gofta ke doxtaron xo-r mom[49] vâ šemâ dom, šemâ âdamon-e zerang-en. har kadon ino-r yag dee dâda-vo ami yake ke u-r bekošta qabuldâr našeda. berafta berafta-vo be yag jây cašme e[50] rasida-vo deraxte beda, deraxte beda vâ unja ke doxtar parizâd hamunja miâmada maške âb mekerda-vo merafta-vo meâmada.

[38] *vâdi* = *padid*; cette forme se trouve dans la prose préclassique.

[39] *cete* = *ce towr*.

[40] *nandonem* = *nemidânim*.

[41] *nankonem* = *nemikonim*.

[42] *joel* = *jâhel* au sens de "jeune."

[43] *biâyn* est une forme de persan commun, au lieu de la forme dialectale *bien*, v. ci-dessus, § 1, note 7.

[44] *u cize ke bimāni hastâ* = "cette chose qui est sans sens," expression euphémistique.

[45] *gâv*: forme du persan commun au lieu de la forme dialectale *ge*.

[46] *am mio* = *az miân*.

[47] *yak šaqqe* = *yek šaqqe-i*.

[48] Le récit est un peu embrouillé et le procédé employé pour tuer le monstre n'est pas clair.

[49] *mom* = *mixâham*.

[50] *cašme e* = *cašme-ye âb*. A la ligne suivante, *âb* est une forme du persan commun au lieu de *e*, forme locale.

[11] be hamunja rasida-vo deraxt-e bane[51] beda vâ amunja. de caquk biâmada, de kaftar[52] ru-e derax šeda gofta ke aho âdam te ke inja-i, var qaltida-i,[53] hâlâ doxtar parizâd bexâmad,[54] mašk-e âb xâke-vo[55] bexâma, amu deraxt-a takko xâdâ,[56] xâgo:[57] ey deraxt-e bisamar me har vax biâmadom te yag bâr samar nadâdi, te u dam jibon xo-r per naxot kešmeš koni berizi ke i gir šu, te u-r begiri, agar na xo nantuni[58] u-r begiri.

[12] i sar xo-r harkat dâda, kaftaro goftan: a, cera sar xo-r harkat dâdi tâ mâ panâ našem? i berafta panâ šeda-vo i pesara sar derax šeda-vo dida ke ana i le i ju xo cerâqrizo še, uqzar jele[59] vâ xo gol-o golbana[60] le ju biâmad. sar derax še-o i doxtar biâmad hami deraxt-a bogoroft-o takko dâd gof: to xo samar nadâri uqzar ke me biâmadom xo yak samar-e xub bidi . . .

[13] ceni naxoto-r i pesar berext ke doxtar jam kone. i pešt-e xo-r var had-e derax dešt-o tend-o[61] ten naxoto-r jam meke,[62] i az sar derax ta[63] âmad-o i-r bogorof. i-r bogoroft-o beraft-o beraf xed i. gofteš ke aha me xozgâr[64] dârom, me hâlâ pedar-o mâdar me miâ-vo te-r mokoše,[65] inja[66] vâ ce kâr-â? gofteš: ce kâr dâri? me can farsax râ biâmadam vâ bude[67] te ke ana te-r bebarom.

[14] xed am[68] beraftan beraftan-o gof ke ey bâbâ mâ kojâ merem? âxer mâ hici nadârem, serâe nadârem, xone nadârem, mâ ce kâr konem? beraftan sar cašme e degare vâ-nšestan xed am-o hami pesara sar xo-r ru zoni dešt. gof ke te ce kâr dâri? hâlâ dega haminja bâš-o bini ke ce serâe vâ-râsta mešu.

51 *bane < bana + -e.*
52 *de caquk, de kaftar*: la conteuse se reprend.
53 *var qaltida = derâz kašide.*
54 *bexâma(d) = (be)xâhad âmad.*
55 *xâke = xâhad kard.*
56 *xâdâ = xâhad dâd.*
57 *xâgo = xâhad goft.*
58 *nantuni = nemitavâni.*
59 *jele = jelow.*
60 *gol-o golbana = naqš-o negâr.* La construction n'est pas claire.
61 *ten(d) = tond.*
62 *meke = mikard.*
63 *ta = tah.*
64 *xozgâr = xâstgâr.*
65 *miâ, mokoše*: au singulier au lieu du pluriel.
66 *inja* = "ceci."
67 *vâ bude (buda + -e) = barâ-ye, be xâter-e.*
68 *xed am = bâ ham.*

[15] cešon xo-r vâ kerd did ke serâe-vo xona-vo zendegoni ârâsta še-vo ke hama ciz . . . bād biâmadan-o xed am zendegoni kerdan. zendegoni kerdan-o ana yag gašt xed am ceni gardeš mekardeš yak pirzâl-e šār-e Lut ke biâmad var unja nemâšome, gof ke ey, me yak pirzâluke-om,[69] me-r râ nanden?[70]

[16] i pirzâl biâmad dar xone ino gof ke me amru var[71] inja eftâdâm,[72] me-r jam bokonen. goftan: bale, cera jam nankonem? i biâmad-o i-r jam kerdan-o non-o cerâe dâdan-vo gofteš ke me-r yak lahâfuke[73] beden ke vâ xo da xe[74] šom-o i da xâb še.

[17] seb ke še biâmad be i xona gof: xed am tâ berem yag gardeše bokonem tu kuco. gof: xeyli xob. âxer da xâb-an, mâ cete uno-r bugzârem?[75] gof: berem, hâlâ bexemma.[76] biâmadan o xed am gardeše kerdan-o i xânem gof ke ana ma ceni marde dârom ke ana matarsom ke az gorde u[77] harkat nankonom ke agar az gorde u harkat konom tu gorde u yak cize hastâ ke agar kase bekašed-e[78] hami zud nafas-eš[79] kanda mešu.

[18] beraftan-o i bâr konâr hamu ju didan kaštie tu âb-â-vo gofteš: xed am biâ tu hami kešti šem. i, zaneka i-r tu kešti kerd o zanjir-a be dar endâxt-o var hami tu âb xed am zadan beraftan. var tu âb zadan beraftan-o[80] be yag jâe rasidan-o didan ke hazâr tâ vâ pâdešâ xabar beber[81] ke ana doxtar-e parizâd-a biârdeš.

[19] i-r beber tu serâ xo. yakke biâmad gof ke doxtar-e parizâd-a pirzâl biârda-vo goftan ke i-r biâren. i-r biârdan-vo vâ hamu pâdešâ dâdan. i gof: me šuare dârom, šemâ cete ceni kâre mokonen? gof ke hâlâ i dam te-r az u šuar ce kâr-

69 *pirzâluk*: diminutif.
70 *nanden = nemidehid*.
71 *var = bar*.
72 *eftâdâm = oftâde-am*.
73 *lahâfuk*: diminutif.
74 *xe = xâb*. La conteuse emploie ici côte à côte la forme locale et celle du persan commun.
75 *da xâb-an, uno*: pluriel de politesse.
76 *bexemma = (be)xâhim âmad*.
77 *gorde u = pahlu-ye u*.
78 *bekašed-e = bekašad-eš, bekašad ân-râ*. La chose en question doit être une sorte de talisman qui le tient en vie. Au vu de la similitude de ce récit avec celui de *Jāntīgh va chihilgīs* (voir note no. 1), la "chose" en question doit être le poignard qui protège la vie du jeune homme.
79 *nafas-eš* est une forme de persan commun.
80 *var tu âb zadan beraftan* = "se mirent à partir sur l'eau."
81 *beber = (be)bord*.

â? i dam dega i-r vâ i dâdan-vo dega mâ xo az unja biâmadom vâ xo, dega nafāmidom ke ce kâr kerdan. ana amiqzar bale.[82]

TRADUCTION

[1] Il y avait un roi. Ce roi se maria et resta plusieurs années sans enfant. Un derviche vint un soir dans sa maison et récita des incantations. Le roi lui dit: "Si vous faites des incantations—depuis des années nous n'avons pas eu d'enfant,—[si] vous faites des incantations de sorte que nous ayons des enfants, eh bien, quand vous reviendrez, nous vous donnerons tout ce que nous connaîtrons de digne de vous." Le derviche s'exécuta (litt. vint) et après quelque temps Dieu donna un enfant au roi (litt. à celui-ci). [Le derviche] dit: "S'il est mort, gardez-le, et s'il est vivant, gardez-le."

[2] Deux semaines [après] qu'il fut venu au monde, cet enfant mourut. [Le roi] le garda. Le derviche dit: "Qu'avez-vous fait de l'enfant?" Il répondit: "Nous l'avons gardé pendant quelques jours; [comme] vous n'êtes pas venu, on est allé l'enterrer." Alors il alla au bord de la rivière et vit que, oui, on le gardait. Il le ressuscita. L'enfant ressuscita. [Le roi] dit: "Qu'est devenu le derviche, que nous lui donnions quelque chose?" On répondit: "Le derviche s'est enfui, il est parti."

[3] Alors on garda l'enfant et il alla à l'école (litt. devint écolier). Or (litt. alors) son père était riche (litt. avait de telles choses): il avait des entrepôts, des chambres. Il dit: "Holà, attention que cet enfant n'ouvre pas les portes [de peur] qu'il ne tombe amoureux, car s'il entre et qu'il voie l'image de la fille des fées, il est à craindre qu'il ne s'enfuie de chez nous et ne s'en aille."

[4] L'enfant un jour alla en promenade avec son serviteur il [lui] dit: "Ouvre les portes." Il ouvrit les portes et [le jeune homme] vit que, oh la la, sur les murs sont gravées des images telles que sur le champ il perdit conscience et mourut.

[5] Il mourut, et le serviteur alla en informer le roi: "Point de mire du monde, tuez-moi ou faites-moi grâce (litt. si vous me tuez ou si vous me faites grâce), votre fils m'a pris de force la clef, il a ouvert la porte, et voilà qu'il est mort là-bas." Le roi dit: "Allez le chercher. S'il est mort, vous l'enterrerez. Hé, que puis-je faire? Tu n'aurais pas dû faire ça."

[82] *mâ xo* . . .: formule de fin de conte.

[6] Ils allèrent le charger sur leur dos et le rapportèrent. Le jeune homme ressuscita. Le voilà [donc] là. Il prit ses vêtements et partit en courant. Il partit en courant, et il alla, il alla, il arriva à un village. Il arriva à un village et vit que dans ce village il y avait un tumulte, une agitation. Il dit: "Eh bien, que se passe-t-il dans votre village?"

[7] On lui dit: "Voici, dans notre village est apparue une chose qui mange les gens, mange les moutons, mange les bêtes." Il reprit: "Quel genre d'être est-ce, quel genre de chose?" On lui dit: "Maintenant nous ne savons pas, nous n'osons pas l'approcher." Deux jeunes gens arrivèrent là près de lui. Il dit: "Où allez-vous?" Ils dirent: "Nous allons, nous allons pour trouver des épouses." Il dit: "J'ai le même souci que vous: moi aussi, je vais avec (litt. pour) le même souci." Ils dirent tous les trois: "Venez, vous aussi," [c'est-à-dire] les deux jeunes gens et celui que le derviche avait ainsi ressuscité.

[8] Il alla donc et dit: "Allons (litt. viens que nous allions), moi, cet être, quoi que ce soit, je le tuerai. Rassemblez mes compagnons." On rassembla leurs compagnons. Il y avait un roi, on lui dit: "Roi, un homme (litt. un tel homme) est apparu [qui] dit: moi, cette chose indicible, je vais la tuer."

[9] Alors il alla, on le mena auprès du monstre marin (litt. baleine)—c'était un monstre marin, un monstre marin.- Quand il arriva auprès du monstre marin, il dit: "Venez, il y a un boeuf, un boeuf gras. Vous le couperez en deux par le milieu et vous m'apporterez la moitié que je la jette dans la gueule du monstre, de sorte qu'il meure." Ils s'exécutèrent (litt. allèrent allèrent). Quand [le monstre] souffla, il le frappa dans la gueule et le tua. On vint le dépecer.

[10] Le roi dit: "Je veux vous donner mes filles, vous êtes des hommes intelligents." Il leur donna à chacun un village, mais celui qui avait tué le monstre n'accepta pas et s'en alla. Il alla et arriva à une source [où] il y avait un arbre. Il y avait un arbre à cet endroit, où la fille des fées venait remplir d'eau une outre; elle allait et venait.

[11] Il arriva là. Il y avait là un arbre, un térébinthe. Deux moineaux, deux pigeons perchés sur l'arbre dirent: "Hé l'homme, toi qui es là vautré, la fille des fées va venir, elle va emplir d'eau une outre, et elle va venir secouer cet arbre et dire: O arbre stérile, si souvent que je sois venue, tu n'as pas une fois donné de fruit. Toi alors tu rempliras tes poches de pois et de raisins secs et tu les répandras de sorte qu'elle soit occupée [à les ramasser], et tu l'attraperas; sinon, tu ne pourras pas l'attraper."

[12] Il se leva (litt. remua sa tête). Les pigeons dirent: “Hé, pourquoi te lèves-tu avant que nous soyons à l’abri?” Ils se mirent à l’abri et le garçon grimpa dans l’arbre. Il vit que voilà le bord du cours d’eau qui s’illumine, tant de merveilles sont venues au bord du ruisseau en avant [de la fille des fées?]. Il était monté (litt. monta) dans l’arbre et la fille vint prendre cet arbre et le secouer et dit: “Tu n’as pas de fruit, si souvent que je sois venue pour que tu donnes un bon fruit . . .”

[13] Le garçon répandit les pois de telle sorte que la fille les ramasse. Elle se tenait le dos vers l’arbre et ramassait les pois en toute hâte. Lui descendit de l’arbre et l’attrapa. Il l’attrapa et s’en alla, s’en alla avec elle. Elle dit: “Oho, j’ai des prétendants, mon père et ma mère vont venir te tuer, que veut dire ceci (litt. ceci est pour quoi)?” Il dit: “Qu’est-ce qui ne va pas (litt. quelle affaire as-tu)? J’ai parcouru tant de farsakhs pour toi, pour t’emmener.”

[14] Ensemble ils allèrent, ils allèrent . Il dit: “Voyons, où allons-nous? Nous n’avons rien enfin, pas de maison, pas de chambre, que pouvons-nous faire?” Ils allèrent s’installer ensemble auprès d’une autre source d’eau. Le garçon se tenait la tête sur les genoux. Elle lui dit: “Qu’est-ce que tu as? Ne bouge pas et vois quelle maison va être apprêtée.”

[15] Il ouvrit les yeux et vit qu’étaient apprêtés une maison, une chambre, de quoi vivre et toutes choses. Ensuite ils vécurent ensemble. Ils vécurent ensemble et voilà que, une fois qu’ils se promenaient ensemble ainsi, une affreuse vieille (litt. une vieille du pays de Lout) vint les trouver un soir et dit: “Hé, je suis une pauvre vieille, ne me laisserez-vous pas entrer?”

[16] Cette vieille vint donc à leur porte et dit: “Je me trouve aujourd’hui ici, accueillez-moi.” Ils dirent: “Oui, pourquoi ne t’accueillerions-nous pas?” Elle entra et ils l’accueillirent et lui donnèrent à manger. Elle dit: “Donnez-moi une petite couverture que je me couche.” Elle se coucha.

[17] Le matin elle vint à leur chambre et dit [à la jeune femme]: “Allons ensemble faire une promenade dans les rues.” [La jeune femme] dit: “Très bien, mais enfin il (mon mari) est couché; comment pouvons-nous le laisser?” La vieille dit: “Allons-y, nous reviendrons tout de suite.” Elles s’en allèrent et firent une promenade ensemble. Le jeune dame dit: “C’est que j’ai un mari tel que je crains que, si je m’éloigne de ses côtés, [il arrive malheur, car] il y a dans ses flancs une chose telle que si quelqu’un la tire, son souffle lui est bientôt enlevé.”

[18] Elles allèrent et alors (litt. cette fois) elles virent au bord de la rivière un bateau qui était sur l'eau. La vieille dit: "Viens, allons ensemble sur ce bateau." Elle, la bonne femme, emmena l'autre sur le bateau, elle enleva l'amarre et elles prirent le large ensemble. Elles prirent le large et elles arrivèrent à un endroit, [où] elles virent que mille personnes portèrent au roi la nouvelle que [la vieille] avait amené la fille des fées.

[19] Elle (?) l'emmena dans sa maison. Quelqu'un vint dire que la vieille avait amené la fille des fées. [Le roi] dit: "Amenez-la." On l'amena et on la donna à ce roi. Elle dit: "J'ai un mari, comment pouvez-vous faire (litt. faites-vous) une telle chose?" Il dit: "A présent qu'as-tu à faire de ce mari?" Alors donc on la lui donna. Et moi je suis partie de là et je ne sais pas ce qu'ils ont fait. Voilà, c'est tout, oui.

SUMMARY

Since our first meeting at Tehran University's Faculty of Letters almost fifty years ago, Iraj Afshar and I have never ceased to entertain a friendly exchange of information and publications. I here dedicate to him a modest fruit of one of my dialectological field trips in Iran as a token of fond memories. It is a folk tale recorded in 1963 in the village of Gīv, located a few dozen kilometers to the south of Bīrjand. As a specimen of the local language a form of Khorasanian Persian—it exhibits a number of peculiarities, some of which, interestingly, are already found in prose texts of the preclassical period of Persian literature.

Persian Printing and Publishing in England in the 17th Century

Geoffrey Roper

THE ORIGINS AND EARLY DEVELOPMENT OF PERSIAN printing in England, as elsewhere, are inseparable from those of Arabic printing. A general survey of the latter has been given in an earlier article,[1] and the purpose here is to consider further the earliest attempts at printing Persian texts, and the introduction of specifically Persian type-forms. This in turn is of course closely linked with the development of Persian studies in Britain and the rest of Europe, which was the subject of an important survey by the celebrated dedicatee of this volume.[2]

The first English scholar to make serious attempts to include texts in the Arabic script in his publications was the celebrated 17th-century jurist and antiquary John Selden (1584–1654). In 1614 he published a treatise called *Titles of honor* in which he introduced a number of "Words of the Eastern tongues," apparently engraved on wood-blocks inserted into the lines of type. These were mostly crude and malformed, with incorrect ligatures and letter-forms. One of the titles is given as "*Firistājanī* [presumably a mistake for *Firistagānī*] = *Prestigiani*, that is, in Persian, *Apostolique*," and this seems to be the first Persian word to appear, in script, in an English publication. All the words were repeated in an index at the end (Fig. 1). The printer was William Stansby of London who produced a second edition in 1631, using slightly larger blocks, with a few improvements and some extra titles, including *Bādishāh*, *Mīrzā* and *Shāh*.[3]

Meanwhile, in 1625 the same printer produced a four-volume set of the famous compendium of travel literature by Samuel Purchas, *Purchas his pilgrimes*.[4] The first volume included a table of exotic alphabets, "cut in Brasse or Wood," one of which is "Persian,"[5] but its somewhat grotesque and mis-shapen Arabic letters do not include any specifically Persian ones. Further on,

[1] Roper 1985.
[2] Afshar 1970; see also Arberry 1942, Dresden 1968 and Ṭāhiri 1974.
[3] Selden 1631, 66, 104, 108–9.
[4] Purchas 1625.
[5] Ibid., 1:185.

however, is a much better engraved reproduction of a Mughal seal, with Persian names within circular panels, in a recognizable *nasta'līq*.[6]

The first use of Arabic movable metal types in England was also by Stansby for Selden in 1635,[7] but the main impetus for scholarly publishing in non-European languages came from William Laud (1573–1645), who was both Archbishop of Canterbury and Chancellor of the University of Oxford. He ordered the acquisition of punches and matrices for Arabic types from Leiden in the Netherlands. These were all, of course, in the *naskh* style of script; Persian *nasta'līq* was beyond the capabilities for the early punch-cutters, even if the level of demand had warranted it. A number of these new types were what is known as "portmanteau" sorts, which include all the possible dots, leaving the printer to file off some of them, as required, to create types for letters such as *b, t, n, j, kh*, etc.[8] This obviously unsatisfactory practice was the bugbear of Arabic and Persian typography in 17th-century England and elsewhere. On the other hand, its flexibility allowed the cutting and casting of Persian letters, with extra dots, which might otherwise have been uneconomic in relation to the level of demand.

The first use of types cast from these matrices was by the Oxford scholar John Greaves (1602–52) who was one of the first two Englishmen to make a serious study of Persian. About 1640 he wrote a Persian grammar, but was frustrated to find that he could not get it published for lack of types.[9] He was, however, a mathematician and astronomer as well as being an Orientalist, and in 1643 was appointed Savilian Professor of Astronomy at Oxford. In the ensuing years, despite being ejected from his chair during the Civil War, he completed and prepared for publication a work on astronomy by his predecessor, John Bainbridge, and to it he appended the text of the astronomical observations of the Persian astronomer Ulugh Beg. This was the first printing in Oxford using Arabic types, and was executed by the University printer Henry Hall.[10] It does not appear to use any specifically Persian sorts; but another text edited and published by Greaves the same year did include the letters *ch* and *p*. In order to obtain them, he had in January 1648 borrowed the University's Arabic matrices, and volunteered to have their defects remedied. He took them

[6] Ibid., 3:591.

[7] Roper 1985, 13.

[8] Morison 1967, 241. Morison's observations are based on an examination of the original punches.

[9] Greaves 1649, f.A2 (Dedication to Selden): "Nonus annus agitur . . . ex quo haec Rudimenta Linguae Persicae in publicam lucem edere in animam induxeram. Sed typis destitutus. . . eum laborem differendum judicavi"; see also Birch 1737, xxxiii; Arberry 1942, 10; and Reed 1952, 59.

[10] Bainbridge and Greaves 1648; cf. Madan 1895–1931, 2:474–5.

to London, had new matrices made for some defective letters (and for the Persian ones), and then had a new font cast (or, probably, more than one),[11] including a new set of Arabic/Persian numerals (the Fig. 4 is the Persian shape).

These Arabic/Persian types were then used by the London printers Miles Flesher and his son James Flesher[12] to print five Persian books written or edited by Greaves, including two tables of longitude and latitude (*zīj*) by Naṣīr al-Dīn Ṭūsī and Ulugh Beg, which were published in 1648.[13] In the same year appeared his long-delayed Persian grammar, *Elementa Linguæ Persicæ*, dated 1649[14] and printed by James Flesher, which exhibits a full Persian alphabet (Fig. 2). To it was appended *Anonymus Persa De siglis Arabum & Persarum astronomicis*,[15] dated 1648 and printed by Miles Flesher. Then in 1650 Greaves went on to publish yet another Persian astronomical text, that of Maḥmūd Shāh Khuljī,[16] and also yet more from Ulugh Beg: *Maqālah dar ma'rifah-i tavārīkh.*[17] This latter, dedicated to the Venetian Republic (perhaps as an oblique gesture to the new republican regime in England), was his most substantial Persian text, consisting of 52 pages (not including the facing Latin translation). Like the grammar, it uses the full alphabet, including *p*, *ch*, and *g* (three dots); but there are some curiously solecistic typographical features such as the substitution of an undotted isolated *q* for *v*, and, most incongruous of all, the separation of the initial *ch* of the word *chūn*, which starts the text, and its enclosure in a decorative foliated panel in the manner of European-language printing of the period. Both these 1650 publications were also printed in London by James Flesher, still using types from the Oxford/Leiden matrices. Greaves died two years later, in 1652.

The 1650s—the republican period—were somewhat fallow years for Oxford scholarship. Little appeared there in Oriental languages during this time, and nothing, as far as can be ascertained, in Persian. But after the restoration of the monarchy in 1660, another Oxford Orientalist, Thomas Hyde (1636–1703), composed a number of Persian verses which he contributed to

[11] Hart [1900] 1970, 182.

[12] For information about them, see Plomer 1907, 75–6.

[13] Ṭūsī 1648. There is no printer's name on this book, but it can hardly have been anyone but Flesher.

[14] Greaves 1649; Birch 1737, xxxiii: "In 1649 [or rather 1648, the Printers usually anticipating part of the following year], he had published at London in 4to, *Elementa Linguae Persicae* . . . he propos'd to have published it nine years before, but wanting type . . . he had been obliged to suspend the edition"; cf. Arberry 1942, 10; Carter 1970, 39.

[15] According to Birch (1737, xxxiv), Greaves had himself met the anonymous author of this work in İstanbul in 1638.

[16] Khuljī 1650 (Birch 1737 erroneously dates it 1652).

[17] Ulugh Beg 1650.

the frequent volumes of poems published to celebrate royal occasions.[18] These made use of the same basic Leiden font, but with a number of extra sorts for Persian which may possibly have been cut and cast by De Walpergen, a type-founder employed by Bishop Fell, the great promoter of University printing in Oxford after the Restoration.[19] Among his plans was an edition of *The History of Tamerlan* in Persian, but this seems never to have been published.[20] However, one authority suggests that these additional types may have been made for Hyde in London before the establishment of the Oxford foundry.[21] However that may be, they appear in *A specimen of several sorts of letters given to the University by Dr. John Fell*,[22] which includes "A supplement to the Arabick alphabet, to print any thing in the Persian, Turkish, and Malayan languages" (Fig. 3). They include *p*, *ch*, *zh*, *g* (with three dots) and *h* with *hamzah*. Some of them, however, especially the initial *p*, are poorly cut and of a clumsy and disjointed appearance. In addition to the royal poems, Hyde also published in 1665 an edition of the tables of longitude and latitude by Ulugh Beg called *Jadāvil-i mavāẓī'-i ṣavābit dar ṭūl va 'arẓ*,[23] in which these types were used by Henry Hall, who had earlier printed Greaves's text of Ulugh Beg.

Along with John Greaves, the other founding father of Persian studies in England was the Cambridge scholar Abraham Whelock (1593–1653), a versatile man who was also the University Librarian and held the newly created lectureships of both Arabic and Anglo-Saxon.[24] He translated the Gospels into Persian and saw them through the press in London, where they were published posthumously in 1657.[25] Like most of Greaves's Persian works, they were printed by James Flesher, using the Leiden/Oxford types, with *p* and *ch*, but no *g*. The edition was financed by Sir Thomas Adams, founder of the Arabic lectureship (later chair) in Cambridge.[26]

Whelock was also involved[27] in the early stages of another Biblical edition, the famous London Polyglot of Brian Walton, the first volume of which

[18] For instance, *Domiduca Oxoniensis*, Oxford 1662; *Epicedia Universitatis Oxoniensis*, Oxford 1669; ditto, 1670; ditto, 1671. Cf. Madan 1895–1931, 3:156–8, 239–42, 249–50 (nos. 2578, 2844, 2845 and 2869).

[19] Morison 1967, 72.

[20] Ibid., 39, citing Fell's correspondence.

[21] Hart [1900] 1970, 183.

[22] *Specimen* 1693.

[23] Ulugh Beg 1665.

[24] For information about his life and career, see Oates 1986, 173–246.

[25] Whelock 1657.

[26] Oates 1986, 209.

[27] Todd 1821, 1:49.

was published in 1653, and which was completed in five volumes in 1657. It was printed by Thomas Roycroft (although James Flesher had printed the original prospectus and specimen),[28] and was the first of the great Polyglots to include a Persian text: Pentateuch and Gospels.[29] A new type was cut and cast for this work, and in appearance it is quite different from the Leiden/Oxford type-face, being generally clearer and more elegant in style.[30] It is also larger, of Great Primer size, and is in fact modeled on that of Savary de Brèves,[31] used in the great Paris Polyglot of 1645, which Walton's version was designed to rival. (The Paris Polyglot, however, contained no Persian). The same types were used for Walton's *Introductio ad lectionem linguarum orientalium*, which has a section entitled "Introductio ad lectionem linguae Persicae"[32] in which the full font is used, including *p*, *ch*, *zh*, and *g* (with three dots). They also appear in *Sol Angliae oriens auspiciis Caroli II regum gloriosissimi*,[33] a volume of odes to celebrate the restoration of the monarchy and to ingratiate the Polyglot scholars, previously patronized by Cromwell, with the new King, Charles II. On folios D1v and D2v is a "Carmen Persicum" (Fig. 4) in which Charles is hailed as *Pādishāh bā Injilīsistān*. This volume was likewise printed by Roycroft who was rewarded by being appointed as the King's printer in the Oriental languages.[34]

The editor of this latter volume was another Cambridge scholar, Edmund Castell (1606–85), his magnum opus was the great *Lexicon heptaglotton*,[35] a dictionary of seven languages, including Persian, using the Polyglot types. The Persian section, attributed to the great Dutch scholar Jacobus Golius along with Castell, displays a full alphabet, including *g* (with three dots). In Cambridge itself, Arabic printing came rather late, and the first Persian text to appear, as far as can be ascertained, was a "Carmen Persicum" by C. Wright, included in a volume entitled *Academiae Cantabrigiensis carmina*. This was printed in 1702 by the University Press, using Arabic types borrowed from the Cambridge printer John Hayes.[36] This 10-line poem was very badly typeset, with wrong letter-forms, and *l* confused with *alif* in a number of places.

[28] Reed 1952, 158.

[29] Darlow and Moule 1903–11, 2:24, no. 1446.

[30] Krek 1971, 20.

[31] French diplomat, Orientalist and typographer, d. 1627. His celebrated Arabic font was acquired by the Imprimerie Royale in Paris.

[32] Walton 1655, 85–95.

[33] Castell 1660.

[34] Plomer 1907, 158.

[35] Castell 1669.

[36] Cf. Forster 1982, 160; McKenzie 1966, 37, 238–9, no. 74.

An apology is also given for the use of Arabic in place of Persian letters, for lack of types.[37] Rather better produced was Simon Ockley's *Introductio ad linguas orientales*,[38] which discusses Persian briefly,[39] and quotes the words *Chān-i Pāk* (using correct Persian letters), which Ockley criticizes as a rendering of "Holy Spirit" in the Polyglot Bible. Both these Cambridge books made use of types modeled, like the Oxford ones, on Dutch originals, and probably of Dutch provenance.[40] But nothing else in Persian, it seems, was printed in Cambridge for the next hundred years or more.

Until the 18th century, the possibilities for printing and publishing Persian texts in England were very restricted, as can be seen from the foregoing survey. This was mainly for economic and financial reasons, since producing the necessary fonts and setting texts with them was expensive. Although there was a growing interest in the study of foreign languages, including Oriental ones, in this period,[41] the demand for Persian texts was still quite low. The universities had no funds to subsidize such editions, and wealthy churchmen, who did sometimes sponsor books in Arabic, for evangelical use among the Arab Christians, or for elucidation of Biblical texts, were generally less interested in Persian. A scholar of substantial private means, like John Greaves, could and did pay to have his works printed, but this was exceptional. Others, like Whelock, could not afford such expense.[42]

In the mid-18th century, however, there was a significant change. The expansion of British commerce and conquest in India brought a substantial new interest in Persian, which was the official and court language of the Mughal empire and many of its successor states. British merchants, administrators and military officers bound for India needed to learn the language, and then to read some of the literature in order to gain a knowledge of the culture of the peoples with whom they had to deal. So there was a new demand for books containing Persian texts, both elementary and for more advanced reading. There was also a new interest in Persian historical works relating to India (and Afghanistan).[43]

[37] "Paucae hic Literae *Persis* propriae (ob defectum Typorum) *Arabicè* pinguntur" - f. Hh1v.

[38] Ockley 1706.

[39] Ibid., 158.

[40] Roper 1985, 20.

[41] Cf. Salmon 1985, passim.

[42] Arberry 1942, 10.

[43] Ibid., 11–7.

This demand was met partly by straightforward commercial publishing, including some in places such as Bristol and Newcastle, outside the established centers of scholarly publishing (London, Oxford, and Cambridge); and partly by the sponsorship of publications by the East India Company itself. This led to the development of new type-faces, including eventually the short-lived *nasta'līq* fonts, which were in turn displaced by Indian and Iranian lithographic texts in the 19th century. But that is another story.

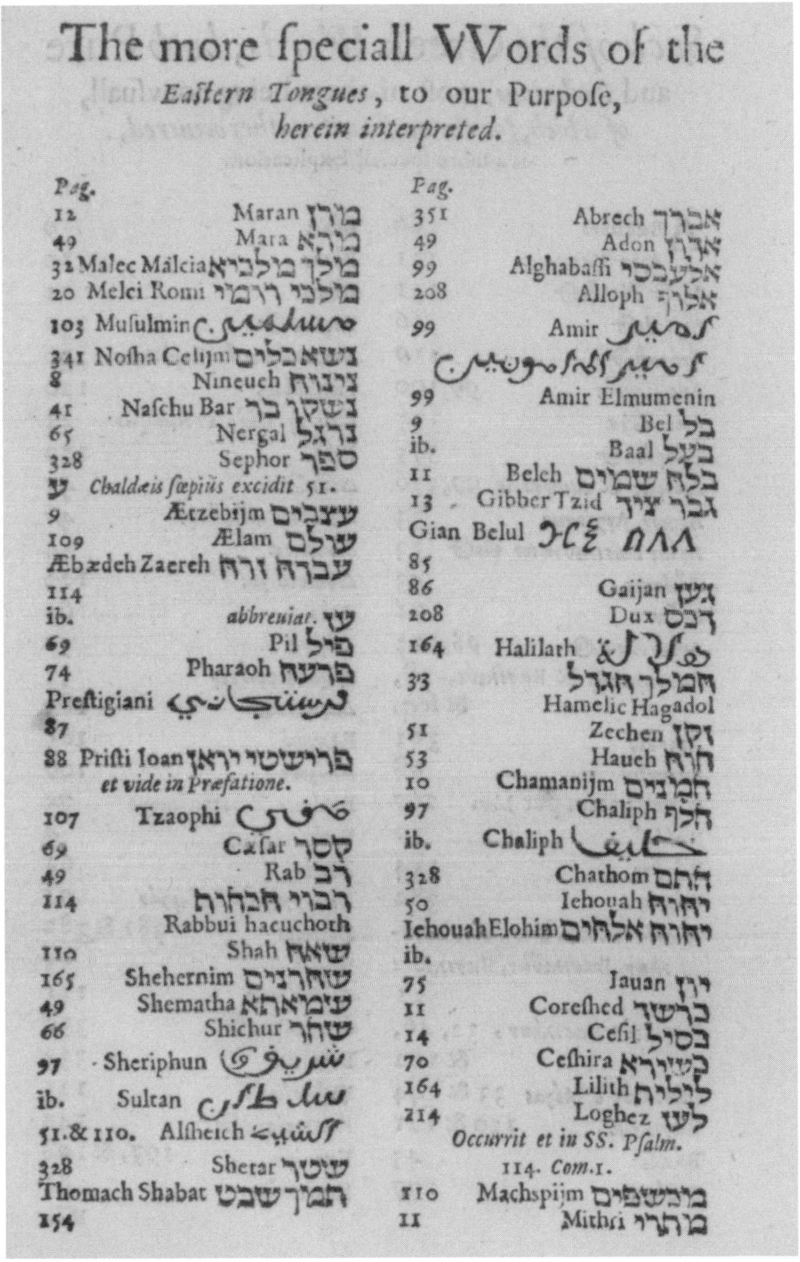

The more speciall VVords of the *Eastern Tongues*, to our Purpose, *herein interpreted.*

Pag.	
12	Maran מרן
49	Mara מרא
32	Malec Málcia מלך מלכיא
20	Melci Romi מלכי רומי
103	Musulmin مسلمين
341	Nosha Celijm נושא כלים
8	Nineueh נינוה
41	Naschu Bar נשקו בר
65	Nergal נרגל
328	Sephor ספר
ע	*Chaldæis sæpius excidit* 51.
9	Æzebijm עצבים
109	Ælam עלם
	Æbædeh Zaereh עבדה זרה
114	
ib.	*abbreuiat.* עז
69	Pil פיל
74	Pharaoh פרעה
	Prestigiani فرستجاني
87	
88	Pristi Ioan פרישטי יואן *et vide in Præfatione.*
107	Tzaophi صوفي
69	Cæsar קסר
49	Rab רב
114	רבוי חבהות Rabbui hacuchoth
110	Shah שאה
165	Shehernim שהרנים
49	Shematha שמאתא
66	Shichur שחור
97	Sheriphun شريف
ib.	Sultan سلطان
51.& 110.	Alsheich الشيخ
328	Shetar שטר
	Thomach Shabat תמך שבת
154	

Pag.	
351	Abrech אברך
49	Adon אדון
99	Alghabassi אלעבבסי
208	Alloph אלוף
99	Amir امير
	امير المومنين
99	Amir Elmumenin
9	Bel בל
ib.	Baal בעל
11	Belch בלח שמים
13	Gibber Tzid גבר ציד
	Gian Belul [illegible]
85	
86	Gaijan גין
208	Dux דכס
164	Halilath
33	המלך הגדל Hamelic Hagadol
51	Zechen זקן
53	Haueh חוה
10	Chamanijm חמנים
97	Chaliph חלף
ib.	Chaliph خليف
328	Chathom חתם
50	Iehouah יהוה
	IehouahElohim יהוה אלהים
ib.	
75	Iauan יון
11	Coreshed כרשד
14	Cesil כסיל
70	Ceshira כשירא
164	Lilith לילית
214	Loghez לעז *Occurrit et in SS. Psalm.* 114. *Com.*1.
110	Machspijm מכשפים
11	Mithri מתרי

Fig. 1. The first Persian word in an English publication: *Firistajānī* (left-hand column, line 18). John Selden. *Titles of honor*, London, 1614, f.Fff2r. Cambridge University Library: Syn.7.61.226. By permission of the Syndics of Cambridge University Library

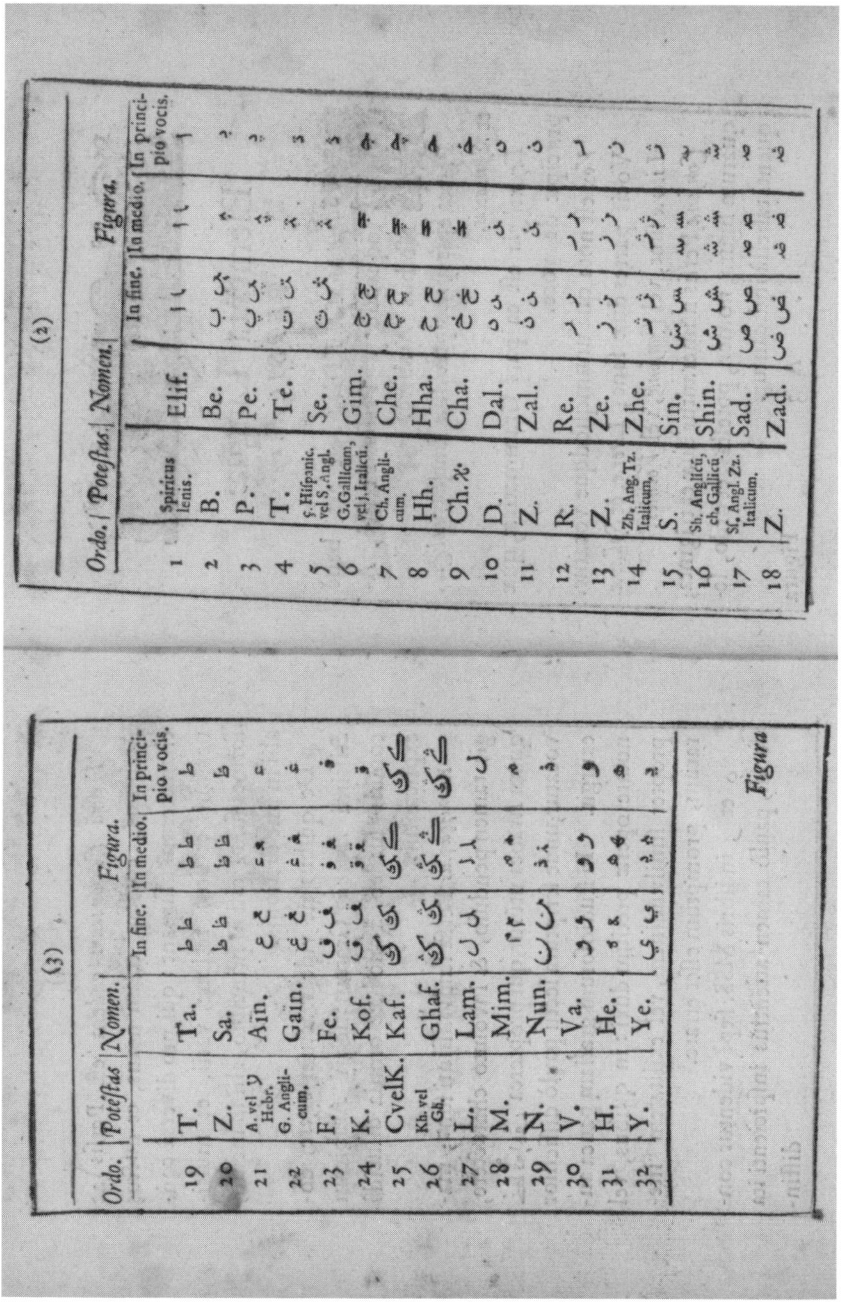

(2)

Ordo.	Potestas.	Nomen.	Figura. In fine.	In medio.	In principio vocis.
1	Spiritus lenis.	Elif.	ا ـا	ـا	ا
2	B.	Be.	ب ـب	ـبـ	بـ
3	P.	Pe.	پ ـپ	ـپـ	پـ
4	T.	Te.	ت ـت	ـتـ	تـ
5	ς. Hispanic. vel S. Angl.	Se.	ث ـث	ـثـ	ثـ
6	G. Gallicum, vel J. Italicū.	Gim.	ج ـج	ـجـ	جـ
7	Ch. Anglicum.	Che.	چ ـچ	ـچـ	چـ
8	Hh.	Hha.	ح ـح	ـحـ	حـ
9	Ch. χ	Cha.	خ ـخ	ـخـ	خـ
10	D.	Dal.	د ـد	ـد	د
11	Z.	Zal.	ذ ـذ	ـذ	ذ
12	R.	Re.	ر ـر	ـر	ر
13	Z.	Ze.	ز ـز	ـز	ز
14	Zh. Ang. Tz. Italicum.	Zhe.	ژ ـژ	ـژ	ژ
15	S.	Sin.	س ـس	ـسـ	سـ
16	Sh. Anglicū, ch. Gallicū	Shin.	ش ـش	ـشـ	شـ
17	Sf. Angl. Zz. Italicum.	Sad.	ص ـص	ـصـ	صـ
18	Z.	Zad.	ض ـض	ـضـ	ضـ

(3)

Ordo.	Potestas.	Nomen.	Figura. In fine.	In medio.	In principio vocis.
19	T.	Ta.	ط ـط	ـطـ	طـ
20	Z.	Sa.	ظ ـظ	ـظـ	ظـ
21	A. vel ע Hebr.	Aïn.	ع ـع	ـعـ	عـ
22	G. Anglicum.	Gaïn.	غ ـغ	ـغـ	غـ
23	F.	Fe.	ف ـف	ـفـ	فـ
24	K.	Kof.	ق ـق	ـقـ	قـ
25	CvelK.	Kaf.	ک ـک	ـکـ	کـ
26	Kh. vel Gh.	Ghaf.	گ ـگ	ـگـ	گـ
27	L.	Lam.	ل ـل	ـلـ	لـ
28	M.	Mim.	م ـم	ـمـ	مـ
29	N.	Nun.	ن ـن	ـنـ	نـ
30	V.	Va.	و ـو	ـو	و
31	H.	He.	ه ـه	ـهـ	هـ
32	Y.	Ye.	ی ـی	ـیـ	یـ

Fig. 2. The Persian alphabet. John Greaves. *Elementa Linguæ Persicæ*, London, 1649 [actually 1648], pp. 2–3. Cambridge University Library: U.19.20. By permission of the Syndics of Cambridge University Library

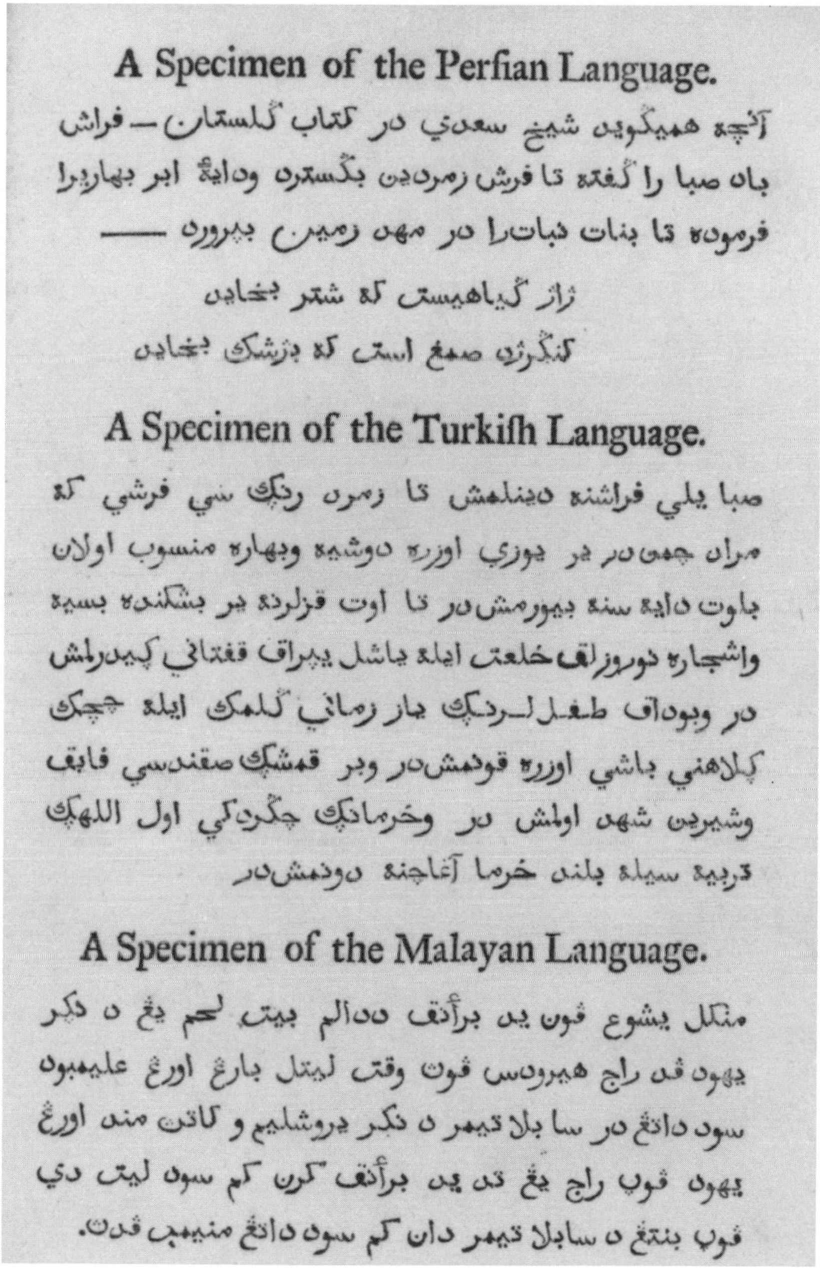

A Specimen of the Perſian Language.

آنچه همیگوید شیخ سعدی در کتاب گلستان — فراش
باد صبا را گفته تا فرش زمردین بگسترد ودایهٔ ابر بهاری را
فرموده تا بنات نبات را در مهد زمین بپرورد ——
زار گیاهیست که شتر بخاید
کنگرش صمغ است که پزشک بخاید

A Specimen of the Turkiſh Language.

صبا یلی فراشنه دینلمش تا زمرد رنگ سنی فرشی که
مران چمن در یر یوزی اورزه دوشیه وبهاره منسوب اولان
بلوت دایه سنه بیورمش در تا اوت قزلرده یر بشکنده بسیه
واشجاره نوروزلق خلعت ایله یاشل یپراق قفتانی کیدرلمش
در وبوداق طفل لـردنک یاز زمانی گلمک ایله چچک
کلاهنی باشی اورزه قونمش در وبر قمشک صقندسی فایق
وشیرین شهد اولمش در وخرمانک چگردکی اول اللهک
دربیه سیله بلند خرما آغاجنه دونمش در

A Specimen of the Malayan Language.

منکل یشوع فون ین برأنق دالم بیت لحم یغ د دکر
یهود فد راج هیرودس فون وقت لیتل بارغ اورغ علیمبون
سوت داتغ در سا بلا تیمر د نکر یروشلیم و کاتن منن اورغ
یهود فوپ راج یغ تد ین برأنق کرن کم سوت لیت دي
فوپ بنتغ د سابلا تیمر دان کم سوت داتغ منیمبه فدن.

Fig. 3. Sample of Persian and other types. *A specimen of several sorts of letters given to the University by Dr. John Fell*, Oxford, 1613, f.d2. Cambridge University Library: Broxbourne.c.39. By permission of the Syndics of Cambridge University Library

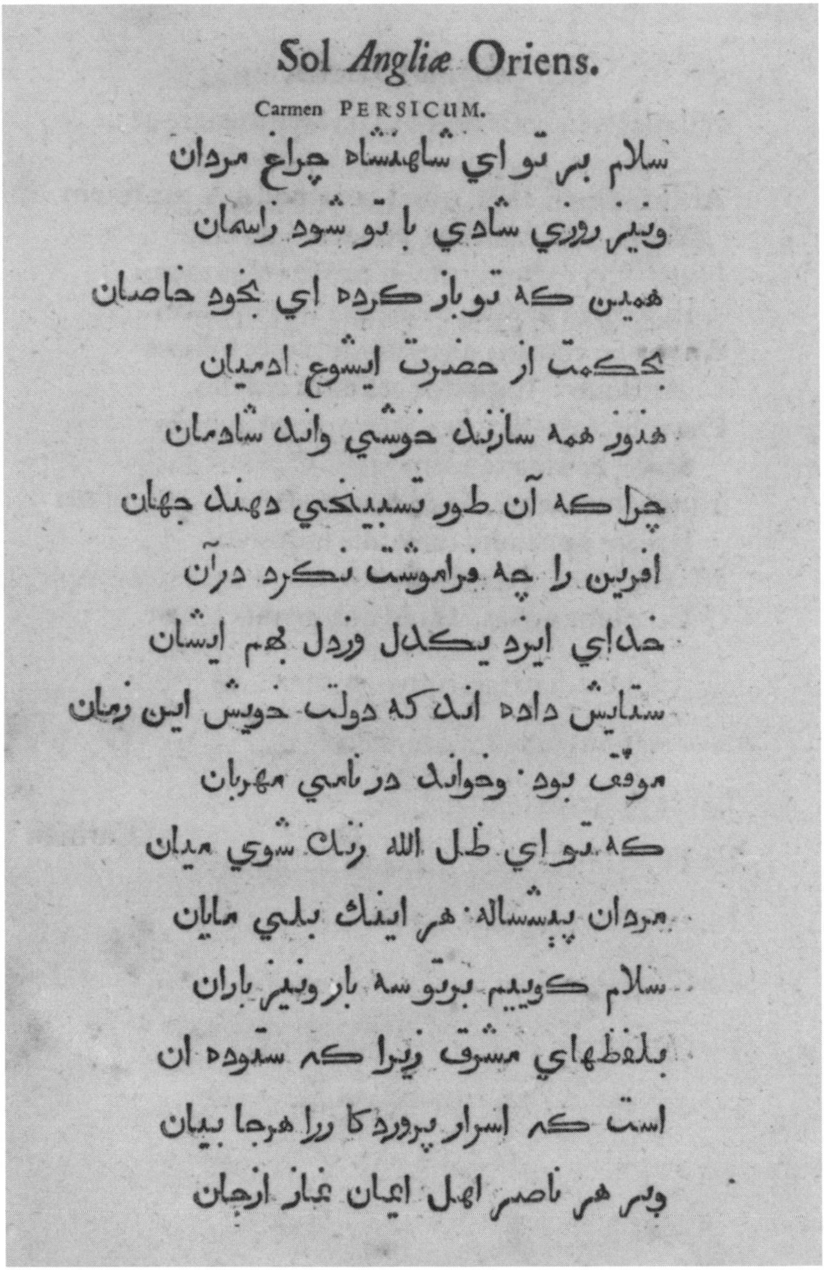

Sol *Angliæ* Oriens.

Carmen PERSICUM.

سلام بر تو اي شاهنشاه چراغ مردان
ونيز روزي شادي با تو شود زاسمان
همين كه تو باز كرده اي بخود خاصان
بحكمت از حضرت ايسوع ادميان
هنوز همه سازند خوشي وانند شادمان
چرا كه آن طور تسبيحي دهند جهان
افرين را چه فراموشت نكرد درآن
خداي ايزد يكدل وزدل بهم ايشان
ستايش داده اند كه دولت خويش اين زمان
موفق بود· وخواند درنامي مهربان
كه تو اي ظل الله زنك شوي ميدان
مردان پيشساله· هر اينك بلبي مايان
سلام كوييم برتو سه بار ونيز باران
بلفظهاي مشرق زيرا كه ستوده ان
است كه اسرار پرورد كا ررا هرجا بيان
وبر هر ناصر اهل ايمان غمار ازجان

Fig. 4. Persian ode to celebrate the restoration of the English monarchy. Thomas Roycroft. *Sol Angliae oriens auspiciis Caroli II regum gloriosissimi*, London, 1660, f.D1v. Cambridge University Library: Broxbourne.d.97. By permission of the Syndics of Cambridge University Library

BIBLIOGRAPHY

AFSHAR, IRAJ. 1970. *Rāhnamā-yi taḥqīqāt-i Īrānī*. Tehran : Markaz-i Barrasī va Mu'arrifī-i Farhang-i Īrān, 1349 Sh.

AHMAD, NAZIR. 1985. *Oriental presses in the world*. Lahore : Qadiria Book Traders.

ARBERRY, ARTHUR J. n.d. *Arabic printing types : a report made to the Monotype Corporation limited*. N.p.

—— 1942. *British contributions to Persian studies*. London, New York : British Council

—— 1948. *The Cambridge school of Arabic*. Cambridge, [England] : University Press.

BAINBRIDGE, JOHN and GREAVES, JOHN. 1648. *Astronomiæ in celeberrima Academia Oxonensi Professoris Saviliani, Canicularia : una cum demonstratione ortus quibus accesserunt, Insigniorum aliquot stellarum longitudines & latitudines, ex astronomicis observationibus Vlug Beigi, Tamerlani Magni nepotis*. Oxford : Henry Hall.

BIRCH, THOMAS. 1737. An historical and critical account of the life and writings of Mr. John Greaves. In *Miscellaneous works of Mr. John Greaves*. Vol. 1, London : J. Hughs for J. Brindley and C. Corbett: i–lxxii.

CARTER, HARRY. 1970. Introduction to *Notes on a century of typography at the University Press, Oxford, 1693–1794*, by Horace Hart. Oxford : Clarendon Press: 1–16, xvi.

CASTELL, EDMUND. 1660. *Sol Angliæ oriens auspiciis Caroli II Regum gloriosissimi*. London : Tho. Roycroft.

—— 1669. *Lexicon heptaglotton : Hebraicum, Chaldaicum, Syriacum, Samaritanum, Aethiopicum, Arabicum, conjunctim, et Persicum, separatim*. London : Thomas Roycroft.

DARLOW, T. H. and MOULE, H. F. 1903–11. *Historical catalogue of the printed editions of Holy Scripture in the Library of the British and Foreign Bible Society*. 2 vols. London : The Bible House.

DRESDEN, MARK J. 1968. Survey of the history of Iranian studies. *Handbuch der Orientalistik* I, i, 4/2: 168–90.

FORSTER, H. 1982. The rise and fall of the Cambridge muses (1603–1763). *Transactions of the Cambridge Bibliographical Society* 8, no. 2: 141–72.

GREAVES, JOHN. 1649. *Elementa linguæ Persicæ*. London : Jacob Flesher.

HART, HORACE. [1900] 1970. *Notes on a century of typography at the University Press, Oxford, 1693–1794*. Reprint with introd. and notes by Harry Carter, Oxford : Clarendon Press.

KHULJĪ, MAḤMŪD SHĀH. 1650. *Astronomica quædam ex traditione Shah Cholgii Persae : una cum hypothesibus planetarum*. London : Jacob Flesher.

KREK, M. 1971. *Typographia Arabica : the development of Arabic printing as illustrated by Arabic type specimens : exhibition held at the Rapaporte Treasure Hall*. Waltham [USA] : [Brandeis University Library].

McKENZIE, D.F. 1966. *The Cambridge University Press 1692–1712 : a bibliographical study*. Cambridge, [England] : Cambridge University Press.

MADAN, FALCONER. 1895–1931. *Oxford books : a bibliography of printed works relating to the University and city of Oxford or printed or published there.* 3 vols. Oxford : Clarendon Press.

MORISON, STANLEY. 1967. *John Fell, the University Press, and the 'Fell' types.* Oxford : Clarendon Press.

OATES, J. C. T. 1986. *Cambridge University Library : a history from the beginnings to the Copyright Act of Queen Anne.* Cambridge, [England], New York : Cambridge University Press.

OCKLEY, SIMON. 1706. *Simonis Ockleii Introductio ad linguas orientales.* Cambridge, [England] : John Owen.

PLOMER, HENRY R. 1907. *A dictionary of the booksellers and printers who were at work in England, Scotland and Ireland from 1641 to 1667.* London : Bibliographical Society.

PURCHAS, SAMUEL. 1625. *Purchas his pilgrimes.* 4 vols. London : William Stansby for Henrie Fetherstone.

REED, TALBOT BAINES. 1952. *A history of the old English letter foundries : with notes, historical and bibliographical, on the rise and progress of English typography.* New ed. revised and enlarged by A. F. Johnson. London : Faber and Faber.

ROPER, GEOFFREY. 1985. Arabic printing and publishing in England before 1820. *British Society for Middle Eastern Studies bulletin* 12, no. 1 (winter): 12–32.

SALMON,V. 1985. The study of foreign languages in seventeenth-century England. *Histoire, épistémologie, langage* 7, no. 2: 45–70.

SELDEN, JOHN. 1614. *Titles of honor.* London : William Stansby.

—— 1631. *Titles of honor.* 2nd ed. London : William Stansby.

A specimen of several sorts of letters given to the University by Dr. John Fell. 1613. Oxford : The Theater.

ṬĀHIRĪ, ABŪ AL-QĀSIM. 1974. *Sayr-i farhang-i Īrān dar Birītāniyā, yā, Tārīkh-i divīst sālah-'i muṭāla'āt-i Īrānī.* Tehran : Anjuman-i Āṣār-i Millī, Isfand 1352 Sh.

TODD, HENRY JOHN. 1821. *Memoirs of the life and writings of the Right Rev. Brian Walton.* 2 vols. London : F. C. & J. Rivington, et al.

ṬŪSĪ, NAṢĪR AL-DĪN MUḤAMMAD. 1648. *Binæ tabulæ geographicæ : una Nassir Eddini Persæ altera Vlug Beigi Tatari.* London : n.p.

ULUGH BEG. 1650. *Epochæ celebriores, astronomis, historicis, chronologis, Chataiorom, Syro-Græcorum, Arabum, Persarum, Chorasmiorum, usitatae : ex traditione Ulug Beigi.* London : Jacob Flesher.

—— 1665. *Tabulae long. ac lat. stellarum fixarum ex observatione Ulugh Beighi : Ex Tribus invicem collatis mss. Persicis jam primum luce ac Latino donavit.* Oxford : H. Hall.

WALTON, BRIAN. 1655. *Introductio ad lectionem linguarum orientalium : hebraicæ, chaldaicæ, samaritanæ, syriacæ, arabicæ, persicæ, æthiopicæ, armenæ, coptæ ...* London : Tho. Roycroft.

WHELOCK, ABRAHAM. 1657. *Quatuor Evangeliorum . . . versio Persica.* London : n.p.

The Waning of Indo-Persian Lexicography : Examples from Some Rare Books and Manuscripts of the Subcontinent

John R. Perry *

AS IS WELL KNOWN, FROM AT LEAST THE 10TH/16TH UP TO the 13th/19th centuries, the most numerous and voluminous Persian dictionaries were compiled in the Indian subcontinent. Classics such as the *Farhang-i Jahāngīrī* (1017/1608–9) and the *Burhān-i qāṭi'* (1062/1652) by emigrants from Iran, the *Sharaf'nāmah-i Manyarī* (ca. 877/1472) and the *Mu'ayyid al-fuẓalā'* (925/1519) by native Muslims, and the *Bahār-i 'Ajam* (1152/1739–40) and several other brilliant works of lexicography and lexicology by the Hindu scholar Lālā Rāy Ṭēk Chand Bahār (d. 1180/1766) established the reputation of Indo-Persian linguistic scholarship in Iran and throughout the eastern Islamic ecumene. The Delhi Sultans, the Mughals and their vassals, and in turn the British, who staffed their civil service on the basis of examinations in the Persian classics, all patronized Persian lexicography and dictionaries to or from Arabic, Turkish, Sanskrit, Urdu, Hindi and other languages. Two important dictionaries by Indians, each of which ran through several editions, the Persian *Shams al lughāt* of 1220/1806 and the Arabic-Persian *Muntahá al-'arab fī lughāt al-'Arab* (first printed between 1252/1836 and 1257/1841), owed their genesis, editing and/or printing to British and European orientalists. All such works used Persian as the linchpin, i.e., the usual source or target language in these combinations, and in other cases the medium of marginal gloss and commentary.

By the latter part of the 13th/19th century, Persianate lexicography had become an Indian cottage industry, and in educated court circles (which had been growing in number) virtually an obsession. Amateur poets and antiquarians of all classes burned the midnight oil compiling glossaries and lexicons, with or without patronage; almost every library in India and Pakistan, from Madras to Hyderabad, Lahore to Peshawar, preserves several of these minor

* I would like to acknowledge my gratitude for research awards from the American Institute of Indian Studies in 1990, and the American Institute of Pakistan Studies in 1995, which enabled me to examine manuscripts and books mentioned here.

works in manuscript (often anonymous, if the first and last pages are missing), their prefaces proclaiming "I always wanted to write a dictionary of X," or "Since the existing dictionaries of X are in various ways inadequate . . ."

In the same period, however, great changes were under way in the fabric of traditional Indian society. Persian was no longer a living language in north India, a fact acknowledged when the British Raj changed the language of government administration from Persian to Urdu in 1837. Persianate Muslim hereditary rulers, dependent now on an alien Christian overlord (especially after being forced to take sides in the "mutiny" of 1857) and jostled by the aspirations of Hindu subjects, began to see themselves as enlightened and progressive. Their scholarly *protégés* naturally tended to follow (in some cases, to lead) this trend toward imitation of British attitudes and techniques and relaxation of the more stringent social and cultural traditions associated with a dominant Islam. Literary reform, political self-assertion, economic and social modernization, women's emancipation (through education) were in the air. These and other intimations of the 20th century are to be found reflected in the authorship, form, and content of some of the dictionaries of the period, at the same time as strictly Persian lexicography was giving way to that of Urdu and other vernaculars.

The traditional arrangement of a Persian or Arabic-Persian dictionary, as established by the middle of the 13th/19th century, was one of three kinds: alphabetical by the final letter of the word (an approximate rhyming dictionary), or alphabetical by initial with or without alphabetical ordering of the second and subsequent letters, or alphabetical by initial but subcategorized alphabetically by the final, and sometimes further by the penultimate, letter of the entry. This last arrangement, which provides the best of both worlds (alphabet-initial for ready reference, and alphabet-final within this scheme, for use as a rhyming dictionary), became the most popular form for Persian and Arabic dictionaries in the 12th/18th and 13th/19th centuries.[1] Whichever ordering was chosen, the subcategorization of lemmata by one or more of the hierarchy *kitāb*, *bāb*, *faṣl* (in later Indian usage, often *ma'a* or *bā* "with" for the second-order lemma) was explicitly stated in often cryptic pseudo-Arabic for each descent, e.g., *bāb al-dāl al-mu'ajjamah, faṣl/ma'a al-taḥtānī: ẕimmī*, etc.

In 1314/1896–7 Shaykh Nūr al-Dīn Muḥammad Yūsuf Ḥakīm of Hyderabad, resident in Allahabad, completed his *Qisṭās al-lughah*, a massive three-volume monolingual Persian dictionary preserved in manuscript in the

[1] Cf. Perry 1993, 250–2, 255.

Asafiyeh Library.[2] The first volume is embellished with a painting of the author, sitting on his porch with a book and a hookah; the last volume ends abruptly at the beginning of the letter *nūn*. In the preface the compiler reveals that he spent three years with Christians (*dar ṣuḥbat-i Tarsāyān*) and learned a good deal, especially from a certain *Farhang-i Pārsī-i Jān*, i.e., Francis Johnson's *A dictionary [of] Persian, Arabic, and English*, published under the auspices of the East India Company in 1852. This work, a revision of John Richardson's dictionary of 1777–80, and in its turn a model for Steingass' Persian-English dictionary of 1892, was in content solidly within the Indo-Persian tradition, its main sources being the *Burhān-i qāṭi'*, the *Haft qulzum* (1229–30/1814–5), and the Persian literary classics.[3] In structure, of course, it followed strictly the alphabetical-by-initial ordering long standard in Europe. This feature was a revelation for the Shaykh, who criticizes at length the overdetermined *bāb*-and-*faṣl* lemmatization of traditional Persian dictionaries for being inefficient and user-unfriendly, and arranges his own work in strict alphabetical order, in two columns, with end-stopped entries and vowelling with diacritical *ḥarakāt*.

Against this momentous innovation must be set the prolixity of the bulky *Qisṭās* (1,686 pages), which is taken up not by citations and source references but by redundant rewording of idioms and Rabelesian lists of *iẓāfah* compounds; it is not, in fact, a very good dictionary. Admittedly, too, the principle of alphabet-initial ordering had been accepted since the *Burhān-i qāṭi'* and had increased during the past century; however, even works which used the system (including the Persian-Arabic-Urdu *Karīm al-lughāt* of 1277/1860–1, and the widely respected Persian citation dictionary *Farhang-i Ānandraj* of Muḥammad Pādshāh, completed and published a few years before the *Qisṭās*, and which also used Johnson) still retained the now redundant announcements of category and the analogical description of vowel patterns. Nūr al-Dīn Ḥakīm, though his work remains unpublished, must nevertheless be credited with first articulating the transition from *bāb* and *faṣl* to the Western method of automatic alphabet-initial ordering which was now *de facto* established.

The most striking example of a princely patron's personally setting the tone and pace for a modernizing literature and lexicography is to be seen in Shāh Jahān Begam, Nawab of Bhopal from 1868 to 1901. The princely state of Bhopal was founded in 1723 by an Afghan adventurer, Dūst Muḥammad

[2] Government Oriental Manuscript Library, Hyderabad, MS 117–9; see Naqvī 1962, 244–6.

[3] For criticism, see Blochman 1868, 41–2; the rest of Blochman's article is a useful, comprehensive, and critical account of Indo-Persian lexicography.

Khān. From 1844 to 1926 it was ruled by three well-educated and strong-willed women, each of whom distinguished herself by loyalty to the British, administrative skill, enthusiasm for public works and social legislation, and literary output. Sikandar Begam (r. 1844–68) reformed the tax system and the police; she appeared in public unveiled and in masculine attire, built the biggest mosque in India, and published an account of her pilgrimage to Mecca in 1863–4. Her daughter Shāh Jahān Begam took after her; her first husband once wounded her with his sword for transgressing purdah, and after his death in 1867 she openly dispensed with the veil. After her second marriage in 1869 to a conservative *mullā*, Sayyid Muḥammad Ṣiddīq Ḥasan Khān (who was styled honorary nawab, and in some histories is wrongly identified as the ruler of Bhopal), she observed purdah. Her consort, the author of some influential religious treatises, was formally degraded by the British on charges of being a Wahhābī and uttering anti-British sentiments—to the annoyance of Shāh Jahān Begam, and perhaps with the connivance of her daughter, who later ruled as Sulṭān Jahān Begam (1901–26). Whatever the truth, mother and daughter were estranged from then on, a situation acknowledged (but not explained) in Sulṭān Jahān Begam's otherwise flattering biography of her mother.[4]

Shāh Jahān Begam used the three printing presses established in Bhopal, and the assistance of the abundant literary and scholarly talent assembled at her court, to publish two *dīvāns* of Urdu poetry, a history of Bhopal, a women's encyclopedia (the *Tahẕīb al-nisvān va tarbiyat al-insān)*, and a six-language dictionary, the *Khazānat al-lughāt*. The latter work, lithographed in two folio-size volumes (1,310 pages) in 1304/1886–7 and surviving in only two copies known to me (at Bhopal and Peshawar), displays its entries in individual cells in six columns per page, in the sequence Urdu, Persian, Arabic, Sanskrit, English, and Turkish. The Urdu, Persian, and Ottoman Turkish words are written in *nasta'līq* and the Arabic in *naskh*; the Sanskrit entries are in *devanagari* and the English in cursive Latin characters, but each is additionally transcribed into Urdu characters. The ordering of the Urdu keywords is alphabet-initial, though retaining the redundant lemmatization into *bāb* for the initial and *bā* to introduce the second letter. Roughly 12,700 Urdu keywords and phrases, and their appropriate equivalents or brief glosses (a total of over 76,000 entries), are given without citations; there are frequent supplementary glosses in Persian (see below), and the occasional reference to Arabic or Persian dictionaries (the *Qāmūs* of Fīrūzābādī and the *Bahār-i 'Ajam*). The principal source for the Urdu, Persian and Arabic entries (co-compiled by one Sayyid Ẕū al-Faqār Aḥmad) appears to have been the *Nafā'is al-lughāt* of

[4] See Sultān Jahān Begam 1926; Ashfaq Ali 1981, 50–90.

Awḥad al-Dīn Bilgrāmī, the first Urdu-to-Persian and Arabic dictionary, which was compiled in 1253/1837–8 and circulated in manuscript until printed at Lucknow in 1315/1897; some sixty percent of the Urdu vocabulary in this work is of Persian or Perso-Arabic provenance.[5]

What was the purpose of such a largely vicarious *tour de force*, and how did it fit into the tradition of Persianate lexicography at this critical period? According to the English preface of Navrosji Hormasji, B.A. (there is of course a similar preface in each of the other five languages), the "Treasury of Words," with its unusual format and Urdu transcription ("Persian characters"), is "the first work of its kind published in India." It includes "many words expressive of Mohammedan customs and manners which cannot be rendered otherwise than by explaining them," and should also be useful "especially to philologists, as it will enable them to mark the resemblance of words and the changes they seem to have undergone in the different languages."[6] Let us accordingly sample the work's features under the rubrics of form, vernacular and cross-cultural vocabulary, women's vocabulary, and interlingual comparison and communication.[7]

The idea of a multi-language dictionary and the "spreadsheet" format are not in themselves original to the *Khazānah*. Edmund Castell's *Lexicon Heptaglotton* of 1669 had glossed six Semitic languages together, and Persian separately, in a similar columnar format. The same grid pattern (six columns per page) was later used by Muḥammad 'Abd al-Majīd in the *Muntakhab al-nafā'is* (printed at Cawnpore, 1338/1920), for Urdu, Persian, and Arabic equivalents, though still adorned with the redundant *bāb–bā* lemmatization.

The cell thereby allotted to an entry is generally insufficient for more than a couple of alternatives or a short phrase (a fact noted by Mr. Hormasji). The *Muntakhab al-nafā'is* solves this problem with the time-honored expedient of a marginal commentary; the *Khazānah* confines itself to ad hoc interlinear glosses or footnotes, most of which distinguish etymology and usage, and indeed provide valuable asides on local Islamic customs. One of the longest and most detailed, incorporating commentary from the *Bahār-i 'Ajam*, supplements the entry on Urdu *mīrzā* or *mirzā* with diachronic and sociolinguistic data concerning Persian and Indo-Persian usage.[8] One good

[5] See Naqvī 1962, 234–6, 225–7. In the copy of the *Khazānah* I examined (Islamiya College, no. 1359) the two volumes are bound together, and pp. 149–52 are bound upside down in reverse sequence.

[6] Shāh Jahān Begam 1886–7, 1:548–9.

[7] English glosses beginning with a capital letter ("A prating woman") reproduce direct quotations from the dictionary; those beginning in lower case are my own and in single quotes.

[8] Cf. Perry 1990, 213, 221.

result of the constricting cell is that it has encouraged the compiler to list polysemous words separately. Thus Urdu *'awrat*, Persian s*harmgāh*, Arabic *'awrah*, English "The pudenda," etc., is distinguished from the Urdu-Hindi metonym *'awrat*, Persian *zan*, Arabic *imra'ah*, English "A woman," etc.; Urdu *mastī*, Persian *mastī*, *nashā*, English "Intoxication" is a distinct entry from *mastī*, Persian *ḥālatī kih murghān va dīgar ḥayvānāt-rā vaqt-i hayajān-i shahvat mībāshad*, English "Lust, wantonness", i.e., 'rut,' or 'must,' as later borrowed from Urdu-Hindi.

The careful vowelling with *ḥarakāt* (replacing the longwinded explanations or analogies of earlier dictionaries, and followed in, e.g., the *Muntakhab al-nafā'is*) distinguishes Indian pronunciation of homographs, such as the characteristic elision of the penult in *qadgh̲an*, Persian *qadaghan*, Arabic *ta'kīd*, English "Injunction," Turkish *ta'kid*, *yazâq* (sic; for *yasâq* or *yâsâq*). This entry, however, also demonstrates succinctly that Indian usage is the touchstone for "Persian" glosses, even where they can be distinguished from an "Urdu" homograph. The Turkic word *qadaghan*, originally a neutral 'command, order' with affirmative or negative connotation determined by the context, as a loanword in Persian of Iran and Central Asia has come to mean 'prohibition; forbidden,' whereas the Indo-Persian and subsequently Urdu reflex of this has specialized in the polar opposite direction, that of 'injunction, corroboration, emphasis.' Both senses are reflected in the Turkish glosses, but only the affirmative meanings of Urdu *qadgh̲an* appear in the Arabic, English, Sanskrit (*šāsanā* 'command, edict, decree') and Persian glosses. The interlinear note also implies that the Persian gloss reflects Indian usage: *lughat-i Turkī ba-ma'nī-i ihtimām-i bādshāhān, va dar Fārsī-i Hindī ba-ma'nī-i ta'kīd musta'mal.*

In other cases, a sharp distinction is drawn between the Urdu-Hindi meaning of an Arabic or Persian etymon and its Persian sense—Indo-Persian, to be sure, but sharing the usage of Iran in a more "literary" register than the vernacular Urdu: *'awrat/zan*, mentioned above, is one example. Another is *risālah*, Persian *tīp*, *fawj*, English "A troop of horse," further annotated as *lughat-i 'Arabī-st ba-ma'nī-i payghām, va dar Urdū-yi Hindī ba-ma'nī-i pārah'ī az lashkar kih zīr-i farmān-i sipah-sālārī buvad, khvāh dū ṣad khvāh dū hazār.* The word was backformed from *risālah-dār* (the next entry in the *Khazānah*), lit. 'commission-bearer,' an Indian cavalry officer in the British army; this opaque piece of jargon appears to have been re-analyzed by illiterate troopers, on the evidence of their eyes, as 'possessor of a troop,' and the document, *risālah*, promptly unseated its suffix to become a cavalry squadron.

Considerable attention is paid to specifically Indian and Indo-Muslim customs and folklore, and Urdu-Hindi idioms; this may be regarded as typical of early Urdu lexicographers, at pains to distinguish and even celebrate a colorful vernacular. Examples include *Musalmānī*, Persian *khatnah*, Turkish *ṣunnat etmek* (sic; for *sunnat*) "Circumcision"; *na'l*, Persian *sang-i zūr*: *chūb-i kandah ba-shakl-i na'l bāshad kih kushtī'gīrān bar sar va dūsh gardānand, va ba-dīn ma'nī dar Hindī va Fārsī musta'mal ast* (an aid to exercise in the traditional gymnasium or *zūrkhānah*); *khicṛā* (related to *khicṛī* 'kedgeree'), Persian *āsh-i 'Āshūrā*: *āshī kih dar 'Āshūrā pazand va bar fuqarā vaqf kunand* (the Turkish equivalent, 'Āshūrā āshi), is similarly explained in the context of pious ritual, whereas the English gloss "A dish made from rice wheat and various sorts of pulse" is merely culinary); *imāmbāṛa*, Persian *Ḥusaynīyah, takyah, ta'ziyah'khānah*, "A building in which the festival of Mohurrum is celebrated"; *fīl-murgh*, Persian (*mākiyān-i/khurūs-i*) *būqalamūn*, "A turkey"; *ḍā'in*, Sanskrit *ḍākinī*, Persian *jigar'khvār*, Turkish *sâḥirah*, "A witch" (glossed in other Indo-Persian dictionaries, usually under the form *jigar'khvārah*, as a woman who can consume children's livers by sheer willpower, and by Platts as an old woman with a reputation for the evil eye); *Turkī tamām hunā*, Persian *Turkī tamām shudan*, "To be humbled," i.e., to be taken down a peg, have one's "Turkishness," or arrogance, squashed); *bhaṛu'ā*, Persian *kus'kish, zan'jalb, qaltabān/qurtaban, qurumsaq, tīr'āvar*: *kasī kih zanān rā ba-mardān rasānad*, "A pimp; a procurer."

In the last example, the compiler may have been piling on the synonyms more for fun than edification. There are other instances of both earthy and innocuous entries or definitions where he, or she, indulges in a display of superfluous erudition: *pād/pādnā*, Persian *gūzīdan, gūz/tīz dādan/zadan*, "Emission of wind downwards; to break wind," etc., is followed by four lines of farting specific to beasts, camels, asses and he-goats. This was clearly inspired by Arabic verbs gleaned from the *Qāmūs*, since the entries for all other languages are simply explicative of these. Similarly derivative of the Arabic entries are a list of twelve gaits (where Persian *kharāmīdan* would have served well in several instances, but is not exploited), and a series of no less than seventeen different terms for types of arrow. It would seem that Her Highness sometimes relaxed her supervision of Sayyid Ẕū al-Faqār Aḥmad.

A cursory examination of the *Khazānah* reveals a number of entries to do with women and their interests, family matters, sexual characteristics and gender roles—enough, I believe, to argue for a consciously feminist perspective on the part of the nominal author, who in her other writings and her personal conduct was a forthright women's liberationist, given the constraints of her milieu. There is the additional fact that women's vocabulary was already an established lexical category in Urdu. Beginning in 1868 the British government offered prizes for authors of "useful works in the vernacular . . . in any branch of science or literature . . . Books suitable for the women of India will be especially acceptable, and well rewarded."[9] Thus stimulated, writers produced works specifically aimed at educating women. These included handbooks of usage, such as the *Hādī al-nisā'* of 1875, a manual of correspondence (*inshā'*) for women by Sayyid Aḥmad Dihlavī, author of the well-known Urdu dictionary *Farhang-i Āṣafīyah*. Sayyid Aḥmad followed this with the popular *Lughāt al-nisā'*, a dictionary of women's words published in 1917 with the help of a subvention from (appropriately enough) Sulṭān Jahān Begam of Bhopal.[10]

Of course, dictionaries by men about women, and dictionaries by women, do not necessarily have anything in common. Shahryār Naqvī to the contrary, the *Khazānah* was not the only, or even the first, Persianate dictionary to be compiled by a woman. The National Museum of Pakistan preserves an interesting manuscript, the *Laṭīf al-lughāt* by Laṭīfah Begam bint Muḥammad Bāqir, written in Bengal about 1720, which bears a note in Urdu by the previous owner (a certain Muẓaffar Ḥasan, prior to 1961) remarking that Indian ladies of two hundred years before were obviously better educated than they are today. Laṭīfah Begam is also the author of the *Jung-i Laṭīfah*, a collection of moral tales in prose and verse.[11] Her dictionary begins with three pages of apparently random Arabic phrases and sayings with literal Persian translations, including the classic of Islamic misogyny *inna kaydakunna 'aẓīm* (Koran 12/28). There follows a glossary of single words of Arabic, Persian, and Turkish provenance into Persian, ordered alphabetically by initial but randomly within this scheme. Definitions are short and in some cases divorced from the intended metaphorical context (e.g., *ẕimma*: *gardan*); there are Indo-Persian shibboleths (*ẕarī'a*: *vasīlah*; *dihqān*: *bādshāh*), and some earthy vernacularisms (*kūn-i kharī*: *aḥmaqī*), but no real sign of a perspective or agenda.

Shāh Jahān Begam includes the following "women's words" in her dictionary: three lines of expressions based on *ultā jānnā* 'to be born feet-first; breech birth'—interesting from a Persian viewpoint here is the use of the non-standard *vāzhūn* and *bāzhgūna* (*zādan*, etc.); *ranḍī*, glossed neutrally in Persian as *zan*, in Arabic as *imra'ah* and English as "A woman," but in Turkish as *orospu* 'whore'—the latter corresponds better with the Hindi-Urdu word, which had been devalued from 'woman' to 'wench' to 'whore'; *buṛhiyā* 'old woman'

[9] Naim 1984, 292–3. (I am indebted to the author for this reference).

[10] The *Lughāt al-nisā'* was reprinted in facsimile in 1988, see Aḥmad Dihlavī [1917] 1988, introd., especially p. 2, for antecedents.

[11] MS "N. M. 1961.1172"; see 'Ārif Nawshāhī 1983, 675.

and the composite *buṛhiyā nihāyat ẓa'īf*, Persian *gandah pīr*, "A decrepit old woman"—here the colorful Persian term, of which the Urdu is merely a gloss, would seem to be the inspiration; *bagvās*, Persian *zan-i bisyār'gū*, "A talkative garrulous woman" and *bagvās-i bīhūda*, Persian *zan-i-bīhūdah'gū va harzah'gū* "A prating woman"; *mardānī*, Persian *mardānah*: *zanī-kih khvud-rā mushābih-i mardān kunad*, "A masculine (woman)" and *mehlā*, Persian *zanānah: kasī-kih ḥarakāt-i zanān kunad va tashābuh ba-zanān paydā kunad*, "Effeminate, womanly," Turkish *pusht*, which is unequivocally a passive homosexual; *nangī*, Persian *zan-i barahnah*, "Naked (a female)", etc.—in each case only the feminine form or adjunct of the adjective is given; *oṛhnī*, Persian *bāshmah*, *bāshūmah*, *bāshām*, *dāmanī*: *chādurī-kih zanān ba-sar andāzand*; *chahārqad*, *chārqad*, "A cloth to cover the head and body of a woman"; *bhiṭnī*, Persian *sar'pistān*, "Nipple"; *pānḍ*, Persian *narūk*: *zanī-kih pistān va shīr nadārad*, "A woman devoid of breasts and milk." Of these, *buṛhiyā*, *bagvās*, *oṛhnī* and *bhiṭnī* later appear in Sayyid Aḥmad's *Lughāt al-nisā'*.

Persian, Sanskrit, and Arabic—the last of which flourished as a medium of Islamic religious and philosophical writing in India during the 13th/19th century, as Persian (prose, at least) declined—were the classical languages appropriate for study by the new Indian scholar-potentate. Of the three modern languages, Urdu was the established vernacular of north India and the Muslim enclaves of the center and south, and the vehicle of poetry and elegant prose, replacing Persian in this function. English was the spoken and written language of the ruling class, of administration and technology, and was soon to be routinely transcribed (in the same system as used in the *Khazānah*) and incorporated wholesale into Urdu as Persian had been. Turkish was the language of the only independent Sunnī Islamic empire, the seat of the caliphate. Where earlier Indo-Muslim lexicographers had preferred to treat Eastern Turkish (Chaghatay), the mother tongue of the Mughal rulers, Western or Ottoman Turkish was now a source of inspiration, patronage and prestige particularly for Hyderabad and Bhopal.[12]

Undoubtedly, a major motive for compiling the dictionary was self-aggrandizement; as demonstrated by the plethora of panegyrics appended to the book (in one of which, by Mawlānā Fidā 'Alī Fārigh, every verse is a chronogram of the date 1304), this weighty work is fundamentally a vanity publication. If, like the *Qisṭās*, it reveals more anticipated shallows than hid-

[12] Among the plaudits received by Shāh Jahān Begam was a firman and a decoration from Sulṭân Abdulhamid, in 1296/1879, to thank her for a contribution to the fund for refugees during the war with Russia, see Sultān Jahān Begam 1926, 299–301.

den depths, it still contains valuable indices both of tradition and transition. Bhopal, it seems, was a staunch outpost of the lexicographical obsession. Shāh Jahān Begam also patronized the *Lughāt-i Shāhjahānī*, an alphabetical Persian-Urdu vocabulary for schoolchildren, compiled in 1295/1878 by Ḥakīm Mawlavī Muḥammad Aḥsan Bilgrāmī; the author asserts in his preface that the traditional *niṣāb*s (rhyming vocabularies, popular in schools of Muslim Asia for almost seven centuries) are a waste of time, and are the reason that Indians do not know proper Persian. The work has remained at Bhopal in manuscript.[13] Finally, the Ḥakīm's pupil Abū al-Naṣr Sayyid ʻAlī Ḥasan Khān Salīm, who was the eldest son of the Begam's second husband Muḥammad Ṣiddīq Ḥasan Khān, produced the *Mavārid al-maṣādir*, a compendium of Arabic and Persian infinitives glossed in Urdu, together with a treatise on transitivity and a list of similes for parts of the beloved's person commonly used in lyric poetry.[14]

The long twilight of Indo-Persian lexicography coincides, happily, with a gradual revival of its Iranian counterpart in the last decades of the Qajar dynasty. Since the first version of Surūrī's celebrated *Majmaʻ al-Furs* of 1008/1599–1600 (written before his visit to India, after which he composed a final version in 1039/1629–30),[15] little of note had been produced in Iran until Riẓā Qulī Khān Hidāyat's *Farhang-i anjuman-ārā-yi Nāṣirī* of 1288/1871. This is a critical but traditional and over-determined work of about 12,000 entries, arranged alphabetically under twenty-four letter-categories called *anjuman*, and extensively supplemented by twelve grammatical and philological essays called *ārāyish* and an appendix of Arabic and Persian phrases with literary citations.[16] Not until the five-volume *Farhang-i Nafīsī* of Nāẓim al-Aṭibbā', completed and updated by 1303 Sh./1924 though not published until 1318–35 Sh./1940–56 (with movable type, and incorporating Latin transcription of keywords), do we have from Iran a modern-style, comprehensive, automatically alphabet-initial dictionary of the vocabulary of Persian literature which uses not only the accumulated lore of Iranian and Indian dictionaries but the Richardson-Johnson-Steingass fusions of the Indo-Persian and orientalist traditions.[17] It is approximately five times as large in scope as its contemporary, the last important Indo-Persian dictionary, the *Farhang-i Niẓām* of Āqā Sayyid

[13] Naqvī 1962, 232–3.

[14] Ibid., 174–6. The work was apparently printed at Agra, in 640 pages, but the date is not given.

[15] Bīnish 1976, pt. 2, 592–3.

[16] See Dabīr Siyāqī 1989, 188–91.

[17] Ibid., 199–201.

Muḥammad ʻAlī Dāʻī al-Islām, lithographed in five volumes at Hyderabad in 1346–58/1927–39.

It has sometimes been regretted that Europe's introduction to Persian language studies came not via the "heartland" of Iran but indirectly, by way of India or the Ottoman Empire or Central Asia in response to the evangelical, commercial or imperial ambitions of particular European countries. All the Persian dictionaries compiled by Europeans from the 15th to the early 20th century focused on the Iranized periphery (with the exception of Ange de Saint Joseph's *Gazophylacium* of 1684, researched in Iṣfahān). It might similarly be argued that, without the direct colonial-imperial presence that in India, especially, encouraged lexicography by both natives and foreigners—and with the mainly one-way brain drain from Iran to India—Iranian scholars were long denied the advantage of cross-fertilization by Indian and European lexicology during this same period of activity. If they retrieved the baton late in the race, however, they are certainly keeping up the pace.

BIBLIOGRAPHY

AḤMAD DIHLAVĪ. [1917] 1988. *Lug̲hatunnisā'*. Reprint, Lahore : Maqbūl Ikaiḍamī.

'ĀRIF NAWSHĀHĪ. 1983. *Fihrist-i nuskhah'hā-yi khaṭṭī-i Fārsī-i Mūzih-i Millī-i Pākistān, Karāchī.* Lahore : Markaz-i Taḥqīqāt-i Fārsī-i Īrān va Pākistān, 1362 Sh.

ASHFAQ ALI. 1981. *Bhopal, past and present : a brief history of Bhopal from the hoary past up to the present time.* Bhopal : Jai Bharat Pub. House ; New Delhi : D. K. Publishers Distributors.

BĪNISH, TAQĪ. 1976. Ravish-i taṣḥīḥ-i mutūn-i Fārsī. *Nashrīyah-'i Dānishkadah-'i Adabīyāt va 'Ulūm-i Insānī* 27: nos. 115 (pāyīz 1354 Sh.): 390–426; 116 (zamistān 1354 Sh.): 561–612.

BLOCHMAN, H. 1868. Contributions to Persian Lexicography. *Journal of the Asiatic Society of Bengal* New ser. 37, pt. I, no. 1: 1–72.

DABĪR SIYĀQĪ, MUḤAMMAD. 1989. *Farhang'hā-yi Fārsī va farhang'gūnah'hā.* Tehran : Isparak, 1368 Sh.

NAIM, C. M. 1984. Prize-winning Adab : a study of five Urdu books written in response to the Allahabad Government Gazette Notification. In *Moral conduct and authority : the place of adab in South Asian Islam.* Ed. Barbara Daly Metcalf. Berkeley : University of California Press: 290–314.

NAQVĪ, SHAHRYĀR. 1962. *Farhang'nivīsī-i Fārsī dar Hind va Pākistān.* Tehran : Idārah-'i Kull-i Nigārish-i Vizārat-i Farhang, 1341 Sh.

PERRY, JOHN R. 1990. Mīrzā, Mashtī and Jūja Kabāb : some cases of anomalous noun phrase word order in Persian. In *Persian and Islamic studies in honour of P. W. Avery.* Ed. Charles Melville. Cambridge : University of Cambridge Centre of Middle Eastern Studies: 213–28.

—— 1993. Early Arabic-Persian lexicography : The asāmī and maṣādir genres. *The Arabist* 6–7: 247–60.

SHĀH JAHĀN BEGAM. 1886–7. *Khazānat al-lughāt.* 2 vols. Bhopal : Maṭba'ah-'i Shāhjahānī, 1304.

SULTĀN JAHĀN BEGAM. 1926. *Hayat-i-Shahjehani : life of Her Highness the late Shahjehan Begum of Bhopal.* Bombay : The Times Press.

The Poetics of *Ḥijāb* in the Satire of Īraj Mīrzā

Paul Sprachman

INTRODUCTION

SMADAR LAVIE'S WORK ON INDIGENOUS LITERARY REACTIONS to Israeli and Egyptian occupation of the Sinai inspired the title of this article. If military rule evinces "a poetics," then certainly the notion of *ḥijāb*, or "veil, curtain" of modesty, "barrier" against illicit stares, and, ultimately, a philosophy of selfhood that values intellectuality and spirituality over the sexual aspects of humanity, can generate one also. By yoking politics and poetics, Lavie was exploring the function of allegory in the poetry of an occupied people, the Mzeina Bedouin of Sinai. Lavie found that the Mzeina allegories conjoined local storytelling and the politics of neocolonialism.[1] This article argues that *ḥijāb* became a lively metonym in Īraj Mīrzā's long satirical poem, *'Ārifnāmah* (composed in 1339/1921), in the same way that Mzeina narrative poeticized geopolitical forces that shaped the lives of the Mzeina people. Thus *ḥijāb* in Īraj's poem is not simply "veiling," an easy target for the "progressive" and anti-clerical intellectuals of early 20th-century Iran, but also the cause of the predatory homosexuality that, the poet felt, plagued Iran. Īraj's satire also expresses the inherent paradox of *ḥijāb*: namely, that in de-eroticizing the human form it eroticizes it in fresh and unexpected ways.

This comparison, of course, in no way implies that Īraj Mīrzā (1290 or 1–1344/1873 or 4–1926), a great-grandson of the Qajar King Fatḥ 'Alī Shāh (r. 1212–50/1797–1834), was a tribal poet laboring under neocolonial military occupation. He was, on the contrary, the *déclassé* scion of a line of royal poets, who, thanks to the patronage of Brigadier General Ḥasan 'Alī Khān Garrūsī, studied at the Tabrīz Polytechnic, traveled abroad, and eventually became a high-ranking Qajar functionary.[2] His poetry emerged during a pe-

[1] Lavie 1990, 338.

[2] Biographical information comes from two sources: Muḥammad Ja'far Maḥjūb's introduction to Īraj's *Dīvān* (Īraj Mīrzā, 1989, introd., 3–58), which records Īraj's date of birth as Ramaḍān 1290 [1873], and, Āryānpūr (1973, 2:383–4), who gives Ramaḍān 1291 [1874]; Mahdī Mujtahidī (1948, 35), citing Īraj's son, gives 1291. 'Abd al-Ḥusayn Zarrīnkūb (1974, 305) finds the source of Īraj's ribaldry in the alienation he experienced when the princely heaven of Qajar revelry disappeared in the middle class world of Iranian constitutional republicanism. The writer thanks Kambiz Eslami for calling these remarks to his attention.

riod of traditional European expansionism in Central Asia, when Russia and Britain were competing for influence and wealth in an Iran weakened by despotism and corruption.

The critical literature on Īraj has slighted the complexity of his poetic uses of the veil. Studies of Iranian women's emancipation typically group Īraj Mīrzā with his contemporaries 'Ārif of Qazvīn (ca. 1300 Q.–1312 Sh./ca. 1882–1934) and Muḥammad Riẓā 'Ishqī (1312–42/1894–1924) as early champions of women's unveiling.[3] In these studies, Īraj's anti-*ḥijāb*ism appears in citations of his printable poetry, which are presented, for the most part, as *prima facie* evidence of intellectual opposition to the veil in Iran.[4] One of the most detailed views of Īraj in English criticizes him along with 'Ārif and 'Ishqī for reducing the veil to a static abstraction and for ignoring or denying the veil's "cultural, social, and psychological complexity."[5] Here I will argue that these citations of Īraj do not do his anti-*ḥijāb*ism justice. His poetry, especially the *'Ārifnāmah,* is too complex to be reduced to the railing of a "progressive" (some would say WOGish[6]) intellectual against the subjugation of women. Such reductive views, which typically oscillate between the two categorical extremes of *ḥijāb*ism and anti-*ḥijāb*ism, leave unexplored Īraj's theory on the relationship between the seclusion of women and pederasty. They also ignore the intricate parable of unveiling which makes up almost one-fifth of the *'Ārifnāmah* and in which *ḥijāb*, as allegory, is anything but static.

*ḤIJĀB*ISM AND ANTI-*ḤIJĀB*ISM : ENDURING ANTIPODES

The first recorded cracks in the seclusion of *ḥaram* women appear in the diary of Nāṣir al-Dīn Shāh's (r. 1264–1313/1848–96) interpreter and minister of publications, I'timād al-Salṭanah (1256–1313/1840–96). His entry for 15 Rabī' II 1313/7 October 1895 records that the Shāh was spending the day outside of

[3] See, for example, Bāmdād 1977, 133; Bayat-Philipp 1978, 304–5; and Nashat 1983, 26. Bayat-Philipp's survey has led to Īraj's inclusion in a broader survey, see Jayawardena 1986, 63, where he appears as "Iraq Mirza."

[4] Typical is Farzaneh Milani's citation of Īraj's famous poem *Dar sar-i dar-i kārvānsarāyī • taṣvīr-i zanī bih gach kashīdand* (High above a caravan-haven • was once the face of a lady graven), see Milani 1992, 30–1; cf. Īraj Mīrzā, 1989, 177–8. Jalāl Matīnī quotes deftly from the *'Ārifnāmah,* avoiding the obscene parts, in his survey of the state of women in Iran from the Constitutional Period until the age of Āyat Allāh Khumaynī, see [Matīnī] 1985, 304–7.

[5] Milani 1992, 30.

[6] "WOGish," Western Oriented Gentelman-ish, here refers to Iranians who traveled abroad or who were exposed to European ideas in Iran, and who were so taken by the West and its liberal ways that they became slavish followers of Westernism. In Īraj's time, such people were *fukul* (i.e., "French collar," *faux col*) and, in more contemporary Persian, *Gharbzadah* (literally "struck by the West" or "Euro-maniac").

Tehran at Surkhah Ḥiṣār, a small village that lacked such basic amenities as a stable, a farrier, and a teahouse. I'timād al-Salṭanah reports that a party of women from the royal *ḥaram* suddenly appeared coming directly from Tehran on horseback, as there were no proper carriages or mounts available to them at Surkhah Ḥiṣār. "They galloped so," he wrote, "that no *chādur* remained on their shoulders and no veil covered their heads; no servant preceded them and no eunuch followed in their wake." This sight causes him to reflect on the moral decline of the Shāh's household and lament that in the good old days such a breach of royal etiquette would have been unthinkable.[7] I'timād al-Salṭanah was such a strict *ḥijāb*ist that he even chastised the Shāh himself for his royal indifference when women cast unveiled glances from roof of the *ḥaram* at horse races run on a track below.[8] He also found the complete freedom with which foreign women behaved while strolling the royal grounds or attending audiences with the Shāh an indication of how morally loose and uncivilized their nations were.[9]

Early 20th-century anti-*ḥijāb*ism also emerged in a diary kept by a member of the Shāh's inner household. Nāṣir al-Dīn Shāh's daughter, Tāj al-Salṭanah (1301 Q.–1314 Sh./1884–1936), offers a detailed account of her secluded life. Her diary differs from other writings by court ladies in that she examined social and political issues that extended beyond the confines of the *ḥaram*. For example, she blames *ḥijāb* for all of Iran's ills: "The source of the ruination of the country, the cause of its moral laxity, the obstacle to its advancement in all areas, is the veiling of women."[10]

While Western emancipationist sentiments and models informed Tāj al-Salṭanah's anti-*ḥijāb*ism,[11] her indictment of the veil is mainly an appeal to indigenous economics and rural practice. She feels that veiling put pressure on poor men to work harder to support their wives and daughters who could not. At the other end of the social spectrum, *ḥijāb*ism caused corruption because it prevented noblewomen from working, thus forcing their husbands to steal to support their wives' expensive tastes. Having traveled into the Iranian countryside, Tāj al-Salṭanah reports, "I saw men and women everywhere working side by side in the villages, the women unveiled."[12] Her view of veiling as an "urban phenomenon"[13] resonates, as we shall see, in Īraj's satire.

[7] I'timād al-Salṭanah 1971, 1035–6.
[8] Ibid., 870.
[9] Ibid., 754, 987.
[10] Tāj al-Salṭanah [1982] 1991, 101 and 1993, 290.
[11] Idem [1982] 1991, 99 and 1993, 285.
[12] Idem [1982] 1991, 101 and 1993, 290.
[13] Idem 1993, 95.

*Ḥijāb*ist and anti-*ḥijāb*ist views were colliding in the feminist newspapers published about the same time the *'Ārifnāmah* was widely read and quoted.[14] In Isfand 1310 Sh./March 1932, a physician from Būshihr criticized the lifting of the veil in *'Ālam-i nisvān* (*Women's world*).[15] Dr. Sayyid Jamāl al-Dīn felt that his country was not morally advanced enough to lift the veil and that calls for unveiling amounted to aping the West. He criticized Iranian women like Tāj al-Salṭanah, who advocated de-*ḥijāb*ization, for seeing merely their own idealized picture of life in the unveiled West and for ignoring the inner corruption of Westerners. Sayyid Jamāl al-Dīn's final argument against unveiling was grounded in his dismal view of morality in Iran. Iranians were, he said, "ruled by the power of their passions"; the veil was a bridle on those passions and unveiling, which he identified as one of the "roads toward progress" (*rāhhā-yi taraqqī*), could take place only when Iranian morality progressed.

Sayyid Jamāl al-Dīn's comments sparked a series of anti-*ḥijābist* responses that were published in *'Ālam-i nisvān*. Muḥammad 'Alī Īravānī, writing from Ābādan, countered with the theological argument, namely that the sources of Islamic law do not mandate the veiling of the face and hands. But he also acknowledged that complete de-*ḥijāb*ization would be against religious law. Like Tāj al-Salṭanah, Īravānī appealed to Iranian rural practice and noted that among the unveiled tribes there was less immorality than among veiled city folk.[16] In other words, he thought that morality had nothing to do with the veil. As we shall see the separation of *ḥijāb*ism from morality is a basic tenet of Īraj's satire.

In another *'Ālam-i nisvān* rejoinder to Sayyid Jamāl al-Dīn, Riẕā Khalīlī relinks *ḥijāb* and morality to argue for unveiling. He saw the veil in all its forms as the source of the increase in immorality, because, like the dark of night it served to cover all sorts of indecencies and scandals.[17] In a continuation of his article, Khalīlī also linked *ḥijāb* to divorce, because it prevented couples from getting to know one another adequately before marriage.[18] The anti-*ḥijābist* arguments of this article amount to a reprise of the *'Ārifnāmah*. Īraj's parable about the woman who keeps tightly veiled while a determined lover, the narrator of the poem, "breaches her nether defenses," mocks the *ḥijābist* notion that the veil is a barrier to immorality.

[14] Janet Afary has surveyed these journals once in English (Afary 1989), and once in Persian (Afary 1993).

[15] *'Ālam-i nisvān* 12, no. 2, Isfand 1310 Sh./March 1932.

[16] *'Ālam-i nisvān* 12, no. 3, Urdībihisht 1311 Sh./May 1932.

[17] *'Ālam-i nisvān* 12, no. 4, Tīr 1311 Sh./July 1932.

[18] *'Ālam-i nisvān* 12, no. 5, Shahrīvar 1311 Sh./September 1932.

The *ḥijāb*ist—anti-*ḥijāb*ist controversy continues to this day in the same diametrical terms. In its capacity to divide and promote demonization, the issue of the veil is comparable to the uncivil pro-life/pro-choice war in the United States. *Ḥijāb*ists charge anti-*ḥijāb*ists with immorality, ignorance, and Wogism. Anti-*ḥijāb*ists accuse their adversaries of being reactionary, anti-modern, and patriarchal. The controversy erupts predictably when the subject of Riẕā Shāh Pahlavī's outlawing of the veil in Day 1314 Sh./ January 1936 arises. In what amounted to an article of faith, Āyat Allāh Khumaynī labeled the act the "Movement of Bayonets," because soldiers were ordered to tear the veils from women's faces.[19] Jalāl al-Dīn Madanī's recent political history sees the anti-veil edict as the act of a west-struck autocrat, who was determined to secularize Iran at all costs.[20] More recently, epitomizing Fariba Adelkhah's *La révolution sous le voile-Femmes islamiques d'Iran*,[21] Āzad Burūjirdī writes that, unlike Adelkhah, "outsiders misunderstand many aspects of contemporary social life in Iran like . . . *ḥijāb*," which is an affirmation of a woman's selfhood whether with *chādur* or without.[22] The forced unveiling of women from this *ḥijāb*ist point of view would amount to depriving them of their womanhood.

Jalāl Matīnī's article *Naẓarī bih vaẓ'-i zanān-i Īrān az Inqilāb-i Mashrūṭīyat tā 'aṣr-i vilāyat-i faqīh* (*The state of women in Iran from the Constitutional Revolution to the age of the vicarate of the jurist*), written to commemorate the 50th anniversary of the outlawing of the veil, presents the traditional anti-*ḥijāb*ist view of that act. He quotes approvingly from a speech Riẕā Shāh gave before his first unveiled audience, which included the Queen and two of the royal princesses: "We must not ignore the fact that [heretofore] half the population of our country did not count; that is, half of our work force was unemployed."[23] The principal source of opposition to unveiling, according to Matīnī, was Iran's clergy. He sees the re-veiling policies of the Islamic Republic as the triumph of that early opposition. The formation of morality squads like the *Gasht-i Ṣār Allāh* (The Vengeance of God Patrol) and *Gasht-i Khvāharān-i Zaynab* (The Sisters of Zaynab Patrol) shows the extent to which clerical *ḥijāb*ism has been institutionalized in the Islamic Republic.[24] Matīnī also observes that, after a sermon by Ḥujjat al-Islām Khāminah'ī, which warned women that if they did not observe "Islamic" *ḥijāb* to the letter, it might force

[19] Tabari, 1983, 63.
[20] Madanī, n.d., 1:243, footnote 1.
[21] Adelkhah 1991.
[22] Burūjirdī 1992–3.
[23] [Matīnī] 1985, 313.
[24] Ibid., 324–5.

their Ḥizb Allāh brothers to react [negatively], vigilantes mounted on motorcycles reacted by shouting "Death to anti-*ḥijāb*ists" (*Marg bar bī'ḥijāb*). Matīnī concludes that in the Islamic Republic, *ḥijāb* is an article of political faith, rather than a principle of modesty.[25]

But, as many writers have pointed out, the politicization of *ḥijāb* (i.e., the birth of *ḥijāb*ism and anti-*ḥijāb*ism) was coincident with the "modernization" or "Westernization" of the Middle East. Leila Ahmed, for example, attributes early Egyptian anti-*ḥijāb*ism to colonialism and classism. She employs an Arabic work *Taḥrīr al-mar'ah* (*The liberation of woman*) by Qāsim Amīn[26] as the archetypal anti-*ḥijābist* tract. After a detailed analysis of the shortcomings of Amīn's arguments, Ahmed concludes that his "assault on the veil represented not the result of reasoned reflection and analysis but rather the internalization and replication of the colonist perception"[27] and that his

> book thus represents the rearticulation in native voice of the colonial thesis of the inferiority of the native and Muslim and the superiority of the European. Rearticulated in native upper-middle-class voice, the voice of a class economically allied with the colonizers and already adopting their life-styles, the colonist thesis took on a classist dimension: it became in effect an attack . . . on the customs of the lower-middle and lower classes.[28]

In Ahmed's view, Amīn was a WOG who, because his class interests coincided with British colonials and Christian missionaries in Egypt, affected a strident but flawed anti-*ḥijāb*ism. Ahmed's classist view of anti-*ḥijāb*ism does not seem to apply in the Iranian case. Riẓā Shāh's edict did not affect merely the lower-middle and lower classes, but the upper classes and royalty as well. According to Milani, who has surveyed the literary record, to many Iranian women, "the veil was a source of respect, virtue, protection, and pride."[29] The anti-anti-*ḥijāb*ism of the upper classes is also found in memoirs written by members of the aristocracy. Sattareh Farman Farmaian, the daughter of a Qajar prince, recalls her mother's bitter reaction to the edict:

> "First Reza Shah attacks the clergy," my mother sobbed, "and now this. He's trying to destroy religion. He doesn't fear God, this evil Shah—may God curse him for it!" As she wept she struggled futilely to hide her

[25] Ibid., 325.
[26] Qāsim Amīn 1899.
[27] Ahmed 1992, 160.
[28] Ibid., 162.
[29] Milani 1992, 35.

> beautiful masses of waist-length black hair under the inadequate protection of a small French cloche.[30]

Farman Farmaian's memoir also shows that even among the upper classes the initial unveiling was superficial and that the veil had achieved the status of a political emblem.[31] After the recision of the Shāh's edict in 1941, she notes, "Women who had felt humiliated by the Shah's dress code put on black *chādur*s and flaunted them in the streets, reveling in the freedom to wear what they wished."[32] Many members of the Iranian upper class like Farman Farmaian's father 'Abd al-Ḥusayn Mīrzā, a noted Anglophile and modernizer in his own right, opposed Riẕā Shāh's edict; while other Qajar aristocrats like Īraj Mīrzā were strongly anti-*ḥijābist*. Classism and colonialism cannot account for this division.

THE POETICS OF *ḤIJĀB*

When *ḥijāb* enters literature or cinema, it achieves dimensions that the *ḥijāb*ist-anti-*ḥijāb*ist debate cannot contain. Anthropologists of veiling have found that in addition to expressing modesty and moral integrity, *ḥijāb* can also be beautifying and sexually suggestive. Unni Wikan discovered, for example, "that one general effect of the *burqa* [Omani mask that can cover the cheeks, nose, upper lips, and eyebrows] is to throw the eyes into relief."[33] Some Omani women with less than attractive foreheads, noses or cheek bones were able to beautify these features with the right *burqa*. In this way, veiling is a paradoxical instrument that at times performs its intended function as a barrier to illicit stares and as a means of expressing moral integrity and intellectual selfhood, and that at other times does just the opposite by inviting scrutiny and speculation.

According to Hamid Naficy this paradox in contemporary Iran, where a rigorous notion of *ḥijāb* has been reinstitutionalized, amounts to a "dialectic" of veiling and unveiling. In his article *Veiled vision/powerful presences : women in post-revolutionary Iranian cinema* he details how the dialectic is practiced:

> In practice, women have a great deal of latitude in how they present themselves to the gaze of the male onlookers, involving body language, eye contact, types of veil worn, clothing worn underneath the veil, and the

[30] Farman Farmaian 1992, 95–6.
[31] Ibid., 128.
[32] Ibid.
[33] Wikan 1982, 98.

> manner in which the veil itself is fanned open or closed at strategic moments to lure or to mask, to reveal or to conceal the face, the body, or the clothing underneath.[34]

When veiling comes to the screen, it develops its own aesthetic, "which governs the actors' behavior, dress, emotional expression, and the narrative structure of a film."[35] Even though the Iranian cinema is regulated by a strict code of modesty, Naficy has found that the paradox of *ḥijāb* emerges in contemporary Iranian films whether Islamic Republican censors allow it or not: "veiled women thus may become highly charged with sexuality, which ironically subverts the purpose of the religious principles of veiling—namely to protect women from becoming sexual objects."[36] The paradox that is integral to *ḥijāb* in all of its manifestations—veiling, unveiling, de-veiling, and re-veiling—is that in de-eroticizing it can eroticize; in muting the sexuality of the *ḥijāb*-ed, it can magnify and enhance it.

Although the parable of unveiling in Īraj Mīrzā's satirical epic *'Ārifnāmah*, on one hand, and the films Naficy cites, on the other, appeared in Iran during two different—virtually converse—periods in Iranian history, they evince a strikingly similar aesthetic. Īraj's parable circulated in an Iran that was about to undergo a state-imposed de-*ḥijāb*ization; whereas modern Iranian cinema operates under a state-imposed re-*ḥijāb*ization. While the two states (the Europeanizing "King of Kings-dom of Iran" of Riẓā Shāh and the de-secularizing "Islamic Republic of Iran" of Āyat Allāh Khumaynī) confine the issue to the traditional antipodes of *ḥijāb*ism and anti-*ḥijāb*ism, poetry and film provide the artistic contexts in which the inherent paradox of *ḥijāb* emerges, producing a poetics or cinematics of veiling.

The 515-line *'Ārifnāmah* is ostensibly aimed at the accomplished poet, singer, lyricist, and pederast of the Constitutional Movement, 'Ārif of Qazvīn, who is often mentioned with Īraj as a proto-feminist. It is actually an epic satire of certain aspects of Iranian culture and society in 1339/1921. It appears that Īraj's old friend 'Ārif visited Mashhad for a performance in that year. Īraj, who had expected the singer to stay with him, was deeply hurt when he accepted the hospitality of the governor of the province at Bāgh-i Khūnī instead. Like many satirists, Īraj vents his spleen on the proximate cause of his anger and draws on that animus to fuel a scathing attack on sanctimony in Iran. The poem attacks 'Ārif for his pederasty and speculates about why the practice

[34] Naficy 1994, 137.
[35] Ibid., 139.
[36] Ibid., 141.

was so common and flagrant on all levels of society (from the lowly *'āmm* to the high-born *'ārif*: a pun on his victim's name that Īraj uses several times):

O Lord, what thing is this pedomania
That plagues Aref and greater Tehrania?
Why is it only in this commonwealth
Does sodomy take place with little stealth?
The European with his lofty bearing
Knows not the ins and outs of *garçon*-tearing.
Since Iran's haven to every donkey buck,
Who else are these asses going to fuck?
If anyone with reason knew this score,
They'd surely yowl a hearty *cri de coeur*:
Until our tribe is tied up in the veil,
This very queerness is bound to prevail.
The draping of the girl with her throat divine
Will make the little boy our concubine.
You see: A cute and cuddly little boy,
Who's ready to become your fawning toy;
Not seen: His sister naked without her wimple,
So there's no hope of doting on her dimple![37]

Īraj was one of the few writers who openly blamed the strict segregation of the sexes demanded by the *ḥijāb*ism of the time for the prevalence of pederasty.

Many parts of the *'Ārifnāmah* echo the anti-*ḥijāb*ism of Tāj al-Salṭanah's memoirs and articles in *'Ālam-i nisvān*, in which the veil is emblematic of the kind of oppression of women that denies them their selfhood. Īraj mocks *chādur*-wearers by accusing them of impersonating vegetables:

Pardon me, but are you some onion ball,
A garlic in chador or praying shawl?
You who're the mirror of God's Divine Splendor,
A turnip sack of undetermined gender?
Bound at both ends when down the lane you careen,
Not like a lady—maybe aubergine?[38]

Here the veil is anything but sexy, but a few lines later the other side of *ḥijāb* emerges:

[37] Sprachman 1995, 82, lines 70–8; Īraj Mīrzā 1989, 78, lines 70–8.
[38] Sprachman 1995, 89, lines 202–4; Īraj Mīrzā 1989, 83, lines 202–4.

Yes, hide your charms from men's unlawful stares;
Don't sell them beauty like forbidden wares.
From head to toe cocooned in silk attire,
You inflame souls—beware *you* don't catch fire.
Your feet in boots, your veil a *faqi* hood,
You bleed anemic blokes of all their blood.[39]

Like some of *'Ālam-i nisvān*'s correspondents, Īraj challenges veiling on doctrinal grounds, and like Tāj al-Salṭanah cites the example of country women who live by a sense of *ḥijāb* that differs markedly from the urban interpretation without succumbing to sin:

Do what the Prophet said was commonplace;
And neither sell your charms, nor hide your face.
It's against Holy Qoran, I am certain,
To hide your hands and face behind a curtain.
This way is not the path to virginity;
Are farts and heads in the same vicinity?
Do rural women and the tribal folks
Conceal their faces using veils and cloaks?
Why aren't *they* subject to filth and lust?
Why isn't *their* bazaar bereft of trust?
The city women reside under tents,
While tenting folk are moved by other bents.[40]

The *'Ārifnāmah* also contains a poem within a poem, a parable with which Īraj illustrates the futility of *ḥijāb*ism. When the narrator was a callow youth, a *ḥijāb*-ed figure captures his heart to such an extent that her seduction becomes his obsession. In this parable, the veil serves to heighten the narrator's sexual appetite for the woman who wears it. It is the "rustling sound" or "suggestive movement" (*khish u fish*) accentuated by the veil that stirs his passion initially.[41] It is the partial concealment of the throat, chin, and lip that makes those and other parts of the body more erotic, as the mere act of walking amounts to a striptease in the eyes of the youthful narrator.[42]

The *ḥijāb*-ed woman's fury turns to passion so long as the sanctity of her veil is not breached. She points out the connection between veiling and marriage[43] and proves the scrupulousness of her *ḥijāb*ism by declaring that even

[39] Sprachman 1995, 89, lines 208–10; Īraj Mīrzā 1989, 84, lines 208–10.
[40] Sprachman 1995, 89–90, lines 213–8.; Īraj Mīrzā 1989, 84, lines 213–8.
[41] Sprachman 1995, 83, line 101; Īraj Mīrzā 1989, 79, line 101.
[42] Sprachman 1995, 83, lines 102–3; Īraj Mīrzā 1989, 79, lines 102–3.
[43] Sprachman 1995, 85, line 135; Īraj Mīrzā 1989, 81, line 135.

her brother-in-law, who would normally be privy to her face, was not allowed a peek.[44] In fact, the lady does protest too much; to the narrator's surprise her resolve melts.[45] While she keeps her hands clamped over her veil, the narrator is free to explore the rest of her body; so long as her facial modesty remains intact, her genital integrity is fair game.[46] Hence the veil becomes an accessory to sexual abandon and permits one of the most explicit descriptions of female genitalia in Persian poetry.[47] Because of its obscenities, this parable is never cited in writing on *ḥijāb*. I offer the following non-literal translation of all the lines so that the poetics of the veil can emerge in context.

'ARIFNĀMAH : THE PARABLE OF ḤIJĀB

Come listen to this tale so you will see
The chador's effect on society.
Those days when I was still a simple boy,
I faced the door of a haramsaroy,
Out came a woman with a rustling sound,
Who made the blood in my veins jump around.
I saw a bit of throat under her clip,
A little chin and hints of lovely lip.
These peaked out from behind her veil as might
Slivers of the moon on a cloudy night.
I approached her and politely salaamed,
And said that some one had just telegrammed.
Doubtful, the fairy-face tried to remember,
Who could the bearer be and who the sender?
"To go into this message on the street,"
"Would be," I said, "coarse and indiscreet.
To all conversation's a time and a place;
To all revelation's honor not disgrace.
Let's go inside and stroll along the hall,
Make the house dance from joy and have a ball."
Before the fairy face could try to refuse,
I shut her mouth with ev'ry trick and ruse.
Repeating "After you's!" I persisted,
More than stubborn, I strongly insisted.
I seized the pretext of that phony call,
And, like it or not, she entered the hall.
But, when the hallway got too crowded soon,
I carried her to the adjoining room.

44 Sprachman 1995, 85, line 137; Īraj Mīrzā 1989, 81, line 137.
45 Sprachman 1995, 86–7, lines 157–64; Īraj Mīrzā 1989, 82, lines 157–64.
46 Sprachman 1995, 87, lines 172–3; Īraj Mīrzā 1989, 82, lines 172–3.
47 Sprachman 1995, 87, lines 174–9; Īraj Mīrzā 1989, 82, lines 174–9.

She sat and used a hundred ploys to flirt,
But her face she kept steadfastly covert.
So I began the most amazing tale;
I had to speak with her—I would not fail.
I told of men at times and women, too,
The things for husbands that the women do.
At times I spoke of Khosrow and Shirin
(Whose infidelities were Byzantine).
I spoke of Rum and lands along the Rhine,
But from the first, 'twas clear what I'd in mind.
Me: yearning to fulfill my heart's desire;
She: thoughts of deciph'ring a phantom wire.
Softly I said, "O my *intime*, my lover,
Rid your face of that mask and uncover.
Why must you hide your beauty from my sight?
I'm not a cat, and you're no mouse to bite.
Aren't we both human beings, anyway,
Fashioned by God from the same mud'n clay?
Speak, listen, look, rise, sit—do what you will,
Sweet soul, we're drawn from the same crucible.
That face of yours was created, you see,
For all mankind to be able to see.
The garden of the soul has women flowers;
Not rose and jonquil beds, but female bowers.
The rose by no means loses its mettle,
If hummingbirds look it in the petal;
Nor's sugar's sweetness somehow nullified,
If honey bees around it flied and flied.
How is a candle's luster more or less,
Were it to reach two folks or a whole mess?
If butterflies alight upon the rose,
The flower is not injured by their toes."
The beauty was so upset by this speech
That up she jumped, and heatedly she screeched,
"Me, unveil illegally? That's taboo!
So take these words and blow them out the kazoo!
The rascals in this town, I do declare!
Al-LAH al-MIGHty, keep them very rare!
Tell me to unveil—hardy har, and, HAR!
The nerve! The brazenness! al-LAH akBAR!
To hell with you! Am *I* some kind of whore,
Who'd appear to the proscribed *sans* chador?
The aim of this whole thing was my disgrace;
I see it all now and spit in your face!
Never would I've experienced husbandhood,
Unless I had kept hidden to those I should.
Get lost you good for nothing little skunk,

How dare you feed me this kind of bunk.
My brother-in-law wished to look,
But even *him* my husband wouldn't brook.
I'm not one of those Tehrani *belles*,
Not one of those you seem to know so well.
Don't try to trap this lovebird, find another;
Save the advice for your sister and mother.
The Griffin builds her nest beyond the trees;
You be content with cooping chickadees.
Even if you were to tear me limb from limb,
My veil would stay, you'd never see my skin!
Why don't your eyes reveal an ounce of shame?
No pumice stone's as hard as your cold mien.
Either you're mad or stoned from too much drinking—
Araq or insanity, that's my thinking.
What a jackass! Today's my lucky day;
A sly young devil has me in his sway!
My, how our times have ebbed and waned!
Not a sign of Islam has remained!
Peeking is sinful, don't you know that's true?
Four fingers are between the grave and you.
You claim that Resurrection is full,
That all the words the Mollas say are bull?
The Mojtaheds don't know what they're about,
That each is a cowardly lying lout?
Consult the Mollas so you'll learn our creed,
For pulpits teach us a lot, indeed.
The night you're on top and I am below,
Monkar and Nakir'll be at our pillow.
They'll pound your head so hard to the bone,
You'll foul your slab of memorial stone."
In sum, of faith she spoke so, on she went
That I was contrite and had to repent.
When this was clear, I uttered not a sound,
And beside her I slowly came around.
I spoke again to claim my innocence,
And beg she forgive this sinner's sins.
I dotted "i"s and crossed a thousand "t"s
To say, "I'm sorry—fucked—forgive me please."
I brought two bowls of salted crispy treat,
And forced her one or two almonds to eat.
Again I softened her resolve of steel,
And slowly diverted her from her zeal.
No more about de-*hejab*ing her face,
Just step by step her arms in my embrace.
From what I did this time I was so sure
She'd be a lioness and growl and roar;

She'd pounce and pound me until flesh she stripped,
And beneath her I crumpled, pussy-whipped;
She'd grab my balls and treat them like two *oeufs*,
Whereupon neighbors would peer from their roofs.
And thus I'd be like some old pair of shoes,
All black and blue, both battered and contused.
But to the contrary, those sparkling wiles,
Although they withdrew, it wasn't by miles.
She became fiercer but not that much harder;
She sharpened not with anger, but with ardor.
From that old rage and intense swings of mood;
I reached the milder, "Wise up, don't be crude."
Her robust swearing and rank obscenities
Soon became, "Softly, my young lad, sit down, please."
As soon as her tie-string began to sag,
My heart, I said, it's nearly in the bag.
My hands caressed that beauty with the love
A Molla showers on his rice pilav.
I tossed her on the carpet like a rose;
Frantic, I raced from her heights to her toes.
My nerves had made me clumsy by surprise;
My hands slipped from her ankles to her thighs.
My heart was racing as she'd buck and rear;
She talked and talked but I would hardly hear.
Her hands: clamped across the veil on her face;
My hands: busy exploring another place.
I said, "You guard the heights, keep the coast clear,
I'll get the bunker ready from down here."
Although her thighs were hard to penetrate,
I was soon staring at that pearly gate.
I saw a budding *kos*, new-blossomed red,
A jonquil cunt, half-asleep in its bed;
Outside, the lemon fragrance of Shiraz,
Inside, the honey-soaked dates of Ahwaz;
Brighter than the face of a believer,
Purer than the breed of a retriever.
Not depilated, but a hairless *kos*
That makes mouths water like sour grape juice.
The rarest cunt of cunts, the smallest bore,
Against my cock its width engaged in war.
With force and blows I got into her stirrup,
Where congress was as sweet as sugared syrup.
In went the head, the woman opened wider,
And placed the rest like her heart deep inside'r.
Yes indeed, cock's a dish that tastes the best,
A cunt in craving it will tear the breast.
But, since her purity was in her visage,

> She kept it tightly veiled from start to finish;
> The hold she had was two-fistedly good,
> Lest she lose something of her "chastitude."
> When of that sweetie I'd all I could eat,
> She cursed my parents and went down the street.[48]

Several elements conspire to produce Īraj's parable of *ḥijāb*. Incorporated in the poem is the basic anti-*ḥijābist* argument that rather than preserving public morality the literal approach to veiling promotes immodesty. The facile assumption fostered by this approach that chastity resides in the face alone is evident in the lady's arguments against unveiling.[49] Also present is the secularist polemic that caricatures the clergy as anti-modern, ignorant, and gluttonous: the misguided woman's authority are *mullās* and *mujtaḥids*[50] and a *mullā*'s appetite for pilav serves as a metonym for the narrator's lust.[51] At the same time, one finds that even during intercourse veiling is an eroticizer and aphrodisiac. While the lady keeps "steadfastly covert," she also manages to find many ways to flirt.[52] The narrator does not succeed in his conquest until he realizes the key to un-chastity: namely, never mentioning *ḥijāb*.[53] So long as the outward sign of modesty is maintained and unnamed, any type of immodesty can flourish beneath it. This paradoxical image in Īraj's poetics of *ḥijāb* is reminiscent of a late 19th-century "women's indoor outfit" pictured in Tāj al-Salṭanah's memoirs.[54] The wife of an Iṣfahānī carpet merchant, Zībā Khānum, is shown in a *charqad* (wimple) that covers her hair, ears, throat, shoulders and the right side of her torso. The left side of her torso from her breast to her hip is exposed. She is also wearing an underskirt that reaches her knees and calf-length stockings. The picture, according to the captionist, is "a telling example of fashionable sensuality in the harem of the affluent." Like the parabolist's conquest, Zībā Khānum's drawstring sags, and, despite her wimple or, perhaps because of it, she is a highly erotic figure. Composed of these elements, the poetics of *ḥijab* invests the veil with a complex dynamic. In Īraj's satire, it can range from a cold abstraction to a warm aphrodisiac to an opaque screen of hypocrisy.

[48] Sprachman 1995, 83–8, lines 99–185; Īraj Mīrzā 1989, 79–83, lines 99–185.
[49] For example, Sprachman 1995, 85, line 134; Īraj Mīrzā 1989, 81, line 134.
[50] Sprachman 1995, 86, lines 147–8; Īraj Mīrzā 1989, 81, lines 147–8.
[51] Sprachman 1995, 87, lines 167–8; Īraj Mīrzā 1989, 82, lines 167–8.
[52] Sprachman 1995, 84, line 113; Īraj Mīrzā 1989, 80, line 113.
[53] Sprachman 1995, 86, line 158; Īraj Mīrzā 1989, 82, line 158.
[54] Tāj al-Salṭanah 1993, 31.

BIBLIOGRAPHY

ADELKHAH, FARIBA. 1991. *La révolution sous le voile : femmes islamiques d'Iran.* Paris : Karthala.

AFARY, JANET. 1989. On the origins of Feminism in early 20th-century Iran. *Journal of women's history* 1, no. 2 (fall): 65–87.

—— 1993. Ta'ammulī dar tafakkur-i ijtimā'ī-siyāsī-i zanān dar Inqilāb-i Mashrūṭah. *Nīmah-'i dīgar* no. 17 (zamistān 1371 Sh.):

AHMED, LEILA. 1992. *Women and gender in Islam : historical roots of a modern debate.* New Haven, CT : Yale University Press.

ĀRYĀNPŪR, YAḤYÁ. 1978. *Az Ṣabā tā Nīmā : tārīkh-i 150 sāl-i adab-i Fārsī.* 5th ed. 2 vols. Tehran : Shirkat-i Sihāmī-i Kitābhā-yi Jībī bā hamkārī-i Mu'assasah-'i Intishārāt-i Firānklīn, 1357 Sh.

BĀMDĀD, BADR OL-MOLUK. 1977. *From darkness into light : women's emancipation in Iran.* Ed. & tr. F. R. C. Bagley. Hicksville, NY : Exposition Press.

BAYAT-PHILIPP, MANGOL. 1978. Women and revolution in Iran, 1905–1911. In *Women in the Muslim world.* Ed. Lois Beck, Nikki Keddie. Cambridge, MA and London : Harvard University Press: 295–308.

BURŪJIRDĪ, ĀZĀD. 1992–3. Inqilāb va vaẕ'-i zan dar Īrān. *Nashr-i dānish* 13, no. 1 (Āẕar va Day 1371 Sh.): 51.

FARMAN FARMAIAN, SATTAREH. 1992. *Daughter of Persia : a woman's journey from her father's harem through the Islamic Revolution.* New York : Crown Publishers Inc.

ĪRAJ MĪRZĀ. 1989. *Dīvān-i kāmil-i Īraj Mīrzā va taḥqīq dar aḥvāl, āṣār, afkār, ash'ār, khānd-n va niyākān-i ū.* 6th ed. Ed. Muḥammad Ja'far Maḥjūb. [Los Angeles] : Shirkat-i Kitāb.

I'TIMĀD AL-SALṬANAH. 1971. *Rūznāmah-'i khāṭirāt-i I'timād al-Salṭanah.* 2nd ed. Ed. Iraj Afshar. Tehran : Amīr Kabīr, 1350 Sh.

JAYAWARDENA, KUMARI. 1986. *Feminism and nationalism in the Third World.* New Delhi : Kali for Women ; London : Zed Books ; Totowa, NJ : Biblio Distribution Center.

LAVIE, SMADAR. 1990. *The poetics of military occupation : Mzeina allegories of Bedouin identity under Israeli and Egyptian rule.* Berkeley and Los Angeles, CA: University of California Press.

MADANĪ, JALĀL AL-DĪN. n.d. *Tārīkh-i siyāsī-i mu'āṣir-i Īrān.* 3rd ed. 2 vols. Qum : Daftar-i Intishārāt-i Islāmī vābastah bih Jāmi'ah-i Mudarrisīn-i Ḥawzah-'i 'Ilmīyah-'i Qum.

[MATĪNĪ, JALĀL]. 1985. Naẓarī bih vaẕ'-i zanān-i Īrān az Inqilāb-i Mashrūṭīyat tā 'aṣr-i vilāyat-i faqīh. *Irān'nāmah* 3, no. 2 (zamistān 1363 Sh.): 301–27.

MILANI, FARZANEH. 1992. *Veils and words : the emerging voices of Iranian women writers.* Syracuse : Syracuse University Press.

MUJTAHIDĪ, MHDĪ. 1948. *Rijāl-i Āẕarbāyjān dar 'aṣr-i Mashrūtīyat.* Tehran : Naqsh-i Jahān, 1327 Sh.

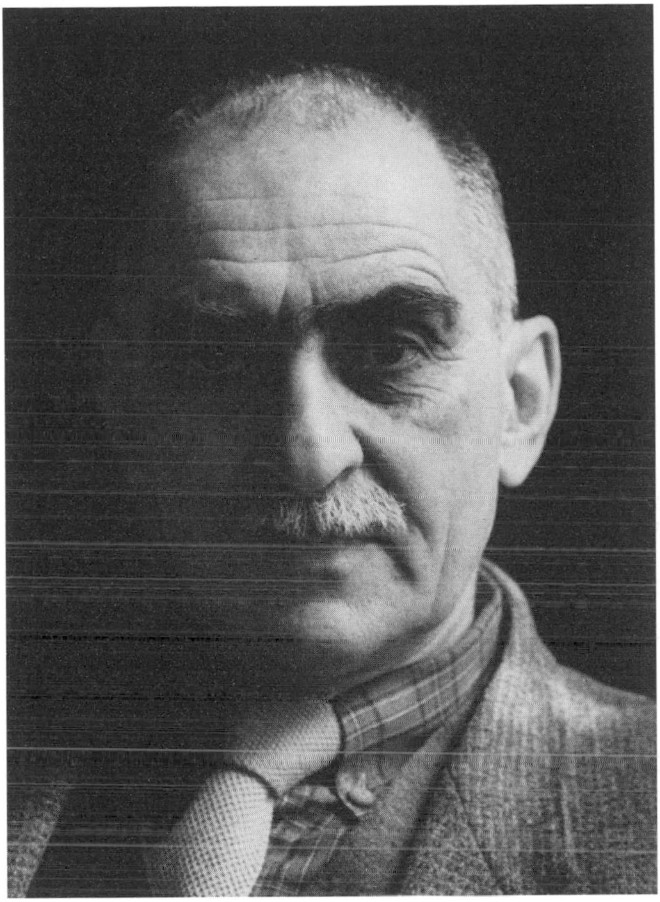

Iraj Afshar

Iran and Iranian Studies